Legal Writing by Design

Legal Writing by Design

A Guide to Great Briefs and Memos

SECOND EDITION

Teresa J. Reid Rambo and **Leanne J. Pflaum**

Legal Skills Professors,
University of Florida Fredric G. Levin College of Law

CAROLINA ACADEMIC PRESS
Durham, North Carolina

Library of Congress Cataloging-in-Publication Data

Rambo, Teresa J. Reid.
  Legal writing by design : a guide to great briefs and memos / Teresa J. Reid Rambo,
and Leanne J. Pflaum. -- 2nd ed.
      p. cm.
  Includes bibliographical references and index.
  ISBN 978-1-59460-859-9 (alk. paper)
1. Legal composition. 2. Legal briefs. 3. Law--United States--Language. I. Pflaum,
Leanne J. II. Title.

  KF250.R35 2012
  808.06'634--dc23   2012036500

Carolina Academic Press
700 Kent Street
Durham, NC 27701
Telephone (919) 489-7486
Fax (919) 493-5668
www.cap-press.com

Printed in the United States of America

To our families for their love and support

Thomas	Thomas
Matthew	Matthew
Lorraine (Mom)	Parker
Carlyn (Dad)	Mary Ella (Mom)
Bill	Sylvester (Dad)
Brennan	

Contents

Acknowledgments

For their help and encouragement, we thank Lorraine Reid; Marge Baker; Glenda Sawyer; our colleagues Henry Wihnyk; Betsy Ruff; Patricia Thomson; Diane Tomlinson; Shira Magerman, and students John Giftos; Bridgit Wenz; Lara Parkin; David Maier; and Doron Weiss. Special thanks to students, Monica Haddad and Sandy Chiu, for exhaustive reading and editing of the second edition, and to Kristine Festa and Patricia Rego for research assistance. We are also most grateful to all our students and teaching assistants for encouraging us to write this book, and allowing us to learn from them. Finally, we gratefully acknowledge our publisher's patience in waiting for this second edition.

Copyright Acknowledgments

Introduction

There was a man who disliked seeing his footprints and his shadow. He decided to escape from them, and began to run. But as he ran along, more footprints appeared, while his shadow easily kept up with him. Thinking he was going too slowly, he ran faster and faster without stopping, until he finally collapsed from exhaustion and died. If he had stood still, there would have been no footprints. If he had rested in the shade, his shadow would have disappeared.

—Benjamin Hoff, *The Tao of Pooh*

The goal of our book is to help you "rest in the shade," at least when it comes to legal reasoning and writing. It's to remind you, in easily understandable terms, that you already know how to reason and how to argue. You've been doing both since you could speak.

We are by nature logical creatures, meeting situations with the memory of how we and others have acted in the past and projecting how we might act in the future. As children, we learned the value of precedent: "Well, Matthew got to stay up *this* late when he was *my age*, so why can't I?" We also learned that there were rules and then there were *RULES*. Just as it was when we were kids, as lawyers, our goal in employing reasoning in a legal writing format is simple: it's to make a point; it's to get what we want.

We hope to give you the confidence and direction to apply to your legal writing the reasoning skills you've spent your life exercising and mastering. We want to demystify the writing process by explaining the logic of deductive, inductive, and analogical reasoning, and by explaining the concept of "relevancy" as a link between rule and fact. We present a common sense approach to understanding and structuring legal analysis.

Effective legal research and oral and written communication are core skills every lawyer must master. You don't have to take our word on this. The importance of these goals in your professional careers is corroborated by a survey cited in an article by Bryant G. Garth & Joanne Martin, *Law Schools and the Construction of Competence*, 43 J. Legal Educ. 469, 488 (1993). That timeless survey asked hiring partners in a large city which skills they expected applicants to bring to the job and which could be developed after hiring. Here are some partial results of that survey:

Skill	Bring	Develop
Library legal research	92	9
Oral communication	91	9
Written communication	90	10
Computer legal research	84	16
Legal analysis and legal reasoning	81	19
Sensitivity to professional ethics	74	25
Counseling	9	91
Ability to obtain and keep clients	8	92
Understanding and conducting litigation	6	94
Negotiation	4	96

(Because of rounding, percentages may not add to 100).

A more recent survey of hiring partners and recruiters in law firms[1] includes **writing** as one of the five basic skills lacking in new attorneys. No matter how well you know the law, that knowledge alone has little value unless you can communicate it effectively. And, to those of you who may be thinking either: (1) I don't need to learn legal writing because I'm going to be a trial attorney; or (2) I already know how to write, allow us to briefly address these thoughts.

First, even those of you who will be trial attorneys will need to know how to write motions and memoranda of law. Second, even though you already know how to write, you likely don't know how to write legal documents, which have their own special structure, format, and citation requirements.

Indeed, the importance and distinctive requirements of legal writing set it apart from other types of writing. The heightened importance of legal writing derives from the critical impact it can have on the lives of the people who are the subject of such writing. Legal writing requires you to be able to analyze a legal issue and to communicate your analysis to others.

Legal analysis generally takes two forms: (1) predictive analysis, and (2) persuasive analysis. The most common type of document used in predictive legal analysis is the legal memorandum, although a client letter providing an opinion on a legal issue is another. The legal memorandum predicts the outcome (favorable or unfavorable) of a legal question by analyzing the authorities governing the question and the relevant facts giving rise to the legal question. It explains and applies the authorities in predicting an outcome, and ends with advice and recommendations. The legal memorandum also serves as a record of the research done for a given legal question on a certain date. Traditionally, and to meet the legal reader's expectations, it is formally organized and written.

On the other hand, a document employing persuasive legal analysis, generally a motion or a brief, attempts to convince a deciding authority to resolve the dispute in

---

1. Katy Montgomery & Neda Khatamee, *What Law Firms Want in New Recruits*, N.Y.L.J. (May 28, 2009).

favor of the author's client. Motions and briefs are submitted to judges, mediators, arbitrators, and others. In addition, a persuasive letter might be sent to the opposing parties in a dispute to persuade them to settle the case. Although a brief, similar to a memorandum, states the legal issues, describes authorities, and applies those authorities in analyzing the facts, the brief's discussion section is framed as an argument. The author argues his or her approach for resolving the legal matter, rather than presenting a neutral analysis.[2]

In both situations, whether writing predictively or persuasively, your job is to evaluate the strength of your client's legal situation and to effectively communicate your case. These two types of analysis and writing tend to overlap: to predict an outcome, the writer must recognize both sides of an argument; and to persuade a decision-maker to accept the client's view, the writer must recognize how the argument will be viewed objectively.

As with any type of writing, what is most crucial is to know the "who" and "why" and "how" of what you are writing. The "who" is your audience, the "why" is the purpose of the communication, and the "how" is the manner in which you write the document.

In the legal arena, the "who" could be a partner in your law firm; a judge or justice for whom you're clerking; a court, mediator, arbitrator, or regulatory body. In short, we're writing for a reader who understands legal reasoning and writing in general, but does not necessarily know the law relevant to a particular problem. Therefore, your job is to educate your reader by explaining the relevant law and how that law applies to the facts of your client's case.

The "why" of legal writing depends on whether you are being asked to provide advice to a law firm partner or a judge for whom you clerk (predictive analysis), or whether your task is to persuade some official body of your client's position (persuasive analysis). The "how" addresses the format, organization and structure of the writing.

Good legal writing is clear, concise, and cohesive. It flows well from point to point. And, it is absolutely accurate and thorough regarding the facts, the law, and how the law applies to a client's case.

Accuracy is critical because a legal document built on a faulty premise, or on the absence of a critical premise, is unprofessional and cannot withstand careful scrutiny. Thoroughness is critical because whether in the realm of predictive or persuasive writing, a legal document must contain the information the decision-maker needs to do his or her job. Thoroughness does not, however, require you to include everything you know about an area of law—remember, you are writing for very busy readers. A thorough legal document includes all that is *relevant*, and nothing extraneous.

Both accuracy and thoroughness require you to comply with all relevant rules governing formatting your document and citing to authority. To control the length and structure of briefs and memos, courts have specific requirements regarding typeface

---

2. Other documents sometimes written by attorneys, not covered by this book but often taught in Legal Drafting courses, include contracts (specifying legal obligations for the parties to the contract); litigation documents such as complaints, answers, certain motions and notices; and various documents involved in the transfer of real or personal property such as wills, trusts, deeds, and bills of sale.

font and size, margins, and page limits. In some courts, even the color of the brief cover or the dimensions of the brief may be specified. Documents submitted electronically are governed by a host of other rules. Failure to follow these requirements can result in the court's rejection of the document and even in the loss of the client's case. In addition, many law firms have internal specific requirements regarding the format and organization of documents. As for citation, legal readers expect, (and courts require), legal authorities to be cited for every statement that relies on a source other than the writer's own ideas. Standardization of citations and abbreviations makes it easier for readers quickly to recognize and identify an authority.

Because we are writing for busy readers, we must make our legal documents clear, concise, and cohesive. Cohesion requires that the entire document be internally consistent, easy to read and digest, and simple. Thus, short sentences and paragraphs, recognizable words rather than "legalese," and transitions moving the reader gently through the document are essential.

These legal writing skills will be new to you, even a bit intimidating, but it is crucial to your career that you learn them. You'll learn how to research in law school, and through the principles explained in this book, will learn how to process and apply that research to produce first-rate written legal analysis. And make no mistake, writing is a **process**—no good legal writer gets it right the first time. You'll find that you must continue to assess, and reassess your position throughout the process, sometimes back-track or even start over, and revise again and again. Writing, and rewriting is the way to produce high quality legal documents.

Through hypotheticals, samples, and commentaries in the upcoming chapters, we'll show you how to *design* a legal analysis or argument and write it in a legal format. Our book, designed primarily for first year law students, but applicable to even seasoned attorneys, focuses both on predictive writing, (explaining the law and predicting an outcome), and on persuasive writing (explaining the law and then convincing the reader of the correctness of your position). We've included some exercises to allow you to apply the new skills you're learning. Although many of the samples rely on predictive legal memoranda, these guidelines apply to persuasive writing as well.

We've divided our book into six **Sections**. In **Section I**, we'll discuss legal rules and reasoning. We'll explore how to select, from an almost limitless number of possibilities, an orderly sequence of statements that lead logically to a conclusion, focusing primarily on analyzing and writing predictively (with a few detours into persuasive analysis). We'll talk a bit about logic, and we'll use terms like *syllogism, premises, analogy, induction, and deduction*, but we won't delve too deeply into any other logic concepts. We'll keep our book user-friendly. Our purpose in discussing the logical underpinnings of "the argument" is simply to *remind* us of *how* we think.

In studying legal reasoning, we've got to keep one paramount principle in mind: writing and reasoning are joined at the hip. We can't write effectively without reasoning effectively. Writing is just a by-product of reasoning. This book explains how to transform thoughts into writing by explaining the link between thinking and writing.

After reviewing the *reasoning* process, we'll see how to transform our thoughts into writing. To that end, in **Section II**, we'll see how to design and write a predictive memo. In **Section III**, we'll explore how to design and write a persuasive brief. Because attorneys must often present their arguments orally, we'll also explore how to design and deliver an effective oral argument. In **Section IV,** we'll discuss the beginning, middle, and end of the writing process; case briefing; citation; and professional ethics. In **Section V,** we'll review the basics of clear and effective writing. Finally, in **Section VI,** we'll show how all of these principles come together in a sample memo and three sample briefs.

In all Sections, we'll go step-by-step through each subject and address strategies that work. (After teaching *thousands* of students, and writing memos and briefs ourselves as practicing lawyers, we've seen what works and what doesn't.) We've included some exercises throughout so you can practice the concepts you're learning, and at the end of most chapters, we've included a chapter review. Our approach, of course, isn't the *only* way to design a well-reasoned legal memo and brief, but we think it's an effective way of doing so. Once you understand the basic principles of analyzing and outlining a legal issue, you may find that you can vary the approach and design of your written analysis to suit your own style. Until you reach this point, however, it's best to stick with the general principles and with the methods we've recommended.

Although we'll highlight some general procedural rules of court practice, we won't get too specific about these. Similarly, although we'll demonstrate some formatting requirements for both legal memos and briefs, it's important that you be aware that the requirements for memos can vary from law firm to law firm; and for briefs, from state to state and court to court. Thus, the most important thing we can tell you in this regard is to always consult the "rule book" before beginning to write. In a law firm you might consult an available firm policy manual, or ask an office manager, managing partner, or an associate for the correct format to follow. In writing a document to a court, you *must* consult the appropriate local practice rules for *that* court. Beyond those requirements, the most important consideration is always the audience for whom you are writing. As such, all your documents should be written with the utmost attention to the readers' needs, as well as to thoroughness, accuracy, and clarity.

The "tone" of our book is conversational; it's how we teach our students. We don't preach, we discuss. And, as you'll see, we also like a good laugh every now and then.

Let's now explore the nature of an argument and the process of reasoning. We'll begin by addressing *rule-based* or *deductive* reasoning, briefly touching on *inductive* reasoning, and then exploring the *hybrid* process (part inductive, part deductive) of *arguing by analogy.* By the end of **Section I,** we'll see how understanding the *design* of the legal argument helps us transform our thoughts into great briefs and memos.

Section I

The Design of Legal Reasoning

"To have ideas is to gather flowers. To think is to weave them into garlands."

—Ann-Sophie Swetchine

Chapter 1

Introduction to Reasoning

§ 1.1   What Is a Rule?

> "A rule is a formula for making a decision."
>
> —Richard K. Neumann, Jr.[1]

Like us, you probably came to law school expecting "the law" to be set out in books, or indeed, carved in stone—your only task being to commit it to memory. Of course, the reality isn't that simple. Laws spring from many sources: constitutions (federal and state); legislative bodies (statutes, ordinances); administrative agencies (regulations); and judges (the "common law" as developed through court cases). A law or rule is simply a statement of what society permits or requires people to do (or not to do) in given circumstances. Roscoe Pound described rules as "precepts attaching a definite detailed legal consequence to a definite, detailed state of facts."[2]

The form of these precepts varies widely. Rules come in many types: commandments, "Thou Shall Not …"; statutes, "gotta have a leash if you walk that dog"; and the common law, i.e., a judge's pronouncement of right and wrong under the circumstances of the case presently before the court. And, as we've stated, rules spring from all branches of the government: executive, judicial, and legislative alike. Thus, the two main sources of law are what we can collectively refer to as statutes (constitutional provisions, statutes, ordinances, and regulations), and the common law (also referred to as judicial precedent, cases, decisions, and opinions). Because statutes are often general and ambiguous in the language used, a court may need to interpret the statute in applying it. In other words, the explanation and application of a statute will often include both the language of the statute itself and a case opinion providing a more specific interpretation of that language. This "compound" interpretation, in turn, would become the "rule" that would apply in resolving the case.

Although we've all learned the tortured route legislative rules take just in being born, that lengthy and careful process doesn't guarantee a sane outcome. Some legislative rules (even without any court interpretation) are downright nutty.

Toto, we're not in Kansas anymore. For example,[3] at one time it was illegal for monkeys to smoke cigarettes in South Bend, Indiana; illegal to punch a bull in the nose in Washington, D.C.; illegal to fish for trout while sitting on the back of a giraffe in Idaho; and illegal to peel an orange in your hotel room in California. Moreover, a Boston, Massachusetts, ordinance mandated that "[a] lodger shall not be lodged for more than seven consecutive nights unless he shall have taken a bath," while a New York Vehicle and Traffic Law instructed that "[t]wo vehicles which are passing each other in opposite directions shall have the right of way." What?

But creating mind-boggling rules is not a task left solely to the legislative branch. Some judicial pronouncements, even from the highest courts, leave us wondering

---

1. Richard K. Neumann, Jr., *Legal Reasoning and Legal Writing: Structure, Strategy, and Style* 9 (6th ed. 2009).

2. Roscoe Pound, *Hierarchy of Sources and Forms in Different Systems of Law*, 7 Tul. L. Rev. 475, 482 (1933).

3. These examples, and many more, were gathered by Leland H. Gregory, III, in *Presumed Ignorant* (1998).

whether we should have gone to medical school after all. For example, in ruling that nude dancing was protected under the First Amendment as a form of expression—fulfilling, of course, the clear intent of old Ben Franklin and the rest of the Framers—Justice Rehnquist stated: "[N]ude dancing of the kind sought to be performed here is expressive conduct within the outer perimeters of the First Amendment, though we view it as only marginally so." *Barnes v. Glen Theatre*, 501 U.S. 560, 566 (1991). Huh? What is an "outer perimeter" of the First Amendment? What does it mean to be only "marginally" within that "outer perimeter"? Are other forms of expression within that "outer perimeter"? Are other forms just hanging on to First Amendment protection by the skin of their teeth? Your guess is as good as ours.

One Florida appellate court, in applying the *Barnes* rule to "offensive sexual conduct which was part of a nude dance," had this to say: "If the simple nude dancing described in *Barnes* was only 'marginally' within the 'outer perimeters of the First Amendment,' then the [sexual acts] here at issue are somewhere on Mars." *State v. Conforti*, 688 So. 2d 350, 355 (Fla. Dist. Ct. App. 1997). Not surprisingly, the court ruled that the conduct in the *Conforti* case (too graphic to describe here but set forth in detail in the case) was *not* protected under the First Amendment.

What are the shores of Gitche Gumee anyway? Fortunately, most rules aren't stated in such paradoxical and vague language as those in the *Barnes* and *Conforti* cases. Still, each word in a rule—especially adjectives and adverbs—is a potential battleground for opposing parties. Take, for example, the following two rules:[4]

(1) to be valid, a will must have the signature of two attesting witnesses,

versus

(2) "The shore of navigable waters which the sovereign holds for public uses is the land that borders on navigable waters and lies between ordinary high and ordinary low water marks. This does not include lands that do not immediately border on the navigable waters, and that are covered by water not capable of navigation for useful public purposes, such as mud flats, shallow inlets, and lowlands covered more or less by water permanently or at intervals, where the waters thereon are not in their ordinary state useful for public navigation. Lands not covered by navigable waters and not included in the shore space between ordinary high and low water marks immediately bordering on navigable waters are the subjects of private ownership, at least when the public rights of navigation, etc., are not thereby unlawfully impaired."[5]

The former rule, stated in straightforward terms, is fairly easy to comprehend. It has very few adjectives (actually just three—"valid," "two," and "attesting") and leaves us asking only a few questions. For example, what constitutes a "signature" and who is an "attesting witness"?

In stark contrast, the latter rule, which seems to go on forever, is riddled with adjectives, adverbs, and other abstract terms. It sounds more like the first few lines

---

4. We thank Todd Messenger for this example.

5. *Lee v. Williams*, 711 So. 2d 57, 59 (Fla. Dist. Ct. App. 1998) (quoting *Clement v. Watson*, 58 So. 25, 26–27 (Fla. 1912)).

from Henry Wadsworth Longfellow's *Hiawatha's Childhood*,[6] than like a legal rule. And like the poem, this rule, spurred on by its less than clear terms, raises a slew of questions.

For example, what are "navigable waters"? What is "ordinary"? What does "immediately border" mean? What does "not capable of navigation for useful public purposes" mean? What does "more or less" mean? And so on and so on. We get the picture … sort of. This one rule, stated in this one case, begets innumerable other rules, stated in innumerable other cases, with each rule and case attempting to define and corral ambiguous terms.

But, in addition to the language used, another important distinction separates these two rules. The former rule, which protects the legitimacy of wills, involves little theoretical or ideological controversy. Presumably, we all want our wills honored, and this rule establishes requirements for giving our wishes legal effect. In contrast, however, the latter rule, which divvies up property rights, is highly controversial. The rule provides the "template" for balancing public-access rights against private ownership interests. Though this latter rule, from *Clement v. Watson*, is seemingly "neutral" in its language, it nonetheless reflects a particular ideological perspective.

Interestingly, the central issue in *Clement* was not a property dispute, but an assault. In *Clement*, a poor man was fishing in a tidal cove when the wealthy property owner told him to leave. The dispute escalated to violence, and the owner assaulted the fisherman. At issue was whether the owner had the right to forcibly eject the fisherman from the property.

To reach an outcome that protected the owner, the Florida Supreme Court held that the owner owned the submerged land, which under long-standing common law had been subject to public ownership. In so holding, the court divested the State of Florida of thousands of acres of tidally influenced land, and, incredibly, the State wasn't even a party to the action. Years later, courts still not only cite *Clement*, but quote its rule in deciding cases involving the ownership of tidally influenced lands. This one rule, not even arising from an "environmental law" case, has had a great impact on environmental issues. Are the shores of Gitche Gumee public or private? "More or less," we guess.

§ 1.2   The Fickle Nature of Rules

"A rose by any other name still smells."
—with our apologies to William Shakespeare

---

6. *"By the shores of Gitche Gumee,*
   By the shining Big-Sea-Water,
   Stood the wigwam of Nokomis,
   Daughter of the Moon, Nokomis.
   Dark behind it rose the forest,
   Rose the black and gloomy pine-trees,
   Rose the firs with cones upon them;
   Bright before it beat the water,
   Beat the shining Big-Sea-Water."

The rule laid bare. Despite how politically charged they may be, who has written them, or the subject they address, most rules share common components. As Professor Richard Neumann has observed, these components are as follows:

> (1) a set of elements, collectively called a test; (2) a result that occurs when all the elements are present (and the test is thus satisfied); and (3) what, for lack of a better expression, could be called a causal term that determines whether the result is mandatory, prohibitory, discretionary or declaratory.... Additionally, many rules have (4) one or more exceptions that, if present would defeat the result, even if all the elements are present.[7]

We've also observed (as many others have before us) two characteristics shared by most rules: (1) almost any rule can be countered with one of equal force; and (2) often the same rule supports both sides of the argument. Welcome to the "wobbly" world of the law—a world with a very shaky foundation. Permit us to explain.

Welcome to the "outer perimeters." In physics, as Newton observed, for every action there's an opposite and equal reaction. This is good; this makes things predictable. Except when we get to the quantum level, physical rules pretty well can describe all of what we see and experience. If we're standing on the Earth and drop a ten pound ball, we can pretty well bet the ball will fall down. We can also pretty well predict the speed at which it will fall, and the impact it will make. If we drop the same ball a hundred times, it will fall a hundred times. There's a real certainty about the outcome.

Because they're so dependable, physical rules are downright comforting. Drop that ball a million times and it'll fall back to Earth a million times. No decree from a judge or act of Congress will change that result. The pattern of action and reaction is the same. Not so with "legal" rules.

Legal rules follow no absolutes. Indeed, almost any rule can be met with an opposing, yet equally convincing, rule. But instead of making things predictable and comforting, this quality leads to the contrary result—it makes the law unstable, unpredictable, and, at times, maddening.

Back in 1950, Karl Llewellyn recognized this principle.[8] Llewellyn analyzed the relationship between twenty-eight pairs of "canons" of statutory construction. He found that for each canon applied by a court to justify an outcome, another recognized canon could be applied to reach the opposite outcome. To return to our "dropping ball analogy," this would be tantamount to a principle that in one out of every two drops, our ball would soar into the sky rather than fall back to the Earth.

But, as if this observation weren't enough, we also find one equally as unsettling: The *same* legal rule often supports *opposite* views. In other words, in many cases either party to a controversy can use the same rule, but reach opposite conclusions. We can explain this result using "scientific" terms: It all boils down to a difference of opinion in how data is measured and interpreted.

---

7. Neumann, *supra*, at 10.

8. Karl Llewellyn, *Remarks on the Theory of Appellate Decision and the Rules or Canons About How Statutes Are to Be Construed*, 3 Vand. L. Rev. 395, 401–06 (1950).

Take, for example, our "nude dancing" case. Imagine a state statute that prohibits public nudity and a First Amendment rule that frowns on laws targeted at the content of expressive conduct. Dancers, wishing to dance nude in a public bar, challenge the statute as violating their First Amendment right to "express" their message of "eroticism." The Court finds that nude dancing is "marginally" protected within the "outer perimeters" of the First Amendment and next has to determine whether the State, nonetheless, can enforce its statute and require the dancers to cover up a bit.

The State agrees that the dancers express a "message of eroticism" but replies that the statute has nothing to do with censoring that message. Rather, the State argues, the statute is concerned only with the "conduct" of nudity. The Court must then decide whether the statute regulates the conduct of nude dancing, or, as the dancers argue, the content of eroticism conveyed by the act of dancing in the nude. In other words, is the statute "content-neutral" and aimed at preventing public nudity; or is it "content-based" and aimed at censoring the message of eroticism such nudity conveys?

In *Barnes v. Glen Theatre*, 501 U.S. 560, 571 (1991), the real case involving this issue, a plurality[9] of the United States Supreme Court ruled in the State's favor, finding that the statute was content-neutral and that its application was constitutional. Applying the rule that the law strongly disfavors statutes targeted at content, the plurality reasoned that "[p]ublic nudity is the evil the State seeks to prevent, whether or not it is combined with expressive activity." *Id.* Thus, because the statute sought to prevent only public nudity, and not to inhibit any message nude dancers wished to convey, the statute didn't violate the First Amendment.

Justice Scalia, in his concurrence, explained this sensitive issue using the reasoned discourse we've come to expect from the highest court in the land:

> [T]here is no basis for thinking that our society has ever shared that Thoreauvian 'you-may-do-what-you-like-so-long-as-it-does-not-injure-someone-else' beau ideal — much less for thinking that it was written into the Constitution. The purpose of Indiana's nudity law would be violated, I think, if 60,000 fully consenting adults crowded into the Hoosier Dome to display their genitals to one another, even if there were not an offended innocent in the crowd.

Id. at 574–75 (Scalia, J., concurring). (Yes, he really said this.)

However, applying this same rule, the Court as easily could have found, as did the dissenting Justices, that the statute was content-based. As one dissenting Justice reasoned:

> It is only because nude dancing performances may generate emotions and feelings of eroticism and sensuality among the spectators that the State seeks to regulate such expressive activity.... The nudity element of nude dancing performances cannot be neatly pigeonholed as mere 'conduct' independent of any expressive component of the dance.

Id. at 592–93 (White, J., dissenting).

---

9. Only three of the nine Justices joined in an opinion announcing the Court's judgment.

Who was correct—the plurality or the dissenters? It's all a matter of opinion. Does the result in the *Barnes* case mean that the Supreme Court has laid down a rule, now set in stone, that all laws regulating public nudity or public nude dancing are constitutional? Absolutely not! The rule expressed in *Barnes* applies only to *that* particular law, *that* particular issue, and *those* particular parties. As soon as a different set of facts (i.e., a new case) arises, the *Barnes* rule at best is but a guiding precept, not a set-in-stone mandate. In other words, the rule of one case will not necessarily remain constant, or even viable, anywhere outside the originating case. The *Barnes* rule applies to the *Barnes* case. Whether, and in what manner, the Court will extend it to other cases are questions only the Court can answer.

We're dealing with Jell-O® and truffles here, not bricks. We hope that courts will apply rules consistently, deciding like cases alike. Indeed, the concept of *stare decisis*[10] mandates that judges keep things on par and stable by deciding like cases in like ways. But, we have no guarantee that such stability will occur. Perhaps this is what caused Oliver Wendell Holmes to remark: "The prophecies of what the courts will do in fact, and nothing more pretentious, are what I mean by the law."[11]

Although lower court judges must follow precedent established by higher courts in their jurisdiction, they decide what is precedent and they're free to decide however they wish on issues of first impression. Moreover, the United States Supreme Court (regarding issues of federal law) and the highest state appellate courts (regarding issues of state law) can decide however they'd like. They can follow precedent, or not. Further, courts of every level can reverse a decision in a pending case or overrule their own prior decisions; in the ultimate of surrealistic enterprises, some can even "depublish" their prior written opinions. In other words, they can issue an order decreeing that an opinion they've issued, which likely is printed in a book sitting on a library shelf, must now be treated as if it never existed. Imagine doing that with a physical rule: "We've decided not to honor the law of gravity today." Yeah, right.

No doubt about it: the law *is* unstable, much more so than many would like to admit. Although the legal consequence of one case may be "definite" as far as the parties to that case are concerned, the law *itself* is anybody's guess. The law constantly changes. Legislators and judges are always tampering with rules—writing new laws or interpreting old ones in new ways to suit the occasion. The bottom line: a "legal" law, or rule, is nothing like a law of physics. It's not a universal "truth."

Legal rules are not inalterable patterns of behavior; they're not instructions on stone tablets. If they were, we'd be out of work. There'd be certainty in the legal universe and no one would need us. We could go into gardening, or brain surgery, or something truly useful.

No, we've got to think of legal rules, not as bricks, but, as, well … as Jell-O®—as pliable, wiggly, masses of slime that we, as lawyers and judges, shape into many forms.

---

10. *Stare decisis* is Latin for "abide by, or adhere to, decided cases." *Black's Law Dictionary* 1577 (revised 4th ed. 1968).

11. Oliver Wendell Holmes, *The Path of the Law*, 10 Harv. L. Rev. 457, 461 (1897).

One of these forms is a case. Each case has its own shape, formed by the "mold" of its particular facts and issue, and filled with the "law" relevant to those facts and issue.

The mold of each case forms the external boundaries, or "holding," of the case. That holding answers the question the issue poses. Whatever law fits into that mold is the court's rule and "reasoning." Whatever law flows out and over the mold is *dictum*. *Dicta* (the plural of *dictum*) are the court's observations on the case which may be interesting (or not) but which aren't necessary to the court's decision on the issue.

Being chocolate lovers, we're also compelled to explain this holding-rule-dicta process in terms of, as Forrest Gump said it, "a box of chocolates." Consider a case as a soft-centered truffle with a hard chocolate shell.[12] The issue and the facts form a "mold." Into that mold, we pour chocolate which takes the shape of the mold, creating a hard shell (i.e., the holding). Into that shell, we pour the truffle filling (i.e., the rule and our legal reasoning). Anything that flows over the shell (i.e., beyond our holding) is *dicta*.

Of course, how we interpret a case determines the shape of our truffle. If we view the issue narrowly, we'll get a different truffle than if we view the issue broadly. Thus, in interpreting a case, we influence its form and content. The following example demonstrates this principle.

Assume that "precedent" Case A and "our" Case B involve incredibly similar issues and facts. Under these circumstances, it's likely that the "shells" (the holdings) of the two cases will also be incredibly similar, as will be the rule and reasoning of each case. The cases "look" alike. We can, in essence, simply "pour" the rule and reasoning from Case A into the shell of our case. Because the facts and issues of the cases are so similar, we shouldn't have any excesses or shortages (of rule and reasoning). However, what happens if the facts and issues differ?

If the facts and issue of our case are variants of Case A, we'll have to make adjustments. The shells of Case A and our case will be dissimilar, and the rule and reasoning of Case A may slosh over or not quite fill the shell of our case. When this happens (and it happens all the time) we adjust the rule and reasoning of Case A to "fit" the shell of our case. In solving our case, we (sometimes subtly, sometimes not) create the rules we then apply. We may "design" a new rule, or reinterpret an existing one. But, whatever we do, the doing of it changes the "law."

We might have changed our mind, but we'll never admit it. An example of this process, i.e., how applying the law changes the law, occurred in *Loper v. New York City Police Department*, 999 F.2d 699 (2d Cir. 1993). In *Loper*, a three-judge panel of the United States Court of Appeals, Second Circuit, (Judges Miner, McLaughlin, and Friedman) considered whether "needy persons," in begging for money, engaged in expressive conduct protected by the First Amendment. The New York City Police Department argued that begging had no expressive elements and that even if it did, the message beggars "convey is entitled only to the 'minimal protection' afforded by the 'outer perimeters of the First Amendment'" *Id.* at 701. Although the court didn't quote the *Barnes* case, we know the origin of that "outer perimeters" language.

---

12. You know "truffles" — those cream-filled candies with a hard chocolate shell. They're definitely not to be confused with any of several subterranean, edible, fungi rooted out by French pigs.

So far, so good. But, the *Loper* court wasn't considering this issue on a clean slate. The Second Circuit had already spoken. Three years earlier, in *Young v. New York Transit Authority*, 903 F.2d 146, 153 (2d Cir. 1990), a three-judge panel (Judges Timbers, Meskill, and Altimari) had found that begging by needy persons did not implicate the First Amendment and was not a form of expression. The *Young* court had said:

> [B]egging is not inseparably intertwined with a 'particularized message.' It seems fair to say that most individuals who beg are not doing so to convey any social or political message.... The only message that we are able to espy as common to all acts of begging is that beggars want to exact money from those whom they accost. While we acknowledge that [other people] generally understand this generic message, we think it falls far outside the scope of protected speech under the First Amendment.... Whether with or without words, the object of begging and panhandling is the transfer of money. Speech simply is not inherent to the act; it is not of the essence of the conduct. Although our holding today does not ultimately rest on an ontological distinction between speech and conduct, we think this case presents a particularly poignant example of how the distinction subsists in right reason and coincides with common sense. To be sure, these qualities ought not to be forsaken in our legal analysis.

Id. at 153–54.

Faced with this — this "precedent" — what was the court in *Loper* to do? How could it possibly find that begging was anything other than, in the words of the *Young* court, "a menace to the common good"? *Id.* at 156. Easily. In *Loper*, the court did an about-face. Distinguishing *Young*, the *Loper* court found that begging, indeed, was expressive activity warranting First Amendment protection. Here's what the court said:

> While we indicated in *Young* that begging does not always involve the transmission of a particularized social or political message, see *Young*, 903 F.2d at 153, it seems certain that it usually involves some communication of that nature. [WHAAAAAT?][13] Begging frequently is accompanied by speech indicating the need for food, shelter, clothing, medical care or transportation. Even without particularized speech, however, the presence of an unkempt and disheveled person holding out his or her hand or a cup to receive a donation itself conveys a message of need for support and assistance.

Loper, 999 F.2d at 704.

There we have it; the same circuit (but with different panels of judges) reached seemingly opposite conclusions on the "same" issue. But, are the conclusions *really* opposite? Is there any way to reconcile (i.e., make sense of) them? We think so.

In describing the *Young* and *Loper* cases, we neglected to mention a very important aspect of each case — the facts! We didn't disclose where the begging in each case had occurred. Should the location of the begging matter? The courts, in the reasoning quoted above, didn't highlight the beggars' location. Nevertheless, is begging "expressive"

---

13. Please pardon our editorial comment. We just couldn't resist.

if conducted in some locations but not expressive if conducted in others? The answer, which explains how we can make sense of both cases, is a resounding "YES."

In the *Young* case, where begging was not protected, beggars were hassling "captive" subway patrons on crowded, inherently dangerous (all those trains whizzing by) platforms. In contrast, in the *Loper* case, where begging was protected, the beggars had come into the light and were hassling people on the public sidewalk (where the pedestrians at least had a fighting chance). As in real estate, location, location, location made all the difference in the judges' opinions.

Consequently, when we're before the Second Circuit and our issue is whether begging is protected expression within the First Amendment, we now must consider both *Young* and *Loper*. Begging on subway platforms or in subway trains is *not* expressive activity (*Young*), while begging on a public sidewalk *is* expressive (*Loper*). But what about begging in other places? Could New York City adopt and enforce an ordinance prohibiting begging — near bus stops? — *in* the streets? — in front of Grand Central Station? And, what if the United States Supreme Court decides that begging is expressive? Does this mean that beggars have the right to beg even in the subway? Or, would that right also depend on location? In other words, would the "right" to beg be limited to only those locations discussed by the Supreme Court in such a case?

These questions and the *Young* and *Loper* cases illustrate what Edward H. Levi noted over fifty years ago: "The rules change as the rules are applied. More important, the rules arise out of a process which, while comparing fact situations, creates the rules and then applies them."[14] When the law doesn't do the facts justice, the law gives way.

Thus, when we alter, even subtly, our analysis of the facts or issue of a case, the law we apply in that case takes on a slightly different shape. (We get a slightly different truffle.) If the facts and issue of our case are similar to a decided case, we readily import — with slight modification — the rule and reasoning of that decided case into the "mold" formed by our case. If, however, our facts and issue are unlike any decided case, we may have to modify substantially an existing rule or design a new one. Multiply this process by case after case and we see why the law changes.

Root around for the truffle. In reading case opinions and in applying them to our case, we, well…, we seek out the "truffle." We seek the form of its shell and the contents of its center. We recognize, however, that the form and those contents may not always be as clearly described as we'd like. In fact, the court's explanation of the case may lead to more than one interpretation. In other words, several possible truffles may exist in one case.

For example, when the *Young* case was decided, we could have read it broadly: "begging is not expressive activity"; or narrowly: "begging on a subway platform or in a subway car is not expressive activity." Until *Loper* came along, we didn't know which of the two interpretations was correct.

As lawyers working with cases, the best we can do is select the interpretation that suits our case. In other words, we interpret the "precedent" case in a manner allowing us readily to import its contents into our case, without making a mess in the process.

---

14. Edward H. Levi, *An Introduction to Legal Reasoning* 3–4 (1948).

In this way, we "pour" the law from one case to the next, sometimes changing it only subtly, sometimes changing it drastically, but always changing it. The law takes shape, but only momentarily, when we grab hold of it and shove it—sometimes kicking and screaming—into a mold formed by the facts and issue of our case. But, because there's no *one* "proper" way of interpreting a case, there's no *one* proper mold, and no *one* proper rule, of the case. Even while seemingly held captive in a case, the rule remains shifty.

Thus, the rule of a case, any case, is not an iron rod or steel infrastructure holding the case upright. It's not a concrete block or a stone tablet. To alter a rule, we don't "bend," "chip away," or "carve" it. We just pour it into a different context (i.e., apply it to new facts) or interpret it differently in the same context (i.e., reexamine it in the context of its stated facts).

We didn't realize this dynamic when we came to law school. We thought the law was stable. We thought judges applied set-in-stone rules to the facts of each case. After all, the law was in a book. It was there to be read and admired, not to be poured from case to case and not to be interpreted a dozen different ways. But as Karl Llewellyn observed: "One does not progress far into legal life without learning that there is no single right and accurate way of reading one case, or of reading a bunch of cases."[15]

We've learned that a host of truffles can exist within any one case. And, equally maddening, any court can come along and "morph" our assorted truffles into homogeneous ones, and vice versa. With one sweeping statement, a court can, in Llewellyn's words, "look over the prior 'applications' of 'the rule' and rework them into a wholly new formulation of 'the true rule' or 'true principle' which knocks out some of the prior cases as simply 'misapplications' and then builds up the others."[16] In other words, from a mixture of truffles, a court can cook up a soufflé.

Judges are searching for truffles, too. Speaking of judges, we should also admit to a few misunderstandings. Before coming to law school, we thought judges knew the law. After all, it was written in books, and judges had those books and those black robes. We thought criminal court judges knew criminal law and civil judges knew divorce and custody law. We thought we'd offend a judge if we attempted to explain a legal principle to His or Her Honor.

We now know that judges can no more keep track of this constantly changing law than can we as lawyers. New rules are created; old laws are reinterpreted. If judges are to know what rules apply in our case, we've got to tell them those rules.

Judges, too, are rooting for truffles. But they aren't asking, "which one single rule or precedent provides the correct answer to this case." No. Judges know rules are pliable, "pourable," if you will. They know there's no single correct answer to a legal problem. The sooner we as lawyers realize this, the sooner we can get on to the business of aiding judges in their jobs. As Llewellyn put it: "The question is: which of the available correct answers will the court select—and why? For since there is always more than one available correct answer, the court always has to select."[17] It's *our* job to help judges choose wisely.

---

15. Llewellyn, *supra*, at 395.
16. *Id.* at 395–96.
17. *Id.* at 396.

§ 1.3   Introduction to Rule-Based Reasoning: The Ashley Montague Hypothetical

The following hypothetical illustrates the familiar design of a legal argument and the intuitive quality of legal reasoning. We've used hypotheticals throughout this book because we believe that to explain reasoning, we must engage in reasoning. Or, as William Shakespeare put it in *Hamlet*: "For to describe true madness, what is it but to be mad?"

Our case. Assume we're students in law school[18] and Ashley Montague, an Appellate Advocacy student, has asked for our help. She wants us to convince Professor Rambo to give her an A in the course. (Of course this is a hypothetical!) Where do we start? With intuition guiding us, we follow the steps discussed below.

§ 1.4   Step # 1: Gather the Facts

Intuitively, we know we must hear Ashley's story before we can argue her case. How well has she performed in the class, and why does she believe she deserves an A? To this end, assume Ashley tells us the following:

> I'm a second semester Appellate Advocacy student with a B- average in all my other courses. I've spent more time working in Appellate Advocacy than any other course, done all reading assignments, attended all classes, and correctly answered just about all questions Professor Rambo asked me in class. I've also completed and passed all assignments, including the research requirements, and have my graded papers as proof. I got an A/B+ on my Appellate Advocacy final brief, and an 'excellent' on my final oral argument. I'll give you my original brief with the grade on it and my original oral argument score sheet marked 'excellent.' That A/B+ really bothers me. I enjoy the class, but I've spent untold weekends writing my brief. I'm afraid I might not get the A I want, and need, to put on my résumé.

Next, we must determine whether Ashley has done enough to merit an A. We must uncover the criteria necessary for receiving an A in Professor Rambo's course. We go to the next step.

§ 1.5   Step # 2: Research and Outline the Rule

We research and analyze the rule stating the requirements Ashley must meet to receive an A. We know intuitively that if Ashley meets these requirements, she deserves that A. This is "deductive" reasoning. That is, based on the evidence, we can deduce that Ashley deserves that A.[19]

---

18. A common "panic dream" of those of us who've made it through to the other side.
19. We address inductive and deductive reasoning in more depth in § 1.8.

The relevant rule is the basis for analyzing any legal issue. We therefore need to understand that rule, and outlining a rule is one of the best ways to achieve the level of understanding we need. We outline for rule for several reasons: (1) to ensure that we have included all parts (i.e., *elements*) of the rule; (2) to understand the interrelationship of the subparts of the rule, if any; (3) to look for key language such as mandatory terms like "shall" or "must"; discretionary terms such as "may"; and structural terms such as "and," "or," "except," "unless," "include," and "exclude." This alphanumeric outline becomes the foundation of our analysis, whether in a predictive memo or in a persuasive brief.

Assume Professor Rambo's "grading policies" state that to receive an A in the course, a student must "demonstrate preparedness in class; satisfactorily complete all assignments; and either write an A final brief, or write an A/B+ final brief and present an excellent final oral argument."

This rule seems simple enough. It has three main requirements or elements, with the last element stated in the alternative or the "disjunctive." A disjunctive rule requires that one of two or more subparts (or elements) be met for the rule to be satisfied. Such a rule usually, but doesn't necessarily, includes the word "or." To keep track of these elements, we create an outline like the following:

Graphic 1.5   **The Rule**

To receive an A in Appellate Advocacy, a student must:
(1) demonstrate preparedness in class;
(2) satisfactorily complete all assignments; and
(3) (a) write an A final brief, **or**
    (b) write an A/B+ final brief and present an excellent final
        oral argument.

Great. Let's go to the next step.

§ 1.6   Step # 3: Personalize the Rule to Fit Our Case and, If Needed, Do More Research

Personalizing a rule means making that rule our own. It means "pouring" an existing rule into the "mold" formed by the facts and issue of our case and seeing what shape the rule takes. **Graphic 1.6** presents one way of doing this:

Graphic 1.6   **The Personalized Rule**

To receive an A in Appellate Advocacy, Ashley must show that she has
(1) been prepared in class *(defined as?)*;
(2) satisfactorily completed all assignments *(defined as?)*; and
(3) (a) has written an A final brief *(defined as?)*, **or**
    (b) has written an A/B+ final brief and presented an excellent
        final oral argument *(defined as?)*.

Notice the importance of the words "and" and "or" in our personalized rule. Ashley deserves an A if she fulfills *either* elements 1, 2, and 3(a) *or* elements 1, 2, and 3(b). As this is a disjunctive rule, she need *not* fulfill the requirements of *both* 3(a) and 3(b). Therefore, we may find that one of these elements (either 3(a) or 3(b)) is irrelevant here; i.e., we don't need to establish it to prove our case.

By personalizing the rule, we change the focus of the rule. We no longer deal with an abstract legal concept applicable to all students. Instead, we care only about Ashley, and our personalized rule reflects that concern. Notice that in personalizing the rule, we are not changing any of the rule's requirements. Instead, we are looking at the rule head-on, warts and all, to see how each element of that rule applies (or doesn't apply) to the facts of our case. But, before we can even begin to apply the rule to Ashley, we need to define its terms. We go to the next step.

§ 1.7   Step # 4: Define the Elements of the Rule

In analyzing what each of the elements of our rule requires, we look for any "hidden" elements, i.e., those requirements for receiving an A we must define through further research. We look especially for adjectives and adverbs, those wonderful bits of language that (because of their inherent ambiguity and pesky need for definition) keep us lawyers employed. (Just consider how many lawsuits would be avoided if the definition of a "reasonable person" was clear.)

What adjectives, adverbs, and other potentially ambiguous terms are lurking, just lying in wait, in our rule? Is there a difference between a "final brief" and a "brief"? Did Ashley tell us her grade on the brief or on the *final* brief? What is an "excellent" oral argument? What is a "final" oral argument? What does "preparedness" encompass? What does "satisfactorily" mean? What is an "A final brief"? What is an "A/B+ final brief"?

We better know the answers to these questions before we go further. We haven't fully thought through a legal rule until we've considered the meaning and impact of its terms. As we'll discuss in Chapter 3, § 3.2, we also pay special attention to how the rule is punctuated. Commas and semi-colons can be very tricky.

However, in law as in life, some terms defy precise definition. What is "love," "happiness," or "liberty"? What's an "outer perimeter"? "Beauty" like "obscenity" is in the eye of the beholder. Some terms, some legal elements, are inherently vague or abstract.

Here, let's assume that we can define all the terms of our rule, except we don't know what "preparedness" means. Do we ignore that element? Absolutely not! We list it as a requirement Ashley must meet, and note that we don't know, but better find out, what it means.

§1.8   Step # 5: Fill in All Gaps in Defining the Rule: Use Inductive Reasoning If Necessary

"The logic of the law is neither entirely deductive nor entirely inductive. It is a circular process."

—Ruggero J. Aldisert[20]

We intuitively understand that if Ashley meets all criteria listed in the rule, Professor Rambo should award her an A. But, how do we prove that Ashley was "prepared"? Professor Rambo's course policies didn't define the term. We can't just assert the point that Ashley was "prepared in class"; we've got to prove it. However, we can't prove anything until we know what to prove. We've gotten ourselves into a vicious circle.

To break free, we let our common sense guide us to a reasonable definition. We know that "prepared" generally means to be ready. With this definition in mind, we cull out of our facts all instances demonstrating Ashley's readiness for class. From those facts, we then "finesse" or create a definition of "preparedness," which, of course, Ashley meets. In other words (and welcome to Oz) we use "inductive" reasoning. Permit us to explain.

In inductive reasoning, we generalize a specific rule from individual instances. But inductive reasoning is nothing new. We use it daily to make cause-and-effect connections.

For example, if we notice that cats bear kittens and never bear dogs; and hens lay eggs, but roosters don't, we induce a rule that "cats, but not dogs, bear kittens; and hens, but not roosters, lay eggs." If we see an egg in a chicken coop, we apply our rule and deduce that the egg came from a hen and not from a rooster. We used inductive reasoning in creating our rule and deductive reasoning in applying it.

But, because inductive reasoning involves generalizing, it isn't foolproof:

Although some things 'just happen so,' we all believe that there are dependable regularities in the world. Everyone believes that if he is hungry and eats food, his hunger will be satisfied; that water will quench his thirst; that fire will warm him; that heat will melt snow and butter; that day will alternate with night. Such beliefs as these are held with varying degrees of strength. They may be mistaken. The thirst of fever is not quenched by water; a dying man is not warmed by the fire. Nevertheless, without believing in some dependable regularities we should not act as in fact we all do. That our expectations are sometimes fulfilled shows that we have learnt that natural happenings can be regarded as having some kind of order; that they are sometimes disappointed reveals our partial ignorance.[21]

Moreover, the accuracy of the rules we induce depends on the quality and quantity of the observations "sampled" and the biases and honesty of the observer. We can't

---

20. Ruggero J. Aldisert, *Winning on Appeal: Better Briefs and Oral Argument* 272 (1996).
21. L. Susan Stebbing, *A Modern Elementary Logic* 169 (1961).

separate ourselves from the problem we're trying to solve. The rule and the rule-interpreter/maker are inextricably joined.

But despite its lack of "absolute" certainty, inductive reasoning helps us, and helps judges, create rules. In synthesizing or comparing cases to formulate common rules, judges reason inductively from the specific to the general. As Justice Cardozo observed: "The common law does not work from pre-established truths of universal and inflexible validity to conclusions derived from them deductively. Its method is inductive, and it draws its generalizations from particulars."[22]

Indeed, the rule in Ashley's case is the result of inductive reasoning. Over time, Professor Rambo examined the qualities shared by students deserving an "A" in her class. She compared these qualities, isolated them, separated them into categories, and transformed this amalgamation into a rule with several elements.

When we apply that rule, we reason deductively. However, when we bridge a gap in that rule and attempt to define an element by discerning a common theme joining individual occurrences—as defining the term "prepared" from the facts Ashley gave us— we create a rule springing from inductive reasoning.

In reasoning inductively, we ask what facts lead to the reasonable conclusion that Ashley was prepared in class? We note that Ashley completed all reading assignments, attended all classes, and correctly answered the majority of questions posed in class. We then identify the common thread running through these individual instances and induce a rule from that commonality. Common to these instances is the quality of "being ready." Thus, we induce that "preparedness" means "to be ready to participate in class discussions." We've got ourselves a working definition. We're ready for the next step.

§ 1.9   Step # 6: Select the Relevant Facts and Apply the Personalized Rule to Those Facts: Use Deductive Reasoning

Before we apply our rule to our facts, we'll take a minor detour to explore some basics of deductive reasoning. We promise not to stray too far off course.

§ 1.9(a)   The Syllogism

In reasoning deductively, we say that if the rule requires Ashley to do 1, 2, and 3 to receive an A, and if the facts demonstrate that Ashley did 1, 2, and 3, then the conclusion is inevitable that she gets that A. This is the classic "syllogism."

As Aristotle, the credited inventor of the syllogism, explained, "'a syllogism is discourse ... in which, certain things being stated, something other than what is stated follows of necessity from their being so.'"[23] He then added, "'I mean by the last phrase that they produce the consequence, and by this, that no further term is required from

---

22. Benjamin N. Cardozo, *The Nature of the Judicial Process* 22–23 (1921).
23. L. Stebbing, *supra*, at 55 (quoting Aristotle, *Analytica Priora* 24b 18).

without to make the consequence necessary.'"[24] He illustrated this principle by the classic example:

> "All men are mortal.
> Socrates is a man.
> Socrates is mortal."

A syllogism, then, is a form of argument containing three different premises (we'll call them the rule premise, the fact premise, and the conclusion), where the conclusion results inevitably from the prior two premises. In "logic" parlance, we refer to these three premises as the following:

Graphic 1.9(a)(1)	Syllogistic Premises
The major (rule) premise: All men are mortal.	The broad proposition that states a general rule for a class of people, things, or actions.
The minor (fact) premise: Socrates is a man.	The narrow proposition confirming that a person, thing, or action is included in the class.
The conclusion: Socrates is mortal.	The result that follows when the rule of the major premise is applied to the person, thing, or action of the minor premise.

Here's where it gets a bit tricky. A "valid" syllogism requires three different "terms" (men, mortal, Socrates). Further, each premise must contain two of the three terms (men/mortal; Socrates/man; Socrates/mortal). So far, so good. Finally, a "bridging" or middle term (men/man) must occur in the rule and the fact premises, but not in the conclusion premise. This bridging term links the rule and the fact premises to the conclusion.

Let's return to our Ashley Montague hypothetical and see how the three premises and three terms there interrelate:

Graphic 1.9(a)(2)	The Ashley Montague Syllogism		
Premise	Term A	Term B bridging term	Term C
1. Rule		Do 1, 2, & 3	to get an A.
2. Fact	Ashley	did 1, 2, & 3.	
3. Conclusion	Ashley		gets an A.

In this syllogism, the three premises are (1) the rule statement, (2) the fact premise, and (3) the conclusion. The three terms are (1) Ashley (term A), (2) the requirements for earning an "A" (term B), and (3) earning an "A" (term C).

---

24. *Id.*

Is this a valid syllogism? Yes! Here's why:

Graphic 1.9(a)(3)	Proof of a Valid Syllogism	
Requirement	**Met ?**	**Proof**
three different premises	✓	premise 1 (rule) premise 2 (fact) premise 3 (conclusion)
three different terms	✓	term A = Ashley term B = doing 1, 2, and 3 term C = earning an "A"
each premise contains two of the three terms	✓	premise 1 = terms B & C premise 2 = terms A & B premise 3 = terms A & C
a bridging term occurs in: premise 1 (rule) and premise 2 (fact), but not in premise 3 (conclusion)	✓	the bridging term is term B [see distribution of terms directly above]

Thus, we could argue as follows that Ashley deserves an A:

> To receive an A in Appellate Advocacy, Ashley must show that she has been prepared in class; satisfactorily completed all assignments; has written an A final brief, or has written an A/B+ final brief and has presented an excellent final oral argument. Ashley was prepared in class; satisfactorily completed all assignments; wrote an A/B+ final brief; and presented an excellent final oral argument. Therefore, Ashley should receive an A in the course.

Observe that we have now written our rule in narrative fashion, the appropriate style for use in legal writing, omitting the letters and numbers we included in our alphanumeric outline. Note, however, that if the rule we are relying upon appears in a legal authority in alphanumeric fashion, we would retain those letters and numbers in our rule, rather than eliminating them.

As we explain in the next section, although this argument is logically sound, it lacks one major requirement of persuasive writing: *proof*. If Professor Rambo is going to give Ashley that A, she needs proof that Ashley has done what we say she's done. Where does proof "fit" within our syllogism? Let's see.

§ 1.9(b)   The "BaRAC" Design: A Syllogism with Attitude

Ba = Bold Assertion
R = Rule
A = Application
C = Conclusion

A purely logical argument, as we've seen conveyed through a syllogism, is all well and good. However, to make a convincing deductive *legal* argument, we do more than just state the premises. We prove them.

The overarching structure we use in this proof is, of course, the syllogism. However, in a legal argument, we need more than just a syllogism—we need a syllogism with guts, a syllogism with "attitude." In other words, we need a syllogism that starts with a bang, ends with a bang, and proves all the steps in-between. We call such a syllogism the "BaRAC" design.[25] BaRAC is the ultimate lawyer's (and judge's) tool; it's the ultimate formula for logical thinking and writing. Here's the design and description of its structure:[26]

Graphic 1.9(b)	The BaRAC Design
Section	**Function**
Bold Assertion	Our stated position; our thesis statement; our conclusion. It's a concrete and specific point concerning our case. There's no equivalent "syllogistic" premise.
Rule	The equivalent to the first (the major or rule) premise of a syllogism. However, unlike the syllogistic rule premise, the **BaRAC** rule statement requires that we prove, and not just state, the rule.
Application	Equivalent to the second (the minor or fact) premise of a syllogism. However, unlike its syllogistic counterpart, the **BaRAC** application section requires us to prove how the rule "fits" our facts.
Conclusion	Equivalent to the third (conclusion) premise of a syllogism. If we've done our job right in stating and explaining the rule, and in applying that rule to our facts, the conclusion inevitably follows.

§ 1.9(c)   Apply the Rule to Our Facts

To return to our Ashley hypothetical, let's focus on proving that Ashley deserves an A. Let's look at the application section, i.e., the reasoning process we use in matching the relevant elements of our rule to our facts. Just how do we demonstrate that Ashley has met the requirements for receiving an A?

First, we orient our reader to the point we'll be arguing by making a "bold assertion" of our position. We boldly state, with (as shown in **Graphic 1.9(c)** on the next page) a separate assertion for each element of the rule, that Ashley has met all requirements for receiving that A. Second, we follow each bold assertion with the relevant facts supporting it. This process of matching element to fact is commonly called "applying the law to the facts" or "reasoning."

---

25. Pronounced "bear ak."
26. We address the BaRAC design in more detail in Chapter 2, § 2.5.

Graphic 1.9(c)	Apply the Rule to the Facts
Personalized Rule	**Relevant Facts**
To receive an A in Appellate Advocacy, Ashley must show that she has:	**Bold assertion:** Ashley deserves an A in Appellate Advocacy.
(1) been prepared in class;	**Bold assertion:** Ashley has been prepared in class; i.e., she has been ready to participate in class discussions. **Facts:** Ashley completed all reading assignments, attended all classes, and correctly answered almost all questions Professor Rambo asked her in class.
(2) satisfactorily completed all assignments; *and*	**Bold assertion:** Ashley has satisfactorily completed all assignments. **Facts:** As her graded papers show, Ashley completed and passed all assignments.
(3)(a) has written an A final brief, *or*	[We have no facts supporting this element but this lack is not fatal to our case. Having written an "A final brief" is an alternative element. If Ashley meets element 3(b), she need not meet element 3(a). In other words, if she meets element 3(b), element 3(a) is irrelevant.]
(3)(b) has written an A/B+ final brief and has presented an excellent final oral argument.	**Bold assertion:** Ashley has written an A/B+ final brief and has presented an excellent final oral argument. **Facts:** As her final brief and final oral argument score sheet show, Ashley received an A/B+ on her final brief and received a score of "excellent" on her final oral argument.

Relevancy. What we're really doing is determining relevancy. We're determining which elements of the rule and which facts of our case we must prove to achieve the result we seek. Those elements and those facts are *relevant*. But, as if we're dealing with something out of *Alice in Wonderland*, the elements determine which facts are relevant and the facts determine which elements are relevant. We're engaged in a two-way process. We're as much applying the rule to the facts as we are applying the facts to the rule. Fine, but how do we do this? Here's how.

We list the elements of our rule. Then we "match," as best we can, the facts to those elements. The facts that match are relevant. Those facts help us prove our case. But, does this mean that the facts that don't match any element aren't relevant? Maybe, … maybe not.

Because the rule is what we, in essence, say it is, we may be able to reinterpret the rule to create a "fit" between our facts and this reinterpretation. Ready for that gardener's job now? This is where legal analysis takes on a Zen-like quality. This is where law becomes more of an "art form" than a logical system.

Let's look at **Graphic 1.9(c)**, one possible way to apply the rule to Ashley's case, again. We now know which facts are and aren't relevant; our rule has defined the scope of useful facts. Although Ashley may want Professor Rambo to know how much time and effort she's spent in the class and how much she'd like to include an A in Appellate Advocacy on her résumé, these facts aren't relevant. They don't "fit" any element of our rule.

We also know which elements of our rule are relevant; our facts have told us. Fortunately, element 3 is stated in the disjunctive; it can be fulfilled by Ashley performing the requirements of either 3(a) or 3(b). Because Ashley did not receive an A on her final brief, we won't rely on element 3(a). That element is legally irrelevant.

We can now say with confidence that Ashley deserves an A. We've applied the rule to our facts and have found a "fit." Our next step is writing our thoughts, showing our work, and persuading our reader to accept the conclusions we've reached.

§ 1.10   Step # 7: Build an Outline of the Argument Using the BaRAC Design

The BaRAC design serves as the overall structure or outline of our analysis of a legal problem, whether we're writing a predictive memo or a persuasive document. Here, as we're advocating on Ashley's behalf rather than simply predicting whether she'll receive an A, our analysis will take the form of a persuasive brief, in which our Bold Assertions are stated as argument points. The rule we have outlined shows up under the "Rule" part of the BaRAC design, often, as here, in narrative rather than in outline format. We can organize Ashley's argument at least two different ways (see the graphics on the next page). In the first outline (**Graphic 1.10(a)**), we discuss the personalized rule and the relevant facts separately; in the second outline (**Graphic 1.10(b)**), we discuss them together.

Each of these outlines adequately conveys our argument. However, neither is very elegant. Both suffer from choppiness, i.e., a lack of cohesion between sentences and paragraphs. We need to smooth out the rough spots by adding transitions — the "glue" words and phrases like "therefore," "moreover," "first," and "second" — that help the reader pass easily from one idea, sentence, or paragraph to the next. (We discuss transitions at length in Chapter 32.) We also need to lend credibility to our argument by citing the sources of the factual and "legal" authorities we rely on. But how do we turn our outline into a written argument? Let's see.

Graphic 1.10(a)	Outline # 1: "Whole Rule" Approach
Main Bold Assertion:	Ashley should receive an A in Appellate Advocacy.
The Personalized Rule:	To receive an A in Appellate Advocacy, Ashley must demonstrate preparedness in class; satisfactorily complete all assignments; and either write an A final brief, or write an A/B+ final brief and present an excellent final oral argument.
Application: Begin with a Bold Assertion	Ashley, a student, has met all requirements for receiving an A in the course.
Follow with the Relevant Facts	Ashley completed all reading assignments, attended all classes, and correctly answered almost all questions Professor Rambo asked her in class.
	As her graded papers show, Ashley completed and passed all assignments.
	As her final brief and final oral argument score sheet show, Ashley received an A/B+ on her final brief, and received a score of "excellent" on her final oral argument.
Conclusion:	Ashley should receive an A in Appellate Advocacy.

Graphic 1.10(b)	Outline # 2: Element-by-Element Approach
Main Bold Assertion:	Ashley should receive an A in Appellate Advocacy.
The Personalized Rule:	To receive an A in Appellate Advocacy, Ashley must demonstrate preparedness in class; satisfactorily complete all assignments; and either write an A final brief, or write an A/B+ final brief and present an excellent final oral argument.
Application: Begin with a Bold Assertion	Ashley, a student, has met all requirements for receiving an A in the course.
The Rule & Relevant Facts Combined Element-by-Element	*Ashley demonstrated preparedness in* class by being ready to participate in class discussions. She completed all reading assignments, attended all classes, and correctly answered almost all questions Professor Rambo asked her in class.
	Ashley satisfactorily completed all assignments. As her graded papers show, Ashley completed and passed all assignments.
	Ashley received an A/B+ on her final brief, and presented an excellent final oral argument. As her final brief and final oral argument score sheet show, Ashley received an A/B+ on her final brief, and received a score of "excellent" on her final oral argument.
Conclusion:	Ashley should receive an A in Appellate Advocacy.

§ 1.11   Step # 8: Write the Argument

The final step in writing our argument is selecting the more persuasive of our outlines and converting it into paragraph form, including transitions and citations to authorities we're relying on. Let's assume that we like Outline # 2 better than Outline # 1 and have written our argument accordingly.

We could have chosen Outline # 1, but we like # 2 better because it links each element of the rule more closely with the facts relevant to that element. Where, as here, we have a multi-element rule, it's easier for our reader to digest our argument in "bite-size" pieces, rather than in one lump. We still, however, have to solve the problem of "proving" our case; i.e., of showing that we've accurately represented both the facts and the law, and have drawn from them correct conclusions.

The best way to show this is to submit to Professor Rambo the documents Ashley has given us. Let's assume that we've assembled copies of these documents, including Ashley's written statement regarding her in-class participation, and have numbered these pages consecutively. We'll call this document our "Record," and we'll cite it in our argument by indicating "R." followed by the page where those facts appear. For example, a citation to page 5 of the Record would look like this: (R.5.). We'll attach this Record as an appendix to the written argument we'll submit. Professor Rambo can then review our argument and the factual record it's based on.

In addition to proving our facts, we also prove the rule we're asking Professor Rambo to accept. We do this by citing the specific source where that rule can be found. In this case, the rule comes from Professor Rambo's course materials, specifically at page 3.[27]

Here's our finished product:

Graphic 1.11	The Written Argument
Bold Assertion	Professor Rambo should award Ashley Montague, a law student enrolled in Appellate Advocacy, an A in the course because Ashley has fulfilled all requirements necessary to receive that grade.
Rule	As the Appellate Advocacy course materials indicate, a student should receive an A if she "demonstrates preparedness in class; satisfactorily completes all assignments; and either writes an A final brief, or writes an A/B+ final brief and presents an excellent final oral argument." (R.3.)
Application Bold Assertion	As the record demonstrates, Ashley has met these criteria.

Graphic continues on next page.

---

27. For reasons unknown to us, lawyers and judges cite pages in legal authority not by stating "*on* page so and so," but by stating "*at* page so and so."

Element 1 Bold Assertion & Proof	Ashley demonstrated her preparedness and readiness to participate in class discussions by correctly answering almost all questions asked of her in class, keeping pace with all reading assignments, and attending all classes. (R.4.)
Element 2 Bold Assertion & Proof	Moreover, as the Record shows, she passed, and thus satisfactorily completed, all course assignments. (R.5.)
Element 3(b) Bold Assertion & Proof	And, although she did not receive an A on her final brief, she was awarded a grade of A/B+ on her final brief, and received a score of "excellent" on her final oral argument. (R.6.)
Conclusion	Accordingly, Ashley has met all criteria for, and Professor Rambo should award her, an A in the course.

With an argument like this, Ashley, indeed, is in safe hands. Her case is as rock solid as it can be. If Professor Rambo accepts the rule and facts as we've stated them here, then she'll be compelled, from the force of our argument alone, to give Ashley that A. If only the practice of law could be this … well, … this *logical.*

§ 1.12 Exercises in Designing and Personalizing Rules

Using the Ashley Montague rule as a guide, design and personalize the rules in Exercises 1–4, separating out the elements of each rule using an alphanumeric outline as needed. There are often several ways to structure a rule, so outline each rule logically, not necessarily as it originally appears, but do not change its meaning. Don't answer the legal question—just design and personalize the rule (see **Graphic 1.6**) and list any additional facts you would need to answer the question.

Exercise 1

Rule: Any person who is of sound mind and who is either 18 or more years of age or an emancipated minor may make a will.

Harold Hunter has just graduated from high school and has decided that he is at a point in life where he needs to make a will. May he prepare a will?

Exercise 2

Rule: When a person marries after making a will and the spouse survives the testator, the surviving spouse shall receive a share in the estate of the testator equal in value to that which the surviving spouse would have received if the testator had died without making a will unless there was a provision waiving this right in a prenuptial or postnuptial agreement, the spouse is provided for in the will, or the will discloses an intention not to make a provision for the spouse.

Rose married David Hill three months after David made his will. Four years later David died, leaving Rose as his widow. Rose wants to take a share of David's estate at least equal in value to the share she would have taken had David died without making a will. May she take that share?

Exercise 3

Rule: A shopkeeper may be held liable for false imprisonment unless the shopkeeper had a reasonable belief that the person has stolen or is attempting to steal merchandise; the shopkeeper detained the person for a reasonable time; and the shopkeeper detained the person in a reasonable manner.

A Macy's store manager thought he saw Ed Jones take a watch from a display and put it into his pocket. The manager called the police. The manager then told Ed that he was not allowed to leave the store until the police arrived. The police arrived at the scene one hour after the manager first approached Ed. May the store be held liable for false imprisonment?

Exercise 4

Rule: Under the Patent Act, a use is public if the inventor gives or sells the invention to at least one person, intends for the invention to be used by that person, places no limitations, restrictions, or injunctions of secrecy on this use, and the invention is so used.

Samuel Barnes applied for a patent for a pair of corset springs in 1866. In 1855, Mr. Barnes had made a pair of corset springs for Mrs. Barnes to wear. Mrs. Barnes wore the corset springs she was given. Was this a public use?

Chapter Review
Introduction to Reasoning

Steps in Analyzing a Legal Issue

Step # 1   Gather the facts.

Step # 2   Research and outline the rule.

Step # 3   Personalize the rule to fit our case and, if needed, do more research.

Step # 4   Define the elements of the rule.

Step # 5   Fill in all gaps in defining the rule: use inductive reasoning if necessary.

Step # 6   Select the relevant facts and apply the personalized rule to those facts: use deductive reasoning following the BaRAC design:

The "BaRAC" design:
A syllogism with attitude

Ba = Bold Assertion
R = Rule
A = Application
C = Conclusion

Step # 7   Build an outline of the argument using the BaRAC design.

Step # 8   Write the argument:

Bold Assertion
Rule
• rule explanation, if necessary
Application
• element 1
  • bold assertion
  • rule
  • application
  • conclusion
• element 2
  • bold assertion
  • rule
  • application
  • conclusion
• element 3
  • bold assertion
  • rule
  • application
  • conclusion
Conclusion

Chapter 2

Reasoning: Deductive, Inductive, and Analogical

"Form is not something added to substance as a protuberant ornament. The two are fused into a unity."

—Benjamin Cardozo[1]

---

1. Benjamin N. Cardozo, *Law and Literature, in* Margaret E. Hall, *Selected Writings of Benjamin Nathan Cardozo* 340 (1947).

§2.1   Deductive Reasoning

As the Ashley Montague hypothetical of Chapter 1 demonstrates, we know how to *argue* because we know how to *think*. There's nothing magical about a deductive argument: it's simply a relationship between premises (statements) where the conclusion logically and inevitably follows. When we're reasoning deductively, we're thinking reflectively—attempting to solve a problem, as opposed to, for example, daydreaming.[2]

L. Susan Stebbing, in her book, *A Modern Elementary Logic*, explained reflective thinking as follows:[3]

> In reflective thinking our thoughts are directed towards an end—the solution of the problem that set us thinking. Thinking is a mental process in which we pass from one thought to another. A thought is an element in this process which requires for its full expression a complete sentence. When one thought is more or less consciously connected with another in order to elicit the conclusion towards which our thinking is directed we are *reasoning*.
>
> Reasoning is a familiar activity; we all reason more or less, badly or well. We connect various items of information and draw conclusions; we judge that, if certain statements are known to be true, then certain other statements are also true and must be accepted. In saying that the latter *must* be accepted we are saying that, *provided we are thinking logically*, we shall accept them; that is to say, we should not be rational beings if we accepted the former statements and rejected the latter.

So, in a nutshell, if we accept that A = B, and that B = C, then the conclusion is inevitable, *provided we are thinking logically*, that A = C. (We could also state the conclusion as C = A.) In other words, the design of deductive reasoning is as follows:

Graphic 2.1(a)   The Design of Deductive Reasoning
If we accept that the legal premise (rule) is true, and if we accept that the fact premise (relevant fact) is true, then we must accept that the conclusion is true.

Revisiting the Ashley Montague hypothetical, if a student must do certain things to receive an A in the course (rule), and if a student did all of those things (relevant facts determined by applying the rule to the facts), then the conclusion is *inevitable* that the student should receive an A.

Let's take a moment to review some of the fundamental logic principles we examined in Chapter 1:

---

2. L. Susan Stebbing, *A Modern Elementary Logic* 2 (1961).
3. *Id.*

Syllogism ↓

3 terms- middle being bridge that connects 1 + 3 making them relevant / true

The Syllogism. When we write a series of statements where the legal and fact premises lead inevitably and logically to the conclusion, we've created a "syllogism." Every syllogism requires three premises:

Graphic 2.1(b)	Every Syllogism Requires Three Premises
	1. The rule
	2. The facts
	3. The conclusion

Moreover, every syllogism requires three terms; and each premise must contain two of the three terms, with a bridging or middle term occurring in the rule and the fact premises, but not in the conclusion premise. This bridging term links the rule and the fact premises to the conclusion.

Graphic 2.1(c)   **Design of the Syllogism**

Premise	Term A	Term B *bridging term*	Term C
Rule		B =	C
Fact	A =	B	
Conclusion	A	=	C

Let's now examine how these terms and premises relate to one another. In a purely "logical" deductive argument (as opposed to a "legal" argument—which we'll get to shortly), the first two premises (rule and fact) are accepted as true without further proof, and the conclusion (the third premise) follows logically and inevitably from the two prior premises. Consider again the following classical syllogism, developed by none other than Aristotle:

Graphic 2.1(d)   **Syllogism**

Rule premise	All men are mortal.
Fact premise	Socrates is a man.
Conclusion	Therefore, Socrates is mortal.

Substituting letters for the three terms in this example, we see the following relationships:

Graphic 2.1(e)		Syllogistic Relationships		
Premise	Term A	Term B *bridging term*	Term C	Relationship
Rule		All men	are mortal.	B = C
Fact	Socrates is	a man.		A = B
Conclusion	Socrates is		mortal.	A = C

The "middle" term—here term B—provides a "bridge" linking the rule and fact premises to the conclusion. This bridging term B (men/man) appears in the first (rule) and second (fact) premises, but not in the conclusion (the third premise).

So far, so good. This logic business isn't so bad. We understand deductive reasoning—we think deductively every day. But, thinking isn't nearly as complicated as explaining how we think. Let's move now to consider the thinking behind another concept we intuitively understand: relevancy.

§2.2   The Role of Relevancy in the Logical Argument

As we've seen, a valid syllogism requires a precise design. We draw a valid conclusion from the rule and fact premises of a syllogism if we use three and *only* three terms in the premises and if we repeat each of those terms *exactly* twice. As we explain below, if we add a fourth term, or if we have no "bridging" or repeating term, the syllogism is invalid and we've got a *relevancy* problem. Understanding this design principle, and what happens when it's breached, helps us formulate valid legal arguments and identify invalid ones—a critical lawyering skill.

For example, the following "syllogism" just doesn't work because it contains a fourth term, and there's no "bridging" term linking the rule and fact premises to the conclusion:

Graphic 2.2(a)	An Invalid "Syllogism": 4th Term Introduced				
Premise	Term A	Term B	Term C	Term D	Relationship
Rule		All men	are mortal.		B = C
Fact	Socrates is			a rock.	A = D
Conclusion	Socrates is		mortal.		???????

What's going on here? The rule speaks only of the mortal "quality" of "men" (or a "man"). It says nothing about the quality of a rock. Therefore, we can't draw a conclusion regarding the quality of a rock from this rule. There's no "match" between the facts (Socrates is a rock) and the rule (all men are mortal). In other words, we have no bridging term linking "Socrates" to "men," so we can't link "Socrates" to "mortal." We have a relevancy problem. The fact that Socrates is a rock is irrelevant where, as here, the rule doesn't include rocks.

Notice also that the following "syllogism" doesn't work:

Graphic 2.2(b)	An Invalid "Syllogism": 4th Term Introduced				
Premise	Term A	Term B	Term C	Term D	Relationship
Rule		All men	are mortal.		B = C
Fact	Socrates			might be a man.	A = D
Conclusion	Socrates		is mortal.		???????

What's going on here? The rule speaks only of the mortal quality of men or a man — not of the mortal quality of one who "might be" a man. Therefore, we can't draw a conclusion regarding the mortal quality of one who might be a man from these premises. We don't have an *exact* bridging term here. Again, we have a relevancy problem.

Let's look now at one more example. The following "syllogism" is invalid for three reasons: (1) there's no middle term providing a bridging function, (2) each term is not repeated twice, and (3) we don't have three different premises.

Graphic 2.2(c)	An Invalid "Syllogism": No Bridging Term			
Premise	Term A	Term B	Term C	Relationship
Rule		all men	are mortal.	B = C
Fact	Socrates		is mortal.	A = C
Conclusion	Socrates		is mortal.	???????

What's going on here? This is a classic "bootstrap" argument. It's a series of statements where the conclusion is assumed in the fact premise instead of flowing from the application of the rule to the facts. We have no bridging term linking Socrates to "men." Instead, our fact premise *assumes* the answer we seek to prove, i.e., that Socrates is mortal. The "argument" is repetitious and "conclusory." Avoid this type of "reasoning" like the plague. It leads nowhere.

Let's move now from the "logical" argument to the "legal" argument.

§2.3 Creating the "Legal" Argument: Adding "Proof"

A purely logical argument, as we've seen conveyed through a syllogism, is all well and good. However, to make a convincing deductive *legal* argument, we must do more than just state the premises. We must prove them.

In a legal argument, we also use syllogisms, but, unlike a purely "logical" argument, we don't just accept that the premises are true. For example, we would not assume that "all men are mortal"—we'd demand proof of that rule. We'd also demand proof of the facts, i.e., that "Socrates is a man."

In a legal argument, we use authorities such as cases, statutes, constitutional provisions, and regulations to "prove" the legal rule. To "prove" the facts involved, we rely only on the facts we know we can prove, citing such sources as affidavits, transcripts, and at the appellate level, the Record on Appeal.[4] We avoid making assumptions of any kind— legal or factual.

The overarching structure we use in this proof is, of course, the syllogism. However, in a legal argument, we need more than just a syllogism—we need, as we explained in Chapter 1, a syllogism with "guts," a syllogism with "attitude." In other words, we need a syllogism that starts with a bang, ends with a bang, and proves all the steps in-between. We use the "BaRAC" design:

Graphic 2.3(a)	Syllogism and BaRAC Compared	
	BaRAC Design	**Syllogism**
	Bold Assertion	No syllogistic equivalent
	Rule	Rule premise
	Application	Fact premise
	Conclusion	Conclusion

For our legal argument to be valid, true,[5] and persuasive, we must do two things:

Graphic 2.3(b)	Steps in Creating a Legal Argument
First:	prove that our rule and fact premises are true:
	step # 1: gather the facts;
	step # 2: research the rule;
	step # 3: personalize the rule to fit our case and, if needed, do more research;
	step # 4: define the elements;
	step # 5: fill in all gaps in defining the rule: use inductive reasoning if necessary; and
Second:	demonstrate how our rule and fact premises logically imply all conclusions we've reached:
	step # 6: select the relevant facts and apply the personalized rule to those facts;
	step # 7: using the BaRAC design, build an outline of the argument; and
	step # 8: write the argument.

---

4. *See* Chapter 13, § 13.6.
5. An argument can be syllogistically valid, yet untrue. For example:
   All lawyers are billionaires. We are lawyers. We are billionaires.

To see how we achieve these two goals, let's look again at the Socrates syllogism. But this time, let's incorporate the design of the syllogism into a very simplified *legal* argument.

§ 2.4   The Socrates Legal Argument

Assume that we're seeking to uphold the trial court's decision that Socrates is mortal. Assume also that we've completed steps #1–5. In other words, we've

Step # 1:	gathered the facts;
Step # 2:	researched the rule; and
Steps # 3–5:	personalized the rule to fit our case. We've also defined the elements and have filled in all gaps in the rule.

The results of steps #1–5 are as follows:

Graphic 2.4(a)   Steps # 1–5: The Socrates Legal Argument

Original Rule	Explanation and Proof of Rule	Personalized Rule
All men are mortal.	The Supreme Court has held that "all men born on this Earth and living their lives upon it, will one day die." *Smythet v. Jones*, 3311 U.S. 99, 105 (2018).	If Socrates is a man born on this Earth and living his life upon it, he will one day die for he would be mortal.
Fact Premise	**Proof of Facts**	
Socrates is a man.	Socrates, a male, was born in Greece, lived in Athens, and currently resides in Pasadena, California. (R.4, 5, 7.) He is a very intelligent and insightful person, who spends most of his day in thought. (R.8.)	

Next (steps # 6 and # 7), we organize this information using the design of the syllogism:

Step # 6:	select the relevant facts and apply the personalized rule to those facts; and
Step # 7:	using the BaRAC design, build an outline of the argument.

Graphic 2.4(b)	Steps # 6-7: The Socrates Legal Argument
Bold Assertion	Socrates is mortal.
Rule	**Original rule and proof of rule:** All men are mortal. *Smythet v. Jones*, 3311 U.S. 99, 105 (2018).
	Rule explanation and proof of that explanation: The Supreme Court has held that "all men born on this Earth and living their lives upon it, will one day die." *Smythet v. Jones*, 3311 U.S. 99, 105 (2018).
	Personalized rule: If Socrates is a man born on this Earth and living his life upon it, he will one day die for he would be mortal.
Application	Socrates is a man, born on this Earth, and living his life upon it.
	Relevant facts and proof of those facts: Socrates, a male, was born in Greece, lived in Athens, and currently resides in Pasadena, California. (R.4, 5, 7.)
Conclusion	Socrates is mortal.

The following is one way to write a legal argument (step # 8) proving that Socrates is mortal:

Graphic 2.4(c)	Step # 8: The Socrates Legal Argument
Bold Assertion **Rule** **[Rule explanation]**	The lower court correctly ruled that Socrates is mortal. The Supreme Court has held that "all men born on this Earth and living their lives upon it, will one day die." *Smythet v. Jones*, 3311 U.S. 99, 105 (2018). Thus, the Court has found that all men are mortal. *See id.*
Application **[Bold Assertion]** **[Application explanation]** **Conclusion**	Here, the Record establishes that Socrates indeed is a mortal male. Socrates, a male, was born in Greece, lived his life in Athens, and currently resides in Pasadena, California. (R.4, 5, 7.) As a man, Socrates, will one day die. *See Smythet*, 3311 U.S. at 105. For this reason, this Court should affirm the lower court's judgment that Socrates is mortal.

§ 2.5   Review: The Socrates Legal Argument

Let's review what we've written in our Socrates argument.

§ 2.5(a)   The "Ba" in BaRAC: The Bold Assertion

The lower court correctly ruled that Socrates is mortal.

The bold assertion is our stated position, the conclusion we want our reader to accept as true and just. We lead with it to frame the issue and to alert the reader to the argument that follows. We leave no question in the reader's mind of our goal.

Please notice that our bold assertion is *not* a generalized statement of the law. Although we want our reader to know and understand the rule we'll be applying, we first want our reader to know the point (about our case) that we're making. Therefore, the Bold Assertion is concrete and specific to our case.

In writing the bold assertion, we follow the wisdom of Sir Winston Churchill: "If you have an important point to make, don't try to be subtle or clever. Use a pile driver. Hit the point once. Then come back and hit it again. Then hit it a third time—a tremendous whack."

After hitting our point, we use the rest of our argument to explain and to prove why this bold assertion is valid and true.

§ 2.5(b)   The "R" in BaRAC: The Rule and Rule Explanation

The Supreme Court has held that "all men born on this Earth and living their lives upon it, will one day die." *Smythet v. Jones*, 3311 U.S. 99, 105 (2018). Thus, the Court has found that all men are mortal. *See id.*

In the rule section, which includes the "rule explanation," we state and explain the applicable legal standard—the legal principle we apply to our facts to reach a conclusion.

Citation. We've cited the relevant case and the specific page number (i.e., 105) in that case where our reader can locate the legal rule: *Smythet v. Jones*, 3311 U.S. 99, 105 (2018). This citation means that the reader can turn to volume 3311 of United States Reports (a publication which prints United States Supreme Court cases) and find the *Smythet* case, beginning at page 99. The *exact* page we call to the reader's attention—the "pinpoint" citation—is page 105. This citation proves that the rule exists and that we're stating it correctly. We've also *quoted* the relevant rule to ensure that we've stated it accurately.

Rule. Further, although we addressed the rule, we did not explain it in detail. We did *not* address the facts of the case (*Smythet*) we cited or the court's reasoning. We omitted these aspects because they weren't necessary to *this* argument. In other words, we didn't need to discuss the facts of the *Smythet* case or the court's reasoning. Instead, we needed only the rule of the case and used only the rule.

However, as we examine in later Chapters, instances arise where we must fully explain a cited case to make a successful argument.[6] In those instances, notably where we argue by analogy, we address the relevant facts, issue, holding, rule, and reasoning of the cited case. In other instances, where we import the reasoning of a cited case into our argument, we explain *that* reasoning. Here, we needed only the rule from the case to complete our argument. Therefore, that is the only portion of the case we addressed.

§ 2.5(c)   The "A" in BaRAC: Application

> Here, the Record establishes that Socrates indeed is a mortal male. Socrates, a man, was born in Greece, lived his life in Athens, and currently resides in Pasadena, California. (R.4, 5, 7.) As a man, Socrates, will one day die. *See Smythet v. Jones*, 3311 U.S. at 105.

In the application section, we discuss the relevant facts of our case and show how they "fit" the stated rule. We start off with a bold assertion of our position. To make our assertions credible, we cite the specific pages in the Record on Appeal or other sources where the facts appear.

The purpose of the application section is to "prove" our factual assertions; i.e., that Socrates is a man. Our rule also requires, so we also must prove, that Socrates was born, and lived his life on Earth. If we fail to prove each of these facts, our argument fails no matter how brilliantly we've stated the rule.

Please notice that our "lead-in" sentence to the application section is itself a bold assertion, just waiting for us to prove it: "Here, the Record establishes that Socrates indeed is a mortal male." But, did we prove it? And, did we state our bold assertion correctly?

Did we prove, as we must, that Socrates is a man? What terms did we use in our bold assertion and proof to *show* that he is a man? Is "male" (the term we used) the same as "man" (the term used in our rule)? Have we made an assumption here? Have we assumed that if Socrates is a "male," he is a "man"? Should we be more precise in the terms we use? If the Record supports us, should we use the term "man," instead of "male"?

The answer is an emphatic: YES! The rule speaks in terms of the mortality of "men," not of the mortality of "males." We argued that Socrates was "male," not that he was a "man." The way we've written the argument, Socrates could be hardware—a type of connector or an electric plug. Of course, the context of our use of the term helps establish that by "male" we meant "man." However, we should rely on precisely crafted terms, rather than on context, to establish the meaning of the terms we employ.

Our argument unquestionably is valid if we match *exactly* the facts with the terms of our rule, i.e., we argue our facts using the same terms the rule requires. If the rule involves a "man or men," then we use the terms "man or men."

---

6. In Chapters 5 and 6, we address this critical subject of how to use cited cases effectively. We discuss, among other topics, the difference between using a case for its rule only, using a case to illustrate a rule, and using a case to argue by analogy. We also illustrate the difference between a rule and a holding.

Further piercing the language in our argument, can we infer that Greece, Athens, and Pasadena are "on the Earth" as required by our rule? Or, must we prove these facts? This raises the important question of what it means to have "legal" and "factual" terms match *exactly* or *close enough*. What role does language play in writing our argument? The answer is—a HUGE role, and one we'll discuss at length in Chapter 3: Language and Relevancy.

§ 2.5(d)   The "C" in BaRAC: Conclusion

For this reason, this Court should affirm the lower court's judgment that Socrates is mortal.

In the conclusion, we tell the reader exactly what we want. For our argument to be persuasive, we must reach a conclusion. Indeed, unless we state a conclusion, we haven't actually argued. Note that the conclusion will often be similar to, or even the same as, our bold assertion.

§ 2.6   The Role of Inductive Generalization in the Legal Argument

Although deductive reasoning is the strongest method of reasoning—the conclusion follows inevitably from the premises—it's not the only way to go. We can also reason inductively. Inductive reasoning is reasoning by example. In other words, from examining the holdings of specific cases, we fashion a generalized rule we then apply to our facts.

We also use inductive reasoning in making *policy* arguments. We consider (from cases, observations, or data) the "rights" and "wrongs," fashion a rule regarding what is "right," and then apply that rule.

Dan Hunter, in an insightful article on the power of inductive inference in law, explains the inductive process as follows:

> Induction is, generally, the process of taking a number of specific cases or instances, classifying them into categories according to relevant attributes and outcomes, and deriving a broadly applicable rule from them. That is, we take a number of isolated experiences and attempt to explain them by a general rule that covers all the instances examined.[7]

Hunter explains that "induction is central to human reasoning":[8]

> For example, prior to any theory about the movements of the heavens, early humans noticed that on day one the sun rose in the east and set in the west. The same thing, they saw, happened on day two, day three, and so on. From many observational instances they were able to induce the rule: 'The sun always

---

7. Dan Hunter, *No Wilderness of Single Instances: Inductive Inference in Law*, 48 J. Legal Educ. 365, 369 (September 1998).

8. *Id.* at 365.

rises in the east and sets in the west.' This rule could then be applied to predict the outcome of unknown, future cases, without having to refer to each past observational instance. If asked whether the sun would rise in the east on a particular day—say, January 1, 2000, in the Justinian calendar that we fol- low—an early human could confidently answer yes.[9]

Let's look at an example of inductive reasoning:

The case of the green apple. Assume that we've been hired to solve the case of the green apple.[10] At issue is whether the green apple goes into a basket. (Seems simple enough; either it does or it doesn't go in.) The holding will be either "yes, the apple goes in" or "no, the apple doesn't go in."

Assume that we've uncovered four cases, described as follows:

Graphic 2.6	Case Holdings — Inductive Generalization
Case	**Holding**
W	Green pears go into the basket.
X	Green bananas go into the basket.
Y	Green marbles go into the basket.
Z	Green fabric goes into the basket.

Although we don't know the rule or reasoning of these cases, we do know their holdings. Using "inductive generalization," we develop a general rule from our cases that green things (pears, bananas, marbles, and fabric) go into the basket. Using this as our rule, we argue deductively that because our green apple is green, it too goes into the basket. We have generalized, or induced, a rule from specific case holdings. The more holdings supporting the rule, the more likely the rule will be accepted.

There is, however, no magic number of cases which will *guarantee* that our generalized rule is correct. In crafting an "induced" rule, the best we can do is establish a sound basis for our generalization. We do this by citing authorities, explaining the relevant common denominator in their holdings, and ensuring that no other aspect of the cases undercuts our generalization. The larger our sample, the better our chance of being correct.

Let's next compare inductive reasoning to reasoning by analogy.

§ 2.7   The Role of Analogy in Legal Argument

We intuitively know how to reason by analogy. We do it whenever we compare one thing to another. In analogical reasoning, we recognize a common form in similar or dissimilar things. We look to how one thing resembles another.

---

9. *Id.* at 369.

10. This hypothetical is ours, but it was inspired by one developed by Lis Keller and reported by Janet Kent Gionfriddo of Boston College Law School in Vol. 12, No. 1 of *The Second Draft* of the Bulletin of the Legal Writing Institute (Nov. 1997).

Analogical reasoning is inherent in the human condition, commonly expressing itself in our language and in court opinions. One example involves *Lucas v. Earl*, 281 U.S. 111 (1930). Before there was such a thing as a "joint" income tax return, Earl, a California lawyer, had contracted with his wife to give her half of all he'd earned, allowing him to be taxed at a lesser rate. The IRS and Justice Holmes, however, would have none of it. After stating that the tax could not be "escaped by anticipatory arrangements and contracts however skillfully devised to prevent the salary when paid from vesting even for a second in the man who earned it," Holmes hit the nail on the head with a beautiful analogy: "[W]e think that no distinction can be taken according to the motives leading to the arrangement by which the fruits are attributed to a different tree from that on which they grew." *Id.* at 115.

We clearly see that tree, those fruits, and how impossible it is to win against the IRS. Justice Holmes's image cuts through reason and goes right to the core of our understanding. The tree can't deny the fruit it's produced. Period. That's the power of analogical thinking.

When we reason by analogy, we recognize a common design in similar or even dissimilar things. We're "reasoning from the particular to the particular, instead of [as in inductive generalization, reasoning] from the particular to the general."[11] Man to tree; earnings to fruit. Unlike inductive reasoning, reasoning by analogy requires us to look not to the "*quantity* of instances, but upon the *quality* of parallelism between things."[12] Man labors to earn money; tree labors to bear fruit.

Moreover, unlike deductive reasoning, reasoning by analogy does not require an exact "match" between rule and fact. Certainly a man is not a tree, but each labors and produces. Being *close enough* hits the target. In analogical legal reasoning, we seek out a common design in a similar or dissimilar case and apply that design to our case. Permit us to explain.

In deductive reasoning, we use the following "formula":

$$\text{If } B = C; \text{ and } A = B; \text{ then } A = C.$$

Graphic 2.7(a)		Deductive Relationships		
Premise	Term A	Term B *bridging term*	Term C	Relationship
Rule		All men	are mortal.	B = C
Fact	Socrates is	a man.		A = B
Conclusion	Socrates is		mortal.	A = C

However, in analogical reasoning, our "formula" takes this shape:

$$\text{If } B \text{ is similar to } C; \text{ and } A \text{ is similar to } B; \text{ then } A \text{ is similar to } C.$$

---

11. Ruggero J. Aldisert, *Winning on Appeal: Better Briefs and Oral Argument* 274 (1996).
12. *Id.* at 275.

As the following graphics illustrate, the design of the underlying argument we're implicitly making when we argue by analogy follows generally the design of a deductive argument. However, we do not mean to imply that analogical reasoning *is* deductive reasoning; it isn't.

Graphic 2.7(b)   Analogical Relationships: General Structure

Rule		Similar cases	should be decided similarly.
Fact	Our case is	similar to a prior case.	
Conclusion	Our case		should be decided similarly to the prior case.

Graphic 2.7(c)   Analogical Relationships: Specific Structure

Rule		Similar cases	should be decided similarly.
Fact	*Our* case	is similar to *Case 1. Case 1* involved *facts* a, b, and c. At *issue* was d. The court *held* e. Employing rule f, the court *reasoned* 1, 2, and 3. *Our* case involves *facts* a, b, and c (or facts very similar to them). At *issue* is d (or a very similar issue to d).	
Conclusion	*Our* case		should be decided similarly to *Case 1.* The court should employ rule f; reason 1, 2, and 3; and hold e.

Thus, in analogical reasoning, we compare our case to a cited case. As lawyers, if we find a precedent case with

(1) the same issue as our issue;

(2) facts similar to our facts;

(3) sound reasoning; and

(4) an outcome favorable to our position —

we've hit the "mother lode." We've found a case "on all fours" with our case. We argue that our court should apply the reasoning and rule of the cited case to our case and reach the same decision. If that case is binding on our court, then we're "home free."

If the cited case has facts and an issue merely similar to our case, we can still reason analogically. However, we'll likely need to explain why the differences between the cases aren't important.

In either circumstance, the very design of the analogical argument requires us to explain the precedent case to our reader, and identify its rule and reasoning. Without this background, our reader can't begin to reason by analogy and can't apply the rule and reasoning of the cited case to our case. When we're drawing comparisons between cases, we've got to first explain those cases. Trees and fruit, we understand. What happened in *Tree v. Fruit*, we don't know unless we're told.

What is reasoning by analogy? In reasoning by analogy, we're extracting the reasoning of the cited case and asking the court to apply that reasoning to our case. The "reasoning" of a cited case is *how* the court applied the rule of the cited case to the facts of the cited case. The reasoning is not the holding (i.e., how the court ultimately answered the issue posed in the case.) Nor is the reasoning the rule of the case. This concept is so vital that we'll say it again: The reasoning of the cited case is *not* the holding of the cited case, and it's not the rule of the cited case. It's *how* the court applied the rule to the facts.

In reasoning by analogy, we apply the reasoning—not just the rule or the holding— of the cited case to our case. Our BaRAC design for reasoning by analogy takes on the following form:

Graphic 2.7(d)	The BaRAC Design in Analogical Reasoning
Bold assertion	This Court should decide this case as the court in *Case X* decided *Case X*.
Rule	Applying the rule that _____, the court in *Case X* reasoned _____.
Application	Similarly, this Court should apply rule _____, and reason _____.
Conclusion	This Court should decide this case as the court in *Case X* decided *Case X*.

To use our "truffle" metaphor, it's not enough to know only what the shell (holding) is. We've got to know what's in the "filling." It's the filling that we "pour" from a cited case into our case. As we'll see in the next section, it's the filling that *defines* the case.

§ 2.8   The Limited Value of the Holding: The Case of the Green Apple

The holding of a case, standing alone, doesn't mean a hill of beans when we're trying to argue by analogy. As we've seen, however in § 2.6, the holding is useful when we're arguing by inductive generalization. The following hypothetical explains these observations.

Our case. Let's return to our case of the green apple. Assume that we've been hired to determine whether the green apple goes into a basket. Assume further that the only law involves two cited cases, described as follows:

Case Holdings
Case #1   The court decided that a green pear goes into a basket.

Case #2   The court decided that a red apple does not go into a basket.

OK. So we know that a green pear goes into a basket but a red apple doesn't. Too bad we don't have a green pear or a red apple in our case.[13] We have, instead, a green apple; we have the "in-between" case that keeps us lawyers employed.

---

13. Warning: this statement is a *red herring*, as we'll soon discuss. It's good practice to read footnotes. Our professors taught us that most of the law was in the footnotes. We think they were right.

The first question we ask in applying these cases is whether they are "binding" on our court.[14] If they are, then our court must follow them. If not, then our court is free to consider them persuasive or not. Of course, consistent with the principle of *stare decisis*, our court should attempt to decide "like cases alike." Let's assume that case #1 and case #2 are from our court, and therefore, are persuasive, but not binding authority, since as pointed out in § 1.2, courts can overrule their own prior decisions.

Can we answer our issue? Can we decide whether that green apple goes into the basket? The answer is a resounding, "NO!" Although we have "precedent" (cases #1 and #2), we don't know the rules and reasoning the court applied in those cases. All we have is the holding of those cases. All we can say is that the one green pear in case #1 went into a basket; and that the one red apple in case #2 did not go into a basket. These holdings, standing alone without any reasoning supporting them, are virtually useless.

Nonetheless, we have a job to do here. We must decide what to do with our green apple. But, to make this decision, we must know what rule applies to our facts.

Can we create a rule? Because the two precedent cases didn't provide any reasoning, we'll have to come up with that reasoning, including a rule, on our own. Can we do this? Can we, mere mortal lawyers, create a rule? Sure we can, and we use inductive reasoning to do so. Can we, however, be certain that the rule we develop or synthesize from these two cases will be correct? Absolutely not. Are we really going to "make up" a rule? Absolutely so. But we can't just throw any rule together.

The rule we develop must be consistent with both case #1 and case #2 and be crafted so that both cases are consistent with each other. In other words, we reconcile these two cases to create a legal "theory" consistent with both precedents and with our case. In reconciling these cases, we're judging what is and what isn't important.

As Stephen Hawking explained in *A Brief History of Time*:

> A theory is a good theory if it satisfies two requirements: it must accurately describe a large class of observations on the basis of a model that contains only a few arbitrary elements, and it must make definite predictions about the results of future observations.

Let's look at seven possible theories, charted in Graphic 2.8 on the facing page, that we might use in deciding our case.

As this example illustrates, the rule and theory of our case "drives" or determines which facts are relevant. If our rule is that all green things go into the basket, then the color green is highly important and highly relevant. The fact that our apple is green determines the outcome of our case.

We also see that the mere holdings of cases do little to help us decide our case. Out of the seven possible theories we've asserted, four may lead to a conclusion. However, out of those four possibilities, the apple stayed out in three instances and went into the basket in one. Which is correct? Who knows?

---

14. We discuss "binding" versus "persuasive" authority in Chapter 5, § 5.2—§ 5.4.

Graphic 2.8   Attempts to Reconcile the Case Holdings, Develop a Rule, and Apply That Rule to Our Case

#	Theory	Logic	Explanation
(1)	color is important: may work	rule	Only green things go in.
		reasoning	Because it was green, the pear (case #1) went in. Because the apple wasn't green (case #2), it stayed out.
		application	Because our green apple is green, it goes in.
(2)	fruit is important: won't work	rule	Fruit may or may not go in.
		reasoning [too indefinite]	Because the pear (case #1) was a fruit, it went in. Because the apple (case #2) was a fruit, it stayed out.
		application	We can't reach a conclusion. Our rule is too indefinite to apply.
(3)	fruit type is important: may work	rule	Only pears go in.
		reasoning	Because the pear was a pear (case #1), it went in. Because the apple wasn't a pear (case #2), it stayed out.
		application	Because our green apple isn't a pear, it stays out.
(4)	shape is important: may work	rule	Only pear-shaped objects go in.
		reasoning	Because the pear was pear-shaped (case #1), it went in. Because the apple (case #2) was not pear-shaped, it stayed out.
		application	Because our green apple is not pear-shaped, it stays out.
(5)	uniqueness is important: may work	rule	Only apples stay out.
		reasoning	Because the pear wasn't an apple (case #1), it went in. Because the apple was an apple (case #2), it stayed out.
		application	Because our green apple is an apple, it stays out.
(6)	context is important: probably won't work	rule	The basket can only hold one thing, and that was the pear of case #1.
		reasoning [questionable]	The basket can only hold one thing; the pear of case #1. Because the basket was filled with the pear of case #1, the apple of case #2 didn't go in. (But, was case #1 decided prior to case #2?) (Is the basket the same?)
		application	Because the basket can hold no more, our apple stays out. (But, is the pear from case #1 still in the basket?) (What assumptions are we making that we shouldn't make?)
(7)	arbitrary: probably won't work	rule	Whatever the judge likes goes in.
		reasoning [questionable]	Because the judge liked the green pear (case #1), it went in. Because the judge didn't like the red apple (case #2), it stayed out.
		application	We can't reach a conclusion in our case of the green apple. We don't know whether the judge likes our green apple or not.

The bottom line. Until we know the reasoning of the court in case #1 and case #2, we can only guess the outcome in our case. We can't reason by analogy here because we don't know the reasoning of the cited cases. Further, we can't use deductive reasoning because we don't know the rule of the cases. Nor can we reason by inductive generalization. Because we have only two "precedents," we don't have a large enough sample to derive a valid, broadly applicable rule.[15]

The case of the green pear. Let's now change the facts. Assume that we're not dealing with a green *apple*, but instead with a green *pear*. Further assume that our green pear is identical to the pear that went into the basket in case #1. Assume also that we know only the holdings of cases #1 and #2. Can we now say with certainty whether our green pear goes into that basket? NO. Surprised? (Not if you've read the footnotes.)

Although we want the law to be "certain" and want to tell our client that because the green pear went into the basket in case #1, so too will *our* green pear—we can't reach this conclusion. Until we know why that green pear went into the basket in case #1, we can't state that our pear will have the same fate.

Through inductive reasoning, we can generalize a rule from case holdings, but—especially where we're dealing with only two cases—we can't be certain that our generalized rule is correct. At best we can only hazard a guess.

Perhaps the green pear went into the basket in case #1 because the judge in that case wanted it to go in. Perhaps case #1 rests on the judge's completely arbitrary decision. Or, perhaps the unique context of case #1 determined the outcome: there was but one basket and but one thing (the pear) that could fill it. Once filled, that's it—*our* pear is out.

Our "green apple" and "green pear" hypotheticals illustrate a fundamental principle: Unless we know the rule of a cited case, we can't convincingly use that case in a deductive or in an analogical argument. Both deductive and analogical reasoning require a starting point: a rule. A holding is not a rule.

Once we have a rule, we can reason deductively. Once we understand how the court applied that rule to the facts of the cited case (i.e., the court's reasoning) we can reason by analogy and apply that cited case to our case. If we want our reader to agree with our analysis, we must prove that our case is similar enough to the cited case to warrant a similar holding. To do this, we've got to tell our reader the relevant facts, issue, holding, rule, and reasoning of the cited cases. We explain *why* that green pear went into the basket and *why* that red apple stayed out.

Although analogical reasoning can be extremely persuasive, it's not without its drawbacks. One problem is that it's an imprecise "science." The key to analogical reasoning lies in recognizing that no two situations will be identical. Indeed, if we ran into a precedent case identical to our case (and with reasoning we could articulate) we'd most likely settle and never take the case to trial or appeal.

The overwhelming majority of the analogical reasoning we do in law does not involve applying "precedent" on "all fours" with our case. (Our truffle isn't identical to an

---

15. Compare this to our hypothetical in § 2.6, where our sample of cases was large enough to induce a rule.

existing one.) Instead, it involves considering the differences and similarities between our case and previously decided cases, and reconciling those differences and similarities. We determine which—the differences or similarities—are more important in deciding our case. That's another way of saying that we make choices involving relevancy.

As Professor H. L. A. Hart put it:

> [T]hough 'Treat like cases alike and different cases differently' is a central element in the idea of justice, it is by itself incomplete and, until supplemented, cannot afford any determinate guide to conduct.... [U]ntil it is established what resemblances and differences are relevant, 'Treat like cases alike' must remain an empty form. To fill it we must know when, for the purposes in hand, cases are to be regarded as alike and what differences are relevant.[16]

In the section below, we explore how to make choices involving relevancy and how to reconcile differences and highlight similarities among rules.

§ 2.9   Designing a Rule from Several Cases: Inductive Reasoning Strikes Again

Deciphering rules. Rules are "if-then" propositions. *If* certain facts are present, *then* a certain legal consequence follows. A rule connects a legal consequence to a generalized fact pattern. In applying a rule to our case, we compare our facts to the generalized statement of facts in the rule. How our facts "fit" the rule's generalized facts determines the outcome of our case. If there's a close enough match between our facts and the rule's requirements, the rule is satisfied.

Often, a rule will be easy to identify, as when it appears as a statute, an administrative regulation, a constitutional provision, or a "rule" of civil procedure. However, as we've already seen, rules derived from judicial opinions can be difficult to identify and to articulate.

In some cases, courts label the rule for us, indicating that the "applicable rule in this case is" so and such. However, in many cases the rule is unclear, and as a consequence, is subject to varying interpretations. The rule is the governing principle under which the case was decided. However, deciphering a rule is difficult, if not impossible, when the court states the rule in vague terms; in the alternative (without indicating which of two or three choices is *the* decisive factor); or as a conglomeration of factors (with no instruction indicating how or whether the factors are to be weighed).

To make matters worse, the rule the court has applied in a prior case was, in essence, derived to "fit" the particular facts of that case. It may or may not have been formulated to apply to situations not present in that case. Indeed, although some do so, courts have no authority to render "advisory" or "hypothetical" opinions concerning issues and facts not before them. They decide only the issue presented on the facts of the "instant" case. Thus, a rule expressed in a case technically is designed to "fit" *only* the

---

16. H.L.A. Hart, *The Concept of Law* 155 (1961).

facts of that particular case. Yet, each case has an impact far greater than the narrow scope of its own facts.

As lawyers, we use prior cases as problem-solving tools. We interpret judicial opinions and extract from them rules relevant to our case. It's a cold day in Miami when our client presents us with a fact pattern and issue identical to a prior case. Instead, the facts and issues we deal with differ from those in the reported cases. It's our job to decipher those precedents, extract from them rules governing our client's case, and suggest an outcome favorable to our client.

Because each prior case deals with a limited factual setting, we often must consult many cases to cover the range of facts and issues present in our case. We then synthesize those cases and design a rule to "fit" our case. When we design a rule in this fashion, i.e., when we derive an applicable rule from specific cases, we engage in *inductive* reasoning. The following exercise illustrates this process. Here's what we consider:

Our green apple case (yet again!). Assume that we're still trying to solve our green apple case. Does *our* green apple go into the basket? Let's further assume that (this time) instead of knowing just the holding of cases, we also know the court's reasoning or at least the factors the court considered important in deciding the precedent cases. Let's also assume that the following four cases were decided by the highest court in our state and are binding on our court.

Case # 1

This case involves but one issue: whether the banana goes into the basket. After careful consideration, we determine that it does. Whether green or yellow, a banana is a soft fruit which easily could be damaged if left unprotected. Accordingly, the trial court acted properly in finding that it should go into the basket.

Case # 2

The coconut, still in its shell, stays out of the basket. Its large size and weight would adversely impact the basket and preclude placing any other object in the basket. Accordingly, we affirm the trial court's judgment finding that the coconut stays out.

Case # 3

The trial court acted correctly in excluding the green cucumber from the basket. The cucumber is bumpy and slick and does not belong in the basket. Moreover, it is a vegetable, and only fruits, to date, have been permitted in the basket.

Case # 4

The orange does not go into the basket, as the trial court correctly found. The orange, brightly colored, will be noticed by customers even without the additional adornment the basket provides.

Let's now fashion a rule for each of these cases. We use inductive reasoning: we generalize a rule from the specific factors the court considered were important.

Graphic 2.9(a)		Inducing a Rule from the Four Cases: Case Comparison Chart		
Case	Fact	Holding	Factors	Rule
#1	banana	in	soft fruit, easily damaged if left unprotected	Soft fruits, i.e., those which could be easily damaged if left unprotected, go in.
#2	coconut	out	in shell, size and weight would adversely impact the basket, precludes placing other items into basket	Weighty (and large) items which adversely impact the basket and preclude placing other objects in the basket stay out.
#3	green cucumber	out	bumpy and slick, a vegetable; only fruits (to date) have been permitted in the basket	Bumpy and slick non-fruit items stay out.
#4	orange	out	brightly colored, noticeable by customers, no need for adornment basket provides	Brightly colored items which will be noticed by customers without the additional adornment the basket provides stay out.

The following is but one possible interpretation of a generalized rule which harmonizes, or makes consistent, the rules of the four cases.

Graphic 2.9(b)	The Generalized, Consistent Rule
case # 1	Soft fruits, such as bananas, which need the basket's protection, go in. However, weighty and large items, such as a coconut in its shell,
case # 2	which could adversely impact the basket and preclude placing other objects into the basket, stay out. Bumpy and slick non-fruit items,
case # 3	such as cucumbers, also stay out; as do brightly colored items, such as oranges, which customers will notice without the additional
case # 4	adornment the basket provides.

Now we have our rule. From factors in an individual case, we induced the rule of *that* case. From the rules of our four cases, we induced an overarching, generalized rule. Here's what we've done:

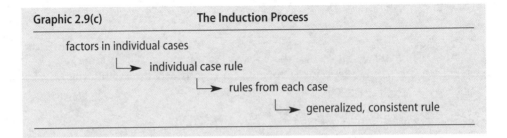

Graphic 2.9(c)	The Induction Process

factors in individual cases
⤷ individual case rule
⤷ rules from each case
⤷ generalized, consistent rule

§ 2.10   Using Deductive and Analogical Reasoning: Applying the Generalized Rule to Our Case

In applying the generalized rule to our green apple case, we use deductive and analogical reasoning. We state the rule, apply it to our facts using analogical reasoning, and reach a conclusion. The following graphic illustrates one of many ways we might apply our generalized rule to our case and what the "syllogism" of our case might look like.

Graphic 2.10(a)   **Applying the Rule to Our Facts**

Premise	Term A	Term B *bridging term*	Term C
Rule		1. Weighty and large items, such as a coconut in its shell, which could adversely impact the structure of the basket and preclude placing any other object into the basket; and 2. Brightly colored items, such as oranges, which customer would notice without the additional adornment the basket provides 3. Soft fruits, such as bananas, which need the basket's protection	 stay out. go in.
Facts	Our green apple	is not weighty, is not large, would not adversely impact the structure of the basket, would not preclude placing other objects in the basket, is not brightly colored, but is a fruit, is soft, and needs the basket's protection.	
Conclusion	Our green apple		goes in.

Please note that we've reorganized the rule by placing the "out of the basket" rules first. Moreover, we didn't address the "cucumber rule" of case #3 because we've decided that this rule, involving non-fruit items, is not relevant to our green apple case. If, however, the court in the cucumber case had found that the green color of the cucumber was significant, then the cucumber case would be relevant. We've also assumed that our apple is not brightly colored.

In the next graphic, we've written this rule application in BaRAC form. For the purpose of illustrating the underlying logic involved in applying the rule to the facts, we've been extremely inclusive here.

Graphic 2.10(b)   Using Deductive and Analogical Reasoning to Apply the Generalized, Consistent Rule

---

Note: Our writing here is in the design of a predictive legal memo.

Bold Assertion	The court will likely find that our green apple should go into the basket.
General Rule	Items which stay out of the basket include: (1) weighty and large items, such as a coconut in its shell, which could adversely impact the basket and preclude placing any other object into the basket; and (2) brightly colored items, such as oranges, which customers will notice without the additional adornment the basket provides. *Case #2; Case #4*. On the other hand, soft fruits, such as bananas, which need the basket's protection, go in. *Case #1*.
Rule Explanation in terms of the personalized rule	If our green apple is weighty enough to adversely impact the basket and preclude placing other objects within, it will stay out. *See Case #2*. It will also stay out if it is "brightly colored" enough for customers to notice without the adornment the basket provides. *See Case #4*. However, if our apple is so soft that it needs the basket's protection, then it will go in. *See Case #1*.
Transition to application bold assertion	Here, we make a choice of importance. That choice is whether the weight, size, and color of the apple are more important than the apple's "softness," i.e., its need for protection. For the reasons below, the court will likely find that the apple's softness is the decisive factor and hold that the apple should go into the basket.
Application **analogical reasoning: weight**	The court will likely find that our green apple is probably not weighty enough to adversely impact the basket. Although it probably weighs more than a banana (*see Case #1*) and is closer in weight to an orange (*see Case #4*), our apple is likely not as weighty as a coconut in its shell. *See Case #2*.
analogical reasoning: size	Moreover, our apple is probably not large enough to preclude placing other items in the basket. The only size the court has mentioned as being too large is that of a coconut in its shell. *See Case #2*. Although our apple is probably closest in size to the orange in *Case #4*,

	that orange was excluded from the basket *on other grounds*, (i.e., not because of its size or weight, but because of its color).
analogical reasoning: color	Further, the court will likely find that our apple is not brightly colored enough to be excluded from the basket. In *Case #4*, the court reasoned that an orange was "brightly colored" and therefore noticeable enough for customers to see without the added adornment of the basket. Unfortunately, the court did not define what it meant by "brightly colored." Nonetheless, a green apple is likely not as "brightly colored" as an orange. Moreover, color does not seem to be as important to the court as other factors. If it were, then the yellow banana in *Case #1* probably should have been excluded from the basket on the "ground" of its "brightness," rather than included on the ground of its "softness."
analogical reasoning: softness	Finally, and as the decisive factor, the court will likely find that our apple needs the protection the basket affords and, for that reason, should go in. Although not as soft as a banana (*see Case #1*), our apple is likely in more need of protection than were the coconut and the orange. *See Case #2*. Common sense tells us that an apple bruises more easily than does a coconut in its shell or an orange. (Because the court in *Case #4* did not mention the "need to be protected" factor in deciding to exclude the orange from the basket, we cannot use that case as authority for this point.)
Conclusion	Based on the above reasoning, the court will likely find that our apple should go into the basket.

Whew! All of this just to decide where to place an apple? You bet! This is the stuff of the law. Reconciling precedents and predicting the court's action is what lawyers do. Are there any clear answers in our green apple case? No. Could we have made a prediction, supported by precedent, that the apple should not go into the basket? Sure. Could most decided cases have "gone the other way"? Absolutely. The irony of the law is that it's supposed to provide certainty, yet it is itself uncertain. Resting on the foundation of language, it has no other choice.

A note on reading cases. Now, when good lawyers (and judges) read a case, they don't sit passively by and think to themselves, "how touching." To the contrary, they read cases actively. They question every word. They make choices as to what is and isn't important in the case, and compare and contrast that case to their case. Unlike law students reading cases in law school to extract the "black letter rule," lawyers read cases within a problem-solving context.

Lawyers, using cases as tools, closely scrutinize language, understanding that one adjective or adverb in a case can make the difference, for example, between whether someone who kills another spends the rest of his life in prison ("premeditated"), is executed ("aggravating circumstances"), or is set free ("self-defense").

In law, life and death decisions literally turn on the meaning of words. Reading the law *is* different from reading other materials. Skipping over an adjective in a John

Grisham novel doesn't amount to much; skipping over an adjective in a case or a statute can be malpractice. To be thorough, we've got to read cases — even those about pears and apples — slowly, deliberately. And, we never make assumptions of fact or law; we always ask "what's not here" as well as "what is here."

In reading the law, we read every footnote and understand every word. If we're unsure, we go to the dictionary. We read the concurring and dissenting opinions. And, if we have time, we even review the briefs filed with the case.[17]

As lawyers, it's our job to make sense of the law and to make the law make sense — one case at a time.

§ 2.11   Exercises — Determining a Legal Rule: Inducing a Rule from Several Cases[18]

Exercise 1. Assume you are a law clerk in the State of Utopia. You know that at least the following crimes are considered felonies in your jurisdiction: arson, assault, murder, rape, and "grand theft auto" (theft of an automobile, truck, or van worth at least $1,000). You also know that burglary is a common law crime in Utopia, but you are unsure of its elements.

In conducting research, you find the following Utopia burglary cases, all of which are "good law," that is, they have not been reversed or overruled. Each of the defendants had been indicted for burglary.

State v. Ash: Defendant Ash, using a crowbar, broke into a house owned by his neighbor at noon on June 30, carrying a can of gasoline and a book of matches. Ash's motion to dismiss the indictment was granted.

State v. Elm: Defendant Elm broke into his neighbor's garage, which was separated from the neighbor's house by a fence, at 10:59 p.m. on July 17, carrying equipment that is used to "hot wire" automobiles. A witness is prepared to testify that she had seen Elm hanging around the scene earlier in the day, at the time that the victim drove his new BMW into the garage. Elm's motion to dismiss the indictment was granted.

State v. Fir: Defendant Fir was estranged from her boyfriend when she entered the house in which they resided by breaking a window at about midnight. Fir was carrying a gun at the time. Witnesses were prepared to testify that they had heard Fir say earlier that evening that she would kill her boyfriend before letting him leave her. Fir's motion to dismiss the indictment was granted.

State v. Oak (Oak I): Defendant Oak entered the victim's home at about 11 p.m. by walking through an open side door. Several women who lived near the current victim's home were prepared to testify that Oak had entered their homes and raped them. Oak's motion to dismiss the indictment was granted.

---

17. Briefs of United States Supreme Court cases are online. Briefs of other cases are available from the individual court.

18. We've made some slight alterations to Exercises 1 and 2 which were developed by Professor Sanford Greenberg. We thank him for allowing us to use them.

State v. Oak (Oak II): Defendant Oak entered a victim's home by opening the garage door at about midnight. Several women who lived near the victim's home were prepared to testify that Oak had entered their homes and raped them. Oak's motion to dismiss the indictment was denied.

State v. Holly: Defendant Holly was a homeless person who spent her days panhandling on a city sidewalk. At about 9:45 p.m. on the first cold night of the season, she entered (through a closed but unlocked window) a home that she believed to be unoccupied, carrying a newspaper, a book of matches, and a bag of wood. After she entered, she used these items to start a fire in the home's fireplace. Just as the fire got going, the owner of the home returned and began calling Holly "a scumbag" and a "leech on society." Holly became enraged and hit the owner over the head with a poker she found next to the fireplace, seriously injuring the owner. Holly's motion to dismiss the indictment was granted.

State v. Maple: At about 11:00 p.m. on March 10, while carrying a Molotov cocktail and a lighter, Defendant Maple broke a glass window of her ex-boyfriend's home and stuck her hand inside to undo the window safety latch. At that moment, her ex-boyfriend, who had heard the glass break, saw her and called the police. Maple's motion to dismiss the indictment was denied.

Based on the above cases, what do you think the elements of burglary are in the State of Utopia? Starting with the cases that *did* satisfy all the elements of burglary (Oak II and Maple) may help you to figure out the rule. Why was each of the indictments other than Oak II and Maple dismissed?

Exercise 2. Now that you know the common law definition of burglary in Utopia, do you think our client, Jill, will be indicted for burglary? What additional information, if any, do you need to answer the question? Here are the facts:

> Jill is a 21-year old woman who was obsessively in love with Jack, the 17-year old boy who lived next door to her. Jill obtained a "love potion," which supposedly released the inhibitions of anyone who drank it. While Jack's parents were away for the evening on the Fourth of July, Jill entered their home at 8:15 p.m. through a closed, but unlocked, sliding screen door. She tricked Jack into drinking the potion by telling him it was a new tropical fruit drink. Rather than becoming amorous, Jack became violently ill and nearly died.

Exercise 3. A Logic Quiz

Please assume the following:

(a) The Crime = element 1 + element 2.

(b) element 1 = X.

(c) element 2 = Y.

Based on these three assumptions, why are the following statements *incorrect*?

(1) Jones should be found guilty of committing the Crime because he met element 1.

(2) Jones did B, therefore he met element 1.

(3) Because the Crime equals element 1 plus element 2, Jones should be found guilty.

Chapter Review
Reasoning: Deductive, Inductive, and Analogical

- "Deductive" reasoning takes the following form: if we accept that A=B, and B=C, then we must accept that A=C. In other words, the conclusion follows inevitably from the prior two premises.

- Relevancy problems occur when we don't have a "fit" between our rule and our facts. The rule ultimately determines which facts are relevant.

- A legal argument requires proof of the rule and proof of the facts.

- "Inductive" reasoning is reasoning by example: from examining the holdings of specific cases, we fashion a general rule consistent with those holdings. Or, from specific factors in a case, we fashion a rule consistent with those factors.

- In reasoning by analogy, we reason from the particular to the particular, recognizing a common form in similar or dissimilar cases. We cannot reason by analogy from a cited case to our case unless we know the court's reasoning in the cited case.

- By following the BaRAC design, as charted below, we can write our argument (using the general form of deductive reasoning) and incorporate both inductive and analogical reasoning where necessary:

The BaRAC Design for Writing Our Argument

Bold assertion	State the point we seek to prove.
Rule	State the rule we use in proving the point. Cite the authority for this rule. We may have to induce this rule from factors the court has discussed in a cited case. Or, we may have to induce a generalized, consistent rule from a series of rules derived from several cases.
Rule Explanation (personalized rule)	Explain what the rule means as it applies to our case, and cite the authority (or authorities) for that explanation.
Application	Bold assertion: assert that the rule applies or doesn't apply to our facts.
Application explanation	Relevant facts and proof of those facts: Explain how the facts "fit" or don't "fit" the rule. Prove all conclusions by citing factual authority. Within this context, i.e., where we are comparing our case to a cited case, we may also be arguing by analogy.
Conclusion	State the point we seek to prove.

Chapter 3

Language and Relevancy

"Words are the most powerful drug used by mankind."

—Rudyard Kipling

" 'When I use a word,' Humpty Dumpty said in rather a scornful tone, 'it means just what I choose it to mean—neither more nor less.'

'The question is,' said Alice, 'whether you can make words mean so many different things.'

'The question is,' said Humpty Dumpty, 'which is to be master—that's all.' "

—Lewis Carroll

§3.1 Language and Relevancy in the Legal Argument

"The difference between the *almost* right word and the *right* word is really a large matter—it's the difference between the lightning bug and the lightning."

— Mark Twain

The fly in the ointment of legal writing is language itself. As lawyers, we have a "love/hate" relationship with it. If language is our stock in trade (and it is), then *relevancy* is what keeps that stock organized—all lined up nice and neat, ordered and orderly. In a purely logical argument, we have no relevancy problems because we express terms and relationships through precise symbols instead of through words. For example, we can write the following argument using nothing but symbols:

Graphic 3.1(a)		The Logical Argument		
Premise	Term A	Term B *bridging term*	Term C	Relationship
Rule		# =	&	B = C
Fact	∧ =	#		A = B
Conclusion	∧ =		&	A = C

In other words, if # equals &, and ∧ equals #, then ∧ equals &. The symbol # is the middle, bridging term allowing us to reach the conclusion that ∧ equals &. The terms are clear. There's no relevancy problem here. We need not interpret any language or make any inferences to reach our conclusion.

However, unlike a purely logical or mathematical argument expressed through precise symbols, we express legal arguments through language, through words. Or as William Shakespeare said in *Hamlet*: "Words, words, words." Of course, old Will also said, "[L]et's kill all the lawyers," but that's literally another story.

For example, if our rule states that "All men are mortal," but our facts tell us that "Socrates is a dog," we can't deduce that "Socrates is mortal"—even if he is. As the graphic below illustrates, we have a relevancy problem.

Graphic 3.1(b)		A Relevancy Problem			
Premise	Term A	Term B	Term C	Term D	Relationship
Rule		All men	are mortal.		B = C
Fact	Socrates is			a dog.	A = D
Conclusion	Socrates is		mortal.		???????

We've introduced into our argument a term (dog) which doesn't appear in our rule. Nor do we have any "bridging" term spanning the gap between the rule and our facts.

To cure this relevancy problem, we either reevaluate the facts or reevaluate the rule—something's got to give. In other words, we alter our argument by (1) better matching the facts to the rule or (2) refining or redefining the rule. Language, of course, is the tool we use to make this adjustment.

Because we can't change the fact that Socrates is a dog, we must change the rule. Here's one solution, which fixes our relevancy problem:

Graphic 3.1(c)	Fixing the Problem by Expanding the Rule			
Premise	**Term A**	**Term B** *bridging term*	**Term C**	**Relationship**
Rule		All men **and dogs**	are mortal.	B = C
Fact	Socrates is	a **dog.**		A = B
Conclusion	Socrates is		mortal.	A = C

Our rule and facts now match. By expanding the rule to encompass dogs, we've solved our relevancy problem.

However, not all cases are as neatly resolved as our example. Most rules, like language itself, are inherently imprecise and messy. Most words have several meanings, and those meanings have several meanings, and so on. Does this mean that all legal arguments are inherently imprecise? Well ... maybe. Because we use language to state rules and to state facts, we may have trouble deriving a precise enough "match"—between our rule and our facts—to make a deductive argument. Well then, just what do we do?

We use our good common sense—that's what we do. For example, the rule in our Socrates hypothetical from Chapter 2 provided that "all men born on this Earth and living their lives upon it, will one day die." *Smythet v. Jones*, 3311 U.S. 99, 105 (2018). Now, to state a valid argument, must we *prove* that Greece and California (the facts we were given regarding Socrates's residence) are "on the Earth"? Or, can we infer that they are? Common sense tells us we *can* make this inference. Understanding this fine line between valid inference and invalid assumption is understanding the "art" of legal writing.

Skilled lawyers have mastered this art. Experience has taught them how to argue. They know, intuitively, which terms do and don't require further explanation and proof. They know the difference between overkill and coming up short. They know which further explanations are necessary and which will only distract readers from the thrust of the argument. They know the fine line between *assuming* too much (i.e., making "conclusory" arguments) and *proving* too much (i.e., presenting a garbled mess of unnecessary information). We know senior partners who, for example, can take five pages of argument, streamline them down to one page, and in the process, strengthen the entire document.[1]

---

1. T. Rambo thanks the best lawyer she knows, Ronald Van Buskirk, for ripping her drafts to shreds, and in the process, teaching her this art.

Skilled lawyers recognize that language and the law are joined at the hip—are one and the same. They understand, at the "gut" level, that the utility and futility of the law lie in the law's ability to be molded and shaped by language itself. Words are our pride and our plague. How we wield them can change the course of our clients' lives.

If we fumble with words, if we're careless and imprecise, we'll blunder and our client will bear the brunt of our mistakes. If, however, we use words with loving care and the delicacy of a surgeon's hand, we give them the force of armies. With them we can pierce any problem, bring light to darkness, and change the course of civilization. Don't believe us? Just read the Magna Carta, the Declaration of Independence, the Constitution, a death penalty judgment, or a stay of execution.

Words are the ultimate paradox—as powerful as they are fragile, as unique as they are common, and as destructive as they are creative. With one word we can empower, with another, we can enslave.

As lawyers, we are professional writers and the power of the word rests with us. Scary? Absolutely. As lawyers, we literally will be putting thoughts into the minds of others. Judges must read what we write. We better take great care in what we say and how we say it.

With these thoughts in mind, we provide the following three guidelines for navigating the "language maze." These aren't canons of statutory construction or methods of interpreting a case. Rather, they're insights into the art of argument.

"A good rule for writers; do not explain overmuch."

—W. Somerset Maugham

Graphic 3.1(d)   Guidelines for Traversing the Language Maze

First

As a general principle, if the factual or legal term in question is an adjective or adverb, chances are we'll need to explain it. It's unfortunate that we can't do as Mark Twain advised: "As to the adjective: when in doubt, strike it out."

For example, a bare assertion that "the defendant acted as a *reasonable* person" is unpersuasive. Why did the defendant act reasonably? A judge, colleague, or client reading that assertion will want to know.

Moreover, unless we explain what "reasonable" means, we can't know which facts are relevant to prove "reasonableness." Unless we explain the term, our argument will be incomplete and conclusory.

Second

On the other hand, if the questionable term is a noun with a commonly understood meaning, we probably don't need to explain it.

For example, in our "Socrates" example from Chapter 2, we did not need to prove that Greece is "on the Earth." We let our common sense guide us; we don't explain the obvious.

Third

Finally, if we can't determine whether we further need to explain a crucial term, we can drop a short footnote clarifying its meaning.[2] We must, however, take care not to abuse footnotes.[3] Too many can be really annoying and distracting.[4]

§ 3.2   How Punctuation Impacts Relevancy

Thus far we've seen how explaining and interpreting a rule can help us solve relevancy problems. What may have been questionably relevant facts can become highly relevant as we uncover the rule's meaning. For this reason, stating the rule correctly and explaining its meaning are critical to writing a valid and persuasive argument.

But problems of relevancy also arise through feeble errors — as feeble as misplacing the humble comma. As the following hypothetical demonstrates, even the slightest misplacement can lead to an irrelevant, erroneous, or incomplete "argument."

Suppose we've been given the following two rules regarding how a student may receive an "A" in the course in Appellate Advocacy:

Graphic 3.2(a)   Precision: The Difference a Comma Makes

Rule #1

A student who does the following will receive an A in the course:
   (a) demonstrates preparedness in class,
   (b) satisfactorily completes all assignments, and
   (c) either writes an A final brief, or
   (d) writes a A/B+ final brief and presents an excellent final oral argument.

Rule #2

A student who does the following will receive an A in the course:
   (a) demonstrates preparedness in class,
   (b) satisfactorily completes all assignments,
   (c) either writes an A final brief or writes a A/B+ final brief, and
   (d) presents an excellent final oral argument.

"Wait a minute," we'd shout indignantly. Then, we'd assert one of the following:

"Rule #1 and Rule #2 are identical; the same. You're just trying to trick us. Not nice, especially considering what we've paid for this...."

Or

"Aha! Punctuation really *does* matter."

---

2. Footnotes are wonderful "CYA" devices.
3. See how the footnote forces the reader to look to the bottom of the page?
4. Isn't this aggravating?

Let's see the difference a comma makes. If we outline Rule #1, we see the following design:

Graphic 3.2(b)	Rule # 1
	To receive an A, a student must do: a, b, and (c or d).

If we outline Rule #2, we get this:

Graphic 3.2(c)	Rule # 2
	To receive an A, a student must do: a, b, c and d.

One little comma changes the rule. Under Rule #1, presenting an "excellent final oral argument" is relevant only if the student received an A/B+ on her final brief. However, under Rule #2, presenting an excellent final oral argument is relevant, regardless of the final brief grade.

Because a misplaced comma in a rule can impact our entire case, we must take special care to check the accuracy of all rule statements. A comma, for example, can determine whether someone recovers a million dollars from an insurance policy or walks away with nothing. A comma can mandate whether someone has committed a crime or has engaged in harmless activity. Just as a paltry pawn in a chess game can cross the board and become a powerful queen, so too can the humble comma change a life or wreak havoc on the unsuspecting.

§ 3.3   Grammar Ain't Wimpy, Neither

Well, it ain't. Throws us off, yes. Sounds like we doesn't know what we is speaking of? Course of.

So let's get it right. Grammar isn't wimpy! Grammar is crucial! Grammar is power!

"Grammar, which knows how to control even kings."[5]

—*Les Femmes Savantes* [1672], act II, sc. vi by Molière

Grammar — there, we've said it again — and we did feel you cringe. Grammar, that subject pounded into us against our will in eighth grade English,[6] is to be embraced, loved, and cherished. Why? Because it's absolutely vital to the law. Grammar is power. It sets the shape and form of language which, in turn, sets the shape and form of the law.

---

5. Sigismund [1368–1437], Holy Roman Emperor, at the Council of Constance [1414] said to a prelate who had objected to His Majesty's grammar, "Ego sum rex Romanus, et supra grammaticam," meaning "I am the Roman king, and am above grammar."

6. In fact, the two examples in this section are, if memory serves us, *from* our eighth grade English class.

Let's look at a simple example of the power of grammar and punctuation. Look at these words:

Graphic 3.3(a)	Example 1: Original
	woman without her man is incomplete

Add a colon, a comma, some capitals, and a period—in other words, put grammar to work on the word, and we get this—a sentence, a thought, a statement:

Graphic 3.3(b)	Example 1: First Variation
	Woman: without her, Man is incomplete.

Use the same words, but change the grammar, the punctuation, and we get an entirely different meaning:

Graphic 3.3(c)	Example 1: Second Variation
	Woman, without her man, is incomplete.

Grammar *is* power! Let's try one more:

Graphic 3.3(d)	Example 2: Original
	Let's eat grandma I'm hungry

Adding two commas, a period, and some capitals, we get the thought:

Graphic 3.3(e)	Example 2: First Variation
	Let's eat, Grandma, I'm hungry.

But, take just one comma out, and ...

Graphic 3.3(f)	Example 2: Second Variation
	Let's eat Grandma, I'm hungry.

There we have it: the same words stated in the same order express two entirely different thoughts. We'll say it again: Grammar is not wimpy; it's not tight-laced. No, in law grammar is power. In the realm of language, it's the one stabilizing force. It adds form, which helps to convey meaning. It's a force we can't ignore.

§ 3.4   But What about the Smoking Monkey?

We also can't ignore how hard it is to convey thoughts through language. As William Shakespeare put it in *Hamlet*, "My words fly up, my thoughts remain below: Words without thoughts never to heaven go." As we like it: "But what about the smoking monkey?" Permit us to explain.

Let's write a law making it illegal for anyone to smoke a cigarette or cigar, that type of (pardon our bias) annoying, repulsive, cancer-inducing thing, in an elevator.

Pretty simple, right? We know what we want to do. We're trying to prohibit an activity *and* provide notice of what's prohibited. We know the result we want, just as we know the result we want when we're writing briefs and memos. But where do we start? What words do we use?

Well, let's try a few possibilities. What if we crafted a statement as follows:

Graphic 3.4(a)	First Try
It's unlawful to smoke in an elevator.	

Seems simple enough; seems to get the point across. But ... who is the actor? Smoke what? In what elevator — public as well as private?

Let's try another version:

Graphic 3.4(b)	Second Try
It's unlawful to smoke a cigarette in a public elevator.	

Well, we still don't have an actor. And we still have problems with the subject of the prohibition: Are we outlawing just cigarettes? What about a pipe or a cigar? Moreover, how is "smoke" defined? Must there be an active inhaling and exhaling? What if the thing is just on fire? And, how is "public" defined? Who is this statute aimed at? And just what does "unlawful" mean? Should we change our verb "to smoke" and our noun "cigarette" to encompass more general categories of actions and objects? If so, how?

We could probably think through this problem better if we followed a simple mnemonic: TARPP.[7]

Graphic 3.4(c)	TARPP
TARPP stands for Thing, Action, Relief, Parties, and Place.	

---

7. Not to be confused with the Troubled Asset Relief Program (TARP), enacted by the United States Treasury Department in 2008. Our use of this mnemonic predates the Treasury's — see the first edition of this book.

Using TARPP, we'd think as follows:

Graphic 3.4(d)	Using TARPP
Thing	cigarette, cigar, pipe
Action	smoking, lighting, exhaling
Relief	prison, fine
Parties	adults, anyone
Place	in a public elevator

However, even using this TARPP framework, we could drive ourselves nuts trying to come up with a statute both specific and general enough to meet our needs. But that's the law business. Playing with words is what it's all about. Here's how the Florida legislature crafted the state's "Don't Smoke in an Elevator" statute:

Graphic 3.4(e)	The Florida Statute

It is unlawful for any person to possess any ignited tobacco product or other ignited substance while present in an elevator. Any person who violates this section is guilty of a misdemeanor of the second degree, punishable as provided in § 775.082 or § 775.083.*

_____

* § 823.12 Fla. Stat. (2009)

Now, what are some problems with this wording? Well, what if we don't "possess" the ignited product? What if we just rest it on the ground? What if we throw a lit cigarette into the elevator but don't ride with it? Or, what if we, upon entering the elevator, hand the cigarette to our monkey, have him hold it while the elevator is in motion, and then retrieve it from him once we've both exited?

And one last question: why did this statute refer us to other statutes? We've all seen statutes do this kind of annoying thing. We do, however, know the answer to this one. Statutes don't like to be read all by themselves so they make us go read other statutes. Chances are, though, that those other statutes will make us read others, and on and on. Welcome to the world of "statutory interpretation"—a world which entails, among other things, staggering through a maze of pages while searching for numbers which in turn refer us to other sets of numbers and more mazes.[8]

So, given this maze of words, how do we have certainty in the law? The answer is: we don't. The best we can do is apply the law to our facts, attempting to fulfill the intent and spirit of the rule we're applying. Case law may step in to help us interpret statutory terms and provide meaning where the statute is silent or ambiguous. Or a case may come along and utterly defeat the statute's plain meaning. When that happens, we scratch our head, take a deep breath, and move on. We rely on our good common sense and let our innate reasoning ability guide us.

_____

8. We address statutory interpretation in more detail in Chapter 11, § 11.7 and § 11.8.

§ 3.5   Exercises

Exercise 1. Using TARPP

Based on the hypothetical set of facts in the Rose and David Hill exercise in Chapter 1, the rule you designed and personalized, and the principles explained in § 1.2, develop some TARPP words you might use in researching to solve the issue in that case.

Exercise 2. Drafting a statute

Try drafting a statute to prohibit smoking in an elevator, making it as simple as possible to achieve the desired result.

Chapter Review
Language and Relevancy

✓ Using language in legal writing is an "art"; with experience we learn how best to deal with the imprecision inherent in words.

✓ Generally, we further explain adjectives and adverbs used in a legal rule but not commonly understood nouns.

✓ Grammar and punctuation are vital forces we can't ignore.

✓ In thinking of legal issues, it's helpful to use the TARPP mnemonic:

Thing, Action, Relief, Parties, and Place.

✓ Always consider the possibility of the "smoking monkey."

Chapter 4

From Reasoning to Writing: Organizing Our Thoughts

§4.1   Organize the Argument by the Rule and Legal Elements

In Chapters 1–3, we addressed the fundamentals of reasoning. In this Chapter, we go one step further and explain how to organize our thoughts so we can readily transform them into writing. How do our syllogisms and BaRAC outlines become paragraphs? Let's see.

Our case. Assume we seek to prove that Jones committed battery when he put poison into a cup of coffee that Smith later drank. Assume further that battery is defined as the "impermissible application of force to the person of another." Did Jones commit battery? And, if he did, how do we express our argument in writing? Here's how.

Let's start with a "global" syllogism expressing our entire case:

Graphic 4.1(a)		The Battery Hypothetical		
Premise	Term A	Term B *bridging term*	Term C	Term D
Rule		the impermissible application of force to the person of another =	battery	
Fact	Jones's action =			put poison into a cup of coffee Smith drank
Conclusion	Jones's action =		???????	Does Term D = Term C?

We can't answer the question yet as to whether Jones committed battery. Why? Because we don't know whether Term D is the same as Term B. In other words, we don't know whether poisoning Smith constitutes "the impermissible application of force to the person of another." It better, or we can't prove our case. But how do we find out? We do further research, that's how.

Assume that we've found that "impermissible" means "acting without the victim's consent," and "application of force to the person of another" means "setting into motion a thing or substance which touches the victim." Assume also that Smith did not consent to being poisoned and that he swallowed the poisoned coffee. We then rethink our argument, as follows:

Graphic 4.1(b)		Revised: The Battery Hypothetical	
Premise	**Term A**	**Term B** *bridging term*	**Term C**
Rule		the impermissible application of force to the person of another =	battery
Rule explanation			
element 1		impermissible application = acting without the victim's consent	
element 2		application of force to another = setting into motion a thing or substance which touches the victim	
Fact	Jones's action =	impermissibly applied force to Smith via poison he put into a cup of coffee Smith drank	
Application of each element		<u>Proof that D = B:</u> Jones acted impermissibly because Smith did not consent to be poisoned.	
		Jones applied force to Smith by setting into motion the poison which Smith touched by drinking.	
Conclusion	Jones's action	=	battery

Within this "global" syllogism, i.e., within our overarching syllogism that proves that Jones did the deed, we have two other syllogisms. The first concerns the "impermissible" element of the rule, while the second relates to the "application of force" element.

Graphic 4.1(c)		Syllogism: Element 1	
Premise	**Term A**	**Term B** *bridging term*	**Term C**
Rule		acting without the victim's consent =	acting impermissibly
Fact	Jones =	acted without the victim's consent.	
Conclusion	Jones	=	acted impermissibly.

Graphic 4.1(d)   Syllogism: Element 2

Premise	Term A	Term B *bridging term*	Term C
Rule		setting into motion a thing or sub-stance which touches the victim =	applying force to the person of another
Fact	Jones =	set into motion a substance (poison) which touched the victim (when Smith drank it).	
Conclusion	Jones	=	applied force to the person of another.

We've now proved that Jones committed battery. Although the general rule did not lead us directly to our conclusion, its explanation did. Learning the specific definitions of each element led us to understand which of our facts were relevant. That process, in turn, led us to conclude that Jones committed the deed. By solving parts of the puzzle—by analyzing each element of the rule—we solved the big picture. How, then, do we write our results into an organized format? Let's see.

The following is one way of incorporating the syllogisms of our case into an outline:

Graphic 4.1(e)   Building a BaRAC Outline of Our Syllogisms

syllogism 1 **"global syllogism"**	Main Bold assertion	Jones committed battery upon Smith.
This is the "overall" syllogism, including the general rule, where we "boldly" state the conclusions we will soon prove.	Rule (general)	Battery is the impermissible application of force to the person of another. *Adam v. Florida*, 40 F.2d 7, 8 (11th Cir. 1999).
	Application	Jones impermissibly applied force to the person of another when he put poison into a cup of coffee Smith later drank.
	Conclusion	Jones committed battery upon Smith.
syllogism 2	Bold assertion	Jones's act was impermissible.
element 1 syllogism Here's where we prove that Jones's act was impermissible.	Rule (specific to element 1)	An impermissible act is one done without the victim's consent. *Art v. Florida*, 999 F. Supp. 181, 184–85 (N.D. Fla. 1999).
	Application (facts specific to element 1)	Jones placed poison in the victim's, Smith's, coffee without Smith's consent.
	Conclusion (specific to element 1)	Therefore, Jones's act was impermissible. [We cannot yet conclude that Jones committed battery; we have not yet proven *each* element required to establish a battery.]

syllogism 3	Bold assertion	Jones applied force to Smith.
element 2 syllogism Here's where we prove that Jones applied force to Smith.	Rule (specific to element 2)	Application of force to the person of another occurs whenever the defendant sets into motion a thing or substance which touches the victim. *Bable v. Florida*, 998 F. Supp. 205, 207–08 (N.D. Fla. 1999).
	Application (facts specific to element 2)	Jones put poison into coffee Smith later "touched" by drinking.
	Conclusion (specific to element 2)	Therefore, Jones applied force to Smith.

We've now designed our argument. We've developed a series of syllogisms (three) proving that Jones committed battery upon Smith. In addition, we now can anticipate some of Jones's arguments. For example, he may allege the following:

Graphic 4.1(f)	**Possible Theories to Escape Liability**

Jones may argue that
(1) he didn't put poison into Smith's coffee;
(2) even if he did put poison into Smith's coffee, he had no specific intent to do so; and
(3) Smith was not harmed by the poison.

Based on our rule of battery, of these three possible arguments, which would vindicate Jones? Why? Hint: as we've defined battery, is *specific* intent (i.e., the "desire" to commit the crime) an element of the crime? No. Is *harm* to the victim an element of the crime? No. By paying attention to the rules governing our case, we can determine which issues, facts, and defenses are relevant.

Let's now write our argument by converting our outline into paragraph form. We begin with a very rough draft, consisting almost entirely of the syllogisms we've stated above:

Graphic 4.1(g)	Very Rough Draft of Battery Argument
	[syllogism 1]
Bold assertion	Jones committed battery on Smith. Battery is the impermissi-
Rule [general]	ble application of force to the person of another. *Adam v. Florida*,
Application	40 F.2d 7, 8 (11th Cir. 1999). Jones impermissibly applied force
	to the person of another when he put poison into a cup of coffee
Conclusion	Smith later drank. Therefore, Jones committed battery.
Application	**[syllogism 2]**
element 1	Jones's act was impermissible. An impermissible act is one
bold assertion	done without the victim's consent. *Art v. Florida*, 999 F. Supp.
rule	181, 184–85 (N.D. Fla. 1999). Jones placed poison in the victim's,
application	Smith's, coffee without Smith's consent. Therefore, Jones's act
conclusion	was impermissible.
element 2	**[syllogism 3]**
bold assertion	Jones applied force to Smith. Application of force to the per-
rule	son of another occurs whenever the defendant sets into motion
	a thing or substance which touches the victim. *Bable v. Florida*,
application	998 F. Supp. 205, 207–08 (N.D. Fla. 1999). Jones put poison, a
	substance, into coffee Smith later "touched" by drinking. There-
conclusion	fore, Jones applied force to Smith.
Conclusion	For these reasons, the jury should find that Jones committed
	battery.

This example shows the elegant design of the legal argument. The argument unfolds like the petals of a flower. Each of the three syllogisms in our outline joins or nests together to form our overarching or "global" argument. In other words, the global argument is *itself* a syllogism, springing from the three syllogisms of our outline. We can readily identify the four sections of the argument as follows:

Bold assertion	Rule	Application	Conclusion

The first paragraph of our argument is the *introductory* BaRAC relating to the entire case. It creates a roadmap for our reader by providing the "big picture." It states the *general rule* and establishes the ultimate conclusions we will prove.

Because we're orienting our reader to the big picture, we explain only the *general rule*. In other words, we don't discuss the meaning of element 1 and element 2 in our first paragraph. If we were to do so, our discussion would either be repetitive (because we discuss each element separately in the body of our argument) or difficult to follow (because we'd be lumping separate elements together).

Although the writing in our draft is choppy and repetitive (the paragraphs are in desperate need of transitions), the syllogisms alone provide a sound framework for our argument. We're on our way to writing our thoughts. In Chapter 7, we address how to transform a series of syllogisms like we have here into a streamlined, polished argument.

But before we leave our battery hypothetical, and at the risk of being repetitive, let's look at one more way to chart or organize our argument. Note that we've omitted citations in this example.

Graphic 4.1(h)	Design of the Battery Argument
GLOBAL BOLD ASSERTION:	**Introduces the entire argument in general terms**
General Bold assertion:	Jones committed battery.
Global Rule:	**States the overarching legal rule**
General Rule:	Battery is the impermissible application of force to
General Application:	the person of another. Jones impermissibly applied force to the person of another when he put poison
General Conclusion:	into a cup of coffee Smith later drank. Therefore, Jones committed battery.
GLOBAL APPLICATION:	**Explains the specific elements and applies those elements to the specific facts**
Discuss/apply the first element:	
Specific Bold assertion:	Jones's act was impermissible. An impermissible act
Specific Rule:	is one done without the victim's consent. Jones
Specific Application:	placed poison in the victim's, Smith's, coffee without Smith's consent.
Specific Conclusion:	Therefore, Jones's act was impermissible.
Discuss/apply the second element:	
Specific Bold assertion:	Jones applied force to Smith. Application of force to
Specific Rule:	the person of another occurs whenever the defendant sets into motion a thing or substance which
Specific Application:	touches the victim. Jones put poison, a substance, into coffee Smith later "touched" by drinking.
Specific Conclusion:	Therefore, Jones applied force to Smith.
GLOBAL CONCLUSION	**States the conclusion for the entire argument**
	Therefore, Jones committed battery.

There we have it. Our legal argument consists of a series of three syllogisms, which nest together to form one larger syllogism. Whether we're looking at the petals or the flower depends on our perspective. We've outlined what we must prove (legally and factually) and the order of proving it. We've made our argument as simple as possible by organizing it around the legal elements.

§ 4.2   No Ping-Ponging Please: Do Not Organize the Argument by Cited Cases

In our battery argument, we organized our argument around bold assertions. We did not organize our discussion around the three cited cases. In other words, we didn't discuss the first case, then apply it; then discuss the second case and then apply it; then discuss the third case and then apply it. As we see in the example below (**Graphic 4.2**), that approach leads to a neck wrenching "ping-pong" style of writing, lacking focus and clarity. It also violates the BaRAC and syllogistic designs, leading our readers to wonder what the heck we're talking about.

Unfortunately, this dizzying "discuss the case—apply the case—discuss another case—apply that other case" approach is very easy to fall into. It doesn't force us to think through *our* case *before* we write. It doesn't require us to make bold assertions about our case which we then prove by discussing the rule and applying it to our facts. Instead, it lets us ramble hither and yon, waltzing through a case discussion, drawing comparisons (maybe), contrasting points (maybe), and, if we're lucky (maybe), reaching a conclusion. This approach provides no roadmap for our reader. It just says, "hang on, here we go, where we'll stop, we don't know."

Let's look at what our battery argument might resemble if we "organized" it around our three cases instead of around the elements of our rule.

Graphic 4.2	Don't Organize the Argument by Cases
First case:	In *Adam v. State*, the defendant had committed battery because he had "impermissibly applied force to the person of another." Jones put poison into Smith's coffee and impermissibly applied force to him.
Second case:	In *Art v. Florida*, the defendant was convicted of battery. The court said that the defendant had acted without the victim's consent and "impermissibly." Jones acted impermissibly in not getting Smith's consent when he put that poison into Smith's coffee.
Third case:	In *Bable v. Florida*, the defendant put something into motion which touched the victim. Jones put poison into Smith's coffee and Smith drank that coffee.
Conclusion:	Similar to the defendants in *Adam*, *Bable*, and *Art*, Jones committed battery.

What a mess! Enough said.

Although rule-based reasoning, as we've used thus far in our battery hypothetical, is helpful and provides a good "backbone" for our argument, it's not the only way to go. We could greatly enhance our argument by providing the court with additional information regarding the meaning of the rules involved.

For example, suppose that the defendant in one of the cases we've cited, *Bable v. Florida*, was convicted of battery for putting poison in his victim's tea. Suppose also that the court's reasoning in the *Bable* case was very persuasive. We would want to share that reasoning with the court in our case. We'd explain the *Bable* court's reasoning and persuade the court in our case to accept that reasoning. In other words, we'd use an argument based on an *analogy* to the *Bable* case. We would use the *Bable* case as "precedent."

In the next chapters, we'll learn how to put not only a rule, but a precedent, to work for us. We'll explore how to read and interpret cases, discuss a cited case, and place our case discussion within our written argument.

Chapter Review
From Reasoning to Writing: Organizing Our Thoughts

✓ Using the general rule, generate a "global" syllogism. Then, develop a syllogism for each element of that rule.

✓ Organize arguments around elements and rules, not around cases.

The BaRAC Design for Organizing a Multi-Element Rule

GLOBAL BOLD ASSERTION	[syllogism 1]
	General Bold assertion
GLOBAL RULE	*General* Rule
	General Application
	General Conclusion
GLOBAL APPLICATION	**[syllogism 2] [first element]**
	Specific Bold assertion
	Specific Rule
	Specific Application
	Specific Conclusion
	[syllogism 3] [second element]
	Specific Bold assertion
	Specific Rule
	Specific Application
	Specific Conclusion
GLOBAL CONCLUSION	

Chapter 5

Sources of Law; Reading and Interpreting Cases

"When is a rule not a rule? Why, when it's used in a case, of course."

— Your Humble Authors

§ 5.1   Sources of Law

In Chapter 1, we introduced the concept of rules and discussed why rules are necessary to understanding and solving a client's problem. Let's now revisit the sources of legal rules (the "law") and see how rules interact with one another. Our goal is to learn how to choose which rules we'll apply in our case.

Our American legal system consists of rules from every branch of government. The United States Constitution, established by a special constitutional convention (which you no doubt learned about in high school civics), and amended over the years, is the highest law of the land. This constitution places limits on all other laws and in turn established the three branches of federal government, each of which also creates law. In addition, each state has its own constitution establishing the various branches of state government.

The legislative branch enacts statutes (or codes or ordinances), the judicial branch creates case law, and the executive branch (which includes administrative agencies) issues executive orders and regulations. In addition, court rules governing the conduct of courts can be created by either the judicial branch or the executive branch, depending upon the jurisdiction. For shorthand purposes, constitutions, statutes, codes, ordinances, and regulations will collectively be referred to as *enacted* law, in contrast to *case* law.

Primary authority is law issued by any branch of government and is divided into two categories: mandatory and persuasive. A *mandatory* authority, meaning one that *must* be applied or followed by the deciding entity in a given situation, is a primary authority controlling the issue in question and may include enacted law, as well as case law from a higher court having jurisdiction over the court deciding the issue. Mandatory authority is also called *binding* authority. Of course, an authority is only mandatory, or binding, when the authority involves the same legal issue and substantially similar facts as the case at issue.[1] A primary authority can also be merely *persuasive*, meaning it *may* be followed by the deciding entity in a given situation but does not have to be. A primary authority that is persuasive, but not binding, arises from an entity that does not have jurisdiction over the entity deciding the issue.

Secondary authority, on the other hand, is never mandatory, but at most, only *persuasive*. Essentially, secondary authorities are either research tools to find primary authority or explanations or critiques of primary authority. Examples of secondary authorities include legal dictionaries, legal encyclopedias, digests, treatises on areas of law (also called hornbooks), restatements of the law, model jury instructions, and legal periodicals, including law reviews. These secondary authorities, although not themselves law, are useful in helping us to find and understand the law.

The following graphics may help you better understand the difference between primary and secondary authorities, and binding and persuasive primary authorities.

---

1. An established hierarchy of mandatory authority exists within both the federal system and within each state. See **Graphic 5.1(b)**.

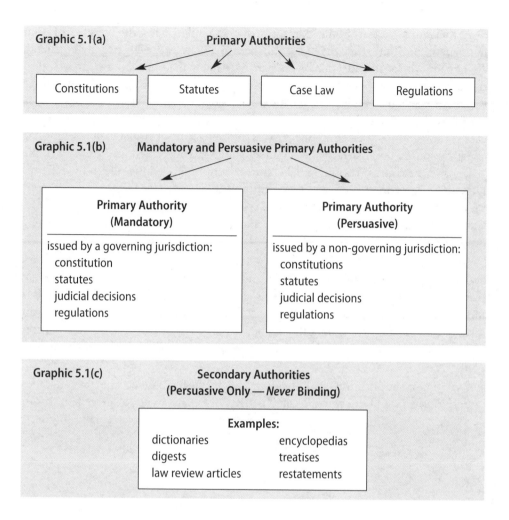

Next, let's see how case law fits within these categories.

§5.2   What Is a Case?

A case, in a nutshell, is a story. It really is. There's a beginning, a middle, and an ending. Something (usually bad) has happened to someone. There's been an injury of some sort: financial, physical, or emotional. Someone is ticked off at someone else and demands "justice." But what we can never forget is that each case involves a *human being*.

In each case, at least one "issue" (often many more) must be decided. The judge or jury is called in to handle the matter, hears from at least both sides, applies a rule or rules to the facts, and decides who wins and who loses. The "judgment," the piece of paper filed with the court announcing the outcome, concludes the trial.

At this point, (at least in the federal system), the judge may write the story of what happened, and that story may be published in a legal reporter, usually entitled a "judgment," or "order." Or, one of the parties (usually the one who lost) may appeal the judgment to a higher court. The parties then go slug it out in appellate court. After that court hears from both sides, the judges or justices write the story of the case. This story usually, but not always, includes the "key facts," the "procedural history" of the case (what action was taken by the lawyers and judges prior to the case reaching the appellate court), the "issue(s)," the "holding" (how the court ruled on the issue(s)), the "rule," and the court's "reasoning" (i.e., how the court applied the rule to the relevant facts). The decision answers the question the issue posed. This decision then may or may not be published in a law reporter. If it is published, we can read it. That's a case. Cases are primary authorities: sometimes mandatory (binding) and sometimes merely persuasive.

But a case doesn't exist in a vacuum. No, that would make this law business too easy and imperil our jobs. Cases exist together and usually build on one another. These "life stories" establish a foundation for what is and isn't acceptable behavior. We like this foundation. We like stability, well, at least the *illusion* of stability, in the law. We want to know the consequences of our actions, and we want assurances that those consequences will remain constant from day to day. The concept of *stare decisis* helps keep things on par.

Stare decisis simply means that judges should decide like cases in like ways. In other words, judges should use an established pattern of behavior (i.e., a "precedent" case), as a guide in deciding the present case. The following five points explain how *stare decisis* works:

Graphic 5.2	*Stare Decisis*: **The Basics**

(1) Judges are empowered to decide only cases lawfully brought to their courts. Judges cannot enact general rules binding on parties not before their courts, nor can they issue advisory or hypothetical opinions.

(2) "Case law" is the law created on a case-by-case basis by courts, including decisions interpreting enacted law. "Common law," on the other hand, is a category of case law developed exclusively through case law without reliance upon enacted law. Torts, property, and contracts cases deal extensively with common law.

(3) "Precedent" means that a prior case is acting as "authority." To put it another way, the prior case establishes a pattern of reasoning or a rule we'll urge the court to accept or reject in our case.

(4) "Binding precedent," also called "mandatory precedent," is a case our court must follow. In contrast, "non-binding precedent," also called "persuasive" precedent, is a case our court is under no duty to accept. Moreover, as long as no binding prece-

dent on point exists to the contrary, any court can reverse its own decision. (This drives lawyers nuts.)

(5) Even in situations involving "binding" precedent, the only aspect of the case a lower court must follow is the "holding." "Legal gravy" — or in Latin terms, *dicta* — doesn't bind the lower court. As lawyers, it's our job to interpret cases, identify the holding, and determine what *is* and *isn't* dicta. As we'll see, drawing these distinctions isn't easy.

Dicta. The term "dictum" and its plural, "dicta," require some further explanation. In essence, dictum is generally used as an abbreviated form of *obiter dictum* (the plural is *obiter dicta*), a Latin term meaning "said by the way." Dicta are collateral remarks or observations made by a court in an opinion that are not a necessary part of the court's holding, even if they happen to be accurate statements of law.

The statements and reasoning of a dissenting opinion also constitute dicta. Under the doctrine of *stare decisis,* statements constituting dicta are not binding. Such statements can, however, be persuasive — particularly if they were written by a court with the power to reverse the court to which we cite such dicta.

Sometimes a court opinion may include dicta when the court lacks jurisdiction to hear a case or dismisses the case on a technicality but nonetheless offers opinions on the merits of the case. Other times a judge may make a side comment to provide context for other parts of the opinion or thoroughly (but unnecessarily) address a relevant area of law. Another example would be where the judge, in explaining a ruling, provides a hypothetical set of facts and explains how he or she believes the law would apply to those facts.

In reaching decisions, courts sometimes quote dicta from prior cases, with or without acknowledging the quoted passage's status as dicta. A quoted passage of dicta may thus become part of the reasoning in a subsequent case, depending on what the latter court actually decided and how that court and others subsequently treat the principle embodied in the quoted passage.

As lawyers, we may need to rely upon dictum in interpreting a case or in explaining an incomplete or ambiguous holding. When we do so, however, we must make it clear that what we are asserting is *not* the holding of the case. We are, of course, also aware that one lawyer's dicta is sometimes treated as the holding by the opposing counsel (and vice versa). But, to maintain our credibility, as lawyers, we must be especially careful not to present dictum as the holding of any case. Indeed, Rule 3.3 of the Model Rules of Professional Conduct governing attorney conduct provides that: "A lawyer shall not knowingly ... make a false statement of fact or law to a tribunal...."

Back to case law. Our job in researching a common law issue, or in researching cases interpreting a statute or constitutional provision, is to find a case involving (1) the same issue as ours and (2) similar facts, or facts which stand in relation to each other as the facts in our case stand to each other. We then determine the precedential *value* of each case and in the event of a conflict among cases, *harmonize* the decisions. In this process, as the following hypothetical demonstrates, we keep our minds open to possible similarities between seemingly unrelated cases.

Nude dancers, again![2] Assume that we're defending dancers convicted of violating a "public indecency" statute. These dancers make their living performing in the nude in a nightclub. We've appealed their conviction on the ground that their nude dancing is *expressive* conduct and that the statute, in prohibiting this form of "expression," violates the dancers' First Amendment speech rights.

Assume further that through our research, we've found three U.S. Supreme Court cases involving defendants convicted for the following:

(1) burning a draft card;
(2) attaching a peace symbol to a U.S. flag; and
(3) burning the U.S. flag.

Do we ignore these cases because they have nothing to do with nude dancing? Absolutely not! Although they involve acts unrelated to nude dancing, each act *is* related to expression. In each case, the Court found that the defendant had been involved in expressive activity.[3] Far from being useless, these cases are highly relevant to our case.

Thus, in researching cases, we don't look solely for cases with facts similar to our case. Rather, we look for cases involving a legal *theory* similar to that we seek to advance. Guided by our theory, we'll better identify the similarities in seemingly disparate cases.

Next in this chapter, we'll discuss the precedential value of cases, examine how to distinguish a holding from a rule, and demonstrate (through a hypothetical) how to develop a rule from a series of cases. In other words, we'll address how to make sense of the law.

§ 5.3   Binding Authority

Although it's rare to find binding precedent for a client's problem, we must be on alert for it. Indeed, we have an ethical duty to disclose such precedents to the court. Which cases, however, are binding? The following provides some *general* guidelines:

Graphic 5.3(a)	State Courts
1. The opinions from a state's highest court bind all other courts of the state, as well as federal courts applying that state's law.	

---

2. See Chapter 1, § 1.1 and § 1.2.

3. *See United States v. O'Brien*, 391 U.S. 367 (1968); *Spence v. Washington*, 418 U.S. 405 (1974); and *Texas v. Johnson*, 491 U.S. 397 (1989).

2. A state's highest court generally follows its own prior opinions but is not required to do so.

3. Opinions from an intermediate appellate court are binding on trial courts within the jurisdiction of the intermediate appellate court.*

4. Opinions of courts from other states or of federal courts, including the United States Supreme Court, are persuasive, but not binding, on issues of *state* law.

* In Florida, for example, the hierarchy of courts is as follows: Florida Supreme Court (highest), district courts of appeal (next highest, or intermediate), and circuit courts (trial courts). The decisions of the Florida Supreme Court are binding on all Florida courts. The decisions of the district courts of appeal, on the other hand, are binding on the trial courts in their district, and, on trial courts in other districts where the governing appellate district court has not yet addressed the point of law. However, one district court of appeal cannot "bind" another district court of appeal. Conflicting opinions among district courts of appeal may be resolved by the Florida Supreme Court.

Graphic 5.3(b)	Federal Courts

1. Opinions from the United States Supreme Court on issues of *federal* law are binding on all federal and state courts. The United States Supreme Court generally follows its own prior opinions but is not required to do so.

2. Opinions from an intermediate federal appellate court are binding on all federal district courts within the jurisdiction of that appellate court.*

3. Opinions from intermediate federal appellate courts and trial courts on issues of federal law are not binding on state courts, although state courts generally give these cases significant weight.

* In the federal system, the hierarchy of courts is as follows: The United States Supreme Court (highest), circuit courts of appeal (next highest, or intermediate), and district courts (trial courts).

Before, however, we argue that a case is binding (or even persuasive), we must *always, always, always,* (did we say always?) *update our authority to ensure that it's still good law.* To update our authorities, we use Shepard's Citations in print, Lexis or Westlaw online, or some other reputable citator. We update case law to make sure it hasn't been reversed or overruled by a higher court, or overruled by a later decision of the same court. We also check to see whether the case has been modified or questioned by a later decision. Similarly, we check statutes. Statutes can be repealed or amended by a later statute or limited, expanded, or found unconstitutional by a later court ruling. No research is complete until we have updated *all* authorities.

But, even if we have found binding precedents and have verified that these cases are still "good law," there's no guarantee that this law will be "consistent." We may find contradictory binding precedents. What then do we do? Here are some suggestions:

Graphic 5.3(c) Resolving Apparent Inconsistencies in Binding Precedent

1. A constitutional provision prevails over an inconsistent statute.

2. A constitutional provision or a statute prevails over an inconsistent regulation promulgated by an administrative agency.

3. A later statute prevails over an earlier statute but not over a constitutional provision, which outranks a statute.

4. A constitutional provision prevails over an inconsistent case law precedent.

5. A statute "overrules" case law established prior to the statute if the case law is inconsistent with the statute. However, statutes can be repealed or amended by a later statute or limited, expanded, or found unconstitutional by a later court ruling.

6. Later decisions generally overrule earlier inconsistent decisions from the same court. The later case may reflect that the rule has "evolved" even if the later decision does not "expressly" overrule the prior case.

7. If the apparently inconsistent case involved more than one issue, and if the dispositive issue is not the issue in our case, we argue that the inconsistent case is not binding on our court and should not prevail.

---

§ 5.4   Persuasive Authority

Although cases *outside our jurisdiction* are not binding precedent, we often include them in our brief or memo as *persuasive* authority. We do this in the following circumstances:

Graphic 5.4(a)   Circumstances for Using Persuasive "Outside" Authority

1. Where the issue is one of first impression in our jurisdiction;
2. Where the case has an extensive (and helpful) policy discussion that does not appear in cases within our jurisdiction;
3. Where the case is factually similar, and those facts are important; or
4. Where the case applies a majority view we want our court to adopt.

Other factors we consider in determining the persuasiveness of authorities and reconciling one case with another are as follows:

Graphic 5.4(b)   Other Considerations in Using Persuasive Authority

1. The level of the court issuing the opinion, the number of judges involved in the opinion, and the author of the opinion.
2. The date of the opinion. The more recent opinion likely reflects the court's current view of the rule.
3. Whether the opinion is published. Published opinions have more persuasive force than unpublished ones.
4. The procedural posture of the case. That is, the point in the judicial process the case reached in the trial court.
5. Whether the opinion is thorough and well-researched.
6. Similarities and differences between the precedent cases and the instant case as to the facts and rules.

As we can see, no one *best* guideline exists for selecting the best case among several persuasive authorities. Our advice is to choose the most recent, well-reasoned case that is factually or theoretically close to our case.

§ 5.5   Determining the Rule of a Case

To predict what a court in our case might do, we look to what courts have done in the past in similar cases. If we like the patterns of thought those other courts have employed, we suggest that the court in our case follow them. If, however, we don't like the outcome of a highly relevant case, we suggest reasons why our court should not reach a similar result. But before we can apply a pattern of thought from a prior opinion to our case, we must understand the rule or rules involved in the prior case. And, as we'll discuss below, that may be a very daunting task.

Unlike legislators, who create laws applicable to a wide range of people and circumstances (i.e., statutes), judges use rules to solve only the dispute of the parties involved in a particular case. In solving that dispute, the judge takes existing rules (either statutory or case-generated) and personalizes them to fit the facts of the "instant" case. The judge then applies these "personalized" rules to the facts.

Because of the doctrine of *stare decisis*, however, personalized rules are also relevant to future cases involving the same or similar issues. Although a future court may not have to follow that prior case, the case nevertheless stands as an example of what one court has done under these circumstances. Under our system of jurisprudence, like cases should be decided alike. Courts should apply the same or similar rule to the same or similar circumstances.

But, articulating *which circumstances* are "similar" or even "relevant" is easier said than done. Facts which may have been highly relevant and crucial to the court's decision may, over time, prove to be insignificant.

The law is constantly evolving; it's in a constant state of flux. It may momentarily slow down when it takes the shape and form of a particular case. However, even then, the rule of that case is subject to interpretation and reinterpretation. A rule is hardly a "rule."

The rule of the *Ciraolo* case. Despite the sprite-like quality of rules, let's try to nail one down and examine it. Let's look at the United States Supreme Court case of *California v. Ciraolo*, 476 U.S. 207 (1986). A copy of this case appears in Chapter 26, along with a sample brief of the case. Look at both the case and the case brief now.

In *Ciraolo*, the Court framed one of the issues as follows: "[W]hether naked-eye observation of the [defendant's backyard] by police from an aircraft lawfully operating at an altitude of 1,000 feet violates an expectation of privacy that is reasonable." *Id.* at 213. Ciraolo, who had pled guilty to a charge of cultivating marijuana, argued that the overflight constituted a search, and violated the Fourth Amendment, because the officers had not obtained a warrant prior to their aerial observations. The Court, after applying Fourth Amendment precedent and personalizing a rule applicable to these facts, ultimately upheld Ciraolo's conviction.

In reaching its holding, the Court engaged in a three-step process. First, it addressed the existing rules (garnered from prior opinions) applicable to the Fourth Amendment issue in the case. Second, it applied those rules to the facts and reached a conclusion. Finally, it summarized the principles it had just applied. Let's look at how the Court used rules throughout this process.

Step # 1. First, addressing existing and relevant Fourth Amendment rules, the Court wrote:

Graphic 5.5(a)	Original Rule (*Ciraolo* case)

The Fourth Amendment protection of the home has never been extended to require law enforcement officers to shield their eyes when passing by a home on public thoroughfares. Nor does the mere fact that an individual has taken measures to restrict some views of his activities preclude an officer's observations from a public vantage point where he has a right to be and which renders the activities clearly visible. *E.g., United States v. Knotts*, 460 U.S. 276, 282 (1983). "What a person knowingly exposes to the public, even in his own home or office, is not a subject of Fourth Amendment protection." *Katz* [*v. United States*, 389 U.S. 347, 351 (1967)].

Notice that this rule says nothing about the circumstance, as in the *Ciraolo* case, where the officers' observations occurred from the air. Here, the law must evolve to keep pace with evolving technology and advancing law enforcement techniques. To decide the *Ciraolo* case, the Court's going to cook up a new truffle.

Let's outline this original rule:

Graphic 5.5(b)   **Outline of Original Rule (*Ciraolo* case)**

1. The Fourth Amendment does not protect what one knowingly exposes to the public.
2. Nor does the Fourth Amendment prohibit an officer from observing activities:
   a. from a public vantage point (i.e., a public thoroughfare);
   b. where the officer has a right to be; and
   c. which renders the activities clearly visible [to the officer's eyes].

Please note that this outline is *our* interpretation of the original rule. Other interpretations may vary. Which is valid? Who knows?

Step # 2. Second, the Court addressed the relevant facts of Ciraolo's case, applied the original rule to those facts, and reached a conclusion. Note, however, that in this process, the Court stressed some aspects of the rule over others. This is only natural. The Court is "pouring" the original rule into the mold formed by the facts and issue of Ciraolo's case. In the process, the rule takes on a shape different from its original version. In applying the rule, the Court is changing the rule.

Note that we use a capital "C" when referring to the United States Supreme Court. Notice too, that when we mention the name of a case, i.e., *Ciraolo*, we italicize or underline it. However, when we discuss the defendant himself, Ciraolo, we do not use underlining or italics.

Graphic 5.5(c)   ***Ciraolo* Court's Application of Original Rule**
and Creation of a Personalized Rule

The observations by Officers Shutz and Rodriguez in this case took place within public navigable airspace, see 49 U. S. C. App. § 1304, in a physically nonintrusive manner; from this point they were able to observe plants readily discernible to the naked eye as marijuana. That the observation from aircraft was directed at identifying the plants and the officers were trained to recognize marijuana is irrelevant. Such observation is precisely what a judicial officer needs to provide a basis for a warrant. Any member of the public flying in this airspace who glanced down could have seen everything that these officers observed. On this record, we readily conclude that [Ciraolo's] expectation that his garden was protected from such observation is unreasonable and is not an expectation that society is prepared to honor.

By outlining the relevant factors the Court addressed in applying the original rule to the *Ciraolo* facts, we see the following personalized rule emerge:

Graphic 5.5(d)   Personalized Rule Derived from Factor Analysis

Officers do not violate the Fourth Amendment where they observe, without a warrant, marijuana plants:

1. from public navigable airspace;

2. in a physically nonintrusive manner;

3. from a point where the activities are readily discernible by the naked eye as marijuana cultivation; and

4. under circumstances in which any member of the public who was flying in the airspace and glanced down, could have seen what the officers observed.

Again, we stress that this is *our* interpretation of the personalized rule. Let's compare this rule to the original:

Graphic 5.5(e)   Comparison: Personalized Rule and Original Rule

Personalized rule derived from factor analysis	Original rule and comments
1. Officers do not violate the Fourth Amendment where they observe, without a warrant, marijuana plants from public navigable airspace;	No such requirement; this is understandable since the earlier cases did not involve observations aircraft. Is this element of the personalized rule equivalent to the original requirement of a "public vantage point" "where the officer has a right to be"?
2. in a physically nonintrusive manner;	No such requirement. Is this element a *new* factor? Must warrantless aerial observations be conducted in a physically nonintrusive manner?
3. from a point where the plants are readily discernible by the naked eye as marijuana; and	No such requirement. Is this element equivalent to the original requirement that the "activities [must be] clearly visible"? What would happen in a future case if the marijuana was visible only with binoculars or only with a thermal imaging device? Would the observations under these circumstances still be legal?
4. under circumstances in which any member of the public who was flying in the airspace and glanced down could have seen what the officers observed.	No such requirement; and there is no requirement in the original rule that any member of the public (even on the ground) would be able to see what the officers saw. However, is this element equivalent to the original element of a "public vantage point"?

Will a later court applying the *Ciraolo* case adopt this four-element personalized rule as *the* "rule"? Which, if any, of these factors is the most important? Must all be present? The answers to these and the above questions are anyone's guess. But to make matters worse, we can't end our analysis of the *Ciraolo* rule here, for the Supreme Court had more to say on the issue.

Step # 3. The Court continued to discuss Fourth Amendment principles in the *Ciraolo* case by stating the following:

Graphic 5.5(f)   **More of the Personalized Rule?**

In an age where private and commercial flight in the public airways is routine, it is unreasonable for [Ciraolo] to expect that his marijuana plants were constitutionally protected from being observed with the naked eye from an altitude of 1,000 feet. The Fourth Amendment simply does not require the police traveling in the public airways at this altitude to obtain a warrant in order to observe what is visible to the naked eye.

Here's an outline of this passage:

Graphic 5.5(g)   **Further Elements of the Personalized Rule?**

Officers do not violate the Fourth Amendment where:

1. private and commercial flight in the public airways is routine;

2. they observe, without a warrant, and visible to the naked eye, marijuana plants;

3. while traveling in the public airways;

4. at an altitude of 1,000 feet.

As this list and the graphic below demonstrate, this last personalized rule differs from the prior one (derived from factor analysis) in the following ways:

1) It adds the element of "in an age where private and commercial flight in the public airways is routine."
2) It uses the term "public airways" instead of "public navigable airspace" to describe the officers' location.
3) It specifies an altitude "of 1,000 feet."
4) It *omits* the "physically nonintrusive" element.
5) It omits the "readily discernible as marijuana" element but mentions marijuana and includes the element of "visible to the naked eye."

6) It omits the "circumstances where any member of the public" could have seen the same thing element.

Graphic 5.5(h)	Different Versions of the Personalized Rule?
Factor analysis	**The Court's further observations**
Officers do not violate the Fourth Amendment where they observe, without a warrant, marijuana plants:	Officers do not violate the Fourth Amendment where:
1. from public navigable airspace;	1. private and commercial flight in the public airways is routine;
2. in a physically nonintrusive manner;	2. they observe, without a warrant and with the naked eye, marijuana plants;
3. from a point where the activities are readily discernible by the naked eye as marijuana cultivation; and	3. while traveling in the public airways;
4. under circumstances in which any member of the public who was flying in the airspace and glanced down could have seen what the officers observed.	4. at an altitude of 1,000 feet.

Now, the questions we, as lawyers, face are: What then *is* the personalized rule? What rule will govern future lower courts facing a similar Fourth Amendment issue? Is it the rule we derived from the Court's factor analysis, or is it the rule we derived from the Court's further statements of Fourth Amendment principles? Or, do we *combine* the two and consider all 8 factors?

Specifically, in deciding whether police conduct constitutes a search, will a future court examine whether the officers' observations were "physically nonintrusive," as the personalized rule derived from factor analysis requires? Or is that element irrelevant, as the Court's further statements seem to suggest?

The answers to these questions are not as clear as we would like. The answers depend upon how broadly or narrowly we, and future courts, read the *Ciraolo* case. And, as we address in the next section, our reading and interpretation of the *Ciraolo* rule will depend in large part on the needs of our client.

§ 5.6   Determining the Theory of a Case

The *theory of the case* is the most simplified, elegant statement we can craft of why the court should agree with our position. We use the word "statement," rather than "rationale," to stress that we must be able to *articulate* our theory using (usually) just a few words. Our theory blends law and justice; it tells the court why what we're asking for is something the court *should* give us. All of our arguments should be consistent with our theory.[4] The following hypothetical illustrates these principles.

The helicopter hypothetical. Assume, in our case, police officers used a helicopter to observe, without a warrant, our client's backyard marijuana garden. Assume further that the helicopter hovered just 200 feet above our client's home, creating extreme noise and stirring up dust. Under those circumstances, and in light of the *Ciraolo* case, what do we argue?

We know that we want to assert that the observation was a warrantless search violating the Fourth Amendment. OK. So far, so good. We also want to highlight the intrusiveness of the observation: the helicopter hovered just 200 feet above our client's home, created extreme noise, and stirred up dust. Is "physical intrusiveness," however, a critical element of the *Ciraolo* rule?

The State argues that it's not. The State asserts that the Court's passing comment that the *Ciraolo* observation was conducted "in a physically nonintrusive manner" was pure dicta and irrelevant to the Court's holding. Who's right? Who knows? Both are credible arguments. Both we and the State can cite to the *Ciraolo* case as authority for our views. (The law *is* tricky.)

How then can we "beef up" our position? Here's a suggestion: we develop a "theory" of the *Ciraolo* case and put it to work in our case.

For example, although we don't know which of the *Ciraolo* factors are the most important, or even necessary, we see a common theme among them.[5] That theme is that the officers made their observations from the "public thoroughfares" (see **Graphic 5.5(a)**), from "public navigable airspace" (see **Graphic 5.5(c)**), or from the "public airways" (see **Graphic 5.5(f)**). As a matter of public policy, these "air spaces" are designed to ensure that air traffic does not adversely impact the property below. Thus, and here's our theory, the warrantless observation in *Ciraolo* was permissible because the officers operated at a height which did not adversely impact the defendant's property. (In *Ciraolo* this was 1,000 feet.)

We then apply this theory to our case and argue that the helicopter—hovering just 200 feet above our client's home, creating extreme noise, and stirring up dust—*did* adversely impact the defendant's property. Under these conditions, we assert, *Ciraolo mandates* that the officers first obtain a warrant.

What will the State argue? The opposite, of course.

§ 5.7   The Holding:
Narrow versus Broad — Take Your Pick
Robinson and *Powell*: Status Crimes?

Not only is it difficult to determine the rule of a case, it's also mind-wrenching to determine the "holding" of a case. The "holding" simply is the court's answer to the

---

4. See Chapter 22, § 22.5(b).

5. Inductive reasoning strikes again! From the Court's factor analysis, we induce a common theme.

dispositive question in the case. For example, if the issue was whether the State violated the defendant's First Amendment rights in arresting him for burning the United States flag during a political protest (when the defendant was using the flag-burning to make a political point), the holding would be either "yes" or "no." Either the State violated the First Amendment (yes) or it didn't (no). However, if the court throws in the proverbial "kitchen sink" in analyzing the issue, determining the precise holding truly can be challenging. Take, for example, two United States Supreme Court cases: *Robinson* and *Powell*.[6]

In *Robinson*, the Court struck down a statute which made it a crime to "be addicted to the use of narcotics." *Robinson v. California*, 370 U.S. 660, 660 n.1 (1962). The Court found that the statute, in criminalizing the "status" of narcotic addiction, violated the Eighth Amendment's protection against cruel and unusual punishment. *Id.* at 666. The Court reasoned as follows:

Graphic 5.7(a)   **The *Robinson* Case**

This statute ... is not one which punishes a person for the use of narcotics, for their purchase, sale or possession, or for antisocial or disorderly behavior resulting from their administration. It is not a law which even purports to provide or require medical treatment. Rather, we deal with a statute which makes the "status" of narcotic addiction a criminal offense, for which the offender may be prosecuted "at any time before he reforms." California has said that a person can be continuously guilty of this offense, whether or not he has ever used or possessed any narcotics within the State, and whether or not he has been guilty of any antisocial behavior there.

It is unlikely that any State at this moment in history would attempt to make it a criminal offense for a person to be mentally ill, or a leper, or to be afflicted with a venereal disease.... But, ... a law which made a criminal offense of such a disease would doubtless be universally thought to be an infliction of cruel and unusual punishment in violation of the Eighth and Fourteen Amendments. [Citation omitted]

We cannot but consider the statute before us as of the same category. In this Court counsel for the State recognized that narcotic addition is an illness. Indeed, it is apparently an illness which may be contracted innocently or involuntarily. We hold that a state law which imprisons a person thus afflicted as a criminal, even though he has never touched any narcotic drug within the State or been guilty of any irregular behavior there, inflicts a cruel and unusual punishment in violation of the Fourteenth Amendment.

Id. at 666–67.

From this case, we can speculate how the Court would rule in future cases involving similar circumstances. For example, the Court probably would find unconstitutional

---

6. *Robinson v. California*, 370 U.S. 660 (1962); and *Powell v. Texas*, 392 U.S. 514 (1968).

any statute which made it a crime to "be mentally ill, or a leper, or to be afflicted with a venereal disease...." We can predict this result even though the Court's language concerning this topic was "dicta"—mental illness, leprosy, and venereal disease were not at issue in *Robinson*.

But, what exactly is the holding of this case? Is it just the few lines following the Court's language "[w]e hold ..."? Or, is it broader, including the factors the Court addressed? For example, is it important that narcotic addiction is considered "an illness"? Is it important that such addiction "may be contracted innocently or involuntarily"? If these factors were important, we could predict that the Court would also strike down a law which made it a crime *to be* an "alcoholic." Alcoholism, after all, is an "illness" and can "be contracted innocently or involuntarily."

But, could the *Robinson* holding be broader? Could we interpret it as meaning that the State could not, consistent with the Eighth Amendment, punish "conduct which is 'a characteristic and involuntary part of the pattern of the disease as it afflicts' the particular individual ..."? *See Powell v. Texas*, 392 U.S. 514, 534 (1968). Does it stand for the even broader proposition that "'[c]riminal penalties may not be inflicted upon a person for being in a condition he is powerless to change'"? *See id.* at 533.

If so, then would a law making it a crime to appear in public "in a state of intoxication" violate the Eighth Amendment? *See id.* at 517. What if such a law were applied against a defendant who was a chronic alcoholic and argued that his appearance in public in a state of intoxication was "'not of his own volition'"? *Id.* Would the holding of *Robinson* apply to these facts? Six years after deciding *Robinson*, the Court in *Powell* said "no" in a 5 to 4 decision.

In *Powell*, the defendant was arrested and convicted of "being in public while drunk." Justice Marshall, upholding that conviction and writing for a plurality of four Justices, distinguished this case from *Robinson*:

Graphic 5.7(b)   **The *Powell* Case**

On its face the present case does not fall within [the *Robinson*] holding, since appellant was convicted, not for being a chronic alcoholic, but for being in public while drunk on a particular occasion. The State of Texas thus has not sought to punish a mere status, as California did in *Robinson*; nor has it attempted to regulate appellant's behavior in the privacy of his own home. Rather, it has imposed upon appellant a criminal sanction for public behavior which may create substantial health and safety hazards, both for appellant and for members of the general public, and which offends the moral and esthetic sensibilities of a large segment of the community. This seems a far cry from convicting one for being an addict, being a chronic alcoholic, being 'mentally ill, or a leper....' [citation to *Robinson* omitted]

Robinson so viewed brings this Court but a very small way into the substantive criminal law. And unless *Robinson* is so viewed it is difficult to see any limiting principle that would serve to prevent this Court from becoming, under the aegis of the Cruel and Unusual Punishment Clause, the ultimate arbiter of the standards of criminal responsibility, in diverse areas of the criminal law, throughout the country.

···

The entire thrust of *Robinson's* interpretation of the Cruel and Unusual Punishment Clause is that criminal penalties may be inflicted only if the accused has committed some act, has engaged in some behavior, which society has an interest in preventing, or perhaps in historical common law terms, has committed some *actus reus*. It thus does not deal with the question of whether certain conduct cannot constitutionally be punished because it is, in some sense, "involuntary" or "occasioned by a compulsion...."

[T]here is a substantial definitional distinction between a "status," as in *Robinson*, and a "condition," which is said to be involved in this case. Whatever may be the merits of an attempt to distinguish between behavior and a condition, it is perfectly clear that the crucial element in this case, so far as the dissent is concerned, is whether or not appellant can legally be held responsible for his appearance in public in a state of intoxication. The only relevance of *Robinson* to this issue is that because the Court interpreted the statute there involved as making a "status" criminal, it was able to suggest that the statute would cover even a situation in which addiction had been acquired involuntarily. [citation to *Robinson* omitted] That this factor was not determinative in the case is shown by the fact that there was no indication of how Robinson himself had become an addict.

Id. at 532–34.

Is Justice Marshall's interpretation of *Robinson* correct? If the *Robinson* Court did not, in Justice Marshall's words, consider the involuntary acquisition of the addiction as a "determinative" factor in the case, then why did the *Robinson* Court address it? Why did the *Robinson* Court compare narcotics addiction to mental illness, leprosy, and disease; highlight that counsel for the State "recognized that narcotics addiction is an illness"; and state, "[i]ndeed, it is apparently an illness which may be contracted innocently or involuntarily"? *Robinson*, 370 U.S. at 667. Doesn't this emphasis show that the Court considered this factor "determinative"?

Moreover, is Marshall's interpretation of *Robinson* one shared by the majority of the Court? Remember, Marshall was writing for just four Justices. Did Marshall just take a bite out of *Robinson*?[7] What would have happened if *Powell* had gone the other way?

Enough questions! Let's see what we *do* know.

From *Robinson* and *Powell*, we know that we can't be convicted under a law which makes our "status" a crime, but we can be convicted for engaging in an act society has an interest in preventing. This, however, raises another question (of course). May the State punish "involuntary conduct that is inextricably related to" one's status? *See Pottinger v. City of Miami*, 810 F. Supp. 1551, 1563 (S.D. Fla. 1992). This question turns on how broadly or narrowly we view the *Robinson* and *Powell holdings*.

Two federal district courts addressing this issue came up with two different answers. Surprised? Of course not.

---

7. Aren't rhetorical questions fun?

In *Pottinger*, the court held that one could *not* be punished for conduct inextricably related to status. *Id.* at 1561. There, homeless plaintiffs sued the City of Miami, contending that their arrests under ordinances prohibiting such actions as "lying down, sleeping, standing, sitting or performing other essential, life-sustaining activities in any public place" violated the Eighth Amendment. *Id.* The court framed the plaintiffs' theory as follows:

> Plaintiffs argue that their status of being homeless is involuntary and beyond their immediate ability to alter and that the conduct for which they are arrested is inseparable from their involuntary homeless status. Consequently, plaintiffs argue, application of these ordinances to them is cruel and unusual in violation of the eighth amendment.

Id.

After addressing the *Robinson* and *Powell* cases, the court reasoned that neither case addressed the issue the *Pottinger* plaintiffs had raised:

Graphic 5.7(c)   **The *Pottinger* Case**

[T]he *Powell* plurality was not confronted with a critical distinguishing factor that is unique to the plight of the homeless plaintiffs in this case: that they have no realistic choice but to live in public places. Justice White identified this distinction in his concurrence [in *Powell*]:

> The fact remains that some chronic alcoholics must drink and hence must drink somewhere. Although many chronics have homes, many others do not. For all practical purposes the public streets may become home for these unfortunates, not because their disease compels them to be there, but because, drunk or sober, they have no place else to go and no place else to be when they are drinking.... For some of these alcoholics I would think a showing could be made that resisting drunkenness is impossible and that avoiding public places when intoxicated is also impossible. As applied to them this statute is in effect a law which bans a single act for which they may not be convicted under the Eighth Amendment — the act of getting drunk.

[citation to *Powell* omitted] Although Justice White joined the majority in rejecting the appellant's challenge to his conviction, he did so only because he found the record insufficient to support the appellant's claim that his alcoholic condition compelled him to appear in public while drunk. [citation omitted] In contrast, ... the record in the present case amply supports plaintiffs' claim that their homeless condition compels them to perform certain life-sustaining activities in public.

[Finding this distinction critical, the *Pottinger* court ruled that the City of Miami's actions had violated the Eighth Amendment:]

> Because of the unavailability of low-income housing or alternative shelter, plaintiffs have no choice but to conduct involuntary, life-sustaining activities in public places. The harmless conduct for which they are arrested is inseparable from

> their involuntary condition of being homeless. Consequently, arresting homeless
> people for harmless acts they are forced to perform in public effectively punishes
> them for being homeless.

Id. at 1563–64.

After *Pottinger*, can a homeless person be arrested in Miami for engaging in sexual activity in public? Bathing in public? Urinating or defecating in public? Being intoxicated in public?

Let's look now at another court which found that one *could* be punished for conduct inextricably related to status, i.e., begging in public. Here's what the court in *Joyce v. City and County of San Francisco*, 846 F. Supp. 843, 857–58 (N.D. Cal. 1994), said on this issue:

Graphic 5.7(d)   **The *Joyce* Case**

On no occasion ... has the Supreme Court invoked the Eighth Amendment in order to protect acts derivative of a person's status. *Robinson* prohibited penalizing a person based on [his] status as having been addicted, whereas the plurality in *Powell* approved a state's prosecution of the act of appearing intoxicated in public. What justified invocation of the Eighth Amendment in one case and not the other was not the difference between drug and alcohol addiction; such distinction is without analytical difference. Rather, the different results were reached because of the distinct targets of the challenged laws — one punished a status, the other an act. Justice Black, concurring in the plurality opinion in Powell, explained,

> [In *Robinson*, we] explicitly limited our holding to the situation where no conduct
> of any kind is involved.... [A]ny attempt to explain *Robinson* as based solely on
> the lack of voluntariness encounters a number of logical difficulties.... [citation]

Plaintiffs' argument that *Powell* would have been differently decided had the defendant been homeless does not reflect the holding of the case and is sheer speculation. While language in Justice White's concurrence can be argued to support that contention, such language was dicta. One can only hypothesize that Justice White would actually have cast his vote differently had the defendant been homeless. Nothing underscores this point more vividly than the fact that Justice White was one of two vigorous dissenters in *Robinson*.

...

The Court must approach with hesitation any argument that science or statistics compels a conclusion that a certain condition [homelessness] be defined as a status. The Supreme Court has determined that drug addiction equals a status, and this Court is so bound. But the Supreme Court has not made such a determination with respect to homelessness, and because that situation is not directly analogous to drug addiction, it would be an untoward excursion by this Court into matters of social policy to accord to homelessness the protection of status.

There we have it. Two different federal district courts reached two different conclusions applying the same two cases. Each court interpreted the cases and drew from them a theory. Each then applied that theory to the facts. To the *Pottinger* court, homelessness was a status; to the *Joyce* court, it wasn't.

Unlike the *Pottinger* court, the *Joyce* court employed "judicial restraint." It narrowly interpreted the *Powell* and *Robinson* holdings, emphasized that Justice White's discussion in *Powell* was dicta, and refused to take an "untoward excursion ... into matters of social policy to accord homelessness the protection of status." 846 F. Supp. at 857–58. Could the *Joyce* court have gone the other way? Absolutely. Can a conviction for the same act violate the Eighth Amendment if performed in the Southern District of Florida but not if performed in the Northern District of California? Absolutely. But, doesn't the Eighth Amendment apply to the entire country? Sure, but only as *interpreted* by the courts. Is this unsettling? It is to us.

Would *Joyce* or *Pottinger* be upheld on review before the United States Supreme Court? Your guess is as good as ours. Were the courts in *Pottinger* and *Joyce* truly addressing a situation not covered by *Powell* and *Robinson*? Or, were they *reinterpreting* those holdings? Did the *Pottinger* court rely too much on White's concurrence? Was that concurrence, as the court in *Joyce* noted, mere dicta? Or, was it appropriate for the court in *Pottinger* to look closely at White's opinion, given that there was no majority opinion in the *Powell* case? Was White's concurrence highly relevant, in that it addressed, even though hypothetically, a *Pottinger*-like issue? But what of White's *dissent* in *Robinson*? Would the plurality in *Powell* at least agree with White's view that a homeless chronic alcoholic could not, consistent with the Eighth Amendment, be arrested for public intoxication?

What of the *next* case? What if a beggar challenges an anti-begging statute under the theory that the statute prohibits him from conducting the "involuntary, life-sustaining" activity of begging? Would arresting him for begging be tantamount to arresting him for his involuntary status of being homeless? Is the conduct of begging harmless and inseparable from a beggar's homeless status? Or, is begging harmful? Is it a voluntary act? Is it distinct from the *Pottinger* acts of sitting, sleeping, and loitering in public? As of this writing, we don't know. Without doubt, though, this is an issue headed (someday) to the Supreme Court.

§5.8   Smoker's Battery?

Let's look at another example of rule interpretation. This time, let's see how advances in scientific research impact the evolution of the law. Take, for example, the law of battery. The Restatement of the Law [Second] Torts (1965) states the common law rule for civil battery as follows:

Graphic 5.8	Civil Battery

An actor is subject to liability to another for battery if

(a) he acts intending to cause a harmful or offensive contact with the person of the other..., and

(b) a harmful contact with the person of the other directly or indirectly results [; or]

(c) an offensive contact with the person of the other directly or indirectly results.

Under this definition, is intentionally blowing or exhaling cigarette smoke onto another person a "battery"? It seems to us that as we (as a society) learn more about the adverse health effects of second-hand smoke, we'll see more lawsuits alleging "smoker's battery." Certainly, to most nonsmokers, cigarette smoke is "offensive."

Further, science is showing that the particulates comprising cigarette smoke *do* make contact and do contain harmful chemicals and carcinogens. Consequently, we could argue that the smoke has the requisite physical properties to make a "harmful contact." In light of new scientific findings and changes in societal attitudes towards smoking, smoker's battery— a theory that might have seemed in the 1980's to be a "law professor hypothetical"—may now be a legitimate cause of action.

Would it also be legitimate to find smokers liable even if they did not specifically "intend" to exhale on any particular individual? Would it be enough for a plaintiff to demonstrate, with substantial certainty, that the exhaled smoke would contact the plaintiff? After all, don't smokers intend to smoke? And aren't smokers aware that their emitted smoke will travel to nonsmokers?

Going further, could a nonsmoker state a cause of action for alleged injuries against an employer who permits co-employees to smoke in an enclosed environment? *See Pechan v. Dynapro, Inc.*, 622 N.E. 2d 108 (Ill. App. 1993). Could we hold parents liable for child abuse for spewing toxic substances, i.e., exhaled cigarette smoke, upon their children? Could we prosecute a case for child endangerment against women who smoke during their pregnancy? Could we state a cause of action for *criminal* battery in any of these examples?

It is highly unlikely that any of the judges fashioning the common law rule of battery ever intended liability to attach to a smoker for the act of smoking. Yet, the words "harmful" and "offensive contact" are broad enough to encompass such a cause of action. Language is at work here, either doing mischief or justice, but always doing something. The "smoking monkey" is lurking around every corner.[8] We stay alert for the *possibilities*—theories, causes of action, defenses—that language offers.

---

8. *See* Chapter 3, § 3.4.

§ 5.9   Discussing Cited Cases: An Introduction

Now that we've gotten a glimpse of how daunting the task of figuring out the rule and holding of a case can be, let's look at the equally daunting task of determining how to *use* a case in making a legal argument.

Reading cases is an *art*, as is *applying* cases in a brief or memo. But reading cases is tricky, and writing about them is trickier still. In writing about a case, we make crucial decisions of relevancy and importance. We determine what aspects of the case to include and what to omit. We extract from the precedent case just what we need and no more. As Albert Einstein stated, "Everything must be made as simple as possible, but not one bit simpler."

One of the most difficult decisions we make in dealing with cases is determining when we have been *simple enough*. In brief and memo writing, cases are tools. We include them *only* if they further our argument or discussion. And, we include *only* those parts relevant to our reasoning. We don't discuss a case just to show that we've found one. In legal writing, space is an exhaustible resource we can't afford to waste.

And we cannot waste our *credibility*. We must be mindful that judges will rely on the cases we've cited. To that end, we must be certain that we accurately state and explain the law. Indeed, as we've seen, rules of professional conduct *require* that we be absolutely candid in our dealings with the court. This candor extends further than many new lawyers realize: we must disclose cases and "any legal authority in the controlling jurisdiction known to the lawyer to be directly adverse to the position of the client and not disclosed by opposing counsel....."[9] This means that even if our opponent did not disclose the particular law/case, and even if the law/case is against our position, we *must* disclose that legal authority to the court. We do so, we analyze the authority, and we show how it doesn't harm our client's case. How? We'll see.

In the next chapter, we'll explore general guidelines for using cases in legal writing. Then, we'll look specifically at where a case discussion "fits" within the design of our written argument. By the end, we'll know the basics of using cases effectively, a skill as important to lawyers as using a scalpel is to surgeons.

§ 5.10   Exercises

§ 5.10(a)   Exercise in Identifying Sources of Law
and Their Precedential Value

Exercise 1. An attorney admitted to the state bar brought an action to recover dues paid to the bar. The bar utilized funds to make financial contributions to political campaigns to which the attorney objected. The issue, presently before the United States Court of Appeals for the Seventh Circuit, is whether the order of the state supreme court integrating

---

9. Model Rules of Prof'l Conduct R. 3.3.

the bar,[10] and thus compelling attorneys to pay dues, was unconstitutional on the ground that it violated the First Amendment right to freely associate.

Determine whether each of the sources listed below is (1) primary or secondary and (2) whether the source is binding or persuasive. A typical answer might be: "Secondary, persuasive."

a. A decision from the U.S. Supreme Court holding that only a legitimate state interest can justify infringing First Amendment rights.

b. A decision from the District Court for the District of Columbia holding that there was no legitimate state interest that justified compelling payment of dues to a union, where the union contributed some of the dues to political campaigns unrelated to the union's purpose.

c. An article published in the University of Florida Law Review discussing unions, arguing that the state has a legitimate interest in compelling certain individuals to join unions, because doing so promotes industrial peace and prevents non-union members from free-riding on the benefits of union bargaining.

d. A decision from the United States Court of Appeals for the First Circuit, holding that only a compelling state interest can justify infringing First Amendment rights.

e. A decision from the United States Court of Appeals for the Seventh Circuit stating, in dicta, that a state bar's compulsory dues provision could be unconstitutional where the bar contributes financially to political causes unrelated to the state bar's purpose.

f. A decision from the Florida Supreme Court holding that the integration of the Florida state bar is constitutional.

g. The First Amendment to the U.S. Constitution, which provides, in relevant part, the rights to free speech and free association.

h. An entry in American Jurisprudence, a legal encyclopedia, explaining that the integration of a state bar has never been held unconstitutional.

i. A treatise on state bars explaining that bars must be cautious in deciding how to spend their money, because compulsory dues may infringe the right to free association.

§ 5.10(b)   Exercises in Identifying and Distinguishing Between Holding and Dictum in a Court Opinion

Exercise 1. Assume our client is Jane Smith. Jane's boyfriend, Bob Atkinson, died on July 27, 2010. Mr. Atkinson, a real estate attorney, had never married, had no children, and left no will, although he and Jane had discussed making wills leaving their respective estates to each other. His only surviving relative was a second cousin with whom he had no contact. Shortly after his death, Jane, who had lived with Mr. Atkinson for ten years, was sorting through his papers in their home office. She found in his desk drawer, among other papers, a sticky note attached to a bank statement with the following written on it:

---

10. When a state requires membership in the state's bar association to practice law within that state, such an organization is called a mandatory, integrated, or unified bar.

"In case something happens to me:
All my $ to Jane Smith
1/13/09
Bob Atkinson"

California Probate Code §6111(a) provides that a holographic will is valid if the "signature and material provisions" are in the testator's handwriting. In addition, courts require that wills demonstrate testamentary intent pursuant to California Probate Code §6111(c): "[a]ny statement of testamentary intent contained in a holographic will may be set forth ... in the testator's own handwriting...."

Read the *In re Estate of Blain*, 295 P.2d 898 (Cal. Ct. App. 4th Dist. 1956) decision located in Appendix A, and decide whether the following statements from the *Blain* court constitute the court's holding or whether the statements are dicta. Label each statement either as holding or dicta.

1. "If, in a document constituting a will, there should appear the statement 'To Jane Doe, my diamond ring' the word 'to' in its particular context would be dispositive, ... but the word 'to' is certainly not a term of art applicable only to testamentary disposition." *Id.* at 901.

2. "It is, of course, elementary that proof of testamentary intent must be made with respect to the very paper proposed before any document may be admitted to probate as a last will and testament.... And the court's finding that there was no testamentary intent is supported by substantial evidence." *Id.* at 901-02.

3. "The suggested integration of the slip of paper in the ring box with the admittedly integrated seven sheets in the envelope, has no such evidentiary support." *Id.* at 903.

Exercise 2. Samuel Barnes applied for a patent for a pair of corset springs in 1866. Mr. Barnes had made a pair of corset springs for Mrs. Barnes in 1855. Mrs. Barnes then wore the corset springs. Believing the 1866 patent was infringed, Mrs. Barnes, as executrix, sued Defendant. According to statute, a patent is invalid if the invention it covers was in public use, with the consent and allowance of the inventor, for more than two years prior to the date of the application for the patent. Defendant argued that Barnes's patent was invalid due to prior public use.

Read the *Egbert v. Lippmann*, 104 U.S. 333 (1881) decision located in Appendix A and decide whether the following statements from the *Egbert* Court are holding or dicta. Label each.

1. "We observe, in the first place, that to constitute the public use of an invention it is not necessary that more than one of the patented articles should be publicly used." *Id.* at 336.

2. "For instance, if the inventor of a mower, a printing-press, or a railway-car makes and sells only one of the articles invented by him, and allows the vendee to use it for two years, without restriction or limitation, the use is just as public as if he had sold and allowed the use of a great number." *Id.*

3. "The effect of the law is that no such consequence will necessarily follow from the invention being in public use or on sale, with the inventor's consent and allowance, at any time within two years before his application; but that, if the invention is in

public use or on sale prior to that time, it will be conclusive evidence of abandonment, and the patent will be void." *Id.* at 337-38.

Exercise 3. Several months ago Hal Hunter graduated from high school. At that time, he decided that he needed to make a will to provide for his long-time girlfriend, Sara Dunn, and their child, in the event that he died. Hal grew up in a terrible home environment and suffered from a severe drug addiction problem that began when he was twelve. He was successfully emancipated from his parents at the age of sixteen and quit using all drugs at that time. However, Hal still had flashbacks from time to time and had suffered some permanent brain damage which may have affected his ability to make logical decisions. Hal wrote out a will leaving all his money, property, and belongings to his best friend Mark Stiles, who told Hal that if Hal left everything to him, he would make sure that Hal's family was taken care of. Last week, at the age of seventeen, Hal died in a car accident. Under Hal's will, Mark Stiles gets all of Hal's estate, giving nothing to Hal's girlfriend Sara, and their child. Sara wishes to contest the will, claiming that Hal lacked testamentary capacity.

Read the *In Re Estate of Edwards*, 433 So. 2d 1349 (Fla. Dist. Ct. App. 1983) decision located in Appendix A, and decide whether the following statements from the *Edwards* court are holding or dicta. Label each.

1. "It is well settled that a testator is determined to be of 'sound mind' when he has the ability to mentally understand in a general way (1) the nature and extent of the property to be disposed of, (2) the testator's relation to those who would naturally claim a substantial benefit from his will and, (3) a general understanding of the practical effect of the will as executed…." *Id.* at 1350.
2. "Viewing the evidence as a whole against the definition of insane delusion as stated in *Hooper*, we cannot disagree with the trial court's conclusion that decedent was not suffering from an insane delusion when he executed the will in question." *Id.* at 1352.
3. "Monomania, sometimes designated paranoia, has reference to a craze or mania for a single object or class of objects." *Id.* at 1351.

Chapter Review
Sources of Law; Reading and Interpreting Cases

- Every case is a story involving a *human being.*
- *Stare decisis* means that judges should decide like cases alike.
- The *common law* is judge-made law.
- *Precedent* means a prior, authoritative case.
- *Binding precedent* is a case our court must follow.
- A *holding* is the court's answer to the dispositive issue in the case.
- The court's *holding* can be narrow or broad, depending on our interpretation of the case.
- *Dicta* is "legal gravy" — factors the court discusses but which aren't necessary to the court's decision.
- *Reasoning* is how the court applied the rule to the facts to reach the holding.
- In researching cases, look for those with facts and an issue similar to ours, *or* for those involving a legal *theory* we seek to advance.
- **Always update every authority used in a brief or memo to ensure that the authority is still good law.**
- A *personalized* rule is the rule the court designs from existing rules to "fit" the facts of the case it is deciding.
- In a single case, the court may state the rule in different ways. It's our job to interpret that rule in a way that is theoretically consistent with the case and best fits our client's needs.
- **Always disclose to the court "any legal authority in the controlling jurisdiction [you know is] directly adverse to the position of [your] client and not disclosed by opposing counsel...."** Model Rules of Prof'l Conduct R. 3.3.
- Language makes the law flexible: never forget that we're dealing with Jell-O® and truffles.

Chapter 6

Using Cases Effectively

Overview. In this Chapter, we'll explore how we use cases in problem solving. To streamline our discussion, we'll refer to the document we're writing as an "argument." Although "argument" is a word used more to describe the function of a brief, we're using the term here to apply both to brief-writing *and* to memo-writing. The truth is that we use the same methods of presenting a case to our reader whether our document is predictive or persuasive. Just *how* we do so is as much logic as it is art.

§6.1   When in Doubt, Cut It Out

"He that hath knowledge spareth his words."

—Proverbs 17:27

When we write, we flip on the computer or grab some paper and face a sea of blank space. We write our first word, then the next, then a deluge. But this space we quickly fill is an exhaustible resource we can't afford to squander. There's no better way to annoy a judge or colleague than by including "flab" in our writing. Every word counts. Every cited case must advance our argument or analysis. There's no room in our brief or memo for the irrelevant or even for the relevant but ineffective. Join us in chanting our mantra: *When in doubt, cut it out.*

Winnow. In writing a memo or brief, we're not writing an encyclopedic summary of the law. Yet, our immediate impulse may be to cite every possibly relevant case to "prove" that our interpretation, or choice, of the controlling rule is correct. After all, we want to impress our reader with our research skills. We want to show, by the dazzling number of cases we've cited, that our interpretation or choice is correct. Too bad: we'd be wrong, dead wrong.

Far from being impressed by a string of multiple citations to (and related discussion of) a host of cases, judges and colleagues will be annoyed, very annoyed. By over-citing, we've shouted out that we haven't done our job. We haven't winnowed our selection of cases down to the *most relevant* precedents.

How do we know if a case is relevant? As we explain in more detail below, the relevancy of a cited case depends on the *function* the case serves in solving the problems presented in *our* case. Unless a cited case (1) states the rule, (2) explains the rule, or (3) provides a pattern of thought we seek to apply in our case, it has no place in our document. A case is relevant only to the degree it serves one of these three functions.

Thus, instead of littering our pages with case after case, and blasting our readers with shotgunned discourse, we use the "silver bullet" approach. We select and address only those cases which go to the heart of the matter. Think of every citation as if it literally attaches the cited case to our brief or memo. Just how thick do we want our document to be?

As Judge Aldisert beautifully illustrated, in citation and in case discussion, *less is more*:

> The time has come for lawyers to simplify, rather than complicate, current legal issues. The time has come to identify clearly the controversy in each case, and to isolate the branch of the law governing that controversy. The first step must be to concentrate on the tree's trunk and its main branches, rather than to fuss over the buds and blossoms which continually sprout and grow, but with the fall will be gone.[1]

Simplify. Our goal in writing is to simplify the legal issues. We accomplish this when we answer the legal problem *before,* and *not while,* we write. As Abraham Lincoln allegedly remarked:

---

1. Ruggero Aldisert, *Winning on Appeal: Better Briefs and Oral Arguments* 208 (1996).

I could not sleep when I got on a hunt for an idea, until I had caught it; and when I thought I had got it, I was not satisfied until I had repeated it over and over again, until I had put it in language plain enough as I thought, for any boy I knew to comprehend.

Taking our cue from Lincoln, nothing but our most distilled thoughts should fill the page. To continue Judge Aldisert's metaphor, legal writing isn't flowery, it's lovingly pruned. If a cited case doesn't advance our client's case, we cut it from our document. And, if we can't explain the case in "language plain enough," it has no place in our writing.

The "light hand" approach. Over the course of practicing law, teaching thousands of law students, and reading thousands of briefs and memos, we've seen just about every imaginable way of discussing a cited case. Some discussions are so cryptic that they're meaningless. Some are so broad that they never make a point. Some pounce right on the point but back away too soon; some stay on the point too long.

To use cases effectively, as contradictory as this seems, we shouldn't rely on them too much. Our legal analysis must stand or fall on its own logic and not on the number of cases we've cited. If we haven't built our analysis on logic and common sense, no amount of cited cases can save it from crumbling. Cases don't support arguments, they simply add a gloss to whatever arguments they complement.

This is why experienced lawyers can write a brief, leave blanks for cases to be filled in by an associate, and nonetheless knock our socks off with the force of their argument. The underlying logic (of course based on a rule), and not the cited cases, packs the punch.

The true art form in discussing cited cases involves a "light hand." We use cases, but only to further a point *we* have made. *We,* not the case, make the point.

How to discuss a cited case. With these ideas in mind, we offer the following (time-, practice-, and student-tested) guidelines for discussing cited cases:

first: Using a *thesis* (i.e., point) *rule sentence,* state why or how the case is relevant. The *thesis rule sentence* is the start of our discussion of the cited case in the *rule (R)* section of BaRAC.

second: Address all relevant (and only relevant) aspects of the cited case and explain the law involved. This is the *rule* and *rule explanation (R)* section of BaRAC.

third: Using a *transitional bold assertion,* state how the cited case (or law developed from several cases/sources) applies to our case, then in the paragraph(s) that follow(s), apply the rule/reasoning of the cited case(s) to our facts. The *transitional bold assertion* is the sentence that begins the *application (A)* section of BaRAC.

Let's look at these three principles in detail.

§6.2   *First:*
Lead with the Point — Thesis Rule Sentence

Thesis rule sentence. In introducing a cited case to our reader, we lead with a transition, a thesis rule sentence, immediately stating, in clear terms, the relevancy or "point" of the case we're citing. This "point" expressly or implicitly states the rule. As stated above, a thesis rule sentence is our starting point for addressing the case in the *rule* section of our analysis, (the *R* in BaRAC).

As needed, we continue to prove and to explain the rule in a successive paragraph (or paragraphs), (the *R = Rule and Rule Explanation* in BaRAC). We're educating our reader regarding the relevant law. In §6.3 below, we explain how to use the cited case in writing our briefs and memos.

Topic sentence vs. thesis rule sentence. While a topic sentence[2] might introduce a general point about the law in a somewhat *neutral* manner, a thesis rule sentence, as we're using the term, specifically tells the reader why the *particular* case we're addressing is relevant. Although we could use a topic sentence for our transition, (and a topic sentence is better than no introductory sentence at all), a thesis rule sentence is stronger and more informative.

Graphic 6.2(a)	Topic Sentence — Thesis Rule Sentence — Transitional Bold Assertion — Bold Assertion
topic sentence	*C.L.B. v. State* [citation] involved a conviction for disorderly conduct.
thesis rule sentence	As *C.L.B. v. State* [citation] illustrates, a disorderly conduct conviction cannot rest on mere words alone.
transitional bold assertion (see §6.4)	Applying *C.L.B.*, this Court should reverse Doe's conviction for disorderly conduct.
bold assertion	This Court should reverse Doe's conviction for disorderly conduct.
flabby ☹ don't do this	*Next, we'll address the critical factor in our analysis conveyed by the* **C.L.B.** *case, a case similar to our case, that the conviction of Doe clearly should be reversed by this Court.* *Why it's wrong:* The boldface portion is flab. *How should we rewrite it?*

Thesis rule sentence vs. transitional bold assertion. While we use a thesis rule sentence to educate our reader about the law involved in solving our client's case, we use a

---

2. A method we all learned in English class of introducing our point in a paragraph or essay.

transitional bold assertion (discussed in more detail in §6.4 below), to state why that law does or doesn't apply *in our case*. In other words, while a thesis rule sentence introduces our discussion of the relevant legal principles, the transitional bold assertion states how or why the law does or doesn't apply to *our facts*. The thesis rule sentence begins the "education" part of our argument (the rule), while the transitional bold assertion begins the "persuasion" part (the application).

Let's see some more examples of thesis rule sentences.

The disorderly conduct hypothetical. Assume that we're explaining the law of "disorderly conduct," and we're introducing a case to address the difference between "illegal" disorderly conduct and "permissible" First Amendment speech. We could write the following:

Graphic 6.2(b)	Thesis Rule Sentence
do this	However, as *C.L.B. v. State* [citation] illustrates, where speech is combined with nonverbal conduct and causes a disturbance or interferes with an arrest, a disorderly conduct conviction may stand. In *C.L.B.*, the defendant was charged with.... [citation]
or do this	However, while a disorderly conduct conviction cannot rest on mere words, where speech is combined with nonverbal conduct and causes a disturbance or interferes with an arrest, a disorderly conduct conviction may stand. *See C.L.B. v. State*, [citation]. In *C.L.B.*, the defendant was charged with.... [citation] *In the above two examples, we've succeeded in orienting our readers.*
☹ *don't do this*	In *C.L.B. v. State*, [citation] the defendant was charged with disorderly conduct.... *why it's wrong: Our reader is lost. We're discussing the facts of the cited case without first establishing any context for those facts. Our reader has no clue why we're addressing the case because we haven't stated the point of the cited case. We might as well start out saying, "A pink elephant walked down the street...."*

Let's try some more examples.

The *Red v. Black* hypothetical. Assume that our client, Smith, is being sued for breach of contract and the issue is whether he had accepted Grey's offer. Assume we've uncovered a case, *Red v. Black*, relevant to the "acceptance" issue. Assume further that we'll use the *Red* case in our brief to argue by analogy. How would we "introduce" *Red* to our reader? Please notice that each correct example introduces the cited case with a bold assertion. This *bold assertion/thesis rule sentence* combination is a very powerful way to begin our discussion of the legal rule.

Graphic 6.2(c)	Thesis Rule Sentence Following a Bold Assertion
do this	No contract was formed in the instant case because Smith did not properly accept Grey's offer. As *Red v. Black*, [citation] illustrates, a contract is formed only upon proper acceptance. In *Red*, Red offered to sell a cow to Black for $500.00 … *Aha! Now we know why the* Red *case is relevant. We know the connection between our client, Smith, and the* Red *case.*
or do this	No contract was formed in the instant case because Smith did not properly accept Grey's offer. A contract is formed only upon proper acceptance. *Red v. Black* [citation].
☹ *don't do this*	No contract was formed in the instant case because Smith did not properly accept Grey's offer. In *Red v. Black* [citation], Red offered to sell a cow to Black. However, …
	why it's wrong: What is the rule of the case, and how does the Red *case relate to our case? There's no tie between our client, Smith, and the cited case.*
☹ *don't do this*	No contract was formed in the instant case because Smith did not properly accept Grey's offer. *Red* is a case that we'll next address in our presentation of this analysis that is factually similar to our case.
	Red is a case that is factually different from our case.
	why these are wrong: These sentences don't tell us how *the case is similar/dissimilar or* why *this similarity/dissimilarity is relevant. They fail to state either expressly or implicitly anything regarding the rule. Moreover, the second sentence is bloated with unnecessary phrases. If we use an unspecific or bloated sentence, rather than a crisp, powerful thesis rule sentence to begin discussing the law, we've wasted space in our document.*

Further examples. In the following, we've also annotated the *purpose* the cited case serves in the rule discussion.

Graphic 6.2(d)	Thesis Rule Sentence Following a Bold Assertion
cited case used to state the rule	Gotham City's Pedestrian Interference Code is void for vagueness because it does not sufficiently describe what behavior is outlawed. A code violates the Fourteenth Amendment if it fails to give adequate notice of what conduct is prohibited and consequently invites arbitrary and discriminatory enforcement. *State v. Wyche*, 619 So. 2d 231, 236 (Fla. 1993).
	note: The name of the code is capitalized as a proper noun. There's no "see" signal before the cite because the rule cited comes directly from the case.

cited case used to state, and then to explain, the rule	Gotham City's Pedestrian Interference Code violates the due process clause of the Florida Constitution because the Code bears no substantial or rational relation to any legitimate governmental interest. "The guarantee of due process requires that the means selected shall have a reasonable and substantial relation to the object sought to be attained and shall not be unreasonable, arbitrary, or capricious." *State v. Saiez*, 489 So. 2d 1125, 1128 (Fla. 1986).
cited case used to state, and then to explain, the rule	Gotham City's Pedestrian Interference Code violates the due process clause of the Florida Constitution because the Code bears no substantial or rational relation to any legitimate governmental interest. "The guarantee of due process requires that the means selected shall have a reasonable and substantial relation to the object sought to be attained and shall not be unreasonable, arbitrary, or capricious." *State v. Saiez*, 489 So. 2d 1125, 1128 (Fla. 1986). In *Saiez*, the Florida Supreme Court struck down, as an unconstitutional exercise of the state's police power, a statute prohibiting the mere possession of machinery designed to reproduce credit cards. *Id.* at 1126. The court reasoned that criminalizing the mere possession of such devices bore no rational relationship to the goal of preventing counterfeiting. *Id.* at 1129. *note: The word "Code" in the second sentence is capitalized as a proper noun.*
cited case used to argue by analogy; case is then addressed in detail	Doe's conviction for simply asking a pedestrian for spare change violates the Eighth Amendment because it criminalizes his "homeless" status. *See Robinson v. California*, 370 U.S. 660, 667 (1962). In *Robinson*, the defendant was convicted of violating a state statute which made it a crime to be addicted to narcotics. *Id.* at 660-61. *note: Do you know why the signal "see" is used here?*
cited case used to argue by counter analogy; case is then addressed in detail	The critical factor, that Doe had no choice but to be homeless and on the streets, distinguishes this case from *Powell v. Texas*, 392 U.S. 514, 517 (1968). In *Powell*, the defendant, appealing a conviction for public drunkenness, claimed that his status as a chronic alcoholic was involuntary, and thus his punishment was cruel and unusual. *Id.*....

Now on to the second principle of discussing a cited case.

§ 6.3   *Second*:
Include Only the Relevant Aspects of the Cited Case

Once we've demonstrated the relevancy of the cited case to our case through a strong thesis sentence, we explain the relevant, *and only the relevant*, aspects of the cited case. How we use the case determines which aspects of the case are relevant.

§ 6.3(a)   *Rule-Only Approach*
Where Only the Rule Is Relevant

If only the rule of the cited case is relevant, that's all we discuss. In other words, if we cite the case *solely* to discuss the rule of the case, and *not* to compare the facts of the cited case to our case, then we don't discuss the facts of the cited case. It's that simple. Really, it is. We address only the rule, and usually we quote the relevant parts of the rule verbatim. Under these circumstances, we're not using the cited case to argue by analogy. Our reasoning focuses only on applying the rule from the cited case to our facts. Our reader just needs to know what that rule is.

If the rule involves factors (elements), we apply them one-by-one, to our facts. If necessary, we create a subheading for each factor. If not, we use transitions to inform our reader that we're moving from one factor to the next.

Judges often use cases in this manner, i.e., to address only the applicable rule. In the following example, Justice Douglas, in reversing the petitioner's conviction for disorderly conduct in *Terminiello v. Chicago*, 337 U.S. 1, 4 (1949), employed this rule-only technique:

Graphic 6.3(a)(1) Rule-Only Approach: Example of Using Cited Cases

As we have noted, the statutory words "breach of the peace" were defined in instructions to the jury to include speech which "stirs the public to anger, invites dispute, brings about a condition of unrest, or creates a disturbance...." That construction of the ordinance is a ruling on a question of state law that is as binding on us as though the precise words had been written into the ordinance. *See Winters v. New York*, 333 U.S. 507, 514; *Hebert v. Louisiana*, 272 U.S. 312, 317.

Justice Douglas did not address the facts or other aspects of the *Winters* or *Hebert* cases because he did not *need* to address them. He cited the cases only for their rules. The facts of these cases were not relevant to his use of these cases. In fact, he could have streamlined his writing by eliminating the second citation. If one citation does the job, there's no need for two.

Here's another example of employing the rule-only (or in this case the *no* rule-only approach). It comes from Judge David Gersten of the Florida District Court of Appeal, Third District. In this mercifully short case, Judge Gersten does not cite *any* cases. He doesn't because there was no reason for him to do so; no authority existed recognizing the point of law the appellant was attempting to advance. We've annotated the case to show its logical — BaRAC — structure.

Graphic 6.3(a)(2)   **Example of the Rule-Only Approach**

---

705 So.2d 976
Charles Edward Stone, Appellant,
v.
The State of Florida, Appellee.
No. 97-237.
District Court of Appeal of Florida,
Third District.
Jan. 28, 1998.

Before SCHWARTZ, C.J., and JORGENSON and GERSTEN, JJ.
GERSTEN, Judge.

introduction and bold assertion

Appellant, Charles Edward Stone ("defendant"), appeals his convictions for robbery and burglary with assault. We affirm because the trial court was not required to conduct an in-court inquiry to determine whether the defendant was aware of the consequences of proceeding to trial as a habitual offender.

rule

There is no authority recognizing the right to an in-court inquiry when a defendant decides to proceed to trial as a habitual offender.

application

Here, the defendant declined two different plea offers and elected to have the case tried.

conclusion

We decline to extend, or even recognize, the right to an in-court inquiry under these circumstances.... Affirmed.

For further examples of the rule-only approach in using cases, please refer to Chapter 2, § 2.4 and Chapter 4, § 4.1.

§ 6.3(b)   *Rule-Plus Approach*
Briefly Explain the Case

For some cited cases, stating just the rule doesn't go far enough, but explaining the rule by fully discussing the case goes too far. If understanding the facts and/or the reasoning of the cited case helps our reader to understand the rule of the case, we use the rule-plus approach; i.e., we briefly discuss those relevant facts and the court's reasoning. We also use this approach where the cited cases don't state the rule as directly as we'd like, requiring us to synthesize or *induce* a rule that does.[3] In each of these circumstances, we can "beef up" our discussion of the rule, yet still conserve space in our

---

3. We address synthesizing cases and inducing a rule in more detail in Chapter 7, § 7.4.

document. We can either explain the information our reader needs by using a few sentences, or by using a *parenthetical*.

A *parenthetical* is an explanatory statement contained in parentheses following a citation.[4] Because writing parenthetical explanations may be foreign to you, we'll focus on this approach to the rule-plus method. As the following examples demonstrate, parentheticals highlight relevant facts, briefly state the holding or reasoning of the cited case, and/or provide short quotations.

Graphic 6.3(b)(1)	Rule-Plus Approach
parenthetical:	The mere testimony of the plaintiff, considered alone, "is not proof of severe emotional distress." *Ford Motor Credit Co. v. Sheehan*, 373 So. 2d 956, 959 (Fla. Dist. Ct. App. 1979) (concluding that the plaintiff's testimony that he had been "extremely worried, upset, and nearly out of his mind for a continuous period of seven hours" was, standing alone, insufficient evidence of severe distress).
a few sentences:	The mere testimony of the plaintiff, considered alone, "is not proof of severe emotional distress." *Ford Motor Credit Co. v. Sheehan*, 373 So. 2d 956, 959 (Fla. Dist. Ct. App. 1979). In *Ford Motor*, the court concluded that the plaintiff's testimony that he had been "extremely worried, upset, and nearly out of his mind for a continuous period of seven hours" was, standing alone, insufficient evidence of severe distress. [citation]
a few sentences:	*See California v. Ciraolo*, [citation]. In *Ciraolo*, the Court reasoned that in shielding, with a ten foot fence, his backyard marijuana plants from ground-level view, the defendant had manifested a subjective expectation of privacy.
parenthetical:	*See Dow*, [citation] (upholding the EPA's warrantless taking of aerial, high resolution photographs of structures in an industrial building complex).
parenthetical:	*But see California v. Greenwood*, [citation] (concluding that in setting out garbage on the public street, the defendant had renounced his expectation of privacy in the contents of the discarded material).
parenthetical:	*See United States v. Place*, [citation] (declaring that the government's use of a specially trained canine to sniff luggage was not a search).

---

4. See Rules B11 and 10.6 of *The Bluebook* for additional information regarding explanatory parentheticals.

parenthetical:	*See Smith v. United States*, [citation] (holding that the government's use of a pen register, which disclosed only dialed telephone numbers and not the content of communications, was not a search).
parenthetical:	*See United States v. Lee*, [citation] (concluding that the government's use of a searchlight, which uncovered contraband from a distance, was not a search).
parenthetical:	*See Dow Chem. Co. v. United States*, [citation] (concluding that "Dow plainly ha[d] a reasonable, legitimate, and objective expectation of privacy within the interior of its covered buildings.").
	note: *Yes, the double periods are proper here. One period ends the quoted sentence, and the other period ends our citation sentence.*
parenthetical:	*See Dow Chem. Co. v. United States*, [citation] (noting that the government's "surveillance of private property by using highly sophisticated surveillance equipment not generally available to the public ... might be constitutionally proscribed absent a warrant.").

The "ing" ending. Note that all of these parentheticals begin with a present participle, what we call "ing" words, such as "concluding," "stating," etc., as specified by *The Bluebook*. Other appropriate present participles for beginning a parenthetical include "holding," "reasoning," "suggesting," and "explaining."

When using the rule-only approach to discuss a cited case, we could also use (1) a series of parentheticals or (2) even a more extended explanation of the cited case(s). In the following opinion, which we've quoted in its entirety, Judge David Gersten used both of these devices (parentheticals and extended discussion), as well as just the rule-only method of discussing cases. We've annotated the opinion to show its "logical" form and have highlighted Judge Gersten's use of parentheticals by italicizing them.

Please note, however, that judges do not always follow the conventions lawyers and students are expected and required to use. For example, the citations in most judicial opinions are not in proper *Bluebook* format. Judges have the freedom to write in their own style. In the case below, for example, Judge Gersten used a present participle to begin some, but not all, of the rule-plus parentheticals he used. His method worked just fine. But we, as lawyers and students, should follow the expected convention and introduce case parentheticals with "ing" words.

Graphic 6.3(b)(2)   Rule-Plus Approach Used in a Judicial Opinion

690 So. 2d 1341

Martha Rae a/k/a Mrs. Ian Nicholas Rae, Appellant,

v.

John F. Flynn, M.D., Appellee.

Nos. 96-1705, 96-1704.

District Court of Appeal of Florida,

Third District.

March 19, 1997.

Before SCHWARTZ, C.J., and GERSTEN, and GREEN, JJ.

GERSTEN, Judge.

introduction

Appellant, Martha Rae ("Rae"), appeals both an order denying her an injunction for protection against repeat violence, and also an order granting her neighbor, appellee, John Flynn, M.D. ("Flynn"), a permanent injunction against repeat violence and prohibiting Rae from housing pets outdoors. We affirm.

bold assertion

This case presents the classic example of escalating neighbor hostilities which could have been avoided through common courtesy, and respect for the peace, quiet, and normal enjoyment to which every property owner is entitled in the use of his or her home. It is unfortunate for both parties as well as the neighborhood and community in general, that instead of attempting to reach an amicable solution to her neighbor's valid complaint regarding a dog nuisance, appellant Rae chose to retaliate. Such actions were properly not condoned by the trial court.

facts

To briefly review the relevant facts, Flynn complained that Rae's dogs were running at large and barking. Rae was thereafter found in violation of Monroe County Code 3-7 for permitting an animal to be a nuisance or run at large. In response, Rae built a 10 foot by 20 foot dog kennel on the common property line between the Rae and Flynn properties. The offensive barking became worse.

Flynn then filed a formal complaint with Monroe County Animal Control and was advised to take photographs and obtain other testimony as corroborating evidence. Flynn took photographs and tape recordings of the nuisance caused by the dogs in the kennel.

Hostilities between the neighbors increased. On May 28, 1996, Flynn filed a petition for injunction for protection against repeat violence seeking to enjoin Rae "from committing any further acts of repeat violence." The petition alleged that Rae was out of control, appeared physically violent, was responsible for slanderous graffiti on the common wall between the residences, and threatened to drive the Flynns out, play loud music, and walk around naked. Rae also threatened that if Flynn came on her property, she would treat him like a burglar and defend herself. At the conclusion of the hearing on Flynn's petition, the parties stipulated to the entry of a permanent injunction against violence.

However, instead of applying the common-sense doctrine of "live and let live," Rae apparently decided to adopt the "live and let's get even" approach. On June 5, 1996, she filed a retaliatory petition for injunction against repeat violence claiming that Flynn was harassing her family, and had trespassed on their property.

After a full evidentiary hearing, the trial court denied the injunction, finding the allegations were not supported by sufficient evidence. The trial court then modified the previous injunction in favor of Flynn, to prohibit Rae from housing any pets outside her property. Having now adopted the "live and let's drag this thing through court forever" doctrine, Rae appeals the injunction order and the order denying her motion for injunctive relief.

general rule: duty of property owner

A residential property owner has a duty not to unreasonably interfere with other persons' use and enjoyment of their property. Reaver v. Martin Theatres of Florida, Inc., 52 So.2d 682 (Fla.1951); Rogers v. City of Miami Springs, 231 So.2d 257 (Fla. 3d DCA), cert. denied, (Fla.1970). As recognized by the Supreme Court of Florida:

> An owner or occupant of property must use it in a way that will not be a nuisance to other owners and occupants in the same community. Anything which annoys or disturbs one in the free use, possession, or enjoyment of his property or which renders its ordinary use or occupation physically uncomfortable may become a nuisance and may be restrained.

Knowles v. Central Allapattae Properties, Inc., 145 Fla. 123, 130, 198 So. 819, 822 (1940) (quoting Mercer v. Keynton, 121 Fla. 87, 163 So. 411, 413 (1935)). The idea behind the law of nuisance, as expressed in the maxim "Sic utere tuo ut alienum non laedas," is that every person has the right to the free use of property so long as the rights of another are not injured. See Pierce v. Riggs, 149 Vt. 136, 540 A.2d 655 (1987); Baum v. Coronado Condominium Association, Inc., 376 So.2d 914 (Fla. 3d DCA 1979) (citing Reaver v. Martin Theatres of Florida, Inc., 52 So.2d at 683). [FN1]

> FN1. This court has further noted: "That mere noise may be so great at certain times and under certain circumstances as to amount to an actionable nuisance and entitle the party subjected to it to the preventive remedy of the court of equity is thoroughly established. The reason why a certain amount of noise is or may be a nuisance is that it is not only disagreeable but it also wears upon the nervous system and produces that feeling which we call 'tired.' That the subjection of a human being to a continued hearing of loud noises tends to shorten life, I think, is beyond all doubt. Another reason is that mankind needs both rest and sleep, and noise tends to prevent both." Baum v. Coronado Condominium Association, Inc., 376 So.2d at 916 (citing Bartlett v. Moats, 120 Fla. 61, 162 So. 477, 479 (1935)).

specific rule regarding barking dogs: rule explanation

Applying these general principle[s] to barking dogs, several courts have held that excessive dog barking which interferes with a neighboring property owner's right to enjoy the use of his or her home constitutes an enjoinable nuisance. See Brewton v. Young, 596 So.2d 577 (Ala.1992) *(noise and odor of dogs that interfered with neighbors' enjoyment of their homes enjoined as private nuisance)*; Connecticut v. Olson, 8 Conn. App. 188, 511 A.2d 379 (1986) *(recognizing dogs that bark excessively as a nuisance)*; Burnett v. Rushton, 52 So.2d 645 (Fla.1951) *(purposefully inciting dog to bark boisterously constitutes private nuisance)*; Allen v. Paulk, 188 So.2d 708 (La.Ct.App.1966) *(early morning barking dog classified as nuisance; plaintiff entitled to injunction where defendant could prevent dog's barking by keeping it in his house).*

Although there is no exact rule or formula for ascertaining when barking dogs rise to the level of a nuisance, relief will be granted where plaintiffs show they are substantially and unreasonably disturbed notwithstanding proof that others living in the vicinity are not annoyed. See Davoust v. Mitchell, 146 Ind.App. 536, 257 N.E.2d 332 (1970); City of Fredericktown v. Osborn, 429 S.W.2d 17 (Mo.Ct.App.1968). Moreover, in these types of cases "[e]ven meager or uncorroborated evidence will support the chancellor's findings if the evidence is of record and properly before the court." Hopkins v. Stepler, 315 Pa.Super. 372, 461 A.2d 1327 (1983).

application to the instant case

Here the trial court found Rae to be maintaining nuisance dogs in violation of the Monroe County Code, [FN2] and that Rae's behavior and threats were a retaliatory response to Flynn's legitimate complaint about the barking dogs. These findings are clearly supported by the record.

FN2. Rae was found in violation of Section 3-7(3) of the Monroe County Code which states: "It is unlawful for any animal owner or keeper to permit, either willfully or negligently, the animal to be a nuisance." Section 3-8 of the Monroe County Code provides that "when the court adjudges an animal to be a nuisance the animals may be removed and/or seized by the [Animal Control] Department."

Under Section 784.046(7)(b), a trial court has broad authority in addition to enjoining acts of violence to also "order such other relief as the court deems necessary for the protection of the petitioner...." § 784.046 (7)(b), Fla. Stat. (1997). In modifying the Flynn injunction, the trial court properly exercised its statutory authority to stop the hostilities by solving the cause of the tensions which was the barking dog problem.

The restrictions imposed on Rae are within the authority of the trial court and are not overbroad. The injunction still permits Rae to maintain her dogs, but requires that she do so in such a manner so as not to disturb Flynn's right to peacefully enjoy his property.

conclusion

Accordingly, because the trial court correctly exercised judicial restraint in crafting a remedy to accomplish the reduction of neighborhood hostilities by the least restrictive means, we affirm the order below.

policy

Finally, we note that Rae would not be the subject of a mandatory injunction and this case would not be before us now, had Rae simply respected her neighbor's legitimate complaint. Neighbors should reasonably resolve their differences without having to abuse the court system.

Affirmed.

SCHWARTZ, C.J., concurs.

GREEN, J., concurs in results only.

Inducing a personalized rule from several cases. Notice that Judge Gersten did not use the cases he cited to reason by analogy. Instead, he used those cases to explain the rules he was applying. Notice how he first developed the general rule regarding a property owner's duty to his/her neighbors, and then how he specifically addressed why that duty applied to an owner's "barking dogs." From these existing rules, he used inductive reasoning to design a personalized rule tailored to *the instant case*. His *induced*, personalized rule was as follows:

> Although there is no exact rule or formula for ascertaining when barking dogs rise to the level of a nuisance, relief will be granted where plaintiffs show they are substantially and unreasonably disturbed notwithstanding proof that others living in the vicinity are not annoyed.

He then applied this rule to the facts and reached a conclusion. He did not provide an expanded discussion of any of the cases he cited, because he did not need to do so. He discussed only the relevant aspects of the cited cases.

An example from the Supreme Court. The Supreme Court often uses this rule-plus method to expand the law by formulating new legal rules. In the following passage, from *Members of the City Council v. Taxpayers for Vincent*, 466 U.S. 789, 805-06 (1984), Justice Stevens did just that. (We've highlighted the new, "induced" rule in italics.)

> In *Kovacs v. Cooper*, [citation omitted], the Court rejected the notion that a city is powerless to protect its citizens from unwanted exposure to certain methods of expression which may legitimately be deemed a public nuisance. In upholding an ordinance that prohibited loud and raucous sound trucks, the Court held that the State had a substantial interest in protecting its citizens from unwelcome noise. [fn. omitted] In *Lehman v. City of Shaker Heights*, [citation omitted], the Court upheld the city's prohibition of political advertising on its buses, stating that the city was entitled to protect unwilling viewers against intrusive advertising that may interfere with the city's goal of making its buses 'rapid, convenient, pleasant, and inexpensive.' [citation omitted] *These cases indicate that the municipalities have a weighty, essentially esthetic interest in proscribing intrusive and unpleasant formats for expression.*

We think, as we stated above, that Justice Stevens "expanded" the law. What do you think?

When a rule applicable to our case has not yet been clearly articulated by any one case (as in the above example), we engage in a similar process of *synthesizing* or designing a *personalized* rule from multiple cases. In other words, we briefly explain the purpose and function of the existing rules, and then we induce a rule which suits our case. If we've adequately explained the existing rules, and if the *personalized* rule we induce is consistent with those rules, our reader will likely accept our "new" rule without further question.

Advancing our interpretation. We also use the rule-plus approach to argue that the court should apply the rule *we* advocate, rather than the rule our opponent advances. An example of this use occurred in *Ward v. Rock Against Racism*, 491 U.S. 781 (1989).

One issue the Supreme Court addressed in *Ward* was how "narrowly tailored" a statute regulating the time, place, or manner of protected speech had to be. The Respondent contended that the tailoring had to be *really, really* narrow, so much so that no least restrictive alternative was available. The Petitioner (i.e., the government), however, countered that this "least restrictive alternative" test applied only to "content-based" speech restrictions, not to the type of "content-neutral" restriction at issue in the case. The Court, in finding for the Petitioner (the government), used the rule-plus approach, as follows, to discredit the Respondent's argument:

> Respondent contends that our decision last Term in *Boos v. Barry*, 485 U.S. 312 (1988), supports the conclusion that 'a regulation is neither precisely drawn nor "narrowly tailored" if less intrusive means than those employed are available.' Brief for Respondent 27. In *Boos* we concluded that the government regulation at issue was 'not narrowly tailored; a less restrictive alternative is readily available.' 485 U.S., at 329[5].... In placing reliance on *Boos*, however, respondent ignores a crucial difference between that case and this. The regulation we invalidated in *Boos* was a content-based ban on displaying signs critical of foreign governments; such content-based restrictions on political speech 'must be subjected to the most exacting scrutiny.' 485 U.S., at 321. While time, place, or manner regulations must also be 'narrowly tailored' in order to survive First Amendment challenge, we have never applied strict scrutiny in this context. As a result, the same degree of tailoring is not required of these regulations, and least-restrictive-alternative analysis is wholly out of place.

Ward, 491 U.S. at 798-99 n.6.

This passage also reinforces what we said in Chapter 1. The law is like Jell-O®. Here, the same term—"narrowly tailored"—used in the context of the First Amendment means two different things. Go figure.[6]

§ 6.3(c)   *The FIHRR Approach*
Use the Cited Case to Reason by Analogy

Graphic 6.3(c)(1)		FIHRR		
F	I	H	R	R
Facts	Issue	Holding	Rule	Reasoning

Analogical reasoning. When we *are* using a cited case to reason by analogy, we *fully* discuss the case.[7] In other words, and subject to the caveats below, we address the

---

5. Please note that Supreme Court Justices do not always follow *The Bluebook* citation rules. Who can blame them?

6. Perhaps there *is* a reason why the study of the Supreme Court's interpretation of the Constitution is lovingly referred to as "Con Law."

7. Please see Chapter 2, § 2.7, where we address the logic involved in reasoning by analogy.

relevant facts, issue, holding, rule, and reasoning of the case. We call this mnemonic the FIHRR method (pronounced "fire"). FIHRR, like the rule-only and rule-plus approaches, is one of several methods for explaining the rule, the "R" in our BaRAC design.

Graphic 6.3(c)(2)	The FIHRR Approach
facts	State the *relevant* facts of the cited case, i.e., the facts the court used in reaching its holding. (Where relevant, include the procedural history of the case.) Cite the pages where those facts appear.
issue	State the *relevant*, precise issue of the cited case and cite the page(s) where the issue appears. Do not state the issue in vague terms. For example, if the case involves a constitutional challenge, don't frame the issue as "whether such and such was unconstitutional." Instead, refer to the specific constitutional issue: "Whether Code 7707 violated the free speech clause of the First Amendment."
holding	State the court's holding and cite the page where that holding appears. (It's surprising how many writers omit the holding.) Remember, a holding is usually very narrow — it answers, usually as "yes" or "no," the dispositive issue in the case. It's also a matter of interpretation: one person's holding may be another person's dicta.[8] *Important*: if we repeatedly use the phrase "the court held," it's likely we're mistakenly referring to the court's reasoning, or to dicta, as a holding.
rule	Accurately state the rule and cite the page(s) where the rule appears. Where the court has clearly articulated the rule, quote (and cite) it. That's right, quote it! By doing so, we ensure that we've stated the rule correctly. Don't, however, fill the page with lines and lines of mind-numbing quotations.
reasoning	Explain the court's reasoning, and cite the page(s) where that reasoning appears. (Novice writers seem to have more difficulty discussing the court's reasoning than any other aspect of a cited case.)
	Remember our theory here: in discussing a cited case using the FIHRR approach, we're asking our court to accept or reject the cited court's reasoning. Therefore, we have to tell our court what that reasoning was. We explain how the court in the cited case applied the rule of the cited case to the facts of the cited case. If we haven't done so, our discussion is worse than useless, wasting valuable space and delivering nothing in return.
	A warning: take special care not to skip steps in explaining the court's reasoning. Don't jump from point A to D without addressing B and C. We may *intuitively* understand this leap, but we can't assume that the court or our colleagues will. If we want our reader to apply the cited court's reasoning to our case, we've got to explain each step in that reasoning.

---

8. *See* Chapter 5, § 5.2.

Caveats. Although we use the FIHRR approach in briefs, we more commonly employ it in memos. The reason for this is two-fold. First, the FIHRR approach takes more space than the rule-only or rule-plus approaches. More so than in a memo, space in a brief is limited. If we can make the same point and as effectively by using the rule-plus method, we do so.

Second, the FIHRR approach is helpful in explaining many different issues arising in the cited case. When we write to inform and predict, as in a memo, this broad-brush approach alerts our colleagues to a range of *possible* ways to interpret the cited case. However, when we write to educate and to persuade, as in a brief, we've already chosen how we'll interpret and how we'll apply the cited case. We don't present the court with probable interpretations. We tell our reader our viewpoint. And, we do so *beautifully*.

However, *and this is important,* whether in a memo or a in brief, in reasoning by analogy, we use the FIHRR approach *only* as a guide. We don't mechanically state the facts, issue, holding, rule, and reasoning of the cited case as if we're writing a mini-book report. This rote approach leads to choppy and clumsy writing.

There may be times when, for example, the issue is *implicit* and we need not state it. In that instance, we might only address the holding, rule, and reasoning of the cited case. Or, we may combine factors by addressing the facts within the context of the holding or by addressing the rule within our discussion of the reasoning. Or, as is very common—especially in memo writing—we may begin discussing the case by addressing its rule or its holding. The bottom line is that we use *only* those aspects of the cited case we need. If an aspect of the FIHRR formula isn't necessary to our discussion of the cited case, we don't include it.

Graphic 6.3(c)(3)	Other Commonly Used Versions of the FIHRR Approach:	
rule, facts, issue, holding, reasoning		RFIHR
holding, reasoning and rule, (implicit issue and implicit facts)		HRR

Let's next look at some examples of the FIHRR approach.

Memo writing. The following example demonstrates how we use the FIHRR approach in explaining a cited case *in a memo.* Transitions are highlighted in bold,[9] and the writing is annotated.

---

9. Please *see* Chapter 32 for a discussion of transitions.

Graphic 6.3(c)(4)   Example of the FIHRR Approach: Memo Writing

bold assertion

introduction to issue

The court will likely conclude that....

rule

last sentence is a thesis rule sentence

Fourth Amendment rights attach where an individual has "manifested a subjective expectation of privacy in the object of the challenged search," and "society [is] willing to recognize that expectation as reasonable." Citation. **This latter element** turns, not on "'whether the individual chooses to conceal assertedly private activity, but instead whether the government's intrusion infringes upon the personal and societal values protected by the Fourth Amendment.'" Citation. *United States v. Ciraolo* [citation] illustrates how the Supreme Court applied this principle to an aerial observation.

facts of cited case

In *Ciraolo*, police, acting on an anonymous tip that marijuana was growing in Ciraolo's backyard, secured a private plane and flew over Ciraolo's house at an altitude of 1,000 feet in navigable airspace. Citation. Trained in marijuana identification, the police readily concluded that marijuana was growing in Ciraolo's yard. Citation. **A few days later,** the officers obtained a search warrant based on their observations, and seized the marijuana plants. Citation. **After** his motion to suppress the evidence was denied, Ciraolo pled guilty to a charge of cultivating marijuana, and then appealed his conviction. Citation.

issue, holding, rule, reasoning of cited case

At issue was whether "naked-eye observation of the curtilage [of Ciraolo's home] by police from an aircraft lawfully operating at an altitude of 1,000 feet violate[d] an expectation of privacy that [was] reasonable." Citation. **The Court held that Ciraolo** did not have a reasonable expectation of privacy to be free of such aerial observation, noting that

> in an age where private and commercial flight in the public airways is routine, it [was] unreasonable for [Ciraolo] to expect that his marijuana plants were constitutionally protected from being observed with the naked eye from an altitude of 1,000 feet. The Fourth Amendment simply does not require police traveling in the public airways at this altitude to obtain a warrant in order to observe what is visible to the naked eye.

Citation.

The Court rejected outright Ciraolo's claim that his curtilage was immune from such observations. Citation. **Reasoning that although** Ciraolo had manifested a subjective expectation of privacy by enclosing his yard with fences, and that privacy expectations are heightened in the curtilage, the Court concluded that Ciraolo's expectation was not one society was willing to accept as reasonable. Citation.

The Court explained that the officers made their observations from a public vantage point, in navigable airspace, where they had a right to be and which rendered the marijuana plants clearly visible to the naked eye. Citation. **Moreover, the Court noted**, the observations were conducted "in a physically non-intrusive manner" and any member of the public flying in that airspace who "glanced down could have seen everything that these officers observed." Citation. **Based on all of these factors**, the Court concluded that no warrant was necessary for the officers' observations in this case. Citation.

application to our case via a transitional bold assertion

Similarly, no warrant was necessary for Officer Smith's observations of the Defendant's backyard marijuana garden. **As the officers in** *Ciraolo*, Officer Smith viewed the Defendant's....

conclusion

For these reasons, the court will likely conclude that....

Referring back to a FIHRR discussion. Please note that if, later in our memo (or in our brief), we again address the *Ciraolo* case, we do not repeat the facts, issue, holding, rule, and reasoning of the case. Instead, we refer our reader back to the pages in our memo or brief where we've addressed those aspects of the case. We introduce our further discussion of the case by stating, for example: "Another issue the Court addressed in *Ciraolo* was whether...." We then address the relevant aspects of this issue.

Please also note how thoroughly we addressed Court's *reasoning* in the *Ciraolo* case. We explained how the Court applied the rule to the facts of the case. We didn't rush through the Court's analysis. Instead, we included all the steps in the Court's reasoning. To the best of our ability, we try to make certain that our reader understands the Court's reasoning.

Addressing only one issue of a multi-issue case. In using a complex cited case with many issues, we address *only* the facts, issue, holding, rule, and reasoning relevant to our case. The *Ciraolo* case was such a complex case. If we're addressing only one aspect of the case, for example, whether Ciraolo had a *subjective expectation of privacy*, we need to alert our reader that we're not addressing all issues. We could do so by stating, i.e.:

> **One of the issues** in *Ciraolo* concerned the defendant's subjective expectation of privacy. Citation. In *concluding* that Ciraolo had demonstrated a subjective expectation, the Court reasoned.... Citation.

Note that we used the term "concluding" instead of "holding." We use "holding" only when addressing the Court's answer to the dispositive issue in the case; i.e., whether the Fourth Amendment was violated. The issue regarding Ciraolo's subjective expectation of privacy is but one preliminary step in the Court's decision-making process.

Brief writing. Let's next see the *design* for using the FIHRR approach in writing a brief.[10] The following two templates illustrate where the FIHRR discussion "fits" within the context of a single-element rule and then within a two-element rule. However, these templates are just that: guidelines. Our writing should be less repetitive and much smoother than that in the following two graphics. Note that these examples do not include the specifics of the facts or the elements of the rule. We omitted this information to focus the examples on the format and organization of the analysis.

Graphic 6.3(c)(5)   The FIHRR Approach
                    Arguing by Analogy: Template of a Single-Element Rule

---

bold assertion; (global rule); (global application); conclusion

    This Court should uphold the trial court's judgment and find that Jones committed the crime. The crime consists of element X. *State v. Carter*, 899 So. 2d 212, 214 (Fla. 20xx). As the Record demonstrates, Jones's actions constituted X; therefore, he committed the crime. (R.1-8.)

rule (bold assertion and thesis rule sentence); then rule, facts, issue, reasoning, and holding of cited case

    By doing a, b, and c, Jones met element X. Element X is fulfilled when an individual does a, b, and c. *Carter*, 899 So. 2d at 215. In *Carter*, the defendant _____. *Id.* at 213. At issue was whether these acts constituted X. *Id.* at 214. Reasoning that the defendant acted with _____ and in a manner evidencing _____, the court found that he had committed X. *Id.* at 214-15. Accordingly, the court upheld his conviction. *Id.*

application (transitional bold assertion); then comparison of relevant aspects of our case to cited case; then conclusion

    Similarly, in the instant case, Jones did _____. (R.3.) Just as the defendant in *Carter*, he also _____. (R.6); *see* 899 So. 2d at 214-15. Taken together, these actions demonstrate that Jones acted with _____ and in a manner evidencing _____. For this reason, Jones met element X and committed the crime. Accordingly, this Court should uphold his conviction.

Can you match the annotations to the actual sentences they refer to in the example? Give it a try. Which of the sentences is the thesis rule sentence? Which is the transitional bold assertion? What transitional words and phrases have we used in the examples? Now on to the next example.

---

10. In Chapter 7, we provide two examples of using analogical reasoning (the FIHRR approach) in brief writing and one example of using it in memo writing.

Graphic 6.3(c)(6)   **The FIHRR Approach**
                        Arguing by Analogy: Template of a Multi-Element Rule

intro.¶:

(global) bold assertion;   This Court should uphold the trial court's judgment, and

(global) rule;   hold that Jones committed the crime. The crime consists of
                                    elements 1 and 2. *State v. Able*, 999 So. 2d 812, 814 (Fla.

(global) application;   20xx). As the Record demonstrates, Jones's actions met

(global) conclusion   both of these elements; therefore, Jones committed the
                                    crime. (R.1-8.)

rule [element 1]

 bold assertion;   First, by committing X, Jones met element 1. Element 1 is

thesis rule sentence;   fulfilled when an individual commits X. *State v. Baker*, 899

the cited case's: facts,   So. 2d 212, 215 (Fla. 20xx). In *Baker*, the defendant _____.

issue,   *Id.* at 213. At issue was whether these acts constituted X. *Id.*

reasoning,   at 214. Reasoning that the defendant acted with _____ and

rule,   in a manner evidencing _____, the court concluded that he

& holding   had committed X. *Id.* at 214-15. Accordingly, the court
                                    upheld his conviction. *Id.* at 216.

application [element 1]

transition bold assertion   Similarly, in the instant case, Jones did _____. (R.3.)

law applied to our facts;   Moreover, just as the defendant in *Baker*, he also _____.
                                    (R.6); *see* 899 So. 2d at 213. Taken together, these actions
                                    demonstrate that Jones acted with_____ and in a manner

conclusion   evidencing _____. For this reason, this Court should con-
                                    clude that Jones committed X and met element 1.

rule [element 2]

bold assertion;   Second, by _____, Jones committed Y, and thus met
                                    element 2. As *State v. Castor*, 777 So. 2d 678, 690 (Fla.

thesis rule sentence;   20xx), illustrates, element 2 is fulfilled when an individual

the cited case's rule,   commits Y. In *Castor*, the defendant did _____ and _____

facts, issue,   while committing _____. *See id.* at 681. At issue was
                                    whether these acts were sufficient to constitute Y for the

reasoning, and   purposes of fulfilling element 2. *Id.* at 683. Reasoning that
                                    the defendant acted with blatant disregard for _____, the
                                    court concluded that the defendant's acts constituted Y,

holding;   and upheld his conviction. *Id.* at 691. This Court should

conclusion   reach the same conclusion in the instant case.

application [element 2]

transition bold assertion;   Here, as did the defendant in *Castor*, Jones acted with

the cited case's   blatant disregard for _____. Not only did he _____, he

reasoning, and rule;   also _____. (R.7-8.) In so doing, Jones exceeded the

conclusion	minimum levels of culpability established in *Castor* to constitute Y and to meet element 2. *See* 777 So. 2d at 691.
(global) conclusion	Because he met elements 1 and 2, Jones committed the crime. For this reason, this Court should uphold his conviction.

Back to the *Pottinger* case. Next, let's see how courts use the FIHRR approach. We'll return to the *Pottinger* case.[11] There, Judge Atkins of the United States District Court, Southern District of Florida, decided, among other issues, that homeless plaintiffs had a legitimate expectation of privacy in personal property they kept in public parks and under public overpasses. In so deciding, Judge Atkins reasoned by analogy to a cited case, *State v. Mooney*, 588 A.2d 145, 153-54 (Conn. 1991), as follows. (We've annotated Judge Atkins's discussion.)

Graphic 6.3(c)(7)	**The FIHRR Approach** **Example of the Court's Use of Analogical Reasoning**
Holding *(implicit issue* *& facts)* *reasoning* *and* *rule*	In *Mooney*, the court found that the homeless defendant had a reasonable expectation of privacy in the contents of his duffel bag and box, which he kept under the bridge abutment where he slept. [citation] In so finding, the court considered society's high degree of deference to expectations of privacy in closed containers, the fact that the containers were located in a place that the defendant regarded as his home and the fact that, because the defendant was under arrest, he could not be at the place he regarded as his home to assert his fourth amendment rights when the search occurred. [citation] Under these circumstances, the court concluded that "society's code of values and notions of custom and civility would cause it to recognize as reasonable the defendant's expectation of privacy in his duffel bag and box." [citation] The court further stated the following:
	[t]he interior of [these items is], in effect, the defendant's last shred of privacy from the prying eyes of outsiders, including the police. Our notions of custom and civility, and our code of values, would include some measure of respect for that shred of privacy, and would recognize it as reasonable under the circumstances of this case.
	[citation]

---

11. 810 F. Supp. 1551, 1572 (S.D. Fla. 1992). *See* Chapter 5, § 5.7, where we address the *Pottinger* case.

transitional Ba Pottinger *case is linked* *to the cited* *case's* *reasoning*	Similarly, the interior of the bedrolls and bags or boxes of personal effects belonging to homeless individuals in this case is perhaps the last trace of privacy they have. In addition, the property of homeless individuals is often located in the parks or under the overpasses that they consider their homes. As in *Mooney*, under the circumstances of this case, it appears that society is prepared to recognize plaintiffs' expectation of privacy in their personal property as reasonable.

Note that Judge Atkins explained, in detail (even quoting), the cited case's reasoning. In other words, he addressed the facts of the cited case while *applying* the court's rule to those facts. After a clear transition directing us to the *Pottinger* case (the case he was deciding), he then applied the cited case's reasoning and reached a conclusion. His writing is clear, precise, and persuasive.

§ 6.3(d)   Where We Are Using the Cited Case to Argue by Analogy and the Case Is "Harmful," Use the *FIHRR* Approach

Unfortunately, not all cases favor our client's position. During our research, we'll come upon a "harmful," or "adverse" case which, at first glance, appears to rip our case apart, limb by limb. What, then, do we do? We can't ignore the case, hoping it'll go away—it won't. If we don't deal with it, our opponent or the court will.[12]

A bud waiting to blossom. The best way to deal with a harmful case is as follows: present our strongest arguments and cases, then deal "head on" with the harmful case by disarming it, and putting it to work for us using *counter*-analogical reasoning. In doing so, we follow the same process as with analogical reasoning. That is, we use the FIHRR approach, but we explain why the cited case is so different from our case that the court in our case should not accept the cited court's reasoning. We don't run from a "harmful" case. Instead, we view such cases not as time bombs waiting to explode, but as buds, waiting to blossom. Here are some guidelines:

Graphic 6.3(d)(1)   **The "Harmful" Case: Guidelines**

(a) If the case is not binding, say so. Then go further and show *why* our court should not follow the case, binding or not.

---

12. Moreover, rules of professional responsibility *require* that if our opponent has not done so, we must inform the court of any case that is binding on our court, similar to our facts and issue, and reaches an outcome unfavorable to the ruling we seek.

(b) If possible, argue factual differences: show why the relevant, critical facts of the case are so distinct from our facts that the case is irrelevant, or at least, unpersuasive.

(c) If possible, argue "issue" differences: show why the issue in the case is so distinct from our issue that the case is irrelevant or unpersuasive. Or, if possible, argue that the precise issue in our case never even arose in the case.

(d) If possible, argue that the court applied the wrong rule and thereby reached the wrong conclusion.

(e) If possible, argue that the court misapplied the correct rule.

(f) If possible, argue that due to time change, attitude changes, and/or unique circumstances, our court should not apply the case.

Logic at work. What we're really saying, in "defusing" a harmful case (*Case X*), is one or more of the following:

Graphic 6.3(d)(2) The Design (Logic) of the "Harmful" Case Argument

bold assertion	*This Court should not follow Case X because of* reason(s) a,b,c,d,e, and/or f above (from Graphic 6.3(d)(1)).
rule	A case possessing characteristics like a,b,c,d,e, and/or f above is poor precedent and should not be followed.
application (*first sentence is a transition BA*)	*Case X* possesses characteristics of a,b,c,d,e, and/or f above. (prove it)
conclusion	Therefore, this Court should not follow *Case X*.

Our goal in dealing with the harmful case is to disarm it and to make it work *for* us. In the sample arguments in Chapter 7, §7.3(a) and §7.3(b), we demonstrate how we can do this. As these samples show, if we do our job correctly, we transform the harmful case into one supporting our argument. Or, as an old Italian proverb instructs, "Since the house is on fire let us warm ourselves."

§6.4
Third:
Tie the Cited Case to Our Case by Leading with a *Transitional Bold Assertion*

After we've explained the (relevant) facts, issue, holding, rule, and reasoning of the cited case, (whether that case is harmful or helpful to our client's position), we then apply the case to our case. Similarly, if we've used the cited case by applying the rule-only or rule-plus approach, we apply that rule. Here's where the third principle of using a cited case comes into play.

We finish our discussion of the cited case by tying that case back to our case with a strong transitional bold assertion, explaining, in a nutshell, how our case "fits" or doesn't "fit" the rule or the reasoning of the cited case. In this sentence, we boldly assert our conclusion regarding how the rule, or, where we argue by analogy, the reasoning, of the cited case applies to our case. We then "prove" that bold assertion by further applying the cited case to our facts. To put it another way, transitional bold assertions are the starting point for the *application* section (the *A* in BaRAC).

Bridging the gap from the cited case to our case. Creating a transitional bold assertion forces us to nail down the precise reason we've included the case we've just discussed. We ensure that our reader can follow our jump from the cited case to our case. Pointed, direct transitional bold assertions evidence clear thinking. Rambling or no transitions evidence just the opposite.

In both brief and memo writing, if we miss this critical step, if we don't "tie" the cited case to our case, we've wasted paper, money, and time. If we begin discussing our case without referring to the cited case, we've left our (now disgruntled) judge or colleague wondering what possible relevance that case has to our case. Why did we bother discussing the cited case if we aren't going to apply any aspect of it to our case? *If we could omit our entire discussion of the cited case without damaging our argument or discussion, then we haven't used the case correctly.*

The following are examples of some good transitional bold assertions directing our reader from the cited case back to our case. For further examples of these types of transition sentences, please see Chapter 32.

Graphic 6.4	Transitional Bold Assertions

"Similarly, there was no contract in the instant case."

"Unlike the offer in *Benton v. Connley*, there is no [state the factual or legal difference] here."

"Unlike *Smith v. Jones*, the instant case does not involve.... The issue here is…, not.… [Then explain why the differences lead to a different result.]"

"Jones relies on *Bruster v. Frank* to support [state Jones's position], but that case is inapplicable here because.…"

In the next chapter, we'll further explore the "thinking" process involved in using cases in our writing. We'll see the role syllogisms and the BaRAC design play in structuring our argument. And, we'll further illustrate where our discussion of a cited case "fits" within the overall design of our reasoning.

§ 6.5   Exercise in Designing a FIHRR, a Rule-plus, and a Transitional Bold Assertion

Our client is Jane Smith, and our firm is located in California, within the jurisdiction of the Third District Court of Appeal. Read the facts in Jane's case, presented in the exercise in Chapter 5, § 5.10(b). Ms. Smith has petitioned the court to have the document she found admitted to probate as the Last Will and Testament of Mr. Atkinson. The case is pending, and the probate court must determine whether the signature and material provisions are in the testator's handwriting, thus satisfying California Probate Code § 6111(a) (West 2010). That section provides as follows:

> 6111(a). A will ... is valid as a holographic will, whether or not witnessed, if the signature and the material provisions are in the handwriting of the testator.

Assume you've found the case of *In re Button's Estate*, 287 P. 964 (Cal. 1930), located in Appendix A. Read that case now.

Exercise 1. Write a FIHRR of the *Button* case for this issue.

Exercise 2. Write a Rule-plus of the *Button* case for this issue.

Exercise 3. Write a strong transitional bold assertion that you'd use to tie the *Button* case to Jane's case in the application section of your BaRAC argument.

We're going to be revisiting Jane Smith's case, so please save your work.

Chapter Review
Using Cases Effectively

- If the cited case doesn't advance our argument or discussion, *omit it.*
- The *relevancy* of a precedent depends on the *function* the case serves in solving our case. Unless a cited case (1) states the rule, (2) explains the rule, or (3) provides a pattern of thought we seek to apply in our case, it has no place in our document.

Follow three guidelines in discussing a cited case:

first:	Using a *thesis* (i.e., point) *rule sentence,* tell the reader why or how the cited case is relevant. This is one of the beginning parts of the *rule* section of BaRAC.
second:	Address all relevant (and only relevant) aspects of the case, and explain the law involved. This is the *rule* and *rule explanation* section of *BaRAC.*

- **rule-only:** Where only the rule is relevant, address only the rule.
- **rule-plus:** Address the rule and any other relevant aspect of the case using either a *parenthetical,* a series of parentheticals, or a more extended explanation of the case. A *parenthetical* is an explanatory statement contained in parentheses following a citation. The rule-plus approach is especially helpful when we're inducing a personalized rule from several cases; or arguing that the court should apply the rule we advocate, rather than the one our opponent advances. Rule-plus can also be used to distinguish adverse or harmful cases. When used in that fashion, be sure to use the appropriate introductory citation signal before the case name. See Rules B4 and 1.2 of *The Bluebook.*
- **FIHRR:** Where the case is useful in arguing by analogy, or we need to distinguish it using *counter*-analogy, use the FIHRR approach and discuss the relevant facts, issue, holding, rule, and reasoning. Remember, the FIHRR approach is a guideline; we don't have to begin with the facts and we don't always include each aspect of the mnemonic. Often, especially in brief writing, the approach works best when we lead with the rule.

third:	Using a *transitional bold assertion,* state how the cited case (or law developed from several cases/sources) applies to our case. Next, apply that law to our facts. This is the beginning and content of the *application* section of BaRAC.

Follow these guidelines in using the three case discussion approaches:

Rule-Only

rule	The rule from the case or other authority is all we need to explain the law to our reader.
how to state the rule	Usually, we just quote the relevant rule.
type of reasoning	Deductive.

suggested application	If the rule involves factors (elements), apply them one-by-one, to our facts. If necessary, create a subheading for each factor. If not, use transitions to inform the reader that we're moving from one factor to the next.

Rule-Plus

rule	We have a general but (surprise!) rather vague rule which we can best define by referring to a variety of cases illustrating that rule.
how to state the rule	State or derive a general rule; then explain that rule by citing, via *parentheticals,* illustrative examples from the cases. Or, include a few sentences to explain the most important aspect(s) of the case.
type of reasoning	*If we must derive the rule from several cases,* we reason inductively in creating the rule; then we reason deductively in *applying* that rule to our facts.
	If a case provides the general rule, we reason deductively in applying that general rule to our facts.
	However, in either situation, we can also reason by analogy by comparing and contrasting the parenthetical or other information from the cited case(s) to our facts.
suggested application	Apply the general rule and reach a conclusion; then support that conclusion by comparing and contrasting the parenthetical or other information to our facts.

FIHRR

rule	We want to import the rule and reasoning from an analogous case into our case.
how to state the rule	State or derive a general rule; then explain that rule by the FIHRR approach. In other words, after stating the general rule, *show how it was applied in the cited case.* Do this by explaining the *relevant* facts, issue, holding, rule, and reasoning of the cited case.
type of reasoning	*If we must derive the rule,* we reason inductively in creating that rule; then reason deductively in applying that rule to our facts.
	If a case provides the general rule, we reason deductively in applying that general rule and reasoning to our facts.
	However, in either situation, we also reason by analogy by comparing and contrasting the cited case to our case.
suggested application	Apply the general rule and reach a conclusion; then support that conclusion by comparing and contrasting the cited case to our case.

Chapter 7

Examples of Using Cases in Writing a Memo or Brief

§ 7.1   From Thinking to Writing: A Step-by-Step Approach

Now that we've explored the role syllogisms and the "BaRAC" design play in structuring our thinking, and the selection process involved in using cases in our writing, let's put all of this learning to use. In this Chapter, we'll address three hypothetical cases. In the first, an example of memo writing, we'll see how to reason by analogy from one cited case. In the second, an example of brief writing, we'll see how to use counter-arguments to strengthen our case. In the last, an example of memo writing, we'll see how to explain a rule we have developed from a series of cases.

§ 7.2   First Example: Memo Writing Using Analogical Reasoning

The Aggravated Assault Case.[1] We represent the State in an appeal from Alex Jones's aggravated assault conviction. Aggravated assault occurs when the defendant commits an assault by using a "deadly weapon." A deadly weapon is "any instrument used in a manner likely to produce death or serious bodily injury."

In our case, Jones admits he committed an assault by throwing a golf shoe at another person. That golf shoe had a rigid leather sole and sixteen sharp, steel cleats. The only issue is whether that assault was "aggravated," i.e., whether a golf shoe is a "deadly weapon."

Assume we're relying on a case from our jurisdiction, *Smith v. State*, holding that the defendant was properly convicted of aggravated assault because he threw a steel-toed boot at another man. In holding that the boot was a deadly weapon, the *Smith* court isolated two factors: the boot's weight and the boot's rigid heel. The *Smith* court reasoned that either of these two factors supported a finding that the boot, when thrown, was a deadly weapon likely to produce death or serious bodily injury. The court noted that the boot's weight made the boot dangerous, and the rigid heel could be used as a blunt instrument. In writing a memo analyzing whether the defendant in our golf shoe case also committed aggravated assault, we could draft our discussion as follows:

Graphic 7.2	The Aggravated Assault Discussion
bold assertion	The court will likely uphold the trial court's judgment that Alex Jones committed aggravated assault in hurling a cleated golf shoe at the vic-
point	tim's head. As *Smith v. State* [citation] illustrates, aggravated assault is an

---

1. This hypothetical is a revision and adaptation of materials developed by our present and former colleagues.

general *rule*	assault committed with a deadly weapon. A "deadly" weapon is a weapon used in a manner likely to produce death or serious bodily injury. [citation] Death or serious bodily injury can be caused by a heavy, rigid, blunt instrument thrown at a victim. [citation]
rule 　facts 　issue 　holding	In *Smith*, the defendant was convicted of aggravated assault for throwing a heavy, steel-toed boot at the victim. [citation] At issue was whether the boot was a "deadly weapon" under the aggravated assault statute. [citation] The appellate court held that it was and affirmed the conviction. [citation]
reasoning 　rule	Reasoning that the boot's steel toe and rigid heel could be used as a blunt instrument, and acknowledging the boot's considerable weight, the court concluded that the boot was used in a "manner likely to produce death or serious bodily injury." [citation] Accordingly, the court held that the boot was a deadly weapon. [citation]
application point	Similarly, the golf shoe here was a deadly weapon. Indeed, the court should consider it as dangerous, and as likely as the boot in *Smith*, to produce death or serious bodily injury.
facts 　and 　reasoning	Even more deadly than the boot in *Smith*, the golf shoe had sixteen pointed steel cleats protruding from its sole. These cleats, sharp enough to pierce the victim's body, made the shoe extremely dangerous. Moreover, although lighter than a boot, the golf shoe also had a leather sole rigid enough to hold those steel cleats. In hurling the golf shoe at the victim's head, Jones used the skin-piercing shoe as a blunt instrument in a manner likely to produce death or serious bodily injury.
conclusion	Accordingly, the court will likely conclude that the golf shoe was used as a deadly weapon, and uphold Jones's conviction for aggravated assault.

We now have a pretty good idea of how to use a case to reason by analogy. Let's turn now to see how to deal with a case which may not be as favorable to our position. Let's explore how to *counter-argue*.

§ 7.3   Second Example: Brief Writing Using Analogical Reasoning and Counter-Argument

The Sentencing Case:[2]

This next case involves a defendant, Williams, who backed out of a plea agreement. The facts of his case, two relevant precedent cases, and two arguments (Williams's and the State's) follow. Which argument is more persuasive?

---

2. This hypothetical is a revision and adaptation of materials developed by our present and former colleagues.

Williams v. State

Williams was charged with aggravated battery for beating a police officer. His lawyer negotiated a plea bargain in which Williams would plead guilty and receive a two-year sentence. However, Williams later changed his mind, demanded a jury trial, and was convicted. At sentencing, the judge said:

> I have little sympathy for you, Mr. Williams. You have been in trouble since you were twelve, and at twenty, you show no sign of changing. You are a menace. Furthermore, you are not very smart. Your lawyer got you a good deal, but you didn't take it. Instead, you demanded a jury trial because you thought you could do better. Well, you have to learn the lesson that when you buck the system, you get the brunt. I sentence you to ten years.

Williams now appeals his ten-year sentence. Two cases, both from the court of appeal in the same jurisdiction, are summarized below.

Case #1:   *Adams v. State*
                          [Prison Sentence Overturned]

Adams was charged with burglary. His lawyer negotiated a plea bargain in which Adams would plead guilty and receive a three-year sentence. However, Adams changed his mind, demanded a jury trial, and was convicted. At sentencing, the judge said:

> Mr. Adams, I am tired of people who put the county to the expense of a trial when they are obviously guilty. Your lawyer arranged a good deal for you. Instead, you required everyone to sit here and listen to you tell a tale. Well, nothing is free. I sentence you to twelve years.

Adams argues that the judge punished him for demanding a jury trial and increased his sentence solely because of that demand. We agree. A mere disparity between a bargained-for sentence and the one imposed at trial does not violate the right to a jury trial. However, in this case, the judge's remarks show that his primary motive for imposing a longer sentence was to punish Adams for demanding a jury trial.

Reversed and remanded for resentencing.

Case #2:   *Brown v. State*
                          [Prison Sentence Upheld]

Brown was charged with sexual battery. His lawyer negotiated a plea bargain in which Brown would plead guilty and receive a five-year sentence. However, Brown changed his mind, demanded a jury trial, and was convicted. At sentencing, the judge said:

> When defendants express a penitent spirit, they are half-way to rehabilitation, and I am inclined to be lenient in sentencing. For that reason, I often give light sentences on guilty pleas. But when a man denies his guilt, and requires the system to go through the motions of proving his guilt, I cannot believe he is re-

morseful, and I cannot believe he is a good candidate for rehabilitation. I think you need a long time to come to terms with your attitude. I sentence you to fifteen years.

Brown argues that the judge punished him for demanding a jury trial and increased his sentence solely because of that demand. We disagree. The judge's remarks show that he properly considered only Brown's potential for rehabilitation in choosing a sentence. Affirmed.

Let's next look at how Williams and the State would craft appellate arguments concerning the resentencing. We've annotated each argument with comments and have identified each aspect of the BaRAC design. In reviewing these arguments, we see the following design emerge:

Graphic 7.3   **Arguing by Analogy**

We follow the process outlined below in writing our argument:*

1. Using the BaRAC design, state our argument in a "nutshell" while introducing our case to our readers:
   - State what the reviewing court should do;
   - Provide a factual "context" for our case;
   - State reasons why the court should rule in our client's favor.

2. State and explain the rule:
   - Extract the rule from a cited case, cite that case, and link it to our case;
   - Explain the relevant facts, issue, holding, rule, and reasoning of the cited case.

3. Apply the rule to our facts:
   - Provide proof of our facts by citing the Record;
   - Because we are arguing by analogy, compare and contrast the cited case to our case.

4. Engage in counter-argument:
   - Introduce, with a strong bold assertion distinguishing the cited case from our case, the rule of the "harmful" case;
   - Distinguish and reconcile the cited case and our case:
   - Explain the relevant FIHRR of the cited case;
   - Compare and contrast the cited case to our case;
   - Reach a conclusion stating why the cited case is not "harmful."

5. Conclude by telling the court exactly what it should do.

---

* We suggest tracking each step of the process outlined in Graphic 7.3 while reading the appellant's and appellee's arguments, to identify statements regarding what the reviewing court should do and to identify the factual context for these statements.

§ 7.3(a)	The Appellant's (Williams's) Argument

bold assertion   This Court should reverse the trial court's judgment and remand this case for resentencing. Williams should receive a new sentencing hearing because his ten-year sentence constitutes punishment for exercising his constitutional right to a jury trial.

Had Williams waived his right to a jury trial by accepting a plea bargain, he would have received a two-year sentence. Instead, he asserted his right, and the trial court imposed a higher sentence than it would have imposed if Williams had pled guilty. Because the court's primary motive in increasing Williams's sentence was to punish him for requesting a jury trial, the court's action violated Williams's constitutional right to a jury trial. Accordingly, a new sentencing hearing is warranted.

rule   A judge may not, as was the case here, increase a sentence to punish a defendant for having demanded a jury trial. *Adams v. State* [citation]. In *Adams*, the defendant had negotiated a sentence of three years in return for pleading guilty to burglary. [citation] After the judge approved the plea agreement, Adams changed his mind, exercised his right to a jury trial, and was convicted. [citation]

Sentencing Adams to twelve years, the judge mentioned the expense and inconvenience Adams had caused by exercising his right to a jury trial. [citation] Indeed, immediately before imposing the twelve-year term, the judge stated, "[N]othing is free." [citation] The appellate court, in reviewing this extended term, read the court's remarks as indicating that the judge's primary motive in increasing the sentence was to punish Adams for his jury demand. [citation] Because this motive was improper, the court remanded the case for resentencing. [citation]

application and conclusion   Similar to the trial court in *Adams*, the trial court here improperly increased the defendant's sentence as punishment for his jury demand. The judge had originally agreed to sentence Williams to a two-year term, if he pled guilty. [citation] However, after Williams requested a jury trial, the judge imposed a ten-year sentence. [citation]

Similar to the trial judge's comments in *Adams*, the judge's remarks here disclose that the court's primary intent was to punish Williams for demanding a jury trial. Not only did the judge mention that Williams had demanded a jury trial, he also stated that Williams needed "to learn the lesson that when you buck the system, you get the brunt." [citation] As the court's comments in *Adams*, the judge's remarks here disclose an intent to punish Williams for the jury demand. Because this intent is improper, this Court should vacate the sentence and remand this case for resentencing.

(counter analysis)   This is not a case where the judge's remarks merely demonstrate concern for the defendant's rehabilitation potential, as in *Brown v. State* [citation], a case cited by the State.
bold assertion

rule   In *Brown*, the trial court had agreed, pursuant to a plea bargain, to impose a five-year sentence for sexual battery, but when Brown demanded a jury trial and was convicted, the judge imposed a fifteen-year term. [citation] However, unlike the sentences in *Adams* and in the instant case, the increased sentence in *Brown* was based on the judge's assessment of Brown's potential for rehabilitation. [citation] The judge expressed that he did not believe Brown was a good candidate for rehabilitation, that Brown had not shown remorse, and that a lack of remorse indicated a lack of penitent spirit. [citation] Because judges properly may consider rehabilitation potential at sentencing, and because the court's remarks in *Brown* focused on rehabilitation, the appellate court upheld the *Brown* sentence. [citation]

application   In contrast, the only remark the court in the instant case made that could possibly be construed as concerned with rehabilitation was that Williams showed "no sign of changing." [citation] The judge's own words show that his primary motive was to punish Williams for demanding a jury trial: "Your lawyer got you a good deal, but you didn't take it. Instead, you demanded a jury trial because you thought you could do better. Well, you have to learn the lesson that when you buck the system, you get the brunt. I sentence you to ten years." [citation]

conclusion   Thus, Williams's request for a jury trial resulted in his increased sentence. Because Williams was punished for exercising a constitutional right, he should receive a new sentencing hearing. Accordingly, this Court should reverse the trial court's judgment and remand this case for resentencing.

Let's turn now to the Appellee's (the State's) argument.

§ 7.3(b)	The Appellee's (The State's) Argument

bold assertion   This Court should uphold Williams's ten-year sentence for the aggravated battery of a police officer. In imposing this sentence, the trial court considered Williams's unlikely potential for rehabilitation. *See Brown v. State* [citation]. The court ruled properly, and this Court should affirm.

rule   *Brown* demonstrates that a judge, just as the trial judge in the instant case, may properly consider a defendant's potential for rehabilitation in imposing a sentence. [citation] In *Brown*, the defendant was charged with sexual battery. [citation] Initially, he agreed to plead guilty in exchange for a five-year sentence. [citation] However, he later revoked his agreement and demanded a jury trial. [citation] The jury found him guilty and the judge sentenced him to fifteen years. [citation] This increased sentence was upheld on appeal. [citation]

In finding the sentence justified, the appellate court noted that sentencing judges may properly consider the defendant's potential for rehabilitation. [citation] The court found it "apparent from the trial court's remarks" that the judge had based the increased sentence on the defendant's low potential for rehabilitation. [citation]

The trial judge had stated:

> "When defendants express a penitent spirit, they are halfway to rehabilitation, and I am inclined to be lenient in sentencing.... But when a man denies his guilt, and requires the system to go through the motions of proving his guilt, I cannot believe he is remorseful, and I cannot believe he is a good candidate for rehabilitation."

[citation]

Even though the trial judge in *Brown* had specifically referred to the defendant's "'requir[ing] the system to go through the motions of proving his guilt,'" the appellate court rejected the argument that the court increased the sentence to punish the defendant for exercising his right to a jury trial. [citation]

application and conclusion

Similarly, the trial court's passing remarks here regarding Williams's demand for a jury trial do not invalidate the court's concern for Williams's rehabilitation potential. The court specifically referred to Williams's poor chances for rehabilitation: "You have been in trouble since you were twelve, and at twenty, you show no sign of changing. You are a menace." [citation] As did the court's comments in *Brown*, these remarks demonstrate that the trial court's primary concern in imposing sentence was Williams's potential for rehabilitation. [citation]

(counter-analysis: including bold assertion, rule, application, and conclusion)

This concern distinguishes the instant case from *Adams v. State* [citation], cited by Williams. In *Adams*, the defendant withdrew his agreement to plead guilty and accept a three-year sentence. [citation] Instead, he demanded a jury trial and was convicted. [citation] The trial judge, never once referring to the defendant's potential for rehabilitation, sentenced Adams to twelve years. [citation]

In imposing this sentence, the judge stated: "'I am tired of people who put the county to the expense of a trial when they are obviously guilty.... [Y]ou required everyone to sit here and listen to you tell a tale. Well, nothing is free.'" [citation]

Finding that the trial court's "primary motive for imposing a longer sentence was to punish Adams for demanding a jury trial," the appellate court reversed and remanded the case for resentencing. [citation]

Unlike the trial court's motive in the *Adams* case, the court's "primary" motive here in imposing sentence was the defendant's potential for rehabilitation. The court expressly considered that Williams had been "in trouble" from an early age, showed "no sign of changing" and was a "menace." [citation] These were all proper factors for the judge to consider in choosing a sentence.

conclusion

Accordingly, this Court should uphold the ten-year sentence William received for the aggravated battery of a police officer.

Going forward. Let's now turn from our example of analogical reasoning (where the rules were clear and our analysis involved applying settled rules to our case), to the situation where we must *develop* (or induce) a rule from several cases, and then apply that rule to our facts. In developing and applying a rule, we consider how to *use* cited cases. Do we use the rule-only method, the rule-plus approach, argue by analogy using the FIHRR design, or use some combination of these approaches? Let's see.

§ 7.4 Third Example: Memo Writing Developing a Rule from Many Cases

The Disorderly Conduct Case

The following hypothetical illustrates that the way we use cited cases depends upon the *function* those cases serve in solving our case.

Our case. We represent the State and are arguing, at the trial court level, against the defendant's Motion for a Judgment of Acquittal. We've been asked to write a memo explaining the law of disorderly conduct as it relates to a specific Florida statute.[3] Assume that our trial court is within the jurisdiction of the Florida Second District Court of Appeal. Assume further that a jury found the defendant, Errin Actor, guilty of disorderly conduct and that the facts are as follows:[4]

During the early morning hours of January 19, 20xx,[5] on two separate occasions, David Glen, Actor's neighbor, was awakened by loud screaming and yelling emanating from Actor's residence. On each occasion, Glen recognized the voice as Actor's, thought that Actor might be engaged in a domestic disturbance, and called the police.

Deputy Ron Omega responded to both of Glen's calls. On the first call, Omega found Actor in her third floor bedroom screaming and disturbing her neighbors. She was also intoxicated and combative. Omega advised her of the complaint and told her to quiet down. Actor complied, and Omega left.

Approximately two hours later, Omega was again called to Actor's residence. All the lights were on, and Actor was screaming and yelling profanities. Meeting Omega outside, Mark Rodgers, Actor's live-in boyfriend, told the officer that Actor was drunk and uncontrollable and had punched Rodgers several times. After examining red marks on Rodgers, Omega entered Actor's apartment. He asked Actor to get dressed (she was unclothed) and placed her under arrest for domestic violence and disorderly conduct. Actor, however, refused to comply.

While Rodgers helped Omega in obtaining clothing for Actor, Actor screamed "F - - K YOU, MARK," and kicked Rodgers full force in the genitals. Based on this testimony, the jury found Actor guilty of disorderly conduct but not guilty of domestic battery. Actor now brings a Motion for Judgment of Acquittal, claiming that the State presented

---

3. Please refer to Chapter 11 for an in-depth look at writing the Discussion Section of a Memo.
4. We thank Marilyn Moran for her help in developing this hypothetical.
5. We have altered the dates referenced in the fact statement, statute, and cases.

insufficient evidence to support the jury's guilty verdict on the disorderly conduct charge. Specifically, Actor claims that her conviction rests on the mere words she uttered and, for that reason, violated her First Amendment right to free speech.

The law. Assume that through our research we've uncovered the following statute and six cases, all existing at the time of Actor's arrest. Assume further that the statute referenced in all the cases has not been amended. Also assume that the *State v. Saunders* case preceded all of the other cases.

Florida Statute

Section 877.03, Florida Statutes (20xx), provides in relevant part:

> Whoever commits such acts as are of a nature to corrupt the public morals, or outrage the sense of public decency, or affect the peace and quiet of persons who may witness them, or engages in brawling or fighting, or engages in such conduct as to constitute a breach of the peace or disorderly conduct, shall be guilty of a misdemeanor of the second degree....

Case Summaries

These summaries also demonstrate one way of "briefing" cases.

State v. Saunders, 339 So. 2d 641 (Fla. 20xx):

Held: The Florida Supreme Court found no probable cause to justify the defendant's arrest for violating section 877.03 where the defendant "hassled" people on a street corner in an attempt to sell them newspapers. However, the court noted that the statute was constitutional, but limited its application to those "words which 'by their very utterance ... inflict injury or tend to incite an immediate breach of the peace' [citations omitted]; or to words known to be false, reporting some physical hazard in circumstances where such a report creates a clear and present danger of bodily harm to others." *Id.* at 644. The court added that it construed "the statute so that no words except 'fighting words' or words like shouts of 'fire' in a crowded theater fall within its proscription...." *Id.*[6]

case	holding	action involved
Saunders Fla. Sup. Ct.	no violation; statute limited to fighting words or false claims of hazards	hassling people to buy newspapers on street corners

K.S. v. State, 697 So. 2d 1275 (Fla. 3d DCA 20xx):

Held: A juvenile's conduct was insufficient to support an adjudication of delinquency for disorderly conduct resulting from a loud, obscene, verbal confrontation with police. When confronted by police, K.S. yelled, "'F--K this, I didn't do anything. This is bull--.'" *Id.* at 1276. The court found that his words were not directed at any crowd "but were instead a coarse expression of frustration at what K.S. perceived was an unjust accusation." *Id.*

---

6. We can't resist the temptation to interrupt here to set the record straight. It's OK to shout "fire" in a crowded theater if the theater *is on fire.* Only fake shouts of "fire" are proscribed, as the court should have noted.

case	holding	action involved
K.S. 3d DCA	no violation; juvenile's words not directed to any crowd	loud, obscene verbal confrontation with police

L.A.T. v. State, 650 So. 2d 214 (Fla. 3d DCA 20xx):

Held: A juvenile's conduct was insufficient to support an adjudication of delinquency for disorderly conduct resulting from a loud, obscene, verbal confrontation with police. When his friend was arrested by police, L.A.T. called upon passersby to protest and yelled: "'You f - - - ing cops, what the hell do you think you're doing? You are full of bull sh - -. This is bull sh - -. This is abuse.'" *Id.* at 215. His words, however, "neither themselves urged the crowd to respond nor actually had that effect. Specifically, they did not 'disturb' or cause anybody to interfere with the arrest or otherwise to breach the peace." *Id.* at 217-18.

case	holding	action involved
L.A.T. 3d DCA	no violation; juvenile's words didn't interfere with arrest and didn't urge crowd to act	loud, obscene verbal confrontation with police

Miller v. State, 667 So. 2d 325 (Fla. 1st DCA 20xx):

Held: The defendant's conduct, occurring within his dwelling, of continuing to "cuss" and to argue after the police told him to calm down, although loud and offensive, did not incite "others to breach the peace or pose an imminent danger to others." *Id.* at 328. "[T]o constitute a violation of section 877.03, there must be evidence of something more than loud or profane language or a belligerent attitude." *Id.*

case	holding	action involved
Miller 1st DCA	no violation; defendant's words didn't incite others to breach the peace or pose an imminent danger to others	loud "cussing," verbal confrontation with police in the defendant's dwelling

C.L.B. v. State, 689 So. 2d 1171 (Fla. 2d DCA 20xx):

Held: A juvenile's nonverbal conduct of interfering with another's arrest supported a delinquency adjudication of disorderly conduct even though his words, "'moth-erf - - ker,'" did not rise to the level of fighting words. Here, the juvenile's actions "actually hindered the arrest of a suspect, amounting to a breach of the peace." *Id.* at 1172. He "repeatedly came so close to the officer and the arrestee that the officer had to repeatedly push him back and tell him to stay away." *Id.* at 1171.

case	holding	action involved
C.L.B. 2d DCA	yes violation; words didn't constitute fighting words but juvenile's actions hindered arrest	loud, obscene verbal confrontation with police and repeatedly coming close to officer while officer was trying to arrest a suspect

Delaney v. State, 489 So. 2d 891 (Fla. 1st DCA 20xx):

Held: A defendant's conduct of precluding an officer from investigating a fight between two suspects by "being loud and abusive, continually interrupting [the officer's] investigation, demanding that [the officer] take a report from him first, yelling obscenities ['you f- - -ing Yankee'] at [the officer], and ignoring [the officer's] request to wait his turn" constituted more than protected speech and was a breach of the peace. *Id.* at 892.

case	holding	action involved
Delaney 1st DCA	yes violation; defendant's actions hindered an officer's investigation	loud, obscene verbal confrontation with police and repeatedly interrupting officer, and ignoring the officer's request to cooperate

All right. Now that we've "found" the law, just how are we to use the statute and these six cases in writing our analysis? Which cases do we use just for the rule? Which do we use for the "rule-plus" in a parenthetical or a few sentences briefly describing a relevant aspect of the case? Which do we discuss at more length, providing the relevant facts, issue, holding, rule, and reasoning (FIHRR)? Which, if any, do we omit?

Although we can offer no absolute answers to these questions, we can provide some guidelines. The following chart illustrates one way of using these cases in writing our memo.

Graphic 7.4(a)	A Case Chart	
case and court	**use of case: rule, rule-plus, or FIHRR and why**	**holding**
Saunders Fla. Sup. Court	rule-only: the facts are not particularly helpful; however, this Florida Supreme Court case is binding on our court and upholds the constitutionality of the disorderly conduct statute. Moreover, it establishes how courts should apply that statute.	no violation
K.S. 3d DCA	rule-only or parenthetical: the facts and the holding are not helpful.	no violation
L.A.T. 3d DCA	rule-only or parenthetical: the facts and the holding are not helpful, except to distinguish that in *L.A.T.*, the court noted that the defendant did not interfere with an arrest.	no violation

case and court	use of case: rule, rule-plus, or FIHRR and why	holding
Miller 1st DCA	rule-only or parenthetical: the facts and the holding are not helpful, except to distinguish that in *Miller*, the defendant merely cussed at the police.	no violation
C.L.B. 2d DCA **our jurisdiction**	FIHRR: the facts, issue, holding, rule and reasoning of *C.L.B.* are relevant to our case. We want our court to apply similar reasoning and find that verbal abuse and physical action establish disorderly conduct.	violation
Delaney 1st DCA	Could use FIHRR: for same reasons as in *C.L.B.*; but if space is limited, employ a limited rule-plus discussion.	violation

Now let's see how to discuss the rules involved in the State's analysis. In other words, let's see how to fashion, from all of these authorities, the rule section of our BaRAC design. Remember, this section is part of the "discussion" section of our memo. We've annotated our writing to highlight our use of rules and cases and used Florida Rules of Citation.

Graphic 7.4(b)	Rule Discussion: State v. Actor
rule	Section 877.03, Florida Statutes (20xx) provides in relevant part:
statute	Whoever commits such acts as are of a nature to corrupt the public morals, or outrage the sense of public decency, or affect the peace and quiet of persons who may witness them, or engages in brawling or fighting, or engages in such conduct as to constitute a breach of the peace or disorderly conduct, shall be guilty of a misdemeanor of the second degree.…
rule **explanation** **rule from** ***Saunders***	This statute, however, has been restricted as it applies to verbal conduct. *State v. Saunders*, 339 So. 2d 641, 644 (Fla. 20xx). In *Saunders*, the Florida Supreme Court narrowed section 877.03 to apply only to those "words which 'by their very utterance … inflict injury or tend to incite an immediate breach of the peace' [citations omitted]; or to words known to be false, reporting some physical hazard in circumstances where such a report creates a clear and present danger of bodily harm to others." *Id.* The court construed the statute "so that no words except 'fighting words' or words like shouts of 'fire' in a crowded theater fall within its proscription…." *Id.*
transition **rule and** **parenthetical** **from *Miller***	In light of *Saunders*, several district courts of appeal have concluded that "there must be evidence of something more than loud or profane language or a belligerent attitude" to violate section 877.03. *See, e.g., Miller v. State*, 667 So. 2d 325, 328 (Fla. 1st DCA 20xx) (holding the defendant did not violate section 877.03 by cursing at the police). Indeed, the courts have overturned disorderly conduct convictions on the ground

parentheticals from *K.S.* and *L.A.T.*

that profane language directed at a police officer is constitutionally pro-tected expression and may not form the basis of a disorderly conduct conviction. *See, e.g., K.S. v. State*, 697 So. 2d 1275, 1276 (Fla. 3d DCA 20xx) (finding that the defendant's words were not directed at any crowd, but "were instead a coarse expression of frustration at what [the defen-dant] perceived was an unjust accusation"); *L.A.T. v. State*, 650 So. 2d 214, 217-18 (Fla. 3d DCA 20xx) (finding that the defendant's words "neither themselves urged the crowd to respond nor actually had that effect. Specifically, they did not 'disturb' or cause anybody to interfere with the arrest or otherwise to breach the peace.").

[rule ex. continued]
transition
lead-in to *C.L.B., Delaney*
facts

While a disorderly conduct conviction cannot rest on mere words, when speech is combined with *nonverbal* conduct which causes a distur-bance or interferes with an arrest, a disorderly conduct conviction may stand. *C.L.B. v. State*, 689 So. 2d 1171 (Fla. 2d DCA 20xx) and *Delaney v. State*, 489 So. 2d 891 (Fla. 1st DCA 20xx) illustrate this distinction.

In *C.L.B.*, an officer was called to investigate a fight. 689 So. 2d at 1173. Once there, the officer determined that one of the adults present should be arrested; however, C.L.B. hindered the officer's attempts to make the arrest. *Id*. Specifically, C.L.B. "repeatedly came so close to the officer and the arrestee that the officer had to repeatedly push him back and tell him to stay away." *Id*. In addition, C.L.B.'s "physical action was accompanied by loud verbal protests and name-calling...." *Id*. It was only after C.L.B. re-fused to calm down and stay away from the officer that the officer ar-rested him for disorderly conduct. *Id*. Based on this behavior, C.L.B. was subsequently adjudicated delinquent for disorderly conduct. *Id*.

holding

On appeal, the Second District Court of Appeal affirmed the adjudica-tion of delinquency for disorderly conduct. *Id*. The court ruled that al-though the First Amendment does not permit the court to impose criminal sanctions against a defendant for merely creating a "scene," C.L.B. had done much more than that. *Id*. at 1171-72. "[H]is actions actu-ally hindered the arrest of a suspect, amounting to a breach of the peace." *Id*. at 1172.

rule

reasoning

lead-in
[rule ex. continued]
Delaney
abbreviated
FIHRR

Similarly, in *Delaney*, the court affirmed the defendant's conviction for disorderly conduct. 489 So. 2d at 892. The court reasoned that the defen-dant's conduct of precluding an officer from investigating a fight be-tween two suspects by "being loud and abusive, continually interrupting [the officer's] investigation, demanding that [the officer] take a report from him first, yelling obscenities ['you f- - -ing Yankee'] at [the officer], and ignoring [the officer's] request to wait his turn" constituted a breach of the peace and was not protected speech. *Id*. at 893.

In writing this discussion section, we relied heavily on a case, *C.L.B.*, from the Second District because that is the court that will ultimately hear our case. We also carefully selected which cases we would "FIHRR" and which we would only mention via "par-entheticals." We *explained* the law. We did not assume that our reader knew the rules involved.

§ 7.5   Using Case Charts to Organize Information

As we saw above in our disorderly conduct hypothetical, we will face instances where the relevant "law" is contained in many different sources. Our task then involves not only finding and understanding the law, but *keeping track* of it. To keep track of the relevant disorderly conduct cases, we chose to use charts to organize important information.

First, we used a chart to reduce each case to its bare essentials, as the following graphic illustrates. (We didn't need an "issue" column because all the cases concerned the same issue.)

case	holding	action involved (facts)

Second, we collected all the cases, and using the following chart, stated how we could use each case in our analysis:

case and court	use rule-only, rule-plus, or FIHRR and why	holding

Trust us; using case charts is an effective way of organizing a vast amount of information. If we don't organize our cases, we'll left with piles of papers (or their equivalent), that we'll likely have to dig through yet again in a frantic effort to "find the law."

We offer one final organizational chart which we've found is very helpful. The § refers to the section in the memo or brief where we will address the case; the "+" means the case is helpful; the "−" means the case is harmful.

case name	court	year	key facts & issue	held	rule reasoning	use rule-only, rule-plus, or FIHRR	§	±

Again, if we don't develop some method of organizing our case notes, chaos reigns. We'll spend hours reading the cases and then countless more re-reading them. If, however, we organize the cases *as* we read them, we'll avoid the "I have all of these cases in piles but can't remember what the heck the piles were for" syndrome.

§ 7.6   Where Do We Go from Here?

We've now completed this reminder of how to reason and argue. We've reviewed the basic principles underlying deductive, inductive, and analogical reasoning, and we've seen how to express our thoughts in writing acceptable to the court and to our colleagues. While others around us might be running about exhaustively trying to escape their "footprints and shadows" of doubt and confusion regarding their writing ability, we can now "rest in the shade," assured, and with the confidence that we can keep pace. We can engage in legal analysis; we can write a legal argument. We've remembered what we already knew.

In the next five sections, we'll see how to apply deductive, inductive, and analogical reasoning to memo writing (**Section II**) and brief writing (**Section III**); we'll explore how we begin writing and how we edit what we've written (**Section IV**); and we'll review the basics of clear and effective writing (**Section V**). Finally, in **Section VI**, we'll see how all of these principles come together in a sample memo and in three sample briefs. Onward!

§ 7.7   Exercise in Designing a Case Chart and Designing a Rule from Multiple Cases

Reread the Jane Smith hypothetical in § 5.10(b) and § 6.5. Ms. Smith has petitioned the court to have the document admitted to probate as the last will and testament of Mr. Atkinson. The court has determined that the signature and material provisions are in the testator's handwriting, thus satisfying California Probate Code § 6111(a) (West 2010). The remaining issue concerns the testamentary intent of the decedent; that is, whether the document is intended to dispose of property after death and thus is a valid will pursuant to California Probate Code § 6111(c).

Assume you have found the following five cases.[1]

> *In re Button's Estate,* **California Supreme Court 1930, 287 P. 964**
>
> Decedent wrote a four-page suicide letter to her ex-husband shortly before taking her life. The letter included the following statement: "I'd like to be cremated. You can have the house on 26th ave. and all the things of value so you won't be out any money on burying me." The court held that the suicide letter was testamentary in character. The court ruled that the basic test of testamentary intent is whether the document is intended to dispose of property after death. The court reasoned that the statement contained "words of gift," and that, to a layman, this statement would

---

1. More complete versions of all these cases are in Appendix A. Note that the citations we've included for these cases are not in proper *Bluebook* format; thus allowing us to give you an assignment to write them in proper *Bluebook* format.

have almost the same significance as if the word "gift" had been used. Moreover, it was clear that decedent had formed the intent to take her life and that the letter was written with the purpose of arranging her affairs after death, because this disposition of property followed her request that she be cremated. It was of little consequence (1) that the statement was contained in a letter rather than in a formally prepared will, (2) that decedent did not include the word "will" in the letter, or (3) that other portions of the letter did not express testamentary intent.

In re Spies' Estate, **California Court of Appeal, Second District 1948, 194 P.2d 83**

The decedent addressed, but did not deliver, the following letter to the secretary of the Brotherhood of Locomotive Firemen and Enginemen:

> "Jan. 12 --45
> Mr. James Yates
> Secy 663 B of L F & E
>
> In case of my death, before my Brotherhood Policy is assign in change of beneficiary it is my wish, that I bequeat $2000.00 of this $4000.00 policy to Patty Lou Smith of 1047 E. Wood St. Decatur, Ill. and Apt's 419 & 421 of Glen Donald's Apt's at Los Angeles, Calif.
>
> Albert P. Spies
> Mrs. W. M. McKay
> (Witness thereto)"

The issue was whether the document was executed with the necessary testamentary intent. The court held that it was. The court reasoned that the words, "In case of my death," the particularity of the description of the beneficiary and the property, and the witness's signature all demonstrated testamentary intent.

In re Estate of Blain, **California Court of Appeal, Fourth District 1956, 295 P.2d 898**

Decedent's safe deposit box contained miscellaneous papers, a sealed envelope marked "Last Will F.B.," and a slip of paper wrapped around a ring on which decedent, an attorney, had written "to Sonia Lambert Frank Blain." Only the contents of the envelope were admitted to probate as decedent's will. One issue was whether the paper wrapped around the ring demonstrated testamentary intent or a disposition of property. The court held that it did not. The court reasoned that the word "to" did not necessarily connote testamentary disposition, and the paper contained no description of property.

In re Estate of Wolfe, California Court of Appeal, First District 1968, 67 Cal. Rptr. 297

A missing person, prior to his disappearance, sent his brother a letter by registered mail which included the following statement:

"[I] am leaveing [sic] my Place in Menlo Park for you"
"[If] I never call for it ... the place is yours"
"[If] I were you I would keep this letter"

The court held that the letter met the requirement of testamentary intent. The court reasoned that the words "am leaveing" [sic] and "for you" constituted a disposition of the "Place." In addition, "[If] I never call for it ... the place is yours" demonstrated a revocable posthumous disposition, because "never" contemplated the testator's eventual death. Finally, sending the letter by registered mail and advising the beneficiary to keep the letter demonstrated that the testator recognized the importance of the letter. The court further noted that a document written by an inexperienced or illiterate person should be construed more liberally than one written by an expert.

In re Estate of Wong, California Court of Appeal, Sixth District 1995, 47 Cal. Rptr. 2d 707

A note was found in decedent's office in a sealed envelope decorated with stickers. The note stated, "All Tai-Kin Wong's → Xi Zhao, my best half TKW, 12-31-92." The issue was whether there was sufficient evidence of testamentary intent. The court found that there was not. The court reasoned that it was impossible to tell what property decedent intended to dispose of by the writing, as there was no description of any property. There were no donative words, such as "give" or "bequeath," to indicate a transfer, and an arrow does not indicate disposition. Furthermore, there was no indication that property should be transferred upon death.

Exercise 1. Design a case chart for the above five cases, including information on how you would use each case in writing a motion to the court on Ms. Smith's behalf regarding the deceased's testamentary intent. Use **Graphic 7.4(a)** and the charts in § 7.5 as guides; for each case, include on the chart the case name, court, and year (can be one column); key facts; holding; rule and reasoning; and how you'd use the case in your motion (rule, rule-plus or FIHRR).

Exercise 2. Design and outline the rule, using the full text of the above five cases in Appendix A, to solve the issue(s) arising in our case on behalf of Ms. Smith. Identify the case or cases you would cite as support for each part of the rule, using proper *Bluebook* format. You do not need to personalize the rule.

Section II

Predictive Analysis: Designing the Legal Memo

Chapter 8

The Legal Memo: Preliminary Matters

"The horror of that moment," the King went on, "I shall never, never forget!"

"You will, though," the Queen said, "if you don't make a memorandum of it."

—Lewis Carroll, *Alice's Adventures in Wonderland*

§8.1   Function and Design

Function. A *memorandum* is a problem-solving document written for a law-trained reader. Memos come in two basic forms. They're *persuasive*, as memos of law accompanying a pleading, informing and persuading the judge to rule in our client's favor. (We examine this type of persuasive writing in **Section III**). Or, they're *predictive*, as an internal office memorandum written for our colleague or client to answer a legal question.[1] This predictive memo is the focus of this section.

Legal memos are result oriented; through them, we predict a likely outcome to a legal problem and advise our client accordingly. Because we write memos at all stages of problem-solving, we must let the reader know what we know and what we don't know. If we lack any information necessary to render an opinion on any issue we were asked to address (and this happens more than we'd like), we say so right in the memo. And, if we make any assumptions of law (which we shouldn't do, but which we must do when our client needs our advice immediately), we identify these assumptions *as* assumptions. In other words, we write an *absolutely credible* document while employing the time-honored device of "covering our," er, "options."

But no matter in what stage in the problem-solving process we write a memo, someone will be relying on our advice. What we say in the memo matters. What we say shapes the course of our client's actions: to sue, or not to sue; to mediate or not to mediate; to settle, or to fight. What we say better be right.

Professionalism. What we do, say, and write also reflects on our firm's reputation.[2] Even if we are "only" law clerks, lawyers likely will rely upon and are responsible for our work, which may be incorporated into documents filed with the court. As officers of the court, with a duty to the legal justice system as well as our clients, we must reveal adverse authority and are prohibited from filing a frivolous claim or making a frivolous argument.[3] Rule 11(a) of the Federal Rules of Civil Procedure states as follows:

> **Signature.** Every pleading, written motion, and other paper must be signed by at least one attorney of record in the attorney's name—or by a party personally if the party is unrepresented. The paper must state the signer's address, e-mail address, and telephone number. Unless a rule or statute specifically states otherwise, a pleading need not be verified or accompanied by an affidavit. The court must strike an unsigned paper unless the omission is promptly corrected after being called to the attorney's or party's attention.

Rule 11(b) further provides:

> **Representations to the Court.** By presenting to the court a pleading, written motion, or other paper—whether by signing, filing, submitting, or later ad-

---

1. If we're clerking for a judge, we may write a "bench memo," analyzing the issues in a case and suggesting an outcome. The principles of writing a law office memo apply equally to writing a bench memo.

2. Although we are not subject to the ethical canons until sworn in as members of the bar, as students we take these ethical responsibilities seriously to ensure that we become the ethical, professional lawyers we should be. See Chapter 27 for further guidance regarding ethics and professionalism.

3. Model Rules of Prof'l Conduct R. 3.1.

vocating it—an attorney or unrepresented party certifies that to the best of the person's knowledge, information, and belief, formed after an inquiry reasonable under the circumstances:

(1) it is not being presented for any improper purpose, such as to harass, cause unnecessary delay, or needlessly increase the cost of litigation;

(2) the claims, defenses, and other legal contentions are warranted by existing law or by a nonfrivolous argument for extending, modifying, reversing existing law or for establishing new law;

(3) the factual contentions have evidentiary support or, if specifically so identified, will likely have evidentiary support after a reasonable opportunity for further investigation or discovery; and

(4) the denials of factual contentions are warranted on the evidence or, if specifically so identified, are reasonably based on belief or a lack of information.

Finally, Rule 11(c) provides for sanctions against a lawyer for violations of the rule, including monetary penalties:

Sanctions.

(1) **In General.** If, after notice and a reasonable opportunity to respond, the court determines that Rule 11(b) has been violated, the court may impose an appropriate sanction on any attorney, law firm, or party that violated the rule or is responsible for the violation. Absent exceptional circumstances, a law firm must be held jointly responsible for a violation committed by its partner, associate, or employee.

. . .

(4) **Nature of a Sanction.** A sanction imposed under this rule must be limited to what suffices to deter repetition of the conduct or comparable conduct by others similarly situated. The sanction may include nonmonetary directives; an order to pay a penalty into court; or, if imposed on motion and warranted for effective deterrence, an order directing payment to the movant of part or all of the reasonable attorney's fees and other expenses directly resulting from the violation.

And make no mistake, the courts frequently impose sanctions on lawyers pursuant to this rule.

Because the memo is a "problem-solving" device, *it will not be entirely objective*, nor should it be. We understand that not all legal writing professors share our view. Some believe that the memo should be an absolutely objective summary of the relevant law. However, based upon years of practicing law, we know otherwise.

Our client is paying us to suggest an answer to a problem. If our memo is so general or "objective" that it fails to identify "the forest for the trees," it's useless. A memo is not a "law review article" spanning the history of legal thought on the subject and then suggesting a million or two reasons why things shouldn't be as they are. Rather, a memo is a working document designed to get a job done. It suggests a path and warns of the mine fields along the way. It counsels; it takes a stand.

Design. Here's the overall design of the memo:[4]

Heading:

    TO: Reader's name
    FROM: Your name
    DATE: The date is important for future research updating.
    RE: Case number; name of client; legal matter; issue
    FILE: Name of our computer file containing this memo

The HEADING (above) identifies the memo's recipient and author, the date, the client's name and file or case number, the legal matter, the issue addressed, and the document's computer file name.

Question Presented: [see Chapter 9]

This is the issue our memo addresses, phrased in easily readable terms which clearly identify the parties and their relationship to each other, as well as the precise legal issue involved.

Brief Answer: [see Chapter 9]

It's just that. Following the BaRAC design, it answers the QUESTION PRESENTED, states the gist of the rule(s) involved, then briefly explains the reasoning underlying the answer.

Facts: [see Chapter 10]

This is the easy-to-follow and self-contained "story" of the relevant facts of our case.

Discussion: [see Chapter 11]

In this section, using the BaRAC design, we identify and discuss the arguments for *both* sides, and predict an outcome on every argument. We explain the law in detail, using headings and subheadings (where necessary) to clarify the discussion and make the document easier to read.

A good way to begin is to restate the issue (clarifying what is and isn't relevant), answer that issue, and then briefly discuss the general rule as that rule relates to our case.

Next, we develop the rule, and apply it to our facts. In other words, we discuss the relevant elements of the rule (usually giving each element its own heading or subheading), and explain how our facts relate to the particular element we are discussing. We then address any counter-arguments our opponent likely will raise and respond to those arguments. We continue in this step-by-step fashion until we have addressed all relevant issues.

---

4. *For proper spacing, capitalization, and formatting, please see the sample memo in Section VI, Chapter 35.* Of course, ours is not the only acceptable memo design. Memo formats vary. We've included here a design which can be readily adapted to any issue.

I. <u>This is how we write headings. They are full sentences, underlined, single-spaced, and can be more than one sentence long. They encapsulate our predictions and suggestions regarding the issue addressed.</u>

Our discussion relevant to Heading I goes here. We follow the BaRAC design in writing it. Notice that the underlining on each line extends only as far as the last character on each line. The period at the end of the last sentence is also underlined.

II. <u>If we have a "I" Heading, we also have a "II" Heading.</u>

Our discussion relevant to Heading II goes here.

Conclusion: [see Chapter 12]

We answer the QUESTION PRESENTED, and we predict what the court likely will do. The CONCLUSION is short and sweet.

Authorities Cited: [see Chapter 12]

Finally, we list all authorities in the form appropriate for the court our case may be before (we check the rules of court to determine this), we list cases in alphabetical order, and we *update* all authorities.

Drafting the memo. Please note that although we have set forth the "sections" of the memo in the order in which they're usually presented, this is not the order in which they're usually drafted. The order for writing memo sections (as for any legal document), is personal to the writer. Some prefer to begin with the Facts, some jump right into the Discussion.

However, no matter which section we write first, all sections must be internally consistent and consistent with all other sections. Nothing is more annoying to a colleague (or indeed to a law professor reading a student's memo), than inconsistent conclusions. Thus, in the course of writing, any time we revise one section, we recheck our other sections to keep them consistent.

In addition to consistency among the sections, the entire memo must be legally and factually accurate; technically flawless (i.e., all quotations, citations, and factual assertions must be accurate); grammatically correct; and easy to read. Finally, we polish our memo by proofreading and editing time and time again until our document is perfect.[5] Remember, our document reflects us. If it's sloppy, ill-conceived, and inarticulate, that's exactly how we'll appear to our colleagues and to our clients.

Because form helps to convey content, we rely on the BaRAC design in writing our memo. We state our Bold Assertion, which in the memo is our prediction, or suggested

---

5. *See* Chapter 24 for editing tips.

path, then follow with the Rule explanation, Application, and Conclusion. In other words, we use the "syllogism with attitude" approach.

However, because the memo is usually not written to advocate a position, but rather to examine options, we discuss counter-arguments more in the memo than we do in a brief. In other words, in our memo we reveal, explain, and chart a course around potential problems. For this reason, the BaRAC design of the DISCUSSION section generally takes the following form:

Graphic 8.1(a)	The BaRAC Design of the Memo's Discussion Section: Single-Element Rule		
bold assertion	State our prediction or suggested course of action.		
rule	State and explain the rule.		
application	Apply the rule to our facts and reach a conclusion. [See Chapter 11]		
counter-argument	bold assertion:	State the counter-argument.	
	rule:	State and explain the rule regarding the counter-argument.	
	application:	Apply the above rule to our facts.	
	conclusion:	Reach a conclusion as to the counter-argument, i.e., "For these reasons, the State will likely assert…."	
response	bold assertion:	State our response to the counter-argument, i.e., "However, we should argue that…."	
	rule:	Discuss any differences in interpreting the counter-argument rule, and/or explain why that rule should not apply to our case.	
	application:	If the counter-argument rule applies to our facts, explain its impact on our case.	
	conclusion:	Reach a conclusion regarding our response to the counter-argument.	
conclusion	State our "overall" conclusion.		

Important point about counter-arguments. When we're dealing with a multi-element rule, we include our counter-argument immediately after our discussion of each element. We do not "save" all counter-arguments for the end of our memo. Rather we address each counter-argument in the context of the element or issue it concerns. Accordingly, the BaRAC design for a multi-element rule is as follows:

Graphic 8.1(b)	The BaRAC Design of the Memo's Discussion Section: Multi-Element Rule	
bold assertion	State our prediction or suggested course of action.	
general rule	State the general rule. Address the specifics of the rule's elements in the application section below.	
application	Concisely apply the general rule to our facts and reach a conclusion. Then explain that conclusion by addressing each element in detail.	
element 1	bold assertion: rule: application: conclusion: counter-argument: bold assertion: rule: application: conclusion: our response: bold assertion: rule: application: conclusion:	
element 2	[repeat **element 1** structure]	
conclusion	State our overall conclusion.	

When done well, a memo is a "mind-reading" device. Through it, our colleagues can literally read our thoughts and understand our reasoning. As we explain in the chapters that follow, we state our ideas and insights so clearly that we leave nothing to misinterpretation. We explain the law so well that we don't send our reader running off to the library to read the cases we've cited or to clarify a point we've made. Our logic (as expressed through the BaRAC design) is so compelling that we or our colleagues can easily transform our memo into a trial brief, an appellate brief, or even a court opinion.

§ 8.2   Preliminary Steps in Writing the Memo

The first, and most critical, step in writing a memo is knowing exactly what we're supposed to do. We don't waste our reader's time (or indeed our own) by addressing irrelevant matters.

Before writing the first word or reading the first case, we determine the memo's:

(1) intended reader,

(2) format,

(3) purpose,

(4) tone and scope,

(5) due date, and

(6) method of submission to our reader.

Essentially, the above list is somewhat of a variation on journalism's information-gathering "five Ws and one H." In journalism these factors are who, what, when, where, why, and how. The axiom is that for a report to be complete, it must satisfy a checklist of six questions, each comprising an interrogative word.

For purposes of writing our memo, we can think of the intended reader as the "who," the format as the "what," the due date as the "when," the method of submission as the "where," the purpose as the "why," and the tone and scope as the "how."

We address each of these aspects except the due date ("when") and the method of submitting the memo ("where") below.

§ 8.2(a)   Step #1: Determine Our Intended Reader

Our intended reader determines the extent to which we define legal concepts in our memo. When our reader is another lawyer experienced in the area of law we're addressing, we likely won't have to explain common legal terms and concepts. However, when the reader is, for example, an expert witness from another field or our client, we define and explain all terms, even those which seem straightforward to us.

§ 8.2(b)   Step #2: Determine the Format

Before beginning our memo, we ask whether our intended readers prefer a certain type of memo format. If they do, we determine exactly what they require and we write our memo conforming to that format. We strongly suggest obtaining a copy of a memo that our readers like and then following that design. However, if our readers have no preference, we suggest following the format of the sample memo in Chapter 35. (This format can easily be edited to form the first draft of a litigation document. In fact, we can see the "footprint" of our sample memo in our sample brief in Chapter 36.)

Computers. We can't leave this topic of "format" without a warning regarding computers. Be extremely careful (indeed, *paranoid* would be appropriate) in saving all work. Don't rely solely on a computer hard drive; save all work externally, and print out a hard copy of all work in progress. Words fail to adequately describe the computer "horror stories" we've heard over the years, the result of which was weeks of work being lost in a flash.

The gremlins living inside the computers (and we know you're there), know exactly when to strike, wreaking havoc at the *most* inopportune time. (Like right before the memo is due.) We think the gremlins sense our increased levels of stress and respond accordingly, but that's only our theory. We'll say it again: back work up on the hard drive, externally, and on paper. The gremlins are waiting....

§ 8.2(c)   Step #3: Determine the Purpose of the Memo

In determining the memo's purpose, we consider the following:

- whether the memo will be used as an internal document for a fellow lawyer or client or whether it will be filed with the court accompanying a pleading;
- the procedural posture of the case (i.e., has a lawsuit already been filed, or are we exploring the possibility of one?);
- the precise issue or issues to be addressed;
- the intended reader (again!);
- whether the reader is looking, in a purely objective sense, at the pros and cons of a given course of action or is looking for a solution to a course of action already undertaken;
- when the memo is due; and
- the approximate time we should spend researching and writing.

It's a fact of life that law firms must keep track of "billable" hours. Very likely, the time we can spend on our memo will be limited. Our time is money. Our client (theoretically) is paying for every minute. We work efficiently and make every minute count.

§ 8.2(d)   Step #4: Determine the Tone and Scope

In determining "tone," we ask how formal our memo should be. Can we refer to ourselves? Can we use informal language such as contractions? If we receive no guidance in this regard, it's best to err on the side of formality (i.e., no contractions and no reference to ourselves).

§ 8.3   Organizing and Outlining

Once we've determined the memo's purpose, intended reader, format, and tone, we're ready to begin organizing our thoughts into a cohesive *theory* and to begin researching our case. We're ready to consider the memo's scope. The following suggest ways to get started:

1. Understand the facts and focus the issue. Before running to the library or hopping online, we *think*. What exactly are the issues to research? What are the relevant facts? To keep our theory and ideas focused, we draft a preliminary Question or Questions Presented. [See Chapter 9]

2. Check the file. We then see if the firm[6] keeps a memo "bank"; that is, a file of memos written by lawyers or law clerks on various topics. Rather than "reinvent the

---

6. By "firm" we mean *any* organization—private or public.

wheel," we see whether a memo in the memo bank has addressed the same or a similar issue as our case. If so, we use that memo as a starting point for our research.

3. Research the law. Using the "TARPP"[7] mnemonic, explained in Chapter 3, § 3.4, we consider what areas to research. We're ultimately looking for "primary" law, that is, constitutional provisions, statutes, regulations, and case law. "Binding" primary authority is the most compelling law we can uncover. But, where no "binding" authority exists, we look outside our jurisdiction to the case law of other jurisdictions, particularly that of "sister" courts.

Alternatively, if we're researching a newly developing cause of action or area, and there are no (or only a handful of) relevant cases, we look to "secondary" sources such as law review articles, "Restatements," and treatises. However, in our memo, we rely on secondary sources only as a last resort. We never cite a law review article or other secondary source when there's a primary source, (e.g., a case, on point).[8]

4. Analyze. Once we've found the relevant authorities, we read these authorities *critically*. By critically, we mean with an eye toward solving our client's issues rather than casually, as we might read a novel. We evaluate their relevance to, and impact on, our client's issues. We evaluate how the various authorities interact. We may discover that we haven't found what we need to address all the issues. Issues that we hadn't initially thought were relevant might now be critical. We may now need to ask our client about additional facts. At this point, we'd backtrack and do additional research.

5. Organize our research. Organization is a tedious, but critical, step in the writing process. If we don't properly organize how we're going to present our analysis, we've wasted our time. Without a well-organized document, we can't adequately inform, and when necessary, persuade our reader. Without good organization, we'll have a messy stream of random thoughts and observations. Thus, when we determine that we have the necessary authorities, we brief our cases, using a full case brief format such as the sample case brief in Chapter 26, or we use case summaries, demonstrated in Chapter 7, § 7.4. We also outline and personalize the rules governing our issues (see Chapter 1, §§ 1.5–1.8). We then coordinate our research results into case charts for each issue, as described in Chapter 7, § 7.5. We break down each chart into the mandatory elements of a governing rule or by factors if the governing rule has factors. We include relevant constitutional provisions, statutes, and cases; list each source by jurisdiction; and comment on the strengths and weaknesses of the cases. We include adverse, as well as favorable, cases. From our case charts, we decide which cases we'll use in our memo or brief.

As you become more experienced, you will likely find that you can skip or condense many of these steps. However, until that time arrives, we recommend that you heed our organizational advice. Moreover, you may find that for some assignments, you won't have time to write a memo. Indeed, you may have to solve a legal problem within hours of receiving the issue you're addressing. Having organized research will enable

---

7. Thing, Action, Relief, Parties, and Place.
8. *See* Chapter 5, §§ 5.1—5.4 regarding types and precedential value of authorities.

you to discuss your findings with your colleagues, employer, or client even though you haven't completed (or even begun) a written memo.

6. Outline our case. Once our research is tidily briefed and charted, what next? Most of us, including your humble authors, resist drafting a formal outline — one with capital and lower case Roman and Arabic numerals and letters and so forth. Such an outline is extremely useful for organizing our research but isn't necessary. If you're comfortable with this type of outlining, that's great — do one for each of the client's issues and use that for writing your document. If, like us, however, you resist formal outlines, you've got to figure out another method for organizing your research.

We prefer to use the BaRAC design for organizing our analysis by creating a "running outline" of the rules involved, and noting how those rules impact our facts. The BaRAC design[9] — Bold Assertion, Rule, Application, Conclusion — is how our reader can best follow and understand legal analysis. Organizing our research in this fashion from the very start will make it quite simple to transform our thoughts into the discussion section of our memo.

We work step-by-step on each part of the document and on each issue. Unless we want to be overwhelmed completely, we don't attempt to write the entire document in one fell swoop. Instead, we compartmentalize our document and work on one manageable "box" at a time.

For each issue, we write the acronym of the BaRAC syllogism vertically down the left side of our paper — creating an "issue box." Chapter 11, § 11.2 explains in detail how we do this. We may have more than one of these syllogisms for each issue, but at least one is needed per issue. When we have multiple issues, we organize and address the issues in their logical order. Chapter 11, § 11.5 explains this process. We deal first with any dispositive issues, i.e., those that the court must decide as a threshold matter. Then, we tackle the issues in order of importance, addressing the most important first. If we follow the BaRAC design, the issue will practically write itself.

We begin with our conclusion on an issue (our Ba) — that is, what we need to prove. We state this as a predicted outcome for a purely objective document such as a memo and as a conclusion or recommendation to the court, for a persuasive document.

Next, we figure out what rule or rules (R) govern the predicted outcome in an objective document or will result in the optimal conclusion for our client in a persuasive document. We ask ourselves whether the rule compels the conclusion we've stated (Ba). If not, we need to revise our conclusion or the rule(s) supporting it. When we're satisfied that our rule or rules will support our conclusion, we use the Rule, Rule-plus, or FIHRR method as appropriate.[10] Like the charts upon which they are based, each BaRAC is organized around the relevant legal rules, not around the cases. Thus, if we have a rule that we'll explain by using multiple cases, we'll have a single Bold Assertion for that issue, and we'll discuss all relevant cases within the Rule section of that BaRAC. Don't worry if these concepts don't quite make sense to you at this point. We explain this process in detail in Chapter 11.

---

9. *See* Chapter 1, § 1.9(b).
10. *See* Chapter 6, §§ 6.3(a)—6.3(d).

Now we apply (A) the rule(s) to our client's facts. For each element or factor of a rule, we match it up with our client's facts. Again, we reassess our conclusion. Is it supportable? If so, we restate our Bold Assertion as our conclusion (C).

We revise our outline to include any additional issues that arise and to divide an issue into subissues where necessary. The outlines contained in **Graphics 8.1(a)** and **8.1(b)** will help keep us on track, as will the Graphics in Chapter 11.

Updating our authorities and revising. This bears repeating: during the course of completing these preliminary steps, and even after we begin writing our memo, we continually (1) update our authorities to determine that they are still valid and (2) evaluate our client's case. We may discover new information—either about the rules governing our issues or about our client's facts. We may discover that there are facts about our client's case that we don't know but *need* to know. When any of these situations occur, we do additional research as needed, and we backtrack to see whether we need to revise earlier steps in our process. We may even abandon conclusions and begin anew. Outlining helps organize and clarify our understanding of the law and the facts. We need to remain willing to revise, or even reverse, prior conclusions we've reached during prior steps.

Needless to say, getting started early on a writing assignment allows us the opportunity to backtrack and revisit prior steps as often as necessary to get the job done right. It also allows us the time to put the document away for a day or two to read it with fresh eyes, as our intended reader will do. In fact, we should read our "final draft" (no matter what document it is) objectively, as if we know nothing about the law or the facts. Have we told our reader what he or she needs to know? If not, we revise our document until we've resolved all lingering doubts.

§8.4   Writing the Memo

Once we have our BaRAC outline, we begin drafting, and redrafting, our analysis. Unlike some types of writing, which we can possibly compose and complete in one effort, legal writing is far more complex. We may find that we need to reread some authorities, reject an authority we initially thought was useful, or find additional authorities to explain parts of the governing legal principles. We may find that we need to explain why we will not be discussing some aspects of the legal rule involved. For example, there may be occasions when we don't need to discuss some of the legal principles because they are clearly satisfied (we briefly say so, and why), clearly not satisfied (we briefly say so, and why), or either not at issue or not within the scope of what we've been asked to address in the memo.

For in-depth pointers on writing the memo, please refer to the following Chapters:

Chapter 9   Question Presented and Brief Answer
Chapter 10   The Facts
Chapter 11   The Discussion
Chapter 12   The Conclusion and Authorities Cited
Chapter 23   The Blank Page: Tips on Getting Started
Chapter 24   Making It Shine: Editing Tips for the Memo and Brief

Chapter Review
The Legal Memo: Preliminary Matters

✓ We ensure that what we write in our memo is absolutely correct, factually and legally. If we're unsure about either the facts or the law, we do more research or clearly state that the information necessary to form an opinion and/or analyze the issue is insufficient. And, if we make any assumptions of law, we identify these assumptions *as* assumptions.

✓ A memo is *not*, and *should not be*, an objective document. Rather, a memo is a self-contained, problem-solving, *predictive* device, written to suggest a path or action and to alert our reader to possible "mine fields" along the way.

✓ The memo follows the BaRAC design and may require us to include *counter-arguments* and our *responses* to those counter-arguments.

✓ Before writing the memo, we consider the "five Ws and one H," that is, the memo's (1) intended reader, (2) format, (3) purpose, (4) tone and scope, (5) due date, and (6) method of submission to our reader.

✓ If working on a computer, we save our work in progress on the hard drive, externally, and on paper. If not, the gremlins will surely get us.

✓ We update all authorities.

✓ We continually re-evaluate our understanding of the facts and the law and revise as necessary. We make certain our memo is internally consistent, legally and factually accurate, technically flawless, and grammatically correct.

✓ Our memo reflects on our professionalism. Whether we appear articulate, smart, and competent depends entirely on what we've written.

Chapter 9

Question Presented and Brief Answer

§9.1   Overview of the Question Presented

Purpose. The Question Presented ("Question") is a query, in easily readable form, concerning the legal issue we've been asked to address. A well-written Question specifically informs the reader of the crucial legal issue (i.e., the ultimate inquiry) and (where relevant) the decisive facts. We write each Question so that with very little editing we can transform it into a thesis sentence. However, as we discuss below in § 9.2, the format of the Question varies depending on whether our memo involves a pure question of law or the application of a legal rule to specific facts.

Context and Format. The Question follows the Heading and precedes the Brief Answer. It's generally one sentence long, (double-spaced) but can be longer. If we have more than one *distinct* Question, we number each Question, using capital Roman numerals. If there's only one Question, we don't number it.

Party Names. To save space, we refer to parties by their last name or designation (e.g., "landlord," "lessee," "plaintiff," or "defendant"). In a criminal case, we refer to "defendant," "state" or "government," and "victim."

Punctuation. If the Question begins with the word "whether," we do not put a question mark at the end of the sentence. However, if the question begins with an appropriate verb, e.g., "should," "does," "may," or "did," we place a question mark at the end.

§9.2   Legal Questions

A pure *legal question* examines the scope or interpretation of a law or legal principle, notwithstanding the facts of our case, and often identifies the jurisdiction in which the question arises.

Design. The design of a legal Question usually takes one of the following forms:

"Whether [jurisdiction] recognizes, allows, permits, prohibits [subject]."

"Does [statute, rule, constitutional provision, case], which [description of statute, rule, constitutional provision, case], violate, undermine, overrule [statute, rule, constitutional provision, case]?"

Graphic 9.2(a)	Designs for a Legal Issue Question Presented		
inquiry word	jurisdiction	verb	subject
whether, did, does, should, may		recognizes, allows, permits, prohibits, prevents	

or

inquiry word	legal rule	description of legal rule	verb	legal rule
whether, did, does, should, may				

Examples of pure legal questions follow:

Graphic 9.2(b)　　　　　　　**Examples: Legal Questions**

I. Whether the State of Florida recognizes the tort of intentional infliction of emotional distress.

II. Does section 796.07, Florida Statutes (20xx), which prohibits sexual activity for hire, violate Florida's Privacy Amendment, Article 1, section 23, of the Florida Constitution?

Graphic 9.2(c)　　　　　　　**Examples Analyzed**

inquiry word	jurisdiction	verb	subject
I. Whether	the State of Florida	recognizes	the tort of intentional infliction of emotional distress.

inquiry word	legal rule	description of legal rule	verb	legal rule
II. Does	Section 796.07, Florida Statutes (20xx),	which prohibits sexual activity for hire,	violate	Florida's Privacy, Amendment, Article 1, section 23, of the Florida Constitution?

Although we don't include facts in a pure legal Question, where we have a statute (as in the second example above), we could include any relevant legislative intent underlying the statute's enactment. For example:

Whether invalidating a surrogacy contract and making a child a ward of the State would defeat the fundamental legislative intent of the Florida Surrogate Parenthood Act, enacted to protect the best interests of children.

Please notice also that we can readily transform our Questions into the following topic sentences (i.e., bold assertions):

I.   The State of Florida recognizes the tort of intentional infliction of emotional distress.

II. Section 796.07, Florida statutes (20xx), which prohibits sexual activity for hire, does not violate Florida's Privacy Amendment, Article 1, section 23, of the Florida Constitution.

§ 9.3   Fact-Based Questions

A fact-based Question examines how a law or legal principle (a constitutional provision, statute, rule, or case) applies to particular facts. It usually takes the following form:

"Whether [legal issue] where [decisive facts]."

For example: "Whether the State of Florida's ban on public nudity is violated by a group of 2-year-olds skinny-dipping at a public beach."

Relevancy. This type of phrasing, where we state the legal issue at the outset—*before* the facts—helps our readers place the decisive facts in context. By stating the issue right away, we don't require our readers to wade through a list of facts before learning why those facts are relevant.

Graphic 9.3(a)	Design for a Fact-Based Question Presented	
inquiry word	**legal point**	**decisive facts**
whether, did, does, should, may		

Several examples of fact-based Questions follow. In determining whether to use names of the parties or generic terms such as husband/wife, employer/employee, we consider (1) whether our reader will recall the names, and (2) which reference makes our Question easier to understand. In the following example, we've used a generic term (chief engineer) instead of a name (Lionell):

Graphic 9.3(b)	Example 1: Fact-Based Question

Whether a complaint states a cause of action for intentional infliction of emotional distress where the plaintiff, the chief engineer of a train, seeks damages for merely witnessing the defendant's physical injury caused when the train ran over and severely injured the defendant, who had purposefully lain down on the railroad tracks.

Graphic 9.3(c)	Example 1: Fact-Based Question Analyzed	
inquiry word	**legal point**	**decisive facts**
Whether	a complaint states a cause of action for intentional infliction of emotional distress	where the plaintiff, the chief engineer of a train, seeks damages for merely witnessing the defendant's physical injury caused when the train ran over and severely injured the defendant, who had purposefully lain down on the railroad tracks.

Note that this fact-based Question specifically identifies a party to the lawsuit, whereas the pure legal Questions above do not.

In a fact-based Question, we may also include the rule, as the following example illustrates:

Graphic 9.3(d)	Example 2: Fact-Based Question
Whether a complaint states a cause of action for intentional infliction of emotional distress, requiring extreme and outrageous conduct intentionally or recklessly causing severe emotional distress to another, where the plaintiff, the chief engineer of a train, seeks damages for merely witnessing the defendant's physical injury, caused when the train ran over and severely injured the defendant who had purposefully lain down on the railroad tracks.	

However, we do *not* include *legal conclusions* in our Question. We save such conclusions for other sections of the memo. For example, we would not conclude, as we have in the following example, that the defendant acted "outrageously" and "intentionally," because such *intentional* actions are elements of the tort of intentional infliction of emotional distress, which we must prove.

Graphic 9.3(e)	Example 3: Don't Do This — Assuming a Legal Conclusion in a Fact-Based Question
Whether a complaint states a cause of action for intentional infliction of emotional distress, where the plaintiff, the chief engineer of a train, seeks damages for severe emotional distress for witnessing the defendant's physical injury caused when the train ran over and severely injured the defendant, who had *outrageously and intentionally* lain down on the railroad tracks.	

Notice that in Example 2, although we've included many facts, the Question is still easy to read. The following example, in contrast, contains *too much* information, making it nearly impossible to follow:

Graphic 9.3(f)   **Example 4: Don't Do This —**
Too Much Detail in a Fact-Based Question

Whether a complaint states a cause of action for intentional infliction of emotional distress, requiring extreme and outrageous conduct intentionally or recklessly causing severe emotional distress to another, where the plaintiff, the chief engineer of a train, seeks damages for his emotional distress, manifested by vomiting, nightmares, weight loss, migraine headaches, sweaty palms, guilt and depression, based on merely witnessing the defendant's physical injury as a result of the train running over and severing the legs of the defendant, after the defendant had purposefully lain down on the railroad tracks to protest the transportation of plutonium on the train.

Whew! Say that in one breath. Of course, eliminating excessive detail is difficult when we must include numerous facts or where the issue is complex. However, under these circumstances, we can use more than one Question and create a separate Question for each element. Or, we can construct one Question, positing the legal query in a main Question and placing the decisive facts or elements in subparts. The following example demonstrates the latter technique:

Graphic 9.3(g)   **Example 5: Fact-Based Question with Subparts**

Did the trial court err in dismissing plaintiff's complaint for intentional infliction of emotional distress for failure to state a cause of action where the complaint alleged facts showing:

(1) that the defendant purposefully lay across railroad tracks in front of an oncoming train, and remained there until he was struck by the train and his legs amputated; and

(2) that the plaintiff, the train's chief engineer and operator, observed the impact and suffered emotional distress, manifesting physical symptoms and resulting in his inability to return to his livelihood as an engineer?

One answer to this exciting question is contained in Chapter 36.

Determining which facts to include. How do we determine which facts to include in a fact-based Question? Here is a suggested method: first, by reading cases in which the same or a similar issue has arisen, we note the decisive facts the courts in those cases relied on. Second, we compare *our* facts to those decisive facts. Finally, we craft our Question focusing on those facts.

If, on the other hand, we're addressing the application of a statute and have no case law on point, we include the facts relevant to the statutory elements we (or our opponent) must prove. The following hypothetical illustrates these principles.

Our case. Assume we represent Ms. Bit Ten, the victim of a dog bite. Bit is a foreigner and does not read or understand English. She wants to hold the dog owners (Mr. and Mrs. Owner) liable for her injuries. Assume further, however, that (1) the Owners had posted a sign on their property which read "BAD DOG"; (2) a statute precludes liability where dog owners post an "easily readable" sign warning "BAD DOG"; but (3) the Owners invited Bit to their property knowing that she could not read English and that she would not understand the sign. In writing our Question, we track the elements of the statute regarding the posting of the "BAD DOG" sign, and we include relevant facts:[1]

Graphic 9.3(h)   **Example 6: The *Bit Ten* Case**

Can Bit Ten, the victim of a dog bite, hold the dog's owners (Owners) liable for her injuries where (1) the Owners posted a "BAD DOG" sign on their property but Ten, a foreigner, could not read or write English; and (2) the Owners knew that Ten could not read English, and invited her to come onto their property?

Let's look next at how we "Answer" our Questions Presented.

§9.4   Brief Answer

Purpose. The Brief Answer ("Answer") is exactly what its name implies: a one or two word response to our Question (e.g., "yes," "no," "probably yes," "probably not," "not enough information to determine"), followed by a concise prediction. As we explain in more detail below, we include the rule we've applied (if not already stated in our Question) and a brief summary of our reasoning. The Answer provides our reader, at the outset, with our conclusion and with a summary of our reasoning. We write it using the BaRAC design.

Predictions. Just how assuredly we state our Answer depends on how confident we are that we've covered every base. In our combined legal experience (over fifty years including law school, clerking, practicing law, and teaching!), we know that *few* legal questions have easy "yes" or "no" answers. Unless we can say the Answer is a straightforward, unqualified, "yes" or "no" (based on the face-to-face client test, that

---

1. Please *see* Chapter 11, § 11.7 and § 11.8 for sample memos addressing Bit Ten's case.

is, whether we can look our client in the eyes and give that Answer being fully aware of the downside), we employ the covering our … "options" theory and err on the side of "hedging" with a "probably" Answer.[2]

Moreover, we leave our Answer in the "probably zone"—meaning we *don't state a percentage prediction.* In other words, we say the court "probably" will do so and so, *not* that there's a "75% chance" of it doing so and so. We're lawyers, not bookies.

Context and Format. The Answer follows the Question, on the same page, and precedes the Facts section. The Answer is double-spaced and spans a paragraph or two. If there's more than one Answer (where we have more than one distinct Question), we number the Answers to correspond to the Questions. The Answer generally doesn't include citations to authority but, instead, summarizes the law governing the issue.

Overview. As with the Question, the Answer may take various forms. However, the Answer and Question are a single concept, to be written and to be read together. Here are some guidelines to ensure we include sufficient, but not too much, information in our Question Presented and Answer:

- Information contained in the Question is not repeated in the Answer.
- Where the Question doesn't include the rule, the Answer should.
- Conversely, where the Question does include the rule, the Answer shouldn't. Thus, the Answer is shorter where the Question includes the rule.
- The Question and Answer must be consistent; where the Question uses names of the parties or generic terms, so should the Answer.

Examples. Let's look at some examples of a Question and corresponding Answer. We've annotated the Answer to show the BaRAC *design*:

Graphic 9.4(a)	**Example 7: Question Presented**

Whether the Town of Micanopy's Ordinance 86 violates the free speech clause of the First Amendment to the United States Constitution, where the ordinance creates a "safety-zone" one hundred feet around a medical facility within which the defendant cannot approach to within eight feet of another person without that person's consent.

Brief Answer

bold assertion	Probably not. The Town of Micanopy's safety-zone ordinance should withstand First Amendment scrutiny, and the defendant's lawsuit will
rule	likely fail. The majority of jurisdictions which have addressed this issue have held such ordinances to be valid, content-neutral regulations placing reasonable restrictions on the place and manner of speech. Here, be-
application	cause the ordinance applies to all speakers without regard to their

---

2. This sentence is a fine example of violating the "one-breath" rule. We look forward to your suggestions on rewriting it.

conclusion	message, it is content-neutral. Further, the ordinance is reasonable because it serves significant government interests, is not substantially broader than necessary to accomplish those interests, and allows ample alternative means for communication. For these reasons, explained in detail below, the court will likely uphold the ordinance.

Notice that the Answer centers on the relevant elements we later address in the memo, but does not address those elements in detail. *We save the detail for the Discussion section.* Let's look next at a Brief Answer to a complex Question.

Graphic 9.4(b)	Example 8: Question Presented

Did the trial court commit reversible error in sentencing Williams to a ten-year prison term? Specifically, did the trial court impose the ten-year sentence to punish Williams for demanding a jury trial?*

Brief Answer

bold assertion rule	Probably yes. Although in sentencing a defendant to prison a judge may consider the defendant's potential for rehabilitation, a judge may not increase a sentence to punish a defendant for having demanded a jury trial.
application	The trial court's remarks here demonstrate that the court's ten-year sentence was higher than the two-year sentence Williams would have received if he had accepted a plea bargain and that the court's primary motive in imposing this increased sentence was to punish Williams for refusing the
conclusion	plea bargain and demanding a jury trial. Because this motive was improper, the court likely committed reversible error in sentencing Williams.

Notice here that the Answer contains a fact not mentioned in the Question: that Williams would have received a two-year sentence if he had agreed to the plea bargain. Because the Question and Answer are read together, we need not repeat facts in both sections. Note also that the two-word response, "probably yes," works for both parts of the question; if it had not, we would have had to revise the phrasing of our Question Presented.

Graphic 9.4(c)	Example 9: Question Presented

Can Bit Ten, the victim of a dog bite, hold the dog's owners (Owners) liable for her injuries where (1) the Owners posted a "BAD DOG" sign on their property but Ten, a foreigner,

---

* Please note that because the second sentence merely *focuses* the first by implying the relevant rule, we do not number them separately. In other words, they are not distinct Questions.

could not read English, and (2) the Owners knew that Ten could not read English and invited her to come onto their property?

Brief Answer

bold assertion **rule**	Probably not. A dog owner is not liable to a person bitten by the dog on the owner's property if the owner posts an easily readable sign warning "Bad Dog," unless the person bitten is a child of "tender years" too young to read the sign and whose presence on the property is foreseeable.
application	Here, the Owners had posted an easily readable "Bad Dog" sign on their property. Despite her inability to read English, Ten, as an adult, will likely
conclusion	not be protected by the "tender years" exception. For this reason, she probably cannot maintain a cause of action against the Owners.

In the above example, our Question is fact-based; it says nothing about the law involved. In contrast, however, our Answer complements the Question by including the relevant rule. The Answer then continues by applying each element of that rule to our facts and by reaching a conclusion. We see this same pattern in the following example.

Graphic 9.4(d)   Example 10: Question Presented

Did the trial court err in dismissing plaintiff's complaint for intentional infliction of emotional distress ("IIED") for failure to state a cause of action where the complaint alleged facts showing:

(1) that the defendant purposefully lay across railroad tracks in front of an oncoming train and remained there until he was struck by the train and his legs amputated; and

(2) that the plaintiff, the train's chief engineer and operator, observed the impact and suffered emotional distress manifesting in physical symptoms and resulting in his inability to return to his livelihood as an engineer?

Brief Answer

bold assertion **rule**	Probably yes. To state a cause of action for IEED, the plaintiff must allege facts demonstrating that (1) the defendant's conduct was extreme and outrageous, (2) the defendant acted with the requisite intent, and (3) the
application	plaintiff suffered severe emotional distress. As discussed below, the plaintiff's complaint adequately alleges facts sufficient to fulfill each of
conclusion	these elements. Accordingly, the trial court erred in dismissing the complaint.

Here, the Question is one of law involving the sufficiency of a complaint, but it also contains relevant facts. The Question is precise and to the point, as is the Answer. The

Answer provides the rule and then states, in *summary* fashion, that the complaint meets that rule. Notice also that we identified, in the Question, the abbreviation (IIED) we used in the Answer.

We could have written the Answer differently by further discussing the facts. However, had we taken this approach, our Answer would have been almost as long as our memo itself. We chose, and correctly so, to save our discussion of the facts alleged in the plaintiff's complaint for the Discussion section of our memo and not to repeat them in the Answer.

A final note. As with the Question, if we draft our Answer early in the research and writing process, we *must* review it after we reach our final conclusions to ensure that it's consistent with those conclusions.

§ 9.5   Exercise in Designing a Question Presented and Brief Answer

Using the Jane Smith hypothetical in (*see* § 5.10(b) and § 6.5), write (1) a Question Presented and (2) a Brief Answer for a memo on Jane's behalf as to the testamentary intent issue.

Chapter Review
Question Presented and Brief Answer

✓ Keep Questions and the Answers easy to read. Questions can be more than one sentence long, divided into subparts, or listed separately. Answers are written in paragraph form, following the BaRAC design.

✓ If there is more than one Question, number Questions and Brief Answers consistently.

✓ Don't include argument or legal conclusions in the Question. Save the conclusions for the Answer.

✓ Questions don't have to start with "whether." If they do, the sentence ends with a period. If the Question begins with "does," "did," "should," or "may," the sentence ends with a question mark.

Whether	.
Does, Did, Should, May	?

✓ Determine whether the Question is purely legal or fact-based. A *legal* Question usually takes one of the following forms:

Designs for a Legal Issue Question Presented			
inquiry word	**jurisdiction**	**verb**	**subject**
whether, did, does, should, may		recognizes, allows, permits, prohibits, prevents	

or

Designs for a Legal Issue Question Presented				
inquiry word	**legal rule**	**description of legal rule**	**verb**	**legal rule**
whether, did, does, should, may				

✓ A fact-based Question usually takes the following form:

Design for a Fact-Based Question Presented		
inquiry word	legal point	decisive facts
whether, did, does, should, may		

✓ The Question and Answer should clearly identify the parties and use consistent terms.

✓ Questions are double-spaced and numbered with Roman numerals (beginning with "I."). However, if there's only one Question, *don't* number it. (You don't want a I. without a II.)

✓ Write each Question so that, with very little editing, we can transform it into a topic sentence (bold assertion).

✓ The Question and Answer complement each other and are written and read as a unit. Information contained in the Question is not repeated in the Answer.

✓ The Answer must *answer* the Question in a one- or two-word response and then explain that answer in BaRAC form.

✓ The Answer must be *brief*.

Practice Pointers: Writing Prompts for the Question Presented

✓ Does [jurisdiction] recognize [action or theory]?

✓ Whether the [court] abused its discretion in [action].

✓ Whether any genuine material issues of fact exist where [state circumstances].

✓ Whether the [court's] entry of summary judgment in favor of [party] was proper where [circumstances].

✓ Whether [statute, law] which prohibits [circumstances] violates [party's] [constitutional right or statutory right].

✓ Whether [court] erred as a matter of law in [action] [circumstances].

✓ Whether the [court] clearly erred in finding [circumstances].

✓ Did the [court] err in granting [party's] motion for summary judgment where [circumstances]?

✓ Did the [court] abuse its discretion in [circumstances]?

Chapter 10

The Facts

"Just the facts, ma'am." (Or, as he really said: "All we want are the facts, ma'am.")

— Sergeant Joe Friday, LAPD
Dragnet

§ 10.1   The Facts: An Overview

Purpose. In the Facts section we tell our reader, through a narrative, the decisive facts in our case, necessary background information, and areas requiring further research.

Context and Format. The Facts follow, usually on the same page, the Brief Answer and precede the Discussion. The Facts are double-spaced and written in paragraph form. Although when corresponding with our clients we respectfully refer to them as Mr., Ms., etc., in writing the Facts we omit those titles to streamline our memo.

Overview. The Facts provide the "story" of our case in a straightforward, unbiased manner without conclusions or argument. We acknowledge disputed facts and clearly state whether decisive facts are proven or only alleged.

Moreover, even though we're probably given the facts by the reader requesting the memo, we still repeat them in this section. By doing so, we ensure that our memo is self-contained. In other words, we unite both facts and law in one document, allowing all readers (present and future), to fully understand our case. Further, by stating the facts we better ensure that *we* understand them, that we haven't overlooked crucial aspects of the "story," and that our reader knows we haven't overlooked anything.

§ 10.2   Level of Detail

Decisive facts. A threshold question in writing the Facts is how much detail to include. The Facts should, at a minimum, include any fact we mention in the "Discussion" section of our memo and all "decisive facts." A decisive fact is one which, as we've learned through our research, could change the outcome of an issue. A decisive fact may be helpful or harmful. In either event, we include it.

For example, assume that in researching the *Bit Ten* case, (see Chapter 9, Graphics 9.3(h) and 9.4(c)), we found the following: (1) a statute exempting from liability for dog bites a dog owner who has posted an "easily readable" "Bad Dog" sign on her premises, and (2) a case interpreting this "easily readable" requirement. The case held that owners who had posted a "Bad Dog" sign were still liable when their dog bit a young child who was a foreseeable victim and who, due to his "tender years," was unable to read the sign.

Based on this research, we now know that the decisive facts in our case include: (1) that the owners had posted a sign reading "Bad Dog," (2) that our client, Bit Ten, is an adult, (3) that Ten could not read the English language, and (4) that the owners had invited Ten to their home knowing that she could not read the English language.

Emotional facts. Even though not decisive, we might also include *emotional* facts. One example is the severity of Ten's injury—the dog bite required thirty stitches and will leave a permanent scar. We know from our research that the severity of the injury doesn't have any bearing on the dog owner's liability. However, human nature being what it is, a court will often find a way for a plaintiff to recover damages for serious injuries. Thus, we include facts which, even though legally irrelevant, might create strong sympathy for our client. By the same token, we include any facts tending to portray our opponent in an adverse or unfavorable light.

Moreover, we include any "unknown," but potentially relevant, facts. Has our client been truthful? Are our potential witnesses credible? We try to predict what facts the court might include in its opinion if our case went to trial, and we include those facts.

♦ We don't sugar-coat anything and we never "slant" the facts. In other words, we alert our reader to possible "land mines" which may be present but not yet fully uncovered. As a Spanish proverb teaches,"Forewarned, forearmed; to be prepared is half the victory."

§ 10.3   Writing the Facts

Process. If we write our Facts *after* we've completed our Discussion section, we have no doubt which facts are and aren't known, decisive, and relevant. However, to write our Discussion, we must first know which facts are relevant; for this reason, it's useful to write the Facts first. However, after writing the Discussion, we then revise our Facts to ensure that we've been complete but not overinclusive.

Organization. In organizing our Facts, we make our story easy to follow and easy to remember. We can choose one of the two most commonly used organizational methods: (1) *the time-line approach*, that is, stating the facts in the order events occurred, or (2) *the thematic approach*, i.e., grouping and discussing facts by their common theme. The nature of the facts themselves usually suggests the best organization—however, when in doubt, the time-line approach is best, unless the facts are complex. Where the facts are complex, i.e., involving different claims or many parties, or where we wish to organize our Discussion around the elements of a cause of action, the thematic approach works best.

Transitions. No matter what approach we use, we don't allow our reader to become "lost" in "time" or "space." We provide clear transitions whenever we shift to a different time or event. Where the facts are complex, headings delineating events, claims, or elements of a rule also are effective "signposting" and orienting techniques.[1] For example, we might include headings such as "Procedural History," or "Events Leading to the Arrest [or other action]," or "Events After the Arrest [or other action]" to orient our reader. Moreover, by using consistent terms in referring to the same person, place, or event, we ensure that our reader stays oriented. For example, if we call our client "Jones," we don't thereafter refer to him as "John" or "the defendant." We call him "Jones" throughout our Fact section.

Record citations. A sample Facts section is located in the sample memo in Chapter 34. (*See also* Chapter 15: "Statement of the Case and Facts" in brief writing). We suggest you turn to those sections before moving on to the next chapter. As you review these documents, note that although record citations must be included in the Statement of the Case and Facts in a brief to a court to substantiate the facts within, record citations

---

1. *See* Chapter 15, § 15.2(b).

may or may not be included in a predictive memo. Some law firms or judges, however, require such citations. Always check first and, if so required, find out what documents to rely upon for your references and how to designate them.

We recommend that you *do* include record cites when available. By including them, you have demonstrated the accuracy of what you are saying. You're also making it easier for you or for another lawyer (or a judge) to transform the information in your memo into a brief or into a legal opinion.

§ 10.4   Exercise in Writing the Facts

Using the Jane Smith hypothetical (see § 5.10(b) and § 6.5), write a Fact statement for a memo on Jane's behalf, being sure to include procedural history.

Chapter Review
The Facts

✓ Include all decisive, background, and "emotional" facts, both harmful and helpful.

✓ Include any as yet "unknown" but potentially relevant and decisive "facts."

✓ Specify whether a "fact" is proven or merely assumed.

✓ Organize the Facts around a time-line or theme; and use transitions (and where necessary, headings) to keep our reader oriented to shifts in space and time.

✓ Use consistent terms in referring to the same person, place, and event.

✓ Double-check that if we refer to a fact in the Discussion section, we also include it in the Facts section.

✓ Determine whether we need to include citations to documents in the record, and if so, how to designate these references.

Chapter 11

The Discussion

§ 11.1   The Discussion: An Overview

Purpose. The Discussion section conveys our overall analysis. We provide the governing rule for each issue; substantiate those rules by citing and explaining authority such as constitutional provisions, statutes, regulations, and case law; and show how we reached each conclusion by applying the rules to our facts.

Context and Format. The Discussion follows the Facts (it can begin on the same page) and precedes the Conclusion. It's double-spaced, written in paragraph form, and includes headings and subheadings, where appropriate. These headings and subheadings are single-spaced, consist of one or more complete sentences, and are written in the style of a bold assertion.

Content. In applying the law to the facts and reaching conclusions on all issues, we acknowledge and probe the weaknesses, as well as the strengths, of our case. We're brutally honest in our assessments, turning over every stone and leaving nothing to chance. If our research discredits our theory of the case, we say so and suggest a new approach. If further research of an issue is warranted, we say so and explain why that research may be significant. If we find gaps in our factual knowledge, we state them and comment on their significance. If any aspect of our reasoning is based on an assumption, either of law or of fact, we state so, clearly and unequivocally. We present our case in the light of the naked truth, warts and all.

Let's look now at the steps preliminary to writing the Discussion section: (1) how to organize this section and (2) how to write the Discussion concisely and cohesively.

§ 11.2   Preliminary Steps in Writing the Discussion: Creating an Outline and Issue Boxes

Before beginning to write the Discussion, we think critically about the scope of our assignment. If we were given a limited point to address, we limit our memo to that point. However, if we were given a problem *to solve,* our work is more difficult. In solving a problem, we develop a *theory* of our case. We think long and hard about our case, and choose, from perhaps many possible solutions, the *best* solution.

Armed with our research results for each issue and subissue, we create an outline of the Discussion. Our outline sets forth each step in our reasoning and demonstrates the relevance of the authorities we rely on. In this way, it provides a cohesive, common sense view of our case. If it doesn't, then we examine its parts to see if changing their order makes our Discussion more understandable or convincing. If we can't arrange the parts into a cohesive whole, we need further analysis, further research, or both.

Here are the steps we take in creating our outline:

1. Begin thinking of possible theories and arguments, including both sides of all issues.

2. Review the facts of our case, and determine what we still don't know, but need to know.

3. Consider which court will likely be hearing our case, and determine which cases our court *must* follow and which cases are merely persuasive. Then choose our strongest cases and rules, and rely on them.

4. Add to our outline the legal and common sense (policy) arguments supporting our position—and citations to the *rules* and *facts* relevant to each point. The sooner we understand the applicable rules, the sooner we can develop a sound theory of our case.

5. Fill in our "running outline" with notes from cases and authorities our research has uncovered. Then transform this rough outline into point headings.

Important. If we fail to use an outline, we'll be left with piles of cases and piles of notes at the "end" of our research. We'll then have to weed through those piles in a frantic effort to connect these cases with the point we want to make. However, if we fill in our outline *as* we research, we'll have an organized view of the cases we'll use, as well as the cases our opponents will likely use against us.

If we find it difficult to create an outline, we start by selecting a portion of our Discussion and organizing that. We start with the easiest issue and then review our research notes to find all facts and cases relating to this issue. After collecting this information, we determine how best to arrange it to advance our Discussion.

We start by crafting point headings, proceed to subheadings (if necessary), and then write topic sentences. We fill in our writing with the authorities to support each point. In this way, we create one "piece" of an outline. We repeat this procedure with our other issues and eventually arrange those pieces in an outline of our entire Discussion.

In arranging our Discussion, we look carefully at each issue and how that issue relates to the other issues. Is any issue dispositive of the others? Must we establish one issue (a "threshold" issue) before we can proceed to the others? Are any issues actually *alternatives*? If so, have we clearly indicated they are alternatives? Which issues are independent? Which are inter-dependent?

We find it easiest when dealing with issues to *compartmentalize* them. In other words, we consider each issue as if we were placing it into a box and dealing only with it. (It's okay for lawyers to be rather obsessive.) The BaRAC design provides the parameters of that box. Here's what the box looks like

Graphic 11.2	Create an "Issue Box" for Each Issue
bold assertion	State our prediction or suggestion.
	Determine the type of rule analysis involved (*see* Chapter 6):[1] (1) rule-only; (2) rule-plus; or (3) FIHRR: reasoning by analogy, we'd use for *each* of the cases we will address.

---

1. See Chapter 6 on Using Cases in Writing a Memo or Brief: General Principles.

rule	State and explain the applicable rule. If the rule is unclear, explain why our interpretation is correct. Cite and address relevant authorities.	
application	Apply the rule to the facts relevant to this issue.	
	bold assertion:	State our prediction or suggestion regarding this issue.
	rule:	If necessary, further explain the rule or its elements.
	application:	Show how the rule applies to our facts.
	conclusion:	State our conclusion.
counter-argument	bold assertion:	State the counter-argument.
	rule:	State the rule relevant to the counter-argument.
	application:	Show how the counter-argument rule does or doesn't apply to our facts.
	conclusion:	State the conclusion for the counter-argument.
response	Respond to the counter-argument, assess its strengths and weaknesses, reach a conclusion on the effect it will have on our case.	
	bold assertion:	State our response to the counter-argument.
	rule:	Discuss any differences in interpreting the counter-argument rule or explain why that rule should not apply to our case.
	application:	If the counter-argument rule applies, explain its impact on our case.
	conclusion:	Reach a conclusion regarding our response to the counter-argument.
conclusion	State what the court will likely rule on this issue.	

Important. Although we've illustrated the above example using a "counter-argument" and a "response" component, please note that our discussion of an issue may not require a counter-argument and a response. If the counter-argument is valid, and/or if we believe that our opponent or the court may rely upon it, we should include it in our discussion. We do not, however, set up a "straw-man" counter-argument (i.e., an argument too weak to stand), just to knock it down.

§ 11.3   Design of the Discussion Section

After we've completed our outline and issue boxes, we're ready to organize and begin writing the Discussion section in a manner that satisfies our theory and our reader. We transform our significant conclusions on the issues into headings and subheadings, written in full sentences. When read together, these headings convey our overarching theory of the case.

Here's the design of the Discussion section:

Graphic 11.3	The Design of the Discussion Section

DISCUSSION:

Here, we include a "global introduction" of our case, written in paragraph form using BaRAC, introducing the issue(s) and subpoints, as applicable. We address how to write this introduction in § 11.4.

I. <u>The first main heading for the case goes here. It's a complete sentence or more, single-spaced, and underlined.</u>

If this section had subheadings, we'd begin with an introductory paragraph (an "umbrella" paragraph), following the BaRAC design, introducing the issue and its subpoints. If this section had no subheadings, we wouldn't need such an introduction.

Next, we discuss the law and facts relevant to issue I. We follow the BaRAC design. We lead with the bold assertion of our prediction or suggestion, followed by the rule and rule explanation, as needed, our application of the rule to our facts, and our conclusion.

We follow this discussion by stating and explaining, using the BaRAC design, any relevant counter-arguments.

We then respond to those counter-arguments, using the BaRAC design, and conclude with our prediction regarding the merits of the counter-argument. We end with our final prediction/conclusion for issue I.

II. <u>The second main heading for the case goes here. It's a complete sentence or more, single-spaced, and underlined.</u>

We discuss the law and the facts relevant to issue II. Because in this example we have subheadings under this heading, we write a short introduction here of the general rule involved and then discuss, in the subheadings below, the specific elements (of the rule) and the specific application of those elements to our facts. We finish our introduction by briefly applying the rule to our facts and reaching a conclusion.

A. <u>Our first subheading goes here. It's a complete sentence or more, single-spaced, and underlined.</u>

We address, in BaRAC form, the law and facts relevant to the issues under this subheading. Using BaRAC form, we then discuss and respond to relevant counter-arguments. We conclude by reaching a final prediction on this issue.

B. <u>Our second subheading goes here. It's a complete sentence or more, single-spaced, and underlined.</u>

We address, in BaRAC form, the law and facts relevant to the issues under this subheading. Using BaRAC form, we follow by discussing, and then responding to, relevant counter-arguments. We conclude by reaching a final prediction on this issue.

§ 11.4 The Global Introduction

We begin the Discussion with a "global" introduction, introducing the overall issue or issues to our reader. Although we may draft these paragraphs when we begin writing our Discussion, we revise them when we've completed our memo to ensure that the introduction accurately summarizes our Discussion.

In Chapter 4, §4.1, we discussed how to organize an *argument* involving a two-element rule. We showed how to formulate the general rule and a "global" BaRAC paragraph, which served as an introduction to the issue.

In writing our memo, we employ a similar introductory technique which encompasses all issues in our memo. These "global" *introductory paragraphs* introduce each issue and its relation to our entire case. They serve the critical role of placing the analysis to follow in context by providing a roadmap of our entire Discussion.

Think of a global introduction as similar to the speech given by a tour director on a bus excursion to an unfamiliar locale. That is, the director *summarizes* the itinerary of the entire trip by organizing that itinerary into its component parts and by explaining all the stops along the way. This summary includes the order in which stops will be made, the reason for this order, and how the stops relate to each other. The director also explains any potentially interesting stops which will not be taken and why. (None of those "outer perimeter" establishments.) Finally, she identifies any related points of interest not covered by the tour but nevertheless of interest to the tourists. Mercifully, however, she does not make us sit through a four or five hour slide show of the highlights of the places we're about to visit.

Let's keep this tour guide in mind when writing our global introductory paragraphs. Summarize the main attractions, and save the details for what's to follow. With this goal in mind, our "global" introductory paragraphs take on the following design:

Graphic 11.4(a) The General Design of Global Introductory Paragraphs[2]

Restate and focus the issue;

State our overall conclusion to the issue (bold assertion);

State and focus the applicable general rule or rules (see explanation below);

Deal with multiple issues if there is more than one issue (see explanation below); and

Briefly explain why the application of the rule to our facts leads to the result we've suggested. Because our reader may jump right to the Discussion section without reviewing the prior sections of our memo, we state our overall conclusion here even though we've already stated it in our Brief Answer.

Explanations

Global introduction: explaining the rule. In explaining the rule, we include how the rule functions in our theory of the case. For example, we may need to address the following:

---

2. The order of these sections depends on the nature of our case. The design we state here is merely a suggested approach.

- whether we must discuss a threshold issue before we can further explain the rule;
- whether we must interpret a statute in a certain manner;
- whether procedural issues will impact our rule selection; and
- whether we, or our opponent, bears the *burden of proof* on the issues.

Global introduction: dealing with multiple issues. In addressing multiple issues, we proceed as follows:

(1) We clearly identify any dispositive issues.

(2) We also explain whether the issues are related, and if so, we tie them together — we show our reader that we understand the issues and their relationship to one another. This connection between issues is crucial.

    Often the outcome or very "life" of one issue turns on the resolution of another. Under these circumstances, we point out this connection using language like the following:

    - "If the court finds [one way on issue one], then it need not address [issues two, three, and four]; however, if the court doesn't find [blank] as to the first issue, it must address these further issues."

    Or, where warranted, we point out that a favorable result on one issue mandates a similar outcome on another issue, as follows:

    - "If the court finds [one way on issue one], then it should reach a similar finding [on issue two]."

(3) Next, in our global introduction, we point out relevant *undisputed* issues, being careful not to make assumptions. We can generally assume (okay, there we go making an assumption after just saying not to!) that our opposing party will dispute all issues. Thus, unless we *know* that an issue is undisputed, we address all relevant issues. However, if we're absolutely certain, after thinking of all the possible arguments by the other side, that an issue is undisputed, we state so, and briefly explain why to our reader.

(4) Further, we explain the order in which we'll address the remaining disputed issues and, if necessary, why we've chosen that order.

(5) Finally, we point out any related issues which we will not address and why. This serves to avoid any misunderstanding and puts our reader on notice of other related issues that merit attention.

Examples of global introductions. As the following examples demonstrate, the nature of our case determines the organization of our global introduction. We offer these examples for your use as potential "templates." See if your case fits any of these patterns.

For some cases, we state the issue, focus the issue, and then state and focus the rule. For others, we follow the more traditional approach of stating the issue, stating the rule, focusing the rule, and then focusing the issue. The bottom line: we employ whichever approach works best in our case. But, whichever approach we take, we still follow the BaRAC design.

Graphic 11.4(b)		Example 1: Global Introduction Case Law Interpretation
restate the issue; and state and focus the rule	**bold assertion** **(of issue)** **rule**	At issue is whether the judge committed reversible error in increasing Williams's sentence from two years to ten years. A judge may not increase a sentence to punish a defendant for having demanded a jury trial. *Adams v. State* [citation]. However, in imposing a sentence, a judge may consider the defendant's potential for rehabilitation. *Brown v. State* [citation].
focus the issue	**application**	The question here turns on whether the judge's comments in Williams's case reflect a genuine concern for Williams's potential for rehabilitation or an impermissible intent to punish him
	conclusion	for having demanded a jury trial. Because the court's comments more strongly reflect the latter, the trial court's sentencing appears to have been improper, and the case will likely be reversed.

Graphic 11.4(c)		Example 2: Global Introduction Statutory Interpretation
restate the issue; focus the issue	**bold assertion** **(of issue)**	At issue is whether Alex Jones committed aggravated assault when he hurled a golf shoe, cleated with sixteen sharp steel points, at the victim's head. Jones admits that he threw the shoe and committed assault, but challenges the lower court's ruling that this assault was aggravated and that the
state the rule	**rule &** **application**	golf shoe was a "deadly weapon." Because, for the reasons set forth below, the court will likely hold that Jones used the shoe in a manner likely to produce death or serious bodily injury,
	conclusion	the court will likely rule for the State and uphold Jones's conviction.

Graphic 11.4(d)		Example 3: Global Introduction Statutory and Case Law Interpretation
restate the issue	**bold assertion** **(of issue)**	Bit Ten wants to know whether she has a cause of action against the Owners for injuries she received when she was bitten by their dog, Buck. In Florida, a dog owner is exempt from
state the rule	**rule**	liability to persons bitten by the owner's dog while on his property, if the owner had posted a warning sign that is (1) "easily readable" and (2) includes the words "Bad Dog." § 767.04, Fla. Stat. (20xx). Section 767.04 provides as follows:

[quote relevant part of the statute's text here]

application

focus the issue

In the instant case, the Owners met the second part of the statute: they had posted a sign with the words "Bad Dog." However, because Ten could not read English, it is questionable whether the Owners's sign met the "easily readable" requirement, and the case turns on how the court will interpret

conclusion

this phrase. For the reasons below, the court will likely conclude that the sign met the statutory requirements, and that the statute precludes Ten's cause of action.

Graphic 11.4(e)   Example 4: Extended Global Introduction: Constitutional Analysis of a Statute

---

bold assertion of issue and conclusion

Our client, Carol Kane, who is terminally ill, wants to know whether, in this case of first impression, her equal protection challenge to Florida's assisted suicide statute, section 782.08, would be successful. That statute prohibits a person from assisting another in self-murder. However, section 765.302(1), Florida's "Living Will Statute," allows a person to direct that life support be withheld or withdrawn. In essence, the "Living Will" statute allows one who is terminally ill to die, while section 782.08 prohibits assisted suicide, even for the terminally ill. Thus, Florida's statutory scheme treats terminally ill patients differently depending on whether they are on life support. For the reasons addressed below, it is likely that Kane's equal protection challenge to section 782.08 will succeed.

focus the issue; roadmap of general rule

This memo assumes jurisdiction in a Florida state court, and addresses *only* the constitutionality of the statute under the Equal Protection Clause of the Fourteenth Amendment. That clause provides that no state shall "deny to any person within its jurisdiction the equal protection of the laws." U.S. Const. amend. XIV. This Clause requires states "to treat in a similar manner all individuals who are similarly situated." *Quill v. Vacco*, 80 F.3d 716, 725 (2d Cir. 1996). However, "disparate treatment is not necessarily a denial of [equal protection]...." *Id.* Where no fundamental right or suspect class is involved, state legislation is presumptively valid if the statutory scheme is rationally related to a legitimate state interest. *See id.*

Because none of the assisted suicide cases decided thus far have found a fundamental right to assisted suicide under the Fourteenth Amendment, this memo will not address whether Kane has a fundamental right to assisted suicide, requiring strict scrutiny analysis rather than the rational relationship test. *See id.* (concluding that the New York statute prohibiting assisted suicide did not impinge on any fundamental rights or involve suspect classifications); *People v. Kevorkian*, 527 N.W.2d 714, 729 (Mich. 1994) (finding no fundamental interest under the Due Process Clause to commit suicide with or without assistance). However, one court, and thus far the only court addressing the issue, held that a statute which prohibited assisted suicide failed the rational relationship test and thus violated the Equal Protection Clause. *See Quill*, 80 F.3d at 729 (concluding that statutes pro-hibiting assisted suicide violated equal protection where other state statutes allowed ter-minally ill patients to refuse or remove life support).

application: focus on our case

The equal protection issue is whether Florida law unconstitutionally distinguishes be-tween terminally ill persons depending on whether they are or are not on life support. *Compare* § 765.302(1) *with* § 782.08. Thus, the issue is whether Kane, who is terminally ill, is being treated differently from terminally ill persons who are on life support systems. Those individuals are permitted, under the Living Will statute, to terminate their life sup-port and hasten their deaths. Kane, however, who is not on life support, cannot obtain medical assistance to end her life. Accordingly, the class in question is that of terminally ill persons.

threshold and subsequent issues focused

However, as a threshold issue the court must first determine whether the Equal Protec-tion Clause even applies to our case. Specifically the court must decide whether the two classes of terminally ill, those on life support and those not on life support, are similarly sit-uated. If the classes are similarly situated, the Equal Protection Clause applies. The court then must determine whether Florida's statutory scheme (§§ 765.302(1) and 782.08) passes rational basis review which requires (1) that the state have a legitimate interest in treating the two classes differently and (2) that this interest is furthered by the statutory scheme. *See Quill*, 80 F.3d at 725.

conclusion

As explained more fully below, the court will likely find that the Equal Protection Clause applies, and that Florida's statutory scheme closely parallels that of New York's in the *Quill* case. Therefore, the court will likely conclude that the State lacks a legitimate interest in treating classes of terminally ill patients differently and the statutory scheme fails rational basis review. Accordingly, Kane's equal protection challenge will likely succeed.

Are you ready to handle such a case? Are you ready, through the words you write, to hold another human being's life or death in your hands?

§ 11.5   Organizing Multiple Issues

After conveying the theory of our case in our global introductory paragraphs, we organize our Discussion point-by-point. Under each heading or subheading, we include only matters relevant to that heading, including supporting authorities. As we explain below, where our memo involves multiple issues, we place the issues in logical order, paying special attention to dispositive, threshold, interrelated, and procedural issues.

Whichever order we employ, our Discussion follows the same order of issues as we've stated in our Questions Presented. If it does not, then we revise the Question and Brief Answer sections to reflect these changes.

§ 11.5(a)   Dispositive Issues

Where our memo involves multiple issues, but one issue is dispositive, we address the dispositive issue first. By "dispositive issue," we mean one that would, if our prediction about it is correct, resolve the case, dispensing with our need to resolve the other issues.

However, the presence of a dispositive issue does not mean we'll have a "one issue" memo and that the other issues are irrelevant. Even though we discuss a dispositive issue first, we still discuss the other issues. Our reader needs to know how our client stands on the other issues for purposes of strategy and possibly settlement value of the case. In discussing the remaining issues, we begin by stating that if the issue we've identified as dispositive proves not to be, then the remaining issues will be relevant.

§ 11.5(b)   Threshold and Interrelated Issues

Our case may involve several issues or elements, the first of which determines how we continue our analysis. This issue or element is a "threshold" matter. Thus, while a dispositive issue is an issue that, alone, can resolve a legal problem, a threshold issue is one which usually is the first of a number of elements in a rule we must resolve before we can continue our analysis. To complicate matters, however, some dispositive issues are also threshold issues. For example, the issue whether Carol Kane (our terminally ill client) in **Graphic 11.4(e)** is in a class protected by the Equal Protection Clause is both a dispositive and a threshold issue. Let's consider some further examples.

Let's return to our "battery" hypothetical from Chapter 4 (**Graphic 4.1**), where battery is defined as "the impermissible application of force to the person of another." Assume further that an "impermissible act" is one done "without the victim's consent." Next, assume that Jones claims that he put poison in Smith's coffee *at Smith's request.* In this case, whether Jones acted without the victim's consent is a threshold issue we address first — before determining whether Jones "applied force" to Smith.

Similarly, let's assume in the aggravated assault hypothetical, addressed in Chapter 7, § 7.2, that Jones (in trouble again!) denies that he's the person who hurled that golf shoe at the victim. In that case, we address first the threshold issue — whether there even *was* an assault, before considering whether the "alleged" assault was "aggravated."

After addressing any threshold issues, we continue our analysis of the issues in logical order; generally, that's the order the elements appear in the rule. If, however, we do not address the elements in the order they appear in the rule, we tell our reader why we are deviating from this order.

§ 11.5(c)   Procedural Issues

In some cases, we address procedural issues before discussing substantive ones. For example, if there's a question regarding the court's jurisdiction over a defendant, and we represent the plaintiff, we address the jurisdictional issue first, before addressing the substantive merits of the lawsuit.

§ 11.5(d)   Other Organizational Methods

Where we don't have any of the considerations addressed in sections 11.5(a)-(c), we organize our Discussion based on the importance of the issues or the usual order in which a legal-trained reader would expect to encounter them. For example, if our case involved a statute with multi-factors or a rule with multiple elements, we'd likely discuss the factors or elements in the order they're stated in the statute or rule.

Let's now look at methods of writing the Discussion.

§ 11.6   Writing the Discussion

In writing the Discussion, our goal is to educate our reader by explaining the law. We accomplish this by presenting analysis supported by the law, logic, and common sense. We also keep in mind that our Discussion section must be self-contained. If there's something our reader needs to know, it better be in our memo.

The number of forms our Discussion could take is virtually unlimited. However, by reviewing examples of Discussions, we can isolate and define common structures and designs. To this end, we present examples of four of the following designs:[3]

(1) Statutory interpretation without case law	§ 11.7
(2) Case law interpretation of a statute	§ 11.8
(3) Case law analysis involving a synthesized rule	§ 11.9
(4) Case law analysis using analogical reasoning	§ 11.10

Each of our examples is based on the following hypothetical case:

The Bit Ten Hypothetical[4]

Our case. We represent Ms. Bit Ten in a lawsuit filed against the Owners for the injuries Ten received from a dog bite. After reading the facts (below), please review the statute, consider whether Ten has a cause of action against the Owners, and anticipate the arguments the Owners's attorney may make in response.

---

3. Note that none of these examples likely would provide a template in which we could simply "plug in" our case. Rather, we've provided these examples as general patterns of each "type" of analysis.

4. This hypothetical was originally developed by our colleague, Patricia Thomson. We thank her for allowing us to modify and use it here. By the way, your humble authors, who both own "International" dogs, have no gripe against Buck. We're actually very sorry he had to get involved in this mess.

The facts. On November 10, 20xx, Bit Ten, age twenty-eight, moved to America from France. She rented an apartment in Gainesville, Florida, and planned to attend the University of Florida College of Agriculture in the Fall of 20xx as a graduate student. During the interim, from January through July 20xx, she planned to take English classes.

Moving to America was difficult for Ten. She could not read English, and could understand only a few words of spoken English. On December 22, 20xx, while shopping at a grocery store, Ten had difficulty being understood by the cashier when inquiring about the price of something in the checkout lane. John and Mary Owner came to her aid. The Owners, who had lived in France for a number of years, were fluent in French. The Owners cleared the matter up for Ten, who neither understood nor read English, and invited her to visit them at their Gainesville home. At some point during the conversation, the Owners also said to Ten: "Oh, by the way, we have a dog."

The Owners have a large German Shepherd named Buck. Although not normally aggressive, Buck has been known to growl at trespassers. To comply with Florida law, the Owners had posted on their front gate a large sign that stated: "WARNING BAD DOG." The Owners have many foreign friends who come to visit, some who read English and some who don't.

The next day, December 23, Ten went to visit the Owners. She noticed the sign posted on the front gate, but she couldn't read it. As Ten approached the front door of the Owners's house, Buck bit her on the leg. The wound required thirty stitches to close, and Ten will have a permanent scar.

§ 11.7   Statutory Interpretation Without Case Law

When we're dealing with a statute which has not yet been interpreted by the courts, our main analytical guide is the language of the statute itself. Our analysis of the above hypothetical demonstrates this principle.

Some assumptions. Assume that we've found a statute providing simply that dog owners are liable for any dog bite unless they have posted a warning sign but that the statute doesn't describe the sign. Bad news for Ten!

In this situation, the court would likely apply the ordinary, plain meaning of the statute to our case. As Ten's attorneys, we'd probably lose, hands down. The Owners *did* have a sign.

However, assume that the following statute was in effect:

The statute.

Section 767.04, Fla. Stat. (20xx) provides:
The owner of any dog that bites any person while such person is on or in a public place, or lawfully on or in a private place, including the property of the owner of the dog, is liable for damages suffered by persons bitten, regardless of the former viciousness of the dog or

> the owner's knowledge of such viciousness. However, the owner is not liable if at the time of any such injury, the owner had displayed in a prominent place on his premises a sign easily readable including the words "Bad Dog."

Now we've got a fighting chance. The statute imposes the requirement that the sign must be "easily readable." We've got ourselves both an adverb and an adjective, and therefore something to argue about. What does "easily readable" *mean*? Your guess is as good as ours. Statutes must be drafted generally to cover many situations—recall our "smoking monkey in the elevator" hypothetical. So, rather than get specific about the dimensions and lettering of the sign, the legislature simply said the sign must be "easily readable."

In this situation, the court would likely apply the ordinary, plain meaning of the statute—that is, if the sign is "readable" by the average "sighted" person, it's "easily readable." As Ten's attorneys, we'd probably lose the case. If, however, we were representing the Owners, we'd rejoice.

Statutory Interpretation. In addition to the "plain meaning rule," courts employ many methods in interpreting statutes when the plain meaning is ambiguous. The following are some of the more common approaches:

(1) *Derive meaning from legislative intent.* Using this method of interpretation, the court reviews the statute's legislative history, such as floor debates or committee reports, to determine what the legislature was trying to accomplish by the statute. With this purpose in mind, the court interprets the statute consistent with that intent.

(2) *Apply various "canons" or principles of statutory construction.* Some, but by no means all, of these canons are as follows:

- a statute is read to achieve its intended purpose (we might need to know the legislative intent to argue this one);
- specific terms in a statute override more general terms;
- related statutes are construed in the same context to create a consistent statutory scheme; and
- a list of specific items excludes other items not listed.[5]

(3) *Compare our statute to a similar statute.* In conjunction with the above, the court might compare a statute to similar statutes that have been interpreted by the courts. In our Bit Ten example, this means the court might analogize to other statutes regarding the posting of signs warning of a potential hazard.

---

5. Karl N. Llewellyn lists twenty-eight such canons and notes that for each of the twenty-eight principles, there are twenty-eight opposite principles. *Remarks on the Theory of Appellate Decision and the Rules or Canons About How Statutes are to be Construed*, 3 Vand. L. Rev. 395, 401–06 (1950). For example, "If language is plain and unambiguous it must be given effect." *Id.* at 403. However, this canon is not to be followed "when literal interpretation would lead to absurd or mischievous consequences or thwart manifest purpose." *Id.*

Here again though, as we warned, the law is like Jell-O® or truffles. Our opponent will no doubt argue in favor of competing legislative history and canons of construction or analogize to different statutes regarding warning signs. We therefore must anticipate and respond to those arguments.

The following is an annotated Discussion section of a memo analyzing the dog bite statute as it relates to Bit Ten's case. The italicized information throughout preceded by the symbol "❖" annotates the discussion.

Sample Discussion Section: Statutory Interpretation Without Case Law

DISCUSSION:

> ❖ *Begin by restating the issue, the conclusion, and follow with the general rule, in this case, the statute.*

Ten wants to know whether she has a cause of action against the Owners for injuries she received when she was bitten by their dog, Buck. For the reasons explained below, it is unlikely that she does.

Under Florida law, dog owners are exempt from liability to persons bitten by their dog if they have a sign posted that is (1) "easily readable" and (2) includes the words "Bad Dog." § 767.04, Fla. Stat. (20xx). The statute provides as follows:

[*Add text of statute here.*]

> ❖ *Next, focus on the part of the legal rule that's relevant to our case. In other words, refine the issue — state specifically what the "battle-grounds" will be in the case.*

Here the Owners met the second element of the statute: they had posted a sign with the words "Bad Dog." However, because Ten could not read English, it is questionable whether the Owners's sign met the "easily readable" requirement. The question thus turns on how the court will interpret this requirement.

> ❖ *Now, predict how the court will interpret the statute and explain our prediction.*

Unfortunately, no Florida cases address the "easily readable" requirement. Nor is there any legislative history on this statute to indicate legislative intent. Therefore, it is likely that the court will apply the plain meaning of the words "easily readable."

As a matter of common sense, the term "easily readable" generally means capable of being seen and read. In other words, the sign must be prominently posted and be of a sufficiently large size and lettering to be read by the average "sighted" person.

This plain meaning interpretation precludes Ten's argument that the "easily readable" requirement is "subjective," i.e., "easily readable" to foreseeable visitors. Because required signs do not normally have to be "universally understood," i.e., written in numerous languages, and because the statute specifically requires the words, in English, "Bad Dog," Ten's argument for a broader interpretation of the "easily readable" requirement lacks merit.

Indeed, if the statute were interpreted this broadly, dog owners could not protect themselves from liability. It would be impossible for an owner to devise a sign which all people, no matter what language they understood or disability they suffered, could "easily read." It is unlikely the legislature intended this result.

> ❖ *Next comes the application and conclusion section. Here's where we discuss how our facts relate to our interpretation of the statute and we reach a conclusion.*

Here, the only known facts regarding the sign are that it was prominently posted and stated: "WARNING BAD DOG." There is no evidence that the sign's lettering was overly small or unreadable. Under these facts, and assuming that the sign's lettering was legible and large enough to be read, the court will likely find that the sign was "easily readable." Because the Owners have complied with the statute, Ten has no cause of action here.

§ 11.8   Case Law Interpretation of a Statute

In § 11.7, we addressed various methods the courts have developed for interpreting statutes where no prior and relevant cases exist. However, where there is case law interpreting our statute we use "analogical" reasoning. In other words, we compare and contrast our case to the cited case(s). If only a few cases are involved, and they apply a similar interpretation of the statute, our job is fairly easy. Where the cases disagree, however, we need to explain the disparate results or reconcile them.

In the following example, we revisit the Bit Ten hypothetical and demonstrate how to use a cited case and analogical reasoning in interpreting the "dog bite" statute.

Assume that we've found the following case, decided after the statute was enacted:

Tot v. Vicious
357 So. 2d 596 (Fla. Dist. Ct. App. 20xx)

PER CURIAM. Appellant Jimmy Tot, age five, timely appeals from a final judgment dismissing his complaint against Sally Vicious, for injuries Tot suffered when he was bitten by Vicious's dog, Sweetie. We reverse.

Although Vicious had posted a sign stating "Warning Bad Dog" in a prominent place as § 767.04 requires, the words were not "easily readable" by the child Tot, who could not read or write. Public policy dictates that society must protect those of tender years. Additionally, Vicious's home was located next door to an elementary school, and thus Vicious had ample warning of the possibility of such an accident.

REVERSED AND REMANDED.

Right, Able, and Good, J.J., concur.

Let's next see how we'd use this case in our Bit Ten hypothetical.

Sample Discussion Section:
Case Law Interpretation of a Statute

<u>DISCUSSION:</u>

❖ *The arguments for both sides are identified and discussed, and an outcome on every relevant argument is predicted. Here's where the law is explained in detail. The italicized information throughout preceded by the symbol "❖" annotates the discussion. We've included subheadings in the application section to help illustrate the discussion and make the document easier to read.*

❖ *Begin by restating the issue and providing an overall conclusion. Then state the general legal rule, in this case, the statute.*

Ten wants to know whether she has a cause of action against the Owners for injuries she received when she was bitten by their dog, Buck. For the reasons below, it is likely that Florida law precludes Ten's action.

In Florida, dog owners are exempt from liability to persons bitten by their dog if they have a sign posted that is (1) "easily readable" and (2) includes the words "Bad Dog." § 767.04, Fla. Stat. (20xx). The statute provides as follows:

[*See* § 11.7]

❖ *Next, focus on the part of the legal rule that's relevant to the case. In other words, refine the issue — state specifically what the "battleground(s)" will be in the case.*

Here, the Owners met the second element of the statute: they posted, in a prominent place on their premises, a sign with the words "WARNING BAD DOG." However, because Ten could not read English, it is questionable whether the Owners's sign met the "easily readable" requirement, and the issue turns on how the court will interpret this phrase. For the reasons below, the court will likely find that the sign met the statutory requirements and that the statute precludes Ten's cause of action.

❖ *Now, explain the specific legal rule — how the courts have interpreted the "easily readable" requirement; use the Tot case. Begin the discussion with the point of the case; follow with the facts, issue, holding, rule, and reasoning.*

❖ *Point — introduction to the case.*

The only case in Florida addressing whether a sign was "easily readable" as required by § 767.04 is *Tot v. Vicious*, 357 So. 2d 596, 596 (Fla. Dist. Ct. App. 20xx). However, as addressed below, the court will likely find that the reasoning of *Tot* is not relevant here.

❖ *Facts.*

In *Tot*, Sally Vicious's dog, Sweetie, bit Jimmy Tot, age five. *Id.* At the time of the attack, Vicious, who lived next door to an elementary school, had posted, in a prominent place on her property, a sign stating, "Warning Bad Dog." *Id.* However, due to his young age, Tot could not read the sign. *Id.* The trial court dismissed Tot's complaint against Vicious, and Tot appealed. *Id.*

> ❖ *Issue, holding, rule (delineate its elements), and reasoning (highlight any ambiguities).*

At issue was whether the sign was "easily readable." *Id.* Reasoning that it was not and reversing the trial court's decision, the court considered two factors. *Id.* First, noting that society must "protect those of tender years," *id.*, the court found that the sign was not easily readable by the five-year-old Tot, who could not yet read or write. *Id.* Second, noting that Vicious's property was located adjacent to an elementary school, the court found that "Vicious had ample warning of the possibility of such an accident." *Id.* Although the court addressed both factors (age and forseeability), the opinion is unclear whether both are necessary to the court's holding.

> ❖ *Next comes the "application" section. Here's where we discuss the elements of the legal rule and explain how our facts relate to those elements. We begin by discussing the first element — the "tender years" doctrine and include a heading to predict the court's conclusion on that issue.*

I. <u>The court will probably conclude that the "tender years" doctrine is irrelevant here and that public policy dictates that the Owners not be held liable.</u>

> ❖ *Here we lead with our conclusion; then explain (i.e., prove) our answer by demonstrating how our facts "mesh" with the legal rule and the facts and policy of the Tot case. We can lead with our client's argument first or with our opponent's argument. In this case, we've led with our opponent's argument because it is likely dispositive.*

> ❖ *Point stated, then our case is compared to Tot.*

The Owners will likely succeed in arguing that the *Tot* holding is irrelevant because the "tender years" doctrine does not apply to Ten. As an adult graduate student, Ten was fully capable of protecting herself. Ten is twenty-eight years old; Tot was only five. *See id.* Although the victims in both cases could not read the sign, the reasons for their inability are critically different. Ten could not read the sign because she had not yet learned how to read English; Tot could not read the sign because he had not yet learned how to read. Public policy protects Tot, who is incapable of protecting himself. In contrast, there is no similar public policy protecting Ten.

> ❖ *Further factual discussion focusing on public policy.*

Moreover, regardless of any sign, the Owners told Ten they owned a dog. Thus, whether she could read or not, Ten was well aware that the Owners had a dog. For these reasons, and because the Owners's sign met all other statutory requirements, the court should not hold them liable.

❖ *Counter-argument addressed: point stated, then prediction made
   and explained.*

Ten, on the other hand, could argue that because of her English illiteracy, she is as vulnerable as a child. She cannot read warning signs and cannot function safely in society without extra protection. Thus, she should be protected, as a matter of public policy, just as a child of "tender years" is protected.

However, this argument will likely fail because it would undercut the very protection the statute was meant to provide to dog owners, that is, to insulate them from liability. If the court accepted Ten's argument, then many groups, including blind persons, illiterate adults, and people who cannot read English, could sue dog owners who had complied with the statute.

Indeed, if the statute were interpreted broadly to cover the instant facts, dog owners could not protect themselves from liability. It would be impossible for an owner to display a sign which all people, no matter what language they understood or disability they suffered, could "easily read." For the reasons above, the court will likely reject Ten's argument and find that the sign was "easily readable."

❖ *Next, we discuss the second element of the legal rule — the "foreseeability" issue. We use a heading to predict the conclusion on that issue.*

II. <u>The court will probably find that Ten's "foreseeability" argument is irrelevant here.</u>

❖ *After leading with our conclusion, we explain (i.e., prove) our answer
   by demonstrating how our facts "mesh" with the legal rule and with
   the Tot case. Here, we've led with our client's argument.*

❖ *Point stated, then our case is compared to the Tot case.*

Ten could assert, in the alternative, that the Owners should be liable because it was foreseeable that she would come into contact with their dog. The court in *Tot*, in finding that liability could be imposed on the dog owner, reasoned that it was foreseeable that potential victims who could not read the sign would come onto the owner's property. *Id.* The court noted that the owner's home was located next door to an elementary school. *Id.* Ten could assert that like the owner in *Tot*, the Owners here "had ample warning of the possibility," *id.*, of their dog biting someone who could not read the "Bad Dog" sign.

❖ *Further factual discussion focusing on the "foreseeable" issue.*

Indeed, in this case, the Owners knew it was more than just "foreseeable," or likely, that someone unable to read the sign would come onto their property. They had many foreign guests who could not read English. Ten should argue that she was a foreseeable victim, and that the Owners knew she could not read English. Therefore, the court should conclude that the sign was not "easily readable" and hold the Owners liable.

❖ *Counter-argument addressed: point stated, then prediction made
   and explained.*

In response, the Owners will likely argue that the foreseeability of potential victims is not an *independent* reason for finding that their sign was not "easily readable." Although the *Tot* opinion is somewhat ambiguous on this point, the phrasing of the opinion helps to support the Owners's claim. In reaching its decision, the court first noted that Tot was protected under the "tender years" doctrine. *Id.* However, the court next stated: "[a]dditionally, Vicious's home was located next door to an elementary school, and thus Vicious had ample warning of the possibility of *such an accident*." *Id.* (emphasis added).

At first blush it may seem that the court's use of the word "additionally" indicates that the foreseeability of potential victims may be a separate factor permitting a court to impose liability under § 767.04. However, the phrase "ample warning ... of *such an accident*" indicates that the foreseeability factor refers back to the previous sentence and concerns the "tender years" doctrine. *Id.* (emphasis added). Thus, the court will likely find that any exemption from the statute's protection under a "foreseeability" theory is limited to victims who fall under the "tender years" doctrine. Because twenty-eight-year-old Ten is not covered by the "tender years" doctrine, the court will likely reject her foreseeability argument.

[In other words, Buck is in the clear!]

§ 11.9   Case Law Analysis Involving a Synthesized Rule

Often we must synthesize, from several cases, a rule governing our case. Examples of this type of analysis appear in Chapter 2, § 2.9 (the green apple hypothetical — who could forget that?), Chapter 7, § 7.4 (the disorderly conduct hypothetical), and Chapter 35 (the Sample Memo). When you're reviewing these examples, please note that the Discussion (rule development) section of the disorderly conduct hypothetical does not include a global introduction. How could we write one?[6] Please review these sections before moving forward.

§ 11.10   Case Law Analysis Using Analogical Reasoning

In analogical reasoning, we draw factual comparisons or distinctions to a cited case to reach a conclusion in our case. We point out similarities when we want our court to reach the same conclusion as a court in a cited case, and point out distinctions when we want our court to reach a different conclusion. Our Bit Ten memo (§ 11.8) employed this technique in comparing Ten's case to the *Tot* case. The following examples also illustrate this type of analysis. To keep the narrative flow easy to follow, we have omitted specific authorities supporting our discussion and instead have inserted the word [citation] where we ordinarily would have cited to authority.

---

6. Of course this is a *rhetorical* question. However, if any of our students really want to write such an introduction, go right ahead.

§ 11.10(a)   Sample Discussion Section:
Case Law Analysis Using Analogical Reasoning
(The Golf Shoe Memo)

<u>DISCUSSION:</u>

✦ *Global paragraph: general rule focused on our facts.*[7]

At issue is whether Alex Jones committed aggravated assault when he hurled a golf shoe, cleated with sixteen sharp steel points, at the victim's head. Jones admits that he threw the shoe and committed assault but challenges the lower court's characterization of the golf shoe as a "deadly weapon" and its ruling that this assault was aggravated. Because, for the reasons set forth below, the court will likely find that Jones used the shoe in a manner likely to produce death or serious bodily injury, the court will likely rule for the State and uphold Jones's conviction.

✦ *Rule explanation: point, facts, issue, holding, rule, reasoning of* Smith.

The State's aggravated assault statute does not define the term "aggravated." [citation] Moreover, although no cases in this jurisdiction involve aggravated assault or simple assault with a golf shoe, *Smith v. State* [citation], involving a boot, is instructive.

In *Smith*, the defendant was convicted of aggravated assault for throwing a heavy, steel-toed boot at the victim. [citation] At issue was whether the boot constituted a "deadly weapon" under the State's aggravated assault statute. [citation] The appellate court held that it did and affirmed the conviction. [citation] Reasoning that the boot's steel toe and rigid heel could be used as a blunt instrument, and acknowledging the boot's considerable weight, the court concluded that the boot was used in a manner "likely to produce death or serious bodily injury." [citation] Accordingly, the court held that the boot was a deadly weapon. [citation]

✦ *Applying* Smith *to our case.*

Similarly, the State should argue that the golf shoe was a deadly weapon because, as the boot in *Smith*, the golf shoe here had characteristics that made Jones's use of the shoe, in the manner employed, "likely to produce death or serious bodily injury." [citation] Indeed, the State should focus on those characteristics of the shoe that make it dangerous.

In comparison to the smooth, leather-soled boot in *Smith*, the golf shoe in the instant case has sixteen steel cleats protruding from its sole. These cleats were sharp enough to pierce the body of the victim. This fact, demonstrating the dangerousness of the shoe, cannot be refuted.

✦ *Jones's counter-argument and our response.*

Jones, however, could argue that the instant case is distinguishable from *Smith* because the golf shoe is much lighter than the *Smith* boot. In response, the State should argue that even assuming that the golf shoe is lighter, the shoe, just as the boot in *Smith*, is rigid. [ci-

---

7. Please *see* Chapter 7, § 7.2 for the facts for this example; assume we represent the State.

tation] Accordingly, despite its lighter weight, the golf shoe, like the boot, could be used, and was used here, as a blunt instrument. Thus, the State should argue, and the court will likely accept, that the golf shoe's physical attributes — its sharp, protruding cleats and rigid leather sole — made it a deadly weapon, capable, as in this case, of being used in a manner likely to produce death or serious bodily injury.

[Note: As mothers of boys, we know that a golf shoe *is* a deadly weapon, whether hurled or not, if, after having been worn to play 18 holes of golf, the shoe is placed in the vicinity of any living creature.]

§ 11.10(b)   Sample Discussion Section: Case Law Analysis Using Analogical Reasoning (The Sentencing Memo)

DISCUSSION:

❖ *Global paragraph: general rule focused on our facts.*[8]

At issue is whether the judge committed reversible error in increasing Williams's sentence from two years to ten years. A judge may not increase a sentence to punish a defendant for having demanded a jury trial. *Adams v. State* [citation]. However, in imposing a sentence, a judge may consider the defendant's potential for rehabilitation. *Brown v. State* [citation]. The question here turns on whether the judge's comments in Williams's case reflect a genuine concern for Williams's potential for rehabilitation or an impermissible intent to punish him for having demanded a jury trial. Because the court's comments reflect the latter, the trial court's sentencing was improper and will likely be reversed.

❖ *Rule explanation: point, facts, issue (implicit), holding, rule, reasoning of* Adams.

The *Adams* case supports a credible argument that the trial court committed reversible error in the instant case. In *Adams*, the defendant had negotiated a three-year sentence in return for pleading guilty to burglary. [citation] After the judge approved the plea agreement, Adams changed his mind and exercised his right to a jury trial. [citation] He was convicted. [citation] Sentencing Adams to twelve years, the trial judge stated:

"I am tired of people who put the county to the expense of a trial when they are obviously guilty.... [Y]ou required everyone to sit here and listen to you tell a tale. Well, nothing is free."

[citation] The appellate court read this language as indicating that the judge's primary motive in increasing the sentence was to punish Adams for his jury demand and remanded the case for resentencing. [citation]

---

8. Please *see* Chapter 7, § 7.3 for the facts for this example; assume we represent Williams.

❖ *Applying* Adams *to our case.*

We should argue that similar to the trial court in *Adams*, the trial court here improperly increased Williams's sentence to punish him for demanding a jury trial. The judge in our case had originally agreed to sentence Williams to a two-year term, if he pled guilty. However, after Williams requested a jury trial, the judge imposed the ten-year sentence to punish him for his request. The judge's remarks, which we cite as proof of this improper, primary motive, are set forth below.

In imposing the ten-year sentence, the judge in our case stated the following:

> I have little sympathy for you, Mr. Williams. You have been in trouble since you were twelve, and at twenty, you show no sign of changing. You are a menace. Furthermore, you are not very smart. Your lawyer got you a good deal, but you didn't take it. Instead, you demanded a jury trial because you thought you could do better. Well, you have to learn the lesson that when you buck the system, you get the brunt. I sentence you to ten years.

[citation] Similar to the trial judge's comments in *Adams*, the judge's remarks here disclose that the court's primary intent was to punish Williams for demanding a jury trial. For this reason, we should argue that Williams's sentence should be vacated and the case remanded for resentencing.

❖ *State's counter-argument and our prediction:* Adams.

The State will most likely counter our argument by claiming that the judge's remarks here did not show that the court's primary motive in imposing the ten-year sentence was to punish Williams for demanding a jury trial. The State will probably point out that the *Adams* case is irrelevant or inconsequential because the trial judge in that case never even once directly referred to the defendant's potential for rehabilitation. [citation] This is a valid argument and points out the most damaging aspect of the *Adams* case. Thus, we should do further research and see if we can find a stronger case than *Adams*. We should look for a case, decided in the defendant's favor, where the judge commented *both* on the defendant's potential for rehabilitation and the defendant's request for a jury trial.

❖ *State's counter-argument and our prediction continued:* Brown *rule explanation.*

The State will probably further argue that similar to the court's remarks in *Brown v. State* [citation], the judge's comments in our case demonstrated that the court's primary concern was the defendant's rehabilitation potential. The *Brown* case, however, is readily distinguishable from our case for the reasons addressed below.

❖ *Facts, issue (implicit), holding, rule, reasoning of* Brown.

In *Brown*, the trial court had agreed to impose a five-year sentence for sexual battery, but when Brown demanded a jury trial and was convicted, the judge imposed a fifteen-year term. [citation] However, unlike the sentences in *Adams* and the instant case, the increased sentence in *Brown* was based on the judge's assessment of the defendant's low potential for rehabilitation. [citation] The trial judge had stated:

> When defendants express a penitent spirit, they are half-way to rehabilitation, and I am inclined to be lenient in sentencing. For that reason, I often give light sentences on guilty pleas. But when a man denies his guilt, and requires the system to go through the motions of proving his guilt, I cannot believe he is remorseful, and I cannot believe he is a good candidate for rehabilitation. I think you need a long time to come to terms with your attitude.

[citation]

Unlike the court's comments in our case, the trial court's remarks in *Brown* established that the higher sentence had not been imposed to punish the defendant for having demanded a jury trial. To the contrary, the judge articulated that he believed Brown was not a "'good candidate for rehabilitation,'" that Brown had not shown remorse, that a lack of remorse indicated a lack of "'penitent spirit,'" and that Brown needed a "'long time'" to consider his attitude. [citation] Because judges properly may consider rehabilitation potential at sentencing, and the court's remarks in *Brown* primarily focused on rehabilitation, the appellate court upheld the *Brown* sentence. [citation]

> ❖ *Applying* Brown *to our case: our response to the State's argument.*

We should argue that in contrast to the trial court's comments in *Brown*, the only remarks by the court in our case that could possibly be construed as concerned with rehabilitation was the offhand comment that Williams was a "'menace'" who had been in trouble since he was twelve, and showed "'no sign of changing.'" [citation] Although the State will argue that these comments demonstrate that the court was concerned with Williams's potential for rehabilitation, we should argue that the judge's own words show that his primary motive was to punish Williams for his jury demand.

The trial court chided Williams:

> Your lawyer got you a good deal, but you didn't take it. Instead, you demanded a jury trial because you thought you could do better. Well, you have to learn the lesson that when you buck the system, you get the brunt. I sentence you to ten years.

[citation]

Unlike the trial court in the *Brown* case, the trial court in our case directly commented on the "good deal" the defendant "didn't take" and on his jury demand. From these comments, we can craft a convincing argument, which the court will likely accept, that if Williams had not exercised his constitutional right to request a jury trial, his sentence would have been eight years shorter.

[Although we're not finished yet, we're closer to being able to "rest in the shade."]

§ 11.11   Exercise in Writing a Discussion Section

Using the Jane Smith hypothetical (*see* § 5.10(b) and § 6.5), write a Discussion section for a predictive memo addressing the testamentary intent issues, using only the California statute and the five cases listed in the exercise in Chapter 7 (§ 7.7). All five cases are located in Appendix A. Use both analogical reasoning (FIHRR) as well as Rule-Plus, and follow *The Bluebook* citation rules.

Chapter Review
The Discussion

No memo is complete until we've edited it at least five times. Five. And, when we review our memo those (at least) five times, we read it as if were reading it for the first time. We read it as if we knew nothing more about our case or the applicable law than what our memo tells us.

We offer below a checklist for drafting and evaluating the most critical aspect of the memo — the Discussion section. But first, we offer four general suggestions relevant to the content of the Discussion:

✓ The Discussion should:

    ✓ contain bold assertions stating the conclusions the court will likely reach on each issue and relevant legal element;

    ✓ include all logical steps necessary to reach our conclusions;

    ✓ provide all critical facts and legal authorities; and

    ✓ contain no unnecessary analysis, words, or phrases.

Checklist for Writing an Effective Discussion Section[9]

Large-Scale Organization: Overall Discussion Section

✓ Begin with an effective global introduction which, following a slightly modified BaRAC design,

    ✓ restates and focuses the issues;

    ✓ states our overall conclusions;

    ✓ states and focuses the general rule or rules; and

    ✓ briefly explains why the application of the rule to our facts leads to the result we've suggested.

✓ State each distinct issue as a separate heading.

✓ Include only discussion necessary to each heading under that heading.

✓ Arrange issues logically.

    ✓ Clearly indicate threshold or dispositive issues *as* threshold or dispositive.

    ✓ Clearly indicate alternative issues as alternatives.

    ✓ Make clear in the headings any interdependence between issues.

    ✓ Place the dispositive or threshold issue first.

    ✓ Unless logic requires otherwise, arrange all issues in an order tracking the elements of the rule.

✓ Check to ensure that if we list the bold assertions from each paragraph, a strong outline of our entire Discussion emerges.

---

9. We thank our colleague Henry Wihnyk for his suggestions regarding this checklist.

Small-Scale Organization: Discussion within a Specific Heading or Subheading
- ✓ Follow each Heading and Subheading with an introductory paragraph which
  - ✓ serves not *as* the analysis, but as a way to *introduce* the analysis;
  - ✓ follows the BaRAC design;
  - ✓ begins with a bold assertion of our position;
  - ✓ states, with proper citation, but briefly, the general rule and relevant facts applicable to the heading;
  - ✓ briefly demonstrates the result of applying that rule to those facts; and
  - ✓ reaches a conclusion on the issue.
- ✓ Follow the BaRAC design in writing the further paragraphs under each heading and subheading. In other words, for each point argued
  - ✓ include a bold assertion;
  - ✓ state and explain the rule;
  - ✓ demonstrate how the rule applies to the facts;
  - ✓ reach a conclusion on the specific issue;
  - ✓ address and respond to relevant counter-arguments; and
  - ✓ edit to eliminate unnecessary analysis, words, and phrases.

Regarding All Paragraphs
- ✓ Make certain each paragraph:
  - ✓ concerns only one topic;
  - ✓ contains sentences which coherently relate to each other and to the topic;
  - ✓ contains a first and last sentence, which when read together, demonstrate consistency and the logical progression of thought; and
  - ✓ flows into the next paragraph effortlessly, with a smooth transition.

Analysis
- ✓ Choose the most effective form of rule development and application for each issue, and ensure that our discussion of cited cases reflects the role the cases play in our analysis:
  - (1) rule-only: factor analysis;
  - (2) rule-plus: the short explanation approach; or
  - (3) FIHRR: reasoning by analogy.
- ✓ Clearly state all rules.
- ✓ Follow the BaRAC structure for all issues.
- ✓ Ensure that each issue is logical, well-developed, internally consistent, and consistent with the overall theory of our case.
- ✓ Explain and distinguish relevant harmful cases and counter-arguments.

Language, Grammar, Spelling, Format, Citation

✓ Carefully choose words to convey our analysis.

✓ Use clear, concrete, and concise language.

✓ Use short sentences.

✓ Do not exceed 1/2 page for paragraphs.

✓ Use transitions effectively.

✓ Ensure that the Discussion is free from grammatical, spelling, citation, and quotation errors.

✓ Follow every quotation with a pinpoint citation.

For further suggestions on editing, *see* Chapter 24.

Detailed Design of the Discussion Section: Example of a Multi-Issue Discussion

DISCUSSION:

global paragraph(s)

I. Main heading written in one or more sentences.

> bold assertion
> rule and rule explanation
> application
> conclusion

counter-argument (if any)

> bold assertion
> rule and rule explanation
> application
> conclusion

response

> bold assertion
> rule and rule explanation
> application
> conclusion

conclusion to heading I.

II. <u>Main heading written in one or more sentences.</u>

> bold assertion
> rule and rule explanation
> application
> conclusion

A. <u>Subheading written in one or more sentences.</u>

> bold assertion
> rule and rule explanation
> application
> conclusion

counter-argument (if any)

> bold assertion
> rule and rule explanation
> application
> conclusion

response

> bold assertion
> rule and rule explanation
> application
> conclusion

conclusion

B. <u>Subheading written in one or more sentences.</u>

> bold assertion
> rule and rule explanation
> application
> conclusion

counter-argument (if any)

> bold assertion
> rule and rule explanation
> application
> conclusion

response

> bold assertion
> rule and rule explanation
> application
> conclusion

conclusion

conclusion to heading II.

Chapter 12

The Conclusion and Authorities Cited

"Mind in its purest play is like some bat
that beats about in caverns all alone,
contriving by a kind of senseless wit
not to conclude against a wall of stone."

—Richard Purdy Wilbur

"Life is the art of drawing sufficient conclusions from insufficient premises."

—Samuel Butler

§ 12.1   The Conclusion

Purpose and Overview. In the Conclusion, we answer the Question Presented and predict what the court will likely do and/or suggest what our client should do. In it, we inform our reader of the likelihood of success and recommend further research or investigation where appropriate. Our Conclusion may also be conditional; that is, we may predict a particular outcome based on our discovery of further facts, on a favorable selection between competing rules, or on a favorable interpretation of established law.

Context and Format. The Conclusion follows the Discussion, on the same page if possible, and precedes the Authorities Cited. It is double-spaced, written in paragraph form, and is shorter than the Brief Answer.

Example. The following is the Conclusion section of our Bit Ten memo.

CONCLUSION:
   Owners are probably not liable for Ten's injuries because they had posted an easily readable "Bad Dog" sign as required by Florida law. The court will likely find that Ten's inability to read English and the Owners's knowledge of that inability are irrelevant here.

For a further example of a conclusion, please *see* Chapter 35.

§ 12.2   Authorities Cited

Purpose. The Authorities Cited section allows our reader to see, at a glance, all citations to all authorities we've cited in our Discussion section.

Context. The Authorities Cited follows the Conclusion, on the same page if possible, and is the last section in our memo.

Format. The Authorities Cited are set forth in citation form appropriate for the court that may hear our case. The Authorities should be divided into categories such as statutes, regulations, and case law, with case law appearing first. Cases are listed in alphabetical order, without regard to jurisdiction. Please *see* Chapter 35 for a sample Authorities Cited section.

Update. All Authorities are updated. Updating is just what it sounds like—checking to ensure that all the sources we use are still "up-to-date"; that is, they are still valid and thus haven't been overturned or superceded. We update as if our job (or grade) is hanging in the balance; it is.

Example. The following is an example Authorities Cited section:

AUTHORITIES CITED:
    Cases
Tot v. Vicious,
        357 So. 2d 596 (Fla. Dist. Ct. App. 20xx)
    Statute
Fla. Stat. § 767.04 (20xx)

Congratulations! You now know the basics of writing a legal memo. The challenge now comes in actually putting your knowledge to work. Writing is a lot like playing tennis. Reading how to hit the ball isn't anything like actually hitting it. Writing, like any sport or art form, takes practice and patience.

§ 12.3   Exercise in Writing the Conclusion and Authorities Cited

Using the Jane Smith hypothetical (*see* § 5.10(b) and § 6.5), do the following:

Exercise 1. Write a Conclusion for the memo.

Exercise 2. Prepare, following *The Bluebook* citation rules, an Authorities Cited section for the memo, using the statute and the five cases.

Section III

Persuasive Analysis: Designing the Brief and Oral Argument

Chapter 13

Introduction to Appellate Advocacy

"If you go in for argument, take care of your temper. Your logic, if you have any, will take care of itself."

—Joseph Farrell

§ 13.1   The Appellate Process

Appellate Advocacy focuses on persuasive writing, brief writing, and oral argument. Our goal in Section III is to explain the appellate process and the following four practical skills:

(1) writing persuasively;

(2) preparing an appellate brief;

(3) presenting an effective oral argument; and

(4) learning good habits of professional practice.

Because of its importance to all aspects of the appellate process, we begin with a discussion of professional practice.

§ 13.2   Professional Practice, Ethics, and Court Documents

In Chapter 27, we discuss many of the ethical and professional duties we owe to our clients based on the Model Rules of Professional Conduct. In addition to these requirements, some specific rules of conduct are directed toward advocates engaged in brief writing and oral argument. We set forth the relevant ones here.

1. Meritorious Claims and Contentions.[1] "A lawyer shall not bring or defend a proceeding, or assert or controvert an issue therein, unless there is a basis in law and fact for doing so that is not frivolous, which includes a good faith argument for an extension, modification or reversal of existing law."

In other words, if there isn't a valid basis for our appeal, we don't pursue it. An action is frivolous if a reasonable, competent lawyer would conclude it is without merit. As the Supreme Court stated in *Neitzke v. Williams*, 490 U.S. 319, 325 (1989), "an appeal on a matter of law is frivolous where '[none] of the legal points [are] arguable on their merits'.... By logical extension, a complaint, containing as it does both factual allegations and legal conclusions, is frivolous where it lacks an arguable basis either in law or in fact."

As advocates, we have an ethical duty to pursue our client's cause to the fullest extent consistent with existing law. The fact that we believe that our client's position will ultimately not prevail does not make an action frivolous so long as we fully inform ourselves about the facts of our client's case and the applicable law, and make only good faith arguments in support of an extension, modification, or reversal of existing law.

2. Expediting Litigation.[2] "A lawyer shall make reasonable efforts to expedite litigation consistent with the interests of the client."

In other words, we meet all court deadlines. We don't unreasonably extend the time for filing our brief or presenting our oral argument.

---

1. Model Rules of Prof'l Conduct R. 3.1.
2. Model Rules of Prof'l Conduct R. 3.2.

3. Candor Toward the Tribunal.[3] "A lawyer shall not knowingly: (1) make a false statement of fact or law to a tribunal or fail to correct a false statement of material fact or law previously made to the tribunal by the lawyer; (2) fail to disclose to the tribunal legal authority in the controlling jurisdiction known to the lawyer to be directly adverse to the position of the client and not disclosed by opposing counsel...."

As officers of the court, we have an absolute duty to tell the court the relevant controlling law, even if harmful to our client, and to correct any prior misstatements we may have made.

4. Fairness to Opposing Party and Counsel.[4] "A lawyer shall not: ... knowingly disobey an obligation under the rules of a tribunal except for an open refusal based on an assertion that no valid obligation exists."

This rule requires us to follow all procedural rules of the court, including those governing the format requirements for our brief, and to meet all deadlines for filing documents.

5. Impartiality and Decorum of the Tribunal.[5] "A lawyer shall not: (a) seek to influence a judge ... or other official by means prohibited by law; (b) communicate ex parte with such a person during the proceeding unless authorized to do so by law or court order."

It goes without saying that we never unlawfully attempt to influence a judge. An *ex parte* communication to a court or judge means one made without notice to the other party. We don't communicate with a judge regarding a pending case without providing notice to the other party. We also provide opposing counsel with copies of everything we file with the court. The Rules of Professional Conduct for Florida Lawyers explains this prohibition in Rule 4-3.5, entitled "Impartiality and Decorum of the Tribunal," as follows:

> (b) Communication with Judge or Official. In an adversary proceeding a lawyer shall not communicate or cause another to communicate as to the merits of the cause with a judge or an official before whom the proceeding is pending except:
>
> (1) in the course of the official proceeding in the cause;
>
> (2) in writing if the lawyer promptly delivers a copy of the writing to the opposing counsel or to the adverse party if not represented by a lawyer;
>
> (3) orally upon notice to opposing counsel or to the adverse party if not represented by a lawyer; or
>
> (4) as otherwise authorized by law.

With these ethical considerations firmly in mind, let's examine the appellate process.

---

3. Model Rules of Prof'l Conduct R. 3.3(a).
4. Model Rules of Prof'l Conduct R. 3.4(c).
5. Model Rules of Prof'l Conduct R. 3.5.

§ 13.3   The Appeal

The case. We all know the story of the Three Little Pigs. Well, let's assume that the Big Bad Wolf has been held liable in a civil action brought by the Third Little Piggy (the one with the brick house). Assume that the Third Little Piggy established at trial that Old Big Bad huffed and puffed and blew in the houses of the First Little and Second Little Piggies, respectively. Assume further that the jury awarded the surviving brother, the Third Little Piggy, a million dollars in a wrongful death action, and the trial court entered a judgment pursuant to that verdict. Wolf is not pleased and, after getting the addresses of all jury members, pursues an appeal.

§ 13.4   Grounds of Appeal

Through his appeal, Wolf challenges the trial court's judgment, and seeks to "reverse" it. Before we return to Wolf's appeal, permit us to address a few background issues.

An appeal is not a retrial of our case. With few exceptions, the appellate court's power is limited to entering an order "affirming," "reversing," or "modifying" the judgment or order being appealed. A "judgment" is a court's final decision regarding the parties' claims in a lawsuit. A judgment may include commands or an award of money damages. For example, a defendant may be permanently prohibited from doing certain acts or, as in Wolf's case, be directed to pay damages. In a criminal case, the judgment may include the court's command that the defendant be sentenced to prison, ordered to pay a fine, or both.

On the other hand, an "order" is a court ruling during a pending case directing that some action be taken or not taken. During a lawsuit, a court enters many orders governing discovery, the court's calendar, evidence that may or may not be used at trial, or temporary or preliminary relief. Some orders have the practical effect of ending a case, such as an order dismissing a complaint for failure to state a cause of action. However, such orders are followed by a final judgment formally recording that final effect.

The "appellant," in our case Wolf, usually asks the appellate court to reverse the lower court's order or judgment and, when appropriate, to "remand" the case back to the trial court for further proceedings. The "appellee," here the Third Little Piggy, normally seeks to "affirm" the judgment or order appealed from. Occasionally, however, both sides are aggrieved by the trial court's action and ask the appellate court, through "cross appeals," to modify the judgment.

However, an appellant cannot base his appeal on any conceivable ground. For example, Wolf can't appeal the judgment against him on the ground that he had a cold the day he testified, and that cold made his voice sound even deeper and gruffer than usual. Instead, he must rely on one or more of the following arguments. He must prove that the trial court, in its judgment or order:

  (1) relied on erroneous facts;

  (2) relied on erroneous conclusions of law; or

(3) misapplied the law to the facts.[6]

Of these three arguments, the first is the most difficult to make and the least often used. Reviewing courts work only from the transcript of prior testimony contained in the *Record on Appeal* and do not receive new evidence. They are, therefore, in a poor position to judge witnesses' credibility. Consequently, they accept the lower court's findings of fact unless (1) the transcript demonstrates that the findings cannot be supported by the testimony, or (2) the "manifest weight of the evidence" compels a finding contrary to the one reached. In our case, Wolf can't bring any new witnesses before the appellate court and will likely lose if he tries to argue that the jury erred in believing the Third Little Piggy's testimony.

Misinterpretation of law is a more fertile ground for a successful appeal. For example, assume a statute, relevant to Wolf's case, forbids any huffing or puffing over an established speed limit. Assume further that trial testimony established that Wolf huffed and puffed at the houses of the First and Second Little Piggies at 10 m.p.h. over that limit, and the judge ruled such conduct constituted negligence. On appeal, Wolf cannot challenge the factual conclusion that his exhalations had exceeded the limit. He can't bring forth a new witness to testify that his huffing and puffing *was* within the limit. However, he could argue a point of law; i.e., that the court erred in instructing the jury *to apply* the law of negligence to his case. We wish him luck.

§ 13.5   An Overview of the Process

A thorough discussion of all aspects of the appellate process would fill volumes — and put us all to sleep. However, to understand the importance of a brief and oral argument, we must understand the process of an appeal. For this reason, we offer the following overview.

We already know what appellate decisions are: they're the cases, called "opinions" or "decisions," we read in casebooks and digests.[7]

Before tackling any appeal, we must understand the structure, organization, and rules of the appellate system in which the appeal occurs. With certain exceptions, a party aggrieved by a trial court's judgment, and by some orders, can appeal to a higher appellate court. There, a judge or a panel of judges determines whether the trial court erred. In the process, the appellate courts interpret and apply the law.

Although an appeal seeks to cure a lower court's error, we can't raise an error for the first time on appeal. With one exception, called "fundamental error," we waive any error we didn't object to at trial.[8] But by objecting at trial to an error, and by obtaining a ruling from the trial court on that objection, we preserve the right to raise that error on appeal. Moreover, any "preserved" ground for appeal that we failed to raise on appeal

---

6. We address this topic in more detail in Chapter 16: Standards of Review.

7. The cases in casebooks are typically, and mercifully, edited for the authors' specific purposes.

8. "Fundamental error," which occurs extremely rarely, is error so critical to justice, or to the outcome of the case, that it must be corrected on appeal even if not objected to at trial.

is waived. Thus, in our case, even if Wolf preserves an issue for appeal by objecting during trial to the trial court's alleged error, that objection is waived if he does not include that point in his brief to the reviewing court.

Wolf must also be aware that appellate courts will generally affirm a "correct" outcome of a case, even if the lower court's rationale in reaching that result was wrong. This principle recognizes the futility of reversing a correct outcome. Further, appellate courts are not inclined to reverse even "actual" error when that error is "harmless." Thus, if Wolf argues an error that did not affect the outcome of his case, he's wasting his time — the court will affirm "harmless error" cases.

To perfect his appeal, Wolf must timely bring his case to the correct court. A party dissatisfied by a trial court ruling or judgment generally has a right to seek review by the appellate court immediately "above" the trial court. In a state, such as Florida, and in the federal system, with two levels of appellate courts, this appeal will be to an intermediate court of appeal. In a state with a one-tiered appellate system, this appeal "as of right" will be to the state's supreme court. Moreover, where a state has two levels of appellate courts, the state's supreme court's jurisdiction may be limited.[9]

In most states, such as Florida, where the question is simply whether a party obtained just treatment by the trial court, the court of last resort is usually an intermediate level (district) appellate court. An appeal to a higher court beyond this one appeal given "as of right" will usually be discretionary — meaning that the highest court may decline to accept the appeal. Thus, Wolf can appeal the trial (circuit) court's judgment to the district court of appeal but cannot seek any further appeal to the Florida Supreme Court unless that court, in its "discretion," agrees to hear his case.[10]

In most intermediate appellate courts, appeals are heard by panels of judges (usually three) rather than by the full court. Occasionally, however, a party who has lost before an intermediate court panel can persuade the full court "*en banc*" (i.e., all of the judges hearing and deciding the case together), on "rehearing" to review the panel's decision. Further, in the United States Supreme Court and state supreme courts (including the New York Court of Appeals — that state's highest court), the full court hears and decides all appeals.

---

9. For example, in Florida, the supreme court's appellate jurisdiction is limited. The court must, under the exercise of "mandatory" jurisdiction, review death penalty orders, decisions of district courts of appeal declaring invalid a state statute or a provision of the state constitution, and, when provided by general law, final judgments entered in bond validation proceedings and actions of state agencies relating to rates or service of utilities. Art. V, §§ 3(b)(1);(2), Fla. Const. The Florida Supreme Court also has limited "discretionary" jurisdiction to review a decision of a district court of appeal declaring a state statute valid, construing a provision of the state or federal constitution, affecting a class of constitutional or state officers, or that expressly and directly conflicts with a decision of another district court or of the supreme court on the same question of law, and questions of great public importance. Art. V, §§ 3(b)(3);(4), Fla. Const.

10. However, a state's highest court in a two-tiered system, such as the Florida Supreme Court, will often exercise its discretionary jurisdiction to address new or unsettled legal issues. For example, a state supreme court may exercise its discretionary jurisdiction to create uniformity in lower court rulings, to acknowledge or reject a cause of action that has been adopted by another jurisdiction, or to define further the elements of a newly recognized cause of action.

§ 13.6   The Steps of the Appellate Process

The Notice of Appeal. The appellate process begins when an "aggrieved" party, i.e., one who is unhappy with the trial court's ruling or judgment, timely "serves" and "files" the appropriate document to commence the appeal.[11] This document is typically styled a "Notice of Appeal," which is directed to, and filed with, the court being appealed *from*. In other words, in our case Wolf files his Notice with the trial court. He goes to the clerk's office of the trial court, hands the clerk the Notice, and pays a filing fee, or does the same electronically. The clerk then assigns the case a number and "files" the Notice of Appeal. Wolf also sends the Third Little Piggy a copy of the Notice.

When the appeal is "as of right," the Notice is usually a simple one-paragraph document, which need not specify the basis for the appeal. However, if the court's jurisdiction is discretionary, the aggrieved party must file a petition, often called a "Jurisdictional Brief," pointing out the alleged errors in the court below, stating why these errors are important, and explaining why the court should accept the appeal. That party, if successful in getting the reviewing court to accept jurisdiction, is then designated the "Petitioner" and the opposing party is designated the "Respondent." The petition is filed with the court being appealed *to*. The denial of a petition for discretionary review precludes further appeal; therefore, the petition's contents are absolutely critical and must be carefully written.

Here's where it gets just a bit tricky. Once Wolf files his Notice with the trial court, all further papers concerning his appeal are filed with the *appellate* court, and bear the case number the appellate court has assigned to the case. Court rules govern how all papers are filed, including what type of cover sheet or "caption" must appear on them. A caption sets forth, among other things, the names of the parties, the court, and the case number.

The Name Game. Depending on court rules, which vary considerably from jurisdiction to jurisdiction, a plaintiff who appeals might, in the appellate caption, become an "Appellant," a "Plaintiff-Appellant," a "Plaintiff-Petitioner," or some other designation. If the appealing party is the "Appellant," the other party is generally the "Appellee," although a few courts call the other party the "Respondent." If the appealing party is the "Petitioner," the other party is always the "Respondent" — not the "Appellee."

An Appellee or Respondent who cross-appeals may, depending on the court, be called a "Cross-Appellant," "Cross-Petitioner," or a "Respondent/Cross-Petitioner." For convenience, and to keep what's left of our sanity, we'll refer to "appellant" as the party initiating an appeal and "appellee" as the party opposing the appeal.

---

11. In general, to "serve" a document means to deliver it to the opposing party; to "file" a document means to deliver it to the court clerk. Court rules mandate how (by what means, i.e., personal delivery, mail, electronic transmission) a document is to be filed.

Timing is Everything. Time limits are critical in appellate practice.

Practice Pointers

🖋 We *must* serve and file the Notice of Appeal or Petition for Discretionary Jurisdiction (Jurisdictional Brief) within the time required by law — and time limits vary from court to court. Failure to do so will result in "dismissal" of our case, "without recourse." Missing the deadline for filing a Notice of Appeal or a Jurisdictional Brief is an absolutely irreparable error. Unless we can demonstrate some extraordinary circumstance, there is no "second chance" to cure or excuse this error. Bottom line: missing this deadline is MALPRACTICE.

If Wolf fails to file his Notice on time, his goose is cooked. In that instance, he'd have to cough (huff?) up a million dollars in damages.

Preparing the Record on Appeal. Assuming that Wolf has timely filed his Notice, he next must ask the *trial court* clerk to prepare and to transmit to the reviewing court the Record (documents, exhibits other than physical evidence, and transcripts) of the trial court proceedings. In other words, he ensures that the documents the appellate court will review are literally assembled, paginated, and transmitted to the appellate court. Unless the Record is simple, this can be a complex, lengthy, and expensive undertaking.

In most appellate courts, the appellant (Wolf) designates the portions of the Record indicating error and pays the clerk to prepare and transmit them to the appellate court. The appellee, in our case the Third Little Piggy, then designates and pays for any additional portions of the Record he wants to include.

Once the Record is prepared, the clerk may send the parties and the appellate court an abridged version, called the "Index to the Record on Appeal," which merely identifies the title of each document in the Record. The appellant reimburses the clerk for any costs of these copies. The actual Record itself — the original pleadings and evidence from the trial court — is usually not duplicated but is eventually sent to the reviewing court. Physical evidence, such as firearms and drugs, usually remains with the trial court.

Using the Index to the Record on Appeal, the attorneys for the parties rely on their own files and the transcripts of hearings or trials, if any, in preparing their briefs. If they are missing any documents, they secure a copy from the clerk.

Citing to the Record. In referring to a trial court pleading or other written exhibit in the Record, we write, for example: (R.150.). This citation refers to page 150 of the Record. We'd cite the trial transcript as (TT.), or something similar, with the appropriate page referenced. Example:

"He drew his chest in, inhaling." (R.3.)

Writing the Briefs. After the clerk sends the Record to the reviewing court and the attorneys receive the Index, the parties finalize their briefs. Each attorney files the brief with the appellate court and "serves it on" (i.e., delivers a copy to) the opposing counsel. The appellant files an "initial brief," followed by the appellee's "answer brief," usually followed by the appellant's "reply brief." Naturally, as with all aspects of an appeal, court rules govern the format, content, and timing of these briefs.

Oral Argument. Following the filing of the briefs, the case may or may not be scheduled for oral argument.[12] Until fairly recently, appellate courts granted oral argument as a matter of course. However, due to increasing appellate case loads, some courts no longer follow this practice. If oral argument is requested and granted, each attorney is allotted a time period, typically around fifteen or twenty minutes, to speak with the judges in open court. Afterwards, the judges typically meet to discuss the case and eventually issue a written opinion (also called a "decision").

§ 13.7 The Function of the Brief and of Oral Argument in Appellate Practice

The brief and oral argument serve different purposes in an appeal. A well-crafted brief provides a decision-making "roadmap" for the court. It sets out in detail the authorities and evidence the court can employ in reaching its decision. *The ideal brief is one the court can adopt, with subtle changes, as its opinion.*

The Oral Argument. As appellate courts are overburdened with increasing caseloads, the importance of the brief in most jurisdictions has vastly transcended the importance of oral argument. In many courts, including the United States Supreme Court, the initial briefs may be up to fifty pages long. Oral argument, however, may only be twenty minutes per side. With the usual questions and interruptions, those twenty minutes may only cover the equivalent of a few pages of the brief.[13] For these reasons, although both the brief and the oral argument are crucial in different ways, most courts have come to rely more heavily upon the briefs.

Nonetheless, the oral argument gives the court the "big picture" and focuses the panel on the most important issues in our case. "Oral argument," though, is a misnomer—we don't argue with the court. Instead, we engage the judges in a dialogue. They ask us questions, we answer. They express their concerns, we do our best to assuage them.

Keep the Overworked Judge in Mind. For each appeal, an appellate judge has a tremendous amount of work to do. The judge must read at least two briefs, not to mention relevant sections of the Record and legal authorities. In complex cases or cases of great public interest where interested parties are allowed to submit "friend of the court (*amicus*) briefs," the judge may also read a half-dozen more briefs. But that's not all. The judge may then be assigned to write the majority or plurality opinion or may write a dissenting or concurring opinion. In addition, the judge will read opinions drafted by other judges. To top it off, the judge also must read and dispose of various motions, deal with other administrative responsibilities, and keep abreast of current law. It's no wonder judges beg lawyers to be concise.

---

12. We address oral argument in detail in Chapter 22.

13. This is in stark contrast to the days when a "brief" in the United States Supreme Court may have been only a few pages long, while the oral argument in the case could continue for days.

Thus, perhaps the most important lesson to learn from this Chapter (aside from *never, never* missing the deadline for filing a Notice of Appeal!) is to write a brief with the *thought continuously in mind* that our intended reader is utterly buried in (often dreadfully boring and complicated or incoherent) briefs and mired in transcripts, opinions, court orders, etc., ad nauseam. Anything we can do to make our brief short and easy to read (even pleasurable if at all possible), will put a smile on the judge's face and undoubtedly benefit our client.

The Brief. Unlike an objective memorandum that informs the reader, an appellate brief both informs and persuades our reader to accept our viewpoint. "Persuading," however, does *not* mean "slanting" the facts or the law. If the court thinks we're playing fast and loose with the law or facts, we'll lose our credibility and never get it back.

The best way to educate the court is to assume that the judges know nothing about our facts or the law involved in our case. A persuasive brief shows how the applicable rules as applied to our facts result in the conclusion we advocate. Recall the analogy to math—we show our work. We write a brief to persuade a judge, not to survey the law. An appellate court doesn't want a "law review" article. Rather, it wants to know how the law, as applied to our facts, mandates the outcome we advocate. Appellate judges are *usually* more interested in doing "justice" than in "doing jurisprudence." If the court concludes that our client's cause is right and just, and that our adversary's is wrong and unjust, we'll probably win.

Not surprisingly, writing a brief requires us to set out the key facts of our case, explain the relevant rules involved, and show how these rules, as applied to our facts, result in the outcome we seek. To do this, we cite all facts, explain the legal rule for each issue argued, and state the relevance of every authority cited. We put BaRAC to work. We teach, we persuade. We engage in the delicious *art* of being a lawyer.

Enough with this preview—on to the brief!

Chapter 14

The Appellate Brief

Brief—the only one-word oxymoron.

—Anonymous

§ 14.1   Purpose of Briefs

The brief is the lifeblood of the law. It's the vehicle that transports a lawyer's thoughts to a judge's brain. What we write in a brief, judges are obligated to read. What we write better be right. Rule 32(d) of the Federal Rules of Appellate Procedure (FRAP) requires that "[e]very brief, motion, or other paper filed with the court must be signed by the party filing the paper or, if the party is represented, by one of the party's attorneys." When we sign a brief, our word is our bond—the brief bears our name and reflects on us personally and professionally.

The brief *is* our case. It's the first glimpse judges get of our client and of us. It's a structured document, supported by reason and common sense, which, if persuasive, takes the judges by the hand and leads them to rule in our favor. As one court explained:

> It is the duty of counsel to prepare appellate briefs so as to acquaint the Court with the material facts, the points of law involved, and the legal arguments supporting the positions of the respective parties.... When points, positions, facts and supporting authorities are omitted from the brief, a court is entitled to believe that such are waived, abandoned, or deemed by counsel to be unworthy.... [I]t is not the function of the Court to rebrief an appeal.

Polyglycoat Corp. v. Hirsch Distributors, Inc., 443 So. 2d 958, 960 (Fla. Dist. Ct. App. 1983).

§ 14.2   Purpose of Procedural Rules
Regarding Briefs

As court documents, briefs must conform to rules of appellate procedure. For example, briefs filed with United States circuit courts must comply with the Federal Rules of Appellate Procedure (FRAP) and any "local" circuit rules. Briefs filed with state courts must comply with both state and local rules. For example, rule 9.210(b) of the Florida Rules of Appellate Procedure requires an initial (petitioner's or appellant's) brief to "contain the following, in order:"

(1) A table of contents listing the issues presented for review, with references to pages.

(2) A table of citations with cases listed alphabetically, statutes and other authorities, and the pages of the brief on which each citation appears....

(3) A statement of the case and of the facts, which shall include the nature of the case, the course of the proceedings, and the disposition in the lower tribunal. References to the appropriate volume and pages of the record or transcript shall be made.

(4) A summary of argument, suitably paragraphed, condensing succinctly, accurately, and clearly the argument actually made in the body of the brief. It should not be a mere repetition of the headings under which the argument is arranged. It should seldom exceed 2 and never 5 pages.

(5) Argument with regard to each issue including the applicable appellate standard of review.

(6) A conclusion, of not more than 1 page, setting forth the precise relief sought.

Judges enforce order (and keep their sanity) through procedural rules like those above governing the brief's format and content. If we break these rules we invite, and deserve, the judge's wrath. As one judge warned in no uncertain terms:

> Since appellate judges are not haruspices [1], they are unable to decide cases by reading goats' entrails. They instead must rely on lawyers and litigants to submit briefs that present suitably developed argumentation with appropriate citations to applicable precedents and to the record below. A party who honors the minimum standards of acceptable appellate advocacy only in the breach frustrates effective review and thereby jeopardizes its appeal.
>
> . . .
>
> Procedural rules are important for two overarching reasons. One reason is that rules ensure fairness and orderliness. They ensure fairness by providing litigants with a level playing field. They ensure orderliness by providing courts with a means for the efficient administration of crowded dockets. In both these respects rules facilitate the tricornered communications that link the opposing parties with each other and with the court.
>
> The second overarching reason why procedural rules are important has a functional orientation: rules establish a framework that helps courts to assemble the raw material that is essential for forging enlightened decisions. In an appellate venue, for example, rules provide the mechanism by which the court, removed from the battlefield where the trial has been fought, gains the information that it requires to set the issues in context and pass upon them. When a party seeking appellate review fails to comply with the rules in one or more substantial respects, its failure thwarts this effort and deprives the appellate court of the basic tools that the judges of the court need to carry out this task.
>
> . . .
>
> The parties to an appeal must recognize that rules are not mere annoyances, to be swatted aside like so many flies but, rather, that rules lie near the epicenter of the judicial process. This case shows why that is so; indeed, we have canvassed the appellant's asserverational array mainly to demonstrate that, even if we were inclined to do [the appellant's] homework—and that is not our place—[the appellant's] substantial noncompliance with the rules would hamstring any attempt to review the issues intelligently. Of course, there must be some play in the joints. No one is perfect, and occasional oversights—fribbling infringements of the rules that neither create unfairness to one's adversary nor impair the court's ability to comprehend and scrutinize a party's submissions—ordinarily will not warrant Draconian consequences. But major infractions or patterns of repeated inattention warrant severe decrees. 'In the long run, . . .

---

1. We had to look this one up. "Haruspices" is the plural form of the Latin noun "haruspex." A haruspex is "a diviner in ancient Rome basing his predictions on inspection of the entrails of sacrificial animals." *Websters New Collegiate Dictionary* (1975).

strict adherence to ... procedural requirements ... is the best guarantee of evenhanded administration of the law.' *Mohasco Corp. v. Silver*, 447 U.S. 807, 826 ... (1980).

Reyes-Garcia v. Rodriguez & Del Valle, Inc., 82 F.3d 11, 12–15 (1st Cir. 1996) (dismissing the appeal with prejudice and retaining jurisdiction to consider the appellee's request for sanctions).

We can't let this passage go without noting how well it was written by Judge Selya. Notice the clear topic sentences, i.e.: "Procedural rules are important for two overarching reasons"; the carefully placed transitions, i.e.: "[i]n both these respects," "[o]f course," "[b]ut"; and the vibrant language: "fribbling infringements,"[2] "Draconian consequences," "hamstring," "forging enlightened decisions," and, our favorite, "rules are not mere annoyances, to be swatted aside like so many flies," and the alliterative "asserverational[3] array." Who says the law has to be dry?

Courts mean what they say when it comes to enforcing rules regarding briefs. Not only may a court "dismiss" an appeal for counsel's failure to file a brief conforming to appellate rules, it can also impose "sanctions"—requiring counsel to satisfy *personally* the expenses, costs, and attorneys' fees the opposing party incurred in dealing with a non-compliant brief. Indeed, imposing sanctions against attorneys is proper as "an exercise of the inherent power possessed by the courts." *Sanchez v. Sanchez*, 435 So. 2d 347, 350 (Fla. Dist. Ct. App. 1983). "[S]anctions are an appropriate means of discouraging parties and their counsel from wasting the time of courts and other litigants by prosecuting appeals in ways that deviate from the rules." *Reyes-Garcia*, 82 F.3d at 16.

Also instructive are the court's comments in *Ernest Hass Studio, Inc. v. Palm Press, Inc.*, 164 F.3d 110, 111 (2d Cir. 1999). In *Hass*, the court imposed an award of attorneys' fees, to be paid by counsel *personally*, as a sanction for filing a deficient brief. The court found that the brief left the reader "without a hint of the legal theory proposed as a basis for reversal" and "create[d] utter confusion...." *Id.* at 112. "Appellant's Brief," the court continued, was "at best an invitation to the court to scour the record, research any legal theory that [came] to mind, and serve generally as an advocate for appellant. We decline the invitation." *Id.*

Indeed, courts are so fed up with shoddy briefs that some are issuing "Orders to Show Cause" why briefs should not be "stricken." For example, Florida's First District Court of Appeal issues such orders, commanding a lawyer who has violated format rules to explain why that brief should not be treated as if it had never been filed. The lawyer must answer that order within ten days by submitting a written response and a corrected brief. Who among us would proudly present one of these orders to our client?

The bottom line: judges expect us, in submitting briefs, to conform with all procedural rules and standards of professionalism.[4] If we breach these rules or standards, we face, and deserve, the judge's sanctions.

---

2. Fribble means to trifle or fool away—as in "she spent the whole afternoon fribbling instead of doing her homework."

3. Apparently from the word "asseverate," which means to assert strongly or seriously.

4. *See* Chapter 13, § 13.2 and Chapter 27 for more detail regarding professionalism.

§ 14.3 How Not to Write a Brief: A Dozen Ways to Lose an Appeal

Any discussion of the purpose of a brief and rules regarding briefs would be incomplete without hearing from Judge Alex Kozinski of the Ninth Circuit Court of Appeals. In a lecture entitled "The Wrong Stuff," he tells how to *lose* an appeal.[5] We, too, have ideas on this, garnered from interviews with appellate judges and years of experience. The following is an amalgamation of the best twelve sure-fire ways to signal to the court that our brief *stinks*.

The Dirty Dozen

(1) Write the biggest, fattest, ugliest brief possible.

Judges we've interviewed confirm that the best way to broadcast that our case is a loser is to write the biggest, fattest, ugliest brief possible. Why say in five pages what we can say in 55? Why slim our case down to two or three pointed, relevant issues—which we might win—when we can bloat our brief with 10 or 12 losers? Throw in the kitchen sink; dilute a perfectly good point with five or six stinkers. Take Goethe's advice: "When ideas fail, words come in very handy." The more the merrier.

(2) Amuse the judge by making our brief impossible to read.

As teachers (as do judges), we just love it when we can't read a brief, or several pages, because the staple blocks the writing; the print is smudged; the print is too light; the paper is so flimsy that it keels over; the type comes off the page onto our hands; or pages are inserted upside-down, out of order, doubled, or just plain missing. The brief *itself* shows us just how much care the writer took in preparing it.

(3) Destroy our credibility before the judge even reads a word by cheating on the page limit and font size.

Computers have added so much fun to the practice of law. With them, we can choose from a seemingly unlimited number of font sizes and styles and cram a 50 page brief into 20 pages. What's more, we can use microprint for footnotes and add, undetected, an extra 30 or so pages. Of course, the rules of procedure say this is a no-no and specify *exactly* the font size and spacing of our brief. But why follow them? Where's the creativity in sticking by the rules?

As Judge Kozinski instructs:

> Chiseling on the type size and such has two wonderful advantages: First, it lets you cram in more words, and when judges see a lot of words they immediately think: LOSER, LOSER. You might as well write it in big bold letters on the cover of your brief. But there is also a second advantage: It tells the judges that

---

5. The text of Judge Kozinski's lecture, "The Wrong Stuff," appears at 1992 B.Y.U. L. Rev. 325. It's required reading in our course. Although Judge Kozinski does not delineate categories of "rottenness" as we've done here, he does address either directly or indirectly the first eight of these "dirty dozen." We thank him for granting us permission to quote portions of his article here.

the lawyer is the type of sleazeball who is willing to cheat on a small procedural rule and therefore probably will lie about the record or forget to cite controlling authority.[6]

(4) Bury our winning argument among a heap of losers.

This is a corollary to rule (1)—write the biggest, fattest, ugliest brief possible. Judges just love a good egg hunt and don't mind it at all when they have to search through page after page to find the *relevant* issue. The more they have to dig, the more they appreciate just what we've done. They'll be sure to share their appreciation with us, one way or the other.

(5) Write our argument so that it is completely unintelligible.

Here are the best five ways to write an unintelligible brief:

(a) Make all paragraphs at least a page long or longer. Judges love the challenge of climbing these walls of words and figuring out just what the heck we're trying to say. They love reading line after line with no rest and don't mind at all that we haven't taken the time to refine our thoughts into distinct paragraphs. Who needs that pesky "tab" key anyway? And isn't stream of consciousness writing much more fun than that stodgy BaRAC style?

(b) Turn all active verbs into nominalizations. "Decided" becomes "made a decision"; "agreed" becomes "reached an agreement"; etc. But don't stop here. Go further: edit out any vibrant language that might keep the judges awake, and replace it with dull, dull, dull "legalese" and "bureaucratese." By commencing in this type of hereinbefore mentioned form of written discourse, we can thereby rest with all assurance that our brief on appeal will be made increasingly longer and that the judges who will be making a determination in our case will in fact be able to partake of their daily allotment of forty winks.

(c) Sneak in sentence fragments. They make reading. Fun and challenging. They also confuse. The issues and keep judges. On their toes.

(d) Drop subjects from sentences, and play the "guess who I'm talking about" game with judges. Or, make the subject unintelligible by relying on "it" so much that it becomes unclear what "it" is.

(e) Rely solely on spell-checking computer programs to catch mistakes. Aft tear awl, anty err ores at wee dew knot ketch will a moose the judge. Four exam pile: "pubic forum" instead off "public forum"; "cod" instead off "code"—that sore off think.

(6) Distract the judge by picking a fight with opposing counsel.

Judges just love getting into the middle of a good fight; after all, they *live* to solve disputes. So, instead of limiting the argument to the merits of our case, attack our opposing counsel—figuratively, of course. Call him or her vile names; say what horrible things he or she has done—in this case or in any other. Go ahead and take up a whole lot of space in the brief by doing this. After all, how much of the merits of our case does the judge *really* need to know?

---

6. *Id.* at 327.

Judge Kozinski tells us how he responds to such "entertainment":

> I often find myself chortling with delight when I read a passage such as this from a recent appellee's brief:
>
> > With all due respect for my colleague, I have to tell this court that it's been told an incredible fairy tale, packed with lies and misrepresentations.
>
> Of course, the other lawyer responded in kind. Pretty soon I found myself cheering for the lawyers and forgot all about the legal issues.[7]

(7) Amuse the judge by picking on his good friend, the trial judge.

Go ahead and vent on the trial judge. Say something bad about him or her just to spice up the argument. Or, show subtle contempt by referring to the court as "the court *below*," "the *lower* court," or "the *mistaken* court." Imagine the chuckle the trial court will get when the appellate judge shows him or her our brief. As Judge Kozinski notes:

> District judges love to laugh at themselves, and you can be sure that the next time you appear in his [or her] courtroom, the judge will find some way of thanking you for the moment of mirth you provided him [or her].[8]

(8) Ignore the law, cite and quote irrelevant materials, and put anything remotely relevant into long block quotations.

Go ahead and assume that the judges know all the law relevant to our case. This makes our brief so much easier to write. All we need do is state the conclusions we want the court to reach and let the judges do all the work finding the law. After all, don't they, not we, write the opinion in the case? Aren't they, not we, public servants? What do their law clerks do, anyway?

Now, there will be a judge, from time to time, who does not appreciate our style. For example, the judge in *Hamblen v. County of Los Angeles*, 803 F.2d 462, 465 (9th Cir. 1986), did not appreciate counsel's brief and imposed *double* costs *and* attorneys' fees as sanctions. The court commented:

> Aside from its form, the substance of the brief is irresponsibly frivolous.... [Counsel's] entire argument, consisting of bare legal conclusions and fragmented, unsupported factual assertions, is a textbook example of feckless lawyering.[[9]] It put the appellees to unnecessary and unwarranted expense in preparing responses and appearing at oral argument.

Id.

Okay ... so what if we *do* feel the urge to throw some law into the mix? (After all, we didn't go through three years of law school for nothing). Well, let's not limit ourselves to only the *relevant* law. Just because the legal issue might be boring doesn't mean our brief has to be. Spice it up with other material, something *we* find interesting. And,

---

7. *Id.* at 328.

8. *Id.* at 329.

9. What a great phrase! "Feckless" means "ineffectual, weak, worthless, irresponsible"—OUCH! *Webster's New Collegiate Dictionary* (1975).

whenever possible, put all our discussion of rules, relevant or not, into long, single-spaced block quotations. Judges expect this—why else do most of them wear glasses?

(9) Don't bother filing our brief on time — the judges are in no hurry to read it anyway.

Judges understand how busy lawyers are; after all, most judges became judges just to get away from the pressures and stresses of practicing law. Judges are state or federal employees and will happily reschedule their calendars to meet our desires. Do they not work for us?

Warnings like the following just come from "insensitive" judges, who care more about our clients than about us:

> We find there is no excuse for an attorney's failure to request an extension of time when it becomes apparent that a brief will not be timely filed.... [Moreover, courts] do not consider counsel's 'heavy case load' good cause for requesting numerous extensions.

Caudle v. State, 478 So. 2d 359, 360–61 (Fla. Dist. Ct. App. 1985). Come on!

(10) Cite headnotes.

Judges realize that lawyers just don't have time to read all of the cases we've cited in the brief. Some cases can be *really* long. They don't mind at all when we rely on and cite headnotes instead of the case itself. After all, the headnotes are correct *most* of the time. It's not the headnote's fault that it was written by an employee of a publishing company (and no offense to that company), rather than by the court. By citing the headnote, we let the judge know how busy we are and that we just haven't had time to read, let alone analyze, the case.

Now some judges actually expect us to *read* the cases we've cited. One "grumpy" judge had this to say about headnotes. (No doubt having their feelings hurt, the folks at the publishing company did not include this passage *as* a headnote.)

> We cannot repeat too often that headnotes are not holdings. We recognize that lawyers are busy people, but careful case analysis is required and frequently reveals the headnote to be a misleading guide to the holding of the court in a particular case.

Forbes v. National Ratings Bureau, Inc., 223 So. 2d 764, 765 (Fla. Dist. Ct. App. 1969).

But this judge failed to realize that citing headnotes can lead to very interesting arguments. For example, headnote 8 in *State v. Bankhead*, 514 P.2d 800, 801 (Utah 1973), reads that " 'dominion and control' *either* means that drug be found on person of accused *or* that accused must have had sole and exclusive possession of narcotic." [Emphasis added.] However, the actual text of the opinion corresponding to headnote 8 reads: "Dominion and control *neither* means that the drug be found on the person of the accused *nor* that the accused must have had sole and exclusive possession of the narcotic." 514 P.2d at 803 [emphasis added]. Isn't this cute?

Finally, and here's a real tribute, by relying solely on headnotes, we might be able to eliminate some pesky grounds of appeal. Headnotes don't always include all relevant aspects of the reported case.

For example, in *Pottinger v. City of Miami*, 810 F. Supp. 1551, 1570 n.30 (S.D. Fla. 1992),[10] the court held "that the City's seizure and destruction of plaintiffs' personal property violates the fifth amendment, which prohibits the taking of private property for public use without just compensation. U.S. Const. amend. V." However, not a word about this finding, or about the Fifth Amendment, appears in any headnote to the case. This means that counsel who read only the headnotes miss an important argument that could be a winner. By not reading the *case*, we may have narrowly pulled our case from the jaws of victory. Won't our clients be grateful?

(11) Misquote and miscite.

There's nothing like a good misquotation or miscitation to spiff up a brief. After all, anyone can *just copy* words from a case or transcript. It takes great effort, which the judges will appreciate, to riddle our brief with misquotations and miscitations. By doing this, we've invited the judges to play "caught ya." Judges just love, as do their clerks, to look up every citation and quotation we've included. And, at oral argument, they'll be sure to tell us just how much they've enjoyed this little game.

(12) Order the court around by telling it that it "must" do this and that.

If all else fails, and it looks like we may win the case, here's what we do: We write our brief in a commanding, disrespectful tone. Tell the court that it "must" do so and so. Give it orders; be forceful. After all, the judges will appreciate that we're stepping up to the plate and will admire our "take charge" attitude. They will, no doubt, be relieved that *we* are now in command, and they can therefore forget all about our case. Indeed, they may be so grateful that they may pass our name and brief along to the Professional Responsibility Committee of the Bar, so that they too, can admire what we've done.

§ 14.4   Overview

Enough about how to lose; let's now see how to write a *winning* brief! In the Chapters below, we discuss the following sections of the brief:

Chapter 15   Statement of the Case and Facts
Chapter 16   Standards of Review
Chapter 17   Questions Presented
Chapter 18   Argument Headings
Chapter 19   Summary of Argument
Chapter 20   The Argument
Chapter 21   The Other Parts of the Brief
  • Caption Page
  • Table of Contents
  • Table of Authorities
  • Opinion Below
  • Jurisdiction

---

10. We address the *Pottinger* case in Chapter 5, § 5.7(a).

- Constitutional and Statutory Provisions
- Conclusion
- Appendix
- Certificate of Service

We also include sample briefs in Chapters 36, 37, and 38.

We've set forth these seven Chapters in the order that we usually create the "section" they address in writing our brief. However, creating a brief is an extremely personal process. Some writers begin, for example, with the "big" picture by writing the Summary of Argument section. By doing this, they concentrate on their theory of the case and the main facts. In contrast, others wait and write the Summary last. Their rationale is that they can't truly understand their theory and main facts until they've worked through their argument by completing all other sections of the brief.

Regardless of which section we tackle first, writing a brief can be a rather maddening exercise. Not only must the brief be technically accurate, i.e., all quotations, citations, and factual assertions must be correct; it also must be easy to read. This means that all sections must be internally consistent and meld readily with all other sections. The only way to write a "seamless" brief is to edit, edit, edit. And, when we think we're done, we edit again.[11]

Unfortunately, the often-quoted image sports journalist Gene Fowler paints of writing is all too true: "Writing is easy. All you do is stare at a blank sheet of paper until drops of blood form on your forehead."

Well, maybe it's not *that* bad. Let's see.

---

11. We discuss editing techniques in Chapter 24.

Chapter Review
The Appellate Brief

✓ Consult the relevant Rules of Appellate Procedure before writing the brief and follow them.

✓ Give the judges a break. Streamline the brief wherever possible; there's no need to take up every inch of allowable space.

✓ Comply strictly with all format rules, especially those regarding page length, font size, lines per page, and binding. If the brief is to be filed electronically, comply with those rules to the letter.

✓ Clearly separate distinct arguments and, whenever possible, place the winning argument first.

✓ Use clear and grammatically correct language. Employ short sentences and short paragraphs. Edit and proofread. Then edit and proofread *again*.

✓ Don't make personal attacks on opposing counsel or judges.

✓ Explain the law and facts involved; cite relevant authorities and the Record on Appeal.

✓ Meet all filing deadlines.

✓ Don't cite headnotes.

✓ Make certain all citations and quotations are accurate.

✓ Use a respectful tone.

✓ Comply with all procedural rules and standards of professionalism. Remember — your name and signature will be on that brief!

Chapter 15

Statement of the Case and Facts

"Let us take things as we find them: let us not attempt to distort them into what they are not.... We cannot make facts. All our wishing cannot change them. We must use them."

— John Henry Cardinal Newman

"Every argument, in court or out, whether delivered over the supper table or made at coffee break, can be reduced to a story. An argument, like a house, yes, like the houses of the three little pigs, has structure. Whether it will fall, whether it can be blown down when the wolf huffs and puffs, depends upon how the house has been built. The strongest structure for any argument is *story*."

— Gerry Spence[1]

---

1. Gerry Spence, *How to Argue and Win Every Time*, 113 (1995).

§ 15.1   Purpose and Context of the Statement of the Case and Facts

Purpose. Through the Statement of the Case and Facts ("Statement"), we persuade the court to rule in our favor by accurately, yet persuasively, telling our client's "story." If we get the court on our side from the start, the court may find a way to rule in our favor. As Saleilles once said, "One wills at the beginning the result; one finds the principle afterwards; such is the genesis of all juridical construction."

Context. In every appeal, the trial court clerk transmits a Record of proceedings to the appellate court.[2] The Record usually consists of all pleadings, motions, and other documents filed in the trial court; the court's opinion; all exhibits and evidence; and testimony transcripts. The Record is the appellate court's sole "official" source of information concerning the trial court's proceedings.

In the Statement, we present the relevant parts of the Record in story-like fashion. The Statement precedes the Summary of Argument and Argument sections but comes after the Table of Contents and the Question(s) Presented sections. The Statement breathes life into our case and reminds the court of the human element involved.

However, the Statement is not the place to *argue*. Indeed, a court may strike a brief containing argument in the Statement. *See Williams v. Winn-Dixie Stores, Inc.*, 548 So. 2d 829, 830 (Fla. Dist. Ct. App. 1989) (striking appellant's initial brief and noting the court's inherent power to strike Statements that are "unduly argumentative and contain matters immaterial and impertinent to the controversy between the parties.").

§ 15.2   Format

The Statement is a persuasive, *but not argumentative*, narrative written in paragraph form. We follow any sentence containing a factual assertion with a citation, described below, to the Record.

§ 15.2(a)   Use Pinpoint Citation for Record Cites

Graphic 15.2	Cite the Record as Follows
record citation placement in a sentence	example:
at the end	It rained. (R.3.)
in the middle	It rained (R.3), and then it snowed. (R.5-6.) *Note:* we do not include a final period within the parentheses enclosing the

---

2. Please *see* Chapter 13, § 13.6 for further information concerning the Record on Appeal.

	record cite when the record cite is followed in this manner by further text.
two citations at the end	It rained, and the wind blew. (R.3, 5.)
end of sentence but before a case citation	(R.3); *Sam v. Deli*, 999 U.S. 555, 557 (2002). *Note:* we do not include a final period within the parentheses enclosing the record cite when the record cite is followed in this manner by further text.
do not use *id.* to refer to a record citation	It rained. (R.3.) As a result, the water level of the stream rose four inches. (R.3.)

We can't stress enough the importance of substantiating each factual assertion by providing "pinpoint" citations to the Record. Indeed, we write the Statement so that we follow *each* sentence, except for those requesting relief, with a Record citation.

Here's what one court said about the appellant's failure to provide such "pinpoint" citations: (Please note, as our annotations point out, that the court also employed the BaRAC design in discussing this issue.)

bold assertion   "We write to call attention to the fact that the citations to the record contained in the initial brief are also inadequate. Rule 9.210(b)(3),

rule   Florida Rules of Appellate Procedure, requires references to the appropriate pages of the record or transcript. Appellant's statement of

application   the case and facts fails to comply with this rule. For example, appellant uses three pages to summarize the testimony he gave at trial. There is not one reference to the record throughout those three pages. At the end of the summary of the testimony, appellant has a parenthetical reference which states 'Williams' testimony, as stated above, is at

conclusion   transcript volume 1, page 94, line 22 to page 160, line 12.' One citation to 66 pages of testimony to support three pages of factual recitation is inadequate for purposes of review of the merits of this appeal."

Williams v. Winn-Dixie Stores, Inc., 548 So. 2d 829, 830 (Fla. Dist. Ct. App. 1989) (granting the appellee's motion to "strike" the appellant's brief).[3]

The added benefit of following each sentence with a Record citation is that this practice keeps us "honest." We won't be able to find a citation for assumptions or for our legal opinions of the case.

---

3. In the *Winn-Dixie* case the appellant was ordered to serve an amended initial brief within ten days which conformed to the court's rules regarding briefs and specifically including pinpoint citations to the record on appeal to substantiate each statement made in the brief. Imagine trying to explain *that* order to your client or employer and spending your *own* time on evenings and weekends to write an amended brief, since you could not ethically charge the client for your own misconduct. And, further imagine how this impacts your reputation with that court, your client, and employer!

§ 15.2(b)   Use Subheadings Where Necessary

Where the Statement is complex, i.e., involving a host of procedural and factual matters, subheadings are extremely helpful. By using subheadings, we alert our reader to a shift in topic or time. These subheadings need not be full sentences and can take the following form:

Procedural History

Events Leading to the Arrest [or other action]

Events Subsequent to the Arrest [or other action]

These subheadings, of course, are not exhaustive. Our goal in using them is to help us tell our client's story.

§ 15.3   Developing a Theory of the Case

"There is nothing more horrible than the murder of a beautiful theory by a brutal gang of facts."

— La Rochefoucald

There are facts and then there are *facts*. Every fact carries with it an agenda, a hidden point of view. There's just no escaping the bias inherent when the observer is the one telling what he or she has observed. Consider the following:

Graphic 15.3	Big, But Not Bad

Since you asked, I'll tell you what really happened in that "First Little Pig" incident. The whole thing started when I was minding my own business, strolling through the woods. Out of nowhere, this little girl in a cape and carrying a basket, ran right smack into me. She wasn't even looking where she was going, and she didn't even apologize. I sure remember that cape — red, made of wool, and scratchy. Now ordinarily, I'm a pretty hardy fellow, but not when it comes to wool. Stirs up my allergies, big time. My nose started to swell up and itch. My eyes began to water, and then the sneezing started. "Sneezeitis giganticus," the doctors call it. Runs in my family. Bad news. I knew the signs; if I didn't get help, I'd sneeze myself to death. We lost Uncle Fred that way. I really needed a phone. This was a 911 event.

Well, I looked around and the only sign of civilization, if you could even call it that, was a house made of straw. The nameplate on the front door read "First Little Pig: Brother of Three." Hoping against hope that this Pig fellow had a phone, I knocked politely on the door. No answer. Then, thinking that maybe my knock wasn't loud enough, and not wanting to just barge in, I hollered as best I could being all stuffed up as I was, "Mister First Little Pig, Mr. First Little Pig, are you in? Please, sir, may I use your phone?" Still no answer. I tried again: "Mr. Pig, Mr. Pig, please let me…."

> Then it happened. A sneezeitis sneeze seized upon me. Before I could turn away, an eruption of volcanic proportion spewed forth — the mother of all sneezes. I was real sorry that the house got in the way. It's amazing how straw crumbles. When I finally caught my breath, there was that First Little Pig, dead. He'd been there the whole time. And you know what? He had *two* phones.

There we have it: Wolf's view of what *really* happened in that fateful encounter. All of these years that view had been kept from us, silenced by the wealthy, pig-industrialists (making their fortune in building construction), who had been controlling the media. Contrary to what we'd been told, Wolf had no intent to kill; he was just an unfortunate victim of circumstances. He was in dire straits, in the throes of a medical emergency. All he wanted was to borrow the phone. It wasn't his fault that he had this terrible allergy. After all, it ran in his family. A full pardon seems in order here.

The very telling of the story demonstrates the injustice that history has heaped upon the "Big Bad Wolf." (Whose *real* name is "Bigdid Wolf." He was named in honor of his maternal grandmother, Lucille Bigdid.) Even without including any legal argument, Mr. B. Wolf convinces us that he's been wronged. He's captured the very essence of writing a Statement: he's told a convincing story and by *juxtaposing* facts,[4] has allowed us, as readers, to reach our own legal and "moral" conclusions.

For example, we can conclude that the First Little Pig was rude (very rude), whereas Wolf, even under these extreme pressures, was the poster-animal for grace and manners. After all, Wolf "knocked on the door," and politely called out to ascertain whether anyone was at home, rather than barge in. The First Little Pig, however, who had "been there the whole time," didn't even have the courtesy to answer the door or to respond to Wolf's needful pleas. The inference is that even though a tragic accident occurred here, this rude little porker got exactly what he deserved.[5]

In our opinion, and in the opinion of an overwhelming majority of the judges we've interviewed, the Statement is one of the most important parts of the brief. It's here that we tell our story, and in so doing, highlight the justice and fairness of our position. Our opponents, of course, will tell that story differently, highlighting the aspects of the case favoring their client. As the Third Little Pig tells it, Wolf didn't accidentally sneeze: he deliberately "huffed and puffed." The judge has the awesome responsibility of reading both stories and determining which one is supported by the truth, law, and justice.

But, in telling our story, we must be absolutely accurate. A lawyer may not "[k]nowingly make a false statement of material fact or law" to a court.[6] Both state and federal rules of procedure mandate that the Statement be written to reflect a "high

---

4. We address juxtaposition in detail in § 15.4(b).

5. Of course, Wolf could do without asking any rhetorical questions; but after all, he's not a lawyer — not yet, anyway.

6. Model Rules of Prof'l Conduct R. 3.3(a)(1).

standard of professionalism." FRAP (11th Cir.) 28-2(I)(ii). This means we include even harmful facts, i.e., facts which are unfavorable to our case. As Thomas Huxley put it: "God give me strength to face a fact though it slay me." FRAP 28-2 mandates that we "state the facts accurately, those favorable and those unfavorable to the party." *Id.*

In addition to the ethical considerations, if we don't "fess up" to the harmful facts in our case, it is a cinch that our opposing counsel will enlighten the court about them. Thus, from a strategic standpoint, there are three important reasons not to omit or misrepresent harmful facts. First, after learning about the harmful facts, either from our opposing counsel or by its own research, the court is then likely to mistrust everything else we write in our brief or say during oral argument. Second, our failure to include harmful facts makes us appear intimidated by those facts and may thus lend them even more credence than they deserve. Third, by not addressing the harmful facts, we lose our opportunity to present them in their best light by presenting *our* interpretation of their effect on the case.

Mainly, however, we tell the court the unvarnished truth because we are professionals, and because it is the right thing to do. We have little to gain and much to lose (our reputations, our case, our jobs, our clients, our Bar membership) by omitting or misrepresenting the facts to a court. Indeed, as the following case illustrates, failure to include a "full and fair statement of facts" can lead to harsh consequences. *See Thompson v. State*, 588 So. 2d 687, 689 (Fla. Dist. Ct. App. 1991).

In the *Thompson* case, appellant challenged the sufficiency of the evidence supporting his conviction for attempted second-degree murder and three counts of aggravated battery. "With full knowledge that his only arguments on appeal concerned the sufficiency of the evidence," appellant distorted the facts by omitting critical information concerning his attack on "C.L.," the victim of the attempted murder. *Id.* at 687. As the appellate court explained:

> The reviewing court relies quite heavily upon the statement of facts contained in the initial brief. This proposition is of necessity particularly true in a case challenging the sufficiency of the evidence. An appellant's statement of the facts must not only be objective, but must be cast in a form appropriate to the standard of review applicable to the matters presented. Appellant's statement of the facts deletes a prior threat made by appellant against [C.L.], appellant's act of breaking down the door to the home, appellant's use of a metal bar to beat [C.L.], appellant's administration of head wounds requiring 40 stitches to close, and finally the state of bleeding unconsciousness to which [C.L.] was rendered by appellant's savage attack upon her with a weapon.

Id. at 689. Good grief!

After casting the facts in this light; i.e., "the state of bleeding unconsciousness to which [C.L.] was rendered by appellant's savage attack upon her with a weapon," the court, not surprisingly, affirmed the appellant's conviction. *Id.* We can never forget that judges, too, are human. Although they must remain impartial, they're not made of stone.

Further, not only must we tell the judge the complete facts, we must also identify *as inferences*, any inferences we've drawn. We never, either through act or omission, misrepresent the truth. We face the stark reality that sometimes the facts are, well, just plain bad. Sometimes an ugly duckling is *really* an ugly duckling.

§ 15.4   Writing the Statement of Facts

§ 15.4(a)   Think Like a Movie Director

In conveying the facts of our case to the court, we think *visually*, as directors filming a movie of our case. Good movies have a consistent theme—a premise or viewpoint which comes shining through all aspects of plot and character development. A good movie also has a defined beginning, middle, and ending.

As a good movie, a good Statement is *thematic*. It springs from, and is supported by, a theory or dominant theme. That theory or theme rings so clearly that it resonates throughout all aspects of our story (and through all sections of our brief). The reader cannot help but hear that we are indeed entitled to the relief we seek. There could be no other just result.

Theory of the case. We cannot, however, create a convincing Statement without first developing a theory of our case. That theory must be absolutely consistent with both the law supporting the relief we seek and with all of our facts. Through our theory, we reduce our case to its most pristine elements. We simplify, and through that simplicity, we create the most compelling of arguments. As Irving Younger explained:

> It has long been understood … that simplicity marks the master.... On the ceiling of the Sistine Chapel, Michelangelo painted a picture of God transmitting the spark of life to Adam and fashioned an image of awesome power. What is it? Simply God's finger touching Adam's. A six-year old can understand it. Only Michelangelo could create it.[7]

And herein lies what we call the "Catch-22" of brief writing. Before we can write a convincing, simplistic, theory-based Statement, we must know all the legal arguments we'll present in our brief. But before we can know all the legal arguments, we must know our theory of the case. But before we can know our theory of the case, we must know the relevant law and the facts. But before we can know that, we must know....

How then *do* we write a Statement? Carefully, very carefully … and in segments. Writing the Statement is an ongoing process. First, we write a draft, including all possibly relevant aspects of the case. Then, we work on the arguments springing from those facts. Next, we go back and review the facts, pruning and expanding where necessary, judging what we keep, add, and extract by what is and isn't relevant to our argument. We become very familiar with the Record. If, in reading through the Record on Appeal we have taken careful notes, we can more easily locate facts to support any additional arguments our research may uncover.

Finally, when we think our argument is complete, we review the facts yet again. This time, we *match* the facts we used in our Argument section to those we've included in

---

7. Irving Younger, *In Praise of Simplicity*, 1984 N.Z. L.J. 277 (1984).

our Statement. We add to our Statement whatever facts we've used in our Argument but haven't yet included in our Statement. We also reassess what facts we haven't used in our Argument and determine whether we can exclude them from our Statement. As Blaise Pascal recognized: "The last thing one discovers in composing a work is what to put first."[8]

Moreover, in writing our Statement, we, as do good directors, carefully consider how to portray shifts in time, the movement of action from place to place, and the transition (where necessary) from one point of view to another. We write as "visually" as possible, painting a picture of the characters and events. As Gerry Spence explained:

> Words that do not create images should be discarded. Words that have no intrinsic emotional or visual context ought to be avoided. Words that are directed to the sterile intellectual head-place should be abandoned. Use simple words, words that create pictures and action and that generate feeling.[9]

§ 15.4(b)   The Fine Art of Juxtaposition

As good movie directors, we portray only the facts relevant to our story. We don't put our readers to sleep by including every excruciating detail. Nor do we pound them over the head with our viewpoint. Instead of telling our readers what to believe, we let them reach that conclusion on their own. We lead them to the gate, open it, invite them to follow us, and then let them do their own walking.

We allow readers to feel as if they've reached their *own* conclusions by using the fine art of juxtaposition. Through juxtaposition, we simply state two or more seemingly inconsistent "facts" and allow the reader to reach the conclusion that "something is wrong here." The beauty of the juxtaposition is that we need not state the point we want our readers to reach; they'll get there on their own. As Blaise Pascal observed: "We are usually convinced more easily by reasons we have found ourselves than by those which have occurred to others."

For example, if we want our readers to conclude that the trial judge erred in reaching a finding of fact, we *could* state: "The trial judge erred in finding that 'the sun was shining brightly' on November 21." However, we would have a hard time finding that particular "fact" in the Record. We might find a Record citation to the judge's comment, but the assertion that the judge erred is not a "fact." We will not find a statement in the Record where the trial judge admitted that he erred in making this finding. There is no such "fact." What we are calling a "fact" is a legal conclusion, an argument. Since the Statement must be "objective," it *cannot* contain such conclusions. How, then, do we spark the idea that the judge erred, without *arguing* that the judge erred? We use juxtaposition.

Here's what we write:

---

8. Blaise Pascal, *Pensees* 347 (A. J. Krailsheimer trans., Penguin Classics 1967).
9. Spence, *supra*, at 104.

Graphic 15.4(b)(1)   Example of Using Juxtaposition

Although clouds filled the sky (R.3), rain was falling at a rate of two inches per hour (R.5), and an eye-witness stated that "this was the worst storm" he had ever seen (R.6), the trial court ruled that "the sun was shining brightly." (R.7.)

Our readers draw their own conclusions: the court erred; there's no way the sun was shining brightly with that kind of storm going on! We've achieved our purpose without arguing. We've allowed our readers to walk right in.

Wolf v. State. Let's put these principles to work by returning to another version of our "Three Little Pigs" case, *Wolf v. State.* Let's assume that Wolf has now been found guilty of *murdering* the First Little Piggy in that blowing-down-the-straw-house incident. Wolf, however, claims he had no intent to kill. He simply had to sneeze. He's now appealing his conviction, claiming that the trial court erred in failing to instruct the jury on excusable homicide. Let's look at a few paragraphs from the parties' Statements, below, and answer the following questions:

- What inferences do we, as readers, draw from these passages?
- What points have the writers stressed?
- What points have they attempted to sublimate (i.e., hide in plain sight)?
- What is the theory of each party's case?

Note that each Statement begins with the party's theory of the case and his express (or implied) request for relief. Although each initial paragraph contains argument, it does so only in the permissible context of asking the court either to affirm or reverse the trial court's decision.

Graphic 15.4(b)(2)   Wolf's Statement

This is a case, not of murder, not of criminal intent, but of the tragic consequences of an allergic nose, faulty building construction, and the trial judge's refusal to instruct the jury on excusable homicide.

Alone in the woods, away from home, and in the throes of a life-threatening medical emergency, Defendant B. Wolf, came upon the home of The Pig. (R.2-3.) Politely and gently, Wolf knocked on The Pig's door; no answer. (R.4.) He then called out, as best he could, imploring The Pig to answer and to let him use a phone; still no response. (R.4.) Not wanting to barge in, he cried out for aid yet a third time, when he was overcome with a sneeze he could not control. (R.5-6.) Tragically, that sneeze caused The Pig's straw house to collapse in on itself and on The Pig, who had been home all the while. (R.7.)

Graphic 15.4(b)(3)   **State's Statement**

This is a case of an opportunistic, cold-blooded killer in search of a ham dinner. The trial court correctly found that there was no "excusable homicide" here and properly refused to instruct the jury on that charge.

On the false pretense of "needing to use the phone," Defendant, The Big Bad Wolf, stormed the house of The First Little Piggy, and demanded entry by pounding on the door. (R.2, 4.) Cowering in fear, The Piggy could not respond, and could only watch in horror though the slats of his home as Big Bad, panting savagely, took a great breath, filling his lungs with air. (R.4-5.) Then, exhaling mightily, Big Bad blew down The Piggy's house, killing him instantly. (R.5-6.) Rummaging through the straw remains, Big Bad found, and then devoured, the pink, plump corpse. (R.7.)

If you were the judge, how would you rule?

§ 15.5   A Flow Chart for Writing the Statement

After we've gathered the facts and developed a theory of our case, we tell our story. Do we organize our facts chronologically, incident by incident, or in some other manner? Our advice is to try different schemes until we find the one that works best. To this end, we offer the following flow chart as a convenient organizational tool. However, we stress that this is simply a guide. Some cases may not readily fit this pattern.

Graphic 15.5   **Flow Chart of Statement**

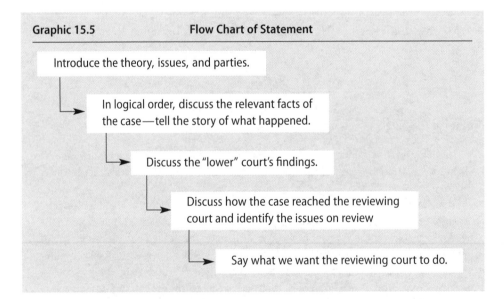

Introduce the theory, issues, and parties.

In logical order, discuss the relevant facts of the case—tell the story of what happened.

Discuss the "lower" court's findings.

Discuss how the case reached the reviewing court and identify the issues on review

Say what we want the reviewing court to do.

Let's look at each of these steps in detail.

§ 15.5(a)　　First: Introduce the Theory, Issues, and Parties

We, not the court's clerk, introduce and explain our case to the court. The judges don't know our client, our issues, or our theory. Although the judges may read the Record on Appeal, they will not independently seek out the facts. Therefore, before launching into a detailed discussion of what happened in our case, we establish, in a paragraph or two, a "context" for our story. We introduce the court to our theory, our client, the issues, and the relief we seek.

As the examples from the *Wolf v. State* case illustrate, establishing our theory at the outset grabs the judge's attention and sets the tone for the story that follows. We know each party's theory simply by reading the opening lines of his Statement:

Graphic 15.5(a)(1)　　　　**Compare These Opening Lines**

"This is a case of an opportunistic, cold-blooded killer in search of a ham dinner. The trial court correctly found that there was no 'excusable homicide' here and properly refused to instruct the jury on that charge."

versus

"This is a case, not of murder, not of criminal intent, but of the tragic consequences of an allergic nose, faulty building construction, and the trial judge's refusal to instruct the jury on excusable homicide."

Advocates are not the only ones who use catchy opening lines to convey the theory of the case. Justices of the United States Supreme Court do it too. For example, Justice Harlan, in *Cohen v. California*, employed an intriguing introduction to the case: "This case may seem at first blush too inconsequential to find its way into our books, but the issue it presents is of no small constitutional significance."[10]

Justice Scalia, in *R.A.V. v. City of St. Paul*,[11] began the Court's opinion, not with a catchy opening line, but with a device as effective — a graphic visual image:

> In the predawn hours of June 21, 1990, petitioner and several other teenagers allegedly assembled a crudely made cross by taping together broken chair legs. They then allegedly burned the cross inside the fenced yard of a black family that lived across the street from the house where petitioner was staying.

This opening compels us to read the case; it grabs our attention. That's exactly what we, as advocates, want to do in the opening lines of our Statement.

---

10. 403 U.S. 15, 15 (1971). At issue in *Cohen* was whether, consistent with the First Amendment, the defendant could be punished for wearing a jacket bearing the words "Fuck the Draft" into a courtroom. The Court held for the defendant, reasoning that "absent a more particularized and compelling reason for its actions, the State may not, consistently with the First and Fourteenth Amendments, make the simple public display here involved of this single four-letter expletive a criminal offense." *Id.* at 26.

11. 505 U.S. 377, 379 (1992).

After our opening lines, we introduce the parties and the legal issues. If a critical authority such as a statute, rule, regulation, or ordinance is involved, we introduce it by quoting its relevant language.

For example, assume that we represented a client who was expelled from a state university for wearing a "costume of hate," a modified version of the Ku Klux Klan uniform. Assume further that the district court of appeal affirmed that expulsion and we are now appealing to the state's supreme court. We might begin our Statement with: "This is a case of a clash between 'political correctness' and First Amendment rights."

We could then write any one of the following three paragraphs introducing our client, the issues, and the law involved:

Graphic 15.5(a)(2)   **3 Different Sample Paragraphs**
                                Introducing Our Case to the Court

---

(1) Petitioner John Doe challenges, as violating his First Amendment rights, the decision of the First District Court of Appeal upholding his expulsion and validating University of Gotham City's Rule 9909. (R.3.) That Rule prohibits.... (R.7.) This Court should hold....

(2) At issue is whether Respondent, the University of Gotham City, can punish Petitioner John Doe, under a University Rule which prohibits "costumes of hate," for wearing a modified version of the "uniform" of the Ku Klux Klan at a public demonstration on campus property. (R.3.) The First District Court of Appeal held the Rule did not violate Doe's First Amendment rights and sustained his one-semester expulsion. (R.3.) This Court should....

(3) After he wore a modified version of the "uniform" of the Ku Klux Klan to a public rally on the University of Gotham City's campus, Petitioner John Doe was expelled from the University for one semester under Rule 9909, which prohibits the wearing of "costumes of hate." (R.3, 7.) At issue is whether his expulsion violated his First Amendment rights to free speech and expression. (R.3.) This Court should hold....

---

§ 15.5(b)   Second: In Logical Order, Discuss the Relevant Facts of the Case — Tell What Happened

Tell the whole story. Next, we discuss the relevant facts in a logical and persuasive (but not argumentative) fashion. If we refer to a fact in any other section of our brief, we mention that fact in our Statement. If, however, our case involves complex facts, such as the results of a study or report, we can refer to that report or study generally in our Statement and save the relevant specifics for our Argument section. (We may also attach the report or study to our brief as an Appendix.)

In logical order, we accurately describe the circumstances surrounding key events, including all relevant — the helpful and the harmful — facts. We have an ethical duty to tell the court the complete story, warts and all.[12]

---

12. *See* ABA Model Rules of Professional Conduct Rule 3.3(a)(1); *see also* ABA Model Code of Professional Responsibility DR7-102(A)(3) and (5).

Cite the Record. Just as we prove a legal rule by citing a case or statute, we prove facts by citing the Record. If we can't cite the Record to verify each assertion, we've likely exaggerated or misrepresented the facts.

For example, assume that the Record states the following: "Doe admitted he was aware of the Anti-Mask Code, and admitted he wore a mask in public." Unless we had additional information, the following statement would be *inaccurate*: "Doe admitted he violated the Anti-Mask Code." No. He admitted only that he had worn the mask in public and that he was "aware" of the Code. He did not admit that he had violated the Code. Similarly, although Wolf admitted that his sneeze ultimately killed the Pig, he did not admit that he *intended* that result.

Because it's easy to extend facts beyond the breaking point to reach unsupported conclusions, we draft our Statement *carefully*. Words are slippery. We guard against using ambiguous terms and unclear sentences. We also verify every fact; if we say a fact appears on a particular Record page, it better be there.

We can refer to the absence of a fact. Although we don't refer to "facts" that aren't in the Record, we can point out the absence of a fact. For example, if our client is appealing his conviction for disorderly conduct, and there was no evidence that he acted inappropriately towards the arresting officer, we could assert: "Although Officer Brown testified to the circumstances leading to Doe's arrest, he did not state or even intimate that Doe attempted to resist the Officer's actions. (R.4-5.)" Further, if we represented the State in *Wolf v. State*, we could assert that "there is no evidence that Wolf called or even attempted to call 911 after the house collapsed in on The Pig."

Use persuasive language. How we characterize actions, of course, depends on who we represent. We use language to paint the exact picture we want the court to see. Returning to *Wolf v. State*, we can portray the same action in vastly different ways.

Did Wolf "visit his neighbor" and "politely knock on the door," or did he "storm the house" and "demand entry by pounding on the door"? Even subtle changes in language impact the image our reader perceives. Our task in writing a Statement is to choose the best words and phrases in telling our client's tale.[13]

For instance, to stress what our client did, or what was done to her, we use precise, exciting, action-packed words. For example, assume that we represent Smith, a victim in a stabbing. We might describe the stabbing as follows: "Jones viciously stabbed Roberta Smith three times in the chest with a foot-long carving knife. (R.5.)" On the other hand, if we represent Jones, we de-emphasize his actions. We write: "The plaintiff was wounded in the incident. (R.5.)" We also de-emphasize what our client has done by using passive voice: "Smith was stabbed by Jones."

We can further de-emphasize our client's actions by using *subordinating* clauses strategically. *Subordination* consists of an "although," "while," or "but" clause followed by a main clause.[14] To de-emphasize an action, we place the damaging fact in the "although" or "while" clause and the favorable fact in the main clause. By putting the subordinate clause first, we stress the favorable fact and not the *un*favorable one.

---

13. Please *see* Section V, Chapters 28-33 on clear and effective writing.

14. We explain this concept in greater detail in Chapter 31, §31.3 and §31.4.

For example, assume that our client, an alcoholic, drinks to excess and is a good worker. To stress his good work and still admit his drinking, we write: "Although Bill drinks, he is a good worker." Or, we state: "Bill drinks, but he is a good worker." Through subordination, we persuade without arguing.

Use short sentences and short paragraphs. A persuasive Statement contains clear sentences and short paragraphs. A judge will get lost in long rambling prose. No judge wants to read a "wall of words." Accordingly, paragraphs should not exceed half a page, and sentences should be short. If, when reading the sentence aloud, we gasp for a breath before reaching the period, the sentence is too long.

Abbreviate repetitive terms. To shorten our Statement, we abbreviate repetitive terms, especially the names of Acts or Laws. For example, the first time we address Florida's Uniform Child Custody Act, we write as follows: Florida Uniform Child Custody Act. Thereafter, refer to it as the Act, or we could use an acronym composed of the first letter of each word.

Use consistent terms. To avoid confusing the judge, we use consistent terms. It's easier for the judge to follow our story if we use the same name for the same party. For example, if we represent Wolf in *Wolf v. State*, we refer to "Wolf" and "The Pig" throughout our Statement. We do not alternately use "Mr. Wolf," "Mr. B. Wolf," and "The Little Piggy." Moreover, although it's good practice to show our clients respect, we save space by calling our client (and the other parties) by their last names, rather than by "Mr.," "Mrs.," "Ms.," or "Miss."

§ 15.5(c)   Third: Address the Relevant Procedural Aspects and, if Relevant, Discuss the Lower Court's Reasoning

Next, we address the procedural aspects of our case and, if relevant, discuss the lower court's holding and reasoning. Remember: the court "reasoned," "acknowledged," "ruled," "found," or "held."[15] It did *not* "admit," "concede," "argue," or "feel." Moreover, a court is an "it," not a "they."

If we represent appellant/petitioner, we point out any relevant inconsistencies in the trial court's reasoning. However, we don't *argue*. We don't say: "The trial court clearly erred when it found that it was not raining." Instead, we use juxtaposition to get our point across. We write: "Although the trial court found that the sky was grey (R.3) and wet droplets were falling (R.4), the court held it was not raining. (R.6.)" Through this method, we avoid argument and avoid reaching legal conclusions. We present the facts and let the reviewing court reach its *own* conclusion that the prior court erred.

§ 15.5(d)   Fourth: Discuss How the Case Reached the Reviewing Court and Identify the Issues on Review

Here, we explain how our case reached the reviewing court and state the issues on review. We include any necessary procedural aspects of the case and, if space permits, quote any certified questions for review.

---

15. Please *see* Chapter 33, § 33.2 for more of these writing prompts.

§ 15.5(e)   Finally: Say What We Want
the Reviewing Court to Do

We conclude with a request for relief, asking the court, for example, to affirm or reverse the lower court's decision. We also include, where relevant, any specific instructions for a remand.

§ 15.6   The Sample Briefs

To illustrate these principles, we've included two sample briefs (in Chapters 36 and 37) containing Statements. Please read (now) these Statements and then return to this section.

Appellant's Initial Brief. The Statement begins, not with a direct statement of the theory of the case, but with a series of paragraphs leading to a graphic visual image. That image conveys our theory. That image introduces the parties as they take their place in the action.

We selected this "narrative" approach for a reason: we want to portray the outrageousness of the defendant's conduct. We want to put the court *on* the railroad tracks with Parker Lionell, the train's engineer. We want to *demonstrate* that Lionell had alleged facts sufficient to state a cause of action for intentional infliction of emotional distress.

Could we have begun our Statement with a precisely crafted summary of our theory? Yes. Should we have? Did we convey our theory *through* the graphic visual image? What do you think?

Appellee's Answer Brief. The Statement begins in a very matter-of-fact style: "At issue is whether the trial court properly dismissed Appellant Parker Lionell's complaint for intentional infliction of emotional distress." But, by the end of the first paragraph, we see Noah Walker's theory: "In this unusual case of first impression, Lionell seeks to hold Walker responsible for the alleged mental distress Lionell suffered at hearing Walker's screams and seeing Walker's blood after the accident." The case, like most appellate cases, isn't so straightforward after all.

§ 15.7   Exercises in Writing a Statement

Using the Hal Hunter hypothetical (see § 5.10(b), Exercise 3), assume that Mark Stiles has appealed a trial court ruling that Hal Hunter lacked testamentary capacity. Write two Statements of the Case and Facts: one favoring Mark Stiles (Appellant) and one favoring Sara Dunn, Hal's girlfriend, (Appellee). Write your Statements using only the facts given in the hypothetical, in light of the *Edwards* case in Appendix A. The *Edwards* case held that a testator is determined to be of "sound mind" when he has the ability to mentally understand in a general way (1) the nature and extent of the property to be disposed of, (2) the testator's relation to those who would naturally claim a substantial benefit from his will, and (3) a general understanding of the practical effect of the will as executed.

Chapter Review
Statement of the Case and Facts

✓ Don't include argument. Any assertion we can't support by citing the Record is likely argument and has no place in the Statement. Lead the reader to a conclusion through *juxtaposition*.

✓ Provide "pinpoint" Record citations for each assertion.

✓ Tell the "full" story; be fair; include harmful and helpful facts. Emphasize the favorable facts and subordinate the unfavorable ones.

✓ Fashion the Statement around a theory or theme which grabs the reader's attention.

✓ Visualize the facts; think like a movie director; write a compelling story.

✓ Review and revise the Statement after writing the Argument section of the brief.

✓ Use subheadings where necessary to alert readers to changes in topic or time.

Guidelines for organizing the Statement:

✓ First, state the theory of the case, or portray a key graphic visual image.

✓ Second, introduce the issues and the parties. Refer to the parties by using consistent and simple terms.

✓ Third, in logical order, discuss the relevant facts; tell what happened. Use vibrant language, but take care not to misrepresent the facts. Pay special attention to making all transitions in time, space, and viewpoint clear to the reader.

✓ Fourth, discuss relevant procedural aspects of the case; and, if relevant, address the "lower" court's reasoning.

✓ Fifth, discuss how the case reached the reviewing court, and identify the issue(s) on review.

✓ Finally, request relief by asking the court to affirm, reverse, or remand.

Chapter 16

Standards of Review

"The standard of review is the keystone of appellate decision-making."

— Judge Harry Pregerson
United States Court of Appeals
for the Ninth Circuit

§ 16.1   Overview: The Standards of Review

Purpose. The "Standard of Review" ("standard") tells the reviewing court the appropriate level of deference it should give to the court below in reviewing that court's decision. That is, the standard involves the nature and degree of error the appellant must prove for the appellate court to reverse the decision.

An appeal is not a retrial. Many attorneys attempt to retry their case when it reaches the appellate level. In so doing, they fail to realize that appellate courts play by different rules than do trial courts. Most appellate tribunals have limited jurisdiction. They can review *de novo*, or independently, certain issues, but they may not second-guess every decision of the trial judge. The rules spelling out these limitations are the "standards of review," and these standards are created by case law or codified in court rules or statutes.

To determine the appropriate standard of review for our issues on appeal, we research the law in our jurisdiction. Jurisdiction is relevant because standards of review differ from state to state and between the states and the federal government. Often, the cases we rely on for the substantive law will also explain the standard of review. However, if these cases do not mention the standard, we look to other jurisdictions that have decided the issue or look to our own jurisdiction on similar issues.

Standard of review versus rule. A standard of review and a "legal standard," or "rule," are not synonymous. A legal standard is the law or rule governing a case. Examples include the statutory definition of murder and common law rules of negligence. Legal standards, of course, are used by *both* trial courts and appellate courts.

In contrast, the standard of review is the measuring stick the reviewing court uses in determining whether a trial court has committed reversible error. Thus, the standard of review is employed *only* by appellate courts (or, less commonly, by trial courts acting in an appellate capacity). The standard of review provides a guideline of what the appellate court can and cannot do to the judgment/result below; that is, how much of a remedy the court can provide our client.

In reviewing any issue on appeal, an appellate judge's first question is likely to be, "What is the standard of review?" In other words, the court is asking, "Just how do we measure the trial court's alleged error?" Unfortunately, many attorneys never answer this question, thereby frustrating the court and losing a strategic opportunity to advance their case. As Judge John Godbold put it, unless counsel is familiar with the relevant standard of review, he may find himself "trying to run for a touchdown when basketball rules are in effect."

Format. Federal appellate courts (and some state appellate courts) require a statement of the standard either "in the discussion of the issue or under a separate heading placed before the discussion of the issues."[1] We state the standard concisely in a few

---

1. See Rule 28(a)(9)(B) of the Federal Rules of Appellate Procedure. See also Fla. R. App. P. 9.210(b)(5). Although some state courts do not require a separate section on the standard of review, every reviewing court must know the standard, and we should, therefore, address it.

sentences, supported by citation to the appropriate authority. For example, we could state: "In this de novo review, this Court should determine as a matter of law that...," or "The trial court abused its discretion when it.... An abuse of discretion occurs where...."

We also state the standard in the Summary of Argument section, and where appropriate, we include the standard at the start of each issue in our Argument. However, if the standard is the same for all issues, we may state it at the beginning of our analysis, in a separate section preceding our Argument section.

Wolf v. State. To illustrate how the standard operates, let's return to *Wolf v. State.* Assume that we represent Wolf. Wolf has been convicted of murdering the First Little Piggy, and seeks to appeal that conviction on the following three grounds:

(1) the jury erred in finding that he had "huffed and puffed" instead of sneezed;

(2) the trial court erred in admitting into evidence an eight-year-old felony conviction for breaking and entering; and

(3) the trial court erred in refusing to instruct the jury on "excusable homicide." After all, Wolf didn't *mean* to blow that house down. A sneeze is a sneeze; accidents *do* happen, and what can you expect when your house is made of straw?

Assume further that Wolf preserved these issues by properly objecting to them at trial.

Before we advise Wolf on the merits of his appeal, we determine what, exactly, he must demonstrate to win a reversal in the appellate court. How will the court determine whether an error of law has occurred? Should the court simply presume that the trial court's rulings were correct? What level of deference will the appellate court give to the trial court's decisions? By identifying and understanding the standard of review applicable to our case, we can answer these questions.

We can tell Wolf that he, as the appellant (i.e., the party seeking reversal), has the "burden" of demonstrating that error occurred in his trial. The lower court's order or judgment is generally presumed correct until the appellant demonstrates that an error sufficiently egregious, i.e., more than harmless, occurred. We can't argue, in a general fashion, that the decision below was somehow wrong or incorrect. Huffing and puffing gets us nowhere. Rather, we must *prove* that the lower court made specific errors. We must *prove* that under the appropriate standard, the appellate court should reverse the decision. What exactly is the appropriate standard? Let's see.

Overview of the standards. Standards of review resemble burdens of proof. At trial, one party bears the burden of proving his or her case by a "preponderance of the evidence"; by "clear and convincing evidence"; or by evidence "beyond a reasonable doubt." On appeal, the appellant has the burden of showing that the jury's findings of facts are not supported by "substantial evidence"; that the trial court's factual findings are "clearly erroneous"; that the trial court "abused its discretion"; or that the trial court erred "as a matter of law."

Graphic 16.1	Standards of Review
Standard	**Description**
clearly erroneous	The trial court clearly erred in its fact finding.
substantial evidence	The jury's verdict or findings are not supported by sufficient evidence.
abuse of discretion	The trial court abused its discretion.
de novo	The trial court made an error of law; i.e., incorrectly interpreted applicable case law or statutes.

Questions of Fact. "Questions of fact" are those decided on the basis of evidence, without reference to the law. Did Wolf sneeze? Was the house made of straw? Did the house collapse? Was the Pig home when Wolf arrived? Did Wolf "huff and puff"?

Questions of Law. In contrast, "questions of law" are those which can be decided without reference to the facts. Assuming that Wolf admits he "huffed and puffed," did his acts meet the statutory definition of murder? Did the trial judge properly follow statutory guidelines in sentencing Wolf to prison?

Mixed Questions of Fact and Law. Mixed questions — involving both law and fact — are the bane of appellate practice. They are questions involving the application of a given law to a given set of facts. Whether the appellate court applies the clearly erroneous standard or *de novo* review depends on the specific case. As the Ninth Circuit explained:

> If the concerns of judicial administration — efficiency, accuracy, and precedential weight — make it more appropriate for a district judge to determine whether the established facts fall within the relevant legal definition, we should subject his determination to deferential, clearly erroneous review. If, on the other hand, the concerns of judicial administration favor the appellate court, we should subject the district court's findings to de novo review. Thus, in each case, the pivotal question is do the concerns of judicial administration favor the district court or do they favor the appellate court.

United States v. McConney, 728 F.2d 1195, 1202 (9th Cir. 1984). Clear as mud. As one court put it: "Mixed questions sometimes are impossible to categorize through sheer logic." *Campbell v. Merit Sys. Protection Bd.*, 27 F.3d 1560, 1565 (Fed. Cir. 1994). Try explaining this to a client.

To make matters even more interesting, even if the appellant satisfies the relevant standard (whatever that is), he doesn't automatically win the appeal. In most cases, he faces the additional burden of demonstrating that the trial court's error affected the outcome. As we'll see, Wolf will rely on three standards of review in pursuing his appeal. Let's look at each standard in more detail.

§ 16.2 Standard of Review for Questions of Fact: Clearly Erroneous or Substantial Evidence

Because appellate judges review only the dry, printed Record, and don't see witnesses eye-to-eye, they're less able than the jury or trial judge to determine *factual* issues such as a witness's credibility. Consequently, standards of review in most jurisdictions require appellate courts to "defer to," that is, to accept as true and correct, the trial court's or jury's factual findings and to reject those findings only when such findings are clearly erroneous or unsupported by substantial evidence.

The terms courts and statutes use to describe this standard differ from jurisdiction to jurisdiction. For example, on the federal level, the standards are whether the trial court's finding of facts were "clearly erroneous"[2] and whether the jury's verdict or findings were supported by "sufficient evidence." *United States v. White*, 81 F.3d 80, 82 (8th Cir. 1996). Florida courts, for example, test both the trial court's and the jury's findings by the "competent evidence" standard; i.e., whether the finding was supported by substantial evidence. *Helman v. Seaboard Coast Line R.R. Co.*, 349 So. 2d 1187, 1189 (Fla. 1977).

These tests reflect the policy that the appellate court should not substitute its judgment for that of the finder of fact:

> If the district court's account of the evidence is plausible in light of the record viewed in its entirety, the court of appeals may not reverse it even though convinced that had it been sitting as the trier of fact, it would have weighed the evidence differently.

Anderson v. Bessemer City, 470 U.S. 564, 573-74 (1985) (reversing the court of appeals' rejection of the district court's factual finding that the city had committed intentional discrimination). Consequently, appellants bear a heavy burden in demonstrating that the trial court or jury made an erroneous factual finding.

Let's see how these principles apply to Wolf's case:

Graphic 16.2　　　　　Clearly Erroneous Standard

We know that The First Little Piggy was killed when his house collapsed in upon him, that Wolf admitted he was present when this tragedy struck, and that Wolf was convicted of the Piggy's murder. One of the questions of fact during the trial was whether Wolf "huffed and puffed" upon the house. Assume that five people testified that Wolf merely sneezed, that Wolf testified that he merely sneezed, but that a thirteen-year-old girl, carrying a basket and wearing a red cape, testified that Wolf had "huffed and puffed." The jury found that Wolf had huffed and puffed. Wolf challenges that finding on appeal.

---

2. *See* Federal Rules of Civil Procedure 52(a)(6).

Is the jury's finding supported by substantial evidence? Probably so. In most jurisdictions, the testimony of a single credible witness constitutes "sufficient evidence" or "substantial evidence." Thus, Wolf is likely to lose on this ground. (Better let the *senior* partner tell him.)

§ 16.3 Standard of Review for Discretionary Rulings: Abuse of Discretion

Court rules and statutes grant trial courts the power to use their judgment in deciding many issues and procedural matters, ranging from issuing injunctions and awarding custody, to excluding relevant evidence. For example, Rule 403 of the Federal Rules of Evidence provides that even relevant evidence *may* be excluded if its probative value is substantially outweighed by the danger of unfair prejudice.[3] Thus, the trial court has great *discretion* in determining whether to exclude evidence. The appellate court will interfere with that exercise of discretion only where the trial court has committed a clear error of judgment.

Let's look further at Wolf's case to see how the reviewing court employs this "abuse of discretion" standard.

Graphic 16.3   **Abuse of Discretion Standard**

Assume that before Wolf's jury trial began, he moved to exclude his eight-year-old felony conviction for breaking and entering.* His attorney argued that the "attenuated probative value" of the conviction was outweighed by the danger of unfair prejudice. The trial court denied the motion, stating that although somewhat tenuous, the conviction reflected upon Wolf's credibility.

In reviewing the trial court's decision, the appellate court is limited to determining whether the trial court abused its discretion in admitting the evidence of Wolf's prior conviction. The appellate court cannot substitute its judgment for that of the trial court, but determines *only* whether the trial court exceeded its discretion. Understandably, courts have struggled to define the precise meaning of an "abuse of discretion."

> An abuse of discretion ... can occur in three principal ways: [1] when a relevant factor that should have been given significant weight is not considered; [2] when an irrelevant or improper factor is considered and given significant weight;

---

3. Florida has a similar provision that applies, in part, to impeaching a witness with prior convictions. *See* § 90.610, Fla. Stat.

   * Into Grandma's house, of course.

and [3] when all proper factors, and no improper ones, are considered, but the court, in weighing those factors, commits a clear error of judgment."

Kern v. TXO Production Corp., 738 F.2d 968, 970 (8th Cir. 1984). (Got to love those adjectives!)

In Wolf's case, the appellate court may well find that no abuse of discretion occurred. In most jurisdictions, prior convictions are admissible to impeach a witness's credibility—the ostensible reason the court here gave for admitting the conviction. Because nothing in the Record indicates that the court considered an "improper factor" in admitting the prior conviction, the appellate court will likely uphold the decision.

On the other hand, if the trial judge had stated he was admitting the prior conviction because "it indicates how Big and Bad the defendant is," then an appellate court might more readily find an abuse of discretion. Under rules of evidence, prior convictions are inadmissible to show a defendant's predisposition to commit the crime in question.

§ 16.4   Standard of Review for Questions of Law: *De Novo*

Although reluctant to interfere with findings of fact, appellate courts will review *de novo*, that is, "anew," the trial court's rulings on legal questions. Appellate courts see their role as interpreting the law and assuring that the "lower" courts apply the law consistently. In deciding a legal question, the appellate court typically (1) relies upon the trial court's findings of fact or upon the parties' stipulation of the facts, (2) determines whether the trial court chose the correct legal rule, and (3) reviews whether the trial court properly applied that rule to the facts. Let's return to Wolf's case to see how this *de novo* standard works.

Graphic 16.4(a)   ***De Novo* Standard**

Assume that the jury, after hearing the evidence, finds the following:

  (a) Wolf, at the least sneezed, and at the most huffed and puffed, upon The First Little Piggy's house;

  (b) The First Little Piggy's straw home collapsed as Wolf stood outside it;

  (c) The First Little Piggy was inside the house when it collapsed; and

  (d) The debris from the collapsing home killed the First Little Piggy.

Assume further that Wolf requested, but the judge refused, to instruct the jury on "excusable homicide," and that the jury found Wolf guilty of murder.

On appeal of his conviction, Wolf could frame the following legal issue:

Graphic 16.4(b)	Possible Issue for *De Novo* Review

Whether the trial court erred in refusing to instruct the jury on excusable homicide where the evidence was undisputed that the victim's death was caused from falling debris resulting from the collapse of his straw house and that the house collapsed when the defendant, at the very least sneezed, and at the most huffed and puffed, upon it.

Here, we have a mixed question of law and fact. (See § 16.1) We would argue that the appellate court should accept the facts as found by the trial court and review whether those facts establish the "intent" necessary for "murder." In other words, we'd ask the court to defer to the trial court's factual findings but reach its own conclusions regarding how to *apply* the relevant legal rules to those facts. Although the trial court is in a better position than is the appellate court to determine factual issues, it is in no better position to determine issues of law. For this reason, we'd argue that the appellate court should decide this issue of law *without deferring* to the trial court.

§ 16.5   Harmless Error

Even if the appellant shows that the trial court erred, the case is not over. The appellant must scale an additional obstacle and show that the error affected the outcome, that is, that the error was "harmful."

In virtually all trials, mistakes occur. Appellate courts recognize that trial judges are not perfect. In the interest of judicial efficiency, appellate judges follow the principle that the trial court's judgment will not be reversed unless the claimed error affected the outcome. Many of the states adhere to this "harmless error doctrine." As Rule 61 of the Federal Rules of Civil Procedure states the principle: "At every stage of the proceeding, the court must disregard all errors and defects that do not affect any party's substantial rights." Fed. R. Civ. P. 61.[4]

In criminal cases, the appellate courts may apply another variation of the harmless error doctrine. If the trial court committed "constitutional error," that is, admitted a defendant's confession that had been obtained in violation of the *Miranda* rule, then on appeal the prosecution must show that the error was harmless "beyond a reasonable doubt." *See Chapman v. California*, 386 U.S. 18, 23-24 (1967).

On the other hand, if the trial court committed "nonconstitutional error," for example, admitted inflammatory photos into evidence, then the appellant must meet the "standard"

---

4. Florida courts, for example, use somewhat different terminology, requiring that the error "result[ ] in a miscarriage of justice." § 59.041, Fla. Stat. In practice, however, Florida appears to follow the same test as the federal courts; i.e., that the party asserting the error must show that if the trial court had not erred, the result would probably have been different. *See McArthur v. Cook*, 99 So. 2d 565, 567 (Fla. 1957).

harmless error test and show that in the absence of the error, he would not have been convicted. Let's see these principles in action in Wolf's case.

Graphic 16.5(a)   **Harmless Error: Constitutional Error**

Assume now in Wolf's case that the police obtained the following statement from Wolf while violating his *Miranda* rights: "Yes, I killed that porker, and if he wasn't already dead, I'd kill him again." Assume further that the trial court admitted that statement over Wolf's specific objection.

Because of the specific "constitutional" nature of this error, the *prosecution*—(the appellee), must show that the error was harmless "beyond a reasonable doubt."

Graphic 16.5(b)   **Harmless Error: Non-Constitutional Error**

Let us now assume that the only error the appellate court found was that the trial court abused its discretion in admitting Wolf's prior breaking and entering conviction.

Under this circumstance, Wolf has to demonstrate that he would not have been convicted if this error had not occurred—a pretty tough standard to meet.

§ 16.6   Strategic Use of the Standards of Review

A good appellate advocate uses standards of review to evaluate the strengths of each issue and the appeal as a whole. In a civil case, if the only error concerns a question of fact which a jury has decided adversely, and the error doesn't appear egregious, we advise our client to cut his losses and forego an appeal. If, on the other hand, the main error concerns the trial court's ruling on a legal question, then the chances of success are greater.

If, however, we represent the appellee and our opponent is relying primarily on a category of error in which the appellate courts generally defer to the trial court, we highlight this point in our argument. Indeed, we highlight this standard even in writing our Questions Presented, as the example below illustrates.[5]

---

5. The Question Presented is the section of our brief where we state the legal issue(s) the brief addresses. We address Questions Presented in Chapter 17.

Graphic 16.6	Strategic Use of Standard of Review: The State's Question Presented

Whether, in trying the defendant for murder, the trial court **properly exercised its discretion** in admitting defendant's eight-year-old felony conviction for breaking and entering.

We also use the standard of review in deciding how to order our arguments on appeal. Because the appellate court has the power to review *de novo* the trial court's rulings on legal questions, legal errors are a more fruitful area for appellants than errors concerning findings of fact or abuse of discretion. Thus, of the original three issues Wolf has alleged on appeal, his best argument is that the trial court erred, as a matter of law, in failing to instruct the jury on excusable homicide.

§ 16.7 Exercise in Identifying the Standard of Review

Exercise 1. Identify the standard of review the court applied in the *Blain* case located in Appendix A.

We end this Chapter with the following review.

Chapter Review
Standards of Review

Standards of Review — Quick Reference

	Clearly Erroneous	Abuse of Discretion	Substantial Evidence	De Novo
type of ruling under review	Questions of fact (trial judge)	Discretionary rulings (trial judge)	Questions of fact (trier of fact, trial judge, or jury)	Question of law (trial judge or lower appellate court judge)
deference given	*Substantial deference:* If the fact findings are plausible, they won't be set aside, even if the appellate court would have reached a different result if sitting as the finder of fact.	*Extreme deference:* Rulings are reversed only if the appellate court is convinced that the trial judge acted arbitrarily or committed a clear error of judgment. E.g., discovery issues; courtroom procedure; some evidentiary issues.	*Extreme deference:* The verdict must stand unless there's no substantial evidence to support it.	*No deference:* The appellate court independently reviews the legal question. E.g., constitutional and statutory questions; summary judgment; jury instructions.
party favored	Appellee	Appellee	Appellee	Appellant
factual examples	Whether Wolf huffed and puffed or merely sneezed.	Whether the trial court abused its discretion in admitting Wolf's prior conviction.	Whether Wolf huffed and puffed or merely sneezed.	Whether the trial court erred as a matter of law in failing to instruct the jury on excusable homicide.

Practice Pointers   Standards of Review

Good lawyers incorporate the proper standard of review into the bold assertion or rule discussion of each issue. Here are some writing prompts for stating the standard:

Writing Prompts

Standard	Prompt
clearly erroneous	"The trial court's findings of fact are clearly erroneous...."
substantial evidence	"The jury's findings of fact are not supported by substantial evidence...."
abuse of discretion	"The trial court abused its discretion in finding...."
de novo [error of law]	"The trial court erred as a matter of law in...."

Chapter 17

Questions Presented

"In law also the right answer usually depends on putting the right question."

—Justice Felix Frankfurter[1]

---

1. *Estate of Rodgers v. Commonwealth*, 320 U.S. 410, 413 (1943).

§ 17.1   Purpose, Context, and Format of the Question Presented

Purpose. In the Question Presented ("Question"), we state in the most persuasive, yet non-argumentative manner possible, the precise legal issues in our case. We frame the Question so that the court not only has a reason to rule in our favor but will *want* to do so.

Context. Because the Question usually appears at the beginning of the brief, before the Statement of the Case and Facts, and before any argument, it serves to introduce our case to the court. This function shapes the nature of the information we place in it.

Format. The Question is doubled-spaced and preceded with a Roman Numeral. However, if there's just one Question, we don't number it. Questions can be more than one sentence long but usually are not.

Punctuation. If the Question begins with the word "whether," we use a period, rather than a question mark, at the end of the sentence. However, if it begins with an appropriate verb, i.e., "should," "does," "may," "did," we place a question mark at the end.

Party Names. Because the court will not yet know the facts of our case when it reads the Question, we usually do not refer to parties by their names. Instead, we use generic terms like "employer/employee," "landlord/tenant," and "husband/wife." In a criminal case, we refer to "defendant," "state" or "government," and "victim."

§ 17.2   The Design of the Question Presented

A Question is an inquiry, not a demand, incorporating a legal rule usually followed by a list of decisive facts. Generally, but not always, the most reliable format for drafting the Question is to begin with the inquiry (the legal basis of the appeal, including the rule) and to list the decisive facts after the inquiry is complete. The decisive facts are usually listed in a series of clauses, each beginning with "where" or "when." As we discuss below, this design makes it easy for the court to transform the Question into a topic sentence favoring our client.

Thus, the Question usually takes the following form:

"Whether [legal issue, including the applicable rule] where/when [decisive facts]."

Graphic 17.2(a)	Design for Questions Presented	
inquiry word	**legal point**	**decisive facts**
whether, did, does,		where
should, may		when

The inquiry *precedes* the decisive facts because the judge will not know which facts are relevant until we establish, through the inquiry, a context for those facts. In establishing this context, we state, or at least imply, the rules governing the result we seek.

In addition, we state the Question in the narrowest form possible. We need only win *our* case, and we frame our issue accordingly. For example, if our case involves only an "as-applied" challenge to a statute—in other words, we're asking the court to reverse our client's conviction—we don't frame our issue as if we were making a "facial" challenge and asking the court to rip the statute from the books. There's no need to be greedy. Winning on a narrow ground is still winning.

Here's an example Question applying the above principles. It's from *Clark v. Community for Creative Non-Violence*, 468 U.S. 288, 289 (1983), in which the Court upheld the application of the statute at issue:

Graphic 17.2(b)   Example of a Question Presented

"[W]hether a National Park Service regulation prohibiting camping in certain parks violates the First Amendment when applied to prohibit demonstrators from sleeping in Lafayette Park and the Mall in connection with a demonstration intended to call attention to the plight of the homeless."

Graphic 17.2(c)   Example Analyzed

Inquiry Word	Legal Point	Decisive Facts
Whether	a National Park Service regulation prohibiting camping in certain parks violates the First Amendment	when applied to prohibit demonstrators from sleeping in Lafayette Park and the Mall in connection with a demonstration intended to call attention to the plight of the homeless.

Please notice the following regarding this Question:

(1) the inquiry *precedes* the decisive facts;

(2) the inquiry includes the legal principles involved (a Park Service regulation and the First Amendment);

(3) the Court refers to the parties by generic terms: "Park Service" and "demonstrators";

(4) although the sentence is long, it's not unwieldy or awkward; and

(5) just by dropping the word "[w]hether," we can easily transform the Question into the following topic sentence or Argument Heading:

"A National Park Service regulation prohibiting camping in certain parks violates the First Amendment when applied to prohibit demonstrators from sleeping in Lafayette Park and the Mall in connection with a demonstration intended to call attention to the plight of the homeless."

In the next section, let's return to our *Wolf v. State* case and look at some more examples of Questions. This time, let's see what *not* to do.

§ 17.3   What Not to Do in Writing the Question Presented

In writing the Question Presented, we must be careful that our zeal to win our case doesn't overcome our obligation to state the Question *objectively*. Specifically, and as explained below, we make certain that we do not present contested issues as if they were uncontested.

Graphic 17.3(a)	The Case of the Big Bad Wolf
	Wolf v. State

Assume that we represent Wolf in his appeal from a conviction for murdering The First Little Pig. Assume further that Wolf challenges the trial court's refusal to instruct the jury on "excusable homicide," i.e., the unintentional, accidental killing of another person (in this case, The Pig). Wolf attempted to prove at trial that he had no intent to kill The Pig. Rather, The Pig's death was an unfortunate accident, the result of faulty building construction and Wolf's uncontrollable sneeze.

In writing the Question on Wolf's behalf, we would *not* say:

Graphic 17.3(b)	Example #1
	Don't Present Contested Issues as if They Were Uncontested

Whether, where defendant clearly had no intent to cause the victim's death, the trial court erred in refusing to instruct the jury on excusable homicide.

We don't include contested issues or facts as if they were uncontested ("the defendant clearly had no intent to cause …"), and we don't slant the Question to this degree.

Although this next version is a little better, we also do *not* write:

Graphic 17.3(c) **Example #2**
Don't Recast Contested Facts or Issues as a Legal Conclusion

Whether, where the overwhelming weight of credible evidence demonstrated that defendant did not intend to cause the victim's death, the trial court erred in refusing to instruct the jury on excusable homicide.

This version, too, contains a legal conclusion — that the evidence was overwhelmingly in favor of Wolf's version of the events.[2]

Let's see a better way of writing Wolf's Question:

Graphic 17.3(d) **Example #3**
Wolf's Question Presented: A Proper Version

Whether the trial court erred in refusing to instruct the jury on excusable homicide where the evidence was undisputed that the victim's death was caused from falling debris resulting from the collapse of his straw house; and that the house collapsed when defendant at the least sneezed, and at the most "huffed and puffed," upon it.

Note that this last Question doesn't unfairly characterize the facts and doesn't assume any legal conclusions. It mentions key facts and the controversial "sneeze versus huff and puff." However, it does not reach a conclusion on the matter. In so doing, the Question presents the "operative" or "decisive" facts, implies the relief sought, and states the legal basis of that relief.

Note also that this last version places the ultimate inquiry (i.e., whether the trial court erred), *before* the decisive facts, making the Question easier to comprehend. If we had placed the facts *before* the inquiry (as in the first and second versions), the judge may not comprehend the significance of the facts at that point and would probably have to reread the Question. The inquiry, stated at the outset of the Question ("[w]hether the trial court erred in refusing to instruct …"), provides the *context* for the facts that follow ("where the evidence was undisputed that …").

Let's next assume that instead of representing Wolf, we now represent the State in *Wolf v. State.* We would write our Question as follows:

---

2. The following Questions are also argumentative and improper because they include legal conclusions:

    I. Should a statute, which no one can understand because it contains vague and ambiguous terms, be struck down as violating the Fourteenth Amendment?

    II. Does Rule 9999, which unlawfully prohibits expressive conduct, violate John Doe's First Amendment right to free speech?

Graphic 17.3(e)   **The State's Question**

Whether the trial court erred in refusing to instruct the jury on excusable homicide where defendant admitted he had (1) destroyed the victim's home; (2) killed the victim in the process; and (3) then devoured the victim for dinner.

Notice the pattern here: the legal issue is framed in the inquiry, followed by the decisive facts. Which facts we stress, of course, depend on which side we represent. Note also that here we've numbered the operative facts. This numbering helps keep the judge on track by making the Question easier to read. Finally, although the Question is persuasive, we haven't fallen into the trap of overstating our case.

§ 17.4   The Complex Case

Often, our case will involve *many* decisive facts. Instead of writing a long, unwieldy sentence incorporating all of those facts, we break our Question into two or more sentences. To do this, we introduce the decisive facts or the terms of the challenged law in one or more sentences and then pose the inquiry in the following sentence.

Although it's preferable to *begin* with the inquiry instead of with the facts, we can't always do so. In complex matters, we may have to begin with the decisive facts to establish a context for the legal issue. The following two examples, from United States Supreme Court opinions, illustrate this multi-sentence format:

(1) From *Coates v. City of Cincinnati*, 402 U.S. 611, 611-12 (1971), in which the Court struck down the challenged ordinance:

Graphic 17.4(a)   **Multi-Sentence Question**
                          Beginning with the Challenged Law

"A Cincinnati, Ohio, ordinance makes it a criminal offense for 'three or more persons to assemble ... on any of the sidewalks ... and there conduct themselves in a manner annoying to persons passing by....' The issue before us is whether this ordinance is unconstitutional on its face."

---

(2) From *Cohen v. California*, 403 U.S. 15, 22 (1971), in which the Court found that the statute, as applied to the appellant, violated the First Amendment:

Graphic 17.4(b)	Multi-Sentence Question Beginning with the Decisive Facts

"Against this [factual] background [explaining Cohen's wearing of a jacket which displayed the words 'F - - K the draft'], the issue flushed by this case stands out in bold relief. It is whether California can excise, as 'offensive conduct,' one particular scurrilous epithet from the public discourse, either upon the theory of the court below that its use is inherently likely to cause violent reaction or upon a more general assertion that the States, acting as guardians of public morality, may properly remove this offensive word from the public vocabulary."

The above example, written by Justice Harlan, also illustrates that the Supreme Court doesn't always present (in fact, it hardly ever does) the Question in an impartial, objective light. We don't use, as the Court used, loaded phrases such as "the issue flushed by this case," imprecise verbs like "excise" (does "excise" mean "prohibit" or "erase"?), or over-the-top adjectives like "scurrilous." Instead, we tie the Question to the legal issue involved (here, the First Amendment) and leave out the rhetoric.

One final note concerning the complex case: if we use more than one Question to convey the issues, we place the Questions in the order in which we address them in the Argument section of our brief. This helps to keep our brief internally consistent.

§ 17.5   Procedure for Writing the Question Presented

Based on the initial review of our case on appeal, we write a preliminary Question (or Questions) Presented. In writing a preliminary Question, we state the legal issue to be resolved and list the critical, undisputed facts. Next, while researching, writing, and rewriting the other parts of our brief, particularly the Argument, we refine our list of facts and add or delete facts from the Question as we better understand the issue. Finally, we construct a final, concise phrasing of the list and join it to the inquiry in sentence form. This process is repeated for each Question in the case.

The following hypothetical and examples illustrate this process.

Graphic 17.5	Title VII Hypothetical

Assume our appeal involves the federal employment discrimination laws (Title VII). Our client is a female associate of a law firm who alleges she was denied partnership because she is a woman. Assume also that she had an exemplary seven-year work record.

Consider the following Question:

Graphic 17.5(a)	First Draft
Whether Title VII applies to law firms.	

This Question falls flat; it tells the judge virtually nothing about our case. Although it introduces the legal principle, it does so only in an abstract way that doesn't endear our client to the court. We have not, but must, show the court the connection between the law, the relief we seek, and our client.

The following version is a little better than the first but is still inadequate:

Graphic 17.5(b)	Second Draft
Whether Title VII prohibits a law firm from denying partnership on the basis of sex.	

This version at least informs the court that these parties disagree regarding the denial of partnership. However, its terms are extremely vague. What does "on the basis of sex" mean? Moreover, the Question leaves our client completely out of the mix. It fails to "preview" *our* argument; indeed, it doesn't even mention our client. It misses the opportunity to begin persuading the court that our position is correct.

Let's look at one more alternative:

Graphic 17.5(c)	Third Draft
Whether Title VII, which prohibits gender discrimination, prohibits a law firm from denying partnership to a female associate who for seven years has had an outstanding work record.	

Now we're on the right track. This Question prepares the court for our argument. The court knows the area of law involved, the main points we'll discuss, and the most important facts in our case.

If we've done our job right in drafting the Question, the court can easily translate it into the topic sentence which begins an opinion in our favor. For example, the court could write: "Title VII, which prohibits gender discrimination, prohibits respondent law firm from denying partnership to appellant, an attorney who for seven years has had an outstanding work record."

§ 17.6   Further Examples of Questions Presented

These examples, with minor revisions, were taken from the briefs and opinions in *Texas v. Johnson*, 491 U.S. 397 (1989). At issue in *Johnson* was whether the State of Texas could, consistent with the First Amendment, prosecute Johnson for burning the American Flag during a political protest demonstration. The State conceded, for purposes of oral argument, that Johnson's actions were "expressive." *Id.* at 405. However, the State asserted that its interests in protecting the flag as a "symbol of nationhood and national unity" outweighed Johnson's speech rights. *Id.* at 407. Because Johnson won in the court below, he is the respondent and the State is the petitioner. (We can't assume that the defendant in a criminal case will always be the petitioner or appellant on appeal.)

While reading these samples, ask whether we can tell which side the writer represents just by the way the Question is phrased. (Please note that although the following Questions appeared in the respective briefs, they did not always appear in the Question Presented section. Some were stated in other sections.) In reviewing the petitioner's Questions, consider whether the Questions sufficiently embody the party's theory; i.e., are the Questions specific enough?

Graphic 17.6(a)   **Petitioner's (State's) Version #1**

"Does the public burning of an American flag during the course of a political demonstration constitute free speech subject to the protection of the First Amendment?"

Graphic 17.6(b)   **Petitioner's Version #2**

"This case presents for determination the question of whether an act of flagburning which occurs during the course of a political demonstration is protected under the First Amendment."

Graphic 17.6(c)   **Respondent's (Johnson's) Version #1**

"I. Whether Tex. Penal Code Ann. § 42.09(a)(3), which penalizes such 'physical mistreat[ment]' of 'a national flag' as the actor 'knows will seriously offend one or more persons likely to observe or discover his action,' facially violates the First and Fourteenth Amendments to the United States Constitution."

"II. Whether Tex. Penal Code Ann. § 42.09(a)(3), as applied to the peaceful burning of an American flag at an overtly political demonstration, an act of symbolic speech closely akin to pure speech, violates the First and Fourteenth Amendments to the United States Constitution."

Graphic 17.6(d)   **Respondent's Version #2**

"The issue in this case is whether the State of Texas (hereinafter 'Texas' or 'The State') can inflict criminal penalties for the peaceful burning of a flag during a political demonstration, under a statute that proscribes such 'physical mistreat[ment]' of the flag as 'the actor knows will seriously offend one or more persons likely to discover his action.'"

Graphic 17.6(e)   **Respondent's Version #3**

"This case presents the question whether, consistent with the First and Fourteenth Amendments to the United States Constitution, a state can criminally convict a person of peacefully burning a flag in an overtly political demonstration, under a statute that hinges punishment on the act's communicative effect on third persons 'likely to observe or discover' it."

Graphic 17.6(f)   **Amicus Curiae in Support of Respondent**

"This case requires the Court to decide whether the State of Texas may punish Gregory Lee Johnson for expressing his political views by publicly burning an American flag."

Graphic 17.6(g)   **The Supreme Court's Version**

"After publicly burning an American flag as a means of political protest, Gregory Lee Johnson was convicted of desecrating a flag in violation of Texas law. This case presents the question whether his conviction is consistent with the First Amendment."

Although the Supreme Court's version is concise, it's not without ambiguity. Was Johnson "convicted" "in violation of Texas law"? In other words, did his conviction *itself* violate Texas law? Or was his "desecrating a flag" "in violation of Texas law"? In other words, did his act of desecrating the flag violate Texas law?

The Court could have made itself clearer by writing: "After publicly burning an American flag as a means of political protest, Gregory Lee Johnson was convicted under a Texas statute prohibiting flag desecration."

Or, the Court could have written: "After publicly burning an American flag as a means of political protest, Gregory Lee Johnson was convicted of violating a Texas statute prohibiting flag desecration."

We suggest refraining from using the phrase "in violation of." It's verbose and often leads to ambiguous sentences. "Violates," "violated," or "violating" is clearer and more concise.

Let's look at one final version of the Question, written by *dissenting* Justice Stevens:

Graphic 17.6(h)	**Dissenting Justice Stevens's Version**
"As the Court analyzes this case, it presents the question whether the State of Texas, or indeed the Federal Government, has the power to prohibit the public desecration of the American flag."	

Interestingly, Justice Stevens mentions neither the "First Amendment," nor the "decisive," *undisputed* fact that Johnson burned the flag "as a means of political protest." He also brings into the case the "Federal Government," even though the case had nothing to do with any federal crime.

§ 17.7 Exercise in Designing a Question Presented

Using the Jane Smith hypothetical (see § 5.10(b) and § 6.5) assume that the trial court held against Jane, and draft a Question Presented for an appellate brief on her behalf. The issue is whether the sticky note attached to the bank statement met the requirement of testamentary intent.

Chapter Review
Questions Presented

✓ Keep Questions easy to read. They can be more than one sentence long, but watch out for long, awkward sentences.

✓ Don't include argument or legal conclusions.

✓ Questions don't have to start with "whether." If they do, the sentence ends in a period. If the Question begins with "does," "did," "should," or "may," the sentence ends with a question mark.

Whether	.
Does, Did, Should, May	?

✓ Unless the Question requires a factual introduction, begin with the legal basis of the appeal and follow that with the decisive facts.

✓ Include a reference to the constitutional provision, statute, or common law cause of action involved.

✓ Include the key facts of our case.

✓ Identify the parties by general description rather than by party designation, since the court may not yet know the facts.

✓ Questions are double-spaced and numbered with Roman Numerals (beginning with "I."). However, if there's only one Question, don't number it.

✓ Refrain from using the phrase "in violation of."

✓ Write each Question so that, with very little editing, the appellate court can transform it into a topic sentence favoring our client.

Practice Pointers   Writing Prompts
Design for Questions Presented

Inquiry Word	Legal Point	Decisive Facts
Whether, Did, Does, Should, May		

- Whether the [court] abused its discretion in [action].
- Whether any genuine material issues of fact exist where [state circumstances].
- Whether the [court's] entry of summary judgment in favor of [party] was proper where [circumstances].
- Whether [statute, law] which prohibits [circumstances] violates [party's] [constitutional right or statutory right].
- Whether [court] erred as a matter of law in [action] [circumstances].
- Whether the [court] was clearly erroneous in finding [circumstances].
- Did the [court] err in granting [party's] motion for summary judgment where [circumstances]?
- Did the [court] abuse its discretion in [circumstances]?

Chapter 18

Argument Headings

§ 18.1   What Are They?

Argument Headings ("Headings") are the most concise, distilled statements possible of the bold assertions comprising our argument. They serve as succinct "headlines" of the argument that follows. In much the same way that an overture introduces an opera, Headings "set the stage" for our reader. Through Headings, we tell the court the legal conclusions it should reach on each issue and the reasons for those conclusions. We provide the court with a self-contained overview of our entire case. Understandably, writing Headings is challenging.

§ 18.2   Context

Headings appear not only in the "Argument" section of our brief, but also in the Table of Contents section. Because the Table of Contents precedes both the Argument and the Statement of the Case and Facts, the Headings embedded in the Table of Contents give the court the *first* overview of our case. There, the Headings appear as an outline of our argument, which the court reads before the Argument or the Statement. For this reason, the Headings must flow together, painting a clear, consistent, and self-contained picture of our case.

In addition, in the Argument section, the text following the Heading must support and ultimately *prove* the conclusions we've stated in the Heading. Although the Headings organize the major points, the argument *itself* guides the reader. If, at the end of each argument, we've proven the conclusion encapsulated in our Heading, our brief appears thorough and our credibility is enforced. If, however, our argument falls short, failing to fulfill the "promise" of the Heading, we've shot ourselves in the proverbial foot.

At this time, please read the Table of Contents in each of the sample briefs in Chapters 36 and 37.

§ 18.3   Format and Design

Main Headings. Each principle point of our argument begins with a Main Heading (preceded by a Roman numeral, if we have more than one Heading) composed of one or more complete sentences entirely in capital letters, single-spaced, and indented on both right and left margins.[1]

Subheadings. If we use Subheadings, they are one or more *complete* sentences, sequentially lettered (A., B., etc.), single-spaced, indented on both left and right margins, and underlined. The underlining stops at, but includes, the period. In other words, the underlining is as follows:

---

1. The format of Argument Headings varies. Some lawyers and judges prefer capitalized main headings. However, some believe that capitalized headings are difficult to read. In your practice of law, we suggest you follow whichever format your employer prefers with respect to capitalization and indention.

A. <u>This is how to underline a Subheading.</u>

B. <u>This is improper.</u>

C. <u>This is also improper.</u>

D. <u>This is also improper.</u>

E. <u>This is improper, too.</u>

Although a single Main Heading is appropriate, a single Subheading is not. If there is a Subheading A., there must also (at least) be a Subheading B. Further, Subheadings enhance, and don't merely repeat, information contained in the Main Heading.

Identical Headings in the Table of Contents and in the Argument Sections. The Headings and Subheadings in the Table of Contents read *identically* to those in the Argument section, and are presented in the same order. Any edits to a Heading *must* be reflected in both sections.

Design. As in writing Questions Presented, generally, but not always, the most reliable format is to begin with the legal basis of the argument and then address the decisive facts. We ensure that the court understands the *relevance* of the decisive facts by placing them *after* the legal point.

One method of writing Headings is to lead with our ultimate conclusion (i.e., "This Court should reverse...," "The trial court erred...," "The complaint states a cause of action...."), followed by the relevant legal point, followed by the words "because" or "where" or "when" (similar to the format for a Question Presented), followed by the key facts relevant to our conclusion. When the standard of review works in our favor, we also include it in our Heading.[2] Yes! Headings are a challenge to write!

Graphic 18.3(a)	Designs for Argument Headings		
Conclusion	**Legal Point**	**Linking Words**	**Decisive Facts**
"This Court should reverse"		"because" "where"	
"This Court should affirm"			
"The trial court erred in"			

or

Subject	Legal Point	Linking Words	Decisive Facts
"The complaint"		"because" "where"	
"The plaintiff"			
"The defendant"			

---

2. Please see Chapter 16: Standards of Review.

The following Headings, from *Wolf v. State*, illustrate these principles:

Graphic 18.3(b)	Argument Heading for Wolf

I. THIS COURT SHOULD REVERSE WOLF'S CONVICTION BECAUSE THE TRIAL COURT ERRED IN REFUSING TO INSTRUCT THE JURY ON EXCUSABLE HOMICIDE. AS THE EVIDENCE DEMONSTRATES, WOLF HAD NO INTENT TO KILL THE PIG. WOLF MERELY SNEEZED, TRAGICALLY CAUSING THE PIG'S STRAW HOUSE TO SELF-DESTRUCT AND COLLAPSE IN ON ITSELF.

The argument on this specific issue follows here. We begin with a bold assertion of our position, follow with the rule, explain the rule, apply that rule to our facts, then reach a conclusion. In other words, we write our argument following the BaRAC design.

Graphic 18.3(c)	Argument Heading for the State

I. THIS COURT SHOULD AFFIRM THE BIG BAD WOLF'S CONVICTION. THE TRIAL COURT PROPERLY REFUSED TO INSTRUCT THE JURY ON EXCUSABLE HOMICIDE WHERE THE BIG BAD WOLF ADMITTED THAT HE HAD DESTROYED THE FIRST LITTLE PIGGY'S HOME, KILLED THE PIGGY IN THE PROCESS, AND THEN DEVOURED THE PIGGY FOR DINNER.

§ 18.4   Main Headings and Subheadings

As these examples from *Wolf v. State* show, a Heading conveys our theory and tells the court why it should rule in our favor. If only one theory supports a favorable ruling on the Question Presented, then we use only one Main Heading. Where we have two

Graphic 18.4(a)	Example Analyzed		
Conclusion	**Legal Point**	**Linking Words**	**Decisive Facts**
This Court should	reverse Wolf's conviction	because	the trial court erred in refusing to instruct the jury on excusable homicide. As the....

or more theories, each of which could support a favorable ruling, we state each in a separate Main Heading, with or without Subheadings as appropriate.

Subheadings are appropriate where our main issue involves several subissues. In those cases (as often occurs when we deal with a tort or crime involving two or more legal elements), we explain the Main Heading by using Subheadings which mirror the legal elements. If, in turn, these Subheadings require further explanation, we use Sub-subheadings to address those points.

To illustrate these principles, let's return to our hypothetical case of *Lionell v. Walker*.[3] Assume that we want to demonstrate that the trial court erred in dismissing our client's (Parker Lionell's) complaint against defendant (Noah Walker) for intentional infliction of emotional distress. Assume further that under the tort of intentional infliction of emotional distress, "[o]ne who by extreme and outrageous conduct intentionally or recklessly causes severe emotional distress to another is subject to liability for such emotional distress, and if bodily harm to the other results from it, for such bodily harm." Restatement (Second) of Torts § 46 (1965).

Crafting our Headings to track the relevant elements of the tort, we write a Main Heading, stating in general terms the trial court's error, followed by Subheadings focusing on each element of the tort:

Graphic 18.4(b)   **Main Heading**

THE TRIAL COURT ERRED IN DISMISSING PARKER LIONELL'S COMPLAINT FOR INTENTIONAL INFLICTION OF EMOTIONAL DISTRESS. THE COMPLAINT SUFFICIENTLY ALLEGED FACTS FROM WHICH A JURY MAY REASONABLY INFER THAT WALKER'S CONDUCT WAS EXTREME AND OUTRAGEOUS, AND INTENTIONALLY OR RECKLESSLY CAUSED LIONELL TO SUFFER SEVERE EMOTIONAL DISTRESS.

Subheadings for Each Relevant Element

A. Walker acted outrageously in lying across railroad tracks, refusing to move from the path of an oncoming train, and causing Lionell to become an unwilling participant in a gruesome mutilation.

B. Walker acted intentionally and recklessly in willfully lying on the railroad tracks in the path of an oncoming train he knew would strike him.

    1. Walker acted intentionally. He knew that distress was certain, or substantially certain, to result from his conduct.

    2. Walker acted recklessly in violating statutes designed to protect others from harm.

C. Walker's outrageous and reckless actions caused Lionell to suffer physical manifestations of severe emotional distress which have prevented Lionell from returning to work as an engineer.

---

3. Please see Chapters 34–38, where we address the facts of this hypothetical.

Notice that the Subheadings add information not stated in the Main Heading. They also state the relevant legal conclusion before addressing the decisive facts.

§ 18.5   Strategies in Writing Argument Headings

Use argument headings as a working outline. If written properly, Headings outline our entire case. (Indeed, the numbering and lettering sequence of our Headings should follow that of an outline.) By using Headings as an outline in writing the brief, we identify gaps in our research and logic. Here's how this process works:

Before writing the Argument section of the brief, we outline the conclusions the court must reach to resolve the case in our favor. We develop syllogisms leading to each of these conclusions. We then fashion those conclusions (or indeed, the entire syllogisms) into Headings.

Under each Heading and Subheading in our outline (but not as part of the Headings themselves) we add citations to relevant authorities and to the Record. In other words, we note where in cases, statutes, or the Record, we can find the legal and factual *proof* for the assertions we've made in the Headings. Through this process, we've created an outline identifying the strengths and weaknesses of our Argument.

Please be aware that some appellate judges become irritated when counsel for the appellee restates and argues issues in a sequence and under Headings different than that used by the appellant without first explaining where, in the appellee's brief, the appellee's response to specific points raised by the appellant can be found. *See Rolling v. State ex rel. Butterworth*, 630 So. 2d 635, 636 n.1 (Fla. Dist. Ct. App. 1994): "An Appellee should address the issues in the same order as they are presented in the Initial Brief so that the court can be certain which arguments are being addressed."

Highlight the central facts, issues, and legal standards. If one or two facts are vital to our argument, we state them in our Heading. Moreover, if a majority of jurisdictions have ruled our way on an issue, we highlight that too:

Graphic 18.5	Highlighting the Legal Standard

I. THIS COURT SHOULD AFFIRM THE TRIAL COURT'S DISMISSAL OF PLAINTIFF'S COMPLAINT. AS HAS EVERY JURISDICTION THAT HAS CONSIDERED THE QUESTION, THIS COURT SHOULD ALSO REFUSE TO RECOGNIZE A TORT OF "MARRIAGE MALPRACTICE."

Use headings to avoid the accidental waiver of a point on appeal. Not only do Headings help us organize and present our argument, they also put the court and opposing counsel on notice of each point we assert on appeal. By using a Heading for each issue, we avoid accidentally waiving an argument. *See Simkins Indus., Inc. v. Lexington Ins. Co.*, 714 So. 2d 1092, 1093 (Fla. Dist. Ct. App. 1998) (finding that a "footnote reference" to an issue in appellant's initial brief did "not elevate the matter to a point on appeal.").

§ 18.6   Common Errors in Writing Headings

Headings are excellent organizational tools, if we use them properly. They can't be so general that we fail to distinguish one issue from another.[4] Nor can they be vague or rambling. The following illustrate five common pitfalls to avoid in writing Headings.

(1) Failing to reach a conclusion. Where is the argument in the example below? These Headings are useless; they don't reach a conclusion on any issue in the case.

Graphic 18.6(a)	Error #1: Failing to Reach a Conclusion

never do this	I. EXPRESSIVE CONDUCT.
	    A. <u>Intent to convey a particularized message.</u>
	    B. <u>Great likelihood that message is understood.</u>

(2) Failing to state an argument. A Heading, like the following, which states only a legal rule, wastes space in our brief. Although the Heading correctly states the law, it fails to state any argument.

Graphic 18.6(b)	Error #2: Failing to State an Argument
don't do this	TO QUALIFY FOR REVIEW UNDER THE TIME, PLACE, AND MANNER TEST, A STATUTE MUST BE DEEMED CONTENT-NEUTRAL.

(3) Failing to provide critical facts. Although the first version of each of these next two general Headings may be correct, each lacks critical facts which would help prove the point. The second version, which provides decisive facts, is more persuasive.

Graphic 18.6(c)	Error #3: Failing to Provide Critical Facts
version #1 **too general**	THE BROWNS DID NOT VIOLATE THE FLORIDA SURROGATE PARENTHOOD ACT.
version #2 **much better**	THE BROWNS DID NOT VIOLATE THE FLORIDA SURROGATE PARENTHOOD ACT BY REIMBURSING SARA SMITH FOR HER PREGNANCY-RELATED EXPENSES BECAUSE SUCH PAYMENT WAS NOT "CONDITIONED UPON THE TRANSFER OF PARENTAL OR CUSTODIAL RIGHTS."

---

4. As one court noted, "the failure to organize arguments under cogent and distinct issues on appeal presents sufficient reason for an appellate court to decline consideration of a matter." *F.M.W. Props. v. Peoples First Fin.*, 606 So. 2d 372, 377-78 (Fla. Dist. Ct. App. 1992).

version #1 too general	DOE'S CONVICTION VIOLATED THE EIGHTH AMENDMENT.
version #2 much better	DOE'S CONVICTION FOR LIFE-SUSTAINING BEGGING VIOLATED THE EIGHTH AMENDMENT BECAUSE IT PUNISHED HIM FOR AN ACT INEXTRICABLY RELATED TO HIS HOMELESSNESS AND TO HIS DESTITUTE STATUS.

(4) Failing to state the rule. A Heading must stand on its own. In other words, it provides readers with information necessary to agree with the Heading's conclusion. The Heading in the example below doesn't stand alone. We can't assume that the judge knows a particular rule or is familiar with a particular statute. We must summarize the rule or statute within the context of the Heading.

Graphic 18.6(d)	Error #4: Failing to State the Rule
don't do this	DOE'S CONDUCT MET THE FIRST ELEMENT OF THE PROTECTED CONDUCT TEST.
much better	BY BURNING AN AMERICAN FLAG AT AN ABORTION RALLY, DOE SATISFIED THE FIRST ELEMENT OF THE "PROTECTED CONDUCT" TEST BY EXPRESSING HIS INTENT TO CONVEY A PARTICULARIZED MESSAGE — THAT HE OPPOSED THE PRESIDENT'S STANCE ON ABORTION.

(5) Failing to omit redundant information. Headings shouldn't be redundant. We don't say the same thing twice. If our main Headings repeat our Subheadings, we pare down those main Headings to more generalized points and let the Subheadings provide the specifics.

Graphic 18.6(e)	Error #5: Failing to Omit Redundant Information
don't do this	DOE'S CONVICTION FOR BEGGING VIOLATES THE DUE PROCESS PROTECTIONS OF THE FLORIDA CONSTITUTION BECAUSE IT IS BEYOND THE SCOPE OF THE CITY'S POLICE POWERS. IT PUNISHES DOE FOR HARMLESS BEGGING, CRIMINALIZES INNOCENT CONDUCT, AND ENCOMPASSES INNOCENT BEHAVIOR. MOREOVER, GOTHAM CITY'S PEDESTRIAN INTERFERENCE CODE SERVES NO LEGITIMATE GOVERNMENTAL INTEREST, BEARS NO SUBSTANTIAL OR RATIONAL RELATIONSHIP TO A LEGITIMATE GOVERNMENTAL INTEREST, AND IS NOT THE LEAST RESTRICTIVE MEANS AVAILABLE. A. Gotham City's Pedestrian Interference Code punishes Doe for harmless begging. B. Gotham City's Pedestrian Interference Code criminalizes innocent conduct. C. Gotham City's Pedestrian Interference Code encompasses innocent behavior. D. Gotham City's Pedestrian Interference Code serves no legitimate governmental interest. E. Gotham City's Pedestrian Interference Code bears no rational relationship to a legitimate governmental interest.
much better	DOE'S CONVICTION UNDER GOTHAM CITY'S PEDESTRIAN INTERFERENCE CODE VIOLATED THE DUE PROCESS GUARANTEE OF ARTICLE I, SECTION 9 OF THE FLORIDA CONSTITUTION BECAUSE THE CODE, AS APPLIED TO DOE'S HARMLESS BEGGING, EXCEEDED THE SCOPE OF GOTHAM CITY'S POLICE POWERS. A. Because it was used to punish Doe's harmless begging, the Code, which prohibits "personal solicitation for the immediate receipt of money," served no legitimate governmental interest. B. Because it criminalized Doe's innocent and harmless begging, the Code bore no substantial or rational relation to a legitimate governmental interest in preventing crime.

(6) Failing to identify alternative issues. If any argument is an alternative to one we have already addressed, we say so in our Argument Heading as well as in the argument itself. If we fail to identify an alternative argument as an alternative, we will confuse the court.

Graphic 18.6(f)	Error #6: Failing to Identify Alternative Issues
don't do this	A. The $30,000 the Browns paid to the surrogate mother to "reimburse" her for such expenses as a two-year membership in an exclusive health club and for designer clothes, constitutes "valuable consideration" and does not fall within the exception in the Act allowing for payment of "pregnancy-related medical or psychological care or treatment." B. The $30,000 payment for the surrogate's "pregnancy-related medical or psychological care or treatment," was conditioned upon the transfer of the surrogate's parental rights. This payment thus constitutes "valuable consideration in exchange for a child" and violates the Act.
much better	A. The $30,000 the Browns paid to the surrogate mother to "reimburse" her for such expenses as a two-year membership in an exclusive health club and for designer clothes, constitutes "valuable consideration" and does not fall within the exception in the Act allowing for payment of "pregnancy-related medical or psychological care or treatment." B. Alternatively, even if the $30,000 payment was for the surrogate's "pregnancy-related medical or psychological care or treatment," the payment was nonetheless conditioned upon the transfer of the surrogate's parental rights. This payment thus constitutes "valuable consideration in exchange for a child" and violates the Act.

§ 18.7   A Warning: How a Judge May Read Headings

Although they're useful tools, Headings don't eliminate the need for our argument to flow logically from one point to the next. Nor do they eliminate the need for bold assertions for each point. The reason for this is a bit disconcerting: some judges read the Headings in the Table of Contents to get an overview of the case and then only glance at the Headings when reading the Argument section of our brief, just as some newspaper readers skim headlines. Does this mean we shouldn't care about Headings? Absolutely not.

Headings force *us* to consider each conclusion the court must reach to rule in our favor. The more we think about each argument, the more distilled we can make it. And, if we can't distill our argument—if we can't make it *simple* as we must do to write a Heading—then something's wrong. As Marquis de Vauvenargues observed: "When a thought is too weak to be expressed simply, simply drop it."

Good advice.

§ 18.8 Examples of Argument Headings from the *Texas v. Johnson* Case

We've taken these examples from briefs filed in *Texas v. Johnson*, 491 U.S. 397 (1989). Please view them with a critical eye, and ask the following:

- Which are more persuasive? Why?
- Could we strengthen them?
- Could we streamline them?
- Do the Headings forcefully convey each party's theory of the case?
- Are the Headings self-contained?
- Do they provide us with enough information to rule in the party's favor?

Please also notice that the petitioner's Headings begin with an "overarching" Heading, which states the ultimate conclusion the petitioner advocates.

Graphic 18.8(a)   From Petitioner's Brief (State of Texas) Arguing That the Court Should Uphold the Defendant's Conviction for Flag Desecration

---

THE PUBLIC BURNING OF AN AMERICAN FLAG DURING THE COURSE OF A POLITICAL DEMONSTRATION DOES NOT CONSTITUTE FREE SPEECH ENTITLED TO THE PROTECTION OF THE FIRST AMENDMENT.

  I. THE FIRST AMENDMENT IS NOT ABSOLUTE; LIMITATIONS MAY BE PLACED ON THE EXERCISE OF FREE SPEECH.

      A. Even if expressive conduct is denominated as speech for purposes of the First Amendment, this classification does not prevent limitations on such expressive conduct.

      B. Expressive conduct is subject to a balancing test in which the individual's right to free speech is weighed against the validity of the governmental regulation sought to be imposed.

      C. Conduct which can be characterized as "symbolic speech" demands a lesser degree of protection under the First Amendment than does verbal or written communication.

  II. THE RIGHT OF THE STATE OF TEXAS TO PRESERVE THE FLAG AS A SYMBOL OF NATIONHOOD AND NATIONAL UNITY IS A COMPELLING STATE INTEREST WHICH SUPERSEDES ANY FIRST AMENDMENT RIGHTS AN INDIVIDUAL MAY HAVE IN EXPRESSIVE CONDUCT.

      A. This Court has yet to answer, in the context of a flag desecration case, the issue of whether a state has a valid interest in protecting the flag as a symbol of nationhood and national unity.

      B. The notion that the state has a valid and substantial interest in protecting the flag as a symbol of nationhood and national unity is neither new nor unusual; rather, it is a view which has found favor with a variety of jurists.

C. Prohibitions against flag desecration neither compel an individual's respect for the flag nor prohibit all forms of an individual's expression of disrespect for the flag.

D. Preservation of the flag as a symbol of nationhood and national unity can be accomplished only by prohibiting severe physical abuse of the flag, most importantly its wanton destruction in a public context.

E. Having shown a danger that threatens the flag as a symbol of nationhood and national unity, it is unnecessary for the state to show the existence of a grave and immediate danger.

III. TEXAS HAS A LEGITIMATE INTEREST IN PREVENTING BREACHES OF THE PEACE WHICH CAN RESULT FROM FLAGRANT ACTS OF FLAG DESECRATION CARRIED OUT IN A PUBLIC CONTEXT.

A. One legislative purpose underlining flag desecration statutes is to prevent a breach of the peace.

1. Prevention of breaches of the peace has been recognized as an important and substantial governmental interest unrelated to suppression of expression in the context of flag desecration cases.

2. The facts of this case support Texas' interest in preventing a breach of the peace even if Texas must demonstrate "imminence" or a "clear and present danger" of public unrest.

B. The Texas Court of Criminal Appeals, by mandating evidence of actual violence before permitting state regulation, has adopted a standard which has not been previously applied and which is stricter than is warranted by First Amendment consideration.

IV. THE FACT THAT JOHNSON'S ACT OF FLAGBURNING OCCURRED AT THE CLIMAX OF A POLITICAL DEMONSTRATION DOES NOT CLOAK HIS ACT WITH GREATER PROTECTION SINCE NO EXCEPTION APPLIES TO § 42.09 FOR AN ACT OF POLITICAL PROTEST.

A. An act of political protest, even if expressive, is entitled to no greater protection than any other act which violates a valid state statute.

B. Johnson's act of publicly burning a United States flag, even if politically motivated, clearly constituted conduct which Texas may proscribe.

1. Section 42.09(a)(3) is "content neutral."

2. There remain alternative avenues of communication.

3. To allow an act of flagburning to go unpunished because it occurred in the context of a political protest creates a "content based" exception to the statute.

V. THAT PORTION OF § 42.09(b) WHICH REQUIRES THAT THE ACTOR KNOW HIS ACTIONS WILL SERIOUSLY OFFEND IS NOT UNCONSTITUTIONALLY OVERBROAD.

A. The language of § 42.09(b) narrowly tailors the statute to punish only flagrant acts of flag desecration carried out in a public context.

B. There is no legislative alternative to § 42.09(b) which justifies the conclusion that it is unconstitutionally overbroad.

C. The "serious offense" language of § 42.09(b) can be excluded and the remainder of the statute given effect under a savings construction.

Graphic 18.8(b)   **From Respondent's Brief (Mr. Johnson):**

I. SECTION 42.09(a)(3) MUST SATISFY STRICT FIRST AMENDMENT SCRUTINY BECAUSE IT PROHIBITS CONDUCT SOLELY ON THE BASIS OF ITS COMMUNICATIVE IMPACT.

II. SECTION 42.09(a)(3) IS UNCONSTITUTIONAL ON ITS FACE.

A. Section 42.09(a)(3) punishes speech solely on the basis of its viewpoint.

B. The "seriously offend" clause of § 42.09(a)(3) proscribes expression solely on the basis of its communicative content, and the asserted state interests do not justify its infringement of expression.

1. The "seriously offend" clause of section 42.09(a)(3) is content-based.

2. The state's interests do not justify § 42.09(a)(3)'s content-based infringement on free expression.

a. Preserving the flag as a symbol of national unity is an impermissible justification for a restriction on expression.

b. Section 42.09(a)(3) is not narrowly tailored to the state's asserted interest in preventing breaches of the peace.

C. Section 42.09(a)(3) is unconstitutionally vague and overbroad.

1. Section 42.09(a)(3) is impermissibly vague.

2. Section 42.09(a)(3) is substantially overbroad.

III. SECTION 42.09(a)(3) IS UNCONSTITUTIONAL AS APPLIED TO THE FLAGBURNING AT ISSUE IN THIS CASE.

A. The flagburning at issue in this case was symbolic speech.

B. Mr. Johnson may have been convicted for his speech and affiliations.

---

§ 18.9   Further Argument Heading Examples

Notice how the following Headings, through careful manipulation of the facts, subtly persuade us to accept each party's viewpoint. We understand the case, and the gist of the relevant statute, even though we haven't yet read the facts. Please notice also which facts each party stresses.

- Which facts, omitted by the Browns, are emphasized by the State?
- How do the Browns refer to the surrogate mother? How does the State?
- Which party argues "policy"?

Graphic 18.9(a)   **Written by Counsel for the Browns**

I. THE BROWNS DID NOT VIOLATE SECTION TWO OF THE FLORIDA SURROGATE PARENTHOOD ACT, WHICH PROHIBITS "VALUABLE CONSIDERATION IN EXCHANGE FOR A CHILD," BY REIMBURSING SARA SMITH FOR THE PREGNANCY-RELATED MEDICAL AND PSYCHOLOGICAL EXPENSES SHE INCURRED AS A SURROGATE MOTHER FOR THEIR CHILD.

   A. The Browns merely reimbursed Sara Smith for expenses she incurred as a result of "pregnancy-related medical and psychological care or treatment" as provided for under the Act.

   B. The Browns' payment of Sara's pregnancy-related expenses was not "conditioned upon the transfer of parental or custodial rights" in the child, and the State has failed to offer any credible evidence to the contrary.

   C. An interest of "primary importance to society," as stated in the preamble of the Act, is protecting the best interests of children. Invalidating the Browns' surrogacy contract and making their child a ward of the State would defeat this fundamental legislative intent.

Graphic 18.9(b)   **Written by Counsel for the State**

I. THE BROWNS' SURROGATE PARENTHOOD AGREEMENT PROVIDES "VALUABLE CONSIDERATION IN EXCHANGE FOR A CHILD" AND VIOLATES THE FLORIDA SURROGATE PARENTHOOD ACT.

   A. The $30,000 the Browns paid to the surrogate mother to "reimburse" her for such expenses as a two-year membership in an exclusive health club and for designer clothes, constitutes "valuable consideration" and does not fall within the exception in the Act allowing for payment of "pregnancy-related medical or psychological care or treatment."

   B. Alternatively, even if the $30,000 payment was for the surrogate's "pregnancy-related medical or psychological care or treatment," the payment was nonetheless conditioned upon the transfer of the surrogate's parental rights. This payment thus constitutes "valuable consideration in exchange for a child" and violates the Act.

§ 18.10 Exercise in Designing an Argument Heading

Using the Jane Smith hypothetical (see § 5.10(b) and § 6.5), assume that the trial court held against Jane, and draft an Argument Heading for an appellate brief on her behalf. The issue is whether the sticky note attached to the bank statement met the requirement of testamentary intent.

Chapter Review
Argument Headings

In general, Headings and Subheadings should:

- ✓ include the governing rule and effectively use key facts;
- ✓ state a legal conclusion and identify the ruling we want;
- ✓ state the reasons for the legal conclusion;
- ✓ when read together, organize the Argument and tell the client's story;
- ✓ persuade the court to act in our favor;
- ✓ set out an entire, forceful, and self-contained outline of our theory; and
- ✓ be written in full sentences, ending with a period.

Bottom Line:

Argument Headings must make an *argument*. A Heading stating only a rule or factual conclusion is useless. A Heading is a *bold assertion* which also explains why a particular principle applies to our case. It stands on its own and provides the court with information necessary to reach the conclusion we advocate.

Practice Pointers   Writing Prompts
Designs for Argument Headings

Conclusion	Legal Point	Linking Words	Decisive Facts
"This Court should reverse affirm" "The court erred in"		"because" "where"	

OR

Subject	Legal Point	Linking Words	Decisive Facts
"The complaint" "The plaintiff" "The defendant"		"because" "where"	

✓ The [court] abused its discretion in [action] because [decisive facts].

✓ The [court] erred in granting [action] where [decisive facts].

✓ The [court] erred in entering summary judgment in favor of [party] because [decisive facts].

✓ [Statute, law] which prohibits [circumstances] violates [party's] [constitutional right or statutory right] because [decisive facts].

✓ The [court] erred as a matter of law in [action] because [decisive facts].

✓ The [court] was clearly erroneous in finding [action] where [decisive facts].

Chapter 19

Summary of Argument

"To go beyond is as wrong as to fall short."

—Confucius

§ 19.1   Purpose, Context, and Format

Purpose. The Summary of Argument ("Summary") is just that—a concise statement of our Argument. Through it we convey the most precise, persuasive, and self-contained version possible of our case. However, the Summary is *not* merely an outline of our assertions or a listing of our Argument Headings. Instead, it's literally a *summary* of the relevant *facts*, *rules*, and *conclusions* addressed in our brief.

Context. The Summary precedes the Argument section and directly follows the Statement of the Case and Facts. It's the section of the brief judges use in quickly familiarizing themselves with our case. It must be compelling, informative, and persuasive.

Format. The Summary is a persuasive narrative, written in paragraph form. It follows the BaRAC design but omits citations to the Record and to authorities. Generally, it shouldn't exceed two to three pages. Indeed, some rules of court mandate that the summary not exceed two pages. At this time, please read the Summary of Argument in each of the sample briefs in Chapters 36 and 37.

§ 19.2   Writing the Summary

The Summary is probably the most difficult to write, yet one of the most important sections of our brief. In it, and following the BaRAC design, we present a concise, self-contained statement of our main conclusions *and the most convincing reasons supporting them*. We introduce our judges to our view of the case and persuade them to accept our conclusions—all within a few pages.

Some attorneys write the Summary before the Argument section, using the Summary as an outline. Others write the Summary after the Argument. We often employ both methods by writing a rough draft of the Summary, then refining it when we've completed the Argument.

§ 19.2(a)   Initial Paragraph

When we have only two to three pages to state our entire argument, the initial paragraph in our Summary better pack a wallop. In it, we introduce the court to *our* case: to our client and to our theory. And, we tell the court, in the simplest terms possible, exactly what it must know to rule in our favor.

The principles that apply to writing a gripping initial paragraph also apply to beginning an oral argument with a bang. For this reason, in the examples below, we've illustrated effective initial paragraphs in briefs, speeches, and oral arguments. Which of the following is the most persuasive? Which contains the most relevant information? Which best conveys the client's theory of the case?

Ways to begin. One way to start the Summary is with the words, "This appeal addresses...."

For example:

Graphic 19.2(a)(1)   **Walker's Initial Paragraph**

---

bold assertion **rule** **application** **conclusion**	This appeal addresses an unusual issue of first impression: Lionell, who unwittingly ran over Walker while operating a freight train, has sued Walker, the injured party, for damages under the theory of intentional infliction of emotional distress. Lionell, who was not physically harmed in the accident, seeks to recover damages resulting from his alleged mental distress at having observed Walker's injury. Although imaginative, Lionell's theory is unsound. As this Court should hold, on *de novo* review, the tort of outrage must involve intolerably atrocious and outrageous conduct intentionally directed at the plaintiff; not, as in this case, political protest leading to the defendant's accidental injury.

Another way to start the initial paragraph is with the phrase, "This case is…," or "This is not a case…," or "This case does not …" and then state the theory. For example:

Graphic 19.2(a)(2)   **Lionell's Initial Paragraph**

---

bold assertion **rule** **application** **conclusion**	This case involves the intentional infliction of emotional distress upon an unsuspecting plaintiff. Appellant Parker Lionell seeks the right to bring his case before the jury; and asks this Court, on *de novo* review, to reverse the trial court's dismissal of his complaint. Lionell's allegations that Appellee Noah Walker's extreme and outrageous conduct intentionally and recklessly caused Lionell to suffer severe emotional distress are sufficient to state a cause for intentional infliction of emotional distress.

Perhaps the most interesting "Summaries of Arguments" we've heard involved the impeachment hearings of President William Clinton. During those hearings, members of the House of Representatives had one, that's right, *one* minute to express their case, pro or con, regarding impeachment. If ever there was a time succinctly to state a theory of a case and argue the merits, that was it. Here's what two Representatives said in their one-minute speeches:

Graphic 19.2(a)(3)   **One Minute Speech: Republican**

By Mr. Rogan:

"Mr. Speaker, the evidence is overwhelming. The question is elementary. The president was obliged, under his sacred oath, faithfully to execute our nation's laws. Yet he repeatedly perjured himself and obstructed justice. Not for any noble purposes, but to crush a humble, lone woman's right to be afforded access to courts. Now his defenders plead for no constitutional accountability for the one American uniquely able to defend or debase our Constitution and rule of law.

When they are old enough to appreciate today's solemnity, I want my young daughters to know that when the last roll was called, their father served in a house faithful to the guiding principle that no person is above the law. And he served with colleagues who counted it a privilege to risk political fortune in defense of the Constitution."

Graphic 19.2(a)(4)   One Minute Speech: Democrat

By Ms. Lee:

"Thank you, Mr. Speaker. I rise to strongly oppose these Articles of Impeachment and this very flawed and undemocratic process. This process and this action are the real crimes against the American people and our democracy. This march to impeachment is an attempt to undo and overthrow a duly elected president and ignores the will of the people. Denying a vote on censure creates the appearance of a one party autocracy, which we condemn abroad and which history has proven can lead to authoritarian rule.

This Republican Party coup underscores that their only goal is to turn back the clock on an agenda that puts people first.... [They seek to] cancel policies that value and support basic human rights, such as a woman's right to choose; a good public education instead of vouchers; that insists on a living wage for working men and women; that protects our environment; that supports a patient's bill of rights; and that preserves Social Security.

The Republican process is cynical and dangerous. It will be recorded that they stood on the wrong side of history. We must restore the public trust and establish a Congress which communicates respect for the people of the United States, the Constitution, and democracy."

Another illustrative example of getting right to the heart of the matter concerned the seemingly uninteresting issue of whether admiralty jurisdiction extended to *limit the liability* of Great Lakes, the owner of a vessel, for damage occurring to several downtown Chicago businesses, including Marshall Fields, a department store. *See Jerome B. Grubart, Inc. v. Great Lakes Dredge & Dock Co.*, 513 U.S. 527 (1995). Great Lakes, while replacing pilings in the bed of the Chicago River, inadvertently damaged the City's old underground freight tunnel system, resulting in the flooding of several businesses, including Marshall Fields.

Here's how counsel for the flooded businesses, Mr. Rosenthal, began his oral argument in the United States Supreme Court:

Graphic 19.2(a)(5)   **Counsel for Flooded Businesses:**
Opening Statement

"Today, the Court is asked to extend admiralty jurisdiction beyond its historic boundaries, the shore and property abutting the shore, and bring it into the basements of downtown Chicago. While we think it extraordinary that there should be Federal admiralty jurisdiction over water in the basement of Marshall Fields, that is what the court of appeals managed to hold, and this morning I will press two points with respect to that holding."

Here's how counsel for Great Lakes, Mr. Roberts (who became Chief Justice of the United States Supreme Court), began:

Graphic 19.2(a)(6)   Counsel for Great Lakes: Opening Statement

---

"The petitioners seek to hold Great Lakes liable for the operations of its vessel on the navigable waters of the Chicago River while that vessel was doing what vessels of its sort normally do on navigable water, maritime repair work. In this instance, replacing pilings in the river."

Both lawyers conveyed their theory of the case masterfully. Both wove the facts into the legal standard effortlessly. Both painted a vibrant and memorable picture of their cases. We see the flooded Marshall Fields basement and ponder how a judge could have ever found that federal law governed there. But we also see the vessel, in the Chicago River, with a crew engaged in repairs, and question how anyone could find otherwise.

§ 19.2(b)   After the Initial Paragraph: A Checklist

To provide the court with enough information in the Summary to agree with the conclusions we've reached, we do the following:

(1) Briefly state the decisive facts—provide the facts necessary to place the issues in context.

(2) Briefly state what the lower court held, whether our court should affirm or reverse, and why.

(3) Briefly state the precise issues and the standard of review for each issue, if different.

(4) Paraphrase the relevant statutes, constitutional provisions, or other governing law (if any).

(5) Explain each step in the argument leading to the conclusion our court should reach. This includes applying the relevant rules to the facts. For each contested

point, include a bold assertion, the rule, how the rule applies to our facts, and a conclusion. Our Summary follows the BaRAC design, but without citations or case explanations.

(6) State what the reviewing court should do—request relief.

§ 19.3   Exercise in Designing a Summary of Argument

Using the Jane Smith hypothetical (see § 5.10(b) and § 6.5) (again!), assume that the trial court held against Jane, and draft a Summary of Argument for an appellate brief on her behalf. The issue is whether the sticky note attached to the bank statement met the requirement of testamentary intent.

Chapter Review
Summary of Argument

✓ The Summary is the place in our brief to convey the heart of our argument. It must be persuasive, complete, self-contained, and *to the point.*

✓ The Summary begins with a strong initial paragraph which introduces the case—the parties, legal issues, and theory—to the court.

✓ The Summary should not exceed 2 or 3 pages (check applicable court rules) and should follow the BaRAC design, but without citations or case explanations.

Practice Pointers	Writing Prompts
	Initial Paragraphs

"This appeal addresses...."

"This is / is not a case...."

"This case involves...."

"In this case, the Court addresses whether...."

"This case requires this Court to determine...."

"[Facts — legal action by the trial court]. At issue is whether...."

"This case involves a clash between...."

"This cases arises from an inevitable conflict between...."

"The First Amendment protects.... However, as this case demonstrates,...."

Chapter 20

The Argument

"The powerful argument begins and ends by telling the truth. Truth is power."

—Gerry Spence

"The successful argument must be one which makes the reader *want* to believe. Something warmer than the cold science of logic is needed to achieve this purpose. Logic may be a means of showing the reader that his preconceived ideas have been wrong; but this is not enough. A man convinced against his will is of the same opinion still. Persuasion must create a desire to believe."

—Frank E. Cooper[1]

---

1. Frank E. Cooper, *Writing in Law Practice* 24 (1963).

§ 20.1   Purpose

Through the Argument, we prove that the legal standards as applied to our facts require (legally and morally) the court to reach the result we advocate. We create, from an almost limitless number of possibilities, an orderly procession of statements leading logically and inevitably to our conclusion.

§ 20.2   Context

The Argument section is the main body of the brief. Here, we either succeed or fail in convincing the court of the legitimacy of our client's claims. For this reason, the Argument must:

(1) be persuasive, backed by logic, and clearly written;

(2) be supported by common sense; and

(3) contain all the information (i.e., legal rules and facts with proper citations to authorities and the Record on Appeal) the judges need to rule in our favor. Indeed, "[w]hen points, positions, facts and supporting authorities are omitted from the brief, a court is entitled to believe that such are waived, abandoned, or deemed by counsel to be unworthy."[2]

Caveat: Because we've already discussed, in prior chapters, techniques for writing effectively, using cases, and employing logic, we deal here only with a few remaining topics particular to the Argument section.

§ 20.3   Format

The following illustrates the *design* of the Argument section:

Graphic 20.3(a)   General Design of the Argument Section
<div align="center">ARGUMENT</div>
[We may, but need not, include a *brief* introduction of the case here (i.e., between the word "Argument" and our first Heading). If we do, we write this introduction in paragraph form.]

---

2. *Polyglycoat Corp. v. Hirsch Distributors, Inc.*, 442 So. 2d 958, 960 (Fla. Dist. Ct. App. 1983).

I. THE FIRST MAIN ARGUMENT HEADING FOR THE CASE GOES HERE. IT'S WRITTEN IN ALL CAPITAL LETTERS AND IS SINGLE-SPACED.

Under this Main Heading, we discuss the law and facts relevant to this argument. We follow the BaRAC design. We lead with the bold assertion of our position, followed by the rule (and rule explanation), our application of the rule to our facts, and our conclusion. We then respond to any relevant counter-arguments.[3]

II. THE SECOND MAIN ARGUMENT HEADING FOR THE CASE GOES HERE. IT'S WRITTEN IN ALL CAPITAL LETTERS AND IS SINGLE-SPACED.

Under this Main Heading, we discuss the law and the facts relevant to this argument. If we have Subheadings under this Heading, we introduce the general rule involved. We then discuss, in the Subheadings below, the specific elements (of the rule) and apply those elements to our facts. Along the way, we respond to any relevant counter-arguments.

A. <u>Our first Subheading goes here. It's written in complete sentences, in lower case, and is underlined.</u>

B. <u>Our second Subheading goes here. It's written in complete sentences, in lower case, and is underlined.</u>

Graphic 20.3(b)   **Detailed Design of the Argument Section: Example of a Multi-Issue Argument**

<u>ARGUMENT</u>

[Introduction optional]

I. MAIN HEADING WRITTEN IN ONE OR MORE SENTENCES.

bold assertion

rule and rule explanation

application

   counter-argument (if any)

      bold assertion

      rule and rule explanation

      application

      conclusion

   response

      bold assertion

      rule and rule explanation

      application

      conclusion

conclusion to heading I.

---

3. We cite the Record on Appeal using the same format as we used in the Statement of the Case and Facts, i.e., (R.3.). See Chapter 15, § 15.2(a).

II. MAIN HEADING WRITTEN IN ONE OR MORE SENTENCES.
introduction:
> **bold assertion**
> **general rule**
> **general application**
> **conclusion**
> A. <u>Subheading written in one or more sentences.</u>
>> **bold assertion**
>> **rule and rule explanation**
>> **application**
>>> **counter-argument (if any)**
>>>> bold assertion
>>>> rule and rule explanation
>>>> application
>>>> conclusion
>>> **response**
>>>> bold assertion
>>>> rule and rule explanation
>>>> application
>>>> conclusion
>> **conclusion to subheading A**
> B. <u>Subheading written in one or more sentences.</u>
>> **bold assertion**
>> **rule and rule explanation**
>> **application**
>>> **counter-argument (if any)**
>>>> bold assertion
>>>> rule and rule explanation
>>>> application
>>>> conclusion
>>> **response**
>>>> bold assertion
>>>> rule and rule explanation
>>>> application
>>>> conclusion
>> **conclusion to subheading B and to heading II**

§ 20.4   Differences Between the Argument Section of the Brief and the Discussion Section of the Memo

In both a memo and a brief, we analyze legal issues while attempting to solve a "problem." Our goal in both documents is to ethically serve the best interests of our client. However, the way we go about doing this differs significantly between memo writing and brief writing.

Audience. When we write a memo, our audience is our client and our colleagues. We suggest a course of action after analyzing the pros and cons of alternatives. We candidly articulate both the strengths and weaknesses of our case and predict how the court will rule on each issue.

In contrast, when we write a brief, our audience is the court, the court's clerk, our opposing counsel, our colleagues, our client, and, potentially, the public.[4] Instead of speaking to our client or a colleague, we speak directly to the court. Rather than suggesting a course of conduct, we convince the court that our way is the *only* way to go. We persuade the court that reason, policy, and, of course, the law, mandate our solution to the problem.

No "hedging." Thus, in brief writing, unlike memo writing, we do not "hedge." We do not write that the court "probably should" do anything or that the facts "seem" to favor our position. Such abstract language weakens our argument. Instead, we use precise, concrete words: "This Court *should* reverse ...";[5] "The statute *provides* ..."; "The Appellant's argument *misstates* the governing rule...." Our client is paying us to *win* the case, not to debate it.

Designing a favorable rule. And because our goal is to win the case and not merely to analyze our options, we also present the legal rule persuasively. *In doing so, however, we never mislead the court or misrepresent the law or the facts.* In a memo, where we analyze the strengths and weaknesses of our client's position, we state the rules in an objective, straight-forward manner. However, in a brief, where we write to win, we present the rules in the light most favorable to our position. We do not simply extract rules from cases as if we were merely "briefing" these cases. Rather, we give serious thought to how, consistent with canons of ethics and principles of professionalism, we can design the rule to favor our client and to obtain the relief we seek.

Recall from §§ 5.2 and 5.3 that we use the strongest (i.e., binding) authority for the rule. Once we've determined the source of our rule, we can use several techniques to phrase the rule in the light most favorable to our position. These techniques include stating the rule broadly or narrowly, stressing the relief sought, addressing policy concerns, and using sentence structure and word choice to emphasize favorable, and to downplay unfavorable, aspects of the rule.

In the following examples, we illustrate how to put these techniques to work. Recall (who could forget?) the dog bite case involving Bit Ten and the Owners.[6] In these examples, we see an objective statement of the "easily readable" requirement of the statute, then Bit Ten's and the Owners's favorable rule interpretations:

---

4. Unless a brief is filed under seal, it's available to the public. Our writing literally becomes a matter of "public record."

5. However, we do not order the court to do our bidding. For example, we do not say, "this Court *must* reverse...." We remain respectful in what we write.

6. See Chapter 11, § 11.6.

Graphic 20.4(a)   **"Objective" Statement of the Rule**

Under § 767.04, Fla. Stat., dog owners are exempt from liability to persons bitten by their dogs if they have a sign posted that is "easily readable" and includes the words "Bad Dog." One court has determined that a sign is not "easily readable" to a child of tender years who cannot read the English language and was a foreseeable victim. *Tot v. Vicious*.

Graphic 20.4(b)   **Bit Ten's Statement of the Rule**

Under § 767.04, Fla. Stat., dog owners are exempt from liability to persons bitten by their dogs if they have a sign posted that is "easily readable" and includes the words "Bad Dog." A warning sign is not "easily readable" where the victim cannot read English and was a foreseeable victim. *Tot v. Vicious*.

Query: Although Bit Ten would, of course, fully explain the *Tot* case in her rule explanation so as not to mislead the court, does her rule statement nonetheless impermissibly cross the line between advocacy and misrepresentation? Note that Bit Ten has emphasized the foreseeability aspect of the rule and has omitted any mention of the tender years doctrine.

Graphic 20.4(c)   **Owners's Statement of the Rule**

Under § 767.04, Fla. Stat., dog owners are exempt from liability to persons bitten by their dogs if they have a sign posted that is "easily readable" and includes the words "Bad Dog." The only case interpreting the statute held that a posted warning sign which states "Bad Dog" is not easily readable where the victim is a child of tender years who cannot read the English language. *Tot v. Vicious*.

The Owners, understandably, have emphasized the limited nature of the *Tot* rule. However, they've omitted any reference to the "forseeability" factor. Were they correct in doing so? Have Bit Ten and the Owners misled the court?

§ 20.5   Organizing Our Thoughts

We write our brief as if we were writing the court's opinion for our case. Our goal is to guide each step of the court's thought processes. We educate the court about our case, then persuade it to accept our conclusions. However, we can't guide another through unfamiliar terrain. We think through each step of our argument before we write it.

This process of thinking through our argument helps us to understand the argument's "logical flow," or the way our ideas and legal authorities combine to support our conclusion. When we understand what we must prove, we work backwards to organize the facts and cases to lead our reader to the result we seek.

An outline is the best method for organizing our thoughts. A strong outline sets forth each step in our reasoning and demonstrates where each authority "fits." It gives us a cohesive, common sense view of our entire case. If our outline doesn't provide this "finished" sense, we examine its parts to see if changing their order improves our argument. If we can't arrange the parts into a cohesive whole, we conduct further analysis, further research, or both.

Here's one way of creating an outline:

(1) Know exactly what the two sides argued below and how the lower court resolved those issues.

(2) Know exactly what the parties are arguing now. Determine the exact issue on appeal and what subissues, if any, are contained in that issue. What is the standard of review? Which precedents must our court follow? Which precedents are merely persuasive?

(3) Begin thinking of possible arguments. Determine exactly what we need to win, and argue only those points. Create a syllogism for each issue.

(4) Begin creating Argument Headings and Subheadings[7]—i.e., our outline.

(5) Know the facts inside and out by reading and analyzing the Record on Appeal. Take notes and summarize important testimony. Insert relevant facts, with citations to the Record, into our outline.

(6) Add to our outline the "legal" and "common sense" (policy) arguments supporting our position *and* citations to the rules and facts relevant to each argument. Also include the arguments, rules, and facts (with citations) our opponent will use and our response to them. State our arguments and our opponent's arguments in BaRAC form.

Important: If we fail to use an outline, we'll be left with piles of cases and piles of notes at the "end" of our research. We'll then have to weed through those piles in a frantic effort to connect cases with arguments. However, if we fill in our outline as we research, and use a case chart (see Chapter 7, § 7.5), we'll have an organized view of the law and facts we'll use, as well as the law and facts our opponents will likely use against us.

If we find it difficult to create an outline of our entire Argument, we can start by selecting a portion and organizing that. (We address how to do this in detail in § 20.6(a)

---

7. We address Argument Headings and Subheadings in Chapter 18.

below.) We craft Argument Headings, Subheadings, and topic sentences. We fill in the outline with authorities supporting each point. In this way, we create our outline, piece by piece, and don't become overwhelmed by the "big picture." We repeat this procedure with our other arguments and eventually arrange those pieces into an outline of our entire case.

§ 20.6   Writing the Argument

In writing the Argument, our goals are to:

(1) educate the court;

(2) persuade the court; and

(3) win the case.

We accomplish these goals by presenting a compelling argument, supported by the law, logic, and common sense. By educating the court on the law and on our facts, we give the court enough information to rule in our favor. But this alone is not enough. We must also give the court a reason to want to rule in our favor. We do this by presenting our case in a compelling, persuasive fashion—highlighting not only the "legal" correctness of our position but the "moral" correctness as well. Through our argument, we show the court that it's not just properly applying the law to our facts, it's also doing justice in the process.

§ 20.6(a)   Create an Outline of "Issue Boxes"

To win our case, we give the court the tools it needs to agree with us. Our argument is a roadmap, directing each of the court's steps. The BaRAC design helps us here by providing the structure to transport the court from point A to point D and through all the points in-between.

But before we express this roadmap to the court, we must internalize and understand it ourselves. We look carefully at each issue and how that issue relates to the other issues. Is any issue dispositive of the others? Must we establish one issue before we can proceed to the others? Are any issues actually alternative arguments? Which issues are independent? Which are dependent? (We address ordering issues in detail in § 20.6(c).)

We find it easiest, when dealing with issues, to compartmentalize them. In other words, we consider each issue as if we were placing it into a box and dealing with it exclusively. Not surprisingly, as the following graphics illustrate, the BaRAC design provides the parameters of that box.

Graphic 20.6(a)(1)	Create an "Issue Box" for Each Issue
standard of review	State the standard of review for the issue.[8]
bold assertion	State how the court should rule on this issue.
type of rule	Determine the type of rule analysis involved:[9] (1) rule-only: factor analysis; (2) rule-plus: the illustrative approach; or (3) fihrr: reasoning by analogy.
rule design	State and explain the applicable rule. If the rule is unclear, explain why our interpretation is correct. Cite and address any relevant authorities.
application	Apply the rule to the facts relevant to this issue.[10] **bold assertion:** State the conclusion the court should reach regarding the application of the rule to our facts. **rule:** If necessary, further explain the rule or its elements. Address relevant authorities. **application:** Show how the rule applies to our facts. **conclusion:** State the conclusion the court should reach regarding the application of the rule to our facts. **counter-arguments:** Discuss and respond to any relevant and harmful arguments and authorities.
conclusion	State how the court should rule on this issue.

By creating a box like this for each issue, we create a "syllogism with attitude" for arguing our case. We know exactly the outcome we seek and exactly how to lead the court to that end.

Here's another version of the issue box, this time without any comments:

---

8. See Chapter 16: Standards of Review.

9. We explain this process in the next section, § 20.6(b).

10. Please see §§ 20.6(c), (d), and (e).

Graphic 20.6(a)(2)	Issue Box		
issue			
standard of review citation[11]			
bold assertion			
rule design general rule citation	❑ rule-only: 　factor 　analysis	❑ rule-plus: 　illustrative 　approach	❑ fihrr: 　analogy
specific rule citation			
application with record and case citations			
counter-argument & response			
conclusion			
updating			

§ 20.6(b)　Determine How to Address the Rule and How to Apply That Rule to Our Facts

We've discussed, in prior chapters, generally how to develop a rule from a statute, case, or multiple cases and how to apply that rule to our facts. These chapters reveal that we can discuss rules and their application to facts in many different ways. But this multitude of discussion options is maddening. It leads many novice writers to throw up, er, their hands in utter frustration. Too many choices, not enough time. How do we know the best way to explain and apply a rule? The answer is: *(drum roll)* ... WE DON'T ... *(sounds of heads clunking against wooden desks, or even worse, computer keyboards)*.

---

11. Cite the rule and authority re the proper standard of review governing the issue.

There's no one best way of explaining and applying any given rule to any given set of facts. However, we have noticed three clear patterns of effective rule development and application: (1) Rule-only: factor analysis; (2) Rule-plus: the illustrative approach; and (3) FIHRR: reasoning by analogy. We review these patterns in the graphics below.

Graphic 20.6(b)(1)	Rule-Only: Factor Analysis
rule	The rule from the case or other authority contains several relatively distinct factors.
how to state the rule	List the factors; i.e., paraphrase or quote the relevant language. See Chapter 6, §6.5(a).
type of reasoning	Deductive.
suggested application	Apply the factors, one-by-one, to our facts. If necessary, create a Subheading for each factor. If not, use transitions to inform the reader that we're moving from one factor to the next.

Graphic 20.6(b)(2)	Rule-Plus: the Illustrative Approach
rule	We have a general, but (surprise!) rather vague rule which we can best define by referring to a variety of cases illustrating that rule.
how to state the rule	State or derive a general rule; then explain that rule by citing, via parentheticals, illustrative examples from the cases. See Chapter 6, §6.5(b).
type of reasoning	*If we must derive the rule from several cases,* we reason inductively in creating the rule; then reason deductively in applying that rule to our facts. *If a case provides the general rule,* we reason deductively in applying that general rule to our facts. *However, in either situation,* we can also reason by analogy by comparing and contrasting the parenthetical examples (from the cited cases) to our facts.
suggested application	Apply the general rule and reach a conclusion; then support that conclusion by comparing and contrasting the parenthetical examples to our facts.

Graphic 20.6(b)(3)	FIHRR: Reasoning by Analogy
rule	We want to import the rule from an analogous case into our case.
how to state the rule	State or derive a general rule; then explain that rule by the FIHRR approach. In other words, after stating the general rule, *show how it was applied in the cited case*. Do this by explaining the relevant facts, issue, holding, rule, and reasoning of the cited case. See Chapter 6, § 6.3(c).
type of reasoning	*If we must derive the rule*, we reason inductively in creating that rule; then reason deductively in applying that rule to our facts.
	If a case provides the general rule, we reason deductively in applying that general rule to our facts.
	However, in either situation, we also reason by analogy by comparing and contrasting the cited case to our case.
suggested application	Apply the general rule and reach a conclusion; then support that conclusion by comparing and contrasting the cited case to our case.

§ 20.6(c)   Brief Any Dispositive Issue First, Then Advance Our Strongest Position

Order our issues. After we create a "box" for each issue, (see Graphics 20.6(a)(1) and 20.6(a)(2)), we then map out how all the boxes fit together. We consider which issues stand independently and which depend on others. We group the dependent boxes together, in the order we must logically present them to the court. We then evaluate each argument, from the strongest to the weakest. We thus order our arguments to best suit our analysis as follows:

> I. dispositive issues
> II. strongest issue
> III. next strongest issue
> IV. weakest issue

Dispositive issue. A "dispositive issue" is one the court must rule on before moving to any other issue. For example, in a contract case, we must first establish that there *was* a contract (the dispositive issue) before we argue that it has been breached. Because dispositive issues determine the fate of other issues, we place them first in our argument.

Our strongest issue. After any dispositive issues, we brief our most compelling argument. The judges' enthusiasm for our argument will be strongest as they begin reading. If we immediately capture their attention and confidence, we make an excellent first impression which carries through to the rest of our brief. Within this issue, we first address any threshold issue(s). In our contract case example above, whether there *was* a contract is both a dispositive issue (i.e., if there was no contract, that could be the end of the case), and a threshold issue because the court would first have to decide whether there *was* a contract before deciding whether it was breached.

Our weakest issue. Every case has a weak issue — some point we wish didn't exist in our case. What do we do about it? We face it, that's what. As trial and appellate attorney Gerry Spence counsels:

> You can expose your weaknesses in a better light than your opponent who will expose them in the darkest possible way. An honest admission, having come from you, not only endows you with credibility, it also leaves your opponent with nothing to say except what you have already admitted.[12]

Again, within this issue, and any others, we first address any threshold issue(s).

Our strongest argument and strongest authority. Within our discussion of each issue, we state our strongest argument first and lead with our strongest authority.

Alternative issues. If any argument is an alternative to one we have already addressed, we say so in our Argument Heading as well as in the argument itself. If we fail to identify an alternative argument as an alternative, we will confuse the court.

Overlapping issues. We also identify any issue that relates back to a prior one. Often, issues overlap. In that event, instead of repeating points, we refer the court back to the pages in our argument where we've already addressed the point. In essence, we incorporate that prior part "by reference." This cuts down on repetitive arguments and streamlines our brief.

Never mislead the court. Please refer to Chapters 5, 6, and 7 regarding evaluating and using cases. We add here a reminder that in dealing with authorities, we can't mislead the court. A common error we've seen among students and lawyers alike involves stating that an issue has been "resolved" when, in fact, the authority cited for that point is non-binding. Stating that an issue has been resolved, when it hasn't been resolved by any case binding in *our* jurisdiction, is unethical.

For example, assume that our case is in the First Circuit, that the case on point is from the Eighth Circuit, and that the Eighth Circuit is the only court that has considered the issue. We could not honestly say:

> "It is settled law that wolves are capable of forming the intent to kill. [citation]"

However, we could introduce the case as follows:

> "In the only decision that has considered the issue, the Eighth Circuit Court of Appeals held that wolves are capable of forming the intent to kill."

If other circuits have considered the issue and arrived at a different conclusion, we acknowledge the opposing view and distinguish those cases from our case.

Primary vs. secondary authority. The court considers the source of legal authority in determining how much weight a particular argument merits. "Primary authority" is

---

12. Gerry Spence, *How to Argue and Win Every Time* 204 (1995).

more persuasive than secondary authority. In briefs that discuss federal statutory issues, primary authority includes not only case law and statutes but also federal regulations and legislative history.

If we have no primary support for our view, then, and only then, do we use "secondary authority." For example, a law review article might provide an excellent discussion of public policy, and can be the source of a creative argument. However, we never use secondary authority in the place of primary authority. For example, if a law review article and a case stand for the same proposition, we cite the case. Naturally, we update all our authorities. (See § 5.3).

The next step. After we've ordered our issues and our authorities, we then carefully consider how to write the initial paragraphs for each issue. We describe this process in the next section.

§ 20.6(d)   Dazzle the Court with a Clear and Persuasive Initial Paragraph

In our initial paragraph and using the BaRAC design, we immediately tell the court the trial court's error (appellant / petitioner) or why the trial court ruled properly (appellee / respondent). Then, we briefly state the general rule involved, the relevant standard of review, the most critical facts, and what we want the reviewing court to do. (We discuss the specifics of the rule and facts in later paragraphs.)

Graphic 20.6(d)(1)	Content of Initial Paragraph(s)
bold assertion	Appellant/Petitioner: State how the lower court erred.
	Appellee/Respondent: State why the lower court ruled correctly.
	Note: If appropriate, include the standard of review in the bold assertion.
rule	Paint a broad picture of our legal theory by stating:
	(1) the relevant standard of review (if not included in the bold assertion); and
	(2) the general rule involved.
application	Briefly apply the rule to the critical facts.
conclusion	Tell the reviewing court what it should do: reverse, affirm, modify, remand, etc.

Graphic 20.6(d)(2)	Example of an Initial Paragraph
bold assertion with standard of review	This Court, on *de novo* review, *see* [citation omitted] should reverse the trial court's judgment, and hold that John Doe's conviction under Gotham City's Anti-Begging Code violates the Eighth Amendment. As
rule	the Supreme Court has held, a person cannot be punished for his or her status. *Robinson v. California*, 370 U.S. 660, 667 (1962). Yet, this is ex-
application	actly what happened here. For simply asking a passerby for "spare change for a homeless man," Doe was convicted and sentenced to ninety days in jail. His peaceful begging, his "crime," was inextricably tied to his status as a homeless person. In punishing Doe for begging,
conclusion	the City punished him for being homeless. Because this punishment violates the Eighth Amendment, this Court should reverse Doe's conviction.

After reading our initial paragraphs(s), the reviewing court should know the exact conflict it's facing. In other words, the court should know (because we've told it), the standard of review and whether the issue involves a clash over (1) applying a *settled* rule to settled facts, (2) interpreting an *agreed-upon* rule and applying that rule to our facts, or (3) selecting the *controlling* rule and applying that rule to our facts.

Important. In the initial paragraph(s), we don't address in detail the rule or the application of that rule to our facts. Our initial paragraphs serve not as the argument but to introduce the argument. We save the details of the argument for subsequent paragraphs or subsections. If our initial paragraphs are filled with details we later repeat in our argument, we'll confuse and bore the court. We'll also waste valuable space in our brief—something we can't afford to do.

We know we've written effective introductory paragraphs if we can separate the bold assertions from each, list them, and in so doing, form a strong outline of our entire argument. Moreover, as the graphic below illustrates, our initial paragraph is effective if the court can, with minor changes, transform it into the opening paragraph of an opinion in our favor.

Graphic 20.6(d)(3)	The Court's Initial Paragraph
bold assertion with standard of review	This Court, on *de novo* review, *see* [*citation omitted*], reverses the trial court's judgment and holds that John Doe's conviction under Gotham City's Anti-Begging Code violates the Eighth Amendment. As
rule	the Supreme Court has held, a person cannot be punished for his or her status. *Robinson v. California*, 370 U.S. 660, 667 (1962). Yet, this is
application	exactly what happened here. For simply asking a passerby for "spare change for a homeless man," Doe was convicted and sentenced to ninety days in jail. His peaceful begging, his "crime," was inextricably

conclusion	tied to his status as a homeless person. In punishing Doe for begging, the City punished him for being homeless. Because this punishment violates the Eighth Amendment, we reverse Doe's conviction.

§ 20.6(e) Address Contrary Points after Advancing Our Position, and Conclude with a Summary of Our Position

As advocates, we anticipate our opponent's arguments and confront damaging precedent through counter-analysis. But this analysis should follow positive arguments for our client. We make *our* argument and support it first, then we distinguish contrary cases.

Just as words placed at the beginning and ending of sentences and paragraphs have the most impact, so too do points made at the beginning and ending of each section of our argument. Therefore, after we acknowledge contrary authority, and either distinguish it or point out its error, we return to our position. Our readers will then remember most clearly the points supporting our position.

§ 20.7   Review Our Brief from the Reader's Perspective

Once we've written a draft of our brief, we review it from the perspective of the judges who will be reading it. Before we do this, however, we need to know something about those judges. We do our homework.

Who are our judges? Assuming that we know who the judges on our panel will be, we research to uncover what, if anything, they've said regarding the issues involved in our case. We also read opinions they've authored on unrelated issues. Through these writings, we get a better sense of our audience.

Educate, then persuade. But, regardless of the information we find, we view our judges as people who are intelligent and familiar with the legal process but who are not familiar with the facts or arguments of our case. When we think of a judge, we likely imagine a legal scholar—a person with expertise. In deference to this expertise, we often skip over the simpler points of our argument, assuming that the judge must know them and that it would be insulting to discuss such simple concepts. *Never make such assumptions!*

In reality, judges don't see omitting steps in the reasoning process as compliments to their ability. Rather, they see an incomplete argument. They question, and rightly so, our ability to reason thoroughly, and they question, as they should, the validity of our conclusions. If we want the judge to accept our conclusions, we include each step of every argument leading to those conclusions. We educate the judge before we persuade her to accept our view.

Don't jump from A to D. Providing the court with incomplete information undermines our efforts to guide the judge's reasoning and cripples our brief. We might as well just shoot ourselves in the foot. One common "the lights are all on but nobody is home" error is to begin a brief by discussing whether a statute applies to our facts without first providing the court with the relevant statutory language or facts.

For example, consider a brief which begins by stating: "The Civil Rights Act of 1964 does not apply to married women." Although judges may know what the Civil Rights Act says generally, they probably don't know the statute's precise wording. If the judge wants to read the language, she's forced to send her clerk to fetch it or to look it up herself; a nuisance considering the number of briefs judges must read.

Another example of incomplete information concerns stating that something is "obvious." Assume that we represent the prosecution in a criminal appeal. Assume further that the crime involved has three elements, but our argument focuses on only one. We do not write: "It is obvious that the prosecution has proved the first two elements of the crime," and then discuss only the last element. Whether the other elements have been proven might be obvious to the prosecution, but it's not obvious to the judge.

Just as the judge knows only what we tell her about our facts, so too, she knows only what we tell her about the cases we cite. If we want the judge to know something about a cited case, we provide that information. We can't assume that the judge has read the cited case and is familiar with its key facts, issue, holding, rule, and reasoning.

Indeed, if, after reading our brief, the judge must read the cited cases to understand their significance to our argument, we've failed. We've wasted space in our brief; we've been ineffective and inefficient. We haven't put those cited cases to work for us.

The bottom line: We write our argument so that it gently takes the judge by the hand, and leads her step-by-step through the analytical process, leading to victory for our client. We write our brief so the court can easily transform it into an opinion ruling in our favor. We write our brief bearing in mind that the only thing obvious to the judge is that we want our client to win. Everything else, we must fully explain.

§ 20.8   Use a Respectful Tone

"He that flings dirt at another dirtieth himself most."

—Thomas Fuller

The tone of our brief reflects our respect for the judge and for the legal system in general. While we appeal to the judge's emotions as well as to reason, we don't make a highly emotional or exaggerated pitch.

Avoid overstatement. Failure to use subtlety in our language can be costly. Characterizing the other side as "vicious," "unscrupulous," or "remorseless" will get us nowhere. It serves only to create resistance to the very characterizations we're trying to establish.

Avoid disparaging other courts. Very few advocates will intentionally attack the court hearing their case. However, the court might consider statements such as "no other conclusion is possible" as an attack, if the court is inclined to reach a different conclusion. Attacks on other courts also raise the ire of our court. Instead of attacking any court or any person, we criticize the court's or person's *reasoning*.

Graphic 20.8	Attack vs. Criticism
this is an attack — don't do it:	"The Eighth Circuit's ridiculous position in *Smith* is totally illogical and can be defended only as ignoring precedent."
this is permissible criticism:	"The court misapplied the doctrine of the *Smith* case."

In some cases, however, the line between "attack" and "vigorous advocacy" is hard to draw. Here's what we recommend: If we can't, face-to-face, repeat to our court, the lower court, or opposing counsel what we've written, then that statement has no place in our brief.

§ 20.9   Do Not Characterize Our Argument as Opinion

Phrases like "my argument," "I will argue," and "the Appellant contends" (when we're counsel for Appellant) are weak and redundant. *Of course* we're contending what's in our brief. It's *our* brief. These editorial comments give the judge the impression that our brief is simply a series of our opinions, rather than well-reasoned conclusions arising from the just and fair application of the law to our facts. We state our position; we don't editorialize.

§ 20.10   Edit Our Work, Then Edit It Again, and Again, and Again, and Again

No argument is complete until we've edited it at least five times. Five. And, when we review our brief those five (at least) five times, we read it as if we were reading it for the first time. We read it as if we knew nothing more about our case or the applicable law than what our brief tells us.

In Chapter 24, we review in detail how to edit our entire brief. In the Chapter Review section below, we offer a checklist for drafting and evaluating the argument section. Here, we offer four general editing suggestions relevant to the content of the argument:

The argument should:

(1) contain strong bold assertions stating the conclusions the court should reach on each issue;

(2) include all logical steps necessary to reach our conclusions;

(3) provide all critical facts and legal authorities; and

(4) contain no unnecessary arguments, words, or phrases.

And of course, it should be *a winner*.

Chapter Review
Checklist for Writing a Persuasive Argument[13]

Organization

Large-Scale Organization: Overall Argument Section

✓ State each ground for relief as a separate Argument Heading.

✓ Include only grounds necessary to the argument.

✓ Arrange issues logically.

✓ Clearly indicate threshold or dispositive issues *as* threshold or dispositive.

✓ Place the dispositive or threshold issue first.

✓ Unless logic requires otherwise, arrange all issues in order of strength.

✓ Acknowledge our weakest arguments.

✓ Clearly indicate, in the Argument Headings, alternative issues as alternatives.

✓ Make clear in the Argument Headings any interdependence between issues.

✓ Check to ensure that if we list the bold assertions from each initial paragraph, a strong outline of our entire argument emerges.

Small-Scale Organization: Argument within a Specific Heading or Subheading

✓ Follow each Heading and Subheading with an initial paragraph which

  ✓ serves not as the argument, but to introduce the argument;

  ✓ follows the BaRAC design;

  ✓ begins with a bold assertion of our position;

  ✓ references the standard of review applicable to the issue;

  ✓ states, with proper citation but briefly, the general rule and relevant facts applicable to the Heading;

  ✓ briefly demonstrates the result of applying that rule to those facts; and

  ✓ reaches a conclusion on the issue.

✓ Follow the BaRAC design in writing the further paragraphs under each Heading and Subheading. In other words, for each point argued,

  ✓ include a bold assertion;

  ✓ state and explain the rule;

  ✓ demonstrate how the rule applies to the facts, and where relevant, discuss counter-arguments and our response;

  ✓ reach a conclusion on the specific issue; and

  ✓ edit to eliminate unnecessary arguments, words, and phrases.

---

13. We thank our colleague Henry Wihnyk for his suggestions regarding this checklist.

Regarding All Paragraphs

✓ Make certain each paragraph:

   ✓ concerns only one topic;

   ✓ contains sentences which coherently relate to each other and to the topic;

   ✓ contains a first and last sentence, which when read together, demonstrate consistency and the logical progression of thought; and

   ✓ flows into the next paragraph effortlessly, with a smooth transition.

Analysis

✓ Choose the most effective form of rule development and application for each issue, based on the role the cases play in our analysis:

   (1) rule-only: factor analysis;

   (2) rule-plus: the illustrative approach; or

   (3) FIHRR: reasoning by analogy.

✓ Clearly state the theory of the case, and ground it in common sense.

✓ Consider the kind of argument most likely to appeal to the particular audience in question, i.e., the judges of our particular court.

✓ Clearly state and explain all rules.

✓ Follow the BaRAC structure for all arguments.

✓ Ensure that each argument is logical, well-developed, internally consistent, and consistent with the overall theory of our case.

✓ Explain and distinguish relevant harmful cases, authorities, and policy arguments.

Language, Grammar, Spelling, Format, Citation

✓ Carefully choose words to create a favorable tone for our argument.

✓ Use clear, concrete, and concise language.

✓ Use short sentences.

✓ Do not exceed 1/2 page for paragraphs.

✓ Use transitions effectively.

✓ Ensure that the argument is free from grammatical, spelling, citation, and quotation errors.

✓ Check that the argument follows the jurisdiction's rules of format (proper margins, font size, etc.).

✓ Follow every quotation or reference to authority with a pinpoint citation.

Chapter 21

The Other Parts of the Brief

This Chapter contains guidelines for writing the "other" sections of the brief. Because these sections are specifically tailored to each case and concern more a matter of "form" than style, we've placed our suggestions in a list rather than in a narrative. All sample sections are in Courier New font. Bear in mind that these are simply examples; as in preparing the other sections of our brief, we would follow all procedural rules of the court to which we are submitting our brief.

§ 21.1 Caption Page

Purpose:

- the cover page of the brief;
- tells the court the information it needs to file and locate the brief.

Context and Content:

- first page of the brief;
- includes the name of the parties, the case number, the court name, counsel's name and address, the document name, and any other information required under court rules; e.g., some courts require counsel to list their State Bar Membership number.

Format:

- no page number;
- some courts require a specific color, differentiating between the Petitioner/ Appellant's brief and the Respondent/Appellee's brief.

The following is an example Caption Page:

Graphic 21.1   **Caption Page**

IN THE
DISTRICT COURT OF APPEAL OF FLORIDA
FIRST DISTRICT

PARKER LIONELL,

       Appellant,

v.   CASE NUMBER: S10

NOAH WALKER,

       Appellee.

_____/

ON APPEAL FROM THE CIRCUIT COURT
FOR THE EIGHTH JUDICIAL CIRCUIT OF FLORIDA

_____

APPELLANT'S INITIAL BRIEF
_____

STEW DENT
Counsel for Appellant, Parker Lionell
250 Bruton-Geer Hall
University of Florida
Gainesville, Florida 32611
352-555-5555

§ 21.2   Table of Contents

Purpose:

- a quick reference guide listing the page number where each argument and section of the brief appears.

Context:

- the second page of the brief, preceded by the cover page and followed by the Table of Authorities.

Format:

- all sections of the brief are listed in capital letters and in the order in which they appear in the brief;
- Argument Headings and Subheadings are listed as they appear in the brief;
- each section, Heading, and Subheading is followed with "dot leaders" ending with the page number of the brief where the section begins;
- all page numbers are aligned against the right margin;
- the page number for the Table of Contents is "ii" (lower-case Roman numeral for "2");
- if the Table extends to more than one page, continue numbering the pages using lower-case Roman numerals ("iii, " etc.), and center these page numbers at the bottom of the page.

The following is an example of a Table of Contents:

Graphic 21.2	Table of Contents

<u>TABLE OF CONTENTS</u>

<u>PAGE</u>

§ 21.3   Table of Authorities

Purpose:

- lists all authorities cited and the pages in the brief where those citations appear.

Context:

- (approximately) the third—"iii" (or fourth—"iv") page of the brief, preceded by the Table of Contents and followed by the Opinion Below section.

Format:

- check court rules for proper format and order of presenting authorities;
- cite each authority in proper form (state or federal citation rules), followed by "dot leaders" aligned against the right margin and ending with the page number(s) of the brief where each authority appears;
- generally, list cases first, *in alphabetical order;*[1]
- separate the name of the case from the rest of the case citation by placing the case name on one line; then, add the rest of the citation on the next line, indenting 5 spaces (see example below);
- skip two lines between each case;
- in citing cases, include only the official citation. In other words, do *not* include all of the pages of the case (past the first page) that we've used in our argument. For example:

Graphic 21.3(a)   **Citing Cases: Table of Authorities**

Don't do this:

Spence v. Virginia,
        457 U.S. 211, **215, 217** (1989) 3, 6

Instead, just give the official citation:

Spence v. Virginia,
        457 U.S. 211 (1989) 3, 6

- be sure all authorities are updated, using Shepard's Citations or an online service;
- when appropriate, include the subsequent history of the case in the citation;
- following the cases, list constitutional and statutory provisions, followed by administrative and procedural rules, followed by secondary authorities;

---

1. Note that *United States v. [name]* is listed under "u" and written out in full; i.e., not *U.S. v. Doe. City of [name]* is listed under "c"; and *State v. [name]* is listed under "s."

- when pervasively citing an authority other than case law, use the term "passim," either italicized or underlined, consistent with the way you have formatted case names, instead of listing an extensive number of pages;

- include all authorities but don't include authorities which appear only as a quotation in another authority. For example, if our brief contains the following quotation, and this is the only time we mention the *Terminiello* case in the brief, do *not* list the *Terminiello* case in the Table of Authorities:

  > "[A] principal 'function of free speech under our system of government is to invite dispute.'" *Texas v. Johnson*, 491 U.S. 397, 408 (1989) (quoting *Terminiello v. City of Chicago*, 337 U.S. 1, 4 (1949)).

  List *Texas v. Johnson* but not *Terminiello v. City of Chicago* in the Table of Authorities.

The following is an example of a Table of Authorities, written to conform to Florida Rules of Citation:

Graphic 21.3(b)   **Table of Authorities**

TABLE OF AUTHORITIES

<u>CASES</u>

    <u>PAGE(S)</u>

<u>Armstrong v. H & C Commc'ns, Inc.</u>,
    575 So. 2d 280 (Fla. 5th DCA 1991) 1

<u>Blakeley v. Shortal's Estate</u>,
    20 N.W.2d 28 (Iowa 1945) 3-4, 6

<u>Dominquez v. Equitable Life Assurance Soc'y</u>,
    438 So. 2d 58 (Fla. 3d DCA 1983),
    <u>approved sub nom.</u>, <u>Crawford v. Dominquez</u>,
    467 So. 2d 281 (Fla. 1985) 4, 7, 10

<u>Ford Motor Credit Co. v. Sheehan</u>,
    373 So. 2d 956 (Fla. 1st DCA 1979) 4, 11, 12

<u>Jefferson Ward Stores, Inc. v. Khorozian</u>,
    519 So. 2d 627 (Fla. 4th DCA 1984) 4

<u>Korbin v. Berlin</u>,
    177 So. 2d 551 (Fla. 3d DCA 1965) 4

<u>Metro. Life Ins. Co. v. McCarson</u>,
    467 So. 2d 277 (Fla. 1985) 1

<u>Sullivan v. deColigny</u>,
    432 F. Supp. 689 (D. V.I. 1977) 2

<u>STATUTES</u>

§ 860.05, Fla. Stat. (20xx) 9

§ 860.09, Fla. Stat. (20xx) 9

<u>COURT RULES</u>

Fla. R. Civ. P. 1.110 1-2

<u>RESTATEMENTS</u>

Restatement (Second) of Torts § 46 (1965) .... <u>passim</u>

§21.4   Opinion Below

Purpose:

- tells the reviewing court where it can locate the text of the opinion (or opinions) rendered by the trial court and/or lower appellate court in our case.

Context:

- begins on a new page following the Table of Authorities and precedes the Jurisdiction section.

Format:

- paragraph(s);
- if any lower court case has been published, cite it;
- if the lower court case has not been published, state the page numbers of the Record on Appeal where the opinion or judgment is located.

Special Note: For some proceedings, the rules of appellate procedure may require counsel to include a copy of the trial court's judgment and/or lower reviewing court's decision in an Appendix. Please see §21.8 for instructions on compiling an Appendix.

The following is an example of an Opinion Below section:

Graphic 21.4   **Opinion Below**

OPINION BELOW

    The final judgment of the Circuit Court for the
Eighth Judicial Circuit is unreported and appears at
pages 1-6 of the Record on Appeal.

---

§21.5   Jurisdiction

Purpose:

- to establish that the reviewing court has jurisdiction to hear the appeal or petition.

Context and Content:

- follows, on the same page, the Opinion Below section and precedes the Question Presented section.
- includes information such as the entry date of the final judgment of the trial court, when the notice of appeal or petition for certiorari was filed, and the constitutional or statutory basis for the reviewing court's jurisdiction.

Format:

- paragraph(s).

The following is an example of a Jurisdiction section:

Graphic 21.5	Jurisdiction

<u>JURISDICTION</u>

The final judgment of the Circuit Court for the Eighth Judicial Circuit was entered on September 6, 20xx. (R.2.) Notice of appeal was timely filed on September 11, 20xx. (R.6.) This Court's jurisdiction is invoked pursuant to Article V, Section 4(b)(1) of the Florida Constitution.

§ 21.6   Constitutional and Statutory Provisions

Purpose:

- references the text of the law involved in our case.

Context and Content:

- follows, on the same page, the Jurisdiction section and precedes the Question Presented section;
- quotes the text of all constitutional and statutory provisions directly involved in the case, including administrative regulations, restatement provisions, codes, ordinances, etc. (If, however, this section is too long to include in our brief, i.e., over two pages, place this information in a separate Appendix. Please refer to § 21.9.)

Format:

- Provisions can be quoted in full or in relevant part, as with the Fourteenth Amendment in the example below. If the quotation is fifty or more words long, indent on both side margins, single-space, and do not use quotation marks;
- if the quotation is less than fifty words long, do *not* indent the margins. Instead, use quotation marks and double-space the text.

The following is an example of a Constitutional and Statutory Provisions section:

Graphic 21.6   **Constitutional and Statutory Provisions**

CONSTITUTIONAL AND STATUTORY PROVISIONS

The Eighth Amendment to the United States Constitution provides:

"Excessive bail shall not be required, nor excessive fines imposed, nor cruel and unusual punishments inflicted."

The Fourteenth Amendment to the United States Constitution provides in relevant part:

"No State shall make or enforce any law which shall abridge the privileges or immunities of citizens of the United States; nor shall any State deprive any person of life, liberty, or property, without due process of law. . . ."

Gotham City, Fla., Code 5505 (20xx) provides:

PEDESTRIAN INTERFERENCE

It shall be unlawful and a misdemeanor (punishable by a maximum fine of $500 and 90 days in jail) for anyone, while upon the public sidewalks or streets in the downtown core of Gotham City, to engage in personal solicitation for the immediate receipt of money. The downtown core is defined as the twenty blocks bordering Main Street to the north, Fifth Street to the south, First Avenue to the east, and Fifth Avenue to the west.

§ 21.7   Conclusion

Purpose and Content:

- tell the reviewing court the precise relief we request and why the court should rule in our favor;
- "ring the bell" and leave the merits and theory of our case resounding in the judge's mind;
- *do not rehash our entire argument*;
- instead, focus on our theory and remind the court that by ruling in our favor, it will be doing the "right thing" as a matter of law and policy.

Context:

- begins on a new page following the Argument section and precedes the Certificate of Service.

Format:

- paragraph(s), not to exceed one page;
- most court rules require counsel to sign the Conclusion and to include a business address.

The following is an example of a Conclusion:

Graphic 21.7	Conclusion

<u>CONCLUSION</u>

The trial court properly dismissed Lionell's complaint for intentional infliction of emotional distress. Though novel, if allowed, the complaint would permit witnesses to an accident who suffered no physical injury themselves to recover damages from the accident victim simply for witnessing the accident. Recognizing that this cannot and should not be the law, the trial court properly dismissed Lionell's complaint. This Court should affirm that dismissal.

Respectfully submitted,
<u>*(signature goes here)*</u>
Matthew Thomas
Counsel for Appellee Noah Walker

---

§ 21.8 Certificate of Service

Purpose:

- to verify that we've given a copy of a document (i.e., our brief and any appendix) to our opponent. The Certificate of Service ensures fairness by requiring the parties to provide each other with any documents they file with the court.

Context:

- attached, as a separate sheet, to the end of each document; i.e., brief, separate appendix. In the brief, begins on a new page following the Conclusion section.

Format:

- Rules of Appellate Procedure and/or Civil Procedure govern format and delivery requirements.

The following is an example of a Certificate of Service:

Graphic 21.8   **Certificate of Service**

<u>CERTIFICATE OF SERVICE</u>

    I certify that a true copy of this brief was furnished to Matthew Thomas, Counsel for Appellee, by hand delivery this 15th day of October, 20xx.

                       (signature goes here)

                       Stew Dent
                       Attorney for Appellant Parker Lionell
                       [Address goes here]
                       [Phone number goes here]
                       Bar No. [goes here]

---

§ 21.9   Appendix

Purpose:

- to provide helpful information too bulky to include in the brief, such as: a copy of the opinion, order, or judgment to be reviewed; relevant sections of transcripts; relevant documents; and the text of relevant legal authorities. Rule 9.220, Florida Rules of Appellate Procedure, permits an appendix to be filed with almost any appellate pleading and requires an appendix in some proceedings.

Context:

- follows the Conclusion and the Certificate of Service.

Format:

- a separate section of the brief or a separate document attached to the brief;
- Rules of Appellate Procedure generally dictate the format. For example, Rule 9.220 of the Florida Rules of Appellate Procedure requires the Appendix to "contain an index and a conformed copy of the opinion or order to be reviewed and [directs that the Appendix] may contain any other portions of the record and other authorities. It shall be separately bound or separated from the petition, brief, motion, response, or reply by a divider and appropriate tab."

Chapter 22

The Oral Argument

"Here comes the orator! with his flood of words, and his drop of reason."

—Benjamin Franklin,
Poor Richard's Almanac (1733)

"Remember, judges are government employees. We help pay their salaries."

—Your Humble Authors

§ 22.1   Purpose and Context of Oral Argument

Purpose. No aspect of being a lawyer has more appeal (no pun intended) than presenting oral argument. It's easily the most exciting, intense, and frightening experience we face as lawyers. However, the term "oral argument" is a misnomer; oral argument is not, in the strict sense of the word, an argument. Our role is not to argue with the judges or debate opposing counsel. To the contrary, in oral argument we engage in a reasoned dialogue, a conversation, with the court.

The purpose of our oral "presentation" is the following:

(1) to persuade the court of the logic of our argument;

(2) to influence and assist the court in reaching the conclusion we seek by giving the court the benefit of our focused thinking on a problem; and

(3) to draw out of the court any nagging doubts it may have regarding our case and answer their concerns.

Context. Oral advocacy plays a crucial role in appeals as well as other courtroom situations. While our brief sets out our arguments in detail, our oral presentation highlights selected crucial points, including the following:

- our strongest and most convincing arguments;

- any arguments we did not sufficiently explain in our brief; and

- any topics judges ask us to address in more depth.

In the following section, we discuss oral argument procedures (at the appellate level), helpful advocacy techniques, and courtroom etiquette.

§ 22.2   Procedural Matters

We must request oral argument. In appeals from final judgments, appellate courts generally, but not always, grant oral argument. In other appellate situations, oral argument may or may not be available. Even in those appeals where oral argument is available, however, the court will not grant it unless a party to the appeal (either side) requests it.

Thus, as appellate counsel, we wrestle with the question of whether to request oral argument. We consider whether it will make a difference or whether the judges have already made up their minds after reading our brief.[1] Although it's difficult to generalize

---

1. One judge has stated that "'I used to ask myself the same question.... From my standpoint here [as an intermediate appellate judge, oral argument] makes a huge difference, and I think it is because the written word is not always accurate or precise even in the hands of the good writer, and in the hands of the poor writer, it is entirely ineffective. Oftentimes there is a point there that simply is not being expressed. With oral argument, within minutes, here it comes; the point is out; and a single question can do it and clear up the confusion that arises from briefs.'" Paul Morris, Oral Arguments and Written Briefs — DCA Judges Comment, *The Florida Bar Journal*, Vol. LXII, No. 5 (May 1988) at 23 (quoting Daniel S. Pearson, former judge of the Third District Court of Appeal of Florida).

when a party should and should not request oral argument, we believe the appellant should, in most cases, request it, while the appellee should not. This is because in cases where the parties have waived oral argument ("no request" cases) some courts may be more likely to summarily affirm the result below.[2] When we do seek oral argument, we submit our request to the court in a separate document from our brief, and serve this "notice" on opposing counsel, normally not later than the time our last brief is due or along with our initial brief, if so required.

§ 22.3   Preparing for Oral Argument

To be effective in oral argument, we must enter into the process with the right "mind-set." As we've said, oral argument is not an "argument." We shouldn't walk into the courtroom expecting a verbal battle. Rather, oral argument is grand theater; it's an art form. Permit us to explain.

§ 22.3(a)   Preparing the Proper "Mind-Set"

Oral Argument is "Grand Theater." Just pause for a moment and consider the setting of the oral argument. Participants and spectators dress up—some wear black robes and sit on elevated platforms, flanked by flags. Some dress in police uniforms and likely bear a weapon. We, too, parade in the costume of the lawyer.[3] But the grand theater of the courtroom doesn't stop with costumes and props.

Language, too, is strange, formal. We address those in the robes as "Your Honor," those in the uniforms as "Officer," and those in the suits as "Counsel." We carefully craft every word, knowing that what we say is being recorded. There's even an audience, listening and watching. Indeed, we know one bailiff who, while opening the doors of a particular San Francisco courtroom each morning would exclaim: "It's showtime." He was dead-on right.

Because of this unique setting, oral argument demands our attention. We can't expect to waltz into the courtroom unprepared and sweep the judges away with the sheer force of our personality. No, oral argument requires much more than the clever turn of a phrase; it requires preparation and a lot of it.

Careful preparation is *essential* to effective oral advocacy. Through it, we achieve the two goals of effective advocacy: communication and persuasion. Persuasion is of course paramount, but if we haven't effectively communicated our message, we can't begin to persuade the court to accept it. For this reason, we develop a strategy for presenting

---

2. Another judge, Winifred Sharp, of the Fifth District Court of Appeal of Florida, suggests that "counsel should never waive argument in a difficult case, because her experience has been that argument has changed the outcome of a significant number of cases. Several judges would go further, suggesting that if counsel deems the case worthy of review, it should be deemed worthy of argument." *Id.*

3. To avoid any "morning of" panic, we strongly suggest preparing our "costumes" at least the night before. Make sure the suit is back from the cleaners and those new shoes have been broken in.

our case to the court *before* we pass through those doors. As Gerry Spence advises: "Prepare until you know every scale on the hide of the fish."[4]

§ 22.3(b) Consider the Panel: "Hot" vs. "Cold" Bench

The best way to prepare for oral argument is to think about our audience, to *image* the court hearing our case. We then frame our presentation to "fit" that court.

At the appellate level, panels of judges hearing our case may come in two "types": a "hot bench" or a "cold bench." A hot bench is prepared; the panel members (or most of them) have read the Record and the briefs and have thought about, or know enough about the case, to pose challenging questions.

In contrast, a cold bench may be unprepared; the panel members may have only read a clerk's "summary" of our case and brief. The cold bench typically has fewer and less probing (or no) questions. Of course, some benches fall in-between these two extremes. And, of course, a cold bench may be prepared but just may not have any questions to ask.

We dread the cold bench. It's unnerving to stand before three (or more) stone-faced judges, not knowing whether they're on our side or violently opposed to our position. In contrast, with a hot bench asking questions, we at least have an idea of the judges' views on the strengths and weaknesses of our case.

As practicing advocates, we prepare for every oral argument by anticipating both types of panels. Because a cold bench allows us to cover more ground, while a hot bench demands more specifics, we prepare separate outlines for each. Although this level of preparation takes extra work, we highly recommend it.

§ 22.3(c) Further Guidelines

Naturally, every case and every oral argument is different, so our preparation and presentation varies from case to case. However, the following eight guidelines, which we discuss in detail below, apply in every situation:

Graphic 22.3(c)(1) Guidelines for Preparing the Oral Argument

(1) Know the Record.
(2) Know the court rules.
(3) Study the briefs.
(4) Know the cases; update authorities.
(5) Decide what to argue and what to omit.
(6) Outline the argument.
(7) Start strong; end strong.
(8) Rehearse the argument.

---

4. Gerry Spence, *How to Argue and Win Every Time* 202 (1995).

1. Know the Record. To be effective advocates, we must *know* the Record — like the back of our hand — including all facts and procedural aspects of our case. Any uncertainty we convey about the facts will annoy the court and seriously weaken our credibility. *There's no excuse for not knowing the facts of our case.* If significant time has elapsed since we've written our brief, we review the facts — either by reviewing the notes we made while preparing our Statement of the Case and Facts or by rereading the Record.

We heed the following advice, by Judge Alex Kozinski, regarding the importance of understanding the facts:

> There is a quaint notion out there that facts don't matter on appeal — that's where you argue about the law; facts are for sissies and trial courts. The truth is much different. The law doesn't matter a bit, *except* as it applies to a particular set of facts. So you will find that judges at oral argument often have a lot of questions about the record. Which makes sense. After all, we can read the cases just as well as you can. Often, one or another of the judges has written the key case, so what can the lawyer really contribute to the panel's understanding of it? [¶] But each case is different insofar as the facts are concerned; where the lawyer can really help the judges — and his client — is by knowing the record and explaining how it dovetails with the various precedents. Familiarity with the record is probably the most important aspect of appellate advocacy.[5]

2. Know the court rules. Woe unto those who fail to study the court's oral argument rules. We can't prepare for oral argument unless we know the critical details, such as the all important one — how much *time* will we be allotted to speak? Some courts will send us their rules after we've requested oral argument or have the rules posted online. If not, we call the clerk's office and request a copy prior to our argument.

We should also *go* to the courtroom several days before our argument to view other oral arguments before the same panel. We see how the court operates, what level of decorum the court expects from counsel, and how best to tailor our argument to those judges.

3. Study the briefs. Oral argument is not like a TV-trial where a surprise witness appears out of nowhere and wreaks havoc on the hero's case. No. Oral argument is a chess game where all the players and their moves are known ahead of time. After all, each party has filed a brief, outlining and explaining in detail that party's strategy for winning the case. The briefs, both ours and our opponent's, are gold mines of information; we study them before oral argument. We reassess the strengths and weaknesses of each party's case and hone in on the aspects we'll highlight to the court. In particular, we point out any important points our opponent has conceded or ignored. We rethink our moves; we play to win.

4. Know the cases; update authorities. In preparing for oral argument, we thoroughly review the important cases cited in *all* briefs. Of course, we can't memorize the details of every case cited, but we can thoroughly understand the issues and reasoning of the most important ones. To keep this information at our fingertips, we create a list of the crucial cases with their citations (in case the court asks), along with a "buzzword" or two to help us remember what the case was about.

---

5. Judge Alex Kozinski, *The Wrong Stuff*, 1992 B.Y.U. L. Rev. 325, 330 (1992).

We also verify that all relevant cases and statutes are "still good law" by updating them. (Although we updated all authorities before we submitted our brief, many months may have elapsed between the time we filed that brief and oral argument.)

If any new and relevant law or case has appeared since we submitted our brief, we file a "Notice of Supplemental Authority" with attached copies of the authority. On the other hand, if an authority we had cited is no longer good law, we tell the court, also through this "Notice."

5. Decide what to argue and what to omit. Due to the strict time limits the court places on oral argument, we must be efficient in our presentation. The following three suggestions help keep our argument concise and on track:

(1) don't repeat exactly what's in our brief;

(2) simplify the argument; and

(3) make our best points first.

We make a grave mistake in attempting to explain all of our arguments in detail. Lengthy explanations are confusing, time consuming, and dull, dull, dull. Instead, we identify one or two major issues or themes, present them with clear, simple logic, and disregard all other points unless the court asks about them.

In the short time allotted for oral argument, we can't educate the court on all that we've researched over a period of weeks (months, or years). If we've done a good job on our brief, the court will have all the details it needs. This is not, however, to suggest that we present an argument touching only the surface of the issues or focusing only on general principles of law. Instead, we carefully select our points, present our strongest arguments first and state them clearly and concisely.

In oral argument, we're teaching the court about our case and the relevant law. As good teachers, we make the complex simple. We crystallize our theory. We pare down our arguments to their most essential elements, and then we simplify them even further. When we've finished this winnowing process, we have a case any intelligent ten-year-old can understand.

6. Outline the argument. This is a must. We can't imagine preparing for or presenting an oral argument without an outline. The outline helps us organize our presentation; see at a glance how our logic develops, and where its strengths and weaknesses lie; and guides us quickly back to our argument after a judge's question has diverted us.

Moreover, if we have an outline and not a word-for-word speech, we can't read our argument to the court. Oral argument is a conversation between counsel and the court. We don't read speeches when we converse; therefore, we don't read to the court.

Our outline is simple, with large type we can see at a glance. We don't "organize" our "outline" into a pile of file cards which will likely fall all over the floor—as we've seen happen.[6] Instead, we put our outline onto a large manila legal folder. We either write on the folder itself or on sheets of paper stapled to the two inside panels. We highlight crucial passages with colored markers to see key phrases and to help us "find our place." We include "buzzwords," summaries, and citations to the critical cases. As we did in our brief, we organize our outline using the BaRAC design.

---

6. The classic example of a case "falling to pieces."

The following is a sample outline from the *Lionell v. Walker* case (see Chapter 36).

Graphic 22.3(c)(2)   Sample Outline Format: Lionell's Oral Argument

Lionell seeks day in court; appeals grant of Walker's motion to dismiss

ba: Complaint states c/a for int. infl. em. dist.: unwilling participant in Walker's attempted suicide

s/r: de novo; & review compl. in light most fav. to Lionell

r: [1] extreme / outrageous
[2] intent or reckless
[3] severe emot. dist.
Restatement; Metro

a: lying in path, allowed train to run over, severe distress

c: reverse and remand — let case proceed

---

ba: Walker: intentional / reckless; stayed on tracks

r: actual desire or reckless; need no specific intent to harm; knowledge of high risk enough; reasonable person std.; also intentional viol. of statute — ***Restatement (& Blakeley)*** can prove by circumstantial evidence—***Williams***

a: W: elicit emotional response; notified paper; speech — "I have to do what I have to do." Reasonable person; violated three RR statutes; willful

c: Allegations sufficient to show intentional/reckless conduct

---

policy:
— not "opening floodgates"
— recognizing legit. c/a
— asking only for day in court

---

ba: Extreme/outrag. conduct —lying in path of oncoming train, refusing to move

r: beyond all bounds of decency; outrageous; jury should decide ***Restatement; Williams; Blakeley***: guest-suicide. ***Others:*** false acc. shop; false statements to 6 yr. old; refusals to pay insurance proceeds; false reports of injuries to relatives; dissolving swimsuit

a: Walker's comments "go through me"; "drastic times require drastic measures" — ignored warning from RR official, whistles

c: T/Ct.'s ruling: "illegal, foolhardy, and extreme" but not outrageous: wrong

---

ba: Severe emotional distress T/Ct. acknowledged: "vomiting, nausea, guilt, depression, headaches, sweaty palms, and nightmares" but found "not severe enough" — applied the wrong legal standard

r: Severe emotional distress = fright, horror, grief, shame, nausea-so severe no reas. person should be expected to endure-intensity & duration — outrageousness is evid. of severity of distress ***Restatement; Sheehan***

a: unwilling participant in W's self-mutilation: guilt, severe migraine headaches, nausea, weight loss, depression, sweaty palms, recurring nightmares, can't work as engineer

c: Severe emotional distress

---

policy:
— if this isn't IIED, then can't imagine what would be

The bottom line is that we don't take a pile of papers with us to the podium. Although we might take our brief, the brief of the opposing party, key cases, and the Record on Appeal, there is rarely time to use these documents during argument. Moreover, flipping through papers while at the podium is distracting and annoying. However, if we do bring these documents with us, we securely fasten them in a tabbed notebook which won't spring open.

7. Start strong; end strong. Like the most interesting briefs, the most interesting oral arguments start strong and end strong. A strong opening grabs the judges' attention and invites the court to listen to what follows. We can't forget that courts hear case after case after case of oral argument—lawyers droning on hour after hour after hour. It's not surprising that after awhile, all cases start to sound alike.

To persuade the court, we first get its attention. The first words we utter, after introducing ourselves and our client, determine whether the court is riveted to our argument or switching on the "cruise control." For suggestions on good openings, please see Chapter 15, § 15.5(a), Statement of the Case and Facts, and Chapter 19, § 19.2(a), the Summary of Argument. In these sections, we examined several examples of solid opening lines.

Just as we start out strong, we end strong, too. We "ring the bell," leaving the court with a reverberating feeling that it's not only doing the right thing legally, but also morally and socially, in ruling for our client. We leave the court feeling good about "letting" us win. To do so, we consider the common sense implications of the court's ruling, know the exact relief we require, and ask for no more than what we need.

We recommend preparing three conclusions: a one-minute conclusion, a thirty-second conclusion, and a ten-second conclusion. The one-minute conclusion is good for a cold bench, that is, when we're not getting many questions. A thirty-second conclusion works well when we're right on schedule; while the short, ten-second version helps when our time has run short because the judges have pounded away the whole time.

8. Rehearse the argument. Finally, we rehearse our argument. The more we rehearse, the more relaxed and effective we'll be. Ideally, we rehearse three days to a week prior to the argument. If we rehearse only the day before argument, we'll be (and should be!) nervous. A sufficient lead-time also allows us to make a list of things we don't know, or haven't thought through thoroughly, and then use our remaining time to fill in gaps in our information.

But whenever we rehearse, it must be under conditions similar to those we'll experience in court. We stand up straight, speak slowly, and limit our gestures to controlled movements. If possible, we practice in front of someone who will interrupt us with questions. We ask our colleagues to read our briefs, listen to our arguments, and ask us tough questions—the tougher the better.

Although we always rehearse the argument, however, we never memorize it—except for the opening first thirty seconds or so. A memorized presentation sounds, and is, stilted. More importantly, it's impossible to deliver a prepared speech when the panel interrupts us with questions. We can't repeat it enough: an oral argument is a "conversation," and a conversation is not a memorized speech.

§ 22.4   Presenting the Oral Argument

Courtroom Procedure. We recommend arriving at the courthouse at least thirty to sixty minutes prior to argument. That way, we're prepared for the unexpected—flat tires, bad traffic, or a rearrangement of the court's calendar because of a canceled argument. Once we're there and have checked the calendar, we can take some quiet moments to compose ourselves and reflect on our presentation.

In the courtroom, appellants (or petitioners) sit to the left of the podium as they face the court; appellees (or respondents) sit to the right. If the judges enter the courtroom after counsel, we stand until the judges are seated. In addition, we stand when addressed by, or addressing, the court.

§ 22.4(a)   Overview of Appellant's Argument

Let the argument begin! When the judges are ready to proceed, the chief judge or justice asks both sides if they're ready. Appellants and appellees respond in turn. The court then directs appellant to proceed. Because appellant has the burden of persuading the court to reverse the outcome, appellant argues first and, by reserving time for rebuttal, last. Appellant doesn't begin speaking until receiving the appropriate word or signal from the court.

Once the judge has signaled us to begin, as appellant, we introduce ourselves and our client and request rebuttal. (Rebuttal must be requested at the beginning of appellant's presentation and generally consists of two to five minutes.) At this point, some appellants present the facts and issues of the case, while others briefly outline their argument before they address the facts.[7]

Next, we highlight the relevant and crucial facts, being as brief as possible.[8] We emphasize, however, the details of any compelling equities in our client's favor.

Here's a sample introduction which effectively introduces counsel and the case to the Court:

Graphic 22.4(a)	Introduction

May it please the Court. My name is Daniel Webster and I represent the plaintiff, Frederick Douglass, in this action. Please reserve two minutes of my time for rebuttal.

The issues before this Court today are: first, whether the territories may recognize human Bondage, and second, whether the Fugitive Act violates the Fifth Amendment. As to the first issue, the facts here present a compelling case for federal management of its territories.

---

7. Outlining the argument prior to stating the facts is particularly helpful where the argument is complex.

8. The appellant is responsible for presenting the facts and procedural history of the case. However, the appellant should also prepare for the likelihood that the judges will waive the statement, allowing appellant to use the full time allotted for argument.

In a dignified manner we emphasize why the trial or lower appellate court incorrectly rejected our client's position. In other words, we tell the court our theory and briefly what we'll argue. As quickly as possible, we get to the heart of our case.

We address points we haven't argued in our brief *only* if the appellee has raised them and *only* if the new argument seriously threatens our case. At the end of our argument we restate our theory and request specific relief. We don't just fade away at the end; we leave the court with a strong impression.

We also pay attention to appellee's argument and to the questions the court asks appellee. Our role isn't over yet; we still have rebuttal.

§ 22.4(b)   Overview of Appellee's Argument

Our role as the appellee is somewhat different from the appellant's, although many of the same rules apply. The appellee may begin with a brief overview of the facts but only if it adds to or modifies the appellant's factual statement. We then present a brief outline of our argument, restate the issue as we see it, convey our theory, and then hit the merits of the case.

Although we respond to the specific points made by appellant, our argument is not simply a point-by-point refutation. Instead, we respond pursuant to *our* theory, beginning with our strongest point.

However, we don't respond to arguments contained in the appellant's brief but not addressed by appellant at oral argument. If these arguments weren't important enough for appellant to address, we certainly don't need to bring them up.

By having carefully listened to the questions the judges asked during the appellant's argument, we have an idea of the judges' concerns. We adapt our argument to address those issues. Where possible, we use the judges' own words to preface our point. For example: "As Judge Baker commented...." Or, "to address Judge Sawyer's concerns...."

At the end of our argument, we sum up our theory and state a prayer for relief. Typically, this involves a simple statement, such as: "For these reasons, we ask the court to affirm the trial court's judgment."

§ 22.4(c)   Overview of Appellant's Rebuttal

As we've stated, as the appellant, we present rebuttal only if we've reserved the allotted time. In rebuttal, we don't raise new points, simply rehash points already covered, or cite new cases (unless we can quickly explain them). Instead, we respond to specific, *damaging* points the appellee made during his or her argument and clarify any misunderstandings the court may have expressed about our case. For this reason, we listen carefully to the appellee's argument, noting the court's main concerns.

As appellant, it's easy to lose momentum when a judge questions us during rebuttal. We respond quickly to the question and move back to our main point. Rebuttal is the "last word" in the case. It may contain the winning point for the appellant *if* it's short and forceful.

§ 22.5   Content of the Oral Argument

§ 22.5(a)   The Court's Concerns

Whether we're appellant or appellee, merely repeating the contents of our brief at oral argument is a waste of the court's time and a missed opportunity to hone in on the strongest points of our case. Judges groan silently (and sometimes audibly!) when we attorneys indicate we're about to regurgitate our brief. In structuring our argument, we anticipate, and then address, the court's concerns. Most likely, the court will be particularly interested in the following:

- whether the legal propositions we espouse apply *only* (or at all) to the specific facts of our case;
- whether our position conforms to the applicable statutes, rules, and judicial precedent;
- whether our case represents a valid exception, if an exception is necessary, to current judicial precedent;
- whether our position is firmly grounded in prevailing public policy considerations and standards of justice;
- whether our position is analytically consistent with the law in related fields;
- whether a ruling in our favor will have far-reaching positive or adverse effects; and
- whether an opinion in our favor could withstand further appellate review.

If we aren't prepared to address each of these concerns, we aren't prepared for oral argument.

§ 22.5(b)   The Theory of Our Case

Our argument is effective only if it presents a clear and workable theory of our case. To demonstrate the soundness of our theory, we

- rely on governing statutes or rules, if their plain language supports our position, and explain how our theory fits within the rule or the statute;
- analogize our facts to similar fact situations; or analogize our legal principle to similar legal principles in related fields of law, and draw from cases in those areas; and
- emphasize the consequences of a ruling either in our favor or against us. We then carry the proposed legal principle to its logical conclusion (e.g., "If this rule is adopted, then a private cause of action will exist for disabled individuals.").
- Finally, we support our legal arguments with policy arguments. We identify ethical or humanistic concerns that favor our position; we strive for an emotional impact if our facts call for it.

The best way to convey our theory to the court during oral argument is to start with that theory. We think the best examples we've seen (in a long, long time) of getting right to the heart of counsel's theory come from a case we've already (Chapter 19) addressed. However, because we're so smitten by these examples, we're repeating them here.

Our illustrative, but actual, case concerned the seemingly uninteresting issue of whether admiralty jurisdiction extended to limit the liability of Great Lakes, the owner of a vessel, for damage occurring to several downtown Chicago businesses, including Marshall Fields, a department store. *See Jerome B. Grubart, Inc. v. Great Lakes Dredge & Dock Co.*, 513 U.S. 527 (1995). Great Lakes, while replacing pilings in the bed of the Chicago River, inadvertently damaged the City's old underground freight tunnel system, resulting in the flooding of several businesses, including Marshall Fields.

Here's how counsel for the flooded businesses, Mr. Rosenthal, introduced his theory of the case to the United States Supreme Court:

Graphic 22.5(b)(1)   Expressing the Theory of the Case:

"Today, the Court is asked to extend admiralty jurisdiction beyond its historic boundaries, the shore and property abutting the shore, and bring it into the basements of downtown Chicago. While we think it extraordinary that there should be Federal admiralty jurisdiction over water in the basement of Marshall Fields, that is what the court of appeals managed to hold, and this morning I will press two points with respect to that holding."

Here's how counsel for Great Lakes, Mr. Roberts (who became Chief Justice of the United States Supreme Court), introduced his theory:

Graphic 22.5(b)(2)   Expressing the Theory of the Case:

"The petitioners seek to hold Great Lakes liable for the operations of its vessel on the navigable waters of the Chicago River while that vessel was doing what vessels of its sort normally do on navigable water, maritime repair work. In this instance, replacing pilings in the river."

Both lawyers conveyed their theory of the case masterfully. Both wove the facts into the legal standard effortlessly. Both painted a vibrant and memorable picture of their case that even a 10-year-old could understand. We see the flooded Marshall Fields basement and ponder how a judge could have ever found that federal law governed there. But we also see the vessel, in the Chicago River, with a crew engaged in repairs, and question how anyone could find otherwise.

§ 22.5(c)   Countering Our Opponent's Arguments

In refuting our opponent's arguments, we identify immediately our points of agreement and then focus on our points of departure. In doing so, we also point out any "distinctions without a difference." This has the effect of making a single narrow issue or two the focus of our case. We cut to the heart of the argument and address the court's questions on these vital issues.

For example, if opposing counsel has distinguished our case from the leading case or has pointed out factors that might render our statutory interpretation incorrect, we meet these arguments head-on. However, if the distinctions have no significant impact on the outcome of the case, we say so, and move on. We don't waste time addressing inconsequential matters.

§ 22.5(d)   Using the BaRAC Design in
Presenting Our Position

Because the BaRAC design is a "syllogism with attitude," it provides a solid model for presenting our oral argument. As in persuasive writing, we use bold assertions to preface each point. First, we tell the court what it should hold. Then we tell the court which rule applies and, if necessary, explain that rule. Next, we apply that rule to our facts and reach a conclusion. Throughout, we include transitional "roadmaps" to keep the court on track—i.e., "first," "in addition," "as to the second issue," "finally."

BaRAC is deductive reasoning. And deductive reasoning is exactly the framework upon which we hang our words.

§ 22.6   Questions from the Bench

A critical aspect of oral argument is the give-and-take occasioned by the court's questions. It's also the part of oral argument that many novices find nauseating. But, rather than shying away from questions, we welcome and embrace them! Questions from the bench show that the judges are paying attention. Questions demonstrate that the judges are engaged in our case.

Responding to questions is the high point of oral argument. In our responses, we convey the essence of our case. We allay any nagging doubts the court may have about ruling in our favor. We emphasize the strengths of our case and the weaknesses of our opponent's. As we discuss below, answering is easy if we do two things: first, treat all questions as *friendly*, no matter how hostile they sound, and second, stick to our theory of the case.

§ 22.6(a) There's No Such Thing as an Unfriendly Question

This is our mantra, our chant. Just as Dorothy repeated, "There's no place like home, there's no place like home," we repeat: "There's no such thing as an unfriendly question; there's no such thing as an unfriendly question." Soon, we'll believe what we're saying.

All questions *are* friendly. In oral argument, we're not being quizzed or interrogated; rather, we're engaging in a dialogue with the court. And, there's nothing intimidating in a dialogue. If we treat all questions as friendly, the "argument" becomes a conversation. The entire dynamic of the event changes. No longer are we rattling off a prepared speech. No longer are we standing up before a judgmental panel of grand inquisitors, who seek to singe us with their every word. Instead, we're demonstrating to an inquisitive, helpful, friendly group of people just how right it is to rule in our favor.

Questions from the bench mean that the judges *are listening to us.* Judges ask questions to ensure they understand our points, to test our theory of the case, and to test the ramifications of what we're asking them to do. Judges also use questions to speak to or to convince their fellow judges of a point. But whatever their motives, judges ask questions because they want answers!

Therefore, we prepare an answer to every conceivable question we might be asked. We repeat: it's not enough to prepare for the question itself; we also prepare for the answer. We never side-step a question; we give an answer no matter how damaging it seems. This may be the only chance we have to deal head-on with the concerns of a decision-maker.

§ 22.6(b) Let the Theory of Our Case Guide Every Answer

If we stick to our theory of the case in answering questions, we can't go wrong. When a judge asks a question, the first thing we consider is how that question "fits" within our theory of the case. We fashion our answer accordingly. Permit us to illustrate this principle via a "war story."

When one of us was just a second year associate, working late at a large San Francisco law firm, a call came in. It was a scientist from a well-known marine animal theme park and zoo. The animal park, which wasn't yet our client, was moving from an old, out-dated facility to a new one, about 70 miles away. The problem: a group of neighborhood homeowners near the new facility opposed the relocation. They were headed to court, at 9:00 the next morning, to secure a temporary restraining order (TRO) to halt further work on the new facility.

The animal park scientist was extremely upset. Scheduled for immediate relocation were the remaining members of a dolphin "family" and an adult whale. Apparently, some members of the dolphin family had already been moved, and it was imperative to the psychological health of the entire dolphin group that they be reunited as soon as possible. Further, provisions had been made for moving the whale—the exiting whale tank had been dismantled; the whale *had* to be moved to the new facility.

After calling a law partner and hoping against hope that he'd take the case, the humble associate was told to handle it. She then called the scientist back to do further research on the matter and was told: "There's nothing more to tell. The whale has to be moved and we can't break up the dolphin family." No, the client couldn't send the TRO papers to her. No, the scientist couldn't accompany her to court. No, there was no economic data to look at. No, there was no information on the homeowners.

So, the next morning at 5:00, the humble associate drives 80 miles to a small courthouse. As the sound of a rattling legal pad echos in her near-empty briefcase, she walks in. There, she sees the other two lawyers, present with about five of their clients. She exchanges pleasantries, gets a copy of the moving papers from them, reads like the wind, and wonders what she's doing in the middle of nowhere representing Flipper.

Soon, the ax falls and the case is called. The homeowners' lawyers go first. The park will cause irrevocable damage to property values; an injunction is needed *now*; etc.; etc.; and etc. The humble associate doesn't even bother taking notes; she doesn't have a clue whether what the lawyers are saying is true. All she's been told is that the whale has to be moved, and you can't break up that dolphin family.

It's her turn to talk. She stands up, she introduces herself. She says the TRO shouldn't be granted. She says some members of a dolphin family have been moved, and the others need to follow right away. She says the original whale tank has been dismantled, and the whale has to be moved. She is interrupted by the judge, a man about 70 years old with a goat-like voice: "Counsel, we will proceed in my chambers, along with the court reporter." She wonders what the h—!

The whole shebang moves into the judge's chambers. The judge hobbles to a throne situated behind a barge-sized desk. The humble associate sits to the left, the homeowners to the right. The judge, peering over the top of his glasses, his eyebrows saluting, leans toward her: "Ms. _____, are you actually asserting before this court the rights of animals? Is that what you're doing here? The rights of animals?" She swallows, she pauses. Then, without a hint of doubt in her voice, she answers slowly and deliberately while eyeing him back: "That's exactly what I am doing, Your Honor. The animals cannot speak for themselves. The whale has to be moved, and you can't break up that dolphin family." She waits, forgetting to breathe, but still eye-balling the judge.

The judge leans back in his throne, pauses a moment, then smiles: "TRO denied." She remembers to breathe. She thanks the judge, shakes the hands of her opponents, and rides back to the big city, wondering what the heck had just happened.

What had happened was that she had *stuck to her theory*. She had no law, no statistics, just a theory. She was speaking for the animals. The whale had to be moved and….

Moral of story: if we can recognize the theory of our case and stick to it, we can answer any question.

§ 22.6(c)   General Practice Pointers
for Answering Questions

The following are general guidelines for answering questions:
- As soon as a judge speaks, we stop—even if we're mid-sentence.

- If we don't understand a question, we politely ask the judge to "rephrase" it.

- Further, even if we know the answer, we pause momentarily and gather our thoughts before answering. Although we're prepared enough that when a judge begins to ask us a question we'll know where she's going with it, we don't butt in—this isn't "Jeopardy®!" We let the judge finish, pause thoughtfully for a second, and then answer. This gives the appearance that we think on our feet and aren't easily stumped. Moreover, if we don't know the answer right away, this pause gives us time to think of one. If we've established a "rhythm" of momentarily pausing before answering, the judges will think our taking a few seconds of quiet reflection is "normal." We maintain the appearance of being in control, even if the question initially has baffled us.

- We also don't nod understandingly as the judge is speaking. This tends to give the impression that we're hurrying the judge and anticipating the rest of the question. When she's finished, we answer.

- Oral argument is not the time to bore the court with strings of citations to cases. When we answer a question, we do so in the context of our case and not through a cited case. Unless the court asks about a specific cited case, we answer in terms of our case alone. If we have time to elaborate, then, and only then, do we bring in another case.

- We also don't state (or even imply) that the answer is obvious. Nor do we act too humbly grateful—e.g., "I'm glad you asked that, Your Honor." We never patronize the court.

- We answer every question directly and concisely. We aren't evasive, and we don't make long-winded speeches.

- We never lose our temper or act disrespectfully to the court.

- Finally, we answer the question the judge has asked, not the question we *wished* the judge had asked.

The key to answering any question is staying true to our theory of our case. If we fashion our answers consistently with our theory, we can't be led astray or "boxed in" to a position we don't mean to assert.

§ 22.6(d) Types of Questions

§ 22.6(d)(1) Yes or No Questions

Generally, we give a simple "yes" or "no" response to a question calling for one and *then* explain our answer. However, we need not be afraid to say something other than simply "yes" or "no"—we say "absolutely not, your honor," if the judge is asking an outlandish question or "absolutely" when we agree with the question.

§ 22.6(d)(2) Hostile Questions

There's no such thing! Turn every question into an opportunity to educate and persuade the panel. For example, if the judge says the *XYZ* case seems to undermine our position, we meet the question head-on without being defensive: "I recognize your

Honor's concern, but there are two very strong reasons why that case doesn't apply here...." A good advocate can disagree with a judge respectfully, yet assertively.

§ 22.6(d)(3)   Friendly Questions

All questions are friendly. Through a friendly question, a judge seeks to validate his reasoning or communicate her position to the rest of the court. We listen carefully so that we don't miss the opportunity to "run" with a friendly question. In other words, we agree with the court and then explain the impact of the court's observation. For example: "Exactly, Your Honor. The Record does reflect that the police officers engaged in a pattern and practice of making traffic stops based primarily on the most observable aspects of the vehicle. Here, the officer did just that...."

§ 22.6(d)(4)   Hypothetical Questions

In a "hypothetical" question, the judge asks us to apply the theory of our case, or an extension of that theory, to an imaginary scenario in an attempt to define the potential ramifications of our position. When judges ask hypothetical questions, they test the limits of our theory. Some hypotheticals are closely related to our facts; some are drastically different. However, no matter what the factual scenario, we answer the question.

When judges pose hypotheticals closely related to our facts, they're likely agreeing with our position and we respond as we would to any such friendly question. When judges pose extremely unlikely hypotheticals, however, they may or may not agree with us. They may be trying to "lead us down the primrose path" and right into the brambles, or not.

In responding, the best we can do is provide a credible answer that doesn't give away our case. We could emphasize, respectfully, that we're only arguing the specific facts before the court. E.g., "Your Honor, the facts you are hypothesizing go beyond what is being considered here. However, under the facts you have presented...." The judge, however, knows that the hypothesized facts are not presently before the court.

A better response is to gently and respectfully remind the court that any ruling can be carried to an extreme, with unacceptable results. But the court knows this, too.

Ultimately, then, the most effective response is to argue the beneficial ramifications of the course we're urging the court to take, and to convince the court that these benefits outweigh any detriments. We reassure the judge that a ruling in our favor *does justice*.

And we better be ready for anything. Here's a transcript from the oral argument before the United States Supreme Court in the "nude dancing" case, *Barnes v. Glen Theatre, Inc.*, 501 U.S. 560 (1991). In that case, the Court found that nude performance dancing implicated the "outer perimeters" of the First Amendment but, nevertheless, could be regulated under an Indiana law prohibiting public nudity. The following is an exchange between the Court and counsel for the dancers:

> QUESTION: You began by using a term—was it dance performance?
> MR. ENNIS: Performance dance. By that I mean dance which is intended as a performance in front of an audience, to distinguish that from recreational dance or dancing at home in your room.

QUESTION: Suppose someone wanted to increase business at the car wash or in a bar and they hired a woman and said, now, you sit in this glass case—and this is an adults only car wash— ... you sit in this glass case and attract the customers. Is that permitted?

MR. ENNIS: Your Honor, I think it would—if was intended as expressive activity, if it was performance dance.

QUESTION: No, it's just what I said. The employer says this is the job, you sit up there.

MR. ENNIS: I think that would trigger First Amendment analysis. Whether the State could ban it or not would depend on the State's justifications.

QUESTION: Well, suppose he said, I've heard the arguments in the Supreme Court and you have to dance. And she said, I can't dance. And he said, just wander around when the music starts to play.

(Laughter.)

MR. ENNIS: Well, your Honor—

...

QUESTION: Now, would one have to analyze the Indiana murder law as a—as valid or invalid under the First Amendment if the murder happens to be performed in the course of a public performance dance? Would we have to consider that a First Amendment case?

MR. ENNIS: Well, let me turn directly to that Justice Scalia. That depends on the State's justifications, assuming this is expressive activity. This statute cannot—

QUESTION: So your answer to my last question is yes, it does turn on the State's justifications.

MR. ENNIS: It does—

QUESTION: That's a First Amendment case, if you kill somebody in the course of dancing.

MR. ENNIS: If someone uses peyote or commits a murder for the purpose of committing—communicating or expressive activity, that would trigger First Amendment analysis. But the State could nevertheless prohibit it.[9]

In other words, if we stick to our theory, we can answer any question.

§ 22.6(d)(5)   Questions Seeking Concessions

We also take care not to concede any harmful points in answering a question. If the judge catches us unaware, it's better to respond with "I don't know," rather than to concede a point we haven't analyzed. We never know when such a concession may come back to haunt us.

However, we must be flexible. We can agree with questions seeking concessions if we can isolate a statement that doesn't hurt our argument. Here's how this technique works—we pick out something in the question that we favor and then point out any distinctions:

---

9. Transcript of Oral Argument at 29-32, *Barnes v. Glen Theatre, Inc.*, 501 U.S. 560 (1991) (No. 90-26).

"Yes, that's correct, Your Honor. Florida is a comparative negligence jurisdiction. But Florida law also provides for a different standard of care regarding uninvited licensees."

We concede honestly, not defensively.

§ 22.6(d)(6)   Questions About Our Weakest Point

Although we don't dwell on the weakest point of our case, we anticipate that the court may have more questions in this area than any other, precisely because it's the weakest link in our argument. When we get such a question (and we will), we respond *effortlessly*. In other words, we know our case so well that we seamlessly answer these questions and return to our argument. Because we know the question is coming, we have no excuse for not preparing an excellent response to it. If we provide a stilted, evasive answer, we've only succeeded in confirming the judge's worst view of our case (and of us).

§ 22.6(d)(7)   Questions About Our Best Case or Best Argument

We're always prepared to tell the court our best case and our strongest argument. Judges are particularly fond of asking these questions for two reasons. First, a "what is your strongest argument?" tends to "cut to the chase" — that is, it highlights the overall strengths and weaknesses of our case. Second, these "generic" questions may cover up a lack of preparation by the judge, yet not expose him or her to embarrassment.

And speaking of not being embarrassed, we move on to the next section — how to present our argument.

§ 22.7   Advocacy Techniques

§ 22.7(a)   Forensics

"Nerves and butterflies are fine — they're a physical sign that you're mentally ready and eager. You have to get the butterflies to fly in formation, that's the trick."

— Steve Bull

We could provide a long laundry list of "DOS" and "DON'TS" here (mostly "DON'TS"), the majority of which are obvious but true, i.e., don't wear a loud tie; don't walk into court unzipped or unbuttoned; don't slouch on the podium; don't read the argument; don't interrupt the judges; don't wander all around the courtroom; etc. However, we think the better approach is to bear in mind that everything we do while in the courtroom must advance our client's case. We consider our mannerisms and behavior in terms of what they convey to the court.

We've seen hundreds of oral arguments, and most of them have gone pretty smoothly. However, we've also witnessed some very strange behavior.

Take, for example, the case of the spontaneous bleeder. One student, an ex-Marine, began to bleed profusely from his mouth during oral argument. It was like an eruption.

But to his credit, he didn't skip a beat. He kept going with his presentation, and, well, as discreetly as he could under the circumstances, swallowed. When we later asked him what had happened, he said he had been eating hard pretzels before oral argument. Apparently, he inadvertently gouged his gum tissue. The rise in his heartbeat and blood pressure during argument, he conjectured, must have started the bleeding.

Our colleague, Henry Wihnyk, also has his share of "experiences." He tells of one student who, after being asked the first question from the bench—and a friendly question at that—responded with an "Oh Jesus," rolled her eyes, and fainted. Fortunately, she quickly came around.

These examples, of course, are extreme and highly unusual. The bottom line is to expect the unexpected. Recognize that oral argument is nerve racking. It is challenging. But, it's also a critical part of what we, as lawyers, do. When done correctly, it's one of the most rewarding aspects of the job.

Here are some pointers on doing it correctly.

Posture. Our posture is straight and confident-appearing. We don't lean on the podium or walk around as we present our argument. Nor do we lock our knees or stand with our feet close together. It's better to stand with our feet several inches apart and our knees somewhat relaxed. That posture gives us better stability and allows the blood to flow more readily throughout our body—especially to our brain.

Position. We also don't turn and face our opposing counsel. We're convincing the court, not counsel, to rule in our favor. Someone is paying our opponent to disagree with us. We're not going to convince him or her of our position; there's no need to try. The judges, not our opponents, are the only game in town.

Gestures. We take care not to make gestures that distract the court from our fascinating argument—no "landing planes" with our hands or shaking our fingers at the judges. Some subtle gestures can be effective, but it's best to test them out by practicing them before a mirror. We don't want to frighten the court.

If our hands seem to have a life of their own, place them on either side of the podium or at the podium's front center. Don't put them in our pockets or clench them together in a death grip. Plant them on the podium.

Voice. Not only do we consider how we look, we also consider how we sound. Before the court can agree with us, it must hear what we have to say. We speak up. We don't yell, but we don't whisper either. We maintain a well-modulated tone. This, however, is often easier said than done.

When we get nervous, our voices tend to express the strain by going up about an octave. We may sound whiny, even though we don't intend to convey that impression. To keep our tone in control, we practice listening to ourselves.

We've also noticed an increasing tonal quality that we call, for lack of a better description, "Valley-talk." Valley-talk occurs when the speaker raises his or her voice at the end of every sentence, regardless of whether the sentence is declarative or interrogative. This manner of speaking, where every sentence *sounds* like a question, is extremely annoying. It conveys the impression that the speaker isn't sure of anything. Studies have shown that up to 97 percent of the communicative impact of speaking is in the tone we use. If our tone is indecisive, unsure, and questioning, that's the impression we'll convey.

Eye-contact. Finally, sincerity and eye contact are vital to persuading—we trust and take seriously those who look us directly and confidently in the eyes. We need to know how the judges are reacting to what we're saying; we need to *look* at them.

§ 22.7(b)   Professional Courtesy

As appellate advocates, we display professional courtesy at all times in and out of court. We address judges and other lawyers respectfully and formally. We refer to intermediate appellate judges as "Judge Smith" or "Your Honor," and to State or United States Supreme Court justices as "Justice." We address opposing counsel by his or her name or as "counsel for the appellant/respondent" but not as "my opponent."

We also are aware of our appearance and our tone of voice. We represent our client. We put on a *class act.* We dress neatly, in formal "courtroom" attire, to show respect for our client and the court. We keep our physical gestures discreet while waiting for the judges or while opposing counsel is addressing the court. Restless movements or sarcastic expressions tell the court that we're not taking the proceedings seriously. Moreover, we don't insult or act contemptuously toward opposing counsel or to the "lower court" judge. Not only is such behavior rude, it's dangerous. We never know how close a relationship a lower court judge or our opposing counsel may have with our judges. The ideal tone we adopt in argument is a thoughtful, respectful one. We don't rant and rave.

§ 22.7(c)   Time

In oral argument, time is crucial. We must be concise; we make every minute count. *There's no requirement, however, that we use all our allotted time.* If we've said what we need to say, we sum up and sit down. If we're leery of doing this, we politely say, "Your Honors, I believe you understand appellant's case and theory. May I ask if the Court has any further questions?" If there are none, we thank the Court and sit down. Yes, we shut up and sit down!

A timekeeper will generally notify us when time is running short. If we find that we're under the minute mark and need a few more seconds (not minutes), we ask the court's permission: "Your Honors, with the court's permission, may I have leave to conclude?" If the court grants us leave, we sum up the particular point we were discussing, request relief, and sit down. We don't argue other points.

However, we can't assume that the court will grant us permission to continue—sometimes courts refuse. In that case, we simply state a one-sentence prayer for relief, thank the court, and sit down.

§ 22.7(d)   Avoid Referring to Ourselves
and Avoid Excessive Emotion

We don't refer to ourselves in presenting our arguments. Phrases like "I will argue" or "my contention" or "my opinion" are inappropriate. It's not our contention, it's our client's. Phrases like "Your Honors, the government argues that" or "Your Honor, Ms. Doe's request is" sound more professional and remind the court who we represent. Better yet, *just make the statement*—the bold assertion—rather than prefacing it with this verbal baggage.

Moreover, we avoid emotion-laden words such as "feel" or "think;" they're ineffective and weaken our argument. Our argument is based on logic and the law, not on emotion. State the point; don't editorialize it.

§ 22.7(e)   The Gutsy Move

Trial and appellate lawyers have their favorite stories of "the gutsy move." This is a tactic that's absolutely effective but achieved only by the most masterful and, well, gutsy, among us. It's an unexpected maneuver during oral argument that drives home the point in the most direct way. Judge Aldisert tells of the gutsy move (our term) of Paul Freund, a Harvard law professor and former deputy U.S. Solicitor General.

> Once when he was arguing a case before the Supreme Court, the justices brought out in their questioning of the petitioner everything he had planned to say. Freund [representing the respondent] walked to the podium and said, 'May it please the court, there is a typographical error on page 10 of our brief.' He made the correction and then said, 'If there are no questions, the government will rely on its brief.' The [C]ourt had no questions and the government prevailed in a unanimous decision. For years afterwards, Justice Felix Frankfurter often would refer to Freund's performance and say: 'Since I have been on the Court, I have heard learned arguments. I have heard powerful arguments. I have heard eloquent arguments. But I have only heard one perfect argument.'[10]

The bottom line: be smart enough to quit while we're ahead, even if we haven't uttered a word. Seizing that moment is making the gutsy move.

---

10. Aldisert, *supra*, at 377-78.

Chapter Review
The Oral Argument

✓ The term "oral argument" is a misnomer; we don't argue with the court, we discuss our case — we converse.

✓ The best way to prepare for oral argument is to practice.

✓ *Every* question from a judge is a *friendly* question.

✓ We've got to know the Record on Appeal — the judges want to know how the law applies to our facts.

✓ We don't read during oral argument.

✓ We let the theory of our case guide every answer. *The whale has to be moved, and we can't break up the dolphin family.*

✓ When a judge speaks, we stop talking.

✓ If a question calls for a "yes" or "no," we answer "yes" or "no" and then explain.

✓ We prepare for both hot (questioning) and cold benches.

✓ We don't prepare a speech; we prepare an outline.

✓ When our time is up, we stop, or ask permission to conclude.

✓ When we have no more to say, we sit down.

Section IV

Beginning, Middle, and Ending

Chapter 23

The Blank Page: Tips on Getting Started

"The act of writing must tie together diffusely located parts of the brain, making writing perhaps the most difficult neurological task a human can undertake."

—Robert Ochsner,
Physical Eloquence and the
Biology of Writing 56 (1990)

§ 23.1   The Ticking Clock

Here we are. We've got our assignment, we have an idea of what's expected of us, we've done our research, we've analyzed, we've briefed our cases, we've outlined and personalized the legal rules, we've created case charts, and we're sitting facing a blank page (or a blank screen). The clock ticks and ticks again and nothing happens. The page is as blank as it was a minute, an hour, ago.

We get up, we move around. Maybe a bit of blood flow to the head will get things going. We return. Nothing.

We start to fret, big time. This thing is due soon, too soon, and we haven't written a word. The words aren't making it from the brain to the hand. Somewhere along the line, the thought is rerouted. We think not of what we should write but that we haven't yet written.

However, the problem is not that we haven't yet written, it's that we haven't yet *thought*. Writing, those words on a page, that act of moving the hand, is nothing more than a byproduct of thought. Writing and thinking are not synonymous, nor do they occur simultaneously. The thought precedes the written word. The written word is merely evidence of the preceding thought. And, without the thought, there is no writing. As Cervantes put it: "It is not the hand but the understanding of a man that may be said to write."

So, when we sit facing the blank page, we're facing the absence of focused thought. We can't force the words to flow. We can only think the thought that will allow the words to escape to our fingers and to the page. But how do we do that? Let's see.

§ 23.2   If Time Permits, Go Away,
Think of Something Else, Then Return

Your humble authors aren't neuro-scientists, psychiatrists, or stress counselors, but we are professional writers, lawyers, and teachers of thousands of students. And here's one thing we know: Stressing over writing never makes the words flow.

When we reach the point where we can't write, when absolutely nothing is flowing, we stop. We go do something else. We give our brain the down-time it needs to *think*.

We, along with most lawyers, have experienced the strange sensation of being engaged in a non-law activity and having a thought concerning a case we're working on emerge seemingly from nowhere. Right there in the middle of paying a bill or getting change from a cashier, our brain flashes with an insight on a topic we didn't even know we were considering. Or, as often happens, we'll awake in the middle of the night with an idea or theory of our case. Our brain, in autopilot mode, has been busy. When it's good and ready, it will reveal its secrets. When this happens, we write like the wind.

§ 23.3   When We Don't Have Time to Wait

More often than not, however, we don't have time to wait for flashes of brilliance to awaken us. We've got to produce, and we've got to produce *now*. Here are two suggestions for getting the thoughts and words flowing.

Start writing, or
start talking.

Start writing. Get comfortable; grab that paper and pen or computer and write. It doesn't matter at first what we say, just say something. Vent if we must. Curse if we must. Just start writing—despoil that nice clean sheet of paper or blank computer screen. Write straightforwardly, the way you talk. In fact, pretend you are telling someone about your case and write it down in just that fashion. You can make it fancy and more formal later. Just get something down on paper or the screen. For example:

> Yeah, right. I'm supposed to complete this **%$! brief by Friday, the 18th. Fat chance. Do they think this is my only case? Do they think this is the only time commitment I have? HA. Defend John Doe from a charge of begging? Of course he was begging. Of course he violated the City's anti-begging ordinance. Just where the *&^% is our case? What does the ordinance prohibit? Personal solicitation for the immediate receipt of money. Ok, he was doing that. Solicitation—that involves speech. Is there really a First Amendment issue here? Was Doe punished simply for asking for some spare change? Is that type of begging a protected form of speech? Should it be? What do the cases say? Well, in *Loper*, the Second Circuit found that begging was a protected form of speech. Ok, how can I use that case? What was its rule? Something about begging being closely akin to charitable solicitation, which the Supreme Court has found is protected under the First Amendment. Let's look at that Supreme Court case.

There—didn't that feel good? If need be, we go on for page after page, "thinking out loud." Then, we read what we've written, organize it into themes, evaluate those themes, and pursue those that pass initial scrutiny. We, in essence, dump our thoughts on the page, then organize and evaluate them.

By doing this, we avoid "mental constipation." That's the condition many writers face when absolutely nothing is flowing. The mistaken belief that they can't put anything but the *exact, finalized* thought on the page paralyzes many would-be writers. They sit, mentally blocked, not writing a word until exactly the right word comes. Of course, it never does. As all writers know, we don't write, we *rewrite*. By letting our thoughts flow, even if in a disorganized and rambling fashion, we create something that we can then rewrite. We've at least allowed the thought to make it to the page.

Start talking. This suggestion is the cousin of the one above. Instead of writing our thoughts, we speak them into a tape recorder, computer, or phone. We vent; we query; and ultimately, we begin to solve the legal problem. We then listen to what we've said and take notes, writing down what's relevant. We then organize this written information, evaluate it, and then start the rewriting process.

§ 23.4   Once We Have Some Idea Where We're Headed, We Compartmentalize Our Analysis and Issues, Then Work Incrementally, Using the BaRAC Design

Once we have something written down, we work step-by-step on each part of the document and on each issue using the BaRAC design.[1] Unless we want to be overwhelmed completely, we don't attempt to write the entire document in one fell swoop. Instead, we compartmentalize our document and work on one manageable "box" at a time.

For each issue, we can write the acronym of the BaRAC syllogism vertically down the left side of our paper—essentially an "issue box."[2] We may have more than one of these syllogisms for each issue, but at least one is needed for each issue. When we have multiple issues, we refer to Chapter 11, § 11.5 for organizing and addressing the issues in their logical order. We deal first with any dispositive issues, i.e., those that the court must decide as a threshold matter. Then, we tackle the issues in order of importance, addressing the most important first. If we follow the BaRAC (bold assertion, rule, application, conclusion) design, the issue will practically write itself.

Graphic 23.4(a) illustrates the essentials of this type of issue box, and **Graphics 23.4(b)** and **23.4(c)** illustrate issue boxes for a single-element rule and a multi-element rule, respectively.

Graphic 23.4(a)	Create an "Issue Box" for Each Issue
bold assertion	State the likely outcome on this issue.
type of rule	Determine the type(s) of rule analysis involved: (1) rule-only: factor analysis; (2) rule-plus: the illustrative approach; or (3) FIHRR: reasoning by analogy.
rule design	State and explain the applicable rule. If the rule is unclear, explain why our interpretation is correct. Cite and address any relevant authorities.
application	Apply the rule to the facts relevant to this issue. bold assertion: State the conclusion the court should reach regarding the application of the rule to our facts. rule: If necessary, further explain the rule or its elements. Address relevant authorities. application: Show how the rule applies to our facts.

---

1. See Chapter 1, §§ 1.9-1.10; refer also to Chapter 8, § 8.2(d) on how to outline our case.
2. See Chapter 11, § 11.2 and Chapter 20, § 20.6(a).

	conclusion: State the conclusion the court should reach regarding the application of the rule to our facts.
	counter-arguments: Discuss and respond to any relevant and harmful arguments and authorities.
conclusion	Restate the likely outcome on this issue.

Graphic 23.4(b)	"Issue Box" for Single-Element Rule
bold assertion	The court should hold __✖__ .
rule and rule explanation	In holding __✖__ , the court employs rule __●__ . [Citation.] Rule __●__ is met when __▲__ occurs. [Citation.] [Explain the rule. Use the rule-only, rule-plus (illustrative approach), or FIHRR (analogy approach).]
application	The court should hold that the requirements of rule __●__ have been fulfilled in this case. In the instant case, __▲__ has occurred. [Record citation.] As the facts demonstrate, … [addressing __▲__]. [Citation to facts.] [Also using the BaRAC design, address any relevant counter-arguments and our response.]
conclusion	For these reasons, the court should hold __✖__ .

Graphic 23.4(c)	"Issue Box" for Multi-Element Rule
bold assertion	The court should hold __✖__ .
rule (general)	In holding __✖__ , the court employs rule __●__ . [Citation.] Rule __●__ is met when __▲__ and __■__ occur. [Citation.] [Explain the rule.]
application	The court should hold that the requirements of rule __●__ have been fulfilled in this case.
element 1 bold assertion	First, __▲__ has occurred in the instant case. [*See* citation.] __▲__ occurs when __□__ . [Citation.]
rule [specific]	[Explain this element of the Rule. Use the rule-only, rule-plus (illustrative approach), or FIHRR (analogy approach).]
application conclusion	In the instant case, as the facts demonstrate __□__ occurred. [Address the facts as they relate to __□__ .]. [Citation to facts.] For this reason, __▲__ occurred in the instant case.*
element 2 bold assertion	Second, __■__ has occurred in the instant case. [Record citation.] __■__ occurs when __★__ . [Citation.]
rule [specific]	[Explain this element of the Rule. Use the rule-only, rule-plus (illustrative approach), or FIHRR (analogy approach).]
application	In the instant case, as the facts demonstrate, __★__ occurred. [Address the facts as they relate to __★__ .]. [Citation to facts.] For this reason, __■__ occurred in the instant case.**
conclusion	

| conclusion | As the above discussion demonstrates, the requirements of __●__ have been met in the instant case. For these reasons, the court should hold __✖__. |

*/** Also using the BaRAC design, address any relevant counter-arguments and our response.

At the very least, these BaRAC outlines give us a direction, a path to follow. We're on our way to writing the document.

Chapter 24

Making It Shine: Editing Tips for the Memo and Brief

"A single word often betrays a great design."

— Jean-Baptiste Racine

"There is no such thing as good writing. There is only good rewriting."

— Justice Brandeis

No document is complete until it shines, until words glisten like waves upon water on a bright, crisp day. Using the techniques outlined below, we eliminate the dull and stagnant aspects of our writing and create a document we're proud to call our own.

§ 24.1   Topic Sentences

- **Have we used topic sentences effectively?**[1]

Topic sentences get to the heart of the matter in record time. All too often, however, writers fail to use them effectively, if at all. Here are some pointers:

(1) Review the document for topic sentences; highlight each one with a colored marker.

(2) Ask whether the topic sentences, when written in the order they appear in the document, create a coherent, logical outline of the document. They should. If they don't, we edit the document until they do.

(3) Do the topic sentences flow together easily? They should.

(4) Circle every transition used in the topic sentences. Then, consider whether that transition is appropriate. For example, have we used "therefore" correctly?

(5) Locate every portion of the document where we discuss cited cases. Have we begun each of these discussions with a sentence clearly stating the point of the cited case? We should. We don't make our reader wait until the end of the discussion to understand the point we're trying to make. The following graphic illustrates this concept:

Graphic 24.1	Using Topic Sentences
don't do this **(no topic sentence)**	In *ABC*, the court held…. Also, in *DEF*, the court reasoned…. Finally, in *XYZ*, the court found…. Therefore, the court has repeatedly stated that….
instead, do this	The court has repeatedly stated that…. For example, in *ABC*, the court held…. Also, in *DEF*, the court reasoned…. Finally, in *XYZ*, the court concluded….
	or
(using parentheticals)	The court has repeatedly stated that…. *ABC* (holding …); *DEF* (reasoning …); and *XYZ* (concluding …).

(6) Locate every portion of the document where, after discussing a cited case, we return to our case. Have we made this shift in discussion clear to our reader by using an appropriate transition? We should.

---

1. By "topic" sentence, we also mean "thesis" or "point" sentence.

§ 24.2   Citation[2]

- **Have we streamlined our citation wherever possible?**

Cut out what we don't need. Excessive citation drags down our writing and bloats our document. Sure, we want to support what we say, but we don't need overkill. If one authority effectively supports our point, why should we add two or three? We shouldn't. Space in legal writing is an exhaustible resource; we don't waste it.

- **Are our citations well-placed?**

Place citations at the end of sentences whenever possible. We know we hate it. We're reading along, really getting into the argument, when suddenly we're trapped in a bog of case names and numbers, volume this and that, this year and that year—our eyes glaze over and we forget the point. The case citation itself has distracted us; it's gotten in the way of the argument.

Graphic 24.2	Using Citations
don't do this	According to the United States Supreme Court, under the test in *Spence v. Washington*, 418 U.S. 405 (1974), the First Amendment protects.... *Id.* at 410–11.
do this instead	The First Amendment protects.... *Spence v. Washington*, 418 U.S. 405, 410–11 (1974).

To eliminate this phenomenon of *citation-interruptus* (so-called "embedded citations"), we place citations at the end of sentences and consolidate citations whenever possible.

- **Are our citations accurate and in the proper form?**

Make certain citations are accurate. When we cite authority, we're saying, "Look, here's the proof of my point. You can believe me." If the citation we provide is wrong, we're saying, "Look, you shouldn't believe a word I have to say because I'm obviously not even careful enough to get the easy things right."

Every citation is an invitation, from us to our readers, to check our veracity. Every citation better be accurate. If we say a certain fact is on a certain page of a certain case, it better well be there.

Make sure citations are in the proper form. But it's not enough just to be accurate. Every citation must also be in the proper form. Rules of Appellate Practice, local rules of court, and other "form-books" may govern how we cite authority. These rules act as a universal translator, assuring some level of consistency in our ability to locate materials in the world of statutes, constitutions, regulations, cases, ordinances, legislative history, law reviews, and you-name-its. If we mix up, for example, the volume number of a case with the page of the case, we've sent our readers on a wild goose chase; they won't be pleased.

---

2. See Chapter 25 for additional information regarding citation.

Moreover, an error in citing may translate into an error in updating, which means Trouble (yeah, with a capital "T"). The bottom line: an error in citing may spell *malpractice*.

§ 24.3   Authorities

- **Have we winnowed our authorities down to the most relevant ones?**

String citations are the hallmark of inexperience. Our court wants to know (1) what binding authority is on point, and (2) whether any cases from this jurisdiction are on point. For example, a federal circuit court of appeal will, after Supreme Court cases, be most interested in cases from that particular circuit. Thus, if we're before the First Circuit, we cite and address relevant Supreme Court and First Circuit cases. If there are none, we say so and then refer to cases from other jurisdictions.

- **Have we streamlined our discussion of relevant authorities?**

Editing our own work is painful, no doubt about it. We've worked diligently on the document, have forgone other activities (i.e., life) to hammer out our best work possible, and then, then, we're told to edit this perfect piece of human achievement. This borders on sacrilege. However, it's got to be done. As Albert Einstein noted: "One can only continue to expect to be read if, as far as possible, one omits everything that is unimportant."

We've found that most of the "fat" in legal writing, other than the stylized fat such as nominalizations and redundancies, lies in the discussion of authority. Some writers think that they must include in their document a "brief" of every case they cite. For example, even if they're only using a cited case to state a rule, they'll go on for a page or two about the facts, issue, holding, rule, and reasoning of that case. This overkill does nothing to advance their argument; it serves only to waste space.

Here are some further suggestions for streamlining our discussion of authority:

- Highlight, with a colored marker, all discussion of cited cases where we address the case in full (the FIHRR approach).

- Ask: do we really need to address this case using the FIHRR approach? Or, can we shorten our document by placing the relevant material into a parenthetical?

  If, following our discussion of this case, we do compare and contrast the cited case to our case (i.e., we are using the cited case to *argue by analogy*) then we can, and should, stick to the FIHRR approach.

  If, however, we find that our application section doesn't include, and doesn't need to include, such a comparison, then we edit our discussion of the cited case. We either pare down our discussion to include only the rule, or we include the relevant aspects of the case in a parenthetical.

- Ask: even if we retain the FIHRR format, can we pare down what we've written?

  Here's an example of streamlining the discussion of a cited case:

Graphic 24.3(a)   **Original Version: 96 Words**

In *Young*, an organization representing homeless people brought a class action against the New York City Transit Authority challenging a regulation prohibiting panhandling and begging in the subways. *Young*, 903 F.2d at 148. At issue was whether the regulation violated the petitioners' First Amendment rights. *Id.* The petitioners claimed that begging and panhandling was a form of expressive conduct protected by the First Amendment. *Id.* The court disagreed and held that begging and panhandling in the subways was not a form of expressive conduct protected by the First Amendment. *Id.* at 153.

The court reasoned....

Graphic 24.3(b)   **Edited Version: 58 Words**

In *Young*, an organization representing homeless people brought a class action against the New York City Transit Authority challenging, as violating the First Amendment, a regulation prohibiting panhandling and begging in the subways. *Young*, 903 F.2d at 148. The petitioners claimed that their activities were "expressive conduct." *Id.* The court disagreed. *Id.* at 153.

The court reasoned....

Continuing with suggestions for streamlining:

- Highlight, with a (different) colored marker, all discussion of cited cases where we address the rule only. Have we provided the complete rule? If not, and if the complete rule is relevant, we add it to our discussion. However, if we've stated (or quoted) the full rule, where only a portion of that rule is relevant, we cut the unnecessary material.

- Highlight, with still another different colored marker, all cases we've cited but haven't discussed. Ask: do we really need these citations? If not, cut them out. If we do need them to support a point, consider whether we should spruce them up by adding, in a parenthetical, the relevant aspect of the case. A case citation standing alone stands idle. A case citation with a parenthetical containing a pithy quote or crucial fact *works*.

- **Have we adequately addressed contrary authorities and policies?**

No document is complete until we've dealt directly and effectively with adverse statutes, cases, and policies. We resist the temptation to slough off, in cursory fashion, our discussion of contrary authorities. Because we can't assume that our reader has read and understood the contrary case, we can't simply mention the case by name and dismiss it with a pat, "*Apple v. Banana* simply does not apply here." Instead, we address the relevant principle of the case (statute or policy) and explain why that principle doesn't apply to our case.

- **Have we updated our authorities?**

We update all our authorities. We update case law to make sure it hasn't been reversed or overruled by a higher court, overruled by a later decision of the same court, or altered by a subsequent statute. We also check to see whether the case has been modified or questioned by a later decision. Similarly, we check statutes. Statutes can be repealed or amended by a later statute or limited, expanded, or found unconstitutional by a later court ruling. No document is complete until we have updated *all* authorities.

§ 24.4   Logic and Persuasion

"Place it before them briefly so they will read it, clearly so they will appreciate it, picturesquely so they will remember it, above all, accurately so they will be guided by its light."

— Joseph Pulitzer

- **Have we used the BaRAC design effectively?**

The BaRAC design is the core design of our argument and analysis. Through it, we help determine not only what our readers think, but how they think. For this reason, we must use it as effectively as possible. Here's one way to help ensure that we've done so.

Take three different colored highlighters (again!). Use one color (e.g., yellow) to highlight every bold assertion and conclusion. Use another color (e.g., green) to highlight every rule and rule explanation. Finally, use the last color (e.g., pink) to highlight every application section. If we're having trouble just determining which section is which, then we need to focus our writing. We probably also need better transition and topic sentences.

Assuming that we're able to distinguish the separate Ba-R-A-C sections, what do we see?

We should see a balanced pattern of color: yellow — Ba, then green — R, then pink — A, then yellow — C. But, what we usually see in novice writing is either (1) the absence of color, notably in the rule and application sections, or (2) a mismash of color: yellow, to green, to pink, back to green, back to pink, maybe a yellow, then a pink, etc.

When we're dealing with the absence of color, this usually means that we haven't provided our reader with a crucial section of the BaRAC design. We may have omitted necessary information. We need to rethink our approach. Have we subtly included a BaRAC section? If so, fine. Or, have we just neglected to include a section? If so, we edit our work to include it.

Ping-Ponging. When we're dealing with a mismash of color, we probably have some "ping-ponging" going on. This occurs most often when we write our argument or analysis using the following "design":

Graphic 24.4(a)	Ping-Ponging
bold assertion	yellow
rule	green
application	pink
a bit more of the rule	green
some more application	pink
some more rule	green
some more application	pink
a conclusion	yellow
some more rule	green
some more application	pink

Correcting this type of error is easy. Normally, we just re-group our writing. We place all the related rule discussion for a particular issue or sub-issue together and follow it with of all the application discussion. We end with the conclusion.

If we find that this regrouping is not effective, we may have a situation where we're attempting to discuss two or more elements of the rule together. If that's what's occurring, we separate our discussion. We address the first element, with a full BaRAC pertaining only to *that* element; then we do the same for the next element. In other words, we create the following:

Graphic 24.4(b)	Creating Order
element **1**	
bold assertion	yellow
rule	green
application	pink
conclusion	yellow
element **2**	
bold assertion	yellow
rule	green
application	pink
conclusion	yellow

- **Are our bold assertions strong?**

We don't want wimpy suggestions; we want bold assertions. Make them strong. Here are some examples of strong, effective assertions. (Assume that we represent the City and that our opponent is Doe.)

Graphic 24.4(c)	Making Assertions Bold

The City has met its burden of proving that....

Doe has the burden of proving, yet has failed to prove, that....

On *de novo* review, this Court should hold that....

The trial court properly exercised, not abused, its discretion in finding....

The trial court correctly dismissed this case after concluding that Doe's complaint....

As a matter of law, Doe's conduct was not....

As the trial court concluded, the facts alleged lead to but one conclusion:....

The trial court also properly found that....

Here, as the trial court found,....

Doe's arguments ignore a fundamental principle; namely,....

- **Have we included any premature conclusions?**

We evaluate each conclusion and ask if it's appropriate. Can we reach the conclusion we've reached, or is our conclusion premature?

Premature conclusions most often appear in the context of a multi-element rule. For example, suppose our rule is as follows:

"Rule __●__ is violated when a defendant does __▲__ and __■__."

Suppose further that we've just finished addressing element __▲__ . We *cannot* yet conclude that rule __●__ has been violated. In other words, the following conclusion is *premature*:

"Because the defendant did __▲__ he violated rule __●__."

We can only reach this conclusion after we demonstrate that the defendant did __▲__ and __■__ .

§ 24.5   Paragraphs

- **Have we streamlined our paragraphs?**

There are few things more foreboding in legal reading than coming upon a seemingly insurmountable wall of words that some call "a long paragraph." When we see such artifices, we cringe. "You expect us to climb that thing?" We shudder. "You've got to be kidding." There, plopped down on the page is a barrier, created by the writer, keeping the reader at bay. And for what purpose? None that we can see. None that anyone has ever been able to explain to us.

When we read, we don't want to mountain climb. Give us little hills to frolic over. Little "white-spaced" valleys to rest in. Keep the paragraphs short—half a page *maximum*.

Short paragraphs mean we've articulated our thoughts and have expressed them in a logical form. We've ordered our ideas and haven't let them pass from the brain to the page in a rambling mass. Readers expect this type of order and resent it if we don't give it to them. When we're trying to convince someone to agree with us, reader resentment is the last thing we want to foster.

- **Do our paragraphs pack a "punch"?**

Can we edit our paragraphs to convey, more directly, our thoughts? Let's examine the following two versions of the opening paragraph from a Statement of the Case and Facts section. The original version conveys necessary information but falls rather flat. The revised version packs a subtle punch, is shorter than the original, and contains more information.

Graphic 24.5(a)   **Original: 102 Words**

In January of 1995, Petitioner, John Doe, was laid off from his employment with Gotham City Motor Works. (R.12.) He was unable to secure steady employment since the layoff (R.12), and his community, Gotham City ("City"), was unable to provide public assistance to all those in need. (R.9.) In hardship and desperation, Doe became homeless and resorted to begging as a means of survival. Although the City could not provide adequate assistance to Doe in his time of misfortune, it nonetheless arrested and prosecuted Doe for conveying his message of need to others within his community. (R.12.)

Graphic 24.5(b)   **Revised: 81 Words**

In January of 1995, Petitioner, John Doe, was laid off from Gotham City Motor Works. Since then, and, through no fault of his own, he has been unable to find work. (R.12.) Making matters worse, Gotham City has refused him public assistance. (R.9.) Homeless and desperate, Doe resorts to begging to survive. (R.8.) On December 20, 1995, fully aware of these circumstances, the City arrested and prosecuted him for asking a pedestrian for spare change. (R.12.)

- **Could we shorten our paragraph by using a list instead of a series of repetitive sentences?**

If we find that our paragraphs contain repetitive clauses concerning the same subject, we consider using a list instead of separate sentences. The following examples illustrate this technique:

Graphic 24.5(c)   **Original: 51 Words**

The Study found that the vast majority of those questioned believe that beggars "pervade the downtown core." The Study also revealed that people believe that beggars commit "most of the area's crime." Moreover, the Study disclosed that people perceive beggars as dissuading "visitors from shopping at the City's Market Place."

Graphic 24.5(d)   **Revised: 33 Words**

The Study found that the vast majority of those questioned believe that beggars "pervade the downtown core", commit "most of the area's crime", and "dissuade visitors from shopping at the City's Market Place."

---

§ 24.6   Sentences

- **Have we streamlined our sentences?**

The same reasons for shortening paragraphs apply to shortening sentences. Readers remember and accept ideas much more readily if we present those ideas bit by bit, instead of in one lump sum. Often, when we are uncertain about what we want to say, our writing gets complicated with lots of commas, semi-colons, and other punctuation. When we think thoroughly about what we want to say, we have an easier time writing short, straightforward sentences. So, shorten those sentences. Clear up any ambiguous passages. Strike out any redundant phrases. Make every word count.

§ 24.7   Quotation[3]

- **Are all quotations accurate and tied to a "pinpoint" citation?**

A surefire way to wreck our credibility is to misquote an authority. After all, if we can't *copy* correctly, how can we analyze correctly? We can't; our readers know this.

---

3. See Chapter 25, § 25.6(c) for additional information regarding quotation.

Checking the accuracy of *all* quotations in our document is boring, tedious, time consuming, and *essential*. By "checking the accuracy" of all quotations, we don't mean giving the source a cursory review. We don't mean relying on our memory that the quotation is accurate. We do mean the following:

- checking our quotation *word for word* (including all punctuation) against the source;
- properly indicating any changes to the quoted material;
- placing the quoted material in the proper form;
- making certain the quoted material makes grammatical sense in the form that we're using it; and
- providing an accurate, page-specific "pinpoint" citation to the quoted material.

§ 24.8 Footnotes

- **Do we need the footnote?**

Footnotes can be very helpful or very annoying. In editing our work, we ask whether we need the footnote. Could we eliminate it entirely? Could we incorporate it into the body of our document? If so, we do so.

Although some lawyers and professors consider footnotes inappropriate, we have no inherent bias against them. In the right instance, they're effective tools in providing information. For example, footnotes are appropriate in the following circumstances:

- to demonstrate, by citing to authorities, that a certain proposition has been widely accepted or criticized by other jurisdictions;
- to dispose of irrelevant authorities or arguments advanced by our opponent or by the trial court;
- to quote relevant passages from statutes, codes, administrative regulations, trial transcripts, etc.;
- to refer to collateral issues, or issues which the court need not reach, which don't merit a fuller discussion; and
- to refer the reader to other relevant sections of our document.

However, we use footnotes, even in the above circumstances, with utmost care. The reason is simple: footnotes break the reader's flow. They send the reader looking down the page and then back up again. An occasional detour is fine; repeated detours are time-consuming, wasteful, and tiring.

But, under no circumstances do we use footnotes to cram in information and evade page limits. Courts know when counsel are doing this and don't appreciate this thinly-disguised form of deceit.

Nor do we use footnotes to make biting remarks about opposing counsel or judges. A footnote *is* part of the document. It's not an aside whispered in private. *Ad hominem* attacks have no place anywhere in our writing.

§ 24.9   Typos or Format Errors

- **Do we have any typos or format errors?**

Submitting a sloppy document is like getting all dressed up for the prom and smelling like manure. Something stinks, and the stink runs deep. No amount of brilliance can quell the smell.

We count only on ourselves to catch typos and to make certain our document complies with all format requirements.[4] Our name, not our secretary's, goes on the document. We bear the burden of refining that document until it reflects our best work.

Proofreading errors not only undermine our credibility, they're embarrassing. Take, for example, two blunders that occurred during the Senate impeachment trial of President Clinton. The first occurred on the first day when the Senators—all 100 of them—signed their oaths to be "impartial." In a flurry of pomp and circumstance, they were each given the pen they had used, which bore the impressive engraving: "Untied States Senator." To make matters worse, the pens had originated from the Senate secretary's office.

The second blunder came from the President's highly paid, highly visible counsel. The cover page to the President's trial memorandum, the chief defense document, read in bold letters: "In re Impeachment of William Jefferson Cinton President of the United States." Ouch!

In proofreading our document, we can't rely on spell-checkers. Although they're wonderful devices, they don't always catch errors, as the following poem illustrates:

Ode to Spell Checkers

I have a spelling checker

I disk covered four my PC.

It plane lee marks four my revue

Miss steaks aye can knot see.

Eye ran this poem threw it.

Your sure real glad two no.

Its very polished in its weigh,

My checker tolled me sew.

A checker is a blessing.

It freeze yew lodes of thyme.

It helps me right awl stiles two reed,

And aides me when aye rime.

Each frays comes posed up on my screen

Eye trussed too bee a joule.

The checker pours o'er every word

---

4. Any errors in this writing are, of course, intentional, to keep you dear readers on your toes.

To cheque sum spelling rule.

Bee fore we rote with checkers

Hour spelling was inn deck line,

Butt now when wee dew have a laps,

Wee are not maid to wine.

And now bee cause my spelling

Is checked with such grate flare,

There are know faults in awl this peace,

Of nun eye am a wear.

To rite with care is quite a feet

Of witch won should be proud,

And wee mussed dew the best wee can,

Sew flaws are knot aloud.

That's why eye brake in two averse

Cuz eye dew want to please.

Sow glad eye yam that aye did bye

This soft wear four pea seas.

Author Unknown

As one commentator has noted: "Readers see misspellings as oddities — like a troop of bald Boy Scouts — and must give their attention to them. Distracted by the oddities, readers find it impossible to follow the sense of the writing."[5]

But not only are typos distracting and annoying, they can constitute malpractice. A misplaced comma, a forgotten semicolon, an inverted dollar amount, an inverted percentage can change the meaning of a contract. As lawyers, we not only read the fine print, we *double-check* the fine print.

Format. Format requirements exist to help our reader read. If a requirement calls for a double-spaced document, we don't submit one spaced any more or any less. If one-inch margins are mandated, we don't cheat with lesser ones. If the font size is 12 point, we use 12 point.

§ 24.10   Consistency

- **Have we used the same name for the same thing?**
- **Are our arguments consistent with our theory?**
- **Have we identified alternative arguments as alternatives?**

Use consistent terms. When referring to persons, places, or things, we use the same term for the same item. If we're inconsistent, we'll lose our reader.

---

5. William L. Rivers, *Writing: Craft and Art* 81 (1975).

In addition, we abbreviate long terms wherever possible. However, before launching into the abbreviation, we introduce the shortened form to our reader.

Stay true to our theory. Our document will fall flat if it advances arguments inconsistent with our theory of the case. Particularly when we're writing a document addressing many issues, we must make certain that we don't contradict ourselves. For example, if our argument on issue #5 cuts the heart out of our argument on issue #2, we've got trouble. We've shot ourselves in the proverbial foot.

Identify alternative arguments as alternatives. Unless we identify alternative arguments as alternatives, we'll have our readers running in circles. If we're arguing in the alternative, we say so, at the outset. But even alternative arguments must remain consistent with our theory of the case.

Chapter Review
Making it Shine: Editing Tips for the Memo and Brief

✓ Have we used topic sentences effectively?

✓ Have we streamlined our citation to cases wherever possible?

✓ Are our citations well-placed?

✓ Are our citations accurate?

✓ Are our citations in the proper form?

✓ Have we winnowed our authorities down to only those that are the most relevant to the court deciding our case?

✓ Have we streamlined our discussion of authorities?

✓ If we've used the FIHRR approach to discuss a cited case, could we instead use the rule-only or rule-plus approach?

✓ If the FIHRR approach is appropriate, can we pare it down?

✓ Have we adequately addressed contrary authorities and policies?

✓ Have we updated our authorities?

✓ Have we used the BaRAC design effectively?

✓ Are our bold assertions strong?

✓ Have we included any premature conclusions?

✓ Have we streamlined our paragraphs?

✓ Do our paragraphs pack a "punch"?

✓ Could we shorten our paragraph by using a list instead of a series of repetitive sentences?

✓ Have we streamlined our sentences?

✓ Is each quotation accurate?

✓ Is each quotation tied to a pinpoint citation?

✓ Do we need the footnote?

✓ Have we eliminated all typos?

✓ Have we complied with all format requirements?

✓ Have we used the same name for the same thing?

✓ Are our arguments consistent with our theory?

✓ Have we identified alternative arguments as alternatives?

Chapter 25

Citation, Quotation, and Style[1]

1. We thank our colleague, Diane Tomlinson, for her suggestions and edits on this chapter.

§ 25.1   Citation and Legal Writing: An Introduction

What is a citation? As with most types of writing, in legal writing we acknowledge when we use ideas other than our own by "citing," i.e., attributing, the authorities we've relied on. A "citation" contains the information necessary to guide our reader to a particular source. In essence, we need to think of a legal citation as a coordinate system — allowing our reader physically or electronically to locate the authority we cite, somewhat similar to the latitude and longitude coordinates for geographic locations. Cases, for example, have a coordinate system (like an address) consisting of a (1) volume number, (2) reporter name or originating source, and (3) page number. With these three bits of information, we can find the case we're looking for, whether we're seeking the case in print in a book or electronically.

Why do we cite? In legal documents, we cite (1) to prove that our statements about the law are true; (2) to show the precedential value of the authority, that is, whether primary or secondary, mandatory or persuasive, supportive or contradictory; (3) to assist the reader in locating the source; and, finally, (4) to attribute the statements and ideas of others, thus avoiding plagiarism. *When we file a document with a court, we cite because the court requires that we do so.* We follow the format the court mandates. But, whether mandated or not, we want to cite authorities to show that our analysis is supported by something other than just our opinion. We also want to avoid plagiarizing any source. Plagiarism, an honor code violation at most law schools, occurs when we use language and ideas of others without giving the authors credit — in other words, plagiarism is stealing! Never, ever, be tempted to follow the advice of an American playwright, raconteur, and entrepreneur:

> "If you steal from one author it's plagiarism; if you steal from many it's research."
>
> — Wilson Mizner

Quoting vs. paraphrasing. Whether we're paraphrasing, quoting, using another's idea, or building upon the analysis of another, we ensure that we always attribute ideas to their source by citing to that authority. *And, when we quote, we use quotation marks and accurately state the original text.* For reasons that we find baffling, some people think (or were taught) to quote using single quotation marks, as follows: 'and.' *This is incorrect!* When we quote, we use double marks, as follows: "and." We use single quotes only when we are quoting a quote, as follows: " 'and.' "

We also ensure, by copious proofreading, that all of the quotations we use are absolutely accurate! We match word-for-word the text in our document with the quoted text. If we can't even copy the original text accurately into our document (so we can present that information accurately to our reader) we've got no business being lawyers.

When we "paraphrase," i.e., when we restate the law or an idea in our own words, we don't use quotation marks, because we're stating, in our own words, the idea expressed by someone else. But, in paraphrasing, we don't just alter a word or two of the source here and there. That "change a word or two" method would likely lead to a valid claim that we've plagiarized the source. When we paraphrase, we express the idea as we understand it, using our own "voice," but staying true to the passage's original meaning.

And, yes, *we cite the original source, giving the author credit for the idea we've discussed.* Whether we quote a passage or paraphrase a passage, we acknowledge that the idea was not our own by citing to the source.

Pinpoint citations. Whether we quote or paraphrase, we "prove" the accuracy of our statement(s) by citing to the precise page of the authority we've relied upon. This specific page citation is variously referred to as a "pincite," "jumpcite," or a "pinpoint" cite (presumably because the reader is being told to "jump" to that page and because a particular page is being "pinpointed"). We'll refer to these as "pinpoint" cites.

A pinpoint cite is always included in case citations unless we're merely introducing the case by name, in which event we include the basic coordinates of the case. If our pinpoint cite includes more than one page, we cite the page numbers properly. Yes, there *are* rules governing how to cite page numbers.

Why citations must be accurate. When we cite an authority, we're saying to our reader, "Look, here's the proof of my point. You can believe me." If the citation we provide is wrong, we're saying, "Look, you shouldn't believe a word I have to say because I'm obviously not even careful enough to get the easy things right. I can't even tell you where I got this information." Every citation is an invitation, from us to our readers, to check our veracity. Every citation better be accurate. If we say a certain fact is on a certain page of a certain case, it better well be there. If we're wrong, it's like we've given out the wrong phone number or the wrong website address.

Why citations must be in the proper format. But it's not enough just to have accurate citations. Every citation must also be in the proper form.

💣* However, in writing their opinions, judges don't necessarily follow the citation format lawyers must follow. In other words, the citations contained in the cases we read are not necessarily in the "proper" format we need to use. Don't rely on the citation form you see in cases.

Rules of Appellate Practice, local rules of court, and other "form-books" govern how we cite authority. These rules act as a universal translator, assuring some level of consistency in our ability to locate materials in the world of statutes, constitutions, regulations, cases, ordinances, legislative history, law reviews, and "you name its." If we mix up, for example, the volume number of a case with the page number of the case, we've sent our readers on a wild goose chase. They won't find our case with the information we've provided. They won't be pleased.

Moreover, an error in citing a case may translate into an error in *updating* the case, which means Trouble (yeah, with a capital "T"). We use the proper citation to check whether our case is still good law. If we don't begin with the proper cite, we can't possibly ensure that our case hasn't been reversed. The bottom line: an error in citing may spell *malpractice.* Indeed:

> "A reputation once broken may possibly be repaired, but the world will always keep their eyes on the spot where the crack was."
>
> —Joseph Hall

§ 25.2   Citation Manuals; Court Rules

For ease and uniformity, the legal citations we use in writing academic articles and court documents follow a standard format. Although several citation manuals exist, the two primary ones are *The Bluebook*[2] and the *ALWD Citation Manual.*[3] Both are challenging, indeed downright daunting, to the novice (and sometimes to the experienced researcher). Still, learning how to cite properly is an inescapable and indispensable part of your legal education. Indeed, if you find citation to be a challenge you readily accept, you may become a "citation guru," i.e., the go-to person for answers to citation questions. If you achieve this level of enlightenment, you'll be amazed at the number of new friends you'll have seeking out your advice.

The following is a quick overview of *The Bluebook* and *ALWD* citation manuals:

The Bluebook. *The Bluebook* (which just happens always to have a blue cover) provides general citation rules applicable to both academic writing (such as in law review articles) and practical writing (such as in memos and briefs). *The Bluebook* is terribly difficult to navigate, even harder to understand, and has too few examples. However, it's been around for a long time and, perhaps because of its longevity, is the manual most widely used by judges and lawyers. Truly, it's worth the effort to master. But, and we don't sugar-coat this, *The Thing* (as one of us calls it) can be absolutely frustrating to use. (Your humble authors were in law school in the late 1970s. Since that time, *The Bluebook* has literally quadrupled in size.)

Inside front and back covers. *The Bluebook*'s inside *back* cover provides a quick reference for court documents and for legal memoranda, while the inside *front* cover provides a quick reference for law review articles. Refer to these covers; they're packed with information.

The Index. Also, don't overlook *The Bluebook*'s Index. The Index is your Rosetta Stone. It's the *second* place you look in trying to answer a citation question. Where's the first? The front or back cover!

The Introduction. The Introduction explains the organization of the book and some general principles of citation. It's worth the read.

The Bluepages. The blue pages (usually in the front), entitled (drum roll, please) the "Bluepages," are primarily for legal practitioners and pertain to court documents and legal memoranda. These pages are invaluable. They provide a quick view of the most used citation forms. They also contain references to related rules and tables located in other parts of the book.

Rules. Following the "Bluepages" are (at least in the 19th edition) twenty-one rules. (These are *not* the same as rules of court.) The first nine are general rules governing

---

2. *The Bluebook: A Uniform System of Citation* (Columbia L. Rev. Ass'n et al. eds., 19th ed. 2010). You'll need to use the most current edition.

3. ALWD & Darby Dickerson, *ALWD Citation Manual: A Professional System of Citation* (4th ed. Aspen Publishers 2010). You'll need to use the most current edition.

citation and style. The second section consists of rules 10 through 21, governing particular sources. The two rules you'll use most often are rule 10 for *cases*, and rule 12 for *statutes*. If a 20th or higher edition of *The Bluebook* has since been published, figure out which rules govern cases and which govern statutes.

Tables. At the end of the rules is a series of tables. Don't overlook these. Don't make the mistake of thinking, "well, if the information in the tables was *that* important, it would be in the text." Trust us. The information you'll find in the tables is crucial. The tables are incredibly important because (1) they provide citation rules for United States and international jurisdictions, both as to case law and to statutes and (2) they list the standard abbreviations for geographical terms, courts, case names, explanatory phrases, and other citation terms.

You truly can't write a properly formatted cite without mastering the information contained in these tables. You can't even begin to write even the *name of the case* you're citing without understanding the information in the tables. You need to know *how* to abbreviate the words listed in the tables and *when* to abbreviate those words. Take a look now (yes, grab *The Bluebook* or *ALWD*), and see if you can locate the rule(s) and tables governing how and when to abbreviate a case name.

ALWD. The *ALWD Citation Manual* is much more user-friendly than *The Bluebook* and includes an abundance of examples to follow. It contains a fast format locator on the inside front cover and a short citation locator on the inside back cover. The *ALWD* manual eliminates distinctions between academic and practical writing. It's divided into six parts, including: introductory material, citation basics, information on how to cite specific print sources, how to incorporate citations into documents, and how to use quotations properly. Finally, it contains appendices that are similar to the tables in *The Bluebook*.

☙ **Local court rules.** *When we're filing a document (i.e., pleadings and memoranda) with a court, we follow the citation rules, called the local rules, of that court.* If those rules aren't available electronically, we contact the clerk's office to get a printed copy. From the very start of the written work we do for a client, we follow the correct citation rules for the court in which our case may be filed. What we write may later be incorporated into a pleading or memoranda, and our citations need to be in the correct format right from the start.

§ 25.3   Understanding and Using Citation: Some Basics

As both manuals explain citation format in depth, we won't do so here. Instead, we'll provide some basic information, advice, and examples. Our focus will be on documents, rather than on law review articles, and the information and the examples (many of which we've invented) are consistent with both *The Bluebook* and *ALWD*, except where noted. Because we most often use constitutions, statutes, and case law in legal writing, we've omitted from this discussion how to cite to books, law review articles, and other sources. We'll focus primarily on cases because they're trickier to cite than constitutions and statutes.

Back to our discussion of citation and the proper use of the "coordinate system" each manual mandates:

Constitutions. For constitutions, this coordinate system includes the abbreviated name of the constitution (U.S. Const. or a state name) and any other necessary information to locate the provision, such as an amendment or article number.

Statutes. For statutes, we include the title number (if the statute has one), the abbreviation of the code's name (U.S. or an abbreviated state name), the code's section number, and year the code was published.

Examples of citations to Constitutions, Statutes, Regulations, and Rules. We've included carets (^) (pronounced 'ka-rət) in the examples below to indicate where a space should be placed, but don't include these in your citations.

Constitutions:

```
U.S.^Const.^amend.^IV
```

```
U.S.^Const.^amend.^XIV,^§^2
```

```
U.S.^Const.^preamble
```

```
Fla.^Const.^art.^I,^§^8
```

U.S. Code and regulations:

U.S. Code	`42^U.S.C.^§^8000^(1999)`
U.S. Code Annotated	`12^U.S.C.A.^§^3256^(West^1999)`
Code of Federal Regulations	`47•C.F.R.^§^73.0009^(1994)`

Federal rules:

```
Fed.^R.^Civ.^P.^12(b)(6)
```

```
Fed.^R.^Crim.^P.^42(b)
```

```
Fed.^R.^App.^P.^3
```

```
Fed.^R.^Evid.^414
```

State statutes and administrative codes:

```
Fla.^Stat.^§^98.436^(1999)
```

```
Fla.^Stat.^Ann.^§^332^(West^1999)
```

```
Fla.^Admin.^Code^Ann.^r.^9C1-99^(1999)
```

Note: the three citations below follow Florida's citation rules:

```
§^98.436,^Fla.^Stat.^(1999)
```

```
§^332,^Fla.^Stat.^Ann.^(1999)*
```

(*Used only for court-adopted rules or references to other non-statutory materials not appearing in an official publication)

```
§^24.436^Fla.^Stat.^(Supp.^1999)
```

Cases. For cases, the basic coordinate system includes the volume number of the reporter, the name of the reporter, and the page number on which the case begins in the reporter, in that order, which would allow our reader to physically or electronically locate the authority. A "reporter" is a bound publication that prints only cases; however, the contents of these reporters are now included on many electronic databases. The same coordinates are used to locate the case physically in a bound reporter and in an electronic database.

First time case is cited. The first time a case (or any authority) is cited in a document, it is cited in full. A full citation of a case includes the following: (1) the case name (did you look at the rule(s) and table(s) re how to abbreviate a case name?); (2) the volume of the reporter (or if the case isn't printed, the source in which the case is reported); (3) an abbreviation of the reporter; (4) the initial page in the reporter where the case begins; (5) the pinpoint page(s) referenced (please look at the rule re how to cite to page numbers); (6) a parenthetical indicating, where necessary, the court that decided the case (abbreviated) and including the year of decision; and (7) subsequent history of the case (when appropriate).

Parenthetical information. Additional information that we may need to include, depending upon the particular case, is parenthetical information relevant to the nature of the decision (plurality, concurring, and dissenting opinions); a parenthetical regarding the weight of authority (an en banc decision or a per curiam opinion); and/or an explanatory parenthetical (a rule-plus) to summarize the holding, to explain the case's relevance to our discussion, or to quote a portion of the opinion.

The case name. We can obtain some of this basic information from the first page of a case as it appears in the bound reporter volume or online in an electronic database. But beware: we can't just write down verbatim what we find there. Some of the information about a case that's included in the published report should not be included in a citation of the case, and many of the citations are *not* in proper form.

For example, we usually can't use the full case name as we find it in a bound reporter or online, because these captions usually include *all* the parties' names in full. Only one party name on each side of the case is included in a proper full cite (consider the "versus" as the dividing line for parties, and note that we use the designation "v." rather than "vs." or "versus").

Moreover, where a party is an individual, only the party's last name is included. Thus, we'd use "Smyth" rather than "Tom Smyth." As always, exceptions to this rule abound. For example, we use abbreviations rather than names for minors, and sometimes for other persons, to protect their identities. We also have to figure out how much of the name to use when a geographical entity, a business, or real property is a party. And we have to determine how to abbreviate the part of the name we do use. Literally pages of the two manuals are devoted to rules regarding how to style the name of a case for citation purposes; therefore, we'll simply advise you to check them. Please refer to *ALWD* rule 12.4, 12.6, and appendix 1 and *The Bluebook*, rules B4, 10, and table 1. Also look at any listed cross-references when you examine a particular rule. For example, the rules of the manuals regarding case names will also refer us to other tables and appendices for abbreviations and other information.

Parallel citations. Sounds like a lot of work to figure it all out, no? Take heart, it used to be even harder. Years ago most citations for state cases required full and short citations to include "parallel citations," i.e., cites to *both* an official reporter and to a commercially published reporter. Now, we generally cite to a single reporter, usually the commercial one, unless the court to which we are submitting a document, or the manuals, require otherwise. And, our citations must be to a reporter, and not to an electronic source, if the case is cited in a reporter. In other words, we use electronic references only when a case is not yet reported in a paper volume.

Example: Full cite to U.S. Supreme Court case. Here's an example of a full case cite to a United States Supreme Court decision.

Graphic 25.3 (a)   Full Cite to United States Supreme Court Decision
Without Pinpoint Cite

<u>Smyth^v.^Jones</u>,^800^U.S.^399^(1999)

Note that the parenthetical includes only the year and no court designation. That's because the reporter in the citation, United States Reports, publishes the decisions of only one court, and thus the reader can tell that the decision is from the United States Supreme Court. (See *ALWD* rule 12.6(e) and *The Bluebook* rule 10.4.) Note, also, that the comma after the case name is *not* underlined.

Example: Full cite to federal case. In contrast, when we're citing a federal case *other* than a United States Supreme Court decision, we include the name of the specific court rather than just the type of court. There are thirteen federal circuit courts of appeal, so if we don't identify the circuit, we aren't giving the reader sufficient information. We do not, however, include the state designation when citing a United States Circuit Court of Appeals case. Note that the abbreviations for the second and third circuits are "2d" and "3d" respectively; the rest follow the usual types of numerical abbreviations such as "1st" and "4th." We don't use superscripts, such as "1st" and "4th."

Similarly, some states have more than one federal district (the federal trial courts), so there, too, we need to identify the district (often "S" for Southern, "E" for Eastern, and so forth). When the state has only one federal district court, however, we need only include the district designation (D) and the state:

Graphic 25.3(b)   Full Cites to Federal Circuit Courts and District Courts
Without Pinpoint Cites

---

federal circuit court cases

correct: <u>United States v. Parizo</u>, 514 F.2d 52 (2d Cir. 1975)

incorrect: <u>United States v. Parizo</u>, 514 F.2d 52 (U.S. Ct. App. 1975)

incorrect: <u>United States v. Parizo</u>, 514 F.2d 52 (2d Cir. Vt. 1975)

incorrect: <u>United States v. Parizo</u>, 514 F.2d 52 (2d Cir. Vt. 1975)

incorrect: <u>United States v. Parizo</u>, 514 F.2d 52 (C.A. Vt. 1975)

federal district court cases

correct: <u>Pottinger v. City of Miami</u>, 810 F. Supp. 1551
(S.D. Fla. 1992)

incorrect: <u>Pottinger v. City of Miami</u>, 810 F. Supp. 1551 (D.
Fla. 1992)

correct: <u>United States v. Botelho</u>, 360 F. Supp. 620 (D.
Haw. 1973)
As Hawaii has only one federal district court, we use only the "D" designation.

Example: full cite to state court case. Similar to a United States Supreme Court cite, when the decision is from a state's highest court, and appears in an official state reporter, the court need not be specified. Note that this rule applies primarily to older decisions published in an official reporter that bears the name of the state. Generally, we include the name of the court. Here's an example, compliments of *The Bluebook*:

<u>Hall v. Bell</u>, 47 Mass. (6 Met.) 431 (1843).

Based on the reporter, and on the lack of a court designation in the parenthetical, the reader can tell that the decision came from the highest court in Massachusetts.

When, however, we cite to a decision in an official reporter that bears the name of the state, but the court is not the highest in the state, we identify the level of the court and still omit the state name itself:

<u>People v. Thomas</u>, 45 Cal. Rptr. 2d 610 (Ct. App. 1995)

Note that California has several courts of appeal (i.e., the intermediate courts in that state). The two manuals differ on whether to provide the specific geographic subdivision of the intermediate state courts. Compare *ALWD* rule 12.6(b)(2) with *The Bluebook* rule 10.4(b). *ALWD* says yes; *The Bluebook* says no, "unless that information is of particular relevance." What do we do? Well, it depends.

Conflicting information. This conflict and others, as well as situations in which neither manual seems to provide the information we need, will arise. To help you out in these conflicting and bewildering situations, we offer the following commonsense advice. When citing, your goal is to provide the requisite amount of information your reader needs to find an authority and to understand how you're using it. With this in mind, we provide the following suggestions for when you're not sure how to cite a source.

First, always consult the citation rules (if any) of your local court to see if they offer any guidance. Second, if the local rules don't offer any advice, then consider whether the information adds anything to the persuasive value of the authority or is something your reader needs to know. In the example of the *Thomas* case above, if we were California practitioners writing a brief to a court in that state, we'd probably include the specific district in our parenthetical because it could affect the persuasive value of the case. On the other hand, if we're practicing in Florida, one California court of appeal likely has the same persuasive value as another, so we'd probably omit that additional information. But, it bears repeating that we'd first check our jurisdiction's citation rules to see if they answer our question.

Whew!!! All that to cite a case? Yes. But fortunately we need only provide one full cite of a case (or other authority) in the text of a document, with the caveat that we also provide a full cite (but without any pinpoint page numbers) in the Authorities Cited section of a memo and in the Table of Authorities section of a brief. Once we've cited the full case in the text, thereafter we can use a short citation format (discussed below in § 25.6(b)).

Some of the basic citation principles for all case citations in a legal document, for both *ALWD* and *The Bluebook,* follow below. For additional information on abbreviations, numerals, symbols, spelling, punctuation, capitalization, spacing, and other aspects of citation, see generally *ALWD* rules 2-5 and *The Bluebook* rules 2 and 6-9.

§ 25.4   Font, Spacing, and Italics

Font. For citations in a legal document use ordinary typeface, such as Courier New or Times New Roman (or whatever your professor recommends or the court requires), usually 12 point font, consistent with the typeface for the text of the document, with upper and lower case letters, not large and small capitals. Times New Roman, which is a proportional font (meaning it doesn't allot the same amount of space for each letter as does a non-proportional font such as Courier New) can distort the spacing in a citation. For this reason, we require our students to use Courier New.

Italics or underlining. Italics, i.e., *slanted type,* or <u>underlining</u> (one or the other, but not both in a document) is required for specific citations or parts thereof. We've included both Courier New and Times New Roman, and both underscoring and italics, in **Graphic 25.4** below to show you the difference in the fonts and spacing. Thereafter, we will use Courier New to maintain proper spacing for all examples. We use underlining, rather than italics, to help show you the correct method for underscoring. Further, we've included carets (^) in the examples to indicate where a space should be placed, but don't include these in your citations. For additional guidance on spacing, see *ALWD* rule 2.2 and *The Bluebook* rule 6.1(a).

Graphic 25.4   Typeface, Underscoring, and Italics Compared

`Courier New:`
<u>`Smyth^v.^Jones,`</u>`^800^U.S.^399^(1999)`
`Smyth^v.^Jones,^800^U.S.^399^(1999)`

Times New Roman:
<u>Smyth^v.^Jones,</u>^800^U.S.^399^(1999)
Smyth^v.^Jones,^800^U.S^399^(1999)

---

§ 25.5   When, Where, and What to Cite

§ 25.5(a)   When and Where to Cite

When not to cite. With a few exceptions, we cite to every sentence when explaining the law. But we don't cite where we point out the absence of a legal principle or authority, such as when we say, for example, "no court has addressed the issue of ..." or "no court has held...." We may also occasionally summarize a general principle without citing, if we follow it up with specific examples which we do cite. However, the better practice is to provide a cite even for the general principle we're addressing. Moreover, *ALWD* rule 43.2(b) allows for the placement of one citation at the end of a single paragraph when all the material within that paragraph comes from the same part of the same source. The *ALWD* rule cautions us not to follow this exception when the section, page, or other subdivision of the cited material changes. We personally wouldn't use this exception, and we discourage you from using it unless it's sanctioned by your professor, managing partner, or judge (if you're a judicial clerk).

Cite placement. The first time we mention a case in the text, the case name is followed with the remaining elements of a full citation, set off by commas. Although it is also proper to skip one space, we skip two spaces between the end of the sentence and the beginning of the citation. The designation "n. 4" refers to footnote 4 of the decision.[4]

```
Battery is the impermissible application of force to
the person of another.^^Adam v. State,^
800^F.^Supp.^712,^714^n.^4^(N.D.^Fla.^1999).
```

Subsequently, we simply refer to the first party's name, with lengthy names appropriately shortened to save space. However, if the first party is a geographic entity (such as "United States" or a state name) or consists of the words "People" or "State," we should generally use the second party's name. For example:

```
In a more recent decision, the court has defined the
impermissible act referenced in Adam to mean an act
done without the victim's consent.^^Art^v.^State,^
999^F.^Supp.^181,^184-85^(N.D.^Fla.^1999).
```

Citation sentence. When the source supports an entire sentence, we place the full citation in its own separate, free-standing, "citation sentence" following the text it supports, beginning with a capital letter and ending with a period. (If you've done as we've suggested, you'll know the rule governing why we cite the pages numbers as we did above!)

Graphic 25.5(a)(1)   Citation Sentence (Full Cite with Pinpoint Cite)

```
The Court has held that all men are mortal.^^Smyth^v.^
Jones,^800^U.S.^399,^401^(1999).
```

When do we and don't we capitalize the "C" in court? Note that we've capitalized the word "Court" in our first sentence because we're referring to the United States Supreme Court. The only times we capitalize the word "court" without providing the name of the court are (1) when we're referring to the United States Supreme Court, and (2)

---

4. Permit us to drop a footnote here pointing out that although footnotes are the preferred method for including cites in academic legal writing, such as law review articles, they should be used sparingly in legal documents.

when we're referring to the court to which we're writing a document (for example, when we say, "Hill respectfully requests this Court to affirm the trial court's decision."). Of course, when we refer to a court by name (as a proper noun) we do capitalize it: United States Court of Appeals for the First Circuit.

Pinpoints, again. The "401" notation in our citation sentence in the graphic above represents the specific pinpoint cite, (the page) of the *Smyth* case where the legal principle is located. The pinpoint cite follows the first page of the source, separated by a comma, and then by one space. More than one pinpoint cite may be included, where appropriate. If the pinpoint cite is the same page as the first page of the case, we repeat that page as follows:

```
Smyth^v.^Jones,^800^U.S.^399,^399^(1999).
```

Citation clause. When we want to combine, in a single sentence, multiple legal principles from different sources, we cite each source directly after the legal principle the source supports. These "citation clauses" are separated from the text by commas, and by semicolons between sources. **Graphic 25.5(a)(2)** illustrates this method.

Graphic 25.5(a)(2)   Citation Clauses (Full Cites with Pinpoint Cites)

```
Battery is the impermissible application of force to the
person of another,^Adam v. State,^800^F.^Supp.^
712,^714^(N.D.^Fla.^1999); and an impermissible act is
one done without the victim's consent.^^Art^v.^State,^
999^F.^Supp.^181,^184-85^(N.D.^Fla.^1999).

All men are mortal,^Smyth^v.^Jones,^800^U.S.^399,^
401^(1999);^Park^v.^Ross,^721^U.S.^444,^444^(1996); and
are capable of great works,^e.g.,^Dunn^v.^Wilson,^
600^U.S.^123,^125^(1990).
```

As the principle "all men are mortal" is derived from two sources, the *Smyth* and *Park* cases, those cites appear in a "string cite" (discussed below) separated by a semicolon. If one of the two cases we cited had provided adequate proof of our rule, we would not have included both cases. The problem with citation clauses is that they tend to interrupt the flow of our analysis. There we are making a point, and then we ask our reader to wade through a bunch of numbers and abbreviations before he/she can move forward. Whenever possible, we avoid citation *clauses*, and use citation *sentences* instead.

§ 25.5(b)   What to Cite

String cites. In both objective and persuasive writing, when we induce a legal principle or rule from more than one source, we may need to cite to multiple authorities in a "string citation." A string citation refers to more than a single source, in which the sources are separated by semi-colons, or periods, as appropriate. See **Graphic 25.6(a)** for an example of a string cite using "introductory signals."[5] Specific rules apply to the order of citations in a string cite: see *ALWD* rule 44.8; *The Bluebook* rules 1.3 and 1.4. Generally, however, we try to avoid lengthy string citations as they're difficult to read and break up the flow of our analysis. Worse yet, they take up valuable space better used for analysis. In any event, if we have a strong case that our court must follow, the other cases are superfluous. That said, string cites are sometimes useful to show that compelling authority supports the rule we're proposing.

In a predictive or objective memo, we can usually cite to one strong case that makes our point rather than to multiple cases. To show that the cited case represents one of several that support the same principle, we can insert the signal "e.g.," before the cite, which means "for example."

Weight of authority (majority, dissenting, concurring opinions). We always cite to the majority opinion in a case when possible. We rarely cite to dissenting opinions, as they're not the law of the case; however, they can be used as persuasive authority. The same rule applies to a concurrence, unless the majority decision depends upon the concurring opinion to constitute a majority, in which case the concurrence (in what sometimes seems like legal magic) then becomes part of the law of the case. (Think about that one!)

Whatever the situation, we *always* indicate that we're citing to other than the majority opinion by including that information in a parenthetical following the citation. See *ALWD* rule 12.5(d) and *The Bluebook* rule B5.14 regarding these types of "weight of authority" parentheticals.

We can also, of course, include an explanatory parenthetical (a rule-plus) as addressed in **Chapter 6, § 6.3(b)**, to include additional information about a case. See *ALWD* rules 46.1, 46.2, and 46.3, and *The Bluebook* rule B5.14 regarding these types of explanatory parentheticals and their appropriate placement in a citation. We also include any relevant "subsequent history," i.e., later action taken by the same or higher court in the case. See *ALWD* rule 12.8 and *The Bluebook* rule B5.15. See examples in § 25.6(a) below.

💣 **No land mines, please.** Finally, to maintain our credibility, and avoid "land mines," we carefully and fully read all cases we've cited. We've seen court documents where lawyers have relied on a "great quote" from a case, only to have been embarrassed to discover that the case itself *held against the position they were asserting*. If we cite to a case, we're inviting our reader to, well, to read the case! That case *itself* better support our position. No citing to headnotes, of course!

§ 25.6   Signals, Short Cites, Quotations

§ 25.6(a)   Signals

In general. Unless our authority directly supports the principle for which we are citing it, or our discussion of the authority clarifies why we're discussing it, we insert a "signal"

---

5. See § 25.6.

before the citation. See *ALWD* rule 44 and *The Bluebook* B4 and rules 1.2, 1.3, and 1.4 for an explanation of signals, their use, and their placement. Note that signals do not always provide accurate information about how we're actually using the case we've cited. For this reason, and because the meaning of some of the standard signals have changed over the years (resulting in confusion), signals are an inadequate substitute for our own analysis of what a case means. For these reasons, we use them sparingly. We always use them, however, when their omission could mislead our reader.

The signal precedes the cite and is separated from the cite by one space. When underlining, do not underline the signal and the cite together—they are two different parts of a citation. Signals may be used before both full and short citations. Where we have more than one authority for which a signal is appropriate, we do not repeat that signal; its use carries through until we introduce a new signal.

Using signals as verbs. We can also avoid these inscrutable abbreviations by using signals as verbs. If so, we neither italicize nor underline the signal, and simply say what we want to tell the reader in plain old simple English. See **Graphic 25.6(a)**. Yes, like that.

Graphic 25.6(a)   **Signals and Signals as Verbs**

Signals:

The equitable defense of laches may bar an action for child support arrears based on extraordinary facts or compelling circumstances.^^See^Dean^v.^Dean,^665^So.^2d^ 244,^247^(Fla.^Dist.^Ct.^App.^1995);^see^also^Hoffman^ v.^Foley,^541^So.^2d^145,^146^(Fla.^Dist.^Ct.^App.^ 1989);^cf.^Moss^v.^Davis,^580^So.^2d^112,^115^(Fla.^ Dist.^Ct.^App.^1993).

Signal as a verb:

The equitable defense of laches may bar an action for child support arrears based on extraordinary facts or compelling circumstances.^^See,^for example,^Dean^v.^ Dean,^665^So.^2d^244,^247^(Fla.^Dist.^Ct.^App.^1995).

We neither underline, nor italicize, signals when we use them as verbs.

Commonly used introductory signals:

no signal	Smith v. Clay, 999 U.S. 325, 327 (1999).
E.g.,	E.g.,^Smith, 999 U.S. at 325.
See, e.g.,	See,^e.g.,^Smith, 999 U.S. at 327.
Accord	Accord^Smith, 999 U.S. at 328.
See	See^Smith v. Clay, 999 U.S. 325, 327–29 (1999).
See also	See^also^Smith v. Clay, 999 U.S. 325, 327 (1999).

<u>Cf.</u>	<u>Cf.</u>^<u>Smith v. Clay</u>, 999 U.S. 325, 327 (1999).
<u>Compare</u> ...	<u>Compare</u>^<u>Smith v. Clay</u>, 999 U.S. 325, 327 (1999)
<u>with</u> ...	<u>with</u>^<u>Doe v. Roe</u>, 878 U.S. 956, 960 (1992).
<u>See generally</u>	<u>See</u>^<u>generally</u>^<u>id.</u> at 327.
<u>Contra</u>	<u>Contra</u>^<u>Smith v. Clay</u>, 999 U.S. 325, 327 (1999).
<u>But see</u>	<u>But</u>^<u>see</u>^<u>Smith v. Clay</u>, 999 U.S. 325, 327 (1999).
<u>But see, e.g.,</u>	<u>But</u>^<u>see,</u>^<u>e.g.,</u>^<u>Smith v. Clay</u>, 999 U.S. 325, 327 (1999).
<u>But cf.</u>	<u>But</u>^<u>cf.</u>^<u>Smith v. Clay</u>, 999 U.S. 325, 327 (1999).

In which of the above cases did we use the long form (full cite)? In which did we use a short cite? Our use of a signal has no effect on our choice of whether we use the long form or short form of a cite. The above are simply examples. So, for instance, we could have used a long form citation introduced by a "<u>see generally</u>" signal, if that was the first time we were citing that particular case. In other words, there is no correlation between using signals and using the long or short form of the cited case. In addition, when the date of a subsequent decision of a case is the same as the date of the original decision, we omit the date from the first parenthetical.

Commonly used explanatory phrases indicating prior or subsequent history and weight of authority:

<u>aff'd,</u>	<u>Seattle v. Bryson</u>, 888 F.3d 1992 (3d Cir. 1999), ^<u>aff'd,</u>^767 U.S. 243 (2000).
<u>cert. denied,</u>	<u>United States v. North</u>, 910 F.2d 843 (D.C. Cir. 2012),^<u>cert.</u>^<u>denied,</u>^866 U.S. 888 (2013).
<u>rev'd,</u>	<u>Seattle v. Bryson</u>, 888 F.3d 1992 (3d Cir. 1999),^ <u>rev'd,</u>^767 U.S. 243 (2000).
<u>modified,</u>	<u>Seattle v. Bryson</u>, 888 F.3d 992 (3d Cir.)^ <u>modified,</u>^888 F.3d 1278 (3d Cir. 1999).
<u>overruled by</u>	<u>Alexport v. Danvey</u>, 698 U.S. 888 (1999),^ <u>overruled</u>^<u>by</u>^767 U.S. 243 (2000).
<u>reh'g denied,</u>	<u>Seattle v. Bryson</u>, 888 F.3d 1992 (3d Cir.),^ <u>reh'g</u>^<u>denied,</u>^888 F.3d 3200 (3d Cir. 1999).

§ 25.6(b)   Short Cites

Authority cited previously. Once we've cited a case (or another authority) in full, thereafter we can refer to it by using a short cite. But do we ever, in the same document, use the full cite again? Well, that depends.

The two manuals disagree as to whether we use only short cites once we've cited an authority in full. *ALWD* notes that some judges and attorneys prefer only one full cite to an authority in a document, while others prefer full citations more often, usually in each new major section of the document. *ALWD* concludes by saying that either is permissible. See *ALWD* rules 11.1 and 11.2.

The Bluebook, in rule B5.2, allows the short form only when (1) the reader unambiguously can understand what is being referenced, (2) the full citation is located in the same general discussion, and (3) the reader will be able to easily locate the full citation.

Whichever format we follow, a short cite must provide sufficient information for a reader to identify and to easily locate the source. See also *ALWD* rules 12.21 and 14.6 and *The Bluebook* rules 4, 10.9, and 12.9 for other information regarding short-form citations.

Id. One of the most ubiquitous short cites used in legal writing is the word "id.," which is similar to the word "ibid." (short for "ibidem" and meaning "in the same place") used in non-legal writing. Id. is an abbreviation for "idem," which means "the same." Id. is appropriately used as a short cite for any source except appellate records and internal cross-references. But, it may only be used when the immediately prior cite is to one source only. The period is always underlined, but whether the word is capitalized or in lower case depends on its placement in the text — that is, lower case when it appears mid-sentence (as in the first sentence in this paragraph) and capitalized when it's used at the start of a citation sentence.

When used standing alone, without a page reference, id. tells the reader that the reference is exactly the same as the citation preceding it. If the source is the same as the preceding citation but we're citing a different page number of the source, we add the word "at" after the word id.. (Yes, two periods are correct here.) After the word "at" we place the page number(s) we're referencing. For example: Id. at 707. If our next cite was to the same source and to the same page, we'd use only id..

And beware, the computer gremlins will invariably capitalize the "at" following the period on the id., so you'll have to watch out for this.

Graphic 25.6(b)(1)   Short Cites for Case Law When There Is No Intervening Cite to Another Source — Using "id."

First full cite of case:

```
All men are mortal, and capable of great things.^^
Smyth^v.^Jones,^800^U.S.^399,^401^(1999).
```

Acceptable short cites in subsequent references to case:

When cite is to the same case and to the same page as the cite immediately preceding it:

```
In Smyth, the Court examined the evidence regarding
the mortality of an individual.^^Id.
```

When cite is to same case immediately preceding it but to a different page:

```
In Smyth, the Court examined the evidence regarding
the mortality of an individual.^^Id.^at^400.
```

When use of <u>id.</u> is inappropriate because there is an intervening citation to a different source, or to multiple sources, other short formats are used. Thus, where we have an intervening citation, we use one of the following options:

Graphic 25.6(b)(2)	Short Cites for Case Law When There Is an Intervening Cite to Another Source

First full cite of case:

```
All men are mortal, and capable of great things.^^
Smyth^v.^Jones,^800^U.S.^399,^401^(1999).
```

Acceptable short cites in subsequent references to case after an intervening cite:

```
In Smyth, the Court examined the evidence regarding
the mortality of an individual.^^800^U.S.^at^401.
```

```
In Smyth, the Court examined the evidence regarding
the mortality of an individual.^^Smyth,^800^U.S.^at^
401.
```

Incorrect: Do NOT do this:

```
In Smyth, the Court examined the evidence regarding
the mortality of an individual.^^Smyth^at^401.
```

Case name. Both manuals approve short cites (where there's an intervening authority) with and without the case name. As a general rule, if the case name is in the sentence, or if there's no ambiguity as to which case is referenced, we don't repeat the case name in the short cite. When it's appropriate to include the case name, as in the second "acceptable short cites" example above, we only use one party's name. Generally, we cite the first party's name unless doing so would create confusion. Confusion can occur when we cite to more than one case with the same name or when the first party is a geographic entity (such as "United States" or a state name) or consists of the words "People" or "State." If our reader will likely be confused, we use the second party's name. Finally, if the name is quite long, we include only as much of it as necessary for our reader to understand which case is cited.

💣 **Verboten: "the case name at page number" format.** The cite to "<u>Smyth</u> at 401" is always incorrect. The reader can't identify and easily locate the source, because our cite lacks the volume and reporter where the case is found.

Note, too, that we never use "*supra*," (meaning "above," or "at an earlier place") and "hereinafter" as short form references for cases, statutes, regulations, and constitutional provisions. We may, however, use these terms to refer to books, legislative hearing, pamphlets, law review articles, and some other sources. Such cites should include the last name of the author of the work or the title, followed by a comma, and the word *supra*. We can use the term "hereinafter" to establish a subsequent shortened method for referring to a previously cited authority, followed by the shortened form in brackets. See *ALWD* rule 11.4 and *The Bluebook* rule 4.2.

Quick review:

- The first time we cite a case, we provide its full citation, including the specific page we're referring to. We end the sentence with a period and skip two spaces.^ ^Cat^v.^Dog,^222^U.S.^25,^26^(1999).^^If our very next citation is to the Cat case, and to page 26, we use id..^^Id.^^If our very next citation is to the Cat case, but to a different page, i.e., not page 26, we use id., but need to use an "at" with the page number indicated.^^Id.^at^27. Then, if our next citation was to the same case at page 27, we would write the following:^^Id.

- Sometimes we use "id." or "id. at" in the middle of a sentence. In that case, here's how we do it. We separate the citation with a comma,^id.,^or^id.^at^28,^then continue with the sentence.

- Let's say that we've cited the Cat case, and then our next citation is not to the Cat case. Let's then say our third citation is to the Cat case. Can we use an "id." or "id. at" to refer to the Cat case? NO, in these circumstances we have an intervening citation. Instead, we need to use a short citation for the Cat case. Here's how we do it.^^Cat,^222^U.S.^at^29. Or, we could write it as follows.^^Cat^v.^Dog,^222^U.S.^at^29. Whatever we do with short citations, we must be consistent, i.e., we either use Cat or Cat v. Dog.

- *Never, ever:* Cat^at^29. *Never, ever:* Cat,^at^29.

- And, when underlining, we underline only the case name, not the comma after the name.

§ 25.6(c)   Quotations

Properly quoting legal sources is one of the toughest tasks for lawyers and students, often because what we're quoting is itself quoting another source. We'll try to address some of the basic and most difficult aspects of quoting, providing examples along the way. Formats for quoting, found in *ALWD* rules 47-49 and *The Bluebook* rule 5, are essentially similar. (We'll note, below, any significant differences.)

To quote, or not to quote? Before we get into the mechanics of quoting, we need to address why it's critical that we keep quotation in our writing to a minimum.

First, we all know that quotations, particularly lengthy ones, slow down our reading, or worse, cause us to skip over the quoted material. Indeed, in reading a student's paper loaded with quotations, we often find ourselves thinking, after the second or third lengthy quote, and seeing another one looming on the page: "Oh not again."

Second, quoting can make us lazy. Instead of fully analyzing the substance of the quote, many students (and lawyers) just parrot the words of a case. The reader feels as if the student/lawyer hasn't done his or her job, and the reader likely would be correct.

Third, long and/or multiple quotations use up valuable space in our document that we likely could better employ in setting out our analysis or argument.

Fourth, our reader expects (and deserves!) our analysis, and we can (and should!) convey our thoughts better than by just quoting a source. Finally, if we quote sparingly, when we do quote, it will pack more of a punch and really capture our reader's attention.

Yes, quote it! That said, there are times when a quote of the original material is absolutely appropriate, indeed, even preferred. We quote (but only relevant language), rather than paraphrase, when

- the source or author of the material would impart significant credibility or precedential value to the material;

- we really (and we mean really!) cannot express the material more concisely and eloquently than the original;

- the interpretation of specific language of a statute or rule governs an issue and the actual phrasing needs to be conveyed; or

- a quote conveys the very essence of the court's reasoning.

Quotations of fifty words or more. We write the 50 word or more quote (and, according to *ALWD*, quotations that exceed four lines of typed text) by placing the quoted material in a "block." To create a "block quote," we single-space the language we're quoting and indent the text on both the left and the right side (double-indent). But, we don't include quotation marks at the beginning and ending of the quoted text. The fact that the text is in the block itself shows that this is the language we're quoting. We set off the block quote with a double line space from the text above and below it. Quotation marks within the quote itself appear as they do in the original. When we need to add a cite after the block quote (where, for example, we didn't include the cite in our introduction to the quote), we place the citation at the left margin after the double-space following the quote. We do *not* place the citation within the block. What's in the block is what we're *quoting*, and we're *not* quoting the citation.

Quotations of fewer than fifty words. To create this type of quote, we double-space the language we're quoting and place it within quotation marks (" "). Our margins are the same as they'd be for any other text. Commas and periods *always* go inside the quotation marks; other punctuation goes inside only when it's part of the original text. Where the quoted material itself contains a quote, we designate the internal quotation with single quotation marks (' ').

Indicating omissions. The manuals contain rules and examples regarding how we indicate that we've altered the original text we're quoting. Below we've included an example of the more commonly used ways of indicating omissions to the original text you're quoting.

Assume that we're working with a document which states the following:

```
Yes, she was an old hag. But, she knew how to have a
good time. She frequntly rode her broomstick happily
off into the distance.6
```

Let's see how we'd indicate omissions in quoting our original.

---

6. We know "frequntly" is misspelled — we'll get to that in a moment.

To show an omission within a quoted sentence, we'd use an ellipsis (...), i.e., three periods separated by spaces, and set off by a space before the first period and after the last period. We'd write:

```
The old hag "rode her broomstick happily . . . into
the distance."
```

We could also write:

```
The "old hag . . . rode her broomstick happily . . .
into the distance."
```

Notice something? We didn't include an ellipsis at the beginning of our quote. English majors shudder at this. We repeat, we would *not* write:

```
The ". . . old hag . . . rode her broomstick happily
. . . into the distance."
```

💣 In legal writing we *never* use an ellipsis to start a quote.

incorrect:

```
The old hag ". . . rode her broomstick happily off into
the distance."
```

correct:

```
The old hag "rode her broomstick happily off into the
distance."
```

When the omitted matter is from the end of a quoted sentence, we include another period to the ellipsis to end the sentence (....”), and we place the end quotation mark after that fourth period. In essence, the ellipsis demonstrates that the sentence we're quoting keeps going, i.e., we're showing that we've cut the sentence short. We'd write:

```
The old hag "rode her broomstick happily . . . ."
```

If we wanted to begin our sentence with something other than the beginning of the quoted sentence, we'd indicate, by using brackets, that we've capitalized a letter that wasn't capitalized in the original. We'd write:

```
"[S]he knew how to have a good time."
```

We also use brackets ([ ]) to show other minor alterations in a quotation, such as the addition or deletion of a word. We'd place in the brackets any word we've added. If we've deleted a word, we'd leave the brackets empty.

We also use the word "[sic]," placed in brackets, to indicate an error in the original material, as follows:

```
"She frequntly [sic] rode her broomstick happily off
into the distance."
```

But we *never* use ellipses or brackets to change the meaning of a quotation.

There we have it. Not exactly citation in a nutshell, but as concise as we can humanly make it. Below, we've included a review of some of the more tricky quotation situations you may face, and a short list of common errors to avoid. Good luck!

§ 25.7   Common Quotation Errors

1. *Omitting the single quotation marks when quoting a quotation:*

wrong: In determining whether conduct is expressive enough to fall within the protection of the First Amendment, this Court should ask "whether [a]n intent to convey a particularized message was present, and [whether] the likelihood was great that the message would be understood by those who viewed it." <u>Texas v. Johnson</u>, 491 U.S. 397, 404 (1989) (quoting <u>Spence v. Washington</u>, 418 U.S. 405, 410-11 (1974)).

We need to show, by the use of single quotation marks, where the Spence *case is quoted.*

2. *Failing to provide the "pinpoint" cite, i.e., the page where the quotation actually appears in the case we're citing (as well as the case quoted within our case):*

wrong: In determining whether conduct is expressive enough to fall within the protection of the First Amendment, this Court should ask "whether '[a]n intent to convey a particularized message was present, and [whether] the likelihood was great that the message would be understood by those who viewed it.'" <u>Texas v. Johnson</u>, 491 U.S. 397 (1989) (quoting <u>Spence v. Washington</u>, 418 U.S. 405 (1974)).

3. *Failing to state that the quotation in fact quotes another case:*

wrong: In determining whether conduct is expressive enough to fall within the protection of the First Amendment, this Court should ask "whether [a]n intent to convey a particularized message was present, and [whether] the likelihood was great that the message would be understood by those who viewed it." <u>Texas v. Johnson</u>, 491 U.S. 397, 404 (1989).

4. *Failing to provide quotation marks of any kind, when we are in fact quoting:*

wrong: In determining whether conduct is expressive enough to fall within the protection of the First Amendment, this Court should ask whether [a]n intent to convey a particularized message was present, and [whether] the likelihood was great that the message would be understood by those who viewed it. <u>Texas v. Johnson</u>, 491 U.S. 397, 404 (1989) (quoting <u>Spence v. Washington</u>, 418 U.S. 405, 410-11 (1974)).

5. *Altering a quotation, without indicating where the text has been altered:*

wrong: In determining whether conduct is expressive enough to fall within the protection of the First Amendment, this Court should ask "whether 'one intends to convey a particularized message . . . , and whether there is a great likelihood that the message would be understood by those who viewed it.'" Texas v. Johnson, 491 U.S. 397, 404 (1989) (quoting Spence v. Washington, 418 U.S. 405, 410-11 (1974)).

6. *Failing to show that we have cut the quotation short:*

wrong: One element in determining whether conduct is expressive enough to fall within the protection of the First Amendment is "whether '[a]n intent to convey a particularized message was present.'" Texas v. Johnson, 491 U.S. 397, 404 (1989) (quoting Spence v. Washington, 418 U.S. 405, 410-11 (1974)).

right: One element in determining whether conduct is expressive enough to fall within the protection of the First Amendment is "whether '[a]n intent to convey a particularized message was present . . . .'" Texas v. Johnson, 491 U.S. 397, 404 (1989) (quoting Spence v. Washington, 418 U.S. 405, 410-11 (1974)).

Note: An ellipsis includes spaces between the "dots" and a space before the first dot and after the last.

7. *Improper use of ellipses:*

wrong: One element in determining whether conduct is expressive enough to fall within the protection of the First Amendment is "'. . . [whether] the likelihood was great that the message would be understood by those who viewed it.'" Texas v. Johnson, 491 U.S. 397, 404 (1989) (quoting Spence v. Washington, 418 U.S. 405, 410-11 (1974)).

wrong: One element in determining whether conduct is expressive enough to fall within the protection of the First Amendment is "'[whether] the likelihood was great that the message would be understood by those who viewed it.'" Texas v. Johnson, 491 U.S. 397, 404 (1989) (quoting Spence v. Washington, 418 U.S. 405, 410-11 (1974)).

§ 25.8   Common Citation Errors to Avoid

1.   Including the year in a short citation.

incorrect   <u>Johnson</u>, 491 U.S. at 404 (1989).

correct   <u>Johnson</u>, 491 U.S. at 404.

2.   Failing to include the reporter in a short citation.

incorrect   <u>Johnson</u>, 491 at 404.

correct   <u>Johnson</u>, 491 U.S. at 404.

3.   Failing to include the volume and reporter in a short citation.

incorrect   <u>Johnson</u>, at 404.

correct   <u>Johnson</u>, 491 U.S. at 404.

4.   Using *id.*: Using a comma, failing to underline the period.

incorrect   <u>Id.</u>, 404. <u>Id</u>. at 404. <u>Id.</u>, at 404.

correct   <u>Id.</u> at 404.

We can't use *id.* if we have an intervening record cite, an intervening cite to another authority, or if the immediately prior cite is to more than one source.

Chapter 26

Case Briefing and Sample Analytical Brief of a Case[1]

Cases. Cases, or judicial opinions (also called decisions) are primary sources of law and provide examples of the method of legal reasoning we use in studying and practicing law. As you have undoubtedly already discovered, some opinions are better examples of legal reasoning than others. Even those opinions edited by an author and published in a law school textbook can be extremely difficult to read and understand. Sometimes the holding is interspersed with dicta.[2] And, although we expect the facts of a case to appear at the start of an opinion, they're sometimes camouflaged in other parts or sprinkled throughout the holding or reasoning of the case. Indeed, we've read cases where the facts didn't appear at all in the majority opinion but rather appeared in a concurrence or dissent in the case. Thus, extremely careful, critical, analytical reading is required in order to fully understand a case.

Case brief. A case brief (or a brief of a case) is a summary of a court's written opinion. We brief cases to help us prepare for class or for a legal writing assignment.[3] The case briefs we write are usually summaries of appellate court opinions (and, on rare occasions, opinions from the appellate division of a state trial court). But, we may also brief published federal trial court judgments, orders, or opinions. As with every type of writing, the method or format for briefing a case depends on (1) the reason for briefing the case, (2) the intended audience, and (3) our personal preferences. The briefs we prepare for classes in law school may be very different from a brief of a case lawyers write when they know that the particular case may be included in a legal document, such as an internal memorandum, or as part of a persuasive pleading or brief to a court. How a case is briefed may also depend on whether the case is simple or complex. A case brief is typically one or two pages, sometimes longer for a complex case.

For whatever purpose a case is briefed, however, the very process of briefing a case can help ensure that we understand that case. In reading and analyzing judicial opinions, we always focus on the opinion itself. Almost every opinion we read, either on-line or in a hard copy reporter, contains, in addition to the opinion itself, additional information added by the publisher. This additional information may include a summary or synopsis

---

1. We thank Thomson Reuters, the copyright holder, for permission to reprint *California v. Ciraolo*, 476 U.S. 207 (1986) in its entirety with our annotations.

2. See Chapter 1, § 1.2, and Chapter 5, § 5.2.

3. A case brief is distinguishable from an appellate or trial brief, which are both formal documents written to a court to persuade the judge(s) to rule in our client's favor.

of the outcome of the case, summaries of the points of law addressed in the case, and other research sources. Although this additional information is useful in researching other authorities, or in helping us to understand the opinion, we never, ever, cite to or rely upon it. The reason we don't is simple: that additional information was not written by the court. Rather, it was written by the commercial publisher of the opinion. We rely on our *own* judgment in interpreting the case.

Interpreting cases can be a daunting task. But, however well or poorly written, a case will usually include some basic parts: the Facts, the legal Issue presented, the Holding, the Rule applied to the facts to reach the holding, and the Reasoning of the court, i.e., the "FIHRR" (pronounced "fire") of a case.[4] Note that although we use the singular here with respect to issue, holding and rule, there may be multiple issues, holdings, and rules in a particular case. Moreover, these basic parts of an opinion may not always be clearly expressed. The opinion may include other information, such as dicta. For this reason, we must sometimes infer (or "deduce") these basic parts of the case.

Each of these parts of an opinion, the FIHRR of a case, merit further explanation as to how we address them in our case briefs.

1. **The Facts.** We generally include only the *relevant* facts, that is, the ones the court used in resolving the case. To determine which are relevant, we ask whether the presence or absence or change of a fact would have changed the outcome of the case. Occasionally we include facts in addition to the relevant ones if those facts help us to better understand the case. We also include the "procedural history" of a case. This procedural history usually includes information about which party sued which other party and for what, the legal basis for the suit, and how the lower court ruled or disposed of the case. One final note: unless we have a reason to vary the order in which we present the facts, we usually present them in chronological order.

2. **The Issue.** As noted above, there may be a single issue or multiple issues in a case, each issue having its own holding, rule, and reasoning. We always analyze each issue separately in our brief. Essentially, an issue states the question that the holding answers. An issue may be clearly expressed in the opinion or implied by the holding and reasoning. Cases included in textbooks for your law courses have often been edited to focus only on the issues pertaining to the topic being addressed, and you will usually need to brief all those issues. In contrast, when briefing cases for use in a legal document, we only brief the relevant issues.

3. **The Holding.** The holding is the answer to a legal issue, and each issue has only one holding. The holding directs the disposition of the case, meaning the outcome or result for the parties, such as affirmance or reversal of the lower court's judgment, and, in the event of a reversal, sometimes a remand to the lower court for further action. Although there's only one holding for each issue, a holding may rely upon more than one reason or rationale. This is why one judge's interpretation of a precedent may be 180 degrees different from another judge's interpretation of the same case.

---

4. See Chapter 6, §§ 6.3(c) and 6.3(d).

4. **The Rule.** The rule is the law the court applied to the facts to reach its holding. The rule may derive from a constitutional provision, statute, rule or regulation, prior case law, or some combination of these sources. When we write the rule in our case briefs, we want to write it as the court presents it in the opinion (i.e., we quote it) rather than paraphrasing it, but in so doing, we also outline it so that we ensure we have included all its elements.[5] We write the rule generically so as to be applicable to the same issue in a future case, rather than with reference to the parties in that particular dispute.

5. **The Reasoning.** Finally, the reasoning or rationale, the "why" and the "because," is the analysis or method the court used in applying the rule to the facts to reach a holding as to an issue in the case. This reasoning is crucial in understanding the actual meaning of the case and how broadly or narrowly the holding of the case will apply in future cases involving a similar issue.[6] Often a court's reasoning will be based not only on precedent but also on public "policy considerations." Policy considerations focus on the societal goals the rule is intended to accomplish and whether that result will be accomplished in the case if the rule is so applied. Judges understand that the way they rule in one case will likely impact many other future cases.

Briefing a case is as individual a process as combing one's hair. Everyone has his or her own style. Some lawyers *never* brief cases; some *always* do. We suggest you start out briefing the cases you're required to read; later, as you become more experienced in reading cases, you may switch to writing short summaries of the cases or highlighting and making margin notations identifying the relevant parts of the opinion. We also suggest that you read through an entire case at least twice before writing your brief. You may not know what's relevant until you've read through the entire opinion.

We read and brief cases bearing in mind why we're studying them, whether preparing for class or solving a client's problem. Thus, as we read and brief each case, we figure out what the case teaches us about the area of law we're analyzing and how the cases fit together. We synthesize, or reconcile, the case law so that it's logical. We ask whether the case is consistent with the previous ones we've read, and we determine how the rule has evolved, i.e., whether it has expanded or become narrower. When solving a problem for a client, we determine how the law as we interpret it furthers the theory of our client's case.

The sample brief. The brief we present here is just a suggestion. Your style of briefing may differ. We simply suggest that you try this method and then adapt it to fit your particular style. We call the sample an "analytical" brief because it's quite detailed. It's the type of brief we'd write if we were trying to explain the case to someone else, i.e., a judge or colleague.

Following the brief, we've included two "case charts." These charts help us organize our research and serve as "mini-briefs" of each case. We've also included the actual text of the case we've briefed—*California v. Ciraolo*, a United States Supreme Court opinion,

---

5. See Chapter 1, §1.5 and Chapter 5, §5.5 for additional information regarding outlining a rule.
6. See Chapter 5, §5.7, for a further discussion of narrow versus broad holdings.

annotated by our colleague Henry Wihnyk to demonstrate the various parts of the opinion.

In reviewing the sample analytical brief, please note the following:

- We state the date the brief was written and the file name in the upper right corner.
- We begin the brief with the correct citation and a narrow holding of the case. We follow all facts, quotations, and discussion points with citations to the pages where the information is located. All citations and quotations are accurate.
- We provide relevant facts, with citations to the specific pages in the case where those facts are discussed.
- We state the general and precise issues as the Court stated them. We also include the Court's dicta re what is *not* at issue.
- We state the precise holding and Court "count" (i.e., 5 to 4 decision). We state the holding in terms of the legal issue.
- We next state the disposition of the case: reversed, overturned, overruled, affirmed, etc. We leave no doubt as to the procedural effect of the decision.
- We fully address the rule and fully discuss the Court's application of the rule and reasoning, followed by arguments the Court rejected.

July 10, 20xx

file: Ciraolobr

<u>California v. Ciraolo</u>, 476 U.S. 207 (1986): Police officers did not violate the Fourth Amendment when (1) without a warrant, (2) with their naked eyes, and (3) from an altitude of 1,000 feet in navigable airspace, they viewed defendant's fenced-in backyard.

I.   <u>FACTS:</u>

Police received an anonymous tip that Ciraolo was growing marijuana in his back-yard—an area completely enclosed by a 6-foot outer fence and a 10–foot inner fence. <u>Id.</u> at 209. This fence, however, prevented the police from being able to observe, from ground level, the contents of the yard. <u>Id.</u> Two officers, who each were trained in marijuana identification, then secured a private plane and flew over Ciraolo's house in navigable airspace at an altitude of 1,000 feet. <u>Id.</u> They readily identified and photographed marijuana plants growing in the yard. <u>Id.</u> A few days later, one of the officers obtained a search warrant "on the basis of an affidavit describing the anonymous tip and [the officers'] observations...." <u>Id.</u> Marijuana plants were later seized pursuant to that warrant. <u>Id.</u> at 210. Ciraolo pled guilty to a charge of cultivating marijuana after the trial court denied his motion to suppress the evidence of the search. <u>Id.</u> The California Court of Appeal reversed, finding that the aerial observation of Ciraolo's yard violated the Fourth Amendment. <u>Id.</u> The California Supreme Court denied review. <u>Id.</u> The United States Supreme Court granted the State's petition for certiorari. <u>Id.</u>

II.   <u>ISSUE:</u>

"[W]hether the Fourth Amendment is violated by aerial observation without a warrant from an altitude of 1,000 feet of a fenced-in backyard within the curtilage of a home." <u>Id.</u> at 209.

> Specifically: "[W]hether naked-eye observation of the curtilage [of Ciraolo's home] by police from an aircraft lawfully operating at an altitude of 1,000 feet violates an expectation of privacy that is reasonable." <u>Id.</u> at 213.

<u>Note:</u> The parties below did not raise, and the Court did not address, the distinct issue of whether a photograph, taken from an altitude of 1,000 feet, and attached as an exhibit to an affidavit in support of a search warrant, raised any Fourth Amendment issues. <u>Id.</u> at 213 n.1.

III. <u>HOLDING:</u>   [5 to 4 decision]

<u>No.</u>   <u>The Fourth Amendment was not violated here.</u> "In an age where private and commercial flight in the public airways is routine, it is unreasonable for [Ciraolo] to expect that his marijuana plants were constitutionally protected from being observed with the naked eye from an altitude of 1,000 feet. The Fourth Amendment simply does not require the police traveling in the public airways at this altitude to obtain a warrant in order to observe what is visible to the naked eye." <u>Id.</u> at 215.

IV. <u>DISPOSITION:</u>

Reversed. Ciraolo had been convicted; the California Court of Appeal had reversed that conviction. Conviction reinstated.

V.   <u>LEGAL RULE:</u>

Fourth Amendment protection arises where:

A. An individual has "manifested a subjective expectation of privacy in the object of the challenged search"; and

Note: This element was not at issue in this case. The State did not challenge the Court of Appeal's finding that Ciraolo met the test of manifesting his subjective intent to maintain the privacy of his marijuana crop. Id. at 211.

B. "[S]ociety [is] willing to recognize that expectation as reasonable." Id.

1. In determining whether the expectation is reasonable, the court must "keep in mind that '[t]he test of legitimacy is not whether the individual chooses to conceal assertedly "private" activity,' but instead 'whether the government's intrusion infringes upon the personal and societal values protected by the Fourth Amendment.'" Id. at 212 (quoting Oliver v. United States, 466 U.S. 170, 181-83 (1984)).

2. Privacy expectations are heightened in the "curtilage" — "an area intimately linked to the home, both physically and psychologically...." Id. at 213. The backyard of one's home is part of the curtilage. Id.

3. However, even in the curtilage, that which is exposed to public view is not subject to Fourth Amendment protection. Id. Thus, "the mere fact than an individual has taken measures to restrict some views of his activities [does not] preclude an officer's observations from a public vantage point where he has a right to be and which renders the activities clearly visible." Id.

VI. APPLICATION—REASONING OF COURT:

A. "Subjective expectation of privacy":

No issue here; Ciraolo possessed a subjective expectation of privacy. Id. at 211-12.

B. "Reasonableness":

Ciraolo's expectation, even though the marijuana was within the curtilage of his home, was not reasonable; therefore, there was no Fourth Amendment violation here. Id. at 212-14. The officers' observations were from a public vantage point where the officers had a right to be and which rendered the marijuana plants clearly visible. Id. at 213. The following factors support this conclusion:

1. The officers' observations took place "within public navigable airspace";

2. The observations were conducted "in a physically nonintrusive manner"; and

3. The officers "were able to observe plants readily discernible to the naked eye as marijuana." Id.

Arguments rejected:

The Court found it irrelevant that the observation from the aircraft was "directed at identifying the plants" and that the "officers were trained to recognize marijuana...." Id. The Court reasoned: "[a]ny member of the public flying in this airspace who glanced down could have seen everything that these officers observed." Id. at 213-14.

The Court, rejecting the dissent's position, noted that Justice Harlan's warnings in <u>Katz</u> regarding future electronic interference with private communications did not apply here. <u>Id.</u> at 214-15. Harlan's observations, said the Court, "were plainly not aimed at simple visual observations from a public place." <u>Id.</u> at 214.

Case Charts. We recommend using a chart, like the following, (or like the one in Chapter 7, § 7.5), to organize cases as we research. Be sure to note, in columns 3, 4 and 5, the pages numbers of the case where we can locate the information.

1	2	3	4	5	6
case name	court – year	key facts & issue	holding & reasoning	rule	how we'll use the case

For individual cases, we can use the following chart. (The "date" notation is for us to indicate when we updated the case.)

citation	updated ☐ date :_____
facts	
issue	
holding	
rule	
reasoning	
use	

Supreme Court of the United States
CALIFORNIA, Petitioner

v.

CIRAOLO.
No. 84-1513.

Argued Dec. 10, 1985.
Decided May 19, 1986.
Rehearing Denied June 30, 1986.
See 478 U.S. 1014, 106 S.Ct. 3320.

Defendant was convicted in the Superior Court, Santa Clara County, Marilyn Pestarino Zecher, J., of cultivation of marijuana, and he appealed. The Court of Appeal, Haning, J., 161 Cal.App.3d 1081, 208 Cal.Rptr. 93, reversed. Certiorari was granted. The Supreme Court, Chief Justice Burger, held that warrantless aerial observation of fenced-in backyard within curtilage of home was not unreasonable under the Fourth Amendment.

Reversed.

Justice Powell filed a dissenting opinion in which Justices Brennan, Marshall and Blackmun joined.

West Headnotes

[1] Searches and Seizures 349 ⌐══26

349 Searches and Seizures

   349I In General

      349k25 Persons, Places and Things Protected

         349k26 k. Expectation of Privacy. Most Cited Cases

Touchstone of Fourth Amendment analysis of lawfulness of search is whether person has constitutionally protected reasonable expectation of privacy. U.S.C.A. Const.Amend. 4.

[2] Searches and Seizures 349 ⌐══26

349 Searches and Seizures

   349I In General

      349k25 Persons, Places and Things Protected

         349k26 k. Expectation of Privacy. Most Cited Cases

In pursuing inquiry into whether expectation of privacy is reasonable, test of legitimacy is not whether individual chooses to conceal assertedly private activity but instead whether government's intrusion infringes upon personal and societal values protected by Fourth Amendment. U.S.C.A. Const.Amend. 4.

[3] Searches and Seizures 349 ⌐══27

349 Searches and Seizures

   349I In General

Margin notes:

The court deciding the case.

This is the name of the case.

The date of the decision.

Citations to location in other reporters.

Summary written by reporter publisher.

Headnotes summarize the legal principles discussed in the case. They are not written by the court.

349k25 Persons, Places and Things Protected

349k27 k. Curtilage or Open Fields; Yards and Outbuildings. Most Cited Cases

That area under observation is within curtilage does not itself bar all police observation. U.S.C.A. Const.Amend. 4.

[4] Searches and Seizures 349 ⚷═══23

349 Searches and Seizures

349I In General

349k23 k. Fourth Amendment and Reasonableness in General. Most Cited Cases

Searches and Seizures 349 ⚷═══25.1

349 Searches and Seizures

349I In General

349k25 Persons, Places and Things Protected

349k25.1 k. In General. Most Cited Cases

(Formerly 349k25)

Fourth Amendment protection of home has never been extended to require law enforcement officers to shield their eyes when passing by home on public thoroughfare. U.S.C.A. Const.Amend. 4.

[5] Criminal Law 110 ⚷═══1222.1

110 Criminal Law

110XXVII Prevention of Crime

110k1222 Prevention and Investigation of Crime

110k1222.1 k. In General. Most Cited Cases

(Formerly 110k1222)

Searches and Seizures 349 ⚷═══25.1

349 Searches and Seizures

349I In General

349k25 Persons, Places and Things Protected

349k25.1 k. In General. Most Cited Cases

(Formerly 349k25)

Searches and Seizures 349 ⚷═══47.1

349 Searches and Seizures

349I In General

349k47 Plain View from Lawful Vantage Point

349k47.1 k. In General. Most Cited Cases

(Formerly 349k47)

Mere fact that individual has taken measures to restrict some views of his activities does not preclude police officer's observations from public vantage point where he has right to be and which renders activities clearly visible. U.S.C.A. Const.Amend. 4.

[6] Controlled Substances 96H ⊙⟳⟳134

96H Controlled Substances

    96HIV Searches and Seizures

        96HIV(B) Search Without Warrant

            96Hk127 Premises, Search of

                96Hk134 k. Open Fields; Curtilage or Yard; Growing Plants.
Most Cited Cases

    (Formerly 138k185(7), 138k185 Drugs and Narcotics)

Searches and Seizures 349 ⊙⟳⟳56

349 Searches and Seizures

    349I In General

        349k53 Scope, Conduct, and Duration of Warrantless Search

        349k56 k. Aerial Surveillance. Most Cited Cases

Police officers' warrantless aerial observation, from altitude of 1,000 feet, of fenced-in backyard within curtilage of home, during which plants readily discernible to naked eye as marijuana were observed, did not violate homeowner's Fourth Amendment rights where home-owner's expectation that his backyard was protected from such obser-vation was unreasonable and was not one that society was prepared to honor. U.S.C.A. Const.Amend. 4.

**1809 *207 *Syllabus* FN*

FN* The syllabus constitutes no part of the opinion of the Court but has been prepared by the Reporter of Decisions for the convenience of the reader. See *United States v. Detroit Lumber Co.*, 200 U.S. 321, 337, 26 S.Ct. 282, 287, 50 L.Ed. 499.

> The numbers correspond to the pages in the other reporters where the case is published.

The Santa Clara, Cal., police received an anonymous telephone tip that marijuana was growing in respondent's backyard, which was enclosed by two fences and shielded from view at ground level. Officers who were trained in marijuana identification secured a private airplane, flew over respondent's house at an altitude of 1,000 feet, and readily identified marijuana plants growing in the yard. A search warrant was later obtained on the basis of one **1810 of the officer's naked-eye observations; a photograph of the surrounding area taken from the airplane was attached as an exhibit. The warrant was executed, and marijuana plants were seized. After the California trial court denied respondent's motion to suppress the evidence of the search, he pleaded guilty to a charge of cultivation of marijuana. The California Court of Appeal reversed on the ground that the warrantless aerial observation of respondent's yard violated the Fourth Amendment.

Held: The Fourth Amendment was not violated by the naked-eye aerial observation of respondent's backyard. Pp. 1811-1813.

(a) The touchstone of Fourth Amendment analysis is whether a person has a constitutionally protected reasonable expectation of privacy, which involves the two inquiries of whether the individual manifested a subjective expectation of privacy in the object of the challenged search, and whether society is willing to recognize that expectation as reasonable. *Katz v. United States,* 389 U.S. 347, 88 S.Ct. 507, 19 L.Ed.2d 576. In pursuing the second inquiry, the test of legitimacy is not whether the individual chooses to conceal assertedly "private activity," but whether the government's intrusion infringes upon the personal and societal values protected by the Fourth Amendment. Pp. 1811-1812.

(b) On the record here, respondent's expectation of privacy from *all* observations of his backyard was unreasonable. That the backyard and its crop were within the "curtilage" of respondent's home did not itself bar all police observation. The mere fact that an individual has taken measures to restrict some views of his activities does not preclude an officer's observation from a public vantage point where he has a right to be and which renders the activities clearly visible. The police observations here took place within public navigable airspace, in a physically nonintrusive manner. The police were able to observe the plants *208 readily discernible to the naked eye as marijuana, and it was irrelevant that the observation from the airplane was directed at identifying the plants and that the officers were trained to recognize marijuana. Any member of the public flying in this airspace who cared to glance down could have seen everything that the officers observed. The Fourth Amendment simply does not require police traveling in the public airways at 1,000 feet to obtain a warrant in order to observe what is visible to the naked eye. Pp. 1812-1813.

161 Cal.App.3d 1081, 208 Cal.Rptr. 93, reversed.

BURGER, C.J., delivered the opinion of the Court, in which WHITE, REHNQUIST, STEVENS, and O'CONNOR, JJ., joined. . POWELL, J., filed a dissenting opinion, in which BRENNAN, MARSHALL, and BLACKMUN, JJ., joined, *post,* p. ——.

Laurence K. Sullivan, Deputy Attorney General of California, argued the cause for petitioner. With him on the briefs were *John K. Van de Kamp,* Attorney General, *Steve White,* Chief Assistant Attorney General, and *Eugene W. Kaster,* Deputy Attorney General.

Marshall Warren Krause, by appointment of the Court, 472 U.S. 1025, argued the cause for respondent. With him on the brief was *Pamela Holmes Duncan.**

These Justices agreed with Justice Burger and make up the majority.

These four Justices disagreed with the majority opinion.

This attorney represented California at oral argument.

This attorney represented the respondent at oral argument.

* Briefs of *amici curiae* urging reversal were filed for the State of Indiana et al. by *Linley E. Pearson*, Attorney General of Indiana, *William E. Daily* and *Lisa M. Paunicka*, Deputy Attorneys General, *Charles A. Graddick*, Attorney General of Alabama, *Charles M. Oberly*, Attorney General of Delaware, *Michael J. Bowers*, Attorney General of Georgia, *Neil F. Hartigan*, Attorney General of Illinois, *Robert T. Stephan*, Attorney General of Kansas, *David L. Armstrong*, Attorney General of Kentucky, *William J. Guste, Jr.*, Attorney General of Louisiana, *James E. Tierney*, Attorney General of Maine, *Francis X. Bellotti*, Attorney General of Massachusetts, *William L. Webster*, Attorney General of Missouri, *Robert M. Spire*, Attorney General-Designate of Nebraska, *Brian McKay*, Attorney General of Nevada, *Stephen E. Merrill*, Attorney General of New Hampshire, *Paul Bardacke*, Attorney General of New Mexico, *Anthony Celebrezze*, Attorney General of Ohio, *LeRoy S. Zimmerman*, Attorney General of Pennsylvania, *Travis Medlock*, Attorney General of South Carolina, *Jeffrey Amestoy*, Attorney General of Vermont, *Gerald L. Baliles*, Attorney General of Virginia, *Kenneth O. Eikenberry*, Attorney General of Washington, and *Archie G. McClintock*, Attorney General of Wyoming; for Americans for Effective Law Enforcement Inc. et al. by *Fred E. Inbau, Wayne W. Schmidt, James P. Manak, David Crump*, and *Daniel B. Hales*; for the Criminal Justice Legal Foundation by *Christopher N. Heard*; and for the Washington Legal Foundation by *Daniel J. Popeo* and *George C. Smith*.

> Many organizations representing both sides of the issue filed "friend of the Court" briefs.

Briefs of *amici curiae* urging affirmance were filed for the American Civil Liberties Union et al. by *C. Douglas Floyd, Alan L. Schlosser*, and *Charles S. Sims*; for the Civil Liberties Monitoring Project by *Amitai Schwartz*; and for the National Association of Criminal Defense Lawyers by *John Kenneth Zwerling*.

*209 Chief Justice BURGER delivered the opinion of the Court.

> This means that Justice Burger authored the majority opinion.

We granted certiorari to determine whether the Fourth Amendment is violated by aerial observation without a warrant from an altitude of 1,000 feet of a fenced-in backyard within the curtilage of a home.

> This is where the text of the Court's opinion starts. This is "the law."

I

On September 2, 1982, Santa Clara Police received an anonymous telephone tip that marijuana was growing in respondent's backyard. Police were unable to observe the contents of respondent's yard from ground level because of a 6-foot outer fence and a 10-foot inner fence completely enclosing the yard. Later that day, Officer Shutz, who was assigned to investigate, secured a private plane and flew over respondent's house at an altitude of 1,000 feet, within navigable airspace; he was accompanied by Officer Rodriguez. Both officers**1811** were trained in marijuana identification. From the overflight, the officers readily identified marijuana plants 8 feet to 10 feet in height growing in a 15- by 25-foot plot in respondent's yard; they photographed the area with a standard 35mm camera.

> The Court details the key facts.

On September 8, 1982, Officer Shutz obtained a search warrant on the basis of an affidavit describing the anonymous tip and their observations; a photograph depicting respondent's house, the backyard, and neighboring homes was attached to the affidavit as an exhibit. The warrant was *210 executed the next day and 73 plants were seized; it is not disputed that these were marijuana.

The procedural history.

After the trial court denied respondent's motion to suppress the evidence of the search, respondent pleaded guilty to a charge of cultivation of marijuana. The California Court of Appeal reversed, however, on the ground that the warrantless aerial *observation* of respondent's yard which led to the issuance of the warrant violated the Fourth Amendment. 161 Cal.App.3d 1081, 208 Cal.Rptr. 93 (1984). That court held first that respondent's backyard marijuana garden was within the "curtilage" of his home, under *Oliver v. United States*, 466 U.S. 170, 104 S.Ct. 1735, 80 L.Ed.2d 214 (1984). The court emphasized that the height and existence of the two fences constituted "objective criteria from which we may conclude he manifested a reasonable expectation of privacy by any standard." 161 Cal.App.3d, at 1089, 208 Cal.Rptr., at 97.

Examining the particular method of surveillance undertaken, the court then found it "significant" that the flyover "was not the result of a routine patrol conducted for any other legitimate law enforcement or public safety objective, but was undertaken for the specific purpose of observing this particular enclosure within [respondent's] curtilage." *Ibid.* It held this focused observation was "a direct and unauthorized intrusion into the sanctity of the home" which violated respondent's reasonable expectation of privacy. *Id.,* at 1089-1090, 208 Cal.Rptr., at 98 (footnote omitted). The California Supreme Court denied the State's petition for review.

The Court announces its holding.

We granted the State's petition for certiorari, 471 U.S. 1134, 105 S.Ct. 2672, 86 L.Ed.2d 691 (1985). We reverse.

The Court summarizes the parties' arguments.

The State argues that respondent has "knowingly exposed" his backyard to aerial observation, because all that was seen was visible to the naked eye from any aircraft flying overhead. The State analogizes its mode of observation to a knothole or opening in a fence: if there is an opening, the police may look.

*211 The California Court of Appeal, as we noted earlier, accepted the analysis that unlike the casual observation of a private person flying overhead, this flight was focused specifically on a small suburban yard, and was not the result of any routine patrol overflight. Respondent contends he has done all that can reasonably be expected to tell the world he wishes to maintain the privacy of his garden within the curtilage without covering his yard. Such covering, he argues, would defeat its purpose as an outside living area; he asserts he has not "knowingly" exposed himself to aerial views.

II

[1] The touchstone of Fourth Amendment analysis is whether a person has a "constitutionally protected reasonable expectation of privacy." *Katz v. United States*, 389 U.S. 347, 360, 88 S.Ct. 507, 516, 19 L.Ed.2d 576 (1967) (Harlan, J., concurring). *Katz* posits a two-part inquiry: first, has the individual manifested a subjective expectation of privacy in the object of the challenged search? Second, is society willing to recognize that expectation as reasonable? See *Smith v. Maryland*, 442 U.S. 735, 740, 99 S.Ct. 2577, 2580, 61 L.Ed.2d 220 (1979).

The bracketed numbers correspond to the head-notes.

The Court announces the rule to be applied in the case.

Clearly-and understandably-respondent has met the test of manifesting his own subjective intent and desire to maintain**1812 privacy as to his unlawful agricultural pursuits. However, we need not address that issue, for the State has not challenged the finding of the California Court of Appeal that respondent had such an expectation. It can reasonably be assumed that the 10-foot fence was placed to conceal the marijuana crop from at least street-level views. So far as the normal sidewalk traffic was concerned, this fence served that purpose, because respondent "took normal precautions to maintain his privacy." *Rawlings v. Kentucky*, 448 U.S. 98, 105, 100 S.Ct. 2556, 2561, 65 L.Ed.2d 633 (1980).

The Court dispenses with the first prong of the *Katz* test because it is not contested.

Yet a 10-foot fence might not shield these plants from the eyes of a citizen or a policeman perched on the top of a truck or a two-level bus. Whether respondent therefore manifested *212 a subjective expectation of privacy from *all* observations of his backyard, or whether instead he manifested merely a hope that no one would observe his unlawful gardening pursuits, is not entirely clear in these circumstances. Respondent appears to challenge the authority of government to observe his activity from any vantage point or place if the viewing is motivated by a law enforcement purpose, and not the result of a casual, accidental observation.

The Court characterizes Respondent's argument as the first step in concluding it had no merit.

[2] We turn, therefore, to the second inquiry under *Katz, i.e.,* whether that expectation is reasonable. In pursuing this inquiry, we must keep in mind that "[t]he test of legitimacy is not whether the individual chooses to conceal assertedly 'private' activity," but instead "whether the government's intrusion infringes upon the personal and societal values protected by the Fourth Amendment." *Oliver, supra,* 466 U.S., at 181-183, 104 S.Ct., at 1742-1744.

Here the court identifies the issue it is considering — the second prong of the *Katz* test.

The Court restates the principle it will apply to the issue.

Respondent argues that because his yard was in the curtilage of his home, no governmental aerial observation is permissible under the Fourth Amendment without a warrant.[FN1] The history and genesis of the curtilage doctrine are instructive. "At common law, the curtilage is the area to which extends the intimate activity associated with the 'sanctity of a man's home and the privacies of life.'" *Oliver, supra, 466 U.S., at 180, 104 S.Ct., at 1742* (quoting *Boyd v. United States, 116 U.S. 616, 630, 6 S.Ct. 524, 532, 29 L.Ed. 746 (1886)*). See 4 Blackstone,

Commentaries *225. The *213 protection afforded the curtilage is essentially a protection of families and personal privacy in an area intimately linked to the home, both physically and psychologically, where privacy expectations are most heightened. The claimed area here was immediately adjacent to a suburban home, surrounded by high double fences. This close nexus to the home would appear to encompass this small area within the curtilage. Accepting, as the State does, that this yard and its crop fall within the curtilage, the question remains whether naked-eye observation of the curtilage by police from an aircraft lawfully operating at an altitude of 1,000 feet violates an expectation of privacy that is reasonable.

> FN1. Because the parties framed the issue in the California courts below and in this Court as concerning only the reasonableness of aerial observation generally, see Pet. for Cert. i, without raising any distinct issue as to the photograph attached as an exhibit to the affidavit in support of the search warrant, our analysis is similarly circumscribed. It was the officer's observation, not the photograph, that supported the warrant. Officer Shutz testified that the photograph did not identify the marijuana as such because it failed to reveal a "true representation" of the color of the plants: "you have to see it with the naked eye." App. 36.

[3][4][5] That the area is within the curtilage does not itself bar all police observation. The Fourth Amendment protection of the home has never been extended to require law enforcement officers to shield their eyes when passing by a home on public thoroughfares. Nor does the mere fact that an individual has taken measures to restrict some views of his activities preclude an officer's observations from a public vantage point where he has a right to be and which renders the activities clearly visible. E.g., **1813 United States v. Knotts, 460 U.S. 276, 282, 103 S.Ct. 1081, 1085-1086, 75 L.Ed.2d 55 (1983). "What a person knowingly exposes to the public, even in his own home or office, is not a subject of Fourth Amendment protection." Katz, supra, 389 U.S., at 351, 88 S.Ct., at 511.

[6] The observations by Officers Shutz and Rodriguez in this case took place within public navigable airspace, see 49 U.S.C.App.§ 1304, in a physically nonintrusive manner; from this point they were able to observe plants readily discernible to the naked eye as marijuana. That the observation from aircraft was directed at identifying the plants and the officers were trained to recognize marijuana is irrelevant. Such observation is precisely what a judicial officer needs to provide a basis for a warrant. Any member of the public flying in this airspace who glanced down could have seen *214 everything that these officers observed. On this record, we readily conclude that respondent's expectation that his garden was protected from such observation is

Margin notes:

Here the Court narrowly states the issue in terms of the determinative facts.

The Court will decide only the issues raised by the parties.

The Court describes its reasoning supporting its conclusion.

The Court announces its conclusion.

unreasonable and is not an expectation that society is prepared to honor.[FN2]

> FN2. The California Court of Appeal recognized that police have the right to use navigable airspace, but made a pointed distinction between police aircraft focusing on a particular home and police aircraft engaged in a "routine patrol." It concluded that the officers' "focused" observations violated respondent's reasonable expectations of privacy. In short, that court concluded that a regular police patrol plane identifying respondent's marijuana would lead to a different result. Whether this is a rational distinction is hardly relevant, although we find difficulty understanding exactly how respondent's expectations of privacy from aerial observation might differ when two airplanes pass overhead at identical altitudes, simply for different purposes. We are cited to no authority for this novel analysis or the conclusion it begat. The fact that a ground-level observation by police "focused" on a particular place is not different from a "focused" aerial observation under the Fourth Amendment.

The dissent contends that the Court ignores Justice Harlan's warning in his concurrence in *Katz v. United States,* 389 U.S., at 361-362, 88 S.Ct., at 516-517, that the Fourth Amendment should not be limited to proscribing only physical intrusions onto private property. *Post,* at ___. But Justice Harlan's observations about future electronic developments and the potential for electronic interference with private communications, see *Katz, supra,* at 362, 88 S.Ct., at 517, were plainly not aimed at simple visual observations from a public place. Indeed, since *Katz* the Court has required warrants for electronic surveillance aimed at intercepting private conversations. See *United States v. United States District Court,* 407 U.S. 297, 92 S.Ct. 2125, 32 L.Ed.2d 752 (1972).

The majority often responds to the dissenting opinion.

Justice Harlan made it crystal clear that he was resting on the reality that one who enters a telephone booth is entitled to assume that his conversation is not being intercepted. This does not translate readily into a rule of constitutional dimensions that one who grows illicit drugs in his backyard is "entitled to assume" his unlawful conduct will not be observed*215 by a passing aircraft—or by a power company repair mechanic on a pole overlooking the yard. As Justice Harlan emphasized,

"a man's home is, for most purposes, a place where he expects privacy, but objects, activities, or statements that he exposes to the 'plain view' of outsiders are not 'protected' because no intention to keep them to himself has been exhibited. On the other hand, conversations in the open would not be protected against being overheard, for the expectation of privacy under the circumstances would be unreasonable." _Katz, supra_, 389 U.S., at 361, 88 S.Ct., at 516-517.

One can reasonably doubt that in 1967 Justice Harlan considered an aircraft within the category of future "electronic" developments that could stealthily intrude upon an individual's privacy. In an age where private and commercial flight in the public airways is routine, it is unreasonable for respondent to expect that his marijuana plants were constitutionally protected from being observed with the naked eye from an altitude of 1,000 feet. The Fourth Amendment simply does not require the police traveling in the public airways at this altitude **1814 to obtain a warrant in order to observe what is visible to the naked eye. FN3

The Court sums up its reasoning supporting the decision.

> FN3. In _Dow Chemical Co. v. United States_, 476 U.S. 227, 106 S.Ct. 1819, 90 L.Ed.2d 226 (1986), decided today, we hold that the use of an aerial mapping camera to photograph an industrial manufacturing complex from navigable airspace similarly does not require a warrant under the Fourth Amendment. The State acknowledges that "[a]erial observation of curtilage may become invasive, either due to physical intrusiveness or through modern technology which discloses to the senses those intimate associations, objects or activities otherwise imperceptible to police or fellow citizens." Brief for Petitioner 14-15.

Reversed.

The procedural outcome of the Court's decision.

These Justices did not agree with the majority.

Justice POWELL, with whom Justice BRENNAN, Justice MARSHALL, and Justice BLACKMUN join, dissenting.

Concurring in _Katz v. United States_, 389 U.S. 347, 88 S.Ct. 507, 19 L.Ed.2d 576 (1967), Justice Harlan warned that any decision to construe the *216 Fourth Amendment as proscribing only physical intrusions by police onto private property "is, in the present day, bad physics as well as bad law, for reasonable expectations of privacy may be defeated by electronic as well as physical invasion." _Id._, at 362, 88 S.Ct., at 516. Because the Court today ignores that warning in an opinion that departs significantly from the standard developed in _Katz_ for deciding when a Fourth Amendment violation has occurred, I dissent.

I

As the Court's opinion reflects, the facts of this case are not complicated. Officer Shutz investigated an anonymous report that marijuana was growing in the backyard of respondent's home. A tall fence prevented Shutz from looking into the yard from the street. The yard was directly behind the home so that the home itself furnished one border of the fence. Shutz proceeded, without obtaining a warrant, to charter a plane and fly over the home at an altitude of 1,000 feet. Observing marijuana plants growing in the fenced-in yard, Shutz photographed respondent's home and yard, as well as homes and yards of neighbors. The photograph clearly shows that the enclosed yard also contained a small swimming pool and patio. Shutz then filed an affidavit, to which he attached the photograph, describing the anonymous tip and his aerial observation of the marijuana. A warrant issued,<u>FN1</u> and a search of the yard confirmed Shutz' aerial observations. Respondent was arrested for cultivating marijuana, a felony under California law.

> FN1. The warrant authorized Shutz to search the home and its attached garage, as well as the yard, for marijuana, narcotics paraphernalia, records relating to marijuana sales, and documents identifying the occupant of the premises.

Respondent contends that the police intruded on his constitutionally protected expectation of privacy when they conducted aerial surveillance of his home and photographed his backyard without first obtaining a warrant. The Court *217 rejects that contention, holding that respondent's expectation of privacy in the curtilage of his home, although reasonable as to intrusions on the ground, was unreasonable as to surveillance from the navigable airspace. In my view, the Court's holding rests on only one obvious fact, namely, that the airspace generally is open to all persons for travel in airplanes. The Court does not explain why this single fact deprives citizens of their privacy interest in outdoor activities in an enclosed curtilage.

II

A

The Fourth Amendment protects "[t]he right of the people to be secure in their persons, houses, papers, and effects, against unreasonable searches and seizures." While the familiar history of the Amendment need not be recounted here,<u>FN2</u> **1815 we should remember that it reflects a choice that our society should be one in which citizens "dwell in reasonable security and freedom from surveillance." _Johnson v. United States,_ 333 U.S. 10, 14, 68 S.Ct. 367, 369, 92 L.Ed. 436 (1948). Since that choice was made by the Framers of the Constitution, our cases construing the Fourth Amendment have relied in part on the common law for instruction on "what sorts of searches the Framers ... regarded as reasonable." _Steagald v. United States,_ 451 U.S. 204, 217, 101 S.Ct. 1642, 1650, 68 L.Ed.2d 38 (1981). But we have repeatedly refused to freeze "'into constitutional law those enforcement practices that existed at the time of the Fourth Amendment's passage.'" _Id.,_ at 217, n. 10, 101 S.Ct., at 1650, n. 10, quoting _Payton v. New York,_ 445 U.S. 573, 591, n. 33, 100 S.Ct. 1371, 1382-83, n. 33, 63 L.Ed.2d 639 (1980). See _United States v. United States District Court,_ 407 U.S. 297, 313, 92 S.Ct. 2125, 2134-2135, 32 L.Ed.2d 752 (1972). Rather, we have construed the Amendment "'in light of contemporary norms and conditions,'" _Steagald v. United States, supra,_ 451 U.S., at 217, n. 10, 101 S.Ct., at 1650, n.10, quoting _Payton v. New York, supra,_ 445 U.S., at

591, n. 33, 100 S.Ct., at 1382-1383, n. 33, in order to prevent "any stealthy encroachments" on our citizens' right to be free of arbitrary official intrusion, *218 _Boyd v. United States,_ 116 U.S. 616, 635, 6 S.Ct. 524, 535, 29 L.Ed. 746 (1886). Since the landmark decision in _Katz v. United States,_ the Court has fulfilled its duty to protect Fourth Amendment rights by asking if police surveillance has intruded on an individual's reasonable expectation of privacy.

> FN2. See, _e.g., Payton v. New York,_ 445 U.S. 573, 583-585, n. 20, 100 S.Ct. 1371, 1378-1379, n. 20, 63 L.Ed.2d 639 (1980).

As the decision in _Katz_ held, and dissenting opinions written by Justices of this Court prior to _Katz_ recognized, _e.g., Goldman v. United States,_ 316 U.S. 129, 139-141, 62 S.Ct. 993, 998-999, 86 L.Ed. 1322 (1942) (Murphy, J., dissenting); _Olmstead v. United States,_ 277 U.S. 438, 474, 48 S.Ct. 564, 571, 72 L.Ed. 944 (1928) (Brandeis, J., dissenting), a standard that defines a Fourth Amendment "search" by reference to whether police have physically invaded a "constitutionally protected area" provides no real protection against surveillance techniques made possible through technology. Technological advances have enabled police to see people's activities and associations, and to hear their conversations, without being in physical proximity. Moreover, the capability now exists for police to conduct intrusive surveillance without any physical penetration of the walls of homes or other structures that citizens may believe shelters their privacy.[FN3] Looking to the Fourth Amendment for protection against such "broad and unsuspected governmental incursions" into the "cherished privacy of law-abiding citizens," *219_United States v. United States District Court, supra,_ 407 U.S., at 312-313, 92 S.Ct., at 2135 (footnote omitted), the Court in _Katz_ abandoned its inquiry into whether police had committed a physical trespass. _Katz_ announced a standard under which the occurrence of a search turned not on the physical position of the police conducting the surveillance, but on whether the surveillance in question had invaded a constitutionally protected reasonable expectation of privacy.

> FN3. As was said more than four decades ago: "[T]he search of one's home or office no longer requires physical entry for science has brought forth far more effective devices for the invasion of a person's privacy than the direct and obvious methods of oppression which were detested by our forbears and which inspired the Fourth Amendment.... Whether the search of private quarters is accomplished by placing on the outer walls of the sanctum a detectaphone that transmits to the outside listener the intimate details of a private conversation, or by new methods of photography that penetrate walls or overcome distances, the privacy of the citizen is equally invaded by the Government and intimate

personal matters are laid bare to view." _Goldman v. United States,_ 316 U.S. 129, 139, 62 S.Ct. 993, 998, 86 L.Ed. 1322 (1942) (Murphy, J., dissenting). Since 1942, science has developed even more sophisticated means of surveillance.

Our decisions following the teaching of _Katz_ illustrate that this inquiry "normally embraces two discrete questions." **1816_Smith v. Maryland,_ 442 U.S. 735, 740, 99 S.Ct. 2577, 2580, 61 L.Ed.2d 220 (1979). "The first is whether the individual, by his conduct, has 'exhibited an actual (subjective) expectation of privacy.'" 442 U.S., at 740, S.Ct., at 2580, quoting _Katz v. United States, supra,_ 389 U.S., at 361, 88 S.Ct., at 516-517 (Harlan, J., concurring). The second is whether that subjective expectation "is 'one that society is prepared to recognize as "reasonable."'" 442 U.S., at 740, —- S.Ct., at 2580, quoting _Katz v. United States,_ supra, 389 U.S., at 361, 88 S.Ct., at 516-517 (Harlan, J., concurring). While the Court today purports to reaffirm this analytical framework, its conclusory rejection of respondent's expectation of privacy in the yard of his residence as one that "is unreasonable," _ante,_ at 1813, represents a turning away from the principles that have guided our Fourth Amendment inquiry. The Court's rejection of respondent's Fourth Amendment claim is curiously at odds with its purported reaffirmation of the curtilage doctrine, both in this decision and its companion case, _Dow Chemical Co. v. United States,_ 476 U.S. 227, 106 S.Ct. 1819, 90 L.Ed.2d 226 and particularly with its conclusion in _Dow_ that society is prepared to recognize as reasonable expectations of privacy in the curtilage, at 235, 106 S.Ct. at ——.

The second question under _Katz_ has been described as asking whether an expectation of privacy is "legitimate in the sense required by the Fourth Amendment." [FN4] *220_Oliver v. United States,_ 466 U.S. 170, 182, 104 S.Ct. 1735, 1742, 80 L.Ed.2d 214 (1984). The answer turns on "whether the government's intrusion infringes upon the personal and societal values protected by the Fourth Amendment." _Id.,_ at 182-183, 104 S.Ct., at 1743-1744. While no single consideration has been regarded as dispositive, "the Court has given weight to such factors as the intention of the Framers of the Fourth Amendment, ... the uses to which the individual has put a location, ... and our societal understanding that certain areas deserve the most scrupulous protection from government invasion." [FN5] _Id.,_ at 178, 104 S.Ct., at 1741. Our decisions have made clear that this inquiry often must be decided by "reference to a 'place,'" _Katz v. United States, supra,_ 389 U.S., at 361, 88 S.Ct., at 516 (Harlan, J., concurring); see _Payton v. New York,_ 445 U.S., at 589, 100 S.Ct., at 1381, and that a home is a place in which a subjective expectation of privacy virtually always will be legitimate, _ibid.;_ see, e.g., _United States v. Karo,_ 468 U.S. 705, 713-715, 104 S.Ct. 3296, 3302-3303, 82 L.Ed.2d 530 (1984); _Steagald v. United States,_ 451 U.S., at 211-212, 101 S.Ct., at 1647-1648. "At the very core [of the

Fourth Amendment] stands the right of a [person] to retreat into his own home and there be free from unreasonable governmental intrusion." *Silverman v. United States,* 365 U.S. 505, 511, 81 S.Ct. 679, 683, 5 L.Ed.2d 734 (1961).

> FN4. In Justice Harlan's classic description, an actual expectation of privacy is entitled to Fourth Amendment protection if it is an expectation that society recognizes as "reasonable." *Katz v. United States,* 389 U.S., at 361, 88 S.Ct., at 516 (Harlan, J., concurring). Since *Katz,* our decisions also have described constitutionally protected privacy interests as those that society regards as "legitimate," using the words "reasonable" and "legitimate" interchangeably. *E.g., Oliver v. United States,* 466 U.S. 170, 104 S.Ct. 1735, 80 L.Ed.2d 214 (1984); *Rakas v. Illinois,* 439 U.S. 128, 143-144, n. 12, 99 S.Ct. 421, 430, n. 12, 58 L.Ed.2d 387 (1978).
>
> FN5. "Legitimation of expectations of privacy by law must have a source outside of the Fourth Amendment, either by reference to concepts of real or personal property law or to understandings that are recognized and permitted by society." *Ibid.* This inquiry necessarily focuses on personal interests in privacy and liberty recognized by a free society.

B

This case involves surveillance of a home, for as we stated in *Oliver v. United States,* the curtilage "has been considered part of the home itself for Fourth Amendment purposes." 466 U.S., at 180, 104 S.Ct., at 1742. In *Dow Chemical Co. v. United States,* *221 decided today, the Court **1817 reaffirms that the "curtilage doctrine evolved to protect much the same kind of privacy as that covering the interior of a structure." *Post,* at 1825. The Court in *Dow* emphasizes, moreover, that society accepts as reasonable citizens' expectations of privacy in the area immediately surrounding their homes. *Ibid.*

In deciding whether an area is within the curtilage, courts "have defined the curtilage, as did the common law, by reference to the factors that determine whether an individual reasonably may expect that an area immediately adjacent to the home will remain private. See, *e.g., United States v. Van Dyke,* 643 F.2d 992, 993-994 (CA4 1981); *United States v. Williams,* 581 F.2d 451, 453 (CA5 1978); *Care v. United States,* 231 F.2d 22, 25 (CA10), cert. denied, 351 U.S. 932, 76 S.Ct. 788, 100 L.Ed. 1461 (1956)." *Oliver v. United States, supra,* 466 U.S., at 180, 104 S.Ct., at 1742. The lower federal courts have agreed that the curtilage is "an area of domestic use immediately surrounding a dwelling and usually but not always fenced in with the dwelling." [FN6] *United States v. LaBerge,* 267 F.Supp. 686, 692 (Md.1967); see *United States v. Van Dyke,* 643 F.2d 992, 993, n. 1 (CA4 1984). Those courts also have held that whether an area is within the curtilage must be decided by looking at all of the facts. *Ibid.*, citing *Care v. United States, supra,* at 25 (CA10 1956). Relevant facts include the proximity between the area claimed to be curtilage and the home, the nature of the uses to which the area is put, and the steps taken by the resident to protect the area from observation by people passing by. See *Care v. United States, supra,* at 25; see also *United States v. Van Dyke, supra,* at 993-994.

> FN6. The Oxford English Dictionary defines curtilage as "a small court, yard, garth, or piece of ground attached to a dwelling-house, and forming one enclosure with it, or so regarded by the law; the area attached to and containing a dwelling-house and its out-buildings." 2 Oxford English Dictionary 1278 (1933).

*222 III

A

The Court begins its analysis of the Fourth Amendment issue posed here by deciding that respondent had an expectation of privacy in his backyard. I agree with that conclusion because of the close proximity of the yard to the house, the nature of some of the activities respondent conducted there, [FN7] and because he had taken steps to shield those activities from the view of passersby. The Court then implicitly acknowledges that society is prepared to recognize his expectation as reasonable with respect to ground-level surveillance, holding that the yard was within the curtilage, an area in which privacy interests have been afforded the "most heightened" protection. *Ante,* at 1812. As the foregoing discussion of the curtilage doctrine demonstrates, respondent's yard unquestionably was within the curtilage. Since Officer Shutz could not see into this private family area from the street, the Court certainly would agree that he would have conducted an unreasonable search had he climbed over the fence, or used a ladder to peer into the yard without first securing a warrant. See *United States v. Van Dyke, supra;* see also *United States v. Williams, 581 F.2d 451 (CA 1978).*

> FN7. The Court omits any reference to the fact that respondent's yard contained a swimming pool and a patio for sunbathing and other private activities. At the suppression hearing, respondent sought to introduce evidence showing that he did use his yard for domestic activities. The trial court refused to consider that evidence. Tr. on Appeal 5-8 (Aug. 15, 1983).

The Court concludes, nevertheless, that Shutz could use an airplane- a product of modern technology-to intrude visually into respondent's yard. The Court argues that respondent had no reasonable expectation of privacy from aerial observation. It notes that Shutz was "within public navigable airspace," *ante,* at 1813, when he looked into and photographed*223 respondent's yard. It then relies on the fact that the surveillance was not accompanied by a **1818 physical invasion of the curtilage, *ibid*. Reliance on the *manner* of surveillance is directly contrary to the standard of *Katz*, which identifies a constitutionally protected privacy right by focusing on the interests of the individual and of a free society. Since *Katz*, we have consistently held that the presence or absence of physical trespass by police is constitutionally irrelevant to the question whether society is prepared to recognize an asserted privacy interest as reasonable. *E.g., United States v. United States District Court*, 407 U.S., at 313, 92 S.Ct., at 2134-2135.

The Court's holding, therefore, must rest solely on the fact that members of the public fly in planes and may look down at homes as they fly over them. *Ante*, at 1813. The Court does not explain why it finds this fact to be significant. One may assume that the Court believes that citizens bear the risk that air travelers will observe activities occurring within backyards that are open to the sun and air. This risk, the Court appears to hold, nullifies expectations of privacy in those yards even as to purposeful police surveillance from the air. The Court finds support for this conclusion in *United States v. Knotts*, 460 U.S. 276, 103 S.Ct. 1081, 75 L.Ed.2d 55 (1983). *Ante*, at 1812.

This line of reasoning is flawed. First, the actual risk to privacy from commercial or pleasure aircraft is virtually nonexistent. Travelers on commercial flights, as well as private planes used for business or personal reasons, normally obtain at most a fleeting, anonymous, and nondiscriminating glimpse of the landscape and buildings over which they pass.[FN8] The risk that a passenger on such a plane might observe *224 private activities, and might connect those activities with particular people, is simply too trivial to protect against. It is no accident that, as a matter of common experience, many people build fences around their residential areas, but few build roofs over their backyards. Therefore, contrary to the Court's suggestion, *ante*, at 1812, people do not " 'knowingly expos[e]' " their residential yards " 'to the public' " merely by failing to build barriers that prevent aerial surveillance.

> FN8. Of course, during takeoff and landing, planes briefly fly at low enough altitudes to afford fleeting opportunities to observe some types of activity in the curtilages of residents who live within the strictly regulated takeoff and landing zones. As all of us know from personal experience, at least in passenger aircrafts, there rarely-if ever-is an opportunity for a practical observation and photographing of unlawful activity similar to that obtained by Officer Shutz in this case. The Court's analogy to commercial and private overflights, therefore, is wholly without merit.

The Court's reliance on *Knotts* reveals the second problem with its analysis. The activities under surveillance in *Knotts* took place on public streets, not in private homes. 460 U.S., at 281-282, 103 S.Ct., at 1085-1086. Comings and goings on public streets are public matters, and the Constitution does not disable police from observing what every member of the public can see. The activity in this case, by contrast, took place within the private area immediately adjacent to a home. Yet the Court approves purposeful police surveillance of that activity and area similar to that approved in *Knotts* with respect to public activities and areas. The only possible basis for this holding is a judgment that the risk to privacy posed by the remote possibility that a private airplane passenger will notice outdoor activities is equivalent to the risk of official aerial surveillance.[FN9] But the Court fails to acknowledge the qualitative difference between police surveillance and other uses made of the airspace. Members of the public use the airspace for travel, **1819 business, or pleasure, not for the purpose of observing activities taking place within residential yards. Here, police conducted an overflight at low altitude solely for *225 the purpose of discovering evidence of crime within a private enclave into which they were constitutionally forbidden to intrude at ground level without a warrant. It is not easy to believe that our society is prepared to force individuals to bear the risk of this type of warrantless police intrusion into their residential areas.[FN10]

> FN9. Some of our precedents have held that an expectation of privacy was not reasonable in part because the individual had assumed the risk that certain kinds of private information would be turned over to the police. *United States v. Miller,* 425 U.S. 435, 443, 96 S.Ct. 1619, 1624, 48 L.Ed.2d 71 (1976). None of the prior decisions of this Court is a precedent for today's decision. As Justice MARSHALL has observed, it is our duty to be sensitive to the risks that a citizen "should be forced to assume in a free and open society." *Smith v. Maryland,* 442 U.S. 735, 750, 99 S.Ct. 2577, 2585, 61 L.Ed.2d 220, (1979) (dissenting opinion).
>
> FN10. The Court's decision has serious implications for outdoor family activities conducted in the curtilage of a home. The feature of such activities that makes them desirable to citizens living in a free society, namely, the fact that they occur in the open air and sunlight, is relied on by the Court as a justification for permitting police to conduct warrantless surveillance at will. Aerial surveillance is nearly as intrusive on family privacy as physical trespass into the curtilage. It would appear that, after today, families can expect to be free of official surveillance only when they retreat behind the walls of their homes.

B

Since respondent had a reasonable expectation of privacy in his yard, aerial surveillance undertaken by the police for the purpose of discovering evidence of crime constituted a "search" within the meaning of the Fourth Amendment. "Warrantless searches are presumptively unreasonable, though the Court has recognized a few limited exceptions to this general rule." _United States v. Karo_, 468 U.S., at 717, 104 S.Ct., at 3304. This case presents no such exception. The indiscriminate nature of aerial surveillance, illustrated by Officer Shutz' photograph of respondent's home and enclosed yard as well as those of his neighbors, poses "far too serious a threat to privacy interests in the home to escape entirely some sort of Fourth Amendment oversight." _Id._, at 716, 104 S.Ct., at 3304 (footnote omitted). Therefore, I would affirm the judgment of the California Court of Appeal ordering suppression of the marijuana plants.

IV

Some may believe that this case, involving no physical intrusion on private property, presents "the obnoxious thing in its mildest and least repulsive form." *226_Boyd v. United States_, 116 U.S., at 635, 6 S.Ct., at 535. But this Court recognized long ago that the essence of a Fourth Amendment violation is "not the breaking of [a person's] doors, and the rummaging of his drawers," but rather is "the invasion of his indefeasible right of personal security, personal liberty and private property." _Id._, at 630, 6 S.Ct., at 532. Rapidly advancing technology now permits police to conduct surveillance in the home itself, an area where privacy interests are most cherished in our society, without any physical trespass. While the rule in _Katz_ was designed to prevent silent and unseen invasions of Fourth Amendment privacy rights in a variety of settings, we have consistently afforded heightened protection to a person's right to be left alone in the privacy of his house. The Court fails to enforce that right or to give any weight to the longstanding presumption that warrantless intrusions into the home are unreasonable. [FN11] I dissent.

> FN11. Of course, the right of privacy in the home and its curtilage includes no right to engage in unlawful conduct there. But the Fourth Amendment requires police to secure a warrant before they may intrude on that privacy to search for evidence of suspected crime. _United States v. Karo_, 468 U.S. 705, 713-715, 104 S.Ct. 3296, 3302-3303, 82 L.Ed.2d 530 (1984).

U.S.Cal.,1986.
California v. Ciraolo
476 U.S. 207, 106 S.Ct. 1809, 90 L.Ed.2d 210, 54 USLW 4471
END OF DOCUMENT

Chapter 27

Ethics and Professionalism

"It isn't the mountain ahead that wears you out — it's the grain of sand in your shoe."

— Robert Service

"It is not what we do, but also what we do not do, for which we are accountable."

— Molière

When we became lawyers in the State of Florida, we raised our hands, as we were required by law to do, and repeated an *oath* in front of a judicial officer. We swore, *to God*, the following:

> *I DO SOLEMNLY SWEAR:*
>
> *I will support the Constitution of the United States and the Constitution of the State of Florida;*
>
> *I will maintain the respect due to courts of justice and judicial officers;*
>
> *I will not counsel or maintain any suit or proceedings which shall appear to me to be unjust, nor any defense except such as I believe to be honestly debatable under the law of the land;*
>
> *I will employ, for the purpose of maintaining the causes confided to me such means only as are consistent with truth and honor, and will never seek to mislead the judge or jury by any artifice or false statement of fact or law;*
>
> *I will maintain the confidence and preserve inviolate the secrets of my clients, and will accept no compensation in connection with their business except from them or with their knowledge and approval;*
>
> *To opposing parties and their counsel, I pledge fairness, integrity, and civility, not only in court, but also in all written and oral communications;*
>
> *I will abstain from all offensive personality and advance no fact prejudicial to the honor or reputation of a party or witness, unless required by the justice of the cause with which I am charged;*
>
> *I will never reject, from any consideration personal to myself, the cause of the defenseless or oppressed, or delay anyone's cause for lucre or malice. So help me God.*

As teachers, we recite this oath to our students the first day of class. We ask who among them have read and understood the federal and state constitutions and will swear to uphold them. (As beginning law students, most have read neither.) We ask who will swear to turn away from unjust causes and defend the defenseless, regardless of the price. We go through each of the promises the oath requires and ask who will uphold them. In doing so, we see in our students' faces the first glint of a sobering realization: this lawyering stuff is serious.

As possessors of, in John Grisham's words, "the power to sue," we take our oath and professional responsibilities to heart. Here, we cannot begin to cover all relevant ethical rules, which fill volumes and touch all areas of professional practice.[1]

We seek here simply to glimpse at what it means to be an ethical, "professional lawyer." The word "profession" comes from the Latin *professio*, meaning to have affirmed publicly. As one legal scholar has explained, "[t]he term refers to a group ... pursuing a learned art as a common calling in the spirit of public service—no less a public service because

---

1. In the United States, every jurisdiction has a formal code of ethics for lawyers, usually based upon the American Bar Association's Model Rules of Professional Conduct. The ABA, which is a voluntary organization for lawyers, does not govern the legal profession; rather, each jurisdiction governs the lawyers practicing in that jurisdiction. In addition, other sources of law regulate lawyer conduct, including the contempt power of courts, rules of procedure and evidence, federal and state administrative law, and of course, malpractice tort law.

it may incidentally be a means of livelihood. Pursuit of the learned art in the spirit of a public service is the primary purpose."[2] A professional traditionally means a person who has obtained a degree in a professional field and, based on the personal and confidential nature of a profession, is held to strict ethical and moral regulations. The term has evolved to describe occupations that require new entrants to take an oath professing their dedication to the ideals and practices associated with a learned calling.

Retired United States Supreme Court Justice Sandra Day O'Connor provided this definition of professionalism:

> To me, the essence of professionalism is a commitment to develop one's skills to the fullest and to apply them responsibly to the problems at hand. Profes-sionalism requires adherence to the highest ethical standards of conduct and a willingness to subordinate narrow self-interest in pursuit of the more fun-damental goal of public service. Because of the tremendous power they wield in our system, lawyers must never forget that their duty to serve their clients fairly and skillfully takes priority over the personal accumulation of wealth. At the same time, lawyers must temper bold advocacy for their clients with a sense of responsibility to the larger legal system which strives, however imperfectly, to provide justice for all.[3]

Former Chief Justice Harold Clarke of the Georgia Supreme Court offered this distinction between ethics and professionalism: "[E]thics is a minimum standard which is *required* of all lawyers while professionalism is a higher standard *expected* of all lawyers."[4]

Essentially, the rules of professional conduct establish *minimal* standards of propriety; they do not define the criteria for ethical behavior. In the traditional sense, persons are not "ethical" simply because they act lawfully or even within the bounds of an official code of ethics. To be ethical, professional lawyers, we must do more than merely follow what is required by law.

The definition of a professional lawyer, adopted by the Professional Committee of the Section of Legal Education and Admissions to the Bar of the American Bar Association, attempts to define this all-too-evasive ideal:

> "A professional lawyer is an expert in law pursuing a learned art in service to clients and in the spirit of public service; and engaging in these pursuits as part of a common calling to promote justice and public good."[5]

This Committee noted the following six characteristics as essential to a professional lawyer:

1. Learned knowledge;
2. Skill in applying the applicable law to the factual context;

---

2. Roscoe Pound, *The Lawyer from Antiquity to Modern Times* 5 (1953).

3. *Meaning of Professionalism*, A.B.A., Prof. Law., Spring, 1989, at 1.

4. John W. Spears, Editor, *Interview with Harold G. Clark, Chief Justice, Supreme Court of Georgia*, Decatur-Dekalb Bar Quarterly, May 24, 1990. *See also Evanoff v. Evanoff*, 418 S.E.2d 62, 63 (Ga. 1992) ("[E]thics is that which is required, and professionalism is that which is expected.").

5. Report of the Professionalism Committee, *Teaching and Learning Professionalism* 6 (1996).

3. Thoroughness of preparation;

4. Practical and prudential wisdom;

5. Ethical conduct and integrity; and

6. Dedication to justice and the public good.[6]

We think each of these characteristics merit further comment.[7]

1. ***Learned knowledge.*** As in life, ignorance of the law is no excuse. We owe our clients an absolute duty of competence. Where we lack competence, we have a duty to refer the case to, or work with, someone who is competent. In other words, if we don't know what we're doing, we have no business doing it.

2. ***Skill in applying the applicable law to the factual context.*** Not only must we know how to find the law, we've got to know what to do with it. We must know how to *reason*, *write*, and *argue*. But even those skills aren't enough.

We've got to know the practical side of practice: how to get to court, court rules, rules of practice, and etiquette. In essence, we must be prepared to file pleadings properly, oversee secretaries and clerical assistants, conduct discovery, engage in skillful negotiations with opposing counsel, and practice courtroom skills and decorum. All the substantive knowledge in the world doesn't mean a hill of beans if we can't apply it. As Aristotle opined: "With regard to excellence, it is not enough to know, but we must try to have and use it.... Excellence is an art won by training and habituation. We do not act rightly because we have virtue or excellence, but we rather have those because we have acted rightly. We are what we repeatedly do. Excellence, then, is not an act but a habit."

3. ***Thoroughness of preparation.*** As lawyers, we research every problem, even if we think we know the law. As we've seen, the law continually changes and evolves. Failure to research the law is malpractice. But our need to prepare doesn't end with the books.

Every aspect of law practice requires research and preparation. The safest, best, and most enjoyable way to represent every client is to always "be prepared" no matter what the task.

4. ***Practical and prudential wisdom.*** This characteristic calls to mind the old poker-playing adage — knowing "when to hold 'em and when to fold 'em." Not every wrong must be "righted" in a court of law. Sometimes the best advice to clients is to cut their losses and let go. Litigation is expensive, stressful, and can literally take over a client's life. The *client's* best interests, and not our personal gain, must be our polestar in all matters.

5. ***Ethical conduct and integrity.*** This characteristic must be our mantra in law practice. To every client, we owe our absolute loyalty, confidentiality, competence, and diligence.[8] As lawyers, we are officers of the court, and at all times must act ethically not only to our clients, but also towards our clients' opponents and their counsel, third parties involved in our clients' affairs, the public in general, and the legal justice system.

---

6. *Id.*

7. See Chapters 13, 14, and 15 for additional ethical requirements associated with writing documents to a court.

8. See Model Rules of Prof'l Conduct R. 1.1, 1.3, 1.6.

As professional lawyers, every action we take and every word we utter and write molds our reputation—for our entire careers. What we do, say, and write also reflects on our firm's reputation. As Abraham Lincoln is alleged to have said, "a lawyer's reputation is his stock in trade." We also like Socrates's thoughts on the matter:

> Regard your good name as the richest jewel you can possibly be possessed of— for credit is like fire; when once you have kindled it you may easily preserve it, but if you once extinguish it, you will find it an arduous task to rekindle it again. The way to gain a good reputation is to endeavor to be what you desire to appear.[9]

Satisfying our duty of ethical conduct to these various entities sounds fine in the abstract, but in practice, can sometimes require a delicate balancing act. We're all aware of the maxim that as lawyers we should zealously represent our clients. This means, however, doing so within the rules of professional responsibility and within the law. But what if zealously representing our client conflicts with our duty to the legal system or to society? On the other hand, isn't a lawyer's duty to the system and society best performed through zealous representation of the client? Unfortunately, the ethical rules in most jurisdictions usually fail to provide clear guidelines on how to resolve these conflicts.[10] The bottom line is that there are no easy answers—we just have to do our very best on a situation-to-situation basis. When in doubt, the following advice from a practitioner should be our default position: "If it turns your stomach even a little bit, don't do it. Period."[11]

We can't leave the topic of ethical conduct without a word or two about civility. Whether or not civility is a specific requirement in any of the ethical canons, we think practicing civility elevates our conduct from merely being ethical to being *professional*. Thus, in addition to ethical conduct, we owe civility to everyone we encounter in law practice, including our opposing counsel. Some lawyers take the approach that litigation is all about winning, but in practice, we learned it's best (and far less stressful) to "play nice." We likely will get what we give. Always saying "no" to reasonable requests from opposing counsel will get us a reputation for being churlish, and result in our fellow lawyers being churlish with us in return. Instead, we learned to try to work out difficulties with opposing counsel—giving a little and getting a little—saving our clients money and saving our own sanity in the bargain.

6. *Dedication to justice and the public good.* Because our ethics must extend beyond just representing our clients, in *every* aspect of our lives we must strive "to do well and to be good." This ethos may require us to engage in *pro bono* work—that is, representing a client without charging a fee, "for the public good." As Désiré-Joseph Cardinal Mercier said: "We must not only give what we *have*; we must also give what we *are*."[12]

---

9. Greek philosopher in Athens (469 BC–399 BC).

10. Note that we can sometimes obtain an "ethics" opinion from our jurisdiction's bar association regarding ethical dilemmas.

11. Mark Herrmann, *The Curmudgeon's Guide to Practicing Law*, 124 (2006). Copyright © 2006 by ABA Publishing. We add that this is a terrific little book which we encourage you to read before beginning the practice of law.

12. Belgian cardinal and educator 1851-1926.

7. *Communication with clients.* We think one final characteristic is essential, and we'll add it to the list: communication with clients.[13] Many, many problems arise from a simple failure to communicate. Communication, it goes without saying (but we'll say it anyway!), involves the fine art of listening as well as talking. This means really listening to what our client has to say and keeping our client informed. We'll say it again — communication is key, as this "war story" illustrates:

One of us once represented a client, a lawyer, who was being sued for malpractice for failing to take *any* action on behalf of his client. The lawyer asserted that he didn't think his firm had undertaken to represent the client. It seems the lawyer had met once with the client, listened to the client's problem, and told the client that he would represent him if the client signed an agreement for representation and provided a retainer. The client did neither, but in a few months, began to send letters asking to hear what progress the lawyer was making on the case. The lawyer, a busy man, was peeved and simply ignored the letters. Eventually, the client sued the lawyer.

We obtained a summary judgment on the lawyer's behalf, but not before valuable time and money had been expended. The whole situation could have been nipped in the bud if the lawyer had responded to the client's letters, inquiring about the signed agreement and retainer. The lawyer learned the hard way Henry W. Longfellow's admonishment: "It takes less time to do a thing right, than it does to explain why you did it wrong."[14]

We end with the best advice we've seen on professionalism and ethics. It comes from attorney Richard S. Masington's "20 Rules for Ethical Behavior," printed in the Florida Bar News.[15] Here they are (we especially like the last one):

1. Behave yourself.
2. Answer the phone.
3. Return your phone calls.
4. Pay your bills.
5. Keep your hands off your client's money.
6. Tell the truth.
7. Admit ignorance.
8. Be honorable.
9. Defend the honor of fellow lawyers.
10. Be gracious and thoughtful.
11. Value the time of your brothers and sisters of the Bar.
12. Give straight answers.
13. Avoid the need to go to court.
14. Think first.

---

13. See Model Rules of Prof'l Conduct R. 1.4.

14. American poet 1807-1882.

15. Florida Bar News, April 1, 1998. We thank Mr. Masington for permitting us to reprint this list.

15. Define your goals:

    (a) Remember that you are first a professional and then a businessman.

    (b) If you seek riches, become a businessman (and hire a lawyer).

16. Remember: There is no such thing as billing 3,000 hours per year.

17. Tell your clients how to behave; if they can't, they don't deserve to have you for a lawyer, and you won't stand for it.

18. Solve problems—don't become a part of the problem.

19. Have ideals you believe in.

20. Tell your mother what you did.

We add one more: If you wouldn't want it done to you, don't you do it.

Section V

The Basics: Designing Clear and Effective Writing

"[A] writer must disguise his art and give the impression of speaking naturally and not artificially. Naturalness is persuasive, artificiality is the contrary...."

—Aristotle's *Rhetoric*

"Keep it simple, stupid."

—Anonymous

In this section, we review the **BASICS** of writing:

B	A	S	I	C	S
Brevity	Artistry	Simplicity	Impact	Cohesion	Style
Chapter 28	Chapter 29	Chapter 30	Chapter 31	Chapter 32	Chapter 33

We deal here with those areas of writing most relevant to legal analysis, discussion, and argument. By becoming familiar with the *designs* addressed, we improve not only the form, but also the content, of our writing. For ease of reference, we've written most of this **Section** in lists or short paragraphs, rather than in a narrative.

Chapter 28

Brevity

§ 28.1   Keep Sentences Short

"[S]ome sentences enjoy all the virtues of grammatical clarity yet remain wordy and graceless. Even when [we] arrange their grammatical bones in all the right ways, they can still succumb to acute prolixity:

> The point I want to make here is that we can see that American policy in regard to foreign countries as the State Department in Washington and the White House have put it together and made it public to the world has given material and moral support to too many foreign factions in other countries that have controlled power and have then had to give up the power to other factions that have defeated them.

That is,

> Our foreign policy has backed too many losers."

—Joseph M. Williams[1]

Important sentences should be short and clear. If a sentence drags, our reader loses energy. If we can't read our sentence aloud in one breath, the sentence likely is too long.

But, of course, for every rule, there's an exception. Take, for example, the following sentences, containing 54 and 66 words, respectively, written by Karl Llewellyn:

> There is the man who loves creativeness, who can without loss of sleep combine risk-taking with responsibility, who sees and feels institutions as things built and to be built to serve functions, and who sees the functions as vital and law as a tool to be eternally reoriented to justice and to general welfare. There is the other man who loves order, who finds risk uncomfortable and has seen so much irresponsible or unwise innovation that responsibility to him means caution, who sees and feels institutions as the tested, slow-built ways which for all their faults are man's sole safeguard against relapse into barbarism, and who regards reorientation of the law in our polity as essentially committed to the legislature.[2]

The bottom line: if we can write like Llewellyn, then we shouldn't follow the "keep it to a single breath" rule; if we can't, the rule applies.

§ 28.2   Eliminate Throat-Clearing Phrases

Many writers believe they must introduce sentences or paragraphs with such "throat-clearing" phrases as "importantly, we should bear in mind that," "a point which the court should consider is," etc. Introductions are important because they ease our reader's mind towards a new idea. However, "empty" introductions like these don't convey information, and they don't tie the new idea to a familiar one. They just waste space.

---

1. Joseph M. Williams, *Style: Ten Lessons in Clarity & Grace* 82 (3d ed. 1989).

2. Karl Llewellyn, *Remarks on the Theory of Appellate Decision and the Rules or Canons About How Statutes are to be Construed*, 3 Vand. L. Rev. 395, 397 (1950).

Instead of saying, "Importantly, we should bear in mind that," we say something *substantive*. For example: "Factors which the court addressed included...." We give our reader information, not empty phrases.

Expletives ("it is," "there are") are also often empty, "throat-clearing" introductions. Instead of saying, "*There are* three people planning to devour the hamburgers," we state, "Three people plan to devour the hamburgers." In doing so, we start our sentence with the subject, rather than with an empty phrase.

§ 28.3   Eliminate "Clearly" and "Obviously"

"Clearly" and "obviously" are almost never appropriate because they serve no useful function. If a point were clear or obvious, we probably wouldn't need to address it. Clearly and obviously we should try to remove such words from our sentences, obviously.

§ 28.4   Eliminate Unnecessary "Hedging" Words

When we can make an unqualified statement, we should do so. Although we'll have to qualify some statements, lawyers often qualify even when it's not necessary, putting "it appears" or "would seem to" into the most straightforward sentences. For example:

> "The evidence *would seem to* contradict the defendant's explanation of his activities."

Well, either it does or it doesn't. If it does, we should say it does.

Usually, lawyers qualify a statement because we're concerned that additional information may render an unqualified statement false. In the example above, the writer may fear that the defendant will later submit a response that will make his explanation consistent with the evidence. If this fear is real, the writer should make the unqualified statement first and then qualify it specifically, e.g.,

> "The evidence contradicts the explanation the defendant offered at the time of his arrest."

§ 28.5   Eliminate Surplus Words

> "Vigorous writing is concise. A sentence should contain no unnecessary words, a paragraph no unnecessary sentences, for the same reason that a drawing should have no unnecessary lines and a machine no unnecessary parts. This requires not that the writer make all his sentences short, or that he avoid all detail and treat his subjects only in outline, but that every word tell."
>
> — Strunk and White[3]

---

3. William Strunk, Jr. and E.B. White, *The Elements of Style* 23 (3d ed. 1979).

"Let thy words be few."

—Ecclesiastes 5:2

The most persuasive briefs and memos are clear and to the point. The words are "few" and those few words "tell." Listed below are common, verbose phrases and suggested ways to write them in a simplified, direct manner.

Graphic 28.5(a)	Use the Simplest Word	
"Use the "bolded" word instead of the words or phrases below the bolded word.		

about	**during**	**probably**
concerning the matter	during the course of	in all likelihood
in reference to		
in regard to	**for**	**should**
in relation to	for the period of	it is important that
with reference to	in favor of	there is a need for
with regard to		
	from	**sometimes**
after	from the point of view of	in some instances
subsequent to	on the basis of	
		then
as	**he**	at that point in time
as far as	he is a person who	
under the classification of		**there**
	here	an instance in which
although	in this case	
despite the fact that	in this instance	**thus**
notwithstanding the fact		for these reasons,
regardless of the fact that	**if**	for this reason
	in the event that	
because		**to**
as a result of the fact that	**in**	for the purpose of
because of the fact that	in terms of	in order to
considering the fact that	in the case of	with a view to
before	**knew**	**until**
before such time as	was aware of the fact that	until such time as,
prior to		
	like	**usually**
by	in the nature of	in the majority of instances
by means of		
in accordance with	**may**	**when**
on the basis of	has the option of	in a situation in which
	it could happen that	in case of
can		on the occasion of
has the ability to	**must**	under circumstances in which
has the capacity for	it is critical that	
has the opportunity to	it is necessary that	**where**
is able to		a situation where
is in a position to	**now**	
	at this point in time	**whether**
		a question as to whether
	often	
	in many instances	**with**
		in connection with

| Graphic 28.5(b) | | Replace Redundant Phrases | |

Time

from	to	from	to
11:00 p.m. at night	11:00 p.m.	early in time	early
12:00 noon	noon	everlasting eternity	eternity
12:00 midnight	midnight	future plan	plan
a period of three months	three months	late time	late
all too soon	soon	never at any time	never
at a later time	later	never before	
at an earlier time	earlier	never since	
at the present time	now	period of time	period
during the course of	during	past history	history
during the day of		plan ahead	plan
during the month of		postponed until later	postponed
during the year of		reflect back	reflect

Distance

from	to
a distance of thirty feet	thirty feet
an area of ten feet	ten feet

Amount

from	to
all of the appellants	all appellants
absolutely everything	everything
absolutely nothing	nothing
both of them	both
each and every	each
each separate	
few in number	few
not very many	
neither of them	neither

Direction

from	to
ascend up	ascend
descend down	descend
revert back	revert
rotate around	rotate

Action

from	to	from	to
acquitted on a charge of	acquitted	merge together	merge
anticipate in advance	anticipate	over exaggerate	exaggerate
argued before the court	argued	permeate throughout	permeate
asked a question	asked	pled guilty to a charge of	pled guilty to
by means of	by	probed into	probed
by reason of		protested against	protested
by virtue of		reiterate again	reiterate, repeat
combine together	combine	suddenly exploded	exploded
completely destroy	destroy	unexpected surprise	surprise
eradicate completely	eradicate	vote in favor of	vote for
indicted on a charge of	indicted	vote in opposition to	vote against
join together	join	without any reason	without reason

Place

from	to
alongside of	alongside
separate and apart from	separate from, apart from

Description

from	to	from	to
a rough estimate	estimate	final aims	aims
absolutely clear	clear	final ultimate outcome	outcome
absolutely true	true	foreign import	import
actual experience	experience	free gift	gift
basic fundamentals	basics	general public	public
bright in color	bright	heavy in weight	heavy
cheap quality	cheap	initial preparation	preparation
confused state	confused	integral part	part
current trend	trend	large in size	large
dishonest in character	dishonest	minor child	child
empty space	space	my own personal opinion	my opinion
end result	result	odd in appearance	odd
expensively priced	expensive	personal friend	friend
extreme in degree	extreme	red in color	red
false pretenses	pretenses	rough in feeling	rough

from	to	from	to
round in shape	round	temporary reprieve	reprieve
shiny appearance	shiny	terrible tragedy	tragedy
specific example	example	true fact	fact
strange type of	strange	usual custom	custom
sudden crisis	crisis	various different	various
sworn testimony at trial	testimony		

Effect

from	to
because of the fact that	because
despite the fact that	despite
except for the fact that	except

Not only can we reduce "wordiness" by replacing a long word or phrase with a shorter one, we can also omit some phrases entirely.

Graphic 28.5(c)	Omit Unnecessary Phrases	
phrase to omit	example of unnecessary phrase in sentence	revised sentence
in order to	He left in order to avoid her.	He left to avoid her.
as everyone knows it is important to note that it must be remembered that it should be noted that it is important that it should be emphasized that it is significant that it would appear that the defendant submits that the defendant asserts that	It is important to note that he left.	He left.
the fact of the matter the heart of the matter	The fact of the matter is that he left.	He left.
it is obvious that it is clear that	It is obvious that he left.	He left.
it is believed that it is generally believed that it is felt that	It is believed that he left to avoid her.	He left to avoid her.

phrase to omit	example of unnecessary phrase in sentence	revised sentence
it is essential that it is crucial that it is critical that	It is essential that he leave.	He must leave.
the basis of before the court	The basis of your argument before the court was that the defendant had left.	You argued that the defendant had left.
Mr.; Mrs.; Ms.; and other titles (if omitting the titles would not be disrespectful)	Mr. Smith and Ms. Jones left.	Smith and Jones left.
in this next section in regard to the next argument	In this next section, we will address the fact that he left.	Moreover, he left.

The following examples illustrate how slight changes in word choice can streamline our writing. Be especially on guard, for example, for phrases taking the following design: "the A *of* B" *such as* "*the conviction of Doe.*" *We can save space and streamline our writing simply by stating* "B's A, *or* "*Doe's conviction.*"

We've included numerous examples of "wordiness" because we believe *bloated* writing is one of the modern plagues. Verbal baggage weighs down ideas, makes sentences sluggish, and drives readers crazy. We implore you to "lighten the load."

Graphic 28.5(d)	Examples of Streamlining Writing
from	**to**
The court emphasized the fact that Doe had been engaged in negligent conduct.	The court emphasized Doe's negligence.
Rod Smith highlighted the issues which were relevant.	Rod Smith highlighted the relevant issues.
The Code, which was enacted in 1990, is applicable to Doe.	The Code, enacted in 1990, applies to Doe.
In order to be held in violation of the Code, one must beg on a street in the City.	To violate the Code, one must beg on a City street.
After it makes a decision regarding a case, the court usually issues an opinion in writing.	After deciding a case, the court usually issues a written opinion.
The begging Doe engaged in was entitled to protection under the First Amendment.	Doe's begging was protected under the First Amendment.
This Court should follow the reasoning of the court in *Young* in the instant case.	This Court should follow the *Young* court's reasoning.

from	to
In one case which deals with the question of whether or not begging can be considered to be expressive conduct, the Federal Second Circuit Court of Appeals	In deciding whether begging is expressive conduct, the Second Circuit
The court found in this manner because	The court decided
In reaching its determination, the Court pointed out	The Court reasoned
Case law as to just what constitutes inherently expressive conduct is somewhat unclear, but in general, it can be stated that the United States Supreme Court has in some instances extended protection to conduct which gives expression to at least a generalized feeling or emotion.	The Court has recognized that conduct which expresses at least a generalized feeling or emotion is inherently expressive.
In *Hurley v. Irish-American Gay, Lesbian, and Bisexual Group*, [citation], one case which illustrates that conduct can be within the inherently expressive conduct classification, the United States Supreme Court made the determination that a parade was an inherently expressive act.	The Court has recognized that conduct, even a parade, can be inherently expressive. *See Hurley v. Irish-American Gay, Lesbian, and Bisexual Group*, [citation].
The Court did state with regards to begging	The Court stated that begging
When evaluating this argument, it is important to keep in mind that this Court should	This Court should
Applying the reasoning of the case of *Village of Schaumburg* to the instant case, the conduct of Doe does not appear to qualify for protection as charitable solicitation. Applying the reasoning of *Village of Schaumburg*, this Court should conclude that Doe's conduct was not charitable solicitation.	Applying the reasoning of *Village of Schaumburg*, this Court should conclude that Doe's conduct was not charitable solicitation.
The conduct of Doe should not be found to fall within the scope of this doctrine. This Court should conclude that Doe's conduct does not fall within this doctrine.	This Court should conclude that Doe's conduct does not fall within this doctrine.
The test to be used in determining whether or not the interest was implicated would be to conduct an examination of the facts and see if the interest of the government was in any manner impaired to a significant degree.	In deciding whether the interest was implicated, this Court should first examine whether the governmental interest was significantly impaired.

from	to
The next step in the determination of whether or not the conviction of Doe should stand involves making a determination as to whether or not the Code is content-based or content-neutral and this Court should find that it is content-based.	This Court should find that the Code is content-based.
The lower court in the instant case here made the finding that the Pedestrian Interference Code was applied to Doe in a manner that was content-neutral in fashion. This instant Court should also uphold that finding of the lower court and make the decision that the Code, being content-neutral, should therefore be subjected to the time, place, and manner test for the determination of whether or not it is a restriction that is reasonable on the right to freedom of speech.	This Court should conclude, as did the trial court, that the City applied the Pedestrian Interference Code to Doe in a content-neutral manner. Accordingly, this Court should subject the Code to time, place, and manner review.
Applying the test to the instant case of Doe, it becomes absolutely clear that the conduct of Doe was not in any way expressive.	This Court should conclude that Doe's conduct was not expressive.
The appeal of Doe of his conviction under the Pedestrian Interference Code of Gotham City should be upheld because Doe cannot challenge with any success the Code on the grounds of the First Amendment.	Upholding Doe's conviction, this Court should conclude that Doe has no First Amendment claim here.

Strunk and White explain that another way of streamlining our writing is to use a concise sentence combining several ideas, rather than to present "a single complex idea, step-by-step, in a series of sentences...." Here is their example of "wordiness" and a rewritten, less verbose version:[4]

Graphic 28.5(e)	Example of Streamlining by Combining Several Related Ideas in One Sentence
verbose	**concise**
"Macbeth was very ambitious. This led him to wish to become king of Scotland. The witches told him that this wish of his would come true. The king of Scotland at this time was Duncan. Encouraged by his wife, Macbeth murdered Duncan. He was thus enabled to succeed Duncan as king. (51 words)"	"Encouraged by his wife, Macbeth achieved his ambition and realized the prediction of the witches by murdering Duncan and becoming king of Scotland in his place. (26 words)"

---

4. Strunk and White, *supra*, at 25.

§ 28.6   Make Affirmative Statements

As these examples show, making affirmative statements also shortens our writing.

Graphic 28.6	Compare

negative	positive
did not grant	denied
did not consider	ignored, overlooked
did not remain the entire time	left early
did not accept	rejected
did not remember	forgot
was not honest	dishonest
had no trust in	distrusted
did not assert rights in	waived
not old enough	too young
did not allow	prohibited
not possible	impossible
not probable	improbable
did not arrive on time	was late
did not have	lacked
did not affirm the case	reversed, overruled
did not violate the provision	honored, complied
not the same	different
not able	unable
not certain	uncertain
could not alter	unalterable
was not secured	unsecured
could not be obtained	unobtainable
did not forward	retained
did not honor the provision	violated
was not occupied	vacant
was not prepared	unprepared
was not included	omitted
was not read	unread
was not written	unwritten
was not spoken	unspoken
did not know	unaware

§ 28.7   Exercises

Exercise 1.

Streamline the following sentences and phrases, without looking at the graphic from which they derive. When you've given them your best shot, then see how you've done.

1. The court emphasized the fact that Doe had been engaged in negligent conduct.

2. Rod Smith highlighted the issues which were relevant.

3. The Code, which was enacted in 1990, is applicable to Doe.

4. In order to be held in violation of the Code, one must beg on a street in the City.

5. After it makes a decision regarding a case, the court usually issues an opinion in writing.

6. The begging Doe engaged in was entitled to protection under the First Amendment.

7. This Court should follow the reasoning of the court in *Young* in the instant case.

8. In one case which deals with the question of whether or not begging can be considered to be expressive conduct, the Federal Second Circuit Court of Appeals

9. The court found in this manner because

10. In reaching its determination, the Court pointed out

11. Case law as to just what constitutes inherently expressive conduct is somewhat unclear, but in general, it can be stated that the United States Supreme Court has in some instances extended protection to conduct which gives expression to at least a generalized feeling or emotion.

12. In *Hurley v. Irish-American Gay, Lesbian, and Bisexual Group*, [citation], one case which illustrates that conduct can be within the inherently expressive conduct classification, the United States Supreme Court made the determination that a parade was an inherently expressive act.

13. The Court did state with regards to begging

14. When evaluating this argument, it is important to keep in mind that this Court should

15. Applying the reasoning of the case of *Village of Schaumburg* to the instant case, the conduct of Doe does not appear to qualify for protection as charitable solicitation.

16. The conduct of Doe should not be found to fall within the scope of this doctrine.

17. The test to be used in determining whether or not the interest was implicated would be to conduct an examination of the facts and see if the interest of the government was in any manner impaired to a significant degree.

18. The next step in the determination of whether or not the conviction of Doe should stand involves making a determination as to whether or not the Code is

content-based or content-neutral and this Court should find that it is content-based.

19. The lower court in the instant case here made the finding that the Pedestrian Interference Code was applied to Doe in a manner that was content-neutral in fashion. This instant Court should also uphold that finding of the lower court and make the decision that the Code, being content-neutral should therefore be subjected to the time, place, and manner test for the determination of whether or not it is a restriction that is reasonable on the right to freedom of speech.

20. Applying the test to the instant case of Doe, it becomes absolutely clear that the conduct of Doe was not in any way expressive.

21. The appeal of Doe of his conviction under the Pedestrian Interference Code of Gotham City should be upheld because Doe cannot challenge with any success the Code on the grounds of the First Amendment.

Exercise 2.

Your task is to write two versions of a letter asking someone (parent, friend, whomever) for money. In the first version, be as wordy, unclear, obtuse (you get the idea) as possible. In the second version, edit the first version to create a streamlined, beautifully edited masterpiece of persuasion.

Chapter Review
Brevity

✓ Are sentences short and to the point?

✓ Can we break long sentences into shorter ones?

✓ Can we omit "throat-clearing" phrases or replace them with phrases conveying information?

Throat-clearing: "it is important to bear in mind that"; "we shall next turn to"; "a point to consider is whether."

✓ Can we omit "clearly" and "obviously"?

✓ Can we eliminate *unnecessary* "hedging" words? (This, of course, depends on whether we're writing a brief or a memo.) But even in a memo, can we be more certain of our conclusions?

Hedging words: "it appears"; "the evidence would seem to"; "the case more or less."

✓ Have we used the simplest word to convey our thought? For example: "by," instead of "in accordance with"?

✓ Have we eliminated redundant phrases? For example: "later," instead of "at a later time."

✓ Have we eliminated unnecessary phrases? For example: "in order to," "it is significant that," "it would appear that."

✓ Have we streamlined our writing? Where appropriate, have we combined several related ideas into one sentence?

Bloated: "in violation of"; "made a decision that"; "is applicable to"; "can be considered to be."

✓ Have we made affirmative statements? For example: "waived," instead of "did not assert rights in."

Chapter 29

Artistry: Choosing the Right Words and Phrases

> "Be still when you have nothing to say; when genuine passion moves you, say what you've got to say, and say it hot."
>
> —D. H. Lawrence

Carefully selecting words is critical in writing persuasively. In writing a predictive memo, we choose words that are fair, balanced, and impartial. However, in writing a persuasive brief, we go for the jugular. Our words are forceful and concrete. We take a stand through the language we use. We write to win.

For example, we might write the following in a memo: "Plaintiff's theory of recovery probably cannot be supported by existing case law." However, we would never put that statement in a brief. It's far too imprecise, too wishy-washy. Instead, we'd take a stand and, if the law supports us, write: "Plaintiff has advanced a position which has no basis in the law and which ignores long-established principles to the contrary."

The following general rules help us select the most effective wording for conveying our thoughts.

§ 29.1   Replace Abstract Words, Phrases, and Concepts with Concrete Examples

Concrete, graphic, and familiar words will most persuasively convey our message. The more specific and concrete the language, the more easily our reader will understand and accept our point. For example, let's compare the following:

Graphic 29.1(a)	Use Concrete Words
abstract	On the reduced income, the family often went hungry.
concrete	Because of the layoff, the family often had to share a bowl of rice for dinner, make a quart of milk last a week, and finally eat Old Bessy.
abstract	The defendant acted rudely to the plaintiff.
concrete	The defendant, extending his middle finger defiantly in the air in the plaintiff's direction shouted: "Mark, you are a cheap, conniving, low-down, pig. We were saving poor Old Bessy for Thanksgiving."
abstract	He exhibited great satisfaction in his action of devouring the meat near the bone.
concrete	He grinned as he gnawed on Old Bessy's bones.

Unavoidably, some legal concepts are abstract—i.e., "equality," "negligence," "injustice," "malice," and "duty." And when a legal concept employs an adjective, things really get murky: "reasonable," "premeditated," "aggravated." Although we can't avoid using these words, we can make them as concrete as possible by tying them to the specific facts of our case. As the following series of statements demonstrates, the more concrete the statement, the more persuasive it becomes.

Graphic 29.1(b)	Add Detail to Create a Concrete Image
vaguest	The defendant violated his duty to the plaintiff.
vague	The defendant violated his duty to warn the plaintiff.
better	The defendant violated his duty to warn the plaintiff of a hidden danger.
best	The defendant violated his duty to warn the plaintiff that Old Bessy had been exposed to Mad Cow disease.

§ 29.2   Use Nouns and Verbs Rather than Adjectives and Adverbs

We make our writing more concrete by using descriptive nouns and verbs rather than adverbs and adjectives. In the examples above, we convey abstract concepts by adverbs (hungry, rudely). In the concrete examples, we use nouns (rice, milk, meat, finger) and verbs (share, extended) to create a more vivid picture.

§ 29.2(a)   Use Forceful Nouns Instead of Intensifying Adjectives

"The adjective is the enemy of the noun."

—Voltaire

Some nouns are stronger than others because they're more graphic, more expressive, or convey a more intense concept. Instead of using these strong nouns, however, we may tend to modify a noun with an intensifying adjective ("strong," "great"). We do this because it's easier to tack on an adjective rather than to think up a more descriptive noun. But, rather than using an adjective to strengthen a weak noun, we heed Voltaire's warning and use a stronger noun instead.

The problem with intensifying adjectives (i.e., very, great) is that they're not at all subtle. Instead of quietly manipulating our gentle reader, they hit him or her over the head with a very great clunk. Adjectives are most effective when we use them merely to describe or to define a noun and not to add emotional intensity.

For example, we may describe a voyage by using adjectives such as "difficult" "terrible," or "painful." However, if we want to convey the arduousness of the voyage, we use a stronger noun. "Expedition" or "ordeal" portray a more vivid image than "difficult voyage." Here are some more examples of using stronger nouns instead of intensifying adjectives:

Graphic 29.2(a)	Use Strong Nouns
weak noun with intensifying adjective	**strong nouns**
great wrong	evil, outrage
a wide view	panorama
great malice	hatred, malevolence
an extremely bad occurrence	disaster, tragedy, catastrophe
great pain	agony, anguish, torment, law school

§ 29.2(b)   Use the Most Forceful Verbs

Verbs carry the action in a sentence, and we choose them with care. They provide the most subtle, and thus the most effective, coloration for our sentences. Statements may be "affirmed" (implies trust), "asserted" (neutral), "alleged" (implies doubt), or "claimed" (weakest yet). The verb "sever" for example, makes a stronger impression than the verbs "cut" or "break." Thus, in editing our writing, we carefully review all verbs to confirm that they convey the impression we intend.

§ 29.2(c)   Replace Forms of "To Be" with More Concrete Verbs

Replacing forms of "to be" (is, am, are, was, were) with more forceful verbs strengthens our sentences. For example:

Graphic 29.2(c)	Replace "To Be" Forms
weak	He was very upset when Old Bessy died.
stronger	He sobbed uncontrollably when Old Bessy died.

In editing our drafts, we should circle every form of "to be." By doing so, we identify these weak verbs and, where appropriate, replace them with stronger ones. We address this concept further below.

§ 29.3   Use Active Voice

The term "active voice" really means "active verbs." To write in active voice is to use the structure "subject-verb-object" (s-v-o). For example, in the sentence: "The family devoured Old Bessy," the "family" is the subject, while "Old Bessy" is the object of the sentence and the (unfortunate) recipient of the verb's action.

Let's compare this structure (s-v-o) with the passive voice: "Old Bessy was devoured by the family." Here, we have a "subject-verb-prepositional phrase" (s-v-p) construction. This passive voice construction weakens the action of the sentence.

However, using the passive voice is a wonderful way to deny responsibility. After all, we can omit the actor from the sentence. For example, we could write, "Old Bessy was devoured." Who devoured her? Who knows? The sentence doesn't tell us. The culprit remains at large.

Graphic 29.3(a)	More Examples of Passive Voice	
A tape of the secret meeting was leaked to the press.	**Who leaked it?**	
Procedures have been followed.	**Who followed them?**	
Old Bessy's bones will be donated to the K-9 club.	**Who will donate them?**	

Although passive voice is appropriate in some circumstances (we discuss those below) it generally weakens the "oomph" value of our sentences. It's wishy-washy. It ducks responsibility. It hides or de-emphasizes the actor. In law, especially in brief writing, we need to know "who did what to whom." Passive voice doesn't do a good job of telling us. It leaves too many questions unanswered, and ambiguity is the antithesis of persuasion.

Graphic 29.3(b)	Put Actors in Sentences
ambiguous	**actor added**
The Code was enacted. (Who enacted it?)	The City enacted the Code.
Doe was held to be in violation of the Code. (Who so held?)	The court held that Doe violated the Code.

Graphic 29.3(c)	And, Make Certain the Actor *Can* Act
The Code sentenced Doe to 90 days in jail. (Can the Code really do that?)	The court sentenced Doe to 90 days in jail.

An easy way to identify passive voice is to circle every "was" or any form of "to be" followed by a verb. To make the sentence active, we omit the "to be" form and, if necessary, add an actor. This is exactly what we've done in the following examples:

Graphic 29.3(d)	Changing Passive Voice to Active Voice	
passive voice		**active voice**
A tape of the secret meeting was leaked to the press.	Who leaked it?	The gremlin leaked a tape of the secret meeting to the press.
Procedures have been followed.	Who followed them?	The vampires followed procedures.
Old Bessy's bones will be donated to the K-9 club.	Who will donate them?	Ralph will donate Old Bessy's bones to the K-9 club.

Bureaucrats, probably more than lawyers, use the passive voice to deny responsibility or to sound like they're not committing themselves. But passive voice is not inherently "bad." Indeed, it's appropriate in the following two circumstances:

Graphic 29.3(e)	Where Passive Voice Is Appropriate
circumstance	**example**
When we *cannot* determine the actor.	Evidence demonstrated that Old Bessy was milked every morning at sunrise.
When the demands of persuasion, etiquette, or good taste require us to conceal or minimize the actor.	A decision was made to terminate Old Bessy.

§ 29.4   Use Base Verbs: Death to Derivative Nouns!

Never use a noun where a verb will do. While verbs concretely convey actions, nouns slothfully signify abstractions. "Complain," we understand; "made a complaint," we ponder.

C. Edward Good in *Mightier Than the Sword* brilliantly illustrated this concept in the following passage:[1]

> Because I am dealing with a mature audience, I feel safe in using my favorite example of nouniness. The noun form wants to avoid issues. The noun form shies away from telling it like it is. The noun form plays it safe and shies away. You don't believe me? Then find a socially acceptable verb describing the sex act. Not out loud, please. The verb form is much too graphic, clinical, or nasty. Instead of [verb]ing, people *make love.* Instead of [verb]ing, people *have relations* or *have sex* or *engage in intercourse.* Never do they [verb]. The closest we've come in the language to [verb]ing, I guess, is the verb *do.* But to tone it down, we follow *do* with the indefinite pronoun *it.*

Here's a trick to help us stop transforming (i.e., nominalizing) the marvelous verb into a run-of-the-mill noun: don't add the following endings to verbs:

Graphic 29.4(a)		Don't Add These Endings to Verbs		
-al	-ance	-ancy	-ant	-ence
-ency	-ent	-ion	-ity	-ment
		Example		
weak	He had a preference for the meat in close *proximity* to the bone.			
stronger	He *preferred* the meat near the bone.			

---

1. C. Edward Good, *Mightier Than the Sword* 44 (1989).

Another trick is to watch out for auxiliary verbs like forms of "to be," "have," "hold," "make," and "take." They morph the powerful verb into the puny derivative noun. For example, by adding "make," we change the vibrant "decide" into the wimpy "make a decision."

Graphic 29.4(b)	Wimpy Derivative Nouns vs. Active Base Verbs
instead of	**use**
a refusal to do so	refused
an invalidation of	invalidated
caused injury to	injured
conducted a cross-examination	cross-examined
conducted an interview of	interviewed
contains a provision that	provides
entered into an agreement	agreed
filed a motion to	moved
gave consideration to	considered
gave recognition to	recognized
granted a continuance	continued
has a preference for	prefers
have an expectation of	expect
have knowledge of	know
held a meeting	met
in agreement that	agree
is a violation of	violates
is binding upon	binds
is dependent upon	depends
made an amendment to	amended
made an appearance	appeared
made an assumption that	assumed
made an inquiry	inquired, asked
made an improvement	improved
made an objection to	objected
made a ruling that	ruled
made a request for	requested
made a study of	studied
made the argument that	argued
made the decision to	decided
made the finding that	found
make a comparison of	compare
make a payment to	pay
placed emphasis on	emphasized
provided treatment of	treated
the approval of	approved
the enforcement of	enforced

the selection of	selected
the suspension of	suspended
took notice of	noticed
reached the agreement that	agreed
reached the conclusion that	concluded
rendered the finding that	found
rendered the holding that	held

§ 29.5   Exercises

Exercise 1.

Graphic 29.4(a) warns that we should not add the listed endings to verbs. In adding those endings, we are creating "nominalizations"—taking a perfectly good verb and transforming it into a wimpy noun. For this exercise, write (using all of the endings in the graphic) two examples using each ending transforming a verb into a noun. For example (and don't use this one or any of the ones listed in § 29.4(a)):

agreed—made an agreement

involved—had an involvement in

Exercise 2.

Write five "to be" words and replace them with more concrete verbs. Don't use any examples given in the Graphics in the Chapter.

Exercise 3.

Write five sentences in passive voice. Then edit those sentences to make them active. Don't use any examples given in the Graphics in the Chapter.

Chapter Review
Artistry: Choosing the Right Words and Phrases

✓ Have we replaced abstract words, phrases, and concepts with concrete ones? Can we add detail to make the sentence concrete?

✓ Have we used descriptive nouns and verbs whenever possible instead of adjectives and adverbs?

✓ Have we replaced forms of "to be" with more concrete verbs?

✓ Have we used active voice?

✓ Have we placed actors in sentences?

✓ Are we certain all our actors can act?

✓ Have we used base verbs, instead of derivative nouns? For example: "injured," instead of "caused injury to"; "prefers," instead of "has a preference for"?

Chapter 30

Simplicity: Avoiding Confusion

§ 30.1   Make Clear What "It" Is and Use "It's" Properly

The puny little word "it," when abused, can wreak havoc in legal writing. It can lead our readers astray; it can create doubt where we need certainty. When we use "it," we better make certain our reader knows exactly what "it" means.

Graphic 30.1(a)	Example: Use of "It"
unclear	**clear**
It cannot be determined whether it applies. (What?)	The court cannot determine whether the Code applies here.

We suggest circling every "it" in our drafts and asking whether we can easily and un-ambiguously identify the noun "it" references. If we can't, we've got to edit!

Graphic 30.1(b)	Example: Use of "It's"
Here's an example of the "it's rule" from *The Elements of Style* by Strunk and White:[1]	
"It's a wise dog that scratches its own fleas."	

"It's" means "it is" or "it has." "Its" is the possessive form of "it." It's very annoying to use "it's" when we mean "its." And we do mean it.

§ 30.2   Make Clear What Each Clause Modifies

"I shot an elephant in my pajamas. How he got in my pajamas, I'll never know."

—The Marx Brothers

A "modifier" describes a verb or a noun. When we misplace a modifier, we run the risk of adding a descriptive phrase to the wrong subject. This leads to confusing (and often humorous) writing.

Here are some examples from students' papers:

---

1. William Strunk, Jr. and E.B. White, *The Elements of Style* 1 (3d ed. 1979).

Graphic 30.2	Misplaced Modifiers[2]

The Board of Education needs the flexibility to decide whether or not to hire convicted felons because they are responsible for protecting the public's economic and safety interests.

This Court determined that there was no proof of abandonment because Ms. Dunn's separated husband may have been capable of caring for her children.

In *Poole*, the child was taken in by the foster parents after her natural mother died under an agreement with her father.

Mary Wood alleged that while wearing an Acme uniform and driving an Acme truck, Jack Martin raped her.

Ms. Powell was replaced by a male worker whose exposure to lead at the levels in the work site would not endanger an unborn child even though his salary was lower.

As in *Millross*, Woodward furnished alcohol at a function which was subsequently consumed by one of its employees.

Tobacco use is legal and there is no rational basis for discriminating against employees who use it for purely economic reasons.

The threat of fiscal annihilation to a financially-strained municipality justifies a policy that prohibits the hiring of potential health hazards as employees.

Dr. Bell testified that he opposes doctors assisting any of their patients to commit suicide for ethical reasons.

Mr. Lark argues that the warrantless search and seizure of his tent is a violation of his constitutional right to unreasonable searches and seizures under the Fourth Amendment.

The nativity scene depicts the birth of Jesus on the steps of City Hall.

The defendant was owner of and employer of women in a laundry.

The nurse stated that during Joe's exam, he expressed a desire to have sexual intercourse with his fiancée in the doctor's presence.

The Fourth Amendment was not violated when an agent for the DEA seized controlled substances from the Defendant who had an expired permit in a national park and had placed his tent in the prohibited area of the park without a warrant.

Here are some more examples from actual newspaper headlines:

Drunk gets nine months in violin case.

Lung cancer in women mushrooms.

Eye drops off shelf.

Teacher strikes idle kids.

---

2. We thank Mary Beth Beazley and Peter Bayer, as well as our colleagues, for sharing these.

Enraged cow injures farmer with ax.

Juvenile court to try shooting defendant.

Two soviet ships collide, one dies.

Two sisters reunited after 18 years in checkout counter.

Kids make nutritious snacks.

Hospitals are sued by 7 foot doctors.

And these, from church bulletins:

The eighth-graders will be presenting Shakespeare's Hamlet this Friday at 7 p.m. The congregation is invited to attend this tragedy.

The concert was a great success. Special thanks to the minister's daughter, who labored the whole evening at the piano, which as usual fell upon her.

Eight new choir robes are needed, due to the addition of new members and to the deterioration of some older ones.

The Reverend Merriwether spoke briefly, much to the delight of the audience.

During the pastor's absence, we enjoyed the rare privilege of hearing a good sermon from Reverend Stubbs.

You get the idea. The best way to avoid confusion is to keep modifiers close to the clause or word being modified.

§ 30.3   Clear Up Vague, Ambiguous, or Awkward Sentences

"The minute you read something and you can't understand it, you can be sure it was written by a lawyer."

—Will Rodgers[3]

In every sentence, pay special attention to the actor's identity, to comparisons we're making to (or involving) the actor, and to pronouns we're using to refer to the actor.

Graphic 30.3(a)	Identify the Correct Actor
unclear	Upon reserving his right to appeal, the trial judge sentenced Doe to 90 days.
reason	Who reserved the right to appeal? Not the trial judge.

---

3. Quoted by Robert B. Smith, *The Literate Lawyer* 18 (2d ed. 1991).

unclear To satisfy the first part of the *Spence* test, that there was an intent to convey a particularized message, this Court should look to Doe's subjective intent.

reason Who satisfies the first part of the *Spence* test? Not the Court.

Graphic 30.3(b)	Make Certain There Is an Actor

unclear In the instant case, by looking at Doe's conduct, there can be no doubt that he communicated a symbolic message.

reason Who is "looking at Doe's conduct"?

unclear Examining Doe's actions, it is clear that his conduct falls under First Amendment protection.

reason Who is "examining"? And, what does it mean for conduct to "fall under First Amendment protection"?

Graphic 30.3(c)	Make Certain the Actor Can Act

unclear Doe has failed to prove that his begging intended to convey a particularized message.

reason Can "begging" intend?

Graphic 30.3(d)	Compare Like Things: We Can't Compare a Case to a Person, Place, or Thing

unclear Like in *Spence*, Doe's cupped hand is a symbolic way of transmitting an idea.

reason Like *what* in *Spence*? What aspect of the *Spence* case are we comparing to "Doe's cupped hand"?

Be wary of the following two patterns, for they lead to faulty comparisons: "Like in *case name*"; and "As in *case name*." To make a valid comparison, we must add a noun, as follows:

Graphic 30.3(e)	Valid Comparisons

"Like [the defendant's **actions**] in *case name*," [the defendant's **actions** here]

"As [the **defendant**] in *case name*," [the **defendant** here]

But don't compare a person to an action or an action to a person. The following are faulty:

Graphic 30.3(f)   **Invalid Comparisons**

"Like the defendant's **actions** in *Adams*, **Jones** did not...."

"As the **defendant** in *Adams*, Jones's **begging**. ..."

Moreover, watch out for those pesky pronouns:

Graphic 30.3(g)   **Clear up Any Ambiguous Pronoun Referents**

unclear   Judges are concerned about their treatment of defendants and their role in society.

reason   Whose "role in society"? Judges or defendants?

Finally, choose the placement of prepositional phrases with care:

"The lawyers argued in their briefs...."

"In their briefs, the lawyers argued...."

Well, perhaps some phrases are just best left *unsaid*.

§ 30.4   Exercises

Exercise 1. Write five sentences where the reader would not know what you are referring to when you use the word "it." See Graphic 30.1(a). Then edit these sentences to correct the error.

Exercise 2. Rewrite the fourteen sentences in Graphic 30.2 to correct the misplaced modifiers and to streamline the sentences.

Exercise 3. Write five sentences where the actor cannot act (as in Graphic 30.3(c)). Then, edit those sentences to correct the error.

Exercise 4. Write five sentences comparing a case to a person, place, or thing (as in Graphic 30.3(d)). Then, edit those sentences to make the comparisons valid.

Exercise 5. Write five sentences using invalid comparisons (as in Graphic 30.3(f)). Then, edit those sentences to correct the error.

Chapter Review
Simplicity: Avoiding Confusion

✓ Have we made clear what "it" refers to?

✓ Have we used "it's" properly? "It's" means "it is" or "it has"; "its" is the possessive of "it."

✓ Have we kept modifiers close to the word or clause being modified?

✓ Is the correct person or thing acting?

✓ Is there an actor in the sentence? Can that actor act?

✓ Have we made valid comparisons? Have we compared cases to cases, people to people, and actions to actions?

✓ Are all pronoun referents clear? Do we know who "he," "she," "it," "they," and "their" refer to?

Chapter 31

Impact: Making Every Word Count

"If indeed you must be candid, be candid beautifully."

— Kahlil Gibran

§ 31.1   Select Words That Create a Favorable Bias

By using words which create a bias favorable to our position, we enhance the impact of our arguments. For example, let's consider the following sentence:

Graphic 31.1(a)	Positive vs. Negative Bias
neutral or positive	**negative**
The letters, if received, were unanswered.	The defendant failed to answer even one of Bob Jones's letters.

In the first sentence, we raise doubt about whether the letters were even received, without actually denying their receipt. Although we acknowledge that they were unanswered, we accuse no specific person. However, in the second sentence, we identify the non-answerer with the dubious title "defendant," while humanizing the plaintiff by stating his full name. We underscore the unreasonableness of the defendant's failure to answer "even one" letter.

Let's look at another example:

Graphic 31.1(b)	Positive vs. Negative Bias
neutral or positive	**negative**
The family killed Old Bessy and then had hamburgers for dinner.	The defendants not only slaughtered Old Bessy, they ground up her carcass, formed that ground meat into hamburgers, browned those hamburgers in a fire, and then feasted upon them.

A warning: In using bias words, we can't take a heavy-handed approach. Our reader will resist any obvious manipulations of language. We avoid sarcastic, disparaging, or over-the-top statements, like those in the last example above. Moreover, we never assert any position we can't substantiate. We'll leave it to you to consider whether the "negative" sentences on the right (below) go too far:

Graphic 31.1(c)	Take Care Not to Go Too Far
neutral or positive	**negative**
Smith and Brown met privately and agreed to cooperate for their mutual benefit.	The unsavory defendants met in secret and made a collusive deal, each seeking a personal advantage.

| The family believed they would starve unless they ate their milk cow. | The gluttonous family couldn't wait to sink their choppers into Old Bessy's tender loins. |

§ 31.2   Use Effective Sentence Structure and Stress Points

"All's well that ends well."

—William Shakespeare

Placing words strategically. We emphasize words by strategically placing them in sentences. The positions carrying the most emphasis are the beginning and the ending. Usually, we use the beginning of the sentence to introduce the actor—the subject of our active verb. The actor is the one "doing," "saying," "holding," "slaying," "devouring."

We also use the ending of the sentence for emphasis. We all know instinctively how important "getting in the last word" or "leaving with a parting shot" can be. Let's consider the following examples:

Graphic 31.2(a)	Which Is Emphasized?
phrase buried in middle of sentence	**phrase placed at beginning or ending**
Dr. Smith said the term pathological killer described the defendant.	Dr. Smith described the defendant as a pathological killer.
Their only choice was to be killed or to obey.	Their only choice was to obey or to be killed.
Old Bessy gave up her life to save the family.	Old Bessy saved the family by giving up her life.
	or
	By giving up her life, Old Bessy saved the family.

We also manipulate points of emphasis by strategically placing transitional words in our sentences. For example, if we wish to stress phrases such as "however," "nevertheless," and "of course," we place them at the beginning of the sentence. However, if we don't wish to emphasize them, we place them in the middle.

Graphic 31.2(b)	Examples of Adding Emphasis Through Word Placement	
phrase is emphasized	**phrase is not emphasized**
However, personal belongings are exempt.	Personal belongings, however, are exempt.
Tragically, Old Bessy had to go.	Old Bessy, tragically, had to go.
However, the hamburgers were delicious.	The hamburgers, however, were delicious.

§ 31.3   Subordinate Unfavorable Facts and Strong Opposing Arguments

We can't ignore the harmful aspects of our case. Indeed, to maintain our credibility, we address the facts and arguments we know our opponent will stress. However, we may use a powerful, yet simple, device called "subordination" to soften their impact.

Subordination consists of an "although," "while," or similar clause followed by a main clause. We place the damaging points in the "although" clause, and the favorable points in the main clause. As the examples below demonstrate, by placing the subordinate clause before the main clause, we stress the favorable point.

Graphic 31.3	Let's Compare These Examples	
favorable facts shout	**damaging facts shout**
Although Bill drinks, he is a good worker.	Although he is a good worker, Bill drinks.
Although the defendant has two convictions, he saved the prison guard from certain death.	Although he saved the prison guard from certain death, the defendant has two convictions.
Although the family ate her, Old Bessie was a good milk cow.	Although Old Bessie was a good milk cow, the family ate her.

§ 31.4   Use Contrasting Elements to Minimize Unfavorable Facts or Arguments

The conjunction "but" is the most powerful contrasting element in the English language. If we use it correctly, we minimize the impact of unfavorable facts or arguments. Here's how we use this device:

(1) insert the *damaging* facts or arguments in a main clause or sentence *before* "but"; then,

(2) insert the *favorable* facts or arguments in a main clause or sentence *after* "but." Let's look at how this is done:

Graphic 31.4	Let's Compare These Examples
favorable facts shout	**damaging facts shout**
Bill drinks, but he is a good worker.	Bill is a good worker, but he drinks.
Jones has two convictions, but he saved the prison guard from certain death.	Jones saved the prison guard from certain death, but he has two convictions.
The family ate Old Bessy, but she was a good milk cow.	Old Bessy was a good milk cow, but the family ate her.

By effectively using subordination, contrasting elements, and other emphasis points, we deal squarely with the weak aspects of our case while persuading our reader to accept our point of view.

§ 31.5   Use Effective Paragraphs

"All length is torture...."

—William Shakespeare

The principles of sentence arrangement also apply to paragraph arrangement: the positions with most impact are the beginning and the ending. As in sentence structure, the beginning is the place for introduction and transition. We bring our reader's mind to a new thought by tying that thought to a familiar one from the previous paragraph.

Once we've previewed the new thought with our opening or topic sentence, we develop our ideas progressively. We explain the details supporting the concept we've introduced. We place the points we wish to emphasize at either the beginning or ending of our paragraph, so our reader will more readily remember them.

This structure of *introduction — explanation — emphasis* minimizes our reader's resistance to our argument. It's the core structure of the BaRAC design.[1] The following example illustrates this concept. Think of the "explanation" section as the equivalent of BaRAC's "rule," and the "emphasis" section as the equivalent of BaRAC's "application."

Graphic 31.5	Introduction — Explanation — Emphasis
introduction	This appeal addresses an unusual issue of first impression: Lionell, who unwittingly ran over Walker while operating a 4021 ton freight train, has sued Walker, the injured party, for damages under the theory of inten-

---

1. Please see Chapter 1 for an explanation of the BaRAC *design*.

explanation	tional infliction of emotional distress. Lionell, who was not physically harmed in the accident, seeks to recover damages resulting from his alleged mental distress at having observed Walker's injury. Although imagi-
emphasis	native, Lionell's theory is unsound. As this Court should hold on *de novo* review, the tort of outrage must involve intolerably atrocious and outrageous conduct intentionally directed at the plaintiff; not, as in this case, political protest leading to the defendant's accidental injury.

introduction	Recognizing the narrow scope of this tort, Florida courts allow recovery only in very limited circumstances involving the most intentionally atro-
explanation	cious and wanton actions. The trial court correctly held that Walker's conduct did not rise to the level the law requires. Walker merely participated in a peaceful political demonstration against nuclear weapons by staging a sit-in upon railroad tracks to protest a train's payload of plutonium — a crit-
emphasis	ical component in nuclear bombs. Tragically, he did not get off the tracks in time, was struck by the train, and is now maimed for life. The trial court correctly held, as should this Court, that his sit-in protest against nuclear weapons did not rise to the level the law requires, as it was not "beyond the bounds of decency" or "utterly intolerable in a civilized society."

The topic sentences (i.e., the first sentences) in the paragraphs above contain the subject of our discussion. They alert our reader to the connection between the ideas that flow from the subsequent sentences. For example, the writer of the argument above seeks to convince the court that our case involves "an unusual issue of first impression" (first paragraph, first sentence), that the tort involved here is "narrow [in] scope" (second paragraph, first sentence), and that "Florida courts allow recovery [under this tort] only in very limited circumstances" (second paragraph, first sentence). The sentences that follow in those two paragraphs explain these topics.[2]

In addition to writing paragraphs with strong topic sentences, we also strive to keep paragraphs short. Just as paragraphs without topic sentences make our readers disoriented, tall "walls of words," i.e., long paragraphs, make our readers heave a heavy sigh as they struggle to overcome the dizziness they feel in reading line after line with no break. Try to make all paragraphs no longer than one-half a page of double-spaced print. By keeping our paragraphs short, we relieve reader stress.[3] And reader stress is the last thing we want when we are trying to convince our audience to accept our legal arguments.

---

2. We also address topic sentences in Chapter 6, §§ 6.1, 6.2, 6.4 and in Chapter 24, § 24.1.

3. We address paragraph length in more detail in Chapter 24, § 24.5.

Chapter Review
Impact: Making Every Word Count

✓ Have we selected words that create a favorable bias?

✓ Have we strategically placed words in sentences to emphasize favorable facts and to de-emphasize unfavorable ones?

✓ Have we used short paragraphs?

✓ Do our paragraphs begin with strong topic sentences?

✓ Do our paragraphs follow the pattern of *introduction — explanation — emphasis*?

Chapter 32

Cohesion: The Power of Transitions

"[T]ransition and connection [is] the art by which one step in an evolution of thought is made to arise out of another: all fluent and effective composition depends on the connections...."

— Thomas de Quincey

§32.1   What Is a Transition?

Although we don't know which came first, the thought or the language used to express it, language is integral to reasoning. Language provides signposts, called "transitions," composed of words, phrases, or sentences which act as bridges between thoughts. Indeed, (there was one) transitions act like the "bridging term" in a syllogism.[1] But, (there was another one) instead of providing a logical connection between premises, transitions provide a "language" connection between thoughts.

Let's examine how these connections operate. We'll start with a sentence containing two thoughts but lacking a transition between them:

> Marilyn is an excellent writer; she was hired by the District Attorney.

Here's the problem: as readers, we don't know whether there's any connection between Marilyn's writing ability and her new job. However, we have no doubt about that connection when we read the next sentence:

> Because Marilyn is an excellent writer, the District Attorney hired her.

The transition "because" tells us that, indeed, Marilyn's writing ability got her the job.

Here's another example. It's a section of an argument written first without transitions and then with transitions. Which is easier to follow?

Graphic 32.1(a)   The Cohesive Force of Transitions

without transitions	with transitions and editing [transitions are in *italics*]
The golf shoe had sixteen steel cleats protruding from the sole. The steel cleats were sharp enough to pierce the body of the victim. The shoe was extremely dangerous. The shoe was lighter than the boot. The shoe had a leather sole which was rigid enough to hold the steel cleats. The shoe had a leather sole which was rigid enough to be used as a blunt instrument. Jones threw the shoe at the victim's head. Jones used the shoe in a manner likely to produce death or serious bodily injury.	*Unlike the boot in Smith,* the golf shoe had sixteen steel cleats protruding from its sole. *These cleats* were sharp enough to pierce the victim's body. *This fact* alone makes the shoe extremely dangerous. *Moreover, although lighter than a boot,* the golf shoe also had a leather sole rigid enough to hold those steel cleats and to be used as a blunt instrument. *Without doubt,* in throwing the golf shoe at the victim's head, Jones used the shoe in a manner likely to produce death or serious bodily injury.

---

1. Please see Chapter 1, §1.9(a) for an explanation of the "bridging term."

The writing in the "without transitions" version is choppy. We stumble over disjointed thoughts and repetitive phrases. In contrast, the version "with transitions" takes us by the hand. We travel with the writer's thoughts smoothly along on a well-outlined path.

Indeed, if you're still not convinced of the power and utility of transitions, please consider this:

Graphic 32.1(b)	Example	
	without transition	**with transition**
	I think, I am.	I think, *therefore* I am.

Need we say more? Of course! In the sections below, we examine three different types of transitions, which we call linking transitions, restatement transitions, and roadmap transitions. Although some transitions overlap categories, for ease of reference, we haven't presented them as overlapping.

§ 32.2   Linking Transitions

The transitions "because" and "therefore" are "linking" transitions; i.e., they link one thought to the next, showing a causal relationship between them. As the following graphic shows, they can also show the connection between thoughts by emphasizing a point ("importantly"); noting exceptions ("however," "although"); concluding or moving the discussion forward ("finally," "next"); noting the passage of time ("then," "now," "later"); providing a sense of location or place ("here," "there"); comparing or contrasting points ("similarly," "in contrast," "for example"); or delineating sequences ("first," "second").

Graphic 32.2(a)		Common Linking Transitions		
		to show time, order, or placement		
above	across from	adjacent to	after	afterwards
as soon as	before	below	beyond	by the time
earlier	eventually	finally	first	formerly
further	furthermore	here	initially	later
latter	meanwhile	moreover	near	next to
next	now	over	prior	recently
second	shortly	simultaneously	since	soon
subsequently	then	there	thereafter	third
ultimately	under	until then	until now	when
while				

to add emphasis and specifics				
above all	actually	after all	allegedly	arguably
at least	but	certainly	clearly	for this reason
for example	fortunately	here	in effect	in that event
in fact	in particular	indeed	inexplicitly	more importantly
nevertheless	nonetheless	notably	of course	primarily
still	surprisingly	to be sure	undoubtedly	unfortunately
without doubt	without question			

to show additions				
additionally	again	also	and	besides
beyond	equally important	further	furthermore	in addition
moreover	once again	similarly	too	

to note exceptions, concessions, or to contrast				
alternatively	contrary to	even though	instead	on the contrary
but	conversely	despite	even so	even if
however	in contrast	in spite of	in place of	nevertheless
no doubt	not only	notwithstanding	on the other hand	otherwise
rather	regardless	specifically	still	there
though	by contrast	to the contrary	under these circumstances	although
unlike	and yet	yet		

to show cause and effect				
accordingly	as a result	because	consequently	for this reason
hence	since	then	therefore	thus

to compare				
also	analogously	applying the same reasoning	applying the same rationale	by analogy
for this reason	for example	for instance	for the same reason	illustrating
in like manner	in this way	likewise	namely	on these facts
similarly	specifically	such as	there	to illustrate

to restate				
as noted	in short	in other words	simply put	to restate
to repeat	to simplify	to clarify	to rephrase	

to conclude				
accordingly	as a result	consequently	finally	hence
in brief	in conclusion	in short	therefore	thus
to summarize	to conclude			

Three caveats. Although these transitions help convey information clearly and logically, they can be misused. For this reason, we offer the following three caveats:

First. The words listed within a category (in the lists above) may not be synonymous. For example, "surprisingly" and "without doubt" both "add emphasis and specifics," but they convey vastly different ideas.

Second. Choosing the wrong transition may confuse our reader more than if we had omitted the transition. For example, let's look at one of the most commonly misused transitions: "therefore."

"Therefore" signals a conclusion. When "therefore" is used, we expect to see a connection between the thought which immediately follows and the proof which preceded that thought; i.e., "I think, *therefore* I am."[2] But we can also misuse "therefore" by employing it when we're not drawing a conclusion. For example, the following would be improper: "I wrote the brief, therefore I'm not certain how the court will decide my case." Instead of a cause-effect relationship, we're attempting to convey doubt or uncertainty. The correct linking transition would be "however": "I wrote the brief, however I'm not certain how the court will decide my case." The linking transition "although" also works: "Although I wrote the brief, I'm not certain how the court will decide my case."

Conversely, we confuse our reader if we use "however" or "although" when we're intending to make a causal connection. "I think, *however* I am" and "I think, *although* I am," are not the ideas we intended to convey. Ironically, the phrase (without transitions), "I think, I am," more accurately conveys our thought than the sentences containing the wrong transition.

Graphic 32.2(b)	Take Care to Choose the Correct Transition
wrong	I think, however I am.
wrong	I think, although I am.
correct	I think, therefore I am.

Third. We must not overuse transitions. Although no clear rules exist regarding when and when not to use a transition, it's highly unlikely that every sentence will require one. In using transitions, we let our common sense guide us. If we read our writing aloud and hear a "jolt," i.e., an interruption in the smooth flow of connected thoughts, we know our reader may stumble, and we need a transition. If, however, the sentences naturally flow together, without any transition, then there's no reason to include one. As the following example shows, unnecessary transitions are annoying:

---

2. René Descartes, *Le Discours de la Méthode IV* (1637).

Graphic 32.2(c)   Take Care Not to Overuse Transitions

In conclusion, nothing goes by luck in composition. In other words, it allows of no tricks. Indeed, the best you can write will be the best you are. For this reason, every sentence is the result of a long probation. Accordingly, the author's character is read from title-page to end. Without doubt, of this he never corrects the proofs.

Here's the passage, more elegant and to the point, as Henry David Thoreau, originally wrote it:

"Nothing goes by luck in composition. It allows of no tricks. The best you can write will be the best you are. Every sentence is the result of a long probation. The author's character is read from title-page to end. Of this he never corrects the proofs."

— Henry David Thoreau

§ 32.3   Substantive Transitions

Instead of bridging ideas with linking transitions, Thoreau, in the example above, used another method of making connections between sentences and thoughts: the "substantive" transition. Substantive transitions are just that: substantive links between thoughts.

If a linking transition is a wooden footbridge, a substantive transition is the steel-cabled Golden Gate Bridge. Substantive transitions make connections by repetition, by restatement, or by providing a "roadmap" or "preview" of the thoughts to follow. Let's examine each of these transition types.

§ 32.3(a)   Repetition Transitions

The first two sentences of § 32.3 above contain an example of a "repetition" transition. We ended that first sentence with the phrase "substantive transition" and began the second sentence by repeating that term. By using this "word bridge" comprised of the same terms, we connected the sentences and the thoughts contained in them.

However, we don't need to repeat terms *exactly* to form a repetition transition. Our goal is to create a bridge between thoughts by overlapping language. We can use the same terms, very similar terms, or pronouns to refer back to the prior term.

Graphic 32.3(a)(1)	Examples of Repetition Transitions
same phrase	Jones committed *the crime*. *The crime* consists of elements x, y, and z.
similar phrase	When the rocket was ignited it *exploded*. *The explosion* caused tremendous damage.
pronoun	We were very excited about seeing *the movie*. *It* was filmed on location at our university.

Case names. We can also use a case name as a repetition transition. This technique is especially helpful where we're explaining a rule. For example, Chief Justice Burger used a case name repetition transition, the *Katz* case, in the following passage from *California v. Ciraolo*, 476 U.S. 207, 211 (1986):

Graphic 32.3(a)(2)	Case Name Repetition Transition

"The touchstone of Fourth Amendment analysis is whether a person has a 'constitutionally protected reasonable expectation of privacy.'" *Katz v. United States* [citation omitted]. *Katz* posits a two-part inquiry: first, has the individual manifested a subjective expectation of privacy in the object of the challenged search? Second, is society willing to recognize that expectation as reasonable? [citation omitted]

Signposts. In legal writing, we often compare our case to other cases. However, if we're not careful, we can easily confuse (and lose) our reader. To avoid this confusion, we alert our reader each time we switch between our case and a cited case. We call these alerts "signpost transitions."

Graphic 32.3(a)(3)	Helpful Signposts	
	cited case	our case
	There	Here
	In that case	In our case
	In [case name]	In the instant case
	As the [court] in [case] held	In the instant case

Note that it is sometimes all right to use the term "our case" in a memorandum written to a colleague or to a senior partner; however, in more formal writing to a court, it's best to use the "instant case."

In using signpost transitions, we choose a transition which unambiguously refers to the case we're addressing. In the following example, the signpost is more confusing than helpful.

Graphic 32.3(a)(4)   An Example of Failing to Use a Clear Signpost

---

In *Miranda*, the Court excluded the confession because the authorities failed to warn the defendant of his constitutional rights. In *this* case, the police failed to warn the defendant of his right to remain silent.

Although the phrase "this case" is a transition, we don't know whether it refers to *Miranda* or to our case. We could unambiguously convey that we were referring to *Miranda* by substituting "that case" for "this case." If, on the other hand, we were referring to our case, we would substitute "the instant case" for "this case." The following illustrates these distinctions:

Graphic 32.3(a)(5)   Signposting

---

referring to a cited case	**referring to our case**
In *Miranda*, the Court excluded the confession because the authorities failed to warn the defendant of his constitutional rights. In *that* case, the police failed to warn the defendant of his right to remain silent.	In *Miranda*, the Court excluded the confession because the authorities failed to warn the defendant of his constitutional rights. In *the instant case*, the police failed to warn the defendant of his right to remain silent.

Indeed, our writing would be even stronger in **Graphic 32.3(a)(5)** if we combined transitions to add the following: "*Similarly, in the instant case*, the police failed to warn...."

§ 32.3(b)   Restatement Transitions

Another way to connect thoughts is through "restatement" transitions. Restatement transitions restate a thought by casting it in a different light, by making concrete a prior, more abstract concept, by renaming the subject, or by classifying or summarizing a group of similar thoughts into one common subject or collective noun. Here's an example:

| Graphic 32.3(b)(1) | Restatement Transition: |
| Making an Abstract Concept More Concrete | |

When we use a repetition transition, we can repeat the last phrase in the preceding sentence as the first phrase in the sentence to follow. *By using this word bridge*, we connect the sentences and the thoughts contained in them.

Making the abstract more concrete. The phrase "by using this word bridge," is a restatement transition. The term "word bridge" restated the process we use in creating a repetition transition. We made more concrete ("word bridge") an abstract concept (the process of creating a repetition transition).

Conveying a bias. Restatement transitions are also wonderful devices for crafting blatantly biased, or subtly persuasive, passages. Consider the following three examples (The restatement transitions are in italics.):

Graphic 32.3(b)(2)	Conveying a Bias

1. **written objectively**
   Accused of breaking the lamp, Matthew was sent to his room. He was allowed to leave after fifteen minutes.

2. **written by "Mom"**
   Accused of breaking the lamp, Matthew was sent to his room. *Punishment befitting the crime*, he was allowed to leave after fifteen minutes.

3. **written by "we know who"**
   Accused of breaking the lamp, Matthew was sent to his room. *Exiled without due process*, he was finally allowed to leave after fifteen minutes.

Addressing a series or summary. Restatement transitions also help us discuss, without being repetitive, a group or series of items, i.e., cases, statutes, or events. For example, we used a restatement transition in the following passage:

Graphic 32.3(b)(3)	Series or Summary

"He illegally interfered with both a railroad vehicle and track, and placed an object capable of causing death or great bodily harm in the path of an oncoming train. *All of these crimes are felonies, punishable by lengthy prison terms.*"

A restatement transition thus can condense or summarize many related concepts into one manageable topic. When a restatement transition performs this function, it often begins with one of the following bridging words: *such, that, these, this,* or *those* followed by a "summarizing" or "classifying" noun.

Great writers make elegant use of restatement transitions. For example, Thoreau used one when he wrote, "The author's character is read from title-page to end. *Of this* he never corrects the proofs." The phrase "[o]f this" restates the subject of "[t]he author's character." Without using a "thus, therefore, or however," Thoreau got his point across.

§ 32.3(c)   Roadmap Transitions

The final type of substantive transition is the "roadmap" transition, used to introduce or preface an idea. We just did it; we just used a roadmap transition. The first sentence of this paragraph alerted us that we'd next discuss the roadmap transition. Another example is the first sentence of the prior paragraph: "Great writers make elegant use of repetitive transitions." That sentence previewed the topic that followed.

Moving from rule to rule application. We also use roadmap transitions when we move from, for example, discussing the law to applying that law to our case. Here's an example of this use from the Supreme Court's opinion in *California v. Ciraolo*, 476 U.S. 207, 215 (1986):

Graphic 32.3(c)(1)   Moving from Rule to Rule Application

"In an age where private and commercial flight in the public airways is routine, it is unreasonable for respondent to expect that his marijuana plants were constitutionally protected from being observed with the naked eye from an altitude of 1,000 feet. The Fourth Amendment simply does not require the police traveling in the public airways at this altitude to obtain a warrant in order to observe what is visible to the naked eye." [citation omitted]
We arrive at the same conclusion in the instant case. Here,…."

Moving from position to position. Roadmap transitions can also alert our reader that we're moving from a statement of our opponent's position to our position:

Graphic 32.3(c)(2)   Moving from Position to Position

Thus, the State urges that because members of the public traveling in navigable airspace can look into the defendant's yard, the defendant had no reasonable expectation of privacy in the contents of his yard.
This line of reasoning, however, is flawed. First, …

Introducing an extended discussion. As the following example illustrates, we can also use roadmap transitions to introduce an extended discussion of a cited case:

Graphic 32.3(c)(3)	To Introduce an Extended Discussion of a Cited Case

In a case remarkably similar to Lionell's, the Iowa Supreme Court held, as this Court should hold, that in causing a plaintiff to view the results of a defendant's self-inflicted wounds, the defendant had acted outrageously. *See Blakeley v. Shortal's Estate* [citation omitted]. In *Blakeley*, the decedent....

As the above examples show, we use roadmap transitions not only to alert our reader to a shift in thought, but also to prejudice our reader's view of the material to follow. Indeed, all transitions can serve this "persuasive" function. For this reason, transitions are not colorless, tasteless glue holding together the layers of our thoughts. Rather, they are vibrant, delicious icing which not only joins, but enhances, our thoughts.

§ 32.4   Using a Variety of Transitions

Hamlet. Examples of the elegant use of linking and substantive transitions abound in literary masterpieces.[3] One of our favorites is from *Hamlet:*

"What a piece of work is a man, how noble in reason, how infinite in faculties, in form and moving, how express and admirable in action, how like an angel in apprehension, how like a god! The beauty of the world! The paragon of animals! And yet to me, what is this quintessence of dust?"

Here, Shakespeare provides a roadmap transition: "[w]hat a piece of work is a man," then follows with restatement transitions, referring to "man" as both "the beauty of the world, the paragon of animals" and as "this quintessence of dust." In so restating Hamlet's thoughts of "man," Shakespeare provides two very different images of the same subject and masterfully conveys Hamlet's mood.

Let's look at one more of Shakespeare's passages. In this famous soliloquy, (did you catch that restatement transition?), Hamlet raises the ancient question of Life, the

---

3. No, this sentence was not a restatement transition intended to compare this humble book to "literary masterpieces." Instead, we intended it as a roadmap transition, previewing the examples that follow.

Universe, and Everything, and in doing so (there's a linking transition) employs a host of substantive—roadmap, repetition, and restatement—transitions:

> "To be, or not to be, that is the question:
> Whether 'tis nobler in the mind to suffer
> The slings and arrows of outrageous fortune,
> Or to take Arms against a Sea of troubles,
> And by opposing end them: to die, to sleep
> No more; and by a sleep, to say we end
> The Heart-ache, and the thousand Natural shocks
> That Flesh is heir to? 'Tis a consummation
> Devoutly to be wished. To die, to sleep,
> To sleep, perchance to Dream: Ay, there's the rub,
> For in that sleep of death, what dreams may come,
> When we have shuffled off this mortal coil,
> Must give us pause. There's the respect
> That makes Calamity of so long life:"

Beautiful! Even the first line uses a roadmap transition: "[t]o be, or not to be," and a restatement transition: "that is the question...." But there are many more: death is recast as "a consummation [d]evoutly to be wished," and the dreaming that comes with the "sleep of death" is restated as "the respect [t]hat makes Calamity of so long life...." We're pretty sure that Hamlet was not speaking of "[t]o be, or not to be" a lawyer, but that's a question we'll leave to the philosophers (or perhaps to our therapists).

Spence v. Washington. Let's return our focus to the role transitions play in legal writing and how they help keep our reader "on track." Compare the next two graphics. The first passage contains only a few transitions, while the second contains the transitions as the Supreme Court originally wrote the passage. This example is from the per curiam opinion in *Spence v. Washington*, 418 U.S. 405, 408-09 (1974). At issue there was whether the defendant's conviction for defacing the United States flag violated the First Amendment. Which excerpt is easier to follow? How do the transitions aid us in understanding the Court's reasoning?

Graphic 32.4(a)   Example with Only a Few Transitions

This was a privately owned flag. It was not the property of any government. The State or National Governments constitutionally may forbid anyone from mishandling in any manner a flag that is public property. Appellant displayed his flag on private property. He engaged in no trespass or disorderly conduct. This case cannot be analyzed in terms of reasonable time, place, or manner restraints on access to a public area. The record is devoid of any risk of breach of the peace. Appellant's purpose was not to incite violence or even stimulate a public demonstration. No crowd gathered. Appellant did not make any effort to attract attention beyond hanging the flag out of his window. The parties stipulated that no one other than the three police officers [who arrested the appellant] observed the flag.

The State and the Washington Supreme Court concede that appellant engaged in a form of communication. The stipulated facts fail to show that any member of the general public viewed the flag. The State's concession is inevitable on this record.... Appellant did not choose to articulate his views through printed or spoken words. It is necessary to determine whether his activity was sufficiently imbued with elements of communications to fall within the scope of the First and Fourteenth Amendments....

Next, let's read this version as it was originally written — with transitions in italics:

Graphic 32.4(b)   **Example with Transitions**

"A *number of factors are important in the instant case. First*, this was a privately owned flag. In a technical property sense it was not the property of any *government*. We have no doubt that the State or National *Governments* constitutionally may forbid anyone from mishandling in any manner a flag that is public *property. But this is a different case. Second*, appellant displayed his flag on private property. He engaged in no trespass or disorderly conduct. *Nor is this a case* that might be analyzed in terms of reasonable time, place, or manner restraints on access to a public area. *Third*, the record is devoid of any risk of breach of the peace. It was not appellant's purpose to incite violence or even stimulate a public demonstration. *There is no evidence* that any crowd gathered or that appellant made any effort to attract attention beyond hanging the flag out of his window. *Indeed*, on the facts stipulated by the parties *there is no evidence* that anyone other than the three police officers [who arrested the appellant] observed the flag.

Fourth, the State concedes, *as did* the Washington Supreme Court, that appellant engaged in a form of communication. *Although* the stipulated facts fail to show that any member of the general public viewed the flag, the State's concession is inevitable on this record.... *To be sure*, appellant did not choose to articulate his views through printed or spoken words. It is *therefore* necessary to determine whether his activity was sufficiently imbued with elements of communications to fall within the scope of the First and Fourteenth Amendments...."

As we see, the first version is more difficult to follow than the second. In the first, there aren't enough "bridges" between sentences and paragraphs to link the writer's thoughts. It's difficult to predict, and then follow, the writer's ideas. In contrast, however, the second version (containing transitions) provides direction; it even begins with a roadmap of the ideas to follow. We understand the logical relationship between the sentences and the thoughts expressed.

Let's look at one more "with/without transitions" example:

Graphic 32.4(c)   **Without Transitions**

Any case involves an aspect of someone's life. The courts and lawyers have intervened to help resolve an error. A trial occurs, facts are gathered, and a judge or jury decides in favor of one party and against the other. The case is taken to the next court — the appellate level.

Graphic 32.4(d)   **With Transitions**

Any case involves an aspect of someone's life. *Something has gone wrong* and the courts and lawyers have intervened to help resolve an error. *Usually,* a trial occurs, facts are gathered, and a judge or jury decides in favor of one party and against the other. *The loser then* takes the case to the next court — the appellate level.

Palsgraf. Let's try another example, this time from the statement of facts in Benjamin Cardozo's opinion in *Palsgraf v. Long Island Railroad Co.*, 248 N.Y. 339, 162 N.E. 2d 99 (1928). This example is loaded with repetition transitions, and a few restatement transitions, which we have italicized. However, there's not a "therefore," "however," "first," or "next" (linking transition) to be found. The writing is exquisite.

Graphic 32.4(e)   *Palsgraf*

Plaintiff was standing on a *platform of defendant's railroad* after buying a ticket to go to Rockaway Beach. A *train* stopped at the *station*, bound for another place. Two *men* ran forward to catch *it*. One of the *men* reached the platform without mishap, though the train was already moving. The other *man*, carrying a package, jumped aboard the *car*, *but* seemed unsteady as if about to fall. A guard on the *car*, who had held the door open, reached forward to help him in, and another guard on the platform pushed him from behind. *In this act*, the *package* was dislodged and fell upon the rails. *It* was a *package* of small size, about fifteen inches long, and was covered by newspaper. *In fact it* contained *fireworks*, but there was nothing in its appearance to give notice of its contents. *The fireworks* when they fell *exploded*. *The shock* of the *explosion* threw down some *scales* at the other end of the platform many feet away. The *scales* struck the plaintiff, causing injuries for which she sues.

Lionell v. Walker. Let's look at one more example which combines repetition, restatement, and linking transitions, taken from an appellate brief in the hypothetical case of *Lionell v. Walker*.[4]

---

4. The complete set of briefs in this case is contained in **Section VI.**

Our hypothetical case involves a rather unusual set of circumstances: The plaintiff, Lionell, who was the chief engineer of a train, is suing the defendant, Walker (a protestor whose legs were severed when the train struck him) for "intentional infliction of emotional distress." Lionell is arguing that Walker, in knowingly remaining on the tracks until the train struck, caused Lionell to suffer severe emotional distress. In essence, Lionell is arguing that Walker had no right to make him an unwilling participant in Walker's self-mutilation. Here's an example combining some portions of Lionell's initial and reply briefs, demonstrating the use of transitions.

Graphic 32.4(f)   **Transitions at Work**

In obstructing the railroad track, Walker violated at least three statutes designed to protect public safety. He illegally interfered with a railroad vehicle (citation omitted); illegally interfered with a railroad track (citation omitted); and illegally placed an object capable of causing death or great bodily harm in the path of an oncoming train. (citation omitted) *All of these crimes are felonies,* punishable by lengthy prison terms. (citations omitted) *Without doubt,* Walker acted recklessly per se.

Despite this, Walker attempts to deny responsibility by asserting a fourth argument: that he did not act recklessly in inflicting any emotional harm because

> [w]hile it might have been foreseeable that Lionell could suffer distress if a close friend or relative was lying on the tracks, Lionell has not alleged that he even knew Walker prior to the incident. Walker did not know, and could not have known, with "substantial certainty" that Lionell would be traumatized by his sit-in, or even by an accidental injury to a complete stranger.

(citation omitted) *This claim, however, that injury to Lionell was unforeseeable because of the lack of any pre-existing relationship between Walker and Lionell, is irrelevant.*

Unlike the tort of negligent infliction of emotional distress, recovery for the tort of *intentional* infliction of emotional distress is not limited to situations "in which the plaintiffs have been near relatives, or at least close associates, of the person" injured by the *defendant.* (citation omitted) *This* makes perfect sense.

A *defendant* who causes a plaintiff to participate in the defendant's mutilation should not escape liability simply because the two are not genetically or socially related. *As the Restatement comments explain,* there is "no essential reason why a stranger who is asked for a match on the street should not recover when the man who asked for it is shot down before his eyes, at least where [the stranger's] emotional distress results in bodily harm." (citation omitted)

Indeed, the Restatement provides an illustration in which recovery is allowed even though the plaintiff and defendant were strangers:

> 21. In the presence of A, a bystander, B quarrels violently with C, draws a pistol, and threatens to kill C. B knows that A is pregnant, and that it is highly probable that his conduct will cause severe emotional distress to A. A suffers severe emotional distress, which results in a miscarriage. B is subject to liability to A.

(citation omitted)

Thus, a familial, or any type of preexisting relationship between Walker and Lionell is irrelevant here. *Without question,* Walker's actions were wilful, and this Court should so find.

This ends (for now) our praise of the transition but not our discussion of language. We'll next explore the concept of *style* and the critical role it plays in crafting elegant arguments.

Chapter Review
Cohesion: The Power of Transitions

✓ Have we effectively used transitions in our writing?

✓ Have we used "therefore" to demonstrate a cause-effect relationship between thoughts?

✓ Have we used linking transitions to emphasize a point, note exceptions, conclude or move the discussion forward, note the passage of time, provide a sense of location or place, compare or contrast points, or delineate a sequence?

✓ Have we used repetition transitions, such as case names, "this case," or "that case," to signpost which case (ours or the cited case), we are addressing?

✓ Have we used restatement transitions to make an abstract concept more concrete, to convey a bias, or to address a series or summary?

✓ Have we used roadmap transitions to preview the discussion for our reader, to move from position to position, or to introduce an extended discussion of a specific point?

✓ Have we used a variety of transitions effectively?

Chapter 33

Style: Writing with Elegance

"Of all those arts in which the wise excel, Nature's chief masterpiece is writing well."

—John Sheffield,
Duke of Buckingham and Normandy
Essay on Poetry (1682)

§ 33.1   Write Parallel Structures

"This principle, that of parallel construction, requires that expressions similar in content and function be outwardly similar. The likeness of form enables the reader to recognize more readily the likeness of content and function."

—Strunk and White, *The Elements of Style*

As legal writers, we deal with complex subjects. Our aim in writing is to make the complex simple. One of the most useful tools we can use to accomplish this goal is parallelism.

To create parallelism, we place a pair or series of words, phrases, clauses, or sentences in similar grammatical structure. The sentence flows easily, undercutting reader resistance to what we're conveying. Let's look at some examples:

Graphic 33.1	Examples of Parallelism	
words	The prosecution acted	unfairly, unethically, and unlawfully.
phrases	The expert witness erred	in his investigation, in his analysis, and in his conclusion.
clauses	A person has knowledge of a fact under the following circumstances: 1. when she has actual notice of it; 2. when she has received notice of it; or 3. when she has reason to know that it exists.	
sentences	In *Camden*, the defendant-employer was a nonprofit legal corporation with fifty employees and with gross annual revenues of over $900,000. In our case, the defendant-employer is a nonprofit hospital corporation with sixty employees and with gross annual revenues of over $1,000,000.	

In the sections below, we'll explore how to write parallel structures. Because we believe the best way to convey this information is to show the difference between parallel and non-parallel structures, we've used many examples. Moreover, because these examples are fairly self-explanatory, we haven't discussed them in detail. Parallel structure, like, well, obscenity, is one of those, "I know it when I see it" occurrences.

§ 33.1(a)   Use the Same Grammatical Form

To write in parallel form, we craft each "branch" of the parallel structure in the same grammatical form. Compare the following two examples (which do not follow parallel structure) with examples in **Graphic 33.1** (which do follow parallel structure). Notice in particular the highlighted (non-parallel) words below:

Graphic 33.1(a)	Non-Parallel Structure
words	The prosecution acted (1) *unfairly,* (2) **with an unethical approach, and** (3) *unlawfully.*
clauses	A person has knowledge of a fact under the following circumstances: 1. when he has actual notice of it; 2. **notice of it was received by him**; or 3. when he has reason to know that it exists.

These passages don't flow as readily as parallel structures. Instead, they "jolt" us; something's "not quite right." This sensation is perhaps best illustrated by the "comfort" we feel in reading "To be, or not to be," compared to the "jolt" we receive in reading "To be, or not being."

§ 33.1(b)   Use the Same Voice

Switching from active voice in one clause of our structure to passive voice in another subtly breaks parallelism. For example:

Graphic 33.1(b)	Avoid Changes in Voice
non-parallel	**parallel**
The defendants should have investigated the story more thoroughly, and the defamatory statement should have been retracted more quickly.	The defendants should have investigated the story more thoroughly, and should have retracted the defamatory statement more quickly.

§ 33.1(c)   Use a List

A list is a particularly helpful parallel structure. We separate causes of action and statutory provisions into their elements, and then focus on the element(s) in issue. Here are some rules for punctuating a sentence using a list:

Graphic 33.1(c)	Rules for Creating a List
(a) Introduce the list with a main clause and a colon: not "The rules are:" but "The rules are as follows:"; (b) in most cases, place semi-colons between the items in the list; and (c) place a conjunction after the next-to-the-last item.	

§ 33.1(d)   Repeat Structural Cues

By repeating structural clues, we signal each branch of the parallel structure.

Graphic 33.1(d)	Using Structural Cues
non-parallel	**parallel**
The court stressed that the plaintiff had invited public inquiry by his conduct, little time had elapsed between his performance and the defamation, and punitive damages would stifle freedom of the press.	The court stressed *that* the plaintiff had invited public inquiry by his conduct, *that* little time had elapsed between his performance and the defamation, and *that* punitive damages would stifle freedom of the press.

§ 33.1(e)   Create Balanced Branches

Besides simplifying the complex, parallelism can help make our writing eloquent. Consider the following:

Graphic 33.1(e)(1)	Balanced Structure
	Give me liberty or *give me death.*

Patrick Henry's famous epigram illustrates balance: both branches of the parallel structure have the same number of words. To achieve *perfect* balance, each branch must have the same number of syllables.

Graphic 33.1(e)(2)	Perfect Balance
imperfect balance	**perfect balance**
As a child the defendant did not have a happy home life. After his father left home to enter the Army, his mother became an alcoholic and accordingly ignored the child.	As a child the defendant did not have a happy home life. *His father abandoned him for the Army. His mother abandoned him for alcohol.*

However, to achieve eloquence, we don't need to put our parallel structures in perfect balance, as John F. Kennedy's famous line illustrates:

Graphic 33.1(e)(3)	Eloquence

Ask not what your country can do for you;
ask what you can do for your country.

If we're within one word or within about two syllables, our parallel structure will have rhetorical impact. Who can forget Johnny Cochran's famous closing argument referencing the glove the killer allegedly wore in the O.J. Simpson criminal case:

Graphic 33.1(e)(4)	Impact

"If it doesn't fit,
you must acquit."

In that one statement, the entire theory of the defendant's case was conveyed, and successfully so.

§ 33.1(f)   Place the Longest Branch Last

In constructing parallel structures, we can't always achieve balance. Most branches won't be the same length. However, we achieve an overall balance by, when logically possible, placing the longest branch of the parallel structure last.

Graphic 33.1(f) When Possible, Place the Longest Branch Last	
unbalanced — longest branch first A person has knowledge of a fact under the following circumstances: 1. when from all the facts known to her at the time in question, she has reason to know that it exists; 2. when she has received notice of it; or 3. when she has actual notice of it.	**balanced — longest branch last** A person has knowledge of a fact under the following circumstances: 1. when she has actual notice of it; 2. when she has received notice of it; or 3. when from all the facts known to her at the time in question, she has reason to know that it exists.

That concludes our review of parallel structure. Let's turn next to another area of writing eloquence—the correct use of "tense"—which is too often ignored in legal writing.

§ 33.2   Use the Correct Tense

Two "rules" govern the use of "tense" in legal writing, and we believe they are (mercifully) simple to remember:

1. Use the past tense in discussing cited cases or the facts of our case; and

2. Use the present tense in discussing an existing legal rule.

Past tense. As the following graphic illustrates, we use the *past* tense to discuss the facts of our case, or to relate the facts, issue, holding, rule, or reasoning of a cited case.

Graphic 33.2(a)	Use the Past Tense in Discussing Cited Cases
incorrect	**correct**
The Court in *Spence* holds	The Court in *Spence* held
	Holding that..., the *Spence* Court
The court finds that	The court found that
	Finding that..., the court
At issue is whether	At issue was whether
The court rules that	The court ruled that
	Ruling that..., the court
The court reasons that	The court reasoned that
	Reasoning that..., the court

The following writing prompts are helpful in discussing cited cases, as well as in addressing our case:

Graphic 33.2(b)	Writing Prompts		
actor	**action**		
the appellant, petitioner, plaintiff, respondent, defendant, appellee:	addressed	alleged	appealed
	argued	articulated	asked
	asserted	attempted	averred
	challenged	claimed	contended
	countered	demanded	failed
	invited	maintained	moved
	proffered	rebutted	remarked
	responded	stated	tried

actor	action		
the court:	addressed	adopted	affirmed
	agreed	amended	applied
	articulated	asked	awarded
	concluded	criticized	decided
	denied	determined	disagreed
	examined	expanded	explained
	fashioned	followed	found
	granted	held	inquired
	limited	maintained	modified
	ordered	overruled	overturned
	proposed	questioned	reasoned
	remanded	responded	reversed
	ruled	stated	upheld

Notice: The court does not *argue.* Advocates argue; the court settles that argument.

Present tense. Finally, in discussing an existing legal rule, i.e., one still in force, we use the present tense.

Graphic 33.2(c)	Discussing the Law
incorrect	**correct**
The Fourth Amendment provided that	The Fourth Amendment provides that

Chapter Review
Style: Writing with Elegance

✓ Have we used parallel structure to emphasize and simplify?

   ✓ Have we used the same grammatical form?

   ✓ Have we used the same voice?

   ✓ Have we used a list?

   ✓ Have we repeated structural clues?

   ✓ Have we created balanced branches?

   ✓ Have we placed the longest branch last?

✓ Have we used the correct tense?

   ✓ Have we used the past tense in discussing cited cases or the facts of our case?

   ✓ Have we used the present tense in discussing an existing legal rule?

Section Review: Section V
The Basics: Designing Clear and Persuasive Writing

Chapter 28:   Brevity

✓ Keep sentences short. §28.1

✓ Eliminate "throat-clearing" phrases. §28.2

✓ Eliminate "clearly" and "obviously." §28.3

✓ Eliminate unnecessary "hedging" words. §28.4

✓ Eliminate surplus words. §28.5

✓ Make affirmative statements. §28.6

Chapter 29:   Artistry: Choosing the Right Words and Phrases

✓ Replace abstract words, phrases, and concepts with concrete examples. §29.1

✓ Use nouns and verbs rather than adjectives and adverbs. §29.2

✓ Use forceful nouns instead of intensifying adjectives. §29.2(a)

✓ Use the most forceful verbs. §29.2(b)

✓ Replace forms of "to be" with more concrete verbs. §29.2(c)

✓ Use active voice. §29.3

✓ Use base verbs—avoid derivative nouns. §29.4

Chapter 30:   Simplicity: Avoiding Confusion

✓ Make clear what "it" is and use "it's" properly. §30.1

✓ Make clear what each clause modifies. §30.2

✓ Clear up vague, ambiguous, or awkward sentences. §30.3

Chapter 31:   Impact: Making Every Word Count

✓ Select words that create a favorable bias. §31.1

✓ Use effective sentence structure and stress points. §31.2

✓ Subordinate unfavorable facts and strong opposing arguments. §31.3

✓ Use contrasting elements to minimize unfavorable facts or arguments. §31.4

✓ Use effective paragraphs. §31.5

Chapter 32:   Cohesion: the Power of Transitions

✓ Use "linking" transitions to link one thought to the next by showing a relationship between them. §32.2

✓ Use the following "substantive" transitions to show substantive links between thoughts: §32.3

    ✓ "Repetition" transitions to create a bridge between thoughts by using overlapping language. §32.3(a)

    ✓ "Restatement" transitions to connect thoughts by making concrete a prior, more abstract concept by renaming the subject, or by classifying or summarizing a group of similar thoughts into one common subject or collective noun. §32.3(b)

✓ "Roadmap" transitions to introduce or preface an idea. § 32.3(c)

✓ Use a mixture of transitions to make writing cohesive and interesting. § 32.4

Chapter 33:   Style: Writing with Elegance

✓ Use parallel structure to emphasize and to simplify. § 33.1

  ✓ Use the same grammatical form. § 33.1(a)

  ✓ Use the same voice. § 33.1(b)

  ✓ Use a list. § 33.1(c)

  ✓ Repeat structural clues. § 33.1(d)

  ✓ Create balanced branches. § 33.1(e)

  ✓ Place the longest branch last. § 33.1(f)

✓ Use the correct tense: § 33.2

  ✓ Use the past tense in discussing cited cases or the facts of our case.

  ✓ Use the present tense in discussing an existing legal rule.

Exercise: How Could We Edit This Passage?

Assume that the following passage is from a brief filed with an appellate court. Relying on the principles addressed in **Section V**, how can we edit it to make it more effective?

> Because the Code focuses on preventing the harmful secondary effects which can arise from aggressive begging, and not on the suppression of a particular viewpoint, the Code is a content-neutral regulation, and is therefore subject to the time, place, and manner test for determining whether or not it is a reasonable restriction on the freedom of speech.

The next step in determining whether or not the conviction of Doe should stand involves making a determination as to whether or not the Code is content-neutral or content-based. If the Code is ultimately and conclusively found to be content-neutral, it will therefore be subjected to the time, place, and manner test under which a determination will be made as to whether or not it is a restriction that is reasonable on the freedom of speech.

The primary question that must be answered in order to determine whether or not a regulation is content-based or content-neutral is whether or not the regulation has sought, or will seek, to regulate a particular message, making it content-based; or seeks to prevent the harmful secondary effects caused by the conduct it forbids, making it content-neutral. Other courts have made the finding that regulations which prohibit the act of begging usually can qualify as being decidedly content-neutral.

In *Chad*, people begged on a sidewalk in Ft. Lauderdale. The Federal Court for the Southern District of Florida found that a regulation banning begging on the sidewalk and beach of the City met the qualification for being content-neutral. The court finds so, because the regulation in question and at issue in this case, seeks to avoid the effects, which were naturally harmful, of disrupting the crucial tourist industry of the City and effecting in a negative way the pleasant atmosphere of the beach, which begging on the beach caused, and did not identify for targeting begging because of any message it apparently sought to convey.

Like the regulation there in this case, the Code in the instant case here is not aimed at the restriction of a message, but rather aims at preventing the harmful secondary effects which begging causes in the area of traffic safety, and should therefore be declared content-neutral. As already discussed, the Code which Doe was arrested for violating was enacted in order to cut down on the significant number of traffic accidents which were being caused by the actions of beggars who were aggressive in the economically vital downtown core of the City. Because the Code is designed in order to aid in the prevention of the statistically proven harmful secondary effects of begging that is aggressive in nature, and is not aiming at the suppression of any message which aggressive begging might be considered to convey, the Code in the instant case here, like the one under consideration in the case of *Chad*, is content-neutral.

Section VI

The Samples[1]

Disclaimer: These samples are just that—samples. They are not offered as examples of "perfect" writing. In fact, each time *we* read them, we find something else to change. (*We thank our publisher for his patience.*) We have used Courier New 12 point font to maintain proper spacing for citations throughout all examples and use underscoring rather than italics to help show you the correct method for underscoring. We've skipped one space between each sentence in the Court Opinion, but have skipped two spaces in the other documents. Either is correct. The current trend is towards a single space.

A special thank you: We thank our good friend and colleague Henry Wihnyk for his help in editing these samples. (If you find any typos, logical inconsistencies, etc. in them, please let *him* know.)

---

1. In all these samples we have used Florida citation rules, supplemented by *The Bluebook,* as required by the Florida Rules of Appellate Procedure Rule 9.800 "Uniform Citation System" because our hypothetical appellate case is situated in a Florida state court.

Chapter 34

Court Opinion

IN THE CIRCUIT COURT FOR THE EIGHTH JUDICIAL CIRCUIT
IN AND FOR ALACHUA COUNTY, FLORIDA

Parker Lionell,   )
)
            Plaintiff,   )
v.   )   Case No.: Sxx
)
Noah Walker,   )
)
            Defendant.   )
_____)

MEMORANDUM OF OPINION AND FINAL JUDGMENT

This case arises under circumstances which this Court
has never before encountered: Plaintiff Parker Lionell, who
operated a train which struck and severely injured Defendant
Noah Walker, seeks to recover damages from Walker for
intentionally causing Lionell to suffer mental distress. The
Court must decide, upon Walker's motion to dismiss, whether
Lionell's complaint states a cause of action for intentional
infliction of emotional distress. Finding that it does not,
and finding that amending the pleadings will not cure the
complaint's defects, the Court dismisses Lionell's complaint
with prejudice.

Findings of Fact

This suit arises out of tragic events occurring on a
semi-remote stretch of railway in Alachua County, Florida.
On April 10, 20xx, a 4021 ton railroad train operated by
Lionell (the chief engineer), ran over Walker, severely
injuring him. Shortly before impact, Walker and two others
had been lying on the tracks to protest the train's cargo:
enriched plutonium used to manufacture nuclear bombs. As the

train approached, the two other protestors leapt aside and
escaped injury. Tragically, the train collided with Walker,
severing both legs below the knees.

On April 9, 20xx, the day before the accident, Walker
notified the local newspaper of his plan to stage a protest
near the train tracks. The next day, a reporter and
approximately twenty bystanders attended the demonstration.
Just minutes before the accident, Walker announced to those
gathered:

> "Pretty soon that train will be coming down these tracks
> carrying death and destruction. The railroad knows this,
> the engineers know this, you know this. But no one does
> a damn thing to stop it. No one's ready to put his butt
> on the line to stop it. The thing goes on and on, on and
> on, on and on -- chugging down the track, chugging down
> our throats. We're choking on it, we're dying from it,
> but no one seems to care. Well I care. Drastic times
> require drastic measures. If it goes any further, it's
> got to go through me."

Pl.'s Compl. ¶ 30. Walker then walked to the train track and
lay down crosswise on it. Two other protestors joined him.

Immediately thereafter, an official of the railroad
approached Walker and pleaded with him to leave the tracks.
The official warned him that the train would not be able to
stop; that Walker would die or be severely injured; and that
interfering with railroad trains or tracks was a felony.
Walker, still astride the tracks, responded: "'I have to do
what I have to do.'" Pl.'s Compl. ¶ 32.

Within three minutes, and before police officers could
arrive, the train appeared, traveling well under the legal
speed limit. Seeing Walker and the other two protestors
lying on the track, Lionell sounded a barrage of warning

whistles, applied the brakes, and took every measure
possible to stop the train. Unfortunately, his and his
crew's efforts failed. The train rolled on: the two other
protestors leapt to safety while Walker was struck.
Tragically, Walker's legs were amputated.

Although Lionell did not see the train strike Walker, he
heard Walker's agonizing cries and saw Walker's blood spew
in a grotesque shower. Stricken by these sounds and sights,
Lionell repeatedly vomited. Shortly thereafter, he
experienced severe migraine headaches, sweaty palms, weight
loss (ten pounds), nausea, guilt, depression, and recurrent
nightmares in which he "relived" his role in the accident.
Although the nausea was short-lived, the severe headaches,
sweaty palms, depression, and nightmares continue. Because
of his distress, he has been unable to return to work as an
engineer, or even board a train.

On July 10, 20xx, Lionell filed the instant complaint
for intentional infliction of emotional distress. On July
31, 20xx, Walker filed a motion to dismiss the complaint in
its entirety, claiming that Lionell's mental distress is not
compensable. At the August 28, 20xx hearing on that motion,
Walker argued that the complaint failed to allege facts
demonstrating (1) that his actions were outrageous; (2) that
he possessed the requisite intent to commit the tort; and
(3) that Lionell's distress was severe.

Conclusions of Law

In judging the sufficiency of the complaint, the Court

3

must consider the facts alleged to be true, read the complaint in the light most favorable to Lionell, and resolve any reasonable doubts in his behalf. Because the Court finds that Lionell has failed to state a cause of action for intentional infliction of emotional distress, and can prove no set of facts supporting his claim which would entitle him to relief, the Court dismisses his complaint with prejudice.

To state a cause of action for intentional infliction of emotional distress, a plaintiff must allege facts demonstrating that the defendant's actions (1) were so outrageous in character and so extreme in degree as to go beyond all possible bounds of decency and are to be regarded as atrocious and utterly intolerable in a civilized community; (2) were performed intentionally or recklessly, in deliberate disregard of a high degree of probability that emotional distress will follow; and (3) caused plaintiff to suffer severe emotional distress which no reasonable person should be expected to endure. See Metro. Life Ins. Co. v. McCarson, 467 So. 2d 277, 278-79 (Fla. 1985) (adopting Restatement (Second) of Torts § 46 (1965) and the Restatement's comments).

Initially determining whether Walker's conduct may reasonably be regarded as so extreme and outrageous as to permit recovery is the court's, not the jury's, function. The jury becomes involved only where reasonable people may hold differing views on whether the defendant's conduct has

4

been sufficiently extreme and outrageous to result in liability. See Restatement (Second) of Torts § 46 cmt. h.

Based on these standards, the Court finds, on three independent grounds, that Lionell's complaint fails to state a claim for intentional infliction of emotional distress. First, the complaint fails to allege facts demonstrating that Walker's actions were "so extreme in degree, as to go beyond all possible bounds of decency, and to be regarded as atrocious, and utterly intolerable in a civilized community." Id. cmt. d. Walker's conduct may have been illegal, foolhardy, and extreme, but it was not outrageous.

Second, the complaint fails to allege facts demonstrating that Walker acted intentionally or recklessly. None of the allegations demonstrate that Walker intended to cause Lionell's mental distress. See E. Airlines, Inc. v. King, 557 So. 2d 574, 576 (Fla. 1990). Because Walker's acts were not directed against Lionell, Walker is not liable for Lionell's alleged distress.

Finally, the complaint fails to state a cause of action for intentional infliction of emotional distress because the mental distress alleged is not severe enough. Lionell's vomiting, nausea, guilt, depression, headaches, sweaty palms, and nightmares can occur without any emotional upset. They do not rise to the level of severity § 46 requires.

For these reasons, the Court holds that Lionell has failed to state a cause of action for intentional infliction of emotional distress; dismisses his complaint with

prejudice; and enters final judgment for Defendant Noah
Walker.

    Dated: September 6, 20xx.

                        /s/ _____

IN THE CIRCUIT COURT FOR THE EIGHTH JUDICIAL CIRCUIT
IN AND FOR ALACHUA COUNTY, FLORIDA

Parker Lionell,   )   Case No.: Sxx
)
          Plaintiff / Appellant,   )
)
v.   )
)
)
Noah Walker,   )
)
          Defendant / Appellee.   )
_____   )

NOTICE OF APPEAL

Parker Lionell appeals to the First District Court of Appeal this Court's final judgment dated September 6, 20xx, dismissing Lionell's complaint with prejudice.

Dated: September 11, 20xx.

                              _____
                              Stew Dent
                              Fla. Bar No.: 23856

                              Counsel for Plaintiff / Appellant
                              Holland Hall
                              University of Florida
                              Gainesville, FL 32611
                              352-555-5555

CERTIFICATE OF SERVICE

I certify that a true copy of this Notice of Appeal was furnished to Matthew Thomas, Counsel for Defendant / Appellee, by hand this 11th day of September, 20xx.

_____
Stew Dent
Counsel for Plaintiff / Appellant

Chapter 35

Legal Memo

TO: L. Pflaum and T. Rambo

FROM: S. Dent

DATE: September 18, 20xx

RE: Case No. Sxx; Lionell v. Walker (IIED) File: memo.r&p

QUESTION PRESENTED:

Did the trial court err in dismissing the complaint of our
client, Parker Lionell, for failing to state a cause of action for
intentional infliction of emotional distress ("IIED") where the
complaint alleged facts showing:

(1)   that Defendant Noah Walker purposefully lay across
railroad tracks in front of an oncoming train and remained there
until the train struck and amputated his legs; and

(2)   that Lionell, who operated the train and observed
the impact, has suffered emotional distress resulting in physical
symptoms so severe that he cannot return to his livelihood as an
engineer?

BRIEF ANSWER:

Probably yes. To state a cause of action for IIED, Lionell
must allege facts demonstrating that (1) Walker's conduct was
extreme and outrageous; (2) Walker acted with the requisite
intent; and (3) Lionell suffered severe emotional distress. As
discussed below, because Lionell's complaint adequately alleges
facts sufficient to fulfill each of these elements, Lionell's
appeal likely should be successful.

FACTS:

On April 10, 20xx, alongside a semi-remote stretch of railway in Alachua County, Florida, a newspaper reporter and twenty bystanders gathered to witness an anti-nuclear protestor named Noah Walker contront a 4021 ton train. The crowd was not there by happenstance; Walker had notified the local paper the day before of his railway protest. That train carried plutonium, a component for nuclear weapons; and Walker meant to stop it.

Minutes before the train arrived, Walker announced to the onlookers:

> Pretty soon that train will be coming down these tracks carrying death and destruction. The railroad knows this, the engineers know this, you know this. But no one does a damn thing to stop it. No one's ready to put his butt on the line to stop it. The thing goes on and on, on and on, on and on — chugging down the track, chugging down our throats. We're choking on it, we're dying from it, but no one seems to care. Well I care. Drastic times require drastic measures. If it goes any further, it's got to go through me.

True to his word, Walker then lay down crosswise on the track, and was joined by two other protestors.

Immediately thereafter, a railroad official arrived and pleaded with Walker to get off the tracks. He told Walker that the oncoming train would not stop; that Walker would die or be seriously injured; and that interfering with railroad trains or tracks was a felony. Despite this warning, Walker remained on the tracks, responding, "I have to do what I have to do."

Within three minutes, the train appeared, traveling well under the legal speed limit. Lionell was the train's chief engineer. When he saw Walker and the two protestors on the tracks, Lionell sounded a barrage of warning whistles, used every

2

braking device available, and did everything humanly possible to stop the train. The other two protestors jumped off the tracks and were unhurt, but Walker remained. Predictably, and tragically, Walker was struck; the train severed both his legs below the knee.

From Lionell's position in the train, he could not see Walker being crushed under the wheels. However, he heard Walker's screams and saw Walker's blood rain down upon the train. Traumatized by these sounds and sights, Lionell vomited repeatedly and uncontrollably. Within days, he was stricken with severe migraine headaches, sweaty palms, nausea, guilt, weight loss of ten pounds, and depression. Even sleep was no sanctuary; he suffered recurrent nightmares reliving his forced role in Walker's attempted suicide. These severe migraines, sweaty palms, depression, guilt, and nightmares continue to plague him. So disabled, he has been unable to return to his livelihood as an engineer. He cannot even board a train. Lionell had no prior history of emotional distress, and indeed, had yearly employment physicals.

Three months later, and still suffering severe distress, Lionell filed suit against Walker for intentional infliction of emotional distress. In that suit, he alleged all of the facts as stated above. On July 31, 20xx, however, Walker filed a motion to dismiss Lionell's complaint for failure to state a claim. On September 6, 20xx, the trial court granted that motion, and dismissed Lionell's complaint with prejudice on three independent grounds.

3

First, the trial court ruled that although "Walker's conduct may have been illegal, foolhardy and extreme," it was not outrageous. Thus, as a matter of law, the trial court held that Walker's actions of lying on the train track in the path of an oncoming train he knew could not stop did not rise to the level of the atrocious and the intolerable.

Second, the court ruled that the complaint failed to allege that Walker had acted with the requisite intent since "Walker's acts were not directed against Lionell . . . ." The court thus held insufficient Lionell's allegations (1) that Walker knew engineers were on the train; (2) that Lionell was on the train acting as chief engineer; (3) that Walker intentionally lay down on the tracks in the path of the oncoming train he knew could not stop; and (4) that Walker had stated, just minutes before the train had struck him, that if "it goes any further, it's got to go through me."

Finally, the court concluded that despite Lionell's continued physical and emotional disabilities resulting from the trauma, his distress was not "severe enough" as a matter of law to warrant recovery. This was so, observed the court, because Lionell's "vomiting, nausea, guilt, depression, headaches, sweaty palms, and nightmares can occur without any emotional upset." On September 11, 20xx, Lionell filed a notice of appeal seeking review of this judgment.

DISCUSSION:

Florida recognizes the tort of IIED as defined in Restatement

(Second) of Torts section 46 (1965) and the comments thereto.
Metro. Life Ins. Co. v. McCarson, 467 So. 2d 277, 278 (Fla. 1985).
Under section 46, "[o]ne who by extreme and outrageous conduct
intentionally or recklessly causes severe emotional distress to
another is subject to liability for such emotional distress, and
if bodily harm to the other results from it, for such bodily
harm." See also Metro., 467 So. 2d at 278-79.

Although the tort of IIED is firmly established, no reported
case in Florida or any other jurisdiction involves a situation
where, as here, a plaintiff who has injured the defendant has then
sued the injured defendant for "outrage" damages. As the comments
to section 46 recognize, however, "the ultimate limits of this
tort are not yet determined," leaving "fully open the possibility
of further development of the law." Restatement § 46 cmt. c. Our
case may give rise to such "further development."

In reviewing a final judgment dismissing a complaint with
prejudice, the appellate court should view the complaint in the
light most favorable to the plaintiff, here Lionell, accepting all
allegations as true. See Sarkis v. Pafford Oil Co., 697 So. 2d
524, 526 (Fla. 1st DCA 1997). Under section 1.110(b) of the
Florida Rules of Civil Procedure, although Lionell must allege
ultimate facts supporting each element of the cause of action, he
need not plead his claim with particularity or specificity. All
he need do is merely outline his position. See Sullivan v.
deColigny, 432 F. Supp. 689, 690 (D. V.I. 1977) (denying
defendants' motion for judgment on the pleadings in an intentional
infliction of emotional distress case, stating that a ruling on

this motion could come only after the plaintiff presented evidence of the defendants' conduct).

Here, Lionell alleged [1] that Walker's act of purposefully lying in the path of an oncoming train was extreme and outrageous; [2] that Walker intentionally or recklessly allowed the train Lionell was operating to run over him; and [3] that Lionell suffered severe emotional distress from being an unwilling participant in Walker's attempted suicide. For the reasons discussed below, I believe these allegations sufficiently state a claim for IIED.

A.   The court will likely conclude that Lionell
     sufficiently alleged that Walker's conduct was
     extreme and outrageous.

Over a hundred years ago, the Florida Supreme Court commented, "[a]n engine-driver seeing an adult upon the track ahead of his engine, or beside the track, has the right to presume that [the person] has possession of his faculties, and that he will obey the instinctive law of self-preservation by getting off the track . . . ." Fla. Cent. & Peninsular R.R. Co. v. Williams, 37 Fla. 406, 426, 20 So. 558, 564 (1896). Although the case did not involve a claim for IIED, the court's implicit common-sense observation applies here. Intentionally failing to get off the tracks when a train is approaching is "outrageous."

Under the Restatement of Torts, conduct is actionable when it is "so outrageous in character, and so extreme in degree, as to go beyond all possible bounds of decency, and to be regarded as atrocious, and utterly intolerable in a civilized community." Restatement § 46 cmt. d. Extreme and outrageous conduct arouses

6

resentment against the actor, and leads people to exclaim, "'Outrageous!'" Id.

Where reasonable people may differ, it is improper for the trial court to decide, as a matter of law, that allegations of outrageous conduct are insufficient. Restatement § 46 cmt. h. Rather, the jury must determine whether the conduct has been sufficiently extreme and outrageous to result in liability. Id. In other words, the trial court decides the issue as a matter of law only when the "facts of a case can under no conceivable interpretation support the tort . . . ." Williams v. City of Minneola, 575 So. 2d 683, 692 (Fla. 5th DCA 1991). However, "where significant facts are disputed, or where differing inferences could reasonably be derived from undisputed facts, the question of outrageousness is for the jury to decide." Id.

The trial court here, however, never gave the jury the chance to determine whether Walker's actions were outrageous. Instead, the court decided as a matter of law that although Walker's conduct "may have been illegal, foolhardy, and extreme," it was not outrageous. We should argue that the court's ruling was wrong.

In a case remarkably similar to Lionell's, the Iowa Supreme Court ruled that in causing a plaintiff to view the results of a defendant's self-inflicted wounds, the defendant had engaged in outrageous and extreme conduct. See Blakeley v. Shortal's Estate, 20 N.W.2d 28, 31 (Iowa 1945). In Blakeley, the decedent was a neighbor and an invited guest who had spent the night in Blakeley's home. Id. at 29. The next day, Blakeley left her

home, leaving the decedent sitting at a table in her kitchen. Id.
When she returned home, she saw the decedent "lying on the floor
with pools of blood about him." Id. He had slit his own throat
with a "skinning" knife, leaving "blood on the floor and about the
room." Id. at 30. In reversing a directed verdict for the
decedent's estate, the court found that the decedent had willfully
created a "gory and ghastly sight" that naturally resulted in
emotional distress worthy of damages. Id. at 31.[1]

In recognizing a cause of action for IIED, Florida courts
have allowed recovery under circumstances far less extreme than
that of Blakeley. For example, in Knowles Animal Hospital, Inc.
v. Willis, 360 So. 2d 37 (Fla. 3d DCA 1978), dog owners sued for
intentional infliction of emotional distress for their mental pain
and suffering where a veterinarian severely burned their dog by
allowing it to remain on a heating pad for a day and a half.
Because of the burn as well as other factors, the dog had to be
put to sleep. Id. at 38. The Third District affirmed a $13,000
verdict in favor of the dog owners, finding such negligence
amounted to "great indifference to the property of the plaintiffs
. . . ." Id. at 38-39; see also La Porte v. Associated Indeps.,
Inc., 163 So. 2d 267, 269 (Fla. 1964) (reasoning that plaintiff's
mental distress was a proper element of recoverable damages in an
action where plaintiff's pet dog was killed by defendant's

---

[1] Notably, there was no "familial" relationship between the
plaintiff and the suicide victim in the Blakeley case.
Blakeley thus helps to demonstrate that a defendant cannot
escape liability simply because he is not related to the
plaintiff. However, if Walker raises this as an issue, we
should conduct more research on this point.

employee in a wrongful, malicious act within plaintiff's sight).

Moreover, despite the Restatement's admonishment that the "extreme and outrageous conduct" element of the tort does not extend to mere insults or indignities, an early Florida decision held that extreme and outrageous behavior existed where the defendant made statements to a six year old child regarding the adulterous conduct of the child's mother. See Korbin v. Berlin, 177 So. 2d 551, 553 (Fla. 3d DCA 1965). There, the court reasoned that the wrongful acts were such as to "reasonably imply malice . . . or great indifference to the rights of others" because they were "intended or reasonably calculated to cause the child 'severe emotional distress.'" Id.

Another Florida court concluded that extreme and outrageous behavior existed where a defendant merely pushed and verbally abused the plaintiff. Jefferson Ward Stores v. Khorozian, 519 So. 2d 627, 627 (Fla. 4th DCA 1984). In Jefferson, a woman was wrongfully accused by store employees of stealing. Id. (Glickstein, J., concurring). Without explaining their actions, the employees chased the woman into the parking lot, verbally abused her, threatened her, pushed her, and dragged her towards the store while a gathered crowd watched. Id. In finding the employees' conduct extreme and outrageous, Judge Glickstein reasoned in his concurring opinion that although liability would not extend to mere insults, indignities, threats, or annoyances, it would extend where a person's actions would incur the resentment of an average member of the community who would be led to exclaim, "outrageous!" Id. at 628.

Florida courts also have allowed recovery in cases involving such outrageous conduct as wrongfully refusing to pay the proceeds of insurance policies, see, e.g., Dominquez v. Equitable Life Assurance Society, 438 So. 2d 58, 61-62 (Fla. 3d DCA 1983), approved sub nom., Crawford v. Dominquez, 467 So. 2d 281 (Fla. 1985); and falsely reporting that one's relatives have been injured, see, e.g., Ford Motor Credit Co. v. Sheehan, 373 So. 2d 956, 958 (Fla. 1st DCA 1979).

Further, the Restatement includes two more examples of actionable, outrageous conduct: [1] threatening to injure the plaintiff and ruin his business; and [2] giving a female plaintiff a bathing suit which the defendant knows is water soluble and which "dissolves while [plaintiff] is swimming, leaving her naked in the presence of men and women whom she has just met." Restatement § 46 illus. 2, 3.

We should argue that Walker's actions are manifestly more extreme, outrageous, and atrocious than any reported Florida decision. Indeed, only the Blakeley case from the Iowa Supreme Court approaches, yet cannot match, the ghastliness of the instant case.

Nonetheless, Walker will likely argue that he was merely engaged in a peaceful political protest which went terribly wrong, and was not engaged in the type of wanton and atrocious conduct required for IIED. As the comments to the Restatement explain:

> It has not been enough that the defendant has acted
> with an intent which is tortious or even criminal, or
> that he has intended to inflict emotional distress, or
> even that his conduct has been characterized by
> "malice," or a degree of aggravation which would

10

entitle the plaintiff to punitive damages for another
tort.

Restatement (Second) of Torts § 46 cmt. d.

Whether a defendant's action is "outrageous" of course
turns on the court's case-by-case assessment. To support
his assertion that his actions were not outrageous, Walker
may cite to cases with utterly atrocious facts, and attempt
to show that his conduct pales in comparison.

For example, one court recognized a mother's claim for
intentional infliction of emotional distress against a
medical examiner who, over the mother's express objection,
removed the eyeballs of her dead three-year-old daughter,
and then falsified an autopsy report on the child, allegedly
intending to cover up his actions. Kirker v. Orange Cnty.,
519 So. 2d 682, 683 (Fla. 5th DCA 1988). In allowing the
mother's claim, the court noted that recovery on this tort
"'is especially appropriate to tortious interference with
rights involving dead human bodies, where mental anguish to
the surviving relative is'" the natural and probable
consequence of the wrong committed. Id. (quoting Kirksey v.
Jernigan, 45 So. 2d 188, 189 (Fla. 1950)).

However, we should stress that IIED is not limited to
just cases involving "dead bodies" or surviving relatives.
Rather, as the above examples demonstrate, the tort extends
to a much wider range of conduct.

In allowing a freight train to run him over, Walker
acted outrageously. Indeed, just before lying down in the
direct path of the approaching train, Walker proclaimed:

11

"[I]f it [the train] goes any further, it's got to go
through me." True to his word, and ignoring warnings from
both a railroad official and from Lionell's barrage of
whistles, Walker allowed himself to be mutilated. On these
undisputed facts, the court will likely conclude that
Lionell sufficiently alleged that Walker's conduct was
outrageous.

B.   The court will likely conclude that Lionell
      sufficiently alleged that Walker's conduct was
      intentional or reckless.

A defendant manifests the requisite intent for IIED not
only (1) where he desires to harm another, but also (2)
where he acts recklessly in doing so. Restatement § 46 cmt.
i (noting that § 46 incorporates the definition of
"recklessness" found in § 500 of the Restatement).

A person acts reckless if

> he does an act . . . knowing or having reason to know
> of facts which would lead a reasonable man to realize,
> not only that his conduct creates an unreasonable risk
> of physical harm to another, but also that such risk is
> substantially greater than that which is necessary to
> make his conduct negligent.

Restatement § 500.

Indeed, Florida case law defines "reckless disregard"
as "the equivalent of intent." Williams, 575 So. 2d at 692.
Moreover, recklessness also exists where one intentionally
violates a safety statute under circumstances creating a
"high degree of probability that harm will result."
Restatement § 500 cmt. e.

12

Illustrations under comment i to section 46 further explain these principles, and provide persuasive examples of intent strikingly similar to that of Walker's:

> 15.   During A's absence from her home, B attempts to commit suicide in A's kitchen by cutting his throat. B knows that A is substantially certain to return and find his body, and to suffer emotional distress. A finds B lying in her kitchen in a pool of gore, and suffers severe emotional distress. B is subject to liability to A.
>
> 16.   The same facts as in Illustration 15, except that B does not know that A is substantially certain to find him, but does know that there is a high degree of probability that she will do so. B is subject to liability to A.

Restatement § 46, cmt. i.

Recognizing that a defendant need not intend to cause harm to be liable for IIED, the Third and Fifth Districts have stated that this tort should "more appropriately be called `outrageous conduct causing severe emotional distress.'" Williams, 575 So. 2d at 690 (quoting Dominquez, 438 So. 2d at 59 n.1). As these courts explain, referring to the tort as one for "intentional infliction of emotional distress" is misleading because this description "'erroneously suggests that the defendant intended to inflict severe mental or emotional distress when, in fact, all that need be shown is that he intended his specific behavior and knew or should have known that distress would follow.'" Id. (quoting Dominquez, 438 So. 2d at 59). As the Blakeley court stated, "[a] wilful wrong may be committed without any intention to injure anyone." 20 N.W.2d at 31.

Thus, a defendant is liable for IIED even if he did not intend to cause harm. It is enough that he realized, or, from

facts which he knew, should have realized, that there was a strong
probability that harm would result, even though he hoped or even
expected that his conduct would prove harmless. Moreover, it is
irrelevant whether a defendant recognized that his conduct was
extremely dangerous; the standard is an objective one. See
Restatement § 500 cmt. a.

In the instant case, in attempting to demonstrate that Walker
acted with the requisite intent, we should include an argument
that Walker violated three Florida statutes designed to protect
others from harm. These statutes, respectively, prohibit the
following: (1) any unauthorized interference with a railroad
track; (2) any unauthorized interference with a railroad vehicle;
and (3) any unauthorized placement of any object capable of
causing death or great bodily injury in the path of a train. §§
860.05, 860.09, and 860.121, Fla. Stat. (20xx).

We should also stress that for Lionell to have stated a cause
of action for IIED against Walker, he need not have shown that
Walker desired to inflict emotional distress. Nor did he need to
show that Walker planned to make Lionell suffer grief, guilt, and
depression. All he needed to show was that Walker willfully lay
down on those railroad tracks in the path of the oncoming train,
and that Walker either (1) knew distress was substantially certain
to result; or (2) deliberately disregarded (by, for example,
violating a statute), a high degree of probability that serious
harm would follow.

The trial court stated, however, and Walker will likely
argue, that "[b]ecause Walker's acts were not directed against

14

Lionell, Walker is not liable for Lionell's alleged distress."
We should respond that this claim applies the wrong legal
standard. In overlooking that Walker can be liable for IIED if
his actions were either intentional or reckless, the trial court
erred in mandating that Walker's actions be directed against
Lionell. The appellate court will likely conclude that Lionell
sufficiently alleged that Walker's conduct was reckless.

C.   The court will likely conclude that Lionell
      sufficiently alleged that his distress was severe.

The comments to section 46 explain that the emotional
distress element of the tort requires that the distress has in
fact resulted, and has been severe. The comments define
"emotional distress" to include "all highly unpleasant mental
reactions, such as fright, horror, grief, shame, humiliation,
embarrassment, anger, chagrin, disappointment, worry, and nausea."
Restatement § 46 cmt. j.

Severe emotional distress is not limited to cases involving
bodily harm "if the conduct is sufficiently extreme and outrageous
. . . ." Id. cmt. k. However, the distress inflicted must be "so
severe that no reasonable man could be expected to endure it. The
intensity and the duration of the distress are factors to be
considered in determining its severity." Id. cmt. j. The court
determines whether severe emotional distress could exist; the jury
determines whether it did in fact exist. Id.

Although severe distress must be proved, "in many cases the
extreme and outrageous character of the defendant's conduct is in
itself important evidence that the distress has existed." Id.;
see also Sheehan, 373 So. 2d at 959. For example, the plaintiff

in <u>Sheehan</u>, after hearing that his children were severely injured,
and being unable to find them, became "extremely worried, upset,
and nearly out of his mind for a continuous period of seven
hours." <u>Id.</u> The court held that Sheehan's suffering, combined
with the defendant's conduct in falsely reporting that Sheehan's
children were seriously injured, provided sufficient evidence of
severe emotional distress to submit the case to the jury. <u>Id.</u>

In the instant case, the trial court concluded as a matter of
law that because Lionell's physical symptoms could "occur in the
absence of any emotional upset" they did "not rise to the level of
severity § 46 requires." Walker will no doubt rely on this line
of argument. However, we should argue that any of the physical
symptoms mentioned in the case law involving IIED <u>could</u> occur in
the absence of any emotional upset. A contrary showing is not
necessary. The trial court failed to recognize that Lionell's
distress, combined with Walker's outrageous conduct, "guarantee
that [Lionell's] claim is genuine . . . ." <u>See</u> Restatement § 46
cmt. k.

Lionell heard Walker's agonizing screams and saw Walker's
blood streaming down. His distress was so intense that he
immediately vomited. Since the incident, he has suffered severe
migraine headaches, nausea, weight loss, depression, sweaty palms,
and recurring nightmares. His guilt and severe distress have
prevented him from returning to his livelihood as an engineer. On
this record, the court should conclude that Lionell sufficiently
alleged "severe emotional distress."

CONCLUSION:

The appellate court will likely hold that Lionell's complaint sufficiently stated a cause of action for IIED and reverse the judgment below.

AUTHORITIES CITED:

Cases

Armstrong v. H & C Commc'ns, Inc.,
    575 So. 2d 280 (Fla. 5th DCA 1991)

Blakeley v. Shortal's Estate,
    20 N.W.2d 28 (Iowa 1945)

Dominquez v. Equitable Life Assurance Soc'y,
    438 So. 2d 58 (Fla. 3d DCA 1983), approved sub nom.,
    Crawford v. Dominquez, 467 So. 2d 281 (Fla. 1985)

Fla. Cent. & Peninsular R.R. Co. v. Williams,
    37 Fla. 406, 20 So. 558 (1896)

Ford Motor Credit Co. v. Sheehan,
    373 So. 2d 956 (Fla. 1st DCA 1979)

Jefferson Ward Stores, Inc. v. Khorozian,
    519 So. 2d 627 (Fla. 4th DCA 1984)

Kirker v. Orange Cnty.,
    519 So. 2d 682 (Fla. 5th DCA 1988)

Knowles Animal Hosp., Inc. v. Willis,
    360 So. 2d 37 (Fla. 3d DCA 1978)

Korbin v. Berlin,
    177 So. 2d 551 (Fla. 3d DCA 1965)

La Porte v. Associated Indeps., Inc.,
    163 So. 2d 267 (Fla. 1964)

Metro. Life Ins. Co. v. McCarson,
    467 So. 2d 277 (Fla. 1985)

Sarkis v. Pafford Oil Co.,
    697 So. 2d 524 (Fla. 1st DCA 1997)

Sullivan v. deColigny,
    432 F. Supp. 689 (D. V.I. 1977)

Williams v. City of Minneola,
    575 So. 2d 683 (Fla. 5th DCA 1991)

Statutes

§ 860.05, Fla. Stat. (20xx)

§ 860.09, Fla. Stat. (20xx)

§ 860.121, Fla. Stat. (20xx)

Court Rules

Fla. R. Civ. P. 1.110(b)

Restatements

Restatement (Second) of Torts § 46 (1965)

Restatement (Second) of Torts § 46 cmt. c

Restatement (Second) of Torts § 46 cmt. d

Restatement (Second) of Torts § 46 cmt. h

Restatement (Second) of Torts § 46 cmt. i

Restatement (Second) of Torts § 46 cmt. j

Restatement (Second) of Torts § 46 cmt. k

Restatement (Second) of Torts § 46 illus. 2

Restatement (Second) of Torts § 46 illus. 3

Restatement (Second) of Torts § 46 illus. 16

Restatement (Second) of Torts § 46 illus. 21

Restatement (Second) of Torts § 500

Restatement (Second) of Torts § 500 cmt. a

Restatement (Second) of Torts § 500 cmt. e

18

Chapter 36

Lionell's (Appellant's) Brief [1]

---

1. Please note throughout these appellate briefs that although *The Bluebook* states that it is customary to use the word "at" in record cites (e.g., R. at 5), in the interest of space, we have eliminated the "at."

IN THE
DISTRICT COURT OF APPEAL OF FLORIDA
FIRST DISTRICT

PARKER LIONELL,

       Appellant,

v.   CASE NUMBER: Fxx

NOAH WALKER,
       Appellee.

_____/

ON APPEAL FROM THE CIRCUIT COURT

FOR THE EIGHTH JUDICIAL CIRCUIT OF FLORIDA

_____

APPELLANT'S INITIAL BRIEF
_____

STEW DENT
Counsel for Appellant, Parker Lionell

250 Bruton-Geer Hall
University of Florida
Gainesville, Florida 32611
352-555-5555

TABLE OF CONTENTS

TABLE OF AUTHORITIES

OPINION BELOW

The final judgment of the Circuit Court for the Eighth Judicial Circuit is unreported and appears at pages 1-6 of the Record on Appeal.

JURISDICTION

The final judgment of the Circuit Court for the Eighth Judicial Circuit was entered on September 6, 20xx. (R.6.) Notice of appeal was timely filed on September 11, 20xx. (R.7.) This Court's jurisdiction is invoked pursuant to Article V, Section 4(b)(1) of the Florida Constitution.

QUESTION PRESENTED

Whether the trial court erred in dismissing plaintiff's complaint for intentional infliction of emotional distress for failure to state a cause of action where the complaint alleged facts showing:

(1) that defendant purposefully lay across railroad tracks in front of an oncoming train and remained until he was struck by the train and his legs were severed; and

(2) that plaintiff, the train's chief engineer and operator, observed the impact and suffered many ailments as a result, including immediate vomiting, subsequent severe migraine headaches, nausea, nightmares, sweaty palms, guilt, weight loss, and depression, resulting in his inability to return to his livelihood as an engineer.

STATEMENT OF THE CASE AND FACTS

Alongside a semi-remote stretch of railway in Alachua
County, Florida, a newspaper reporter and twenty bystanders
gathered to witness an anti-nuclear protestor named Noah Walker,
the Appellee, confront a 4021 ton train. (R.1-2.) The crowd was
not there by happenstance; Walker had notified the local paper
the day before of his railway protest. (R.2.) That train
carried plutonium, a component for nuclear weapons; and Walker
meant to stop it. (R.2.)

Minutes before the train arrived, Walker announced to the
onlookers:

> "Pretty soon that train will be coming down these
> tracks carrying death and destruction. The railroad
> knows this, the engineers know this, you know this.
> But no one does a damn thing to stop it. No one's
> ready to put his butt on the line to stop it. The
> thing goes on and on, on and on, on and on -- chugging
> down the track, chugging down our throats. We're
> choking on it, we're dying from it, but no one seems to
> care. Well I care. Drastic times require drastic
> measures. If it goes any further, it's got to go
> through me."

(R.2 (quoting Pl.'s Comp. ¶ 30).) True to his word, Walker then
lay down crosswise on the track, and was joined by two other
protestors. (R.2.)

A railroad official arrived and pleaded with Walker to get
off the tracks. (R.2.) He told Walker that the oncoming train
would not stop; that Walker would die or be seriously injured;
and that interfering with railroad trains or tracks was a felony.

(R.2.) Despite this warning, Walker remained on the tracks,
responding, "'I have to do what I have to do.'" (R.2 (quoting
Pl.'s Comp. ¶ 32).)

Within three minutes, the train appeared, traveling well
under the legal speed limit. (R.2-3.) Parker Lionell, the
Appellant, was the train's chief engineer. (R.1-2.) When he saw
Walker and the two protestors on the tracks, Lionell sounded a
barrage of warning whistles, used every braking device available,
and did everything humanly possible to stop the train. (R.3.)
Despite his intensive efforts, the train kept rolling. (R.3.)
Two protestors jumped off the tracks and were unhurt, but Walker
remained. (R.3.) The train struck Walker, severing both of his
legs below the knee. (R.3.)

From Lionell's position in the train, he could not see
Walker being crushed under the wheels. But he heard Walker's
screams and he saw Walker's blood. (R.3.) Traumatized by these
sights and sounds, he vomited repeatedly and uncontrollably.
(R.3.) Within days, he was stricken with severe migraine
headaches, sweaty palms, nausea, weight loss, guilt, and
depression. (R.3.) Even sleep was no sanctuary; he suffered
recurrent nightmares in which he relived his forced role in
Walker's attempted suicide. (R.3.) These severe migraines,
sweaty palms, depression, guilt, and nightmares continue to
plague him. (R.3.) So disabled, he has been unable to return to

his livelihood as an engineer. (R.3.) He cannot even board a
train.

Three months later, and still suffering severe distress,
Lionell filed suit against Walker for intentional infliction of
emotional distress. (R.3.) In that suit, he alleged all of the
facts as stated above. (R.1-3.) On July 31, 20xx, however,
Walker filed a motion to dismiss Lionell's complaint for failure
to state a claim. (R.3.) On September 6, 20xx, the trial court
granted that motion, and dismissed Lionell's complaint with
prejudice on three independent grounds. (R.6.)

First, the trial court ruled that although "Walker's conduct
may have been illegal, foolhardy and extreme," it was not
outrageous. (R.5.) Thus, as a matter of law, the trial court
held that Walker's actions of lying on the train track in the
face of an oncoming train he knew could not stop, did not rise to
the level of the atrocious and the intolerable. (R.5.)

Second, the court ruled that the complaint failed to allege
that Walker had acted with the requisite intent since "Walker's
acts were not directed against Lionell . . . ." (R.5.) The
court thus held insufficient Lionell's allegations (1) that
Walker knew engineers were on the train; (2) that Lionell was on
the train acting as chief engineer; (3) that Walker intentionally
lay down on the tracks in the face of the oncoming train he knew
could not stop; and (4) that Walker had stated, just minutes

before the train had struck him, that if "it goes any further, it's got to go through me."   (R.1-3.)

Finally, the court concluded that despite Lionell's continued physical and emotional disabilities resulting from the trauma, his distress was not "severe enough" as a matter of law to warrant recovery.   (R.5.)   This was so, observed the court, because Lionell's "vomiting, nausea, guilt, depression, headaches, sweaty palms, and nightmares can occur without any emotional upset."   (R.5.)

On September 11, 20xx, Lionell filed a notice of appeal seeking review of this judgment.   (R.7.)   Lionell respectfully asks this Court to reverse the trial court's judgment and remand this case for trial.

SUMMARY OF ARGUMENT

This case involves the intentional infliction of emotional
distress upon an unsuspecting plaintiff. Appellant Parker
Lionell seeks the right to bring his case before the jury; and
asks this Court, on *de novo* review, to reverse the trial court's
dismissal of his complaint. Lionell's allegations that Appellee
Noah Walker's extreme and outrageous conduct intentionally and
recklessly caused Lionell to suffer severe emotional distress are
sufficient to state a cause of action for intentional infliction
of emotional distress.

Walker purposefully lay in the path of an oncoming train.
He knew the train was coming; he heard the warning whistles that
Lionell, the train's chief engineer, frantically sounded; he saw
the train approaching, yet he did not move. He allowed the train
to strike him; and in doing so, he made Lionell witness the
brutal maiming of a human body.

Hearing screams and seeing blood, Lionell, helpless and
shocked, shook and vomited uncontrollably. To this day, he
cannot board a train. In recurrent nightmares, he relives the
mutilation and his unwitting role in it. He has lost weight, and
experiences crippling migraine headaches, sweaty palms, guilt,
and severe depression. In one brief moment, his entire world was
changed forever by the outrageous and illegal conduct of one man:
Walker.

Lionell brought this action to hold Walker responsible for the damage he has caused. The trial court, however, granted Walker's motion to dismiss the complaint with prejudice, ruling that Walker had not acted outrageously or with the requisite intent; and that Lionell's distress was not "severe enough." The court erred on all three rulings.

First, the mere recitation of the facts reveals the outrageousness of Walker's conduct. Without doubt, a reasonable person would find that Walker's actions went beyond all possible bounds of decency, and were atrocious and utterly intolerable in a civilized community. Thus, at the very least, this was a jury question.

Second, Walker's intent was also a jury question. Lionell has alleged facts supporting a jury's finding (1) that Walker desired to inflict emotional harm; (2) that he acted with substantial certainty that such harm would result; (3) that he acted recklessly in deliberate disregard of a high degree of probability that harm would follow; and, (4) that he acted recklessly per se by violating statutes designed to protect public safety. Short of Walker's admission of his intent, there is nothing more Lionell could allege.

Finally, Lionell has alleged facts demonstrating that his emotional distress is so severe that no person should be expected to endure it. From the facts alleged, a reasonable person could

easily conclude that he is entitled to damages. For this reason,
Lionell should be entitled to present his case to a jury. The
Court should reverse the trial court's judgment, and remand this
case for further proceedings on the merits.

ARGUMENT

THE TRIAL COURT ERRED IN DISMISSING PARKER LIONELL'S
COMPLAINT FOR INTENTIONAL INFLICTION OF EMOTIONAL
DISTRESS. THE COMPLAINT SUFFICIENTLY ALLEGED FACTS
FROM WHICH A JURY MAY REASONABLY INFER THAT WALKER'S
CONDUCT WAS EXTREME AND OUTRAGEOUS, AND INTENTIONALLY
OR RECKLESSLY CAUSED LIONELL TO SUFFER SEVERE EMOTIONAL
DISTRESS.

Parker Lionell's complaint states a cause of action for
intentional infliction of emotional distress. Under this tort,
"[o]ne who by extreme and outrageous conduct intentionally or
recklessly causes severe emotional distress to another is subject
to liability for such emotional distress, and if bodily harm to
the other results from it, for such bodily harm." Restatement
(Second) of Torts § 46 (1965); see also Metro. Life Ins. Co. v.
McCarson, 467 So. 2d 277, 278-79 (Fla. 1985) (recognizing the
tort of intentional infliction of emotional distress and adopting
section 46 and its comments).[1]

On this review of a judgment granting Walker's motion to
dismiss with prejudice, this Court reviews the complaint in the
light most favorable to Lionell, and accepts as true all
allegations in the complaint. See Armstrong v. H & C Commc'ns,
Inc., 575 So. 2d 280, 280 (Fla. 5th DCA 1991);

---

[1]The Court should also recognize that the law involving this
tort of outrage is "still in a stage of development, and the
ultimate limits of this tort are not yet determined."
Restatement (Second) of Torts § 46 cmt. c. Thus, § 46 leaves
"fully open the possibility of further development of the law,
and [recognizes] other situations [not specifically expressed in
the comments to section 46] in which liability may be imposed."
Id.

Fla. R. Civ. P. 1.110. Under section 1.110 of the Florida Rules

of Civil Procedure, although Lionell must allege ultimate facts

supporting each element of the cause of action, he need not plead

his claim with particularity or specificity. Indeed, all he need

do is outline his position. <u>See</u> <u>Sullivan v. deColigny</u>, 432 F.

Supp. 689, 690 (D. V.I. 1977) (denying defendants' motion for

judgment on the pleadings in an intentional infliction of

emotional distress case, stating that a ruling on this motion

could come only after the plaintiff presented evidence of the

defendants' conduct).

Lionell has alleged (1) that Walker's act of lying in the

path of an oncoming train was extreme and outrageous; (2) that

Walker intentionally or recklessly allowed the train Lionell was

operating to run over him; and (3) that Lionell suffered severe

emotional distress from being an unwilling participant in

Walker's attempted suicide. (R.2.) Without question, these

allegations sufficiently state a claim for intentional infliction

of emotional distress. Accordingly, this Court, on *de novo*

review, <u>see</u> <u>Testa v. S. Escrow & Title, LLC</u>, 36 So. 3d 713, 714

(Fla. 1st DCA 2010), should reverse the trial court's judgment

and remand this case to proceed on the merits.

    A.   <u>Walker acted outrageously in lying across</u>
        <u>railroad tracks, refusing to move from the</u>
        <u>path of an oncoming train, and causing</u>
        <u>Lionell to become an unwilling participant</u>
        <u>in a gruesome mutilation.</u>

The trial court erred in finding that Walker's conduct was

not outrageous, and therefore, not actionable. Conduct causing
emotional distress is actionable when it is "so outrageous in
character, and so extreme in degree, as to go beyond all possible
bounds of decency, and to be regarded as atrocious, and utterly
intolerable in a civilized community." Restatement (Second) of
Torts § 46 cmt. d. Extreme and outrageous conduct is such that
its recitation to average members of the community would arouse
their resentment against the actor, and lead them to exclaim,
"'Outrageous!'" Id.

"[W]here significant facts are disputed, or where differing
inferences could reasonably be derived from undisputed facts, the
question of outrageousness is for the jury to decide." Williams
v. City of Minneola, 575 So. 2d 683, 692 (Fla. 5th DCA 1991).
The trial court decides the issue as a matter of law only where
the "facts of a case can under no conceivable interpretation
support the tort . . . ." Id. Here, the trial court erred in
taking this case from the jury. Reasonable people could
conclude, on these undisputed facts, that Walker exhibited
outrageous conduct in this case.

In a case remarkably similar to the instant case, the Iowa
Supreme Court ruled, as this Court should rule, that in causing a
plaintiff to view the results of a defendant's self-inflicted
wounds, the defendant had acted outrageously. See Blakeley v.
Shortal's Estate, 20 N.W.2d 28, 31 (Iowa 1945). In Blakeley, the
decedent was a neighbor and an invited guest who had spent the
night in Blakeley's home. Id. at 29. The next day, Blakeley

left her home, leaving the decedent sitting at a table in her
kitchen. _Id._ When she returned, she found it difficult to open
the door to her kitchen. _Id._ Pushing the door partially open,
she found the decedent "lying on the floor with pools of blood
about him." _Id._ He had slit his own throat with a "skinning"
knife, leaving "blood on the floor and about the room." _Id._ at
30. In reversing a directed verdict for the decedent's estate,
the court found that the decedent had wilfully created a "gory
and ghastly sight" that naturally resulted in emotional distress
worthy of damages. _Id._ at 31.

Florida courts allow recovery under circumstances far less
extreme than one in which the plaintiff is forced to witness, or
to become an instrument in, the defendant's mutilation. A cause
of action for intentional infliction of emotional distress has
been stated in a case involving false statements made to a six
year old girl regarding sexual activities of her mother, _Korbin
v. Berlin_, 177 So. 2d 551, 553 (Fla. 3d DCA 1965); cases
involving false accusations of shoplifting, _see, e.g._, _Jefferson
Ward Stores, Inc. v. Khorozian_, 519 So. 2d 627, 627-28 (Fla. 4th
DCA 1984); wilful, malicious, and wrongful refusals to pay the
proceeds of insurance policies, _Dominquez v. Equitable Life
Assurance Society_, 438 So. 2d 58, 61-62 (Fla. 3d DCA 1983),
approved sub nom., _Crawford v. Dominquez_, 467 So. 2d 281 (Fla.
1985); and false reports of injuries to relatives, _Ford Motor
Credit Co. v. Sheehan_, 373 So. 2d 956, 958 (Fla. 1st DCA 1979).

Moreover, the Restatement includes two further examples of

4

actionable, outrageous conduct: [1] threatening to injure the
plaintiff and ruin his business; and [2] giving a female
plaintiff a bathing suit which the defendant knows is water
soluble, and which "dissolves while [plaintiff] is swimming,
leaving her naked in the presence of men and women whom she has
just met." Restatement (Second) of Torts § 46 illus. 2, 3.

These examples, including even the suicide in the <u>Blakeley</u>
case, pale in comparison to Walker's conduct. Walker did not
merely falsely accuse Lionell of a crime, give him incorrect
information concerning the well-being or activity of a relative,
fail to honor a fiduciary duty, threaten his business or income,
or play a practical joke on him. Here, Walker committed not only
the outrageous, but the unforgivable. He forced Lionell to
mutilate him. He forced Lionell to suffer not only severe
emotional distress and grief, but excruciating guilt as well.
Without doubt, the mere recitation of the facts of this case
would cause a reasonable person to exclaim, at the least,
"outrageous!"

True to his boast, Walker ignored all warnings – both from
railroad officials and from Lionell's frantic barrage of whistles
– and remained on the tracks, knowing that the train was coming.
(R.3.) Two other protestors who had joined him on the tracks
leapt to safety, while Walker remained. (R.3.) Tragically, the
train hit him, severing both of his legs below the knees –
injuries indicating that he had continued to lie on the tracks
until the moment of impact. (R.3.) Lionell, as chief engineer

5

responsible for operating the train, could do nothing but watch in horror as the train approached Walker, as Walker's screams filled his ears, and as Walker's blood came raining down. (R.3.)

Walker's conduct was outrageous as Lionell's complaint sufficiently alleged.

B.   Walker acted intentionally and recklessly in wilfully lying on the railroad tracks in the path of an oncoming train he knew would strike him.

The trial court erred in finding that Walker did not intend to inflict emotional distress. In reviewing the record in the light most favorable to Lionell, this Court should consider that the defendant's intent "can of course be proved by circumstantial evidence and need not depend on the unlikely possibility of an admission." See Williams, 575 So. 2d at 693.

Intent to inflict emotional distress exists not only where the defendant actually desires to harm another, but where he acts recklessly in doing so. Restatement (Second) of Torts § 46 cmt. i (noting that section 46 incorporates the definition of "recklessness" found in § 500 of the Restatement (Second) of Torts)). As the Fifth District has explained: "[R]eckless infliction of mental suffering is the same as deliberate infliction." Williams, 575 So. 2d at 692; see also Blakeley, 20 N.W.2d at 31 (stating that "[a] wilful wrong may be committed without any intention to injure anyone.").

A defendant acts with the requisite intent to inflict emotional distress where he (1) "intend[s] the wrongful result of

6

his behavior," (2) "without intending harm, [is] able (as a reasonable person) to foresee that the result is certain or substantially certain to result," or (3) "simply act[s] recklessly in deliberate disregard of a high degree of probability that the result will follow." Williams, 575 So. 2d at 692; see also Restatement (Second) of Torts § 46 cmt. i. Where the defendant's conduct involves a "high risk that serious harm will result from it to anyone who is within range of its effect, the fact that he knows or has reason to know that others are within such range is conclusive of the recklessness of his conduct towards them." Restatement (Second) of Torts § 500 cmt. d (1965) (emphasis added).

Thus, for Lionell to state a cause of action for intentional infliction of emotional distress against Walker, he need not show that Walker desired to inflict emotional distress. He need not show that Walker planned to make Lionell suffer grief, guilt, and depression. All he needs to show is that Walker wilfully lay down on the railroad tracks in the path of the oncoming train, and that Walker either (1) knew that distress was certain or substantially certain to result; or (2) deliberately disregarded (as in, for example, violating a statute prohibiting such conduct) a high degree of probability that emotional distress would follow. See Dominquez, 438 So. 2d at 59 n.1. Contrary to the trial court's finding, Lionell has met this standard.

7

1. <u>Walker acted intentionally. He knew that</u>
    <u>distress was certain, or substantially</u>
    <u>certain, to result from his conduct.</u>

A reasonable person would know with substantial certainty
that Lionell, forced to participate in Walker's mutilation, would
endure tremendous anxiety, fear, and grief. As a matter of law,
Walker's premeditated and deliberate conduct sufficiently
demonstrates that he acted intentionally.

Illustrations 15 and 16 under comment i of Restatement § 46
provide examples of intent and recklessness strikingly similar to
Walker's wilfulness:

> 15. [intent] During A's absence from her home, B
> attempts to commit suicide in A's kitchen by cutting his
> throat. B knows that A is substantially certain to return
> and find his body, and to suffer emotional distress. A
> finds B lying in her kitchen in a pool of gore, and suffers
> severe emotional distress. B is subject to liability to A.

> 16. [recklessness] The same facts as in Illustration
> 15, except that B does not know that A is substantially
> certain to find him, but does know that there is a high
> degree of probability that she will do so. B is subject to
> liability to A.

To have acted "intentionally," Walker need not have lain
upon the tracks with the specific desire to harm Lionell.
Indeed, it is irrelevant whether Walker knew that Lionell was in
the train, whether Walker had ever met Lionell, or whether Walker
recognized that his conduct was extremely dangerous. "It is
enough that he [Walker] [knew] or ha[d] reason to know of
circumstances which would bring home to the realization of the
ordinary, reasonable [person] the highly dangerous character of
his conduct." Restatement (Second) of Torts § 500 cmt. c. "An

objective standard is applied to him, and he is held to the realization of the aggravated risk which a reasonable man in his place would have [known]. . . ." Id. at cmt. a.

Like the conduct described in these illustrations, Walker's conduct was premeditated and deliberate, and therefore, intentional. From the outset, Walker's aim in holding a protest on the railroad tracks was to engage in risky conduct to elicit an emotional response from observers. He made certain there would be observers by notifying the local paper the day before his protest. (R.2.)

Indeed, just before lying on the tracks, Walker proclaimed to the onlookers: "'Pretty soon that train will be coming down these tracks carrying death and destruction. The railroad knows this, the engineers know this, you know this. But no one does a damn thing to stop it.'" (R.2.) Like a saboteur, Walker intended to shock his audience. He even boasted that the train would have "'to go through'" him. (R.2.) And, despite a railroad official's desperate warning that the train could not stop, and that Walker would die or be severely injured, Walker boasted: "'I have to do what I have to do.'" (R.2-3.)

Thus, as Lionell's complaint alleges, Walker was acutely aware of the danger he was undertaking. He knew he could be mutilated and he knew others would view that mutilation. Walker thus acted intentionally.

9

2.   <u>Walker acted recklessly in violating</u>
      <u>statutes designed to protect others</u>
      <u>from harm.</u>

Walker acted recklessly in intentionally violating three
Florida Statutes (20xx) designed to protect others from harm:
section 860.05, prohibiting unauthorized interference with a
railroad track; section 860.09, prohibiting unauthorized
interference with a railroad vehicle; and section 860.121,
prohibiting placement of any object capable of causing death or
great bodily injury in the path of a railroad train.

Such interference with the railway is a felony, and although
violating a statute does not by itself make Walker's acts
reckless, it does so where, as here, the statutes are (1)
intentionally violated, and (2) that violation involves a "high
degree of probability that serious harm will result."
Restatement (Second) of Torts § 500 cmt. e. Because Walker's
conduct met both of these requirements, it was reckless.

First, as discussed above, Walker intended to lie down on
those tracks. This is undisputed. And, while his fellow
protestors leapt to safety, he remained – another undisputed
fact. Thus, this Court should readily find that Walker indeed
intended to violate the statutes.

Second, it is beyond dispute that Walker's actions involved
a "high degree of probability that serious harm" would result,
not just to himself, but to others as well. See id. Making a

10

volatile situation even more potentially dangerous, the train was carrying plutonium. (R.2.) That Walker himself was harmed is irrelevant. In lying on those tracks, Walker violated the law. He endangered passengers and train personnel. He endangered bystanders, especially those who may have tried to rescue him. He acted recklessly.

On these facts, this Court should find that Lionell's allegations demonstrate Walker's intent to inflict emotional distress.

C. Walker's outrageous and reckless actions caused Lionell to suffer physical manifestations of severe emotional distress, preventing Lionell from returning to work as an engineer.

The trial court erred in finding that Lionell's emotional distress was insufficient to state a cause of action. Although the trial court acknowledged that Lionell had suffered emotional distress in the form of "vomiting, nausea, guilt, depression, headaches, sweaty palms, and nightmares," it found that this distress was "not severe enough" because these ailments could "occur without any emotional upset." (R.5.) However, recovery under Florida law depends on different considerations than simply whether manifestations of distress can emanate from only one source. See Sheehan, 373 So. 2d at 959. As a matter of law, the trial court applied the wrong legal standard; Lionell has sufficiently alleged severe emotional distress.

Emotional distress includes all "highly unpleasant mental

reactions, such as fright, horror, grief, shame, humiliation, embarrassment, anger, chagrin, disappointment, worry, and nausea." Restatement (Second) of Torts § 46 cmt. j. Although severe emotional distress may be manifested by bodily harm, section 46 is not limited to cases involving bodily harm. "[I]f the conduct is sufficiently extreme and outrageous there may be liability for emotional distress alone, without such harm." Id. at cmt. k; see Sheehan, 373 So. 2d at 959.

Nevertheless, the conduct must be severe: "The law intervenes only where the distress inflicted is so severe that no reasonable [person] could be expected to endure it. The intensity and duration of the distress are factors to be considered in determining its severity." Restatement (Second) of Torts § 46 cmt. j. And, although severe distress must be proved, "in many cases the extreme and outrageous character of the defendant's conduct is in itself important evidence that distress has existed." Id.; see Sheehan, 373 So. 2d at 959.

For example, in Sheehan, the defendant, Ford Motor Credit, was trying to track down Sheehan because he was delinquent on a debt. 373 So. 2d at 958. Posing as a hospital employee, Ford's agent called Sheehan's mother and told her that Sheenan's children had been in a serious car accident and the hospital was trying to find him. Id. After receiving this news, Sheehan became "extremely worried, upset, and nearly out of his mind for

12

a continuous period of seven hours" while he tried to determine where his children were and the extent of their injuries. Id. at 959. The court held that Sheehan's suffering, when combined with the defendant's conduct, provided sufficient evidence of severe emotional distress to submit the case to the jury. Id.

Lionell's allegations also meet this standard. Walker's outrageous conduct and Lionell's distress, as described in Lionell's complaint, "guarantee that [Lionell's] claim is genuine . . . ." Restatement (Second) of Torts § 46 cmt. k. Unlike the defendant in Sheehan, Walker did not merely lie to Lionell, telling him that Lionell had struck a person on the track. Here, Walker went much further.

Callously, Walker made Lionell an unwilling participant in a grisly suicide attempt. As Walker deliberately lay on the tracks, Lionell feverishly, but in vain, attempted to stop the train. (R.3.) As the train struck Walker, Lionell heard Walker's agonizing screams and saw Walker's blood streaming down. (R.3.) Lionell's distress was so intense that he immediately vomited. (R.3.)

Since the incident, Lionell's distress has continued to manifest itself as severe migraine headaches, nausea, weight loss, depression, sweaty palms, and recurring nightmares. (R.3.) Lionell's guilt and this severe distress have prevented him from returning to his livelihood as an engineer. (R.3.) He cannot even board a train. (R.3.) Lionell's distress is genuine,

severe, and meets the Restatement section 46 standard. the trial

court erred in finding otherwise.

<u>CONCLUSION</u>

If forcing an unwilling plaintiff to participate in the mutilation of a living human body does not constitute outrageous conduct entitling the plaintiff to damages, then the tort of "outrage" does not exist in this State.

When Walker forced Lionell to mutilate him, he caused Lionell extreme emotional distress. Yet, the trial court dismissed this case with prejudice on the pleadings. Lionell, traumatized, severely depressed, suffering intense migraine headaches, and forced to relive his role in this tragedy in recurring nightmares, has been denied even his day in court. Because Lionell's complaint sufficiently states a cause of action for intentional infliction of emotional distress, Lionell respectfully requests this Court to reverse the trial court's judgment and remand this case for trial on the merits.

Respectfully submitted,

_____

Stew Dent
Counsel for Appellant, Parker Lionell

250 Bruton-Geer Hall
University of Florida
Gainesville, Florida   32611
352-555-5555

Bar Number: 26437

CERTIFICATE OF SERVICE

    I certify that a true copy of this brief was furnished to Matthew Thomas, Counsel for Appellee, by mail this 23rd day of December, 20xx.

Stew Dent
Counsel for Appellant, Parker Lionell

250 Bruton-Geer Hall
University of Florida
Gainesville, Florida   32611
352-555-5555

Bar Number: 26437

Chapter 37

Walker's (Appellee's) Brief

IN THE

DISTRICT COURT OF APPEAL OF FLORIDA

FIRST DISTRICT

PARKER LIONELL,

        Appellant,

v.   CASE NUMBER: Fxx

NOAH WALKER,

        Appellee.

_____/

ON APPEAL FROM THE CIRCUIT COURT

FOR THE EIGHTH JUDICIAL CIRCUIT OF FLORIDA

_____

APPELLEE'S ANSWER BRIEF

_____

MATTHEW THOMAS
Counsel for Appellee, Noah Walker

888 Park Avenue
University of Florida
Gainesville, Florida 32611
352-555-1234

TABLE OF CONTENTS

TABLE OF AUTHORITIES

OPINION BELOW

The final judgment of the Circuit Court for the Eighth Judicial Circuit is unreported and appears at pages 1-6 of the Record on Appeal.

JURISDICTION

The final judgment of the Circuit Court for the Eighth Judicial Circuit was entered on September 6, 20xx. (R.6.) Notice of appeal was timely filed on September 11, 20xx. (R.7.) This Court's jurisdiction is invoked pursuant to Article V, Section 4(b)(1) of the Florida Constitution.

QUESTION PRESENTED

Whether the trial court erred in dismissing, on the pleading and with prejudice, a complaint for intentional infliction of emotional distress against the defendant where the plaintiff seeks damages for witnessing the defendant's physical injury.

STATEMENT OF THE CASE AND FACTS

At issue is whether the trial court properly dismissed
Appellant Parker Lionell's complaint for intentional infliction
of emotional distress. Lionell seeks damages for alleged mental
distress arising out of a railroad accident which occurred in
Alachua County, Florida, on April 10, 20xx. (R.1-2.) Appellee
Noah Walker was hit by the train Lionell was operating, and
sustained severe injuries as both of his legs were severed below
the knees. (R.2.) In this unusual case of first impression,
Lionell seeks to hold Walker responsible for the alleged mental
distress Lionell suffered based on hearing Walker's screams and
seeing Walker's blood after the accident. (R.1-3.)

On the day of the accident, Lionell was the chief engineer
of a train carrying plutonium. (R.1-2.) Walker strongly opposes
nuclear weapons, for which plutonium is a critical element.
(R.2.) To protest the train's passage, he and two others staged
a sit-in on the tracks. (R.2-3.) Walker had informed the local
newspaper in advance of his demonstration, and a reporter joined
the group of about twenty onlookers near the track. (R.2.)

Walker made a short speech regarding the devastating effects

of plutonium, and expressed his hope of impeding the train's
progress. (R.2.) He and his fellow protesters then laid down on
the tracks. (R.2.) A railroad official told them that it would
be very difficult for the train to stop before reaching them, and
that it was a felony to interfere with the train. (R.2.)

The train, traveling at a lawful speed, soon approached.
(R.3.) Lionell attempted to stop the train, but failed. (R.3.)
The two other protesters avoided injury. (R.2.) Tragically, the
train struck Walker. (R.3.)

Although Lionell heard Walker's screams and saw his blood,
he did not actually see the train hit Walker. (R.3.) Lionell,
safe within the 4021 ton train, suffered no physical injuries as
a result of the impact. (R.3.) However, he became nauseous and
vomited. (R.3.) Subsequently, Lionell alleges he experienced
short-lived nausea and lost ten pounds. (R.3.) He also
complains of sweaty palms, headaches, guilt, depression, and bad
dreams, all of which he attributes to the accident. (R.3.)
Finally, he alleges that because the accident traumatized him, he
can no longer work as an engineer. (R.3.)

The trial court dismissed Lionell's suit with prejudice,
reasoning that the complaint failed to state a cause of action
for intentional infliction of emotional distress. (R.6.) The
court concluded that Lionell's complaint, as a matter of law, did

not meet the requirements of Restatement (Second) of Torts § 46 (1965). (R.4.) The court reasoned § 46 requires that the tortfeasor's actions must (1) be "so outrageous in character and so extreme in degree as to go beyond all possible bounds of decency and are to be regarded as atrocious and utterly intolerable in a civilized community"; (2) be "performed intentionally or recklessly, in deliberate disregard of a high degree of probability that emotional distress will follow"; and (3) "cause[] plaintiff to suffer severe emotional distress which no reasonable person should be expected to endure." (R.4.)

The trial court concluded that Lionell's complaint failed to sufficiently allege facts to support all three essential elements. First, the complaint did not demonstrate that Walker's actions were "outrageous." (R.5.) Second, it did not demonstrate that Walker acted intentionally or recklessly because "[n]one of the allegations demonstrate that Walker intended to cause Lionell's mental distress" and "Walker's acts were not directed against Lionell . . . ." (R.5.) Third, Lionell's alleged injuries were too minor to merit legal redress, because they were ailments which "can occur without any emotional upset." (R.5.) The trial court properly dismissed Lionell's complaint, and this Court should affirm that judgment.

SUMMARY OF ARGUMENT

This appeal addresses an unusual issue of first impression: Lionell, who unwittingly ran over Walker while operating a freight train, has sued Walker, the injured party, for damages under the theory of intentional infliction of emotional distress. Lionell, who was not physically harmed in the accident, seeks to recover damages resulting from his alleged mental distress at having observed Walker's injury. Although imaginative, Lionell's theory is unsound. As this Court should hold, on *de novo* review, the tort of outrage must involve intolerably atrocious and outrageous conduct intentionally directed at the plaintiff; not, as in this case, political protest leading to the defendant's accidental injury.

Recognizing the narrow scope of this tort, Florida courts allow recovery only in very limited circumstances involving the most intentionally atrocious and wanton actions. The trial court correctly found that Walker's conduct did not rise to the level the law requires. Walker merely participated in a peaceful political demonstration against nuclear weapons by staging a sit-in upon railroad tracks to protest a train's payload of plutonium – a critical component in nuclear bombs. Tragically, he did not get off of the tracks in time, was struck by the train, and is now maimed for life. The trial court correctly found, as should this Court, that his sit-in protest against nuclear weapons did not rise to the level the law requires, as it was not "beyond the bounds of decency" or "utterly intolerable in a civilized

x

community."

The trial court also properly held that Lionell's complaint
failed to demonstrate that Walker acted with the intent the law
requires because Walker did not intend to be hit by the train.
Walker's statement, "[i]f it goes any further, it's got to go
through me," rhetorically expressed his commitment to protest
nuclear weapons, not his intent to be run over by an oncoming
train. As the context of his speech demonstrates, Walker was
referring to the process of nuclear arms build-up having "to go
through him," not the train itself. Because Walker did not
intend to be struck, he could not, as a matter of law, have acted
recklessly or intentionally. The trial court correctly found
that Lionell's complaint was insufficient on this ground.

Finally, the trial court correctly held that Lionell's
alleged sweaty palms, nausea, weight loss, guilt, depression,
headaches and bad dreams were evidence of distress, but were
insufficient to establish the severe emotional distress the tort
of outrage requires. Tellingly, Lionell does not allege that he
can support these claims at trial with medical testimony.
Indeed, he does not claim that he even consulted a doctor
concerning his alleged distress. For these reasons, the trial
court dismissed his case, and this Court should affirm that
judgment.

ARGUMENT

LIONELL, ENGINEER OF THE TRAIN THAT RAN OVER WALKER,
HAS FAILED TO STATE A CAUSE OF ACTION FOR INTENTIONAL
INFLICTION OF EMOTIONAL DISTRESS. HE HAS FAILED TO
DEMONSTRATE THAT WALKER'S CONDUCT WAS EXTREME AND
OUTRAGEOUS; THAT WALKER INTENDED TO HARM LIONELL; AND
THAT LIONELL SUFFERED SEVERE EMOTIONAL DISTRESS AS A
RESULT OF WALKER'S CONDUCT.

The trial court correctly dismissed this case after holding

that the complaint failed to state a claim for intentional

infliction of emotional distress. To state a claim for the tort

of "outrage," Lionell must demonstrate not only that (1) Walker's

actions were "extreme and outrageous" beyond all possible bounds

of decency, but also that (2) Walker "intentionally or

recklessly" caused Lionell to suffer (3) severe emotional

distress beyond what any reasonable person could be expected to

endure. See Metro. Life Ins. Co. v. McCarson, 467 So. 2d 277,

278-79 (Fla. 1985) (adopting § 46, Restatement (Second) of Torts

(1965) and comments thereto). Because Lionell's complaint fails

to demonstrate these three factors, this Court, on de novo

review, should affirm the trial court's judgment dismissing this

case with prejudice. See Testa v. S. Escrow & Title, LLC, 36 So.

3d 713, 714 (Fla. 1st DCA 2010).

    A.   Lionell's complaint fails to demonstrate that
        Walker's conduct in staging a political
        protest on the train track was extreme and
        outrageous.

As a matter of law, Walker's conduct was not sufficiently

extreme and outrageous to hold Walker liable for Lionell's

alleged distress. Liability for intentional infliction of
emotional distress exists only where "the conduct has been so
outrageous in character, and so extreme in degree, as to go
beyond all possible bounds of decency, and to be regarded as
atrocious, and utterly intolerable in a civilized community."
Restatement (Second) of Torts § 46 cmt. d (1965). In other
words, the case must be one in which an average member of the
community would, after hearing the facts, not only resent the
actor, but would cry "'outrageous.'" Id.

Whether Walker's conduct may reasonably be regarded as so
extreme and outrageous as to permit Lionell's recovery is the
court's, not the jury's, decision. See id. at cmt. h; Ponton v.
Scarfone, 468 So. 2d 1009, 1011 (Fla. 2d DCA 1985) (noting that
the "subjective response of the person who is the target of the
actor's conduct is not to control" the question of the conduct's
outrageousness). Thus, the trial court evaluates whether, as a
matter of law, Walker's conduct was so extreme.

In this case of first impression, this Court must decide
whether a plaintiff can seek "outrage" damages for witnessing the
defendant's accidental physical injuries. Although imaginative,
this cause of action does not and should not exist. The reason
is simple: the tort of outrage must involve intolerably atrocious
and outrageous conduct; not, as in this case, political protest
leading to tragic consequences. As the comments to the
Restatement explain:

It has not been enough that the defendant has acted

2

with an intent which is tortious or even criminal, or
that he has intended to inflict emotional distress, or
even that his conduct has been characterized by
"malice," or a degree of aggravation which would
entitle the plaintiff to punitive damages for another
tort.

Restatement (Second) of Torts § 46 cmt. d.

Recognizing the narrow scope of this tort, Florida courts
allow recovery only in very limited circumstances involving the
most atrocious and wanton actions. For example, one court
recognized a mother's claim for intentional infliction of
emotional distress against a medical examiner who, over the
mother's express objection, removed the eyeballs of her dead
three-year-old daughter, and then falsified an autopsy report on
the child, allegedly intending to cover up his actions. Kirker
v. Orange Cnty., 519 So. 2d 682, 683 (Fla. 5th DCA 1988). In
allowing the mother's claim, the court noted that recovery on
this tort "'is especially appropriate to tortious interference
with rights involving dead human bodies, where mental anguish to
the surviving relative is'" the natural and probable consequence
of the wrong committed. Id. (quoting Kirksey v. Jernigan, 45 So.
2d 188, 189 (Fla. 1950)).

In another case, the defendant funeral home acted
outrageously in mishandling a body and in misidentifying human
remains. Smith v. Telophase Nat'l Cremation Soc'y, Inc., 471 So.
2d 163 (Fla. 2d DCA 1985). In Smith, the funeral home, late in
picking up the plaintiff's deceased husband's body, forced Smith
to be in her home with the corpse four to five hours longer than

3

necessary. Id. at 165. Then, approximately a week after the
body was to have been cremated, the funeral home turned over to
Smith the remains of someone other than her husband. Id. Smith
discovered the error when, at the end of a "pilgrimage" on which
she had spread ashes at several sentimental locations in three
different states, she found bridgework – which did not belong to
her husband – among the remains. Id. at 165-66. The funeral
home had deposited the true remains at sea, contrary to the
decedent's express wishes. Id. at 166. The Smith court had no
trouble concluding that the funeral home had acted outrageously.
Id.

In another example of outrageous conduct, a debt collector
posing as a hospital employee falsely communicated that she was
trying to locate the debtor / plaintiff to tell him that his
children had been in a serious automobile accident. Ford Motor
Credit Co. v. Sheehan, 373 So. 2d 956, 958 (Fla. 1st DCA 1979).
As a result of this communication, the plaintiff spent seven
frightening hours frantically calling hospitals and police
departments until he finally learned that the information was
false. Id. The following day, the debt collector's independent
contractor repossessed the plaintiff's car. Id. The court
affirmed the jury's verdict assessing damages for intentional
infliction of emotional distress, noting that the extreme and
outrageous nature of the debt collector's cruel hoax ensured that
the plaintiff's distress was real and severe. Id. at 958-59.

As a final example, a court permitted a disabled man to

4

recover "outrage" damages from an insurance company which had intentionally refused to make payments on his legitimate claim, verbally threatened him with legal action, and forced him into bankruptcy. <u>Dependable Life Ins. Co. v. Harris</u>, 510 So. 2d 985, 988-89 (Fla. 5th DCA 1987). In allowing the plaintiff's claim, the court concluded that the insurance company's conduct was outrageous "because of its fiduciary relationship with [the plaintiff], its economic strength and power [over him], and [his] sickness . . . and need for . . . the disability payments which [the company] wrongfully withheld." <u>Id.</u> at 989.

In stark contrast, Walker's peaceful political demonstration against nuclear weapons pales in comparison to these examples of "outrageous" conduct. Walker did not egregiously mishandle the dead body of Lionell's relative; deceptively place Lionell in agonizing fear for the safety of a child; or wantonly breach a fiduciary duty clearly owed to Lionell. Rather, Walker engaged in a political protest which, tragically, resulted in a terrible accident maiming him for life.

Walker's sit-in protest against nuclear weapons was not "beyond the bounds of decency" or "utterly intolerable in a civilized society." Restatement (Second) of Torts § 46 cmt. d. Indeed, non-violent sit-in demonstrations have been an accepted form of political protest for years. <u>See</u> <u>Brown v. Louisiana</u>, 383 U.S. 131, 141-42 (1966) (holding that a sit-in by African American students in a "whites only" library to protest segregation constituted protected First Amendment speech).

Without question, an utterly intolerable tragedy resulted here, but the tragedy was to Walker alone.

As the trial court reasoned, the facts alleged lead to but one conclusion: Walker's conduct "may have been illegal, foolhardy, and extreme, but it was not outrageous." (R.5.) Accordingly, the court found, as a matter of law, that Lionell did not meet the strict threshold for stating a claim of outrage, and that this case did not merit further litigation. This Court should find that the trial court acted properly in dismissing, with prejudice, Lionell's complaint.

B. <u>Walker, in lying across the railroad tracks, neither intended to inflict emotional distress on Lionell nor acted in reckless disregard of a high degree of probability that Lionell's distress would follow.</u>

The trial court properly found that Lionell's complaint failed to demonstrate that Walker intended to harm Lionell. To satisfy the "intent" element of the tort of outrage, Lionell must show that Walker (1) desired to inflict severe emotional distress; (2) acted knowing such distress was certain or substantially certain to result; or (3) acted recklessly, "as that term is defined in [Restatement] § 500, in deliberate disregard of a high degree of probability that the emotional distress will follow." Restatement (Second) of Torts § 46 cmt. i; <u>id.</u> at § 500. Because Walker did not intend to be struck by the train, he could not, as a matter of law, have acted with the requisite intent.

6

1.   <u>Walker did not intend the train to hit him</u>
     <u>and therefore could not have been certain or</u>
     <u>substantially certain that any distress would</u>
     <u>result from his conduct.</u>

Lionell has failed to demonstrate that Walker desired to
inflict severe emotional distress upon him, or that Walker acted
knowing that such distress was certain or substantially certain
to result. Indeed, Walker's failure to "take 'appropriate'
action to" remove himself from the tracks constitutes at most,
mere negligence, not intentional conduct. <u>See</u> <u>E. Airlines, Inc.</u>
<u>v. King</u>, 557 So. 2d 574, 576 (Fla. 1990) (holding that the
plaintiff, in alleging that the airline had failed to take
appropriate action to correct a mechanical problem, stated, at
most, a claim for negligence but not for intentional infliction
of emotional distress). Walker's statement, "'[i]f it goes any
further, it's got to go through me'" (R.2) merely rhetorically
expressed his commitment to protesting nuclear weapons, not his
intent to be run over by an oncoming freight train.

As the context of his speech demonstrates, Walker was
referring metaphorically to the process of nuclear arms build-up
having "'to go through him,'" not literally to the train itself:
"'The thing goes on and on, on and on, on and on – chugging down
the track, chugging down our throats. We're choking on it, we're
dying from it, but no one seems to care . . . . If it goes any
further, it's got to go through me.'" (R.2.) Walker was not
attempting to end his life, and nothing Lionell has alleged

7

demonstrates otherwise. Because Walker did not intend for the
train to hit him, he could not have desired to inflict severe
emotional distress upon Lionell (or anyone else), nor could he
have known that such distress was certain or substantially
certain to result.

This lack of intent thoroughly distinguishes this case from
Blakeley v. Shortal's Estate, 29 N.W.2d 28 (Iowa 1945), cited in
Appellant's Initial Brief. In Blakeley, the decedent fully
intended to commit suicide, and it was that suicide which led to
the plaintiff's harm. Id. at 31. At issue was whether the facts
presented a jury question as to the decedent's wilfulness in
inflicting emotional harm on the plaintiff. Id. The court,
holding for the plaintiff, found that there was sufficient
evidence of the decedent's wilfulness. Id. The court reasoned
that the jury could find either that the decedent's act was
"'intentional, or . . . done under such circumstances as evinced
a reckless disregard for the safety of others, and a willingness
to inflict the injury [emotional distress] complained of.'" Id.
(quoting S. Ry. Co. v. McNeeley, 88 N.E. 710, 712 (Ind. App.
1909)) (emphasis added).

Here, in contrast to the Blakeley decedent, Walker neither
intended to harm himself nor to inflict emotional distress upon
anyone else. Lionell has failed to allege facts demonstrating
that Walker either desired to inflict emotional distress, or that
Walker acted knowing that such distress was certain or
substantially certain to result. Accordingly, this Court should

affirm the trial court's judgment dismissing Lionell's complaint with prejudice.

> 2. <u>Because Walker did not intend the train to hit him, he did not intentionally violate any statute designed to protect others from harm.</u>

As a matter of law, because Walker did not intend the train to hit him, he could not have acted recklessly. For an act to be reckless, even when a statutory violation allegedly is involved, (1) the act <u>itself</u> must be intended, and (2) the act "must involve an easily perceptible danger of death or substantial physical harm" to others. Restatement (Second) of Torts § 500 cmts. a and b (emphasis added).

Restatement section 500 defines "reckless disregard" of another's safety as behavior which would lead "reasonable [people] to realize, not only that [their] conduct creates an unreasonable risk of physical harm to another, but also that such risk is substantially greater than that which is necessary to make [their] conduct negligent." <u>Id.</u> at § 500. "Conduct cannot be in reckless disregard of the safety of others <u>unless the act or omission is itself intended</u>, notwithstanding that the actor knows of facts which would lead any reasonable [person] to realize the extreme risk to which it subjects the safety of others." <u>Id.</u> at cmt. b (emphasis added).

Thus, it is not enough for Lionell to claim that Walker intended to sit on the train tracks and that Walker violated railway safety statutes. Lionell must further demonstrate that

Walker intended to be hit by the train; and that he cannot do.

Moreover, Lionell cannot show that Walker's conduct met the second element of "recklessness," i.e., that it involved an "easily perceptible danger of death or substantial physical harm" to others. Id. at cmt. a. As Restatement (Second) of Torts § 500, comment e explains:

> In order that the breach of the statute constitute reckless disregard for the safety of those for whose protection it is enacted, the statute must not only be intentionally violated, but the precautions required must be such that their omission will be recognized as involving a high degree of probability that serious harm will result.

(Emphasis added.)

While Walker's lying on the tracks did pose the risk of serious harm to himself, it did not threaten harm – serious or not – to Lionell. It was not "easily perceptible" that Lionell, safe within the confines of a freight train, would suffer any harm, let alone "death or substantial physical harm." It would be incredulous for Lionell to assert that he, literally encased in a 4021 ton train, was in any physical danger from Walker's conduct. To hold otherwise would permit witnesses to an accident who suffered no physical injury themselves to receive damages from the accident victim simply for viewing the accident.

Finally, while it might have been foreseeable that Lionell could suffer distress if a close friend or relative was lying on the tracks, Lionell has not alleged that he even knew Walker prior to the incident. See Habelow v. Travelers Ins. Co., 389

So. 2d 218, 220 (Fla. 5th DCA 1980) (affirming the dismissal of a wife's action for intentional infliction of emotional distress, and calling that claim "attenuated," where the offensive conduct had been directed towards the plaintiff's husband, and not toward the plaintiff herself). Walker did not know, and could not have known, with "substantial certainty" that Lionell would be traumatized by his sit-in, or even by an accidental injury to a complete stranger.

Because Lionell has failed to demonstrate that Walker acted with the intent necessary to state a claim for intentional infliction of emotional distress, this Court should affirm the trial court's judgment dismissing this action with prejudice.

C.   Lionell's alleged physical symptoms are insufficient evidence of the severe emotional distress required for a plaintiff to state a claim for intentional infliction of emotional distress.

This Court should affirm the trial court's judgment dismissing this action because Lionell's alleged injuries are not severe enough to meet the section 46 requirement of "severe emotional distress." This Court determines "whether on the evidence severe emotional distress can be found . . . ." Restatement (Second) of Torts § 46 cmt. j. "The law intervenes only where the distress inflicted is so severe that no reasonable [person] could be expected to endure it." Id.; see also Sheehan, 373 So. 2d at 959 (observing that the plaintiff's testimony that he had been "extremely worried, upset, and nearly out of his mind

11

for a continuous period of seven hours" was, standing alone, insufficient evidence of severe distress).

Lionell's bad dreams and headaches are insignificant compared to the "severe distress" the law requires. They pale in comparison, for example, to the distress the Telophase plaintiff suffered when she discovered that she had spread a stranger's remains on sites with sentimental value to her and to her deceased husband. 471 So. 2d at 165 (describing the plaintiff's distress in terms of "graphic nightmares" followed by "severe emotional and physical consequences for which she required medical attention."). Moreover, sweaty palms and slight weight loss would have been a welcome alternative to the Sheehan plaintiff's seven anxiety-filled hours spent trying to discover the condition of his supposedly seriously-injured children. 373 So. 2d at 958 (finding that the outrageous character of the defendant's conduct was evidence that the distress had existed).

Further, an occasional sleepless night and pangs of guilt pale in intensity and duration to the "severe mental depression and distress" the Dependable Life Insurance plaintiff suffered when he was forced into bankruptcy by the defendant's failure to pay a legitimate disability claim. 510 So. 2d at 987 (holding that the plaintiff established his severe distress through his own testimony, as well as through the testimony of a psychiatrist and another physician).

Here, as the trial court found, Lionell's alleged physical symptoms – his sweaty palms, nausea, weight loss, guilt, depression, headaches and bad dreams – were evidence of distress, but were insufficient to establish the severe emotional distress the tort of outrage requires. (R.5.) Tellingly, although Lionell alleges that he has suffered these ailments, he does not allege that he can, at trial, support these claims with medical testimony. Indeed, he does not allege that he even consulted a doctor concerning them.

Although Lionell no doubt has suffered emotional distress due to his role in Walker's injuries, he has failed to demonstrate that his distress is, as a matter of law, so severe that "no reasonable [person] could be expected to endure it." Restatement (Second) of Torts § 46 cmt. j. For this reason, Lionell's complaint fails to state a cause of action for intentional infliction of emotional distress, and this Court should affirm the trial court's judgment dismissing this case with prejudice.

CONCLUSION

The trial court properly dismissed Lionell's complaint for intentional infliction of emotional distress. Though novel, if allowed, the complaint would permit witnesses to an accident who suffered no physical injury themselves to recover damages from the accident victim simply for witnessing the accident. Recognizing that this cannot and should not be the law, the trial court properly dismissed Lionell's complaint with prejudice. This Court should affirm that dismissal.

Respectfully submitted,

_____

Matthew Thomas
Counsel for Appellee, Noah Walker

888 Park Avenue
Gainesville, Florida 32611
(352) 555-1234

14

<u>CERTIFICATE OF SERVICE</u>

I certify that a true copy of this brief was furnished to Stew Dent, Counsel for Appellant, by mail this 27th day of January, 20xx.

_____

Matthew Thomas
Counsel for Appellee, Noah Walker

888 Park Avenue
Gainesville, Florida 32611
(352) 555-1234
Bar Number: 00765

Chapter 38

Lionell's Reply Brief

IN THE
DISTRICT COURT OF APPEAL OF FLORIDA
FIRST DISTRICT

PARKER LIONELL,

                Appellant,

v.   CASE NUMBER: Fxx

NOAH WALKER,
                Appellee.

_____/

ON APPEAL FROM THE CIRCUIT COURT

FOR THE EIGHTH JUDICIAL CIRCUIT OF FLORIDA

_____

APPELLANT'S REPLY BRIEF
_____

STEW DENT
Counsel for Appellant, Parker Lionell

250 Bruton-Geer Hall
University of Florida
Gainesville, Florida 32611
352-555-5555

TABLE OF CONTENTS

TABLE OF AUTHORITIES

<u>ARGUMENT</u>

LIONELL'S COMPLAINT STATES A CAUSE OF ACTION FOR
INTENTIONAL INFLICTION OF EMOTIONAL DISTRESS.

By purposefully lying in the path of an oncoming freight
train, Walker transformed a political protest into an illegal and
outrageous attempt to punish the railroad and its engineers,
including Lionell, for transporting a cargo of plutonium. In so
doing, he changed, utterly for the worse, Lionell's life.

In refusing to leave the tracks and in allowing himself to
be struck by the train, Walker forced Lionell, the train's chief
engineer, into becoming an unwilling participant in Walker's
mutilation. Walker forced Lionell, who frantically sounded
warning whistles and did everything humanly possibly to stop the
train, to hear Walker cry out and to see Walker's blood stream
down as the train ripped both of his legs from his body.

Lionell, plagued by the memory of these horrific sights and
sounds, has been unable to return to his livelihood as an
engineer. In recurrent nightmares, he relives the mutilation and
his unwitting role in it. He has lost weight, experiences
crippling migraine headaches, endures sweaty palms, and suffers
severe guilt and depression. In one brief moment, his entire
world was changed forever by the outrageous and illegal conduct
of one man.

1

In an attempt to make Walker take responsibility for the damage he has caused, Lionell brought this action for intentional infliction of emotional distress. The trial court, however, granted Walker's motion to dismiss the complaint with prejudice, holding that Walker's actions had not been outrageous; that Walker had not acted intentionally or recklessly in causing Lionell's distress; and that Lionell's distress was not "severe enough" to prevail on his claim of intentional infliction of emotional distress. (R.5-6.) The court, however, erred on all three conclusions. This Court, on *de novo* review, should reverse the trial court's judgment of dismissal, and allow this case to proceed to trial.

A.   Lionell has alleged facts demonstrating that Walker's actions were outrageous.

Although Walker correctly states the rule defining "outrageous" conduct, he fails to apply that rule correctly. See Appellee's Answer Br. at 1-6. He asserts that there is no reported case involving a situation where, as here, a plaintiff who has injured the defendant has then sued the injured defendant for "outrage" damages; and that such a cause of action "does not and should not exist." Id. at 2. His claim, however, overlooks two important points.

First, it is irrelevant that there is no reported case involving a similar fact pattern. The Restatement (Second) of

2

Torts section 46, which defines this cause of action, recognizes
that the law in this area "is still in a stage of development,
and the ultimate limits of this tort are not yet determined."
Restatement (Second) of Torts § 46 cmt. c (1965); see Appellant's
Initial Br. at 1 n.1.

Second, it is irrelevant whether Walker, the wrongdoer, was
injured by his wrongdoing. A wrongdoer who commits an
egregiously harmful and tortious act should not then be permitted
to claim his own injury as an affirmative defense. Yet, that is
exactly what Walker is attempting to do here. It is Walker who
knowingly laid down in front of the oncoming train.

Walker engaged in violent conduct resulting in the
mutilation of a living human body. The fact that the body he
mutilated was his own does not change the outrageousness of the
act or the fact that his actions caused debilitating harm to
Lionell.

B.   Lionell has alleged facts demonstrating that
     Walker acted wilfully, intending to inflict
     emotional distress or acting in reckless
     disregard of a high degree of probability
     that such distress would follow.

Walker claims that he cannot be held accountable here
because he did not act with the intent or recklessness section 46
requires. He makes four claims, none of which has any merit.

First, he asserts that Lionell must not only allege that

3

Walker intended to sit on the tracks, but that "Walker intended
to be hit by the train; and that he cannot do." Appellee's
Answer Br. at 9. Second, he claims that "[a]s a matter of law,
because Walker did not intend the train to hit him, he could not
have acted recklessly." Id. at 8.

These claims, however, ignore a fundamental principle: to
establish intent to commit the tort of outrage, Lionell need not
allege that Walker intended to be hit by the train, or that
Walker intended to inflict emotional distress. Lionell need only
allege that Walker intended to lie on those tracks and knew, or
should have known, that distress would follow. See Dominguez v.
Equitable Life Ins. Soc'y, 438 So. 2d 58, 59 n.1. (Fla. 3d DCA
1983), approved sub nom., Crawford v. Dominguez, 467 So. 2d 281
(Fla. 1985). This, Lionell has done. See Appellant's Initial
Br. at 8-9.

Third, Walker asserts that he could not have acted in
deliberate disregard of a high degree of probability that
emotional distress would follow because "[i]t was not 'easily
perceptible' that Lionell, safe within the confines of a 4021 ton
train, would suffer any harm, let alone 'death or substantial
physical harm.'" Appellee's Answer Br. at 10. Walker also
claims that he did not act recklessly in violating any statutes,
since the only safety risk he posed was to himself. Id.

4

However, these claims ignore the fact that Walker posed a foreseeable safety risk not only to himself, but to Lionell, train passengers, and to bystanders. Where, as here, the defendant's conduct involves a "high risk that serious harm will result from it to anyone who is within range of its effect, the fact that he knows or has reason to know that others are within such range is conclusive of the recklessness of his conduct towards them." Restatement (Second) of Torts § 500 cmt. d (1965) (emphasis added).

Yet, Walker attempts to deny responsibility by asserting a fourth argument: that he did not act recklessly in inflicting any emotional harm because

> [w]hile it might have been foreseeable that Lionell could suffer distress if a close friend or relative was lying on the tracks, Lionell has not alleged that he even knew Walker prior to the incident. . . . Walker did not know, and could not have known, with "substantial certainty" that Lionell would be traumatized by his sit-in, or even by an accidental injury to a complete stranger.

Appellee's Answer Br. at 10-11. This claim, however, is irrelevant.

Unlike the tort of negligent infliction of emotional distress, recovery under § 46 for intentional infliction of emotional distress is not limited to situations "in which the plaintiffs have been near relatives, or at least close associates, of the person" injured by the defendant. Restatement

(Second) of Torts § 46 cmt. l; <u>see also</u> <u>Champion v. Gray</u>, 478 So. 2d 17, 19-20 (Fla. 1985). This distinction makes perfect sense.

A defendant who causes a plaintiff to participate in the defendant's mutilation should not escape liability simply because the two parties are not genetically or socially related. As the Restatement comments explain, there is "no essential reason why a stranger who is asked for a match on the street should not recover when the man who asks for it is shot down before his eyes, at least where [the stranger's] emotional distress results in bodily harm." Restatement (Second) of Torts § 46 cmt. l.

Thus, a familial, or any type of preexisting relationship between Walker and Lionell is irrelevant. Without question, Walker's actions were wilful and intentional.

C.   <u>Lionell has alleged facts demonstrating that his emotional distress is so severe that it manifested itself in bodily harm.</u>

Although Lionell need not prove that his emotional distress resulted in bodily harm, it clearly did. Lionell's vomiting, nausea, weight loss, sweaty palms, debilitating migraine headaches, guilt, and depression all constitute bodily harm. Indeed, his distress was so severe that he could not return to work as an engineer. <u>See</u> <u>Harris v. State</u>, 509 So. 2d 1299, 1302 (Fla. 1st DCA 1987), <u>aff'd</u>, 531 So. 2d 1349 (Fla. 1988) (observing, in a criminal case, that severe, recurring

nightmares, headaches, and depression, causing the plaintiff's
inability to return to work, constituted "discernible physical
manifestation resulting from [ ] psychological trauma"); see also
Restatement (Second) of Torts § 436A cmt. c (1965) ("[l]ong
continued nausea or headaches may amount to physical illness,
which is bodily harm; and even long continued mental disturbance
. . . may be classified by the courts as illness, notwithstanding
their mental character").

No person should be expected to endure the severe distress
and guilt Walker has caused Lionell to suffer. Lionell is
entitled to damages here. At the least, he is entitled to
present his evidence of injury to the jury. The trial court
erred in dismissing this case on the pleadings.

CONCLUSION

Walker forced Lionell to mutilate him; Lionell suffered extreme emotional distress as a result; yet the trial court dismissed this case for intentional infliction of emotional distress before Lionell had the opportunity to present any evidence. Because that dismissal with prejudice on the pleadings was in error, Lionell respectfully requests this Court to reverse the trial court's judgment and remand this case for trial on the merits.

Respectfully submitted,

_____

Stew Dent
Counsel for Appellant, Parker Lionell

250 Bruton-Geer Hall
University of Florida
Gainesville, Florida 32611
352-555-5555

CERTIFICATE OF SERVICE

I certify that a true copy of this brief was furnished to Matthew Thomas, Counsel for Appellee, by mail, this 25th day of February, 20xx.

_____

Stew Dent
Counsel for Appellant, Parker Lionell

250 Bruton-Geer Hall
University of Florida
Gainesville, Florida 32611
352-555-5555
Bar Number: 26437

Appendix

Cases Used in Exercises[1]

---

1. We gratefully acknowledge permission from the copyright holder, Thomson Reuters, to reprint these cases in their entirety.

In re Button's Estate

209 Cal. 325, 287 P. 964
Supreme Court of California 1930

CURTIS, J.

*965 This is an appeal from an order denying probate of a document in the form of a letter claimed by the proponent to be the last will and testament of Grace Edna Button, deceased. The letter in question was unquestionably entirely written and dated by the deceased Grace Edna Button during her lifetime. It was found in the same room in which her dead body was discovered after the deceased had presumably taken her own life. It was dated, 'San Francisco, Calif. August 25-1928,' and was addressed to Dear, dear Daddy.' The letter consisted of four pages written on both sides of two leaves of paper. On the left margin of the last page were written the words, 'Love from 'Muddy.'' It is conceded that the letter addressed to 'Dear, dear Daddy' was written and addressed to the proponent, who at one time had been the husband of the deceased, but a final decree of divorce had been granted to the parties on April 4, 1928. There were living at the date of the death of said deceased two children of said parties who had been born during said marriage, one Ralph James Button, Jr., who was then fourteen years of age, and the other, Robert Henry Button, who was eight years old. The letter was evidently written in contemplation of death, and its contents show an unmistakable purpose on the part of the decedent to take her own life, which purpose was successfully accomplished shortly after, and on the day, the letter was written. The letter contains expressions of deep affection of the writer for her former husband and her two sons. In it she reproaches herself,

and expresses deep regret that she had failed to respond to her domestic responsibilities and thus to bring happiness to the family circle. She implores her former husband to care for, protect, and train their two boys, that the latter may 'grow up strong men for Uncle Sam.' A few excerpts from this letter will indicate the feelings of the deceased toward her former husband and her two children: 'I can only think of you, you, you, you, and I am ruining our boys' lives.' 'Keep your loving arms around them (the boys) and protect them as I know you will and always have.' 'I wish I could meet you in heaven just to be near you and the children.' 'I'd like to go down that 'long long trail' with you and our dear boys.' In the body of the letter and toward the end of the second of its four pages is found the following paragraph: 'I'm wearing you out dear and when I am gone you can just breathe one long sigh of contentment. I'd like to be cremated. You can have the house on 26th ave. and all the things of value so you won't be out any money on burying me.'

This provision the proponent contends is testamentary in character and that by it the deceased intended to and did devise to him the house situated on Twenty-Sixty avenue in the city of San Francisco, together with other articles of value belonging to her. No one appeared in the trial court to contest the petition of proponent, but said court nevertheless denied said petition. After the taking of this appeal the trial court appointed a guardian ad litem to represent said minors on the hearing of this appeal, and said guardian has appeared herein and filed a brief in reply and in opposition to the brief of the proponent and appellant.

*966 It is first contended by said guardian that the letter, which the proponent claims is the last will of the decedent, does not conform to the demands of section 1277 of the Civil Code, in that it is not signed as required by the terms of said section. This section of the Code defines an holographic will, and among other requirements of the section is the provision that it must be signed by the testator. We have already called attention to the fact that the letter was not signed at the end of at the close thereof, but that on the left margin of the last page of the letter the words 'Love from 'Muddy'' were written. It is not disputed but that these words were written by the deceased herself. The evidence further shows without conflict that the deceased was affectionately known by the proponent and by her children as 'Muddy' and that they called her by that name. While the section of the Code just referred to requires that an holographic will must be signed by the testator, it makes no requirement that in signing it the testator must use his legal or true name.... We think from the facts in this case, as the same are construed and understood in the light of the foregoing authorities, that the signing of the name 'Muddy' to the letter in question by the decedent was a sufficient signature to meet the requirements of section 1277 of the Civil Code.

The guardian ad litem makes a further objection to the signature of the deceased, and contends that, as it was written not at the end or close of the letter, but on the margin of the last page thereof, it was not written for the purpose or with the intent that it should

there serve as a 'token of execution' or as a signature to said letter. The decisions of this court and those of other jurisdictions so far as they have been called to our attention negative this claim on the part of the guardian....

The rule enunciated by these decisions is correctly stated ... in the following words: 'Where a will has been signed by the testator, it is sufficient even though the signature is not in the place on the instrument where usually such a writing is signed, viz., at the end of the document.... Of course, this statement is subject to the qualification that the signature of the testator, if not subscribed to the will-that is, if it is not at the end of the instrument, the usual place for the signature in such cases-then it must so appear from the document itself that the signature was thus placed 'with the intent that it should there serve as a token of execution' as to afford 'a positive and satisfactory inference' to that effect.'... We feel that these words may be fittingly applied to the facts in the present action. That the deceased wrote the word 'Muddy' on the margin of the last page of the letter for the purpose of finishing and closing the letter with her signature seems so apparent to us that it would be a waste of words to present any argument to support this statement. The photostatic copy of the letter attached to the transcript on appeal before us shows that the deceased in writing the letter had used the entire last page of the paper for the written portion of the letter, and that the only unused portion of the page was a narrow space along the left margin of this page. On this she wrote, 'Love from 'Muddy.'' No other conclusion can be reached from these facts than that the deceased by writing her name on the margin of the last page of the letter intended thereby to sign the letter as effectually as if she had signed the same at the end or close thereof.

The further contention is made by the guardian ad litem that the letter of the decedent is not testamentary in character, and therefore cannot serve the purpose of the last will of the deceased. In this connection the guardian ad litem calls attention to the fact that the letter contains over seven hundred words and but twenty-four of them are claimed to constitute a will; that nowhere in the whole letter does the writer mention the word 'will'; and that nowhere outside of said twenty-four words is there to be found any language indicating in the faintest degree that the writer intended to make a will by the terms of which she was disinheriting her two *967 sons. That the writer of the letter devoted by far the greater portion thereof to matters other than that of disposing of her property cannot, we think, have any bearing upon the question as to whether or not that portion of her letter which does deal with her property constitutes a testamentary disposition of said property. The letter was undoubtedly intended by the decedent to be a farewell letter to the man who had formerly been her husband. It would have been indeed strange, in view of the circumstances under which the letter was written, had the decedent simply mentioned her property and designated the person or persons whom she desired to have the same upon her death. The fact that she referred to many personal and family matters with which she was deeply concerned in the same letter in which she stated that the proponent could have the house and other things of value belonging to her would not in any way render this disposition of her property ineffectual, nor would it in any man-

ner change the character of such disposition. That she did not mention the word 'will' in any part of her letter is neither conclusive nor even persuasive that she did not intend to make a testamentary disposition of her property. 'No particular words are necessary to show a testamentary intent. It must appear only that the maker intended by it to dispose of property after his death.'... That she did not refer to her property nor indicate any intention to dispose of it in a manner which would result in disinheriting her two boys except in the twenty-four word paragraph above quoted presents no good or legal reason why this paragraph of her letter should not be given effect and construed according to its clear intent. If in one part of her letter she has expressed an intent to make a testamentary disposition of her property, it is a matter of little or no consequence that she did not in other portions of her letter make reference to such intent. This is especially true when there is nothing in her whole letter which in the slightest degree conflicts with or casts doubt upon her intention as expressed in the above-mentioned paragraph.

On the other hand, the proponent contends that the letter clearly shows an intention on the part of the deceased to make a testamentary disposition of her property. In order for a document to be the last will and testament of a deceased person, it must, in addition to meeting all other legal requirements, clearly show that the decedent intended it to take effect only after his death, and it must satisfactorily appear therefrom that the decedent intended by the very paper itself to make a disposition of his property in favor of the party claiming thereunder.... 'It is undoubtedly the general rule ... oft repeated, that the true test of the character of an instrument is not the testator's realization that it is a will, but his intention to create a revocable disposition of his property to accrue and take effect only upon his death and passing no present interest.'

We are of the opinion that the document in question, the letter written by the deceased, and particularly that paragraph thereof quoted above, meets the test prescribed by the rule announced.... That she intended that it should take effect only after her death is manifest. The purported disposition of her property follows a request that her body be cremated. She undoubtedly had then formed the intent to take her life, and the whole letter shows unmistakable evidence that it was written with the avowed purpose of arranging her affairs after death. Having intended that the letter, or at least that portion thereof which deals with her property, should take effect only after her death, the only remaining question is whether the decedent in any part of said letter has made, or intended to make, a disposition of that portion of her property referred to in her said letter.

The fact that the words, which the proponent claims to be a testamentary disposition of her property, were contained in a letter and were not set forth in a formally prepared will, does not detract from their testamentary character. The books are full of cases holding that letters under proper circumstances may be testamentary in character, and accordingly they have been proved and judicially determined to be testamentary dispositions of the property of the testator....

'You can have the house * * * and all things of value' are words of gift as direct and certain as if the testatrix had said, 'I give you the house and all things of value.' They perhaps might not have been used by a trained lawyer had he been called upon to draw the decedent's will, but to a layman they have practically the same legal significance as if the word 'gift' had been used. The contents of the letter show that she felt that she had been a burden to her former husband and that she exceedingly regretted that fact. She was asking a further favor of him that *968 he might attend to the final disposition of her body after her death by means of cremation, and that this last request of hers might not be an additional burden upon him, she gave him the house and other articles of value, 'so you won't be out any money in burying me.' The record does not disclose the value of the house and other property mentioned in her letter, but evidently she considered that they were of sufficient value to meet the expense of her funeral. If it be assumed that the value of the property given the proponent exceeded, even to a considerable extent, the expense of cremating the body of the deceased, that fact could not be held to change the plain meaning of the words, or defeat the disposition which she had thereby made of her property. It may well be that she gave the property to her former husband, not only to reimburse him for the expense incident to the final disposition of her body, but also to provide a home for her boys, whose custody and care she had committed to the proponent, their father.

The argument is made that as the letter is filled with expressions of love for her two sons that it is not reasonable to suppose that she would disinherit them in favor of her divorced husband. If this were all that the letter contained, there might be some force to the argument. But the letter further shows, not only that the decedent had a deep and abiding affection for her former husband, but that she relied exclusively upon him to care for her two boys when she was gone. It also shows that she had every confidence in the proponent that he would act as a true father to her children, for after requesting him to 'keep your loving arms around them and protect them,' she added, 'I know you will and always have.' What would be more natural for the mother under these circumstances than to give to the man, the father of her children, for whom she had such a deep affection, and into whose care she had so confidently intrusted the future welfare of her sons, the little property that she possessed that he might be the better able to carry out the trust imposed in him? It is not necessary, however, for us to resort to further argument as to the intent of the decedent. We are satisfied that the plain terms of the letter, written under the circumstances shown, can leave no doubt, but that the decedent intended to give, and did give to the proponent the property mentioned in the letter, and that this gift having been made with the intent that it should take effect upon her death is clearly a testamentary disposition of the property of the deceased in favor of the proponent.

This disposes of all points of any merit raised on the appeal. The judgment is therefore reversed, with directions to the trial court to enter an order admitting to probate the letter in question as the last will and testament of Grace Edna Button, deceased.

We concur: WASTE, C. J.; RICHARDS, J.; PRESTON, J.; SEAWELL, J.; SHENK, J.

In re Spies' Estate

86 Cal.App.2d 87, 194 P.2d 83
District Court of Appeal, Second District, California 1948

*84 MOORE, Presiding Justice.

Albert P. Spies executed his last will and testament March 7, 1930. It left testator's entire estate to his wife. She predeceased him on December 10, 1944, and the will contained no appropriate provision for the disposal of his estate to his survivors. On January 12, 1945, he wrote, dated and signed with his own hand the following instrument:

'Jan. 12-45
Mr. James Yates
Secy 663 B of L F & E

In case of my death, before my Brotherhood Policy is assign in change of beneficiary, it is my wish, that I bequeat $2000.00 of this $4000.00 policy to Patty Lou Smith of 1047 E. Wood St. Decatur, Ill. and Apt's 419 & 421 of Glen Donald's Apt's at Los Angeles, Calif.

Albert P. Spies

Mrs. W. M. McKay
(Witness thereto)'

The addressee of the letter is Mr. James Yates, secretary of Lodge 663 of the Brotherhood of Locomotive Firemen and Enginemen. The letter was not delivered but was found in testator's effects after his death. The witness thereto, Mrs. W. M. McKay, was a neighbor and a practical nurse who attended testator in his last illness and with whom he frequently discussed his affairs. Patty Lou Smith is the daughter of a sister of decedent's wife. Eight brothers and sisters survived decedent, seven of whom are appellants herein and one is administratrix with will annexed. Mr. Spies was in poor health at the time of the demise of his wife and he became progressively worse until his death on February 8, 1945.

At a hearing and trial without a jury the superior court found that the holographic *85 instrument of January 12, 1945, was duly executed with testamentary intent and admitted it to probate as a codicil to testator's last will and testament.

Appellants' sole contention on appeal is that the instrument, viewed either alone or in the light of the circumstances of its execution, does not evidence sufficient testamentary intent to warrant its admission to probate as a will or codicil.

It is axiomatic that the intent of a testator so far as is possible should control in the interpretation of his will. This is accordingly the basic rule of construction to which all others must yield.... When a will is open to two constructions, one of which makes it valid and the other illegal, the construction which sustains it should be followed.... Of two modes of interpretation the one which will prevent intestacy is preferred.... If the prerequisite testamentary intent does not appear from the face of the instrument itself, reference may be made to the circumstances of its execution, and the language will be construed in the light of those circumstances.... The application of the foregoing principles to the questioned instrument and its attendant circumstances demonstrates the correctness of the order of the trial court in the instant case.

The opening words of the contested letter, to wit, 'In case of my death,' indicate clearly that the decedent intended thereby to direct the distribution of his estate in the event of his death. That phrase dramatically expresses the contingency upon which the gift is to take effect. By reason of his years and the recency of the passing of his wife he must have realized that his days were limited and his bequest to her had lapsed. In this he was correct: his decease occurred less than a month from the date of the instrument. His wife's decease was a sufficient incentive to prompt him to make an immediate disposal of his property. Nor only was it natural for him to designate another legatee but his original will shows that his policy was to make disposal by will. Other evidences of a testamentary dispositive intent are apparent in the particularity of the description of the beneficiary as well as of the property involved, and by the fact that the decedent caused Mrs. McKay to sign the instrument as a witness.

These circumstances impel the deduction that the deceased intended by the writing to effect a transfer of his property at death according to his desires....

For the purpose of satisfying the requisite formalities of a holographic will the added signature of a witness may be disregarded as surplusage if the part written by the testator is complete and sufficient ... but such witnessing may be indicative of an intention at its writing to make it dispositive in character.

The circumstances of the execution of the letter further indicate the presence of the necessary testamentary intent. Mrs. McKay testified that the decedent frequently prefaced his remarks with 'if anything happens to me'; that he referred to Patty Lou Smith by name and said that he loved her as if she were his daughter; that he was going to change the beneficiary of his will from his wife to his niece. Such prior declarations of intent to make a will are admissible when the attempt is not to explain an ambiguity but to show the testamentary character of a letter.... Thus the trial court properly concluded that the letter was testamentary in character and that the decedent had the requisite testamentary intent when he wrote and signed it.

The cases cited by appellant are not pertinent. In both *86 ... the court held that the true test of the character of an instrument purporting to bequeath property is not the testator's realization that it is a will, but whether he intended to create an effective though revocable transfer of his property to take effect only upon his decease while passing no present interest. In [one case] ... the court sustained a finding that the purported holographic will was not entirely written by the deceased. In [another case] ... the court declined to disturb a finding of the trial court as to testamentary intent, no error having been shown in the court's application of established rules of law in deriving its determination of factual issues.

The order is affirmed.

McCOMB and WILSON, JJ., concur.

In the Matter of the Estate of Blain

140 Cal.App.2d 917, 295 P.2d 898
District Court of Appeal, Fourth District, California 1956

*899 CONLEY, Justice pro tem.

These are appeals from two complementary judgments denying probate to an alleged integral portion of a holographic will and determining that a granddaughter of the decedent, who is his sole surviving heir at law, is entitled to take the whole of his estate, valued at more than $115,000, to the exclusion of the devisees and legatees named in the will.

The decedent, Frank Blain, and his wife Wanda Berta Blain had one child, Carol, who married Otto Lambert; their only child is Sonia Lambert. The Blains had executed a property settlement agreement and an interlocutory decree of divorce had been issued to them about six months before the happening of an airplane accident in which Mrs. Blain and Mr. and Mrs. Lambert were killed. This left Sonia as the only lineal descendant of Frank Blain; the girl went to live in Los Angeles at the home of Mrs. George Wakefield, sister-in-law of Mrs. Lambert, but she occasionally visited with her grandfather, Frank Blain; he operated certain of the Tulare properties which her mother, father and grandmother had left her and accounted for the income to Sonia's guardian, F. Kenneth Hamlin; the guardianship estate shortly before Mr.

Blain's death was valued in excess of $120,000.

Frank Blain died on February 7, 1953. Prior to the commencement of the proceedings leading to the decrees from which the appeals are taken, his will was admitted to probate. It consisted of seven separate *900 sheets, each of which was wholly in his own handwriting and dated and signed by him; these seven sheets were found in his safe deposit box in the Bank of America at Visalia folded together and enclosed in a sealed envelope which was endorsed in the handwriting of the decedent, 'Last Will F. B.'. Three of these complete pages were dated June 1, 1949, and four of them April 9, 1952; each of six of the seven parts of the will as admitted to probate dealt with a separate devisee or legatee, and the seventh directed the sale of an additional parcel of real property for the payment of inheritance taxes and probate expenses. Sonia Lambert was not mentioned in any of the seven sheets.

If the will as admitted to probate is the complete will of decedent, there can be no question but that Sonia Lambert was a pretermitted heir entitled to the whole estate of her grandfather by virtue of the provisions of Section 90 of the Probate Code:

'When a testator omits to provide in his will for any of his children, or for the issue of any deceased child, whether born before or after the making of the will or before or after the death of the testator, and such child or issue are unprovided for by any settlement, and have not had an equal proportion of the testator's property bestowed on them by way of advancement, unless it appears from the will that such omission was intentional, such child or such issue succeeds to the same share in the estate of the testator as if he had died intestate.'

Sonia Lambert is not provided for in the will admitted to probate, and in fact is not mentioned in it in any way; there is no proof or even contention that she was previously provided for by the grandfather in any settlement or by way of advancement; there is nothing in any of the seven pages to indicate that the omission of all provision for the grandchild and only heir at law of the testator was intentional. Pursuant to Section 222 of the Probate Code she would have inherited all of the decedent's property if he had died intestate. Therefore, it is clear that if the will as admitted to probate was the entire will of Frank Blain, the court's decree determining heirship is correct, and Sonia Lambert is entitled to inherit all of the real and personal property owned by him.

The entire case thus turns on the question whether the court erred in denying the petition for the probate of the alleged integral portion of the will; this petition was filed by Bettie Treaster, a niece of Frank Blain, and one of the devisees named in the will admitted to probate; the alleged integral portion of the will is admittedly in the handwriting of the decedent and consists of five words, including the signature, as follows: 'to Sonia Lambert Frank Blain' written on a small piece of paper which was wrapped around a dinner ring worth $120 and enclosed in a small ring box found in the bank safe deposit box of decedent, which also contained miscellaneous papers of

Mr. Blain and the sealed envelope marked 'Last Will F. B.' in which had been placed the seven sheets of the will as admitted to probate.

This court's enquiry must be: was there substantial evidence to support the trial court's findings that the document in question '* * * was not made or executed in the manner provided by law for the execution of a holographic will', that it '* * * is not testamentary in character, contains no testamentary disposition, and exhibits no testamentary intent,' that it '* * * cannot be related to the last Will and Testament of said deceased, either by sequence of thought, physical proximity, physical attachment, or continuity of purpose' and the judgment that it formed no part of the will of Frank Blain. For in a contested proceeding in probate the limitations imposed upon an appellate court's review of the facts are the same as in any other civil case. As is said ... :

"It is an elementary * * * principle of law, that when a verdict is attacked as *901 being unsupported, the power of the appellate court begins and ends with a determination as to whether there is any *substantial* evidence, contradicted or uncontradicted, which will support the conclusion reached by the jury. When two or more inferences can be reasonably deduced from the facts, the reviewing court is without power to substitute its deductions for those of the trial court.' (Italics added.) ... The rule quoted is as applicable in reviewing the findings of a judge as it is when considering a jury's verdict.'...

The foregoing rules have been applied to judgments in cases where the conflict in the record was between inferences which the trier of fact might draw ... and in cases specifically involving the question of integration....

Unless the piece of paper with the five words on it can be integrated with the will as admitted to probate, ... it cannot pretend to any consideration as a holographic will; it is fatally defective in form in that it bears no date; and strict compliance with the requirements of Section 53 of the Probate Code as to handwriting, date and signature is absolutely essential.... The trial court's finding that it '* * * was not made or executed in the manner provided by law for the execution of a holographic will' is incontestably true, unless there was integration with the seven written pages in the envelope.

Has the trial court substantial support in the record for the finding that this proposed portion of the will 'is not testamentary in character, contains no testamentary disposition, and exhibits no testamentary intent'? We think that a fair consideration of the record compels an affirmative answer. The writing itself 'to Sonia Lambert Frank Blain' contains no description or specification of any property.... A holographic will must be complete in itself; there is no authority given by the code section or decided cases to incorporate physical objects as part of the dispositive instrument. But even if the trier of fact had taken the unauthorized step of saying that the words referred to the ring, the court had before it evidence that the ring was already the property of Sonia through inheritance from her grandmother, and that Frank Blain was merely holding it for her; with this background of fact, the words 'to Sonia Lambert' could be inferred to mean 'This is the property of Sonia Lambert, deliver it to her.' If, in a document constituting a will, there should appear the statement 'To Jane Doe, my diamond ring' the word 'to' in its particular context would be dispositive, ... but the word 'to' is certainly not a term of art applicable only to testamentary disposition. It is a common word used in sundry circumstances. Letters, telegrams, packages are often addressed with the word 'to' preceding the name of the addressee, and the inference could be drawn by the trier of fact from the circumstances developed in the record that no disposition by way of will was intended.

It is, of course, elementary that proof of testamentary intent must be made with respect to the very paper proposed before any document may be admitted to *902 probate as a last will and testament.... And the court's finding that there was no testamentary intent is supported by substantial evidence.

It should be noted in passing that the principle of interpretation that the law favors testacy over intestacy, ... is usually only operative when the existence of testamentary intent has already been ascertained, 'and the subject-matter of the doubt is one of construction. Where there is a doubt as to the existence of the *animus testandi* the rule in favor of testacy is not applicable'.... [a]nd a rule of construction can never serve to create a will where one does not exist.

The testimony of the witness Harriet Young that on one occasion Mr. Blain showed her the ring and said he was going to leave it to his granddaughter and 'he was fixing it to take it to the Safe Deposit Box that day' does not, ... relate to oral declarations of a testator with relation to an existing written instrument as tending to show the intent with which it

was executed, but rather to a mere intention at some time in the future to make a will; in any event, this evidence only furnishes a conflict with other evidence, direct and indirect, which it was the trial court's duty to resolve.

Finally, in our consideration of the findings, we ask: Was the trial court justified under the record in finding that there was no integration of the slip of paper in the ring box with the seven sheets in the envelope, or, using the language of the court, that the slip of paper '* * * cannot be related to the last Will and Testament of said deceased, either by sequence of thought, physical proximity, physical attachment, or continuity of purpose?'

[I]t is said:

> 'In the law of wills, integration, as distinguished from incorporation by reference, occurs when there is no reference to a distinctly extraneous document, but it is clear that two or more separate writings are intended by the testator to be his will.... Thus several writings, connected by sequence of thought..., folded together ... or physically forming one document ... have been admitted to probate as constituting an holographic will.'

The seven sheets of paper constituting the will as admitted to probate, each of which was complete in itself as to date, signature and handwriting, were nevertheless properly considered as one will under the very theory of integration which appellant invokes. The seven writings were in close physical proximity, were physically attached by being folded together, and the sequence of thought and continuity of purpose are apparent through the reading of the documents and by the fact that all of these sheets *903 were enclosed by the testator in a sealed envelope bearing the endorsement in his own handwriting 'Last Will F. B.'

The suggested integration of the slip of paper in the ring box with the admittedly integrated seven sheets in the envelope, has no such evidentiary support. The slip of paper was physically excluded from everything outside of the ring box; even the ring box was not attached physically in any way to the envelope containing the seven sheets. Both closed ring box and sealed envelope were in a bank safe deposit box with numerous other papers, all of which would normally be kept in a bank vault. There is no reference direct or indirect in any of the seven pages in the will envelope to the paper in the ring box, or to the ring, and there is, of course, no reference by any wording on the slip of paper to the will envelope or its contents.

We have been unable to find any case which would authorize an extension of the doctrine of integration to include the slip of paper from the ring box. The three cases principally relied upon by appellant, ... deal with differing factual situations which furnish a basis for the application of the doctrine. In [case one] ... the testatrix declared all three papers to be her will, they were folded in proper and chronological sequence and placed in an envelope; shortly before the death they were at her direction placed together in a sealed envelope; she indicated on the first sheet that the other sheets would carry out her purpose of making a complete testamentary disposition and the 'continuity of the context is manifest'. In [case two] ... the will was on two sheets of paper, and both sides of the first sheet were written on by the testator; it is apparent from their contents that the testator intended all written parts to constitute his will. 'Both parts are wholly testamentary in character; they are integrated by their context; they are congruous, continuous, and make a consistent whole; they were obviously written for the single purpose of disposing of the testator's estate.' In [case three] ... the testator stated that both pieces of paper on which he had written constituted his will and then affixed his signature to one; he kept the papers together and handed an envelope containing them to his chief beneficiary and executrix. These cases differ factually from the instant case and constitute no authority to warrant a reversal of the judgment.

Entirely outside of the writings themselves, the record shows that Frank Blain did not intend to leave any part of the substantial estate referred to in the will to his granddaughter, for he expressed himself as believing that she already had inherited sufficient property from her father, mother and grandmother; he wished to have his sister, niece, nephews and friends receive the land and personalty specified in the seven pages of his will. But, unfortunately, the testator knew just enough about probate law to think he could safely prepare his own will; by acting for himself he saved an attorney's fee amounting to perhaps ten dollars and caused a loss to his intended devisees and legatees of well over a hundred thousand; 'a little learning is a dangerous thing.'

The orders and judgments appealed from are affirmed.

BARNARD, P. J., and GRIFFIN, J., concur.

In the Matter of the Estate of Wolfe

260 Cal.App.2d 587, 67 Cal.Rptr. 297
District Court of Appeal, First District, California 1968

RATTIGAN, J.

*298 The question presented by this appeal is whether a handwritten letter is admissible to probate as its author's holographic will. The letter, which is in a barely legible scrawl, reads as follows (strikeouts by the author shown, within brackets):

'Redwood City Calif
July 29-1927
'R 1 Box 317

'Mr. Herman Wolfe

'Dear Brother I will drop you a few lines this morn. this leaves me OK hope you all are the same kid I am flat broke except my place I (a) have not got no job here yet so I am (leaveing) leaveing to hunt work I dont know where I am going but if I ever make enough money to get Stamps I will *299 write you again but do not write untell you here from me it might be

'2

best for you to write Elsie the rest of the folk is enjoying life very well not so good here for me. We sold the store at Palo Alto I am leaveing my Place in Menlo Park for you if I never call for it (it) the place is yours it is rented now $22.50 per month the rent is due on the 5th of each month but you might (a) hafto

give Elsie part to Colect it you can write about that if you

'3

ever take a notion to come to Calif you will have a place to live in. say I am leaveing my trunk with Elsie but if she dont want it here she will send it to you it has all my pictures in it and ever thing that belongs to (illegible strikeout) me in it if they want to sell the place and all get to gether go ahead and you can have my part of it and all that the Estate

'4

owes me on Papa expence when I came back there at his death Elsie knows all about it as she went part of it I have a note of it in my trunk I must close for this time do not know when I will write again do not write me write Elsie

'Lots of love to Brother Herman from Ernest Wolfe

'PS if you want to sell the Place in Menlo Park go [a] head and sel it but do not

'5

sell it to buy the place back ther for you will loose money on it but if you thank that would be the best go head (three illegible strikeouts)

'6

'I never come back untell I get an nother Start. Ernest

'if I were you I would keep this letter'

When the letter was offered for probate, it was accompanied by the envelope in which it was apparently mailed. In the same handwriting as the letter, the envelope's face reads:

'Mr. Herman Wolfe

R. 1. Box 22 Gardon Tex'

On the reverse side of the envelope, also in the same handwriting, there is written:

'5 days return to R. 1. Box 317 Redwood City Calif'

Postmarks and hand-stamped legends on the envelope indicate that it was mailed to its Texas addressee by registered mail on July 29, 1927.

Respondent offered the letter for probate as the will of Ernest Wolfe, 'a missing person,' asserting that Herman Wolfe is Ernest's devisee under the will. Respondent acted-and still acts-on behalf of an adult child of Herman, who is now deceased. Appellant, one of several collateral heirs of Ernest, appeared below in opposition to the petition for probate. Her opposition was based upon the contentions, among others, that the letter was not a will because it did not reflect testamentary intent on Ernest's part and

that it failed to meet the formal requirements of a holographic will....

The appeal is from the probate court's order admitting the letter (with the envelope) to probate as Ernest's will. Appellant does not challenge the court's finding that the instrument was, in form, a valid holographic will. The sole question on the appeal is, as appellant states, 'Whether the letter ... meets the requirement of testamentary intent.'

Where a trial court's interpretation of a written instrument turns upon the credibility of conflicting extrinsic evidence admitted in aid thereof, we are bound by the interpretation reached.... We are free to make our own interpretation, however, if the trial court (1) admitted no extrinsic evidence, *300 (2) made its determination upon incompetent evidence, or (3) acted upon evidence which was not in conflict.... Appellant states that 'No evidence, either oral or documentary, was presented to the (probate) Court' when the petition for probate was heard. While this may be literally true, it is apparent that the court considered certain extrinsic facts in interpreting the letter to be Ernest Wolfe's will.

Some of the extrinsic facts reached the probate court in the form of uncontroverted allegations in the parties' pleadings and briefs below: others had been adjudicated in a previous probate proceeding. None of the facts is disputed, and the evidence of none is in conflict. We are therefore free to make our own interpretation of the letter.... So doing, however, we must consider the extrinsic facts agreed upon below, because of their obvious relevance to the issue of Ernest's testamentary intent. Including them, the facts shown are as follows:

On and before July 29, 1927, Ernest Wolfe was a resident of San Mateo County. He owned real property in Menlo Park. He was single and had no children, never having married. Herman Wolfe was Ernest's brother. Herman was alive on July 29, 1927, but has since died. On that date, Ernest wrote and mailed the above quoted letter to Herman. The letter was entirely written, dated and signed in Ernest's handwriting. On or about July 29, 1927, Ernest left his last place of residence, disappeared, and has not been seen or heard of since. In 1965, he was adjudicated to be a missing person within the meaning of chapter 2 of division 2a of the Probate Code....

Our interpretation of the letter is guided by the following principles: an instrument may be admitted to probate as a will if it appears from the instrument's terms, viewed in the light of the circumstances of its execution, that it was executed with testamentary intent....

The burden of proving the necessary element of testamentary intent rests upon the proponent of the alleged will....

The basic test of testamentary intent is not the testator's realization that he was making a will, but whether he intended by the document in question to create a revocable disposition of his property to take effect only upon his death.*301 Thus, a document written in the form of a letter, and which meets formal holographic requirements (as the letter before us does), will be admitted to probate if the requisite testamentary intent appears....

If testamentary intent adequately appears, a document's testamentary character is not affected by the fact that it in-

cludes nontestamentary matters.... No particular words are necessary to show testamentary intent.... When an instrument shows on its face-as in the case of the letter before us-that it was written by an inexperienced or illiterate person, it may be construed more liberally than if it had been drawn by an expert....

Under the foregoing rules and the known circumstances in which Ernest Wolfe wrote the letter of July 29, 1927, we interpret it as his will. He wrote '(I) am leaveing my Place in Menlo Park for you(.)' The words 'for you' sufficiently qualify 'am leaveing' to demonstrate that Ernest intended the verb to effect a disposition of the 'Place,' and not to refer to his departure from it. Use of the word 'leave' in a dispositive sense, although not conclusive ... has been recognized as sufficient evidence of testamentary intent....

Ernest also wrote '(I)f I never call for it * * * the place is yours (.)' Had he made a 'call for it' in later years, his previous testamentary disposition of the place would have been revoked. The question here is not whether a 'call' for the property would have actually effected a revocation of the disposition made in 1927, but whether Ernest intended that result. The word 'never' encompassed the reach of eternity, which included the inevitable event of Ernest's death. The passage quoted therefore imparted both (1) revocability and (2) posthumous effect as requisite elements of Ernest's testamentary intent.

Ernest made the disposition in favor of his brother, with whom the letter itself showed him to have been on close and affectionate terms ('Lots of love to Brother Herman * * *'). It does not appear that anyone else occupied a position superior to Herman as an object of Ernest's testamentary bounty, or that anyone would have held such position in the event of his intestacy....

We also note that Ernest, sending the letter by registered mail and admonishing Herman relative to its safekeeping ('(I)f I were you I would keep this letter'), thereby indicated his awareness of the letter's importance and character. Such perception, appearing from a similar admonition, has been recognized as evidence of testamentary intent in a written instrument....

*302 Appellant argues that the letter does not show testamentary intent on the writer's part because, telling Herman that 'this leaves me OK,' it indicates that Ernest was not *in extremis*. Where a document or the circumstances of its execution have showed that its author was *in extremis*-in the sense of anticipating imminent death-the fact has been considered significant in the interpretation of the document as his will.... The absence of the same fact has contributed to an opposite conclusion ... but its absence is not decisive where the document in question shows testamentary intent apart from considerations of the testator's health.

Moreover, the term ' *in extremis*' is not exclusively applicable to an actor's anticipation of imminent death. It characterizes any situation in which the actor is 'in extremity'... or in 'extreme circumstances.'... Ernest's letter stated that 'I am flat broke except my place I * * *. have not got no job here yet so I am * * * leaveing to hunt work * * * not so good here for me * * *' The situation depicted appears to have been one of 'extreme circumstances' which found Ernest *in extremis* in an economic sense, although not anticipating imminent death. Other language in the letter ('I dont know where I am going * * * do not write * * * do not know when I will write again * * * I never come back untell I get an nother Start') indicates sufficient uncertainty of the future to have motivated Ernest to make a testamentary disposition of his property.

Appellant further contends that Ernest, by the letter, intended only to convey to Herman a 'current interest,' or a 'defeasible estate,' in his property. The argument is based upon several passages in the letter, each of which-read by itself-suggests that Ernest intended to vest in Herman only the right to collect rent ('(The place) * * * is rented now $22.50 per month the rent is due on the 5th of each month but you might hafto give Elsie part to Colect it'); or to occupy the property ('(I)f you ever take a notion to come to Calif you will have a place to live in'); or to sell it ('PS if you want to sell the place in Menlo Park go * * * head and sel it * * * (etc.)').

But Ernest's dire economic straits, narrated in the letter as cited above, suggest that he was not in a position-and therefore did not intend-to make a present conveyance of everything of value that he owned ('I am flat broke except my place'). Each of the isolated passages quoted appears to have been advisory rather than dispositive, and the advice given in each instance (relative to Herman's collecting rent, occupying the property, or selling it) was entirely consistent with Herman's ownership of the property as its devisee. Accordingly, appellant's contention of each such passage must yield to our overriding interpretation of the letter-reached from its full context and heretofore discussed-that Ernest intended to make a testamentary disposition, effective upon his death and not as of the letter's date.

The order appealed from is affirmed.

DEVINE, P. J., and CHRISTIAN, J., concurred.

Estate of Tai-Kin WONG, Deceased

40 Cal.App.4th 1198, 47 Cal.Rptr.2d 707
District Court of Appeal, Sixth District, California 1995.

*708 WUNDERLICH, Associate Justice.

In this case we review the trial court's decision that a document containing eight words, seven of them proper names and an appellation, constituted a holographic will.

Tai-Kin Wong (Tai) was a successful 44-year-old businessman who until just before death had a history of good health. He was living with his girlfriend Xi Zhao (Xi), and he enjoyed a close and loving relationship with his large family. On New Year's Eve in 1992, he took ill and died in a hospital emergency room of unexplained causes. Sometime after his death, found in his office was a sealed envelope, decorated with stickers and containing a handwritten note which read "All Tai-Kin Wong's → Xi Zhao, my best half TKW 12-31-92." This document-containing no subject, no verb, no description of property, and no indication of its subject matter or purpose-was found by the trial court to be a holographic will, passing Tai's entire estate to Xi. Tai's father, Kok-Cheong Wong (appellant)[1] brought this appeal. For the rea-

Petitioner's Exhibit 1

sons stated below, we will reverse the judgment.

FACTS/PROCEDURAL HISTORY

At the time of his death, Tai was 44 years old. He had never married and he had no children. For the previous three years, he and Xi had lived together in Saratoga. Tai and Xi had met in 1987 at a scientific conference. They fell in love and began to live together in 1989 after Xi received her doctorate in cell biology. They lived together until the time of Tai's death on New Year's Eve.[2]

---

1. At oral argument Mr. Wong's attorney stated that Mr. Wong has died. Tai's siblings have been substituted as appellants.

2. Whether Xi lived with Tai during the latter months of 1992 was disputed bitterly, as was every other significant fact in this case.

When Xi relocated to California to be with Tai, she turned down several job offers that were more attractive than the one she accepted at Stanford University. Previously she had visited Tai in California and they had kept in close touch. She immediately moved into his house in Saratoga and worked at her full-time job at Stanford. Tai, meanwhile, was engaged in running a company he founded with his brother, Danny Wong (Danny) called Baekon, Inc. Xi helped Tai run Baekon, working for Baekon in the evenings and on weekends. In 1990 Tai and Xi founded a new company, Transgenic Technologies, Inc. (TTI) which they owned equally. Tai worked every day at TTI in Fremont, developing the new business. Baekon was wound down; Danny transferred his interest in the business to Tai.

Tai and Xi thus lived together and worked together for the last three years of Tai's life. Whether their love relationship was flourishing or floundering was disputed at trial. Though supposedly lovers, on the day of Tai's death, New Year's Eve, they had arranged to dine separately-Tai with his close friend, Dr. Jianmin Liu and his girlfriend, and Xi with a man she describes as then a casual social acquaintance, Brien Wilson, a local attorney.

The evidence Xi introduced tended to show that she was close to Tai's family, indeed, practically accepted as a member of it. After Mr. Wong came home from the hospital following a stroke, Tai and Xi took care of him four nights a week, Monday through Thursday. Mr. Wong viewed Xi as his son's companion,*709 and presented her with gifts of money, traditionally given only to family members in Chinese families.

When Tai died on December 31, 1992, it was in the throes of an illness which was similar in its symptoms to sicknesses that had afflicted him two or three times earlier that month.... Doctors were unable to diagnose his illness, but wished to do a test which Tai declined. On December 31st, he again became ill, was taken to the hospital by ambulance, and died with the same symptoms....

Meanwhile, Xi was having dinner with Brien Wilson at a fancy French restaurant in Los Gatos. She had concealed from Tai the fact that she was dining on New Year's Eve with Brien Wilson, a man she moved in with two and one-half months after Tai's death. After dinner, she returned to the Saratoga house, and shortly after her arrival she received a call from Dr. Liu informing her that Tai was in the hospital. (Dr. Liu testified he never did reach Xi on the telephone. Rather, she called him at the hospital after Tai's death.) According to Xi, when she arrived at the hospital, close to midnight, Tai was already dead. While Tai had some symptoms similar to those that characterized his illness 10 days earlier, the cause of death was mysterious and has never been determined.

The questioned document or purported will was discovered in the following way: Xi made no effort to find a will at the residence she shared with Tai. Instead, on January 18, 1993, two weeks after Tai's funeral, Xi, Roy Tottingham (then a business consultant to TTI and now vice-president), Dr. Gin Wu (a TTI employee) and Heston Chau (an old friend of Tai's) searched Tai's office. Xi had asked Danny Wong to help go through Tai's papers, but he refused to do it. These four people, then, including Xi, divided the papers into business documents and personal papers and placed them in separate boxes.

During this search they found a sealed envelope in one of Tai's desk drawers, but Xi could not remember which one nor who saw it first. The upper left hand corner contained Tai's address label, the center of the envelope bore two stickers: a rainbow with the words "You're Special," and a rainbow with the words "Love You." This sealed envelope was placed in the box of Tai's personal papers which itself was sealed. Later the sealed box was placed in Xi's office where it remained unopened.

Dr. Victor Vurpillat, (the co-CEO of TTI when Tai was alive), opened the box in Xi's office sometime later. The only item he removed from the box was the envelope with the stickers. Vurpillat took the envelope and the following day he and Roy Tottingham met with TTI's attorney, together with a *710 probate attorney, John Willoughby, who opened the envelope....

Xi filed a petition for probate of the purported will. Xi was first appointed personal representative and Tottingham was appointed special administrator for the purpose of handling Tai's real estate and voting his shares of stock. Mr. Wong, from whom the family had kept word of Tai's death for some six weeks because of Mr. Wong's poor health, filed the will contest on May 14, 1993.

CONTENTIONS OF PARTIES

Appellants contend: the document admitted to probate is not a valid will, because as a matter of law, the words in the document cannot constitute a will and because there is not sufficient evidence of testamentary intent. Appellants also contend that the trial court erroneously excluded decedent's statements regarding his feelings toward respondent and also erred in granting respondent's motion to quash certain deposition subpoenas. Respondent Xi disputes each contention.

DISCUSSION

The document the trial court found to be a will reads as follows: "All Tai Kin Wong's ø Xi Zhao, my best half." Beneath are the initials "TKW" and the date "12-31-92." The document is completely handwritten.

The parties dispute the standard of review. Whether the questioned document can constitute a will as a matter of law is a legal question subject to independent review.... .If the document can constitute a will, the finding that it expresses testamentary intent is subject to a substantial evidence review....

A holographic will is one entirely in the writing of the testator. The requirements are that it be signed, dated, and that it evidence testamentary intent. (See Prob.Code, § 6111.) The trial court resolved the issue of whether the will was in the writing of the testator in favor of proponent Xi. Clearly the document is dated at the bottom. Regarding the third requirement, Witkin says "[I]t must appear that decedent intended to make a testamentary disposition *by that particular paper,* and if this cannot be shown it is immaterial that his testamentary intentions were [or would have been] in conformity with it." ...

No particular words are required to create a will. "Thus, a letter or other informal document will be sufficient if it discloses the necessary testamentary intent, i.e., if it appears that the decedent intended to direct the final disposition of his property after his death. *The surrounding circumstances may be considered in reaching a conclusion on this issue.* [Citations.]" ... In other words, if it is not completely clear that the document evidences testamentary intent, it is possible to resort to extrinsic evidence of the surrounding circumstances in order to provide it.... *711

In resolving the central issue in this case, we reviewed many cases to study the sorts of documents courts have interpreted to be wills, and the sorts of applicable extrinsic circumstances considered. Briefly we review some of these cases.

In *Estate of Spitzer* ... the testator was ill. He wrote his brother regarding the property he wanted to go to his wife and daughter. The extrinsic circumstances indicating the letter was meant to be a will were that he told both his brother and his neighbor that he was making a will and sending it to his brother.

In another case the decedent Beffa wrote "I sign and [transfer] ... [this] Deed" and some other things to his aunt.... Beffa committed suicide while in the midst of dissolving a partnership. He lived with his aunt to whom he was very close. The question was what appears from the face of the instrument; it appeared that Beffa intended the described property to go to his aunt. He left the document in the safe at the business, and nondelivery tends to show that it was a will.

In *Estate of Button* ... decedent wrote a long letter to her ex-husband, immediately before she committed suicide. The document was found in the same room in which she was found. In it she said " 'I'd like to be cremated. You can have the house on 26th ave. and all things of value so you won't be out any money on burying me.' " While the letter went on for many pages and covered many subjects including how ex-husband should care for the parties' son, still the court found these few words at the end of the letter to be a valid holographic will.

During military service, a seaman wrote a letter to his friend saying: "[I]n case *Davie Jones* gets me out in the South Pacific ocean in other words lost at Sea," a certain person was to have his property. (*Estate of Taylor* ... italics in original.) Although Taylor contemplated death in battle during wartime, he returned from the war safely, and acknowledged and republished his will. He repeatedly told the beneficiary that the third party to whom he wrote the letter was holding the will and that she would receive his property. The court held it was a valid will. One issue considered was whether the will was conditional on his dying at sea. The court found that although the possibility of dying at sea was the occasion for the making of the will, the testator reaffirmed it repeatedly after he came back alive from serving in the Navy....

Perhaps one of the most extreme examples of a court's finding a document to be a holographic will is *Estate of Smilie*.... The decedent, long having quarreled with his wife and stepdaughter, wrote a somewhat illiterate letter to his close friend Max describing a recent altercation and stating he didn't want the stepdaughter to get anything. Smilie wrote: " 'I want you to see that all my bills are paid and that Dot does not get thing. I want you to have all of my after my bill are.'"... Observing the principle that one cannot supply words into a will in order to make it have testamentary intent, but that striking certain words as surplusage *712 is permissible, the court found a valid holographic will. The sentence was changed to read "'I want you to have all.'"...

Finally, we discuss a case which in some ways is most on point. In *Estate of Blain* (1956) 140 Cal.App.2d 917, 295 P.2d 898, the decedent, Frank Blain, executed a holographic will and put it in his safety deposit box. The will failed to mention his only heir, Sonia Lambert, and nothing in the will indicated that the omission was intentional. Thus, she was presumptively entitled to inherit the entire estate as a pretermitted heir. However, one of the devisees under the holographic will contended that a piece of paper, wrapped around a dinner ring in the safety deposit box, containing the words " 'to Sonia Lambert Frank Blain,' " was an integral part of the will. If so, provision was made for the natural object of Blain's bounty (Sonia), so that the remainder of the holographic will giving all of his property to others would have been valid.... .The trial court thus grappled with the issue of whether the paper containing the five words including the signature could constitute a document that was testamentary in character, and whether it could be integrated into the seven-page holograph. The trial court found the document was not testamentary in character, it contained no testamentary disposition and exhibited no testamentary intent.... Reviewing the sufficiency of the evidence, the appellate court agreed. It pointed out that the document contained no description or specification of any property, and that a holographic will must be complete in itself....

In other words, the document must contain some indication that it is intended to convey something upon death, or it is not a will. Testamentary intent may be found when the decedent uses words indicating a transfer of specified property upon the death of the testator.... But when the document itself does not express an intention to convey property upon death, it does not exhibit the intent necessary for a will.... Evidence before the court indicated Sonia's grandmother had left Sonia the ring and Blain was only holding it for her. Such extrinsic evidence as there was, then, tended to show the ring already belonged to Sonia, and Frank Blain's writing only indicated that it was hers, not that he was giving it to her.... Thus, Frank Blain's attempt to disinherit his only heir was unsuccessful. Because he did not specifically disinherit her in the holographic will, the will was invalid and she took the entire estate....

We can see that the instant case thus differs from even the existing similar cases. In most of the cases just discussed, we find descriptions of property and words expressing donative intent. In the cases in which it is a little bit doubtful whether the proffered document is a will, we often have the express statement of the decedent, made shortly before death, that decedent has written his or her will and provided for decedent's loved ones in a certain letter or in a certain document. Clearly such direct extrinsic evidence is extremely probative on the question of whether a document is a will. In the instant case, we have no such helpful extrinsic evidence.

Appellants contend the document admitted to probate cannot, as a matter of law, constitute a will. We agree.

We consider this document which is offered as a holograph to be unique. The document consists of eight handwritten words-five of them constituting two proper names and three of them constituting an appellation, one arrow, a date and initials at the bottom. This series of words contains no recognizable subject, no verb and no object. The trial court below found these words constituted a valid holographic will under California law, the import of which was to bequeath all of decedent's estate to Xi. We conclude that it simply does not contain words sufficient to constitute a valid will.

*713 No particular words are required to create a will.... But every will must contain operative words legally sufficient to create a devise of property.... In this case, the words are either absent or are so ambiguous in meaning that it is impossible to tell what, if anything, is meant to be given, much less that it is intended to be a transfer of property upon death.

First, no words describe the property allegedly meant to be bequeathed, or even that it is property which is the subject of the note. In attempting to determine the meaning of this first phrase the question is, all of Tai-Kin Wong's what? The trial court found that the absence of a "what" meant all of Tai's property but there is nothing in the document that supports that speculation.

Nor does the document contain any donative words-not "give," "bequeath," "will," or even "want Xi Zhao to have." Instead of a word that indicates a gift or transfer of some sort, Xi contends that the arrow is meant to transfer Tai's entire estate to her upon his death. However, an arrow is not a word at all. It is a symbol with no fixed meaning, either in the general community or as used by the decedent himself. As such, it does not have one meaning which allows it to be used in place of a word, nor can it be used to supply any meaning to the words around it.

Appellants did not find, nor have we, a single case in which a symbol has been used in place of words indicating donative intent in a will. In fact, we have not found a case in which a symbol of no fixed meaning has been used in any material clause of a will. The Probate Code itself assumes that words will be used to create a will. (See, e.g., §6162[: "The words of a will are to be given their ordinary and grammatical meaning...".) The entire purpose of a will is to express the decedent's wishes for disposition of his or her property after death. If there are insufficient words in the document to do that, or if there are no words at all but ambiguous symbols, the decedent has failed in his or her purpose even if decedent did intend to write a will. The document in this case falls into that category; it simply does not contain operative words legally sufficient to accomplish a transfer of property upon death. Because this first issue is dispositive, we need not address appellants' other assignments of error.

DISPOSITION

Because the questioned document cannot constitute a will as a matter of law, the judgment is reversed and the trial court is directed to enter judgment in appellants' favor. Costs to appellants.

BAMATTRE-MANOUKIAN, Acting P.J., and MIHARA, J., concur.

In re The ESTATE OF Francis N. EDWARDS, deceased.

433 So.2d 1349

Florida Fifth District Court of Appeal. 1983

*1350 ORFINGER, Chief Judge.

The issue on appeal is whether the decedent had testamentary capacity when he executed his last will and testament. The trial court rejected a petition to revoke probate of the will and we affirm.

Francis N. Edwards died in Leesburg, Florida, on November 3, 1981. His last will, dated October 29, 1981, devised his entire estate to the appellee Richard Freeman, a casual employee of five years. Soon after the will was admitted to probate, the testator's mother and sisters filed a Petition for Revocation of Probate and for Establishment of Probate of a Prior Will dated June 23, 1981. After a hearing, final judgment was entered denying the petition for revocation and this appeal followed.

Appellants contend that Francis N. Edwards lacked testamentary capacity to execute his last will six days before his death. It is well settled that a testator is determined to be of "sound mind" when he has the ability to mentally understand in a general way (1) the nature and extent of the property to be disposed of, (2) the testator's relation to those who would naturally claim a substantial benefit from his will and, (3) a general understanding of the practical effect of the will as executed....

By pre-trial stipulation, the parties here established that Francis N. Edwards understood in a general way both the nature and extent of his property to be disposed of by his will and who the members of his family were at the time the will was *1351 executed. Therefore, the only element of testamentary capacity remaining for consideration was whether Edwards understood the practical effect of the will as executed. Appellants specifically contend that Francis Edwards was suffering from organic brain syndrome and insane delusions when he executed his last will and, thus, lacked the necessary testamentary capacity.

The testator had a history of chronic heart disease, dating back to at least 1972, when he suffered a heart attack. On June 17, 1981, he underwent quadruple bypass heart surgery and was discharged from the hospital on July 2, 1981. Appellants argue that there was more than sufficient evidence that the testator's arteriosclerosis had progressed to such a state that it affected his mental capacity. There was medical testimony from decedent's personal physician to the effect that the decedent was not of sound mind at the time he executed his will because of his arteriosclerotic condition. However, there was other medical testimony from two physicians who saw the testator on November 2 and 3 of 1981, a few days after the execution of his will, both of whose testimony would justify the finding that the testator did have testamentary capacity at the time he executed his will and that there was no indication of brain cell damage or cell death. Finally, two psychiatrists testified to the testator's capacity. Respondent's psychiatrist described the effect of organic brain syndrome upon signatures, concluding that Francis' signature did not differ from one found on his 1979 will and neither signature indicated organic brain syndrome. Even petitioners' own psychiatric expert testified that the testator understood the practical effect of the will. Finally, the attorney who drew the will and employees in his office testified that the testator appeared in full possession of his faculties when the will was executed and understood the effect of the will. We hold that this evidence was more than sufficient to support the trial court's finding that decedent had the testamentary capacity to execute the will in question.

In furtherance of their argument that decedent suffered from insane delusions, appellants refer to a series of incidents which they contend is evidence of Francis Edwards' lack of testamentary capacity due to insane delusion, such as his mistrust of his own family and his suspicion of people in general, including customers at his place of business.

"Insane delusion" was defined by the Florida supreme court with great specificity..:

> Monomania, sometimes designated paranoia, has reference to a craze or mania for a single object or class of objects. The subject of it may be perfectly sane as to all other objects. As with an insane delusion, monomania presupposes a species of mental disease. A mere belief in a state of facts, however imperfect or illogical, will not support an insane delusion. It must be the offspring of an unsound and deranged condition of the mind. Any belief which arises from reasoning from a known premise, however imperfect the process may be, or how illogical the conclusion reached, is not an insane delusion. If one of normal faculties can put himself in the place of the subject of an insane delusion and can see how he could believe that which he is charged with believing and still be in full possession of his faculties, an insane delusion is not established; neither will such a delusion be supported on undue prejudice if based on any kind of reasoning.

> An insane delusion has been defined as a spontaneous conception and acceptance as a fact, of that which has no real existence except in imagination. The conception must be persistently adhered to against all evidence and reason. It has also been defined as a conception originating spontaneously in the mind without evidence of any kind to support it, which can be accounted for on no reasonable hypothesis, having no foundation in reality, and springing from a diseased or morbid condition of the mind.

> Therefore, any belief which arises from reasoning based upon a known premise, however imperfect the process may be or however *1352 illogical the conclusion reached, is not an insane delusion. What is significant is not the truth or falsity of the belief, but rather whether such belief arose from reasoning from a known premise.... It must also appear that the persons having a special claim to the testator's bounty are the object of the alleged delusions of the testator....

As the trial judge indicated in his well-reasoned final judgment, there apparently has only been one Florida decision actually revoking a testator's will on the basis of an insane delusion. That case, *In re Estate of Hodtum,* 267 So.2d 686 (Fla. 2d DCA 1972), involved a decedent who executed a will leaving the residue of his estate to the Masonic Lodge of which he was a member. Soon thereafter, under the belief that the Masons had expelled him as a member, Hodtum removed the Lodge as a beneficiary of his will. His attorney, after checking these claims, advised the decedent that there was no basis for his belief. Nevertheless, the testator persisted in his belief and eventually had another attorney draw up a new will which was admitted to probate, but later revoked. On appeal, the appellate court affirmed, pointing out that there was *no* evidence to establish *any* basis for the decedent's belief.

[5] Contrary to *Hodtum,* there is some basis *sub judice* for the testator's actions and his mistrust of his family. In fact, the appellants' own psychiatrist testified that there was a basis for the testator's feelings, beliefs and fears against his family. The evidence also indicated that the testator had always been suspicious and secretive and always protective of his property. The trial court found that decedent " ... was naturally and justifiably concerned about shoplifting in the operation of his business due to the nature of that business and the physical layout of his store." Decedent was upset when some of his family members entered his property without his permission during one of his hospital stays, and on one occasion had ordered one of his brothers off his property. He suspected that an earlier break-in and robbery at his property had been engineered by another brother. He mentioned these incidents to the lawyer who drew the will in question here.

The trial court found other instances of differences between decedent and his siblings, including correspondence requesting that they stay off his property. Whether we agree that his feelings towards his brothers and sisters were justified is not the point at issue. What is determinative is the fact that those feelings arose from reasoning or a known premise. They had real existence and did not exist only in decedent's imagination. Viewing the evidence as a whole against the definition of insane delusion ... we cannot disagree with the trial court's conclusion that decedent was not suffering from an insane delusion when he executed the will in question. As we agree with the trial court on the issue of testamentary capacity, we need not consider appellants' other issues which only become viable if the testator's last will was held to be invalid.

AFFIRMED.

COBB and FRANK D. UPCHURCH, Jr., JJ., concur.

Egbert v. Lippmann

104 U.S. 333

Supreme Court of the United States 1881

*333 MR. JUSTICE WOODS delivered the opinion of the court.

This suit was brought for an alleged infringement of the complainant's reissued letters-patent, No. 5216, dated Jan. 7, 1873, for an improvement in corset-springs.

The original letters bear date July 17, 1866, and were issued to Samuel H. Barnes. The reissue was made to the complainant, under her then name, Frances Lee Barnes, executrix of the original patentee.

*334 The specification for the reissue declares:—

"This invention consists in forming the springs of corsets of two or more metallic plates, placed one upon another, and so connected as to prevent them from sliding off each other laterally or edgewise, and at the same time admit of their playing or sliding upon each other, in the direction of their length or longitudinally, whereby their flexibility and elasticity are greatly increased, while at the same time much strength is obtained."

The second claim is as follows:—

"A pair of corset-springs, each member of the pair being composed or two or more metallic plates, placed on one another, and fastened together at their centres, and so connected at or near each end that they can move or play on each other in the direction of their length."

The bill alleges that Barnes was the original and first inventor of the improvement covered by the reissued letters-patent, and that it had not, at the time of his application for the original letters, been for more than two years in public use or on sale, with his consent or allowance.

The answer takes issue on this averment and also denies infringement. On a final hearing the court dismissed the bill, and the complainant appealed.

As the second defense above mentioned, it is sufficient to say that the evidence establishes beyond controversy the infringement by the defendants of the second claim of the reissue.

We have, therefore, to consider whether the defense that the patented invention had, with the consent of the inventor, been publicly used for more than two years prior to his application for the original letters, is sustained by the testimony in the record.

The sixth, seventh, and fifteenth sections of the act ... as qualified by the seventh section of the act ... were in force at the date of his application. Their effect is to render letters-patent invalid if the invention which they cover was in public use, with the consent and allowance of the inventor, for more than two years prior to his application. Since the passage of the act of 1839 it has been strenuously contended *335 that the public use of an invention for more than two years before such application, even without his consent and allowance, renders the letters-patent therefor void.

It is unnecessary in this case to decide this question, for the alleged use of the invention covered by the letters-patent to Barnes is conceded to have been with his express consent.

The evidence on which the defendants rely to establish a prior public use of the invention consists mainly of the testimony of the complainant.

She testifies that Barnes invented the improvement covered by his patent between January and May, 1855; that between the dates named the witness and her friend Miss Cugier were complaining of the breaking of their corset-steels. Barnes, who was present, and was an intimate friend of the witness, said he thought he could make her a pair that would not break. At their next interview he presented her with a pair of corset-steels which he himself had made. The witness wore these steels a long time. In 1858 Barnes made and presented to her another pair, which she also wore a long time. When the corsets in which these steels were used wore out, the witness ripped them open and took out the steels and put them in new corsets. This was done several times.

It is admitted, and, in fact, is asserted, by complainant, that these steels embodied the invention afterwards patented by Barnes and covered by the reissued letters-patent on which this suit is brought.

Joseph H. Sturgis, another witness for complainant, testifies that in 1863 Barnes spoke to him about two inventions made by himself, one of which was a corset-steel, and that he went to the house of

Barnes to see them. Before this time, and after the transactions testified to by the complainant, Barnes and she had intermarried. Barnes said his wife had a pair of steels made according to his invention in the corsets which she was then wearing, and if she would take them off he would show them to witness. Mrs. Barnes went out, and returned with a pair of corsets and a pair of scissors, and ripped the corsets open and took out the steels. Barnes then explained to witness how they were made and used.

This is the evidence presented by the record, on which the *336 defendants rely to establish the public use of the invention by the patentee's consent and allowance.

The question for our decision is, whether this testimony shows a public use within the meaning of the statute.

We observe, in the first place, that to constitute the public use of an invention it is not necessary that more than one of the patented articles should be publicly used. The use of a great number may tend to strengthen the proof, but one well-defined case of such use is just as effectual to annul the patent as many.... For instance, if the inventor of a mower, a printing-press, or a railway-car makes and sells only one of the articles invented by him, and allows the vendee to use it for two years, without restriction or limitation, the use is just as public as if he had sold and allowed the use of a great number.

We remark, secondly, that, whether the use of an invention is public or private does not necessarily depend upon the number of persons to whom its use is known. If an inventor, having made his device, gives or sells it to another, to be used by the donee or vendee, without limitation or restriction, or injunction of secrecy, and it is so used, such use is public, even though the use and knowledge of the use may be confined to one person.

We say, thirdly, that some inventions are by their very character only capable of being used where they cannot be seen or observed by the public eye. An invention may consist of a lever or spring, hidden in the running gear of a watch, or of a ratchet, shaft, or cog-wheel covered from view in the recesses of a machine for spinning or weaving. Nevertheless, if its inventor sells a machine of which his invention forms a part, and allows it to be used without restriction of any kind, the use is a public one. So, on the other hand, a use necessarily open to public view, if made in good faith solely to test the qualities of the invention, and for the purpose of experiment, is not a public use within the meaning of the statute....

*337 Tested by these principles, we think the evidence of the complainant herself shows that for more than two years before the application for the original letters there was, by the consent and allowance of Barnes, a public use of the invention, covered by them. He made and gave to her two pairs of corset-steels, constructed according to his device, one in 1855 and one in 1858. They were presented to her for use. He imposed no obligation of secrecy, nor any condition or restriction whatever. They were not presented for the purpose of experiment, nor to test their qualities. No such claim is set up in her testimony. The invention was at the time complete, and there is no evidence that it was afterwards changed or improved. The donee of the steels used them for years for the purpose and in the manner designed by the inventor. They were not capable of any other use. She might have exhibited them to any person, or made other steels of the same kind, and used or sold them without violating any condition or restriction imposed on her by the inventor.

According to the testimony of the complainant, the invention was completed and put into use in 1855. The inventor slept on his rights for eleven years. Letters-patent were not applied for till March, 1866. In the mean time, the invention had found its way into general, and almost universal, use. A great part of the record is taken up with the testimony of the manufacturers and venders of corset-steels, showing that before he applied for letters the principle of his device was almost universally used in the manufacture of corset-steels. It is fair to presume that having learned from this general use that there was some value in his invention, he attempted to resume, by his application, what by his acts he had clearly dedicated to the public.

"An abandonment of an invention to the public may be evinced by the conduct of the inventor at any time, even within the two years named in the law. The effect of the law is that no such consequence will necessarily follow from the invention being in public use or on sale, with the inventor's consent and allowance, at any time within the two years before his application; but that, if the invention is in public use or on sale prior to that time, it will be conclusive evidence of *338 abandonment, and the patent will be void." ...

We are of opinion that the defense of two years' public use, by the consent and allowance of the inventor, before he made application for letters-patent, is satisfactorily established by the evidence.

MR. JUSTICE MILLER dissenting.

The sixth section of the act of July 4, 1836, c. 357, makes it a condition of the grant of a patent that the invention for which it was asked should not, at the time of the application for a patent, "have been in public use or on sale with the consent or allowance" of the inventor or discoverer. Section fifteen of the same act declares that it shall be a good defense to an action for infringement of the patent, that it had been in public use or on sale with the consent or allowance of the patentee before his application. This was afterwards modified by the seventh section of the act of March 3, 1839, c. 88, which declares that no patent shall be void on that ground unless the prior use has been for more than two years before the application.

This is the law under which the patent of the complainant is held void by the opinion just delivered. The previous part of the same section requires that the invention must be one "not known or used by others" before the discovery or invention made by the applicant. In this limitation, though in the same sentence as the other, the word "public" is not used, so that the use by others which would defeat the applicant, if without his consent, need not be public; but where the use of his invention is by his consent or allowance, it must be public or it will not have that affect.

The reason of this is undoubtedly that, if without his consent others have used the machine, composition, or manufacture, it is strong proof that he was not the discoverer or first inventor. In that case

he was not entitled to a patent. If the use was with his consent or allowance, the fact that such consent or allowance was first obtained is evidence that he was the inventor, and claimed to be such. In such case, he was not to *339 lose his right to a patent, unless the use which he permitted was such as showed an intention of abandoning his invention to the public. It must, in the language of the act, be in public use or on sale. If on sale, of course the public who buy can use it, and if used in public with his consent, it may be copied by others. In either event there is an end of his exclusive right of use or sale.

The work public is, therefore, an important member of the sentence. A private use with consent, which could lead to no copy or reproduction of the machine, which taught the nature of the invention to no one but the party to whom such consent was given, which left the public at large as ignorant of this as it was before the author's discovery, was no abandonment to the public, and did not defeat his claim for a patent. If the little steep spring inserted in a single pair of corsets, and used by only one woman, covered by her outer-clothing, and in a position always withheld from public observation, is a public use of that piece of steel, I am at a loss to know the line between a private and a public use.

The opinion argues that the use was public, because, with the consent of the inventor to its use, no limitation was imposed in regard to its use in public. It may be well imagined that a prohibition to the party so permitted against exposing her use of the steel spring to public observation would have been supposed to be a piece of irony. An objection quite the opposite of this suggested by the opinion is, that the invention was incapable of a public use. That is to say, that while the statute says the right to the patent can only be defeated by a use which is public, it is equally fatal to the claim, when it is permitted to be used at all, that the article can never be used in public.

I cannot on such reasoning as this eliminate from the statute the word public, and disregard its obvious importance in connection with the remainder of the act, for the purpose of defeating a patent otherwise meritorious.

Index

References are to sections unless otherwise noted.

CASES CITED OR REFERENCED